T0332462

Advanced Methods and Applications in Chemoinformatics:

Research Progress and New Applications

Eduardo A. Castro
Research Institute of Theoretical and Applied Physical–Chemistry (INIFTA), Argentina

A. K. Haghi
University of Guilan, Iran

ENGINEERING
SCIENCE REFERENCE

Senior Editorial Director:	Kristin Klinger
Director of Book Publications:	Julia Mosemann
Editorial Director:	Lindsay Johnston
Acquisitions Editor:	Erika Carter
Development Editor:	Myla Harty
Production Editor:	Sean Woznicki
Typesetters:	Milan Vracarich, Jr.
Print Coordinator:	Jamie Snavely
Cover Design:	Nick Newcomer

Published in the United States of America by
Engineering Science Reference (an imprint of IGI Global)
701 E. Chocolate Avenue
Hershey PA 17033
Tel: 717-533-8845
Fax: 717-533-8661
E-mail: cust@igi-global.com
Web site: http://www.igi-global.com

Library of Congress Cataloging-in-Publication Data

Advanced methods and applications in chemoinformatics: research progress and new applications / Eduardo A. Castro and A.K. Haghi, editors.
    p. cm.
  Includes bibliographical references and index.
  Summary: "This book provides innovative coverage on the growth of educational, scientific, and industrial research activities among chemists and chemical engineers and provides a medium for mutual communication between international academia and the industry"--Provided by publisher.
  ISBN 978-1-60960-860-6 (hardcover) -- ISBN 978-1-60960-861-3 (ebook) -- ISBN 978-1-60960-862-0 (print & perpetual access) 1. Cheminformatics. I. Castro, E. A. (Eduardo Alberto), 1944- II. Haghi, A. K.
  QD39.3.E46.A38 2011
  542'.85--dc23
                                    2011028266

British Cataloguing in Publication Data
A Cataloguing in Publication record for this book is available from the British Library.

All work contributed to this book is new, previously-unpublished material. The views expressed in this book are those of the authors, but not necessarily of the publisher.

Editorial Advisory Board

Table of Contents

Detailed Table of Contents

Chapter 1

    Santanab Giri, Indian Institute of Technology Kharagpur, India
    Arindam Chakraborty, Indian Institute of Technology Kharagpur, India
    Ashutosh Gupta, Udai Pratap Autonomous College, India
    Debesh Ranjan Roy, Indian Institute of Technology Kharagpur, India
    Ramadoss Vijayaraj, Central Leather Research Institute Chennai, India
    Ramakrishnan Parthasarathi, Central Leather Research Institute Chennai, India
    Venkatesan Subramanian, Central Leather Research Institute Chennai, India
    Pratim Kumar Chattaraj, Indian Institute of Technology Kharagpur, India

In the present chapter, density functional theory based reactivity indices are applied as chemical descriptors in QSAR analysis for ecotoxicological studies on a group of aromatic compounds. Two sets of aromatic compounds have been chosen to model ecotoxicity. First set comprises 97 electron-donor aromatic compounds and 77 electron-acceptor aromatic compounds studied on Tetrahymena pyriformis. The second set consists of 19 chlorophenol compounds studied for Daphnia magna, Brachydanio rerio and Bacillus. It is observed that a very simple descriptor like atom counting (number of non-hydrogenic atoms) along with other descriptors like electrophilicity index and (ground state) energies of the molecule, provide the best QSAR model for the toxicity of the first set of compounds. For the second set of compounds, it is found that the descriptors consisting of atom counting and group philicities together give the best QSAR models.

Chapter 2

    Francisco Torrens, Universitat de València, Spain
    Gloria Castellano, Universidad Católica de Valencia San Vicente Mártir, Spain

Algorithms for classification and taxonomy bases on criteria, e.g., information entropy. The feasibility of replacing a given molecule by similar ones in the composition of a complex drug is studied. Some local anaesthetics currently in use are classified using structural properties. In taxonomy the detailed comparison of the sequences of biomolecules, proteins or nucleic acids, allows the reconstruction of a molecular phylogenetic tree. The method is applied to the classifications of (1) indazolols (against Trichomonas vaginalis), (2) fullerenes and fullerite, (3) living and heat-inactivated lactic acid bacteria against cytokines, (4) phylogenesis of avian birds and 1918 influenza virus, (5) local anaesthetics, (6) transdermal-delivery percutaneous enhancers, (7) quantitative structure–activity relationship of anti human immunodeficiency virus (HIV) compounds, (8) HIV inhibitors, e.g., thiocarbamates, N aryloxazolidinone 5 carboxamides and styrylquinolines, (9) antimalarial aryltriazolylhydroxamates, (10) N aryl N (3 aryl 1,2,4 oxadiazol 5 yl) amines against prostate cancer, antimitotic 2 phenylindole 3 carbaldehydes against breast cancer and anti tubulin agents against gastric cancer with indole ring. The entropy contributions may be studied with the equipartition conjecture. It is not within the scope of our simulation method to replace biological tests of drugs or field data in palaeontology, but such simulation methods can be useful to assert priorities in detailed experimental research. Available experimental and field data should be examined by different classification algorithms to reveal possible features of real biological significance.

Chapter 3

Bakhtiyor Rasulev, Jackson State University, USA
Danuta Leszczynska, Jackson State University, USA
Jerzy Leszczynski, Jackson State University, USA

Nanomaterials are becoming an important component of the modern life and have been the subject of increasing number of investigations involving various areas of natural sciences and technology. However, theoretical modeling of physicochemical and biological activity of these species is still very scarce. The prediction of the properties and activities of 'classical' substances via correlating with molecular descriptors is a well known procedure, i.e. QSAR. In spite of this, the application of QSAR for the nano-materials is a very complicated task, because of "non-classical" structure of nanomaterials. Here, the authors show that an application of the QSAR methods for nanomaterials is nevertheless possible and can be useful in predicting their various properties and activities (toxicity). We briefly explained how the physico-chemical properties can be predicted for nanomaterials. Furthermore, we also demonstrated how the biological activity, particularly toxicity, can be modeled and predicted for the series of nanoparticles, by applying the quantum-chemical methods in combination with the nano-QSAR.

Chapter 4

Laurent A. Baumes, CSIC-Universidad Politecnica de Valencia, Spain

The data mining technology increasingly employed into new industrial processes, which require automatic analysis of data and related results in order to quickly proceed to conclusions. However, for some applications, an absolute automation may not be appropriate. Unlike traditional data mining, contexts deal with voluminous amounts of data, some domains are actually characterized by a scarcity of data, owing to the cost and time involved in conducting simulations or setting up experimental apparatus for data collection. In such domains, it is hence prudent to balance speed through automation and the utility of the generated data. The authors review the active learning methodology, and a new one that aims at generating successively new samples in order to reach an improved final estimation of the entire search space investigated according to the knowledge accumulated iteratively through samples selection and corresponding obtained results, is presented. The methodology is shown to be of great interest for applications such as high throughput material science and especially heterogeneous catalysis where the chemists do not have previous knowledge allowing to direct and to guide the exploration.

Chapter 5

Abdelmalek Amine, Tahar Moulay University & Djillali Liabes University, Algeria
Zakaria Elberrichi, Djillali Liabes University, Algeria
Michel Simonet, Joseph Fourier University, France
Ali Rahmouni, Tahar Moulay University, Algeria

In order to identify new molecules susceptible to become medicines, the pharmaceutical research has more and more resort to new technologies to synthesize big number of molecules simultaneously and to test their actions on given therapeutic target. This data can be exploited to construct the models permitting to predict the properties of molecules not yet tested, even not yet synthesized. Such predictive models are very important because they make it possible to suggest the synthesis of new molecules, and to eliminate very early in the the molecule's search process the molecules whose properties would prevent their use as medicine. The authors call it virtual sifting. It is within this framework that research by similarity is registered. It is a practical approach to identify molecules candidates (to become medicines) from the data bases or the virtual chemical libraries by comparing the compounds two by two. Many statistical models and learning tools have been developed to correlate the molecule's structure with their chemical, physical or biological properties. The large majority of these methods start by transforming each molecule in a vector of great dimension (using molecular descriptors), then use a learning algorithm on these vectorial descriptions. The objective of this chapter is to study molecular similarity using a particular type of neural networks: the Kohonen networks (also called "SOM" Self- Organizing Maps), applying the nearest neighbor algorithm to the projection of the molecules (coordinates) in the constructed MAP.

Chapter 6

Lionello Pogliani, Università della Calabria, Italy

Valence molecular connectivity indices are indices based on the concept of valence delta, δ v, that can be derived from general chemical graphs or chemical pseudographs. A general graph or pseudograph is a graph with multiple edges and loops and it can be used to encode, through the valence delta, chemical entities like the sigma-, pi- and non-bonding n-electrons. Two other graph-theoretical concepts that can also be derived from chemical pseudographs are the intrinsic (I) and the electrotopological state (E) values that are the main tools used to define the valence delta of the pseudoconnectivity indices, I,S. Complete graphs can, instead, be used to encode, through a new type of valence delta, the core electrons of any type of atoms in a molecule. The connectivity indices either valence connectivity or pseudoconnectivity indices are the starting point to develop, by the aid of a dual procedure, the dual connectivity indices, i.e., the dual connectivity, valence connectivity and pseudoconnectivity indices. The dual indices show the interesting property that not only some of them can assume negative values but also that they can cover a wide range of numerical values. Graph concepts can also be used to deal with the problem of the hydrogen contribution in hydrogen depleted chemical graphs, which are the normal type of graphs used in chemistry. For this purpose a perturbation parameter can be introduced into the definition of the valence delta that allows to differentiates among compounds with similar hydrogen-suppressed chemical graphs but different number of hydrogen atoms, like CH3F and BH2F. The new definition of the central parameter of the molecular connectivity theory, the valence delta, consent to define of a completely new set of connectivity indices, which can be distinguished by their configuration and that can advantageously be used to model different properties and activities of compounds.

Chapter 7

    Mihai V. Putz, West University of Timişoara, Romania
    Ana-Maria Putz, Timisoara Institute of Chemistry of Romanian Academy, Romania

The logistic temporal solution of the generalized Michaelis-Menten kinetics is employed to provide a quantum basis for the tunnelling time and energy evaluations of Brownian enzymic reactions. The mono-substrate and mixed inhibition cases are treated and the associated quantum diagrams of the reaction mechanisms are depicted in terms of intermediate enzyme complexes. The methodology is suited for practically controlling of the enzymic activity throughout absorption spectroscopy.

Chapter 8

    Željko Debeljak, University of Zagreb, Croatia
    Marica Medić-Šarić, University of Zagreb, Croatia

During the last few decades the number of available molecular descriptors has grown exponentially. A reduced set of descriptors, containing only relevant descriptors, enables better understanding of the interaction between the molecule and some biological entity and in turn, it enables more reliable molecular modeling and chemical database mining. As a consequence, many new off-line and on-line descriptor selection methods have emerged. Overview of the most important feature selection methods, their advantages, disadvantages and applications in SAR and QSAR is given.

Chapter 9

    D. Shanthi, Madura College, India
    L. Rajendran, Madura College, India

The system is considered here with two chemical species, the reactant a and autocatalyst b. The Gray-Scott model of cubic-autocatalysis with linear decay is coupled with diffusion and considered in a one-dimensional reactor (a reactor-diffusion cell). Steady-state and non steady- state concentration profiles of the reactant and autocatalyst in Gray-Scott model are obtained using He's Homotopy pertuburation method for small values parameters. A satisfactory agreement with analytical and numerical results are noted.

Chapter 10

Pablo R. Duchowicz, INIFTA, CCT La Plata-CONICET, Argentina

Eduardo A. Castro, INIFTA, CCT La Plata-CONICET, Argentina

Present chapter reviews the application of Quantitative Structure-Activity Relationships for the treatment of molecules involving thousands of atoms, such as proteins, nucleic acids (DNA, RNA), or polysaccharides. This is a new developing area of interest in Chemoinformatics, and it is expected to have a growing number of applications during the forthcoming years. Among the several points to be addressed during the modeling of macromolecules, the most important one appears to be the accurate representation of the chemical structure through numerical descriptors. It has to be noticed that descriptors based on optimized three-dimensional geometry are difficult to specify, and it is also a drawback the fact that the experimental geometry is not available. However, different experts in the field have been generalizing the employment of classical types of topological descriptors in macromolecular systems.

Chapter 11

Alan Talevi, CCT La Plata CONICET, Argentina

Eduardo A. Castro, INIFTA, CCT La Plata CONICET, Argentina

Luis E. Bruno-Blanch, CCT La Plata CONICET, Argentina

The universe of known organic chemical compounds has grown exponentially during the last 50 years, which greatly increases the probability of finding chemotherapeutic agents which interact selectively with any given molecular target. Traditional systematic pharmacological screening of available drug-like compounds has, however, can not keep the pace with the uninterrupted growth of the chemical space. The last 20 years have thus witnessed the emergence of novel high throughput screening technologies conceived to explore the vast chemical universe in an efficient manner, among them, virtual or in silico screening.

In this chapter,the authors analyze virtual screening advantages and the classification of virtual screening approaches. They also discuss the current and potential importance of virtual screening for drug development in Latin America. Finally, they present a brief overview on virtual screening perspectives.

Chapter 12

Hamid Dadvar, University of Guilan, Iran

Farhad E. Ghodsi, University of Guilan, Iran

Saeed Dadvar, Isfahan University of Technology, Iran

In this chapter, the sol-gel made titanium dioxide nanostructured thin films deposited on special substrates such as glasses, mica, steels, textiles, fibers, and other organic/inorganic substrates were reviewed. Through this review, several distinctive properties such as optical, electrical, photocatalytic, morphological, and mechanical properties of TiO_2 nanostructured thin films were described. Also, a wide range of practical application of TiO2 nanostructured thin films such as dye-sensitised solar cells, optical coatings, humidity and gas sensors, selfcleaning, dielectric, and antibacterial surfaces were discussed in details. Dip and spin coating techniques were demonstrated as suitable methods for deposition of thin films. It has been shown that properties of such films can be affected by type of coating technique, stabilizer, precursor material, solvents, pH and viscosity of precursor solution, aging, and etc. Finally, Successive Interference Fringes Method (SIFM) was presented as a simple method for the determination of optical constants and thickness of TiO2 thin films from single transmission measurements.

Chapter 13

The chapter surveys mostly original work of the authors on the application of the electrostatic potential at nuclei (EPN) as a reactivity index in quantifying hydrogen bonding as well as different reactions of organic compounds. The EPN index was defined and introduced by E. B. Wilson (1962). However, it was first applied as a reactivity index much later in works from our laboratory (Bobadova-Parvanova & Galabov, 1998; Galabov & Bobadova-Parvanova, 1999; Dimitrova, Ilieva, & Galabov, 2002; Cheshmedzhieva, Ilieva, Hadjieva, Trayanova, & Galabov, 2009; Galabov, Cheshmedzhieva, Ilieva, & Hadjieva, 2004; Galabov, Ileiva, & Schaefer, 2006; Galabov, Nikolova, Wilke, Schaefer, & Allen, 2008; Galabov, Ilieva, Hadjieva, Atanasov, & Schaefer, 2008; Koleva, Galabov, Wu, Schaefer, & Schleyer, 2009). Numerous applications showed that the EPN index, an accurate quantum mechanical quantity, predicts with remarkable accuracy the energy shifts accompanying hydrogen bonding. The theoretically evaluated EPN descriptor correlates also excellently with experimental and theoretically evaluated kinetic parameters for a number of important organic reactions. Based on these findings an efficient computational approach for the evaluation of substituent constants was developed.

Chapter 14

Computer sciences have deeply changed the way by which we make science or produce knowledge. With the era of computers and the development of computer science, quantum chemists were among the first scientists to explore the potentialities of the new tool, and even to collaborate in its development. In this way, they also became participants in what many dubbed as the Second Instrumental Revolution in chemistry. Deeply involved into this research field, QSAR methods are powerful tools to create knowledge on toxicology and drug design, among others. There are several epistemological questions to be analyzed in order to understand the truth and scientific value of their research results (from in silico to wet laboratories and vice versa).

Chapter 15

Computational techniques are widely used in the chemoinformatics and bioinformatics. Most of the drugs produce their effect by interacting with the target molecules via different interactions. However, these interactions are tough to be calculated without use of robotics techniques. The potentials of these drugs depend upon their binding affinity. Due to huge number of such drugs, the measurement of their relative potency is a hard task. In present chapter the authors have discussed about some most common techniques which are widely used in bioinformatics and chemoinformatics.

Chapter 16

J. M. Villalba, Universidad de Castilla-la Mancha, Spain
R. Varón, Universidad de Castilla-la Mancha, Spain
E. Arribas, Universidad de Castilla-la Mancha, Spain
R. Diaz-Sierra, UNED, Spain
F. Garcia-Sevilla, Universidad de Castilla-La Mancha, Spain
F. Garcia-Molina, Universidad de Murcia, Spain
M. Garcia-Moreno, Universidad de Castilla-la Mancha, Spain ·
M. J. Garcia-Meseguer, Universidad de Castilla-la Mancha, Spain

The symbolic time course equations corresponding to a general model of a linear compartmental system, closed or open, with or without traps and with zero input are presented in this chapter. From here, the steady state equations are obtained easily from the transient phase equations by setting the time towards infinite. Special attention is given to the open systems, for which an exhaustive kinetic analysis has been developed to obtain important properties. Besides, the results are particularized to open systems without traps. The software COEFICOM, easy to use and with a user-friendly format of the input of data and the output of results, allows the user to obtain the symbolic expressions of the coefficients involved in the general symbolic equation and all the information necessary to derive the symbolic time course equations for closed or open systems as well as for the derivation of the mean residence times.

Kunal Roy, Jadavpur University, India
Rudra Narayan Das, Jadavpur University, India

Development of predictive models has been accepted as an important strategy to aid in toxicity screening of chemicals, determination of physicochemical as well as other biological activity of new molecules, and also in the generation and optimization of lead compounds in rational drug discovery process. The journey of QSPR started with the development of various property-based and two-dimensional descriptors to model various physicochemical and biological properties (including toxicity). Topological descriptors contain significant information encoded in the molecular structure. Extended topochemical atom (ETA) indices, a relatively new class of topological descriptors, are the focus point in this chapter. ETA indices contain important information regarding the nature of the atoms, bonds, atomic electronic environment and consider the contribution of different functional groups, molecular fragments, and branching to the response as evidenced by different reports showing their successful application in modeling different endpoints including toxicity, drug activity, and physicochemical properties. Extensive research is still going on for the refinement of the ETA indices by the incorporation of some novel parameters, and future reports on ETA indices will include these new indices.

Preface

Using computational techniques and methods, chemoinformatics aims to study and solve complex chemical problems. The collection of topics in this book aims to reflect the diversity of recent advances in chemoinformatics with a broad perspective which may be useful for scientists as well as for graduate students and engineers.

The main objective of this book is to provide innovative chapters on the growth of educational, scientific, and industrial research activities among chemists and chemical engineers and provides a medium for mutual communication between international academia and the industry. Reporting new methodologies and important applications in the fields of chemical informatics as well as includes the latest coverage of chemical databases, this book aims to present leading-edge research from around the world in the dynamic field of chemoinformatics.

Advanced Methods and Applications in Chemoinformatics: Research Methods and New Applications is made up of 17 chapters which will provide insight on this very topic as a whole.

Chapter 1 introduces quantitative structure activity relationship (QSAR) as a mathematical representation of biological activity in terms of structural descriptors. The chapter will present density functional theory based reactivity indices are applied as chemical descriptors in QSAR analysis for ecotoxicological studies on a group of aromatic compounds.

Chapter 2 indicates that the feasibility of replacing a given molecule by similar ones in the composition of a complex drug is studied. In taxonomy the detailed comparison of the sequences of biomolecules, proteins or nucleic acids, allows the reconstruction of a molecular phylogenetic tree.

Chapter 3 explains that nanomaterials are becoming an important component of the modern life and have been the subject of increasing number of investigations involving various areas of natural sciences and technology. However, theoretical modeling of physicochemical and biological activity of these species is still very scarce.

Chapter 4 reviews the active learning methodology, and a new one that aims at generating successively new samples in order to reach an improved final estimation of the entire search space investigated according to the knowledge accumulated iteratively through samples selection and corresponding obtained results, is presented. The methodology is shown to be of great interest for applications such as high throughput material science and especially heterogeneous catalysis where the chemists do not have previous knowledge allowing to direct and to guide the exploration.

Chapter 5 studies molecular similarity using a particular type of neural networks: the Kohonen networks (also called "SOM" Self- Organizing Maps), applying the nearest neighbor algorithm to the projection of the molecules (coordinates) in the constructed MAP.

Chapter 6 is a QSAR/QSPR study with a graph-theoretical centered on a vertex degree based on simple, general (or pseudograph), and complete graphs has shown the ability of the, connectivity, pseudoconnectivity and dual indices to achieve a quite good model of activities (*LogP*) in six different media and of four properties of two different and highly heterogeneous classes of compounds.

Chapter 7 explains that the logistic temporal solution of the generalized Michaelis-Menten kinetics is employed to provide a quantum basis for the tunnelling time and energy evaluations of Brownian enzymic reactions. The mono-substrate and mixed inhibition cases are treated and the associated quantum diagrams of the reaction mechanisms are depicted in terms of intermediate enzyme complexes.

Chapter 8 provides an overview of the most important feature selection methods, their advantages, disadvantages and applications in SAR and QSAR is given.

Chapter 9 presents the approximate analytical and numerical solution of cubic autocatalytic reaction-diffusion equations. There is a great deal of interest in chemical reactions which exhibit oscillatory solutions. These oscillations occur due to feedback in the system either chemical feedback such as autocatalysis or temperature feedback due to non-isothermal reaction.

Chapter 10 reviews the application of Quantitative Structure-Activity Relationships for the treatment of molecules involving thousands of atoms, such as proteins, nucleic acids (DNA, RNA), or polysaccharides. This is a new developing area of interest in Chemoinformatics, and it is expected to have a growing number of applications during the forthcoming years. Among the several points to be addressed during the modeling of macromolecules, the most important one appears to be the accurate representation of the chemical structure through numerical descriptors. It has to be noticed that descriptors based on optimized three-dimensional geometry are difficult to specify, and it is also a drawback the fact that the experimental geometry is not available.

Chapter 11 analyzes virtual screening advantages and the classification of virtual screening approaches. Also discussed is the current and potential importance of virtual screening for drug development in Latin America. Finally, the authors present a brief overview on virtual screening perspectives.

Chapter 12 generalizes the sol-gel made titanium dioxide nanostructure thin films deposited on special substrates such as glasses, mica, steels, textiles, fibers, and other organic/inorganic substrates were reviewed. Through this review, several distinctive properties such as optical, electrical, photocatalytic, morphological, and mechanical properties of TiO_2 nanostructured thin films were described.

Chapter 13 surveys the application of the electrostatic potential at nuclei (EPN) as a reactivity index in quantifying hydrogen bonding as well as different reactions of organic compounds. Numerous applications showed that the EPN index, an accurate quantum mechanical quantity, predicts with remarkable accuracy the energy shifts accompanying hydrogen bonding.

Chapter 14 explains the era of computers and the development of computer science, quantum chemists were among the first scientists to explore the potentialities of the new tool, and even to collaborate in its development. In this way, they also became participants in what many dubbed as the Second Instrumental Revolution in chemistry.

Chapter 15 discusses some of the most common techniques which are widely used in bioinformatics and chemoinformatics. Most of the drugs produce their effect by interacting with the target molecules via different interactions. However, these interactions are tough to be calculated without use of robotics techniques.

Chapter 16 presents the symbolic time course equations corresponding to a general model of a linear compartmental system, closed or open, with or without traps and with zero input. Special attention is given to the open systems, for which an exhaustive kinetic analysis has been developed to obtain important properties.

Chapter 17 focuses on extended topochemical atom (ETA) indices, a relatively new class of topological descriptors. ETA indices contain important information regarding the nature of the atoms, bonds, atomic electronic environment and consider the contribution of different functional groups, molecular fragments, and branching to the response as evidenced by different reports showing their successful application in modeling different endpoints including toxicity, drug activity, and physicochemical properties.

With this collection, this book will provide innovative chapters on the growth of educational, scientific, and industrial research activities among chemists and chemical engineers and provides a medium for mutual communication between international academia and the industry.

Eduardo A. Castro
Research Institute of Theoretical and Applied Physical-Chemistry (INIFTA), Argentina

A. K. Haghi
University of Guilan, Iran

Chapter 1
Modeling Ecotoxicity as Applied to Some Selected Aromatic Compounds:
A Conceptual DFT Based Quantitative–Structure–Toxicity–Relationship (QSTR) Analysis

Santanab Giri
Indian Institute of Technology Kharagpur, India

Ramadoss Vijayaraj
Central Leather Research Institute Chennai, India

Arindam Chakraborty
Indian Institute of Technology Kharagpur, India

Ramakrishnan Parthasarathi
Central Leather Research Institute Chennai, India

Ashutosh Gupta
Udai Pratap Autonomous College, India

Venkatesan Subramanian
Central Leather Research Institute Chennai, India

Debesh Ranjan Roy
Indian Institute of Technology Kharagpur, India

Pratim Kumar Chattaraj
Indian Institute of Technology Kharagpur, India

ABSTRACT

In the present chapter, density functional theory based reactivity indices are applied as chemical descriptors in QSAR analysis for ecotoxicological studies on a group of aromatic compounds. Two sets of aromatic compounds have been chosen to model ecotoxicity. First set comprises 97 electron-donor aromatic compounds and 77 electron-acceptor aromatic compounds studied on Tetrahymena pyriformis. The second set consists of 19 chlorophenol compounds studied for Daphnia magna, Brachydanio rerio and Bacillus. It is observed that a very simple descriptor like atom counting (number of non-hydrogenic

DOI: 10.4018/978-1-60960-860-6.ch001

atoms) along with other descriptors like electrophilicity index and (ground state) energies of the molecule, provide the best QSAR model for the toxicity of the first set of compounds. For the second set of compounds, it is found that the descriptors consisting of atom counting and group philicities together give the best QSAR models.

INTRODUCTION

The quantitative structure activity relationship (QSAR) is a mathematical representation of biological activity in terms of structural descriptors of a series of homologue molecules (Hansch, Leo & Taft, 1991)(Gao, Katzenellenbogen, Garg & Hansch, 1999)(Franke, 1984)(Gupta, Singh & Bindal, 1983)(Gupta, 1991)(Karelson, Lobanov & Katritzky, 1996). The main objective of QSAR is to look for new molecules with required properties using chemical intuition and experience transformed into a mathematically quantified and computerized form (Karelson, Lobanov & Katritzky, 1996). Once a correlation is established, the structure of any number of compounds with desired properties can be predicted. Thus QSAR methodology saves resources and expedites the process of development of new molecules and drugs (Hansch, Hoekman, Leo, Weininger & Selassie, 2002). Success of QSAR not only rests on the development of new drug molecules but, also in exploring the prediction of toxicological and, ecotoxicological activities, biological activity, biodegradability and environmental activities of various molecules (Hansch, Hoekman, Leo, Weininger & Selassie, 2002)(Hansch, Maloney, Fujita & Muir, 1962). Because the experimental determination is time-consuming and expensive, QSAR is widely used as an alternative.

QSAR models are also utilized for the regulation of industrial chemicals. In many countries including United States, legislation allows for the wide use of QSAR (Zeeman, Auer, Clements, Nabholz & Boethling, 1995). These observations have prompted the search for new QSAR tools and therefore the study of applications of molecular

modeling methods, from pharmaceutical sciences to ecotoxicology. Use of quantum chemical descriptors in the development of QSAR has received rave attention due to their reliability and versatility of prediction (Parr & Yang, 1989)(Chermette, 1999)(Geerling, De Proft & Langenaeker, 2003)(Chattaraj, Nath & Maiti, 2003). Specifically, toxicity of various chemical compounds and associated biochemical processes have been related to their molecular structures. In this context, the structure-activity relationships (SARs) based on electrophilicity (ω) is shown to be promising. It has been found (Parthasarathi, Padmanabhan, Subramanian, Maiti & Chattaraj, 2003) (Parthasarathi, Padmanabhan, Subramanian, Sarkar, Maiti & Chattaraj, 2003) that the interaction between a toxin and a bio-system is essentially through a charge-transfer process supplemented by a variety of non-covalent interactions including stacking. Hence, the importance of global and local electrophilicities as well as the conformational flexibility of the toxins in understanding the toxicity of those molecules is well acclaimed.

Conceptual density functional theory (DFT) (Parr & Yang, 1989)(Geerlings, Proft & Langenaeker, 2003)(Chattaraj, 2009)(Chattaraj & Giri, 2009) based quantum-chemical descriptors have become quite successful in explaining physicochemical properties (Giri, Roy, Bultinck, Subramanian & Chattaraj, 2008), biological activities (Parthasarathi, Subramanian, Roy & Chattaraj, 2004), and toxicity(Roy et al., 2006) (Padmanabhan, Parthasarathi, Subramanian & Chattaraj, 2006) of diverse classes of chemical compounds and drug molecules. Chemical potential (Chattaraj, 2009) (μ), electronegativity(Parr, Donnelly, Levy & Palke, 1978) (χ), chemical hardness(Pearson, 1997) (η), and electrophilicity index(Parr, Szentpaly & Liu, 1999)(Chattaraj, Sarkar & Roy, 2006)(Chattaraj & Roy, 2007) (ω) are some of the global reactivity descriptors within the DFT framework(Parr& Yang, 1989) (Geerlings, Proft & Langenaeker, 2003)(Chattaraj, 2009)(Chattaraj & Giri, 2009). It is found that the electrophilicity index (ω) and its local counterpart, philicity, are successful towards explaining the toxicity of various polyaromatic hydrocarbons(Roy, et al., 2006)(Padmanabhan, Parthasarathi, Subramanian & Chattaraj, 2006) (PAHs). Simple descriptors, like atom counting in terms of number of non-hydrogenic atoms (N_{NH}), besides other descriptors such as ground state energy of a molecule are also successful in the prediction of toxicity (Giri, Roy, Bultinck, Subramanian, Chattaraj, 2008)(Chattaraj, et al. 2007)(Roy, et al. 2007). Arsenic toxicity has also been successfully explained (Roy, Giri & Chattaraj, 2009) by using electrophilicity index and atom counting as descriptors. Biological activities of a series of testosterone and estrogen derivatives have been successfully rationalized (Padmanabhan, Parthasarathi, Subramanian & Chattaraj, 2006)using electrophilicity index. Electrophilicity index and group philicity are also utilized to predict various physicochemical properties, e.g., pKa of carboxylic acids and substituted phenols, boiling point of alcohols (Roy, et al. 2006), etc. Quantum chemical descriptors (QCDs) have also been employed in the study of toxicity of different organic chemicals (Parr, Donnelly, Levy & Palke, 1978)(Pearson, 1997). Chattaraj et al have recently proposed a new dual descriptor, net electrophilicity $(\Delta\omega^{\pm})$ which is a measure of the electrophilicity of a system relative to its own nucleophilicity. The newly proposed descriptor, $\Delta\omega^{\pm}$, have been found to be quite versatile in developing effective quantitative structure-toxicity based regression models for a host of halogen, sulfur and chlorinated aromatic compounds. While the associated R^2, R^2_{CV} and R^2_{adj} values for the set of inorganic halogen and sulfur compounds gave the best-fit

regression data with net electrophilicity $(\Delta\omega^{\pm})$, for the other set consisting of the chlorinated aromatic compounds, both the electrophilicity (ω) and the net electrophilicity $(\Delta\omega^{\pm})$ have performed hand-in-hand and have provided comparable values. The utility of the newly proposed dual descriptor, $\Delta\omega^{\pm}$ in constructing effective QSAR based structure- activity- relationship models is thus well validated. The details of this work have been already published as an article elsewhere (Gupta, Chakraborty, Giri, Subramanian & Chattaraj, 2010).

The present study is yet another attempt, to search for the descriptors, which possess the potential to predict the toxicity level of different sets of aromatic compounds in a more accurate and less time demanding manner. The compounds, selected for the present study, have been divided into two sets. The first set consists of 174 aromatic compounds, which are further classified as 97 electron-donor and 77 electron-acceptor aromatic compounds. QSAR models have been developed for such compounds against *Tetrahymena pyriformis*. The second set consists of 18 chlorophenol compounds which have been studied against *Daphnia magna*, *Brachydanio rerio* and *Bacillus* respectively.

Tetrahymena pyriformis is a teardrop-shaped, unicellular, ciliated freshwater protozoan about 50 mm long. They are very common in aquatic habitats and are non-pathogenic, have a short generation time and can be grown to high cell density in inexpensive media. They are one of the generally used ciliated protozoa for laboratory research (Akers, Sinks & Schultz, 1999)(Schultz, 1997) (Cronin & Schultz, 2001)(Dimitrov, Mekenyan, Sinks & Schultz, 2003). In this ciliate species, diverse endpoints can be used to originate the cytotoxic effects and xenobiotics. Experimental determination of toxicological and biochemical endpoints as well as the human health endpoints is a difficult task. Hence, QSAR modeling of the toxicity of aromatic compounds on the *T. pyriformis* is of vital importance in investigating its toxicity, in terms of its inhibitory growth concentration, using the predictive power of electrophilicity and local philicity indices. Various studies have been made to estimate the predictive potential of the quantum chemical descriptors for modeling the toxicity of organic compounds on *T. pyriformis* (Parthasarathi, Subramanian, Roy & Chattaraj, 2004)(Padmanabhan, Parthasarathi, Subramanian & Chattaraj, 2006)(Roy, Parthasarathi, Subramanian & Chattaraj, 2006)(Roy, Parthasarathi, Maiti, Subramanian & Chattaraj, 2005). In the present study, the possibility of prediction power of a simple descriptor like atom counting of number of non-hydrogenic atoms (N_{NH}) along with other descriptors is explored for modeling the toxicity of aromatic compounds on *T. pyriformis*. A large number of selected 174 aromatic compounds containing electron-donor compounds like phenols and electron-acceptor compounds like nitrobenzenes and benzonitriles are chosen with their toxicity values in terms of 50% inhibitory growth concentration (IGC_{50}) to verify their toxic potency(Schultz, 1997)(Cronin & Schultz, 2001) against *T. pyriformis* in the light of number of non-hydrogenic atom (N_{NH}) descriptor and other descriptors like electrophilicity index and (total Hartree-Fock) energy (E_{HF}) of the molecule.

The second set of compounds consists of chlorophenols. Phenol and its derivatives are found to be most toxic among various organic water pollutants because of their carcinogenic properties(Della, Monaco, Pinto, Pollio, Previtera & Temussi, 2001)(Garg, Kapur, Hansch, 2001). The adverse effects of phenolic compounds have also been found on some useful bacteria (nitrification bacteria, bacteria in sediment, etc.) in nature (Dean-Ross & Rahimi, 1995) (Strotmann & Eglsaer, 1995). Phenolic compounds are also present in wastewaters of paper and pulp, pesticides, dyes, textiles, pharmaceutical, plastic, rubber, tanning and petroleum industries. They are also present in domestic effluents and vegetation decay.

In dyestuffs, pesticides and biocides, chlorophenols (CPs) from mono- to pentachlorine-substituted compounds, are widely used as synthetic intermediates. They occur as industrial wastes and direct pollutants in the environment and are relatively soluble in water and detectable in rivers, ponds and soil (Verschueren, 1996). They can also be produced by environmental degradation of more complex molecules such as phenoxyacetic acids and chlorobenzenes. It has been found that toxicity of CPs increases with an increase in the number of chlorine atoms and gets reduced by the chlorine atoms substituted at the ortho-position (Cohen, Gamliel & Katan, 1988). It has been observed in case of studies in fish that the toxicity of CPs increases with an increasing number of chlorine atoms, and the toxicity of CPs having the same number of chlorine atoms, decreases in the order of non-, mono-, and di-ortho-CPs. Thus, it is necessary to evaluate the hazards on non-target organisms in the environment. In an earlier study, we had analyzed the reactivity/toxicity on chlorophenols against *Daphnia magna*, *Brachydanio rerio* and *Bacillus* respectively, using DFT-based descriptors (Padmanabhan, Parthasarathi, Subramanian & Chattaraj, 2006). In the present study, we analyze the potential of other descriptors like number of non-hydrogenic atom (N_{NH}) along with other quantum chemical descriptors towards the prediction of toxicity of chlorophenols against *Daphnia magna*, *Brachydanio rerio* and *Bacillus* respectively. For the current study, the experimental ecotoxicological data of CPs chosen for QSAR analysis are as follows: (i) EC_{50} on *Daphnia magna*, effective concentrations causing 50% immobilization of daphnia after 24 h of exposure (Devillers & Chambon, 1986); (ii) LC_{50} on *Brachydanio rerio*, lethal concentrations for 50% of fish after 24 h of exposure(Devillers & Chambon, 1986); and (iii) IC_{50} on *Bacillus* sp. TL81, effective concentrations of the toxicant causing 50% inhibition of the bacterial dehydrogenase activity (Liu, Thomson & Kaiser, 1982) (Ribo & Kaiser, 1983). The ecotoxicity modeling is carried out by building the QSAR models with experimental toxicity values as dependent variables and number of non-hydrogenic atoms (N_{NH}) and group philicities (ω_g^+, ω_g^-) as independent variables for the series of CPs.

The chapter is organized as follows: first a brief description of theoretical details and methods for data analysis are given. Afterwards, computational details for geometry optimization are given. In the Result and discussion section, the important regression models developed for the various inorganic halogen, sulfur compounds and the chlorinated aromatic compounds in a recent study (Gupta, Chakraborty, Giri, Subramanian & Chattaraj, 2010) have been reported. Further, for the current study we discuss the first set of compounds consisting of 174 electron-donor and electron-acceptor molecules. For the second set, we discuss the set of compounds containing chlorophenols. The last part of the paper contains some concluding remarks.

THEORETICAL DETAILS

Parr and co-workers have defined (Parr, Szentpaly & Liu, 1999) global electrophilicity index (ω) as a measure of the decrease in energy due to the maximal transfer of electrons from a donor to an acceptor system. It has also been used in understanding the reactivity of the human immunodeficiency virus type-1 (HIV-1) against a variety of electrophilic agents (Maynard, Huang, Rice & Covell, 1998). It is defined as follows:

$$\omega = \frac{\mu^2}{2\eta} = \frac{\chi^2}{2\eta} \qquad (1)$$

where μ is the chemical potential (negative of the electronegativity, χ), a Lagrange multiplier associated with the normalization of density, defined as in eq (2)(Parr, Donnelly, Levy & Palke, 1978). To save the computational time, chemical potential and chemical hardness have been calculated using Koopmans' theorem (Koopmans, 1933) as

$$\mu = -\chi = \left(\frac{\partial E}{\partial N}\right)_{v(\mathbf{r})} \approx -\frac{I+A}{2} \approx \frac{E_{HOMO} + E_{LUMO}}{2} \qquad (2)$$

and

η is the hardness given by[24]

$$\eta = \frac{1}{2}\left(\frac{\partial^2 E}{\partial N^2}\right)_{v(\mathbf{r})} = \frac{1}{2}\left(\frac{\partial \mu}{\partial N}\right)_{v(\mathbf{r})} = \frac{I-A}{2}$$
$$= \frac{E_{LUMO} - E_{HOMO}}{2} \qquad (3)$$

In the above definitions for an N-electron system with total energy E and external potential $v(\mathbf{r})$, I and A are respectively the ionization potential and the electron affinity whereas E_{HOMO} and E_{LUMO} are the energies of the highest occupied and lowest unoccupied molecular orbitals respectively.

The local reactivity descriptor, Fukui function is defined as(Yang & Parr)

$$f(\mathbf{r}) = \left(\frac{\partial \rho(\mathbf{r})}{\partial N}\right)_{v(\mathbf{r})} = \left(\frac{\delta \mu}{\delta v(\mathbf{r})}\right)_N \qquad (4)$$

Since the above derivatives are discontinuous, three different types of Fukui functions have been defined (Yang & Mortier, 1986)(Lee, Yang & Parr, 1988).

$$f^+(\mathbf{r}) = \rho_{N+1}(\mathbf{r}) - \rho_N(\mathbf{r}) \qquad (5a)$$
for nucleophilic attack

$$f^-(\mathbf{r}) = \rho_N(\mathbf{r}) - \rho_{N-1}(\mathbf{r}) \qquad (5b)$$
for electrophilic attack

$$f^0(\mathbf{r}) = [\rho_{N+1}(\mathbf{r}) - \rho_{N-1}(\mathbf{r})] / 2 \qquad (5c)$$
for radical attack

Chattaraj et al (2003) have proposed a generalized concept of philicity at a given atomic site *k*. The condensed-to-atom variants of it for the atomic site *k* have been written as

$$\omega_k^a = \omega f_k^a \qquad (6)$$

where α = +, -, and 0 refer to nucleophilic, electrophilic, and radical attacks, respectively. The index ω_k^α varies from atom to atom in a molecule, but the sum of any ω_k^α over all the atoms is conserved.

The condensed philicity summed over a group of relevant atoms is defined as the "group philicity". It is expressed as(Parthasarathi, Padmanabhan, Elango, Subramanian & Chattaraj, 2004)

$$\omega_g^a = \sum_{k=1}^{n} \omega_k^a \qquad (7)$$

where n is the number of atoms coordinated to the reactive atom, ω_k^α is the local philicity of the atom, ω_g^α is the group philicity obtained by adding the local philicity of the nearby bonded atoms, and α = +, -, and 0 refer to nucleophilic, electrophilic, and radical attacks, respectively.

The net electrophilicity ($\Delta\omega^\pm$)(electrophilicity of a system relative to its own nucleophilicity), a new dual descriptor proposed recently by Chattaraj et al (2009) is a measure of the electron accepting power relative to the electron donating power of a given species and has been proven to be a better descriptor in explaining the electrophilic power of any species.

The mathematical genesis of net electrophilicity ($\Delta\omega^\pm$) stems from an earlier idea of the concept of the electroaccepting (ω^+) and electrodonating (ω^-) powers enunciated by Gazquez and co-workers (Gazquez, Cedillo & Vella, 2007). Gazquez et al have defined the latter quantities as follows:

$$\omega^+ = \frac{A^2}{2(I-A)} \qquad (8a)$$

$$\omega^- = \frac{I^2}{2(I-A)} \qquad (8b)$$

They have also described ω^+ and ω^- in an alternative manner[56] as:

$$\omega^+ = \frac{(I+3A)^2}{16(I-A)} \qquad (8c)$$

$$\omega^- = \frac{(3I+A)^2}{16(I-A)} \qquad (8d)$$

Accordingly, Chattaraj et al proposed the following definition of the net electrophilicity:

$$\Delta\omega^\pm = \omega^+ - (-\omega^-) = \omega^+ + \omega^- \qquad (9)$$

Thus, two possible values of net electrophilicity ($\Delta\omega^\pm$) based on equations 8a – 8d are possible and the same have been utilized to build effective regression equations for the inorganic halogen and sulfur containing molecules and aromatic chlorinated compounds.

The global interactions between the constituents A and B are determined by the parameter ΔN (charge transfer), which represents the fractional number of electrons, transferred from system A to the system B, and is represented by (Parr & Pearson, 1983):

$$\Delta N = \frac{\mu_A - \mu_B}{2(\eta_A + \eta_B)} \qquad (10)$$

where μ_A, μ_B and η_A, η_B are the chemical potentials and chemical hardnesses of systems A and B respectively.

METHODS FOR DATA ANALYSIS

The quantitative structure-activity relationships (QSARs) are developed (Mathlab, 1999) using least square error estimation method (Penrose, 1995). Initially, linear/multi-linear regression analyses are performed using experimental toxicity as a dependent variable and various combinations of the selected descriptors as independent variables. Internal validations of the model have been performed using cross-validation(Chatterjee, Price & Hadi, 1999)(Lucic & Trinajstic, 1999) and all the systems are assessed with the coefficients of determination (R) and the variance adjusted for degrees of freedom (R^2_{adj}). The predictivity of the regression models is assessed by the leave-one-out cross-validation coefficient of determination (R^2_{CV}) which is given by

$$R^2_{CV} = 1 - \frac{\sum_i (Y_i^{pred} - Y_i^{obs})^2}{\sum_i (Y_i^{pred} - Y^{mean})^2} \qquad (11)$$

where Y_i^{obs}, Y_i^{pred} and Y_i^{mean} are observed, predicted and the observed mean values of the dependent variables respectively.

Computational Details

Geometries of all of the 174 aromatic molecules considered in the first set are minimized at the Hartree-Fock (HF) level of theory with the 6-31 G(d) basis set with the aid of the Gaussian 98 program package (Frisch et al, 1998). The geometries of the selected 19 CPs of the second set of compounds are optimized using Becke's three parameter hybrid density functional, B3LYP/6-31G (d)(Becke, 1998)(Lee, Yang & Parr, 1988) (Hariharan & Pople, 1973). All the geometries of the compounds in two sets are characterized by harmonic vibrational frequencies which confirmed

that the structures obtained are minima on the potential energy surface as they are associated with zero NIMAG (number of imaginary frequencies) values. Electrophilicity and local philicity values are obtained using the standard working equations as explained in previous studies(Parthasarathi, Padmanabhan, Subramanian, Maiti & Chattaraj, 2003)(Padmanabhan, Parthasarathi, Subramanian & Chattaraj, 2006).

In one of the previous studies (Roy, Parthasarathi, Subramanian & Chattaraj, 2006) for the first set of compounds, local parameters were considered for their potential to act as possible descriptor for ecotoxcity determination. However, in the present study, only the global parameters are considered for investigating the potential of global descriptors in describing the toxicity of chosen set of compounds. For the second set of compounds, Hirshfeld population scheme (Stockholder partitioning scheme)(Hirshfeld, 1977) has been used to calculate the Fukui function values as implemented in the DMOL[3] package[1] and as also described in our previous study(Padmanabhan, Parthasarathi, Subramanian & Chattaraj, 2006). In all cases, the optimized structure of N electronic system has been used for the calculation of (N+1) or (N-1) electronic system. To simplify the analysis, selected compounds in the first set are classified as either of electron donating or of accepting nature, based on the information obtained, by calculating the charge transfer between them and the nucleic acid bases (adenine, thymine, guanine, cytosine and uracil)(Dimitrov, Mekenyan, Sinks & Schultz, 2003). Similarly, the second set of compounds containing chlorophenol, is found to act as electron acceptor, based on the previous study on the calculation of the charge transfer (Roy, Parthasarathi, Subramanian & Chattaraj, 2006).

Results and Discussion

The first set of 174 aromatic compounds have been segregated as 97 electron donors and 77 electron acceptors based on their charge transfer

Table 1. Regression models, coefficient of determinations and the standard deviations with the various combinations of N_{NH}, ω and E_{HF} for the complete set of aromatic donor compounds in the Hartree-Fock level of calculations

Regression Model	R^2_{CV}	R^2	R^2_{adj}
$Log(IGC_{50})^{-1} = 0.4749 \times \omega - 0.1377 \times N_{NH} + 1.0872$	0.126	0.164	0.156
$Log(IGC_{50})^{-1} = -0.0005 \times E + 0.1906 \times N_{NH} - 0.7078$	0.742	0.754	0.752
$Log(IGC_{50})^{-1} = 0.0200 \times \omega - 0.00005 \times E - 0.0136 \times N_{NH} - 0.4953$	0.754	0.765	0.763

ability towards various nucleic acid bases (Roy, Parthasarathi, Subramanian & Chattaraj, 2006). Quantitative-structure-toxicity-relationship models have been developed against *T. pyriformis* for electron donor aromatic phenol compounds and electron acceptor nitrobenzene and benzonitrile compounds. In an earlier work, a similar study was conducted with electrophilicity index and philicity as the descriptors(Roy, Parthasarathi, Subramanian & Chattaraj, 2006). However, in the present study, the role of other descriptors such as electrophilicity index, energy of the molecule and atom counting has been explored to know their capability as possible descriptors in the prediction of toxicity against *T. pyriformis*. The role of atom counting descriptor in analyzing the toxicity level is well established (Giri, Roy, Bultinck, Subramanian & Chattaraj, 2008) (Chattaraj et al, 2007)(Roy et al, 2007). Further this descriptor is very inexpensive and fast since it requires no computation.

Regression models have been developed for both the electron donor aromatic compounds and electron accepting aromatic compounds using partial least square error estimation method to correlate selected descriptors with toxicity values.

Electron donor aromatic compounds, consisting mainly of phenols in the first set of molecules, are initially explored for their toxicity determination against *T. pyriformis*. Regression models developed are shown in Table 1. The two parameters consisting of electrophilicity index and atom counting index (N_{NH}) do not yield good results ($R^2_{CV} = 0.126$), whereas, the same with energy

(ground state Hartree-Fock) of the individual molecule and atom counting descriptor, show reasonably good statistical results ($R^2_{CV} = 0.742$) clearly highlighting the major role of energy and atom counting indices. However, on incorporating these three indices in one regression model, better results are obtained ($R^2_{CV} = 0.754$). This again substantiates the reasoning, that the descriptors, consisting of ground state energy of the molecule as obtained with quantum chemical calculation carried out at the Hartree-Fock level and atom counting are major contributors in the determination of toxicity levels of aromatic electron donor molecules. Since, calculation of atom counting index and energy of the individual molecule requires less time consumption in comparison to electrophilicity index, the regression equation as obtained with these two descriptors seems to be a good model. However, we have utilized three parameter model containing electrophilicity index, atom counting index and energy of the molecule in plotting the graph (Figure 1a and Figure 1b) on account of its being having better R^2_{CV} value. A statistical histogram plot for each type of aromatic groups showing the predicting ability of the toxicity values by the conceptual DFT based electrophilicity index along with atom counting index and the Hartree-Fock energy is reported in Figure 1b. It is interesting to note from Figures 1a, 1b and also from Table 2, that among the 97 aromatic compounds, the best matching experimental and calculated results are obtained in case of chlorophenols and its derivatives.

Figure 1. a) Calculated versus Experimental Log (IGC$_{50}$)$^{-1}$ values and the b) histogram representation of the same of all the electron donor compounds taken together

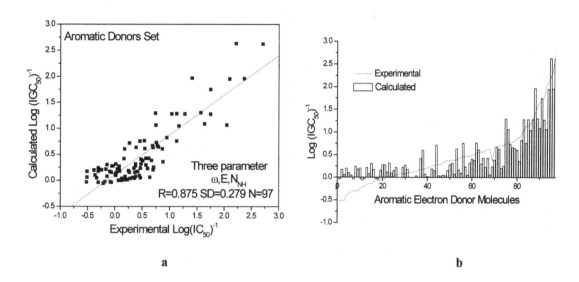

a
b

Among the electron-acceptor aromatic compounds considered in the first set of compounds, various regression models have been developed as shown in Table 3. It can be seen that two parameter model containing the indices like atom counting and energy of the molecule gives better result (R^2_{CV} = 0.760) in comparison to two parameter model containing atom counting index and electrophilicity index (R^2_{CV} = 0.516), highlighting again the major role played by atom counting and energy parameter in comparison to electrophilicity index in the prediction of toxicity levels. On consideration of all of the above three parameters together, regression equation so obtained, shows marginal improvement with R^2_{CV} value of 0.797. Like in case of electron donor aromatic compounds, here also it is found that good results can be obtained with computationally less expensive Hartree-Fock energy index and atom counting index which does not require much computational resources. However, in the present study, QSAR model has been developed for three parameters consisting of electrophilicity index, atom counting index and Hartree-Fock energy descriptor on account of its having better

statistical result. The plot between experimental and calculated toxicity value is shown in Figure 2a and its statistical histogram is shown in Figure 2b. As is observed in case of electron donor aromatic compounds, here also, it is found that chlorine containing nitrobenzene and its various chloro derivatives have very close experimental and calculated values (Table 4). Thus, it is seen that chlorine containing aromatic compounds act as better sets of model molecules for their ecotoxicity investigation.

It is, therefore, seen in the present investigation of the first set of aromatic compounds, containing electron donor and electron acceptor molecules that the index like atom counting and Hartree-Fock energy of the molecule act as good descriptors in describing the toxicity values. However, better QSAR results are obtained with incorporation of electrophilicity index along with the above two descriptors. In order to ascertain the usefulness of our present proposed QSAR model, we compare our present results with previously reported results[37]. On comparison, it is found, that the three parameter QSAR model proposed by us containing electrophilicity index, Hartree-Fock

Table 2. Experimental and calculated values of Log (IGC$_{50}$)$^{-1}$ for the complete set of aromatic electron donor compounds with Tetrahymena pyriformis

| No. | Molecules | Log(IGC$_{50}$)$^{-1}$ | | No. | Molecules | Log(IGC$_{50}$)$^{-1}$ | |
		Exp.[a]	Calc.[b]			Exp.[a]	Calc.[b]
1	3-Aminophenol	-0.52	-0.036	50	3-Methoxysalicylaldehyde	0.38	0.277
2	Salicylic acid	-0.51	0.169	51	Salicylhydroxamic acid	0.38	0.31
3	2-Methoxyphenol	-0.51	0.058	52	3-Fluorophenol	0.38	0.071
4	3-Hydroxyacetophenone	-0.38	0.195	53	2-Chloro-5-methylphenol	0.39	0.632
5	2-Ethoxyphenol	-0.36	0.099	54	Salicylaldehyde	0.42	0.168
6	3-Methoxyphenol	-0.33	0.044	55	5-Amino-2-methoxyphenol	0.45	0.09
7	2-Methylphenol	-0.30	-0.040	56	2,3-Dinitrophenol	0.46	0.753
8	3-Ethoxy-4-methoxyphenol	-0.30	0.235	57	2,6-Difluorophenol	0.47	0.232
9	4-Hydroxyacetophenone	-0.30	0.175	58	4-Isopropylphenol	0.47	0.048
10	Salicylamide	-0.24	0.200	59	Ethyl-3-hydroxybenzoate	0.48	0.313
11	Phenol	-0.21	-0.059	60	2-Amino-4-nitrophenol	0.48	0.404
12	4-Cresol	-0.18	-0.026	61	3-Nitrophenol	0.51	0.375
13	3-Acetamidophenol	-0.16	0.21	62	2,6-Dinitrophenol	0.54	0.762
14	4-Methoxyphenol	-0.14	0.076	63	4-Chlorophenol	0.55	0.611
15	Isovanillin	-0.14	0.3	64	Ethyl-4-hydroxybenzoate	0.57	0.294
16	3,5-Dimethoxyphenol	-0.09	0.168	65	4-Methyl-2-nitrophenol	0.57	0.42
17	4-Aminophenol	-0.08	-0.031	66	2,4-Difluorophenol	0.6	0.223
18	3-Methylphenol	-0.06	-0.039	67	α,α,α-Trifluoro-4-cresol	0.62	0.422
19	3-cyanophenol	-0.06	0.151	68	4-Propylphenol	0.64	0.057
20	Methyl-3-hydroxybenzoate	-0.05	0.274	69	4-Nitrosophenol	0.35	0.232
21	3-methoxy-4-hydroxybenzaldehyde	-0.03	0.273	70	2-Nitrophenol	0.67	0.382
22	4-Ethoxyphenol	0.01	0.116	71	2-Chloro-4,5-dimethylphenol	0.69	0.666
23	3-ethoxy-4-hydroxybenzaldehyde	0.02	0.312	72	4-Chloro-2-methylphenol	0.7	0.628
24	4-Fluorophenol	0.02	0.093	73	4-Butoxyphenol	0.7	0.199
25	2-cyanophenol	0.03	0.146	74	2-Hydroxy-4,5-dimethylacetophenone	0.71	0.25
26	4-hydroxypropiophenone	0.05	0.215	75	2,6-Dichlorophenol	0.74	1.291
27	2,4-dimethylphenol	0.07	-0.003	76	2-Chloromethyl-4-nitrophenol	0.75	1.061
28	2,5-dimethylphenol	0.08	-7E-04	77	3-Chloro-5-methoxyphenol	0.76	0.726
29	2-hydroxyacetophenone	0.08	0.22	78	2-Amino-4-chlorophenol	0.78	0.66
30	Methyl-4-hydroxybenzoate	0.08	0.268	79	4-Chloro-3-methylphenol	0.8	0.64
31	3-Hydroxybenzaldehyde	0.09	0.173	80	3-Chlorophenol	0.87	0.605
32	3,5-Dimethylphenol	0.11	0.002	81	4-Amino-2-nitrophenol	0.88	0.352
33	3,4-Dimethylphenol	0.12	-0.004	82	2,5-Dinitrophenol	0.95	0.822
34	2,3-Dimethylphenol	0.12	0.003	83	2,4-Dichlorophenol	1.04	1.275
35	2,4-Diaminophenol	0.13	0.033	84	3-Chloro-4-fluorophenol	1.13	0.757
36	2-Ethylphenol	0.16	0.005	85	2,5-Dichlorophenol	1.13	1.281
37	Syringaldehyde	0.17	0.414	86	2-Amino-4-chloro-5-nitrophenol	1.17	1.044

continued on following page

Table 2. Continued

		Log(IGC₅₀)⁻¹				Log(IGC₅₀)⁻¹	
		$Log(IGC_{50})^{-1}$				$Log(IGC_{50})^{-1}$	
38	2-chlorophenol	0.18	0.603	87	2,3-Dichlorophenol	1.28	1.276
39	2-Fluorophenol	0.19	0.072	88	2,4,6-Trichlorophenol	1.41	1.966
40	4-Ethylphenol	0.21	0.016	89	3,5-Dichlorophenol	1.57	1.298
41	3-Ethylphenol	0.23	0.008	90	4-Chloro-6-nitromcresol	1.64	1.085
42	Salicylaldoxime	0.25	0.183	91	2,4-Chloro-6-nitrophenol	1.75	1.746
43	4-hydroxybenzaldehyde	0.27	0.151	92	3,4-Dichlorophenol	1.75	1.272
44	3,4-Dinitrophenol	0.27	0.715	93	4-Chloro-2-nitrophenol	2.05	1.062
45	2,3,6-Trimethylphenol	0.28	0.036	94	2,4,5-Trichlorophenol	2.10	1.949
46	2,4,6-Trimethylphenol	0.28	0.031	95	2,3,5,6-Tetrachlorophenol	2.22	2.631
47	2-Allylphenol	0.33	0.051	96	2,3,5-Trichlorophenol	2.37	1.957
48	2,3,5-Trimethylphenol	0.36	0.037	97	2,3,4,5-Tetrachlorophenol	2.71	2.619
49	2-Amino-4-*tert*-butylphenol	0.37	0.152				

[a] Experimental toxicity values obtained from Ref. 32, 33. [b] Calculated toxicity values with ω, E and N_{NH} parameters.

Table 3. Regression models, coefficient of determinations and the standard deviations with the various combinations of N_{NH}, ω and E_{HF} for the complete set of aromatic acceptor compounds in the Hartree-Fock level of calculations

Regression Model	R^2	R^2_{cv}	R^2_{adj}
Log $(IGC_{50})^{-1} = 0.2932 \times ω + 0.3064 \times N_{NH} - 3.3329$	0.541	0.516	0.535
Log $(IGC_{50})^{-1} = 0.2932 \times E + 0.3064 \times N_{NH} - 3.3329$	0.771	0.760	0.768
Log $(IGC_{50})^{-1} = 0.5176 \times ω - 0.00004 \times E + 0.0680 \times N_{NH} - 1.8687$	0.807	0.797	0.805

Figure 2. a) Calculated versus Experimental Log (IGC₅₀)⁻¹ values and the b) histogram representation of the same of all the electron acceptor compounds taken together

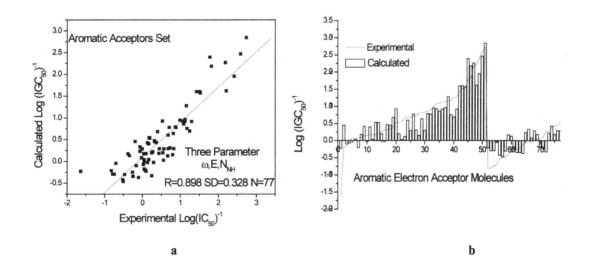

a   b

Table 4. Experimental and calculated values of Log (IGC₅₀)⁻¹ for the complete set of aromatic acceptor compounds with Tetrahymena pyriformis

No.	Molecules	Exp.[a]	Calc.[b]	No.	Molecules	Exp.[a]	Calc.[b]
		$Log(IGC_{50})^{-1}$				$Log(IGC_{50})^{-1}$	
1	*2-Nitrobenzoic acid*	-1.64	-0.229	40	1,2-Dinitrobenzene	1.25	0.693
2	3-Nitrobenzamide	-0.19	0.455	41	1,4-Dinitrobenzene	1.3	0.917
3	2-Nitrobenzyl alcohol	-0.16	-0.1	42	2,4,6-Trichloronitrobenzene	1.43	1.598
4	3-Nitroaniline	0.03	-0.069	43	2,3,4-Trichloronitrobenzene	1.51	1.598
5	2-Nitrotoluene	0.05	-0.005	44	2,4,5-Trichloronitrobenzene	1.53	1.571
6	3-Nitrotoluene	0.05	0.033	45	2,3,4,5-Tetrachloronitrobenzene	1.78	2.394
7	2-Nitroaniline	0.08	-0.202	46	2,3,5,6-Tetrachloronitrobenzene	1.82	2.183
8	4-Nitrobenzyl alcohol	0.1	0.177	47	2,4,6-Trichloro-1,3-dinitrobenzene	2.19	2.263
9	3-Nitrobenzaldehyde	0.14	0.422	48	1,2-Dinitro-4,5-dichlorobenzene	2.21	1.616
10	Nitrobenzene	0.14	-0.027	49	4,6-Dichloro-1,2-dinitrobenzene	2.42	1.952
11	2-Nitrobenzaldehyde	0.17	0.401	50	2,4,5-Trichloro-1,3-dinitrobenzene	2.59	2.467
12	4-Nitrotoluene	0.17	0.039	51	2,3,5,6-Tetrachloro-1,4-dinitrobenzene	2.74	2.842
13	4-Nitrobenzamide	0.18	0.538	52	4-Cyanopyridine	-0.82	-0.214
14	4-Nitrobenzaldehyde	0.2	0.531	53	2-Cyanopyridine	-0.79	-0.294
15	4-Fluoronitrobenzene	0.25	0.194	54	3-Cyanopyridine	-0.74	-0.296
16	1,3-Dimethyl-2-nitrobenzene	0.3	-0.026	55	3-Cyano-4,6-dimethyl-2-hydroxypyridine	-0.7	-0.048
17	3-Nitroacetophenone	0.32	0.468	56	Benzonitrile	-0.52	-0.426
18	5-Hydroxy-2nitrobenzaldehyde	0.33	0.451	57	2-Aminobenzonitrile	-0.5	-0.464
19	Methyl-4-nitrobenzoate	0.4	0.68	58	3-Aminobenzonitrile	-0.47	-0.304
20	3,5-Dinitrobenzyl alcohol	0.53	0.926	59	4-Cyanobenzamide	-0.38	0.17
21	4-Nitroanisole	0.54	0.194	60	1,2-Dicyanobenzene	-0.34	0.128
22	2,3-Dimethylnitrobenzene	0.56	0.025	61	4-Fluorobenzonitrile	-0.26	-0.249
23	3-Nitroanisole	0.67	0.122	62	3-Tolunitrile	-0.25	-0.346
24	2-Chloro-6-nitrotoluene	0.68	0.601	63	2-Tolunitrile	-0.24	-0.348
25	2-Chloronitrobenzene	0.68	0.289	64	4-Tolunitrile	-0.1	-0.373
26	Ethyl-4-nitrobenzoate	0.71	0.779	65	3-Chlorobenzonitrile	-0.06	0.23
27	3-Chloronitrobenzene	0.73	0.305	66	Methyl-4-cyanobenzoate	-0.06	0.33
28	4-Ethylnitrobenene	0.8	0.147	67	3-Cyanobenzaldehyde	-0.02	0.077
29	4-Chloro-2-nitrotoluene	0.82	0.638	68	4-Chlorobenzonitrile	0	0.286
30	4-Nitrophenetole	0.83	0.29	69	4-Cyanobenzaldehyde	0.04	0.175
31	6-Methyl-1,3-dinitrobenzene	0.87	0.79	70	3-Methoxybenzonitrile	0.05	-0.177
32	1,3-Dinitrobenzene	0.89	0.775	71	4-Methoxybenzonitrile	0.1	-0.226
33	2,4-Dichloronitrobenzene	0.99	0.949	72	4-Amimobenzonitrile	0.25	-0.33
34	2,3-Dichloronitrobenzene	1.07	0.926	73	2-Chlorobenzonitrile	0.28	0.218
35	3,4-Dinitrobenzyl alcohol	1.09	0.859	74	Ethyl-4-cyanobenzoate	0.37	0.429
36	2,5-Dichloronitrobenzene	1.13	0.925	75	2-Amino-5-chlorobenzonitrile	0.44	0.179
37	3,5-Dichloronitrobenzene	1.13	0.961	76	3-Nitrobenzonitrile	0.45	0.287
38	3,4-Dichloronitrobenzene	1.16	1.275	77	4-Nitrobenzonitrile	0.57	0.285
39	4-Nitrobenzyl chloride	1.18	0.754				

[a] Experimental toxicity values obtained from Ref. 32, 33. [b] Calculated toxicity values

energy index and atom counting index (R^2_{CV} = 0.797) describes marginally better results in comparison to earlier reported results for electrophilicity and philicity indices (R^2_{CV} = 0.795)[37].

In the second part of our work, a set of eighteen compounds of chlorophenols is studied against *Daphnia magna*, *Brachydanio rerio* and *Bacillus* respectively. Along with these 18 chlorophenol compounds, one compound named 2,3,4,6-tetrachlorophenol (2,3,4,6-TTP), whose experimental toxicity value is unknown, has been also considered and its experimental toxicity value has been predicted. The optimized structures of various CPs are shown in Figure 3 along with atom numbering. Table 5 depicts the calculated values of chemical potential (μ), chemical hardness (η), electrophilicity index (ω), number of non-hydrogenic atoms (N_{NH}) and group philicities (ω_g^+, ω_g^-) for the series of selected CPs. Group philicity is obtained by adding the local philicity of the relevant atoms, that is, nearby bonded atoms. In the present study, the functional group atoms (-OH) along with their nearby bonded atoms (C_1 atom; Figure 4) are considered and their respective summed local philicities ($\Sigma\omega^+$ and $\Sigma\omega^-$) are taken as group philicities (ω_g^+, ω_g^- with g as C_1OH). It is interesting to note that with an increase in the number of chlorine atoms, the electrophilicity index increases, however, the increase is not that substantial, implying that chlorine atoms do not withdraw electrons drastically more towards it from the phenolic system, nor do they contribute electrons more towards phenolic ring as expected because of the resonance effect. The same is also reflected in the group philicity values (Table 5) wherein, there is a marginal increase in group electrophilicity and group nucleophilicity (ω_g^+, ω_g^-) with an increase in the number of chlorine atoms.

In an earlier study, it has been shown that the value of ω depends on the number of chlorine substitution on CPs (Padmanadbhan, Parthasarathi, Subramanian &Chattaraj, 2006). Hence, with the selected CPs, monochlorophenol (MCP) has minimum chemical reactivity and pentachloro-phenol (PCP) has the maximum chemical reactivity. It has also been shown that ω_g^+ and ω_g^- exhibit an increase in their values with an increase in the number of chlorine substitutions. In the present study, a very simple and inexpensive descriptor – atom counting has been selected along with ω, ω_g^+ and ω_g^-.

QSTR ANALYSIS

In the present chapter, QSTR studies are carried out for analyzing the toxicity of CPs on three selected species, viz. *D.magna, B.rerio and Bacillus*. We discuss them individually.

CP vs. D. magna

Various regression models having different indices are proposed for the toxicity prediction of CPs against *D. magna* (Table 6). They have been obtained using experimental toxicity Log $(EC_{50})^{-1}$ (Devillers &Chambon, 1986) against *D. magna* as a dependent variable and various combinations of the selected descriptors as independent variables as carried out on selected set of 18 CPs. It is observed that the best regression model obtained is with electrophilicity index (ω), atom counting (N_{NH}) and group electrophilicity descriptors (ω_g^+) (R^2 = 0.901; R^2_{CV} = 0.872). Calculated toxicity values of 18 set of CPs are shown in Table 7. The plot between observed Log $(EC_{50})^{-1}$ and calculated Log $(EC_{50})^{-1}$ value for CPs against *D. magna* (Figure 4a) shows a correlation coefficient of 0.949. Utilizing the above three parameter model, Log $(EC_{50})^{-1}$ toxicity level of 2,3,4,6-TTP (2,3,4,6-tetrachlorophenol) is predicted to be 2.10 mmol L^{-1}.

CP vs. B. rerio

Linear regression analyses using experimental toxicity Log $(LC_{50})^{-1}$ (Devillers &Chambon, 1986) (Liu, Thomson, Kaiser, 1982) against *B. rerio* as a dependent variable and various combinations of

Figure 3. Optimized structures along with atom numbering for the series of CPs

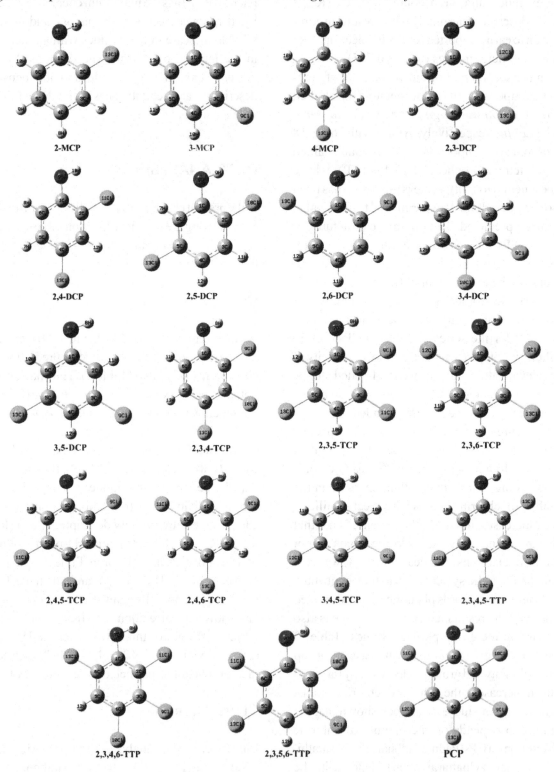

Table 5. Calculated conceptual Density Functional Reactivity Descriptors (in a.u.) for the series of CPs from the B3LYP/6-31G(d) method

Molecule	Number of non-hydrogenic atoms	Chemical Potential	Chemical Hardness	Electrophilicity index	Group Philicity	
	(N_{NH})	(μ)	(η)	(ω)	$\omega_g^+ (C_1OH)$	$\omega_g^- (C_1OH)$
2-MCP	8	-0.1213	0.1083	0.0679	0.0084	0.0183
3-MCP	8	-0.1223	0.1087	0.0688	0.009	0.0174
4-MCP	8	-0.1193	0.1045	0.0680	0.0089	0.0174
2,3-DCP	9	-0.1314	0.1068	0.0808	0.0095	0.0207
2,4-DCP	9	-0.1306	0.1028	0.0829	0.0097	0.0200
2,5-DCP	9	-0.1330	0.1063	0.0832	0.0098	0.0175
2,6DCP	9	-0.1317	0.1065	0.0814	0.0090	0.0201
3,4-DCP	9	-0.1293	0.1034	0.0808	0.0099	0.0187
3,5-DCP	9	-0.1352	0.1084	0.0843	0.0104	0.0212
2,3,4-TCP	10	-0.1376	0.1015	0.0932	0.0103	0.0212
2,3,5-TCP	10	-0.1425	0.1057	0.0960	0.0108	0.0203
2,3,6-TCP	10	-0.1396	0.1038	0.0938	0.0099	0.0181
2,4,5-TCP	10	-0.1394	0.1015	0.0957	0.0106	0.0202
2,4,6-TCP	10	-0.1400	0.1013	0.0967	0.0101	0.0220
3,4,5-TCP	10	-0.1387	0.1026	0.0937	0.0109	0.0208
2,3,4,5-TTP	11	-0.1460	0.1005	0.1060	0.0111	0.0220
2,3,4,6-TTP	11	-0.1458	0.0995	0.1068	0.0107	0.0215
2,3,5,6-TTP	11	-0.1484	0.1033	0.1065	0.0104	0.0198
PCP	12	-0.1518	0.0987	0.1167	0.0110	0.0231

the selected descriptors as independent variables are carried out on the selected set of 18 CPs (Table 8). It is observed that atom counting descriptor along with group philicity descriptors (ω_g^+ and ω_g^-) is capable of explaining maximum coefficient of correlation (0.962) in data with a cross-validated squared correlation coefficient R^2_{CV} of 0.910 (Table 8). Experimental Log $(LC_{50})^{-1}$ and Calculated Log $(LC_{50})^{-1}$ toxicity values corresponding to this model are shown in Table 9 and the corresponding plot is shown in Figure 4b. Therefore, this model is utilized in the prediction of Log $(LC_{50})^{-1}$ toxicity level of 2, 3, 4, 6-TTP, which is found to be 2.54 mmol L^{-1}.

CP vs. Bacillus

Table 10 depicts the various regression models of 18 CPs against *Bacillus* as obtained using experimental toxicity Log $(IC_{50})^{-1}$ (Cohen, Gamliel & Katan, 1988)(Devillers & Chambon,1986) as a dependent variable and various combinations of the selected descriptors as independent variables. It is found that the three parameter model consisting of atom counting (N_{NH}), electrophilicity index (ω) and group electrophilicity index (ω_g^+) is the best QSAR model having maximum coefficient of correlation of 0.976 and R^2_{CV} of 0.938. Based on this model, calculated Log $(IC_{50})^{-1}$ toxicity values are obtained as shown in Table 11. The corresponding plot (Figure 4c) shows the experimental Log $(IC_{50})^{-1}$ versus calculated Log $(IC_{50})^{-1}$ toxicity

Figure 4. Plots between experimental and calculated toxicity of CPs against (A) D. magna, (B) B.rerio, and (C) Bacillus

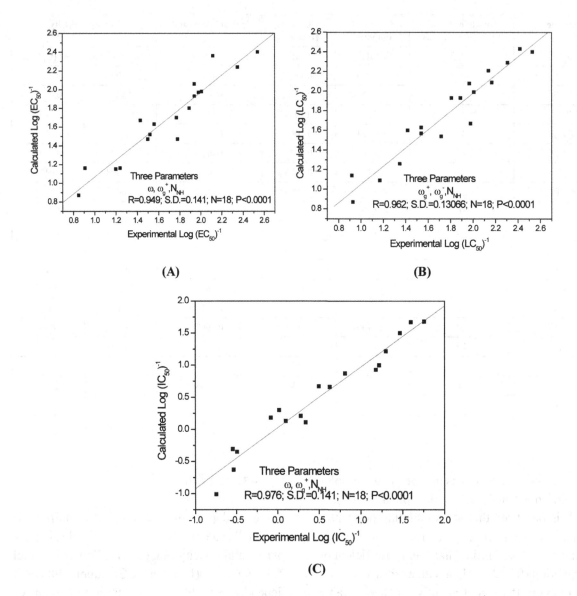

(A)   **(B)**

(C)

Table 6. Regression models for the toxicity [Log(EC$_{50}$)$^{-1}$] against D. magna using various descriptors for a training set of 18 CPs

No.	Regression Equations	R^2	R^2_{CV}	R^2_{adj}
1	$Log(EC_{50})^{-1} = 0.3502 \times N_{NH} - 1.6499$	0.693	0.631	0.674
2	$Log(EC_{50})^{-1} = 35.0540 \times \omega - 0.0832 \times N_{NH} - 0.6195$	0.706	0.645	0.687
3	$Log(EC_{50})^{-1} = 476.3392 \times \omega_g^+ + 0.0597 \times N_{NH} - 3.6298$	0.882	0.851	0.875
4	$Log(EC_{50})^{-1} = 70.5670 \times \omega_g^- + 0.2705 \times N_{NH} - 2.2957$	0.726	0.670	0.709
5	$Log(EC_{50})^{-1} = 454.7832 \times \omega_g^+ + 35.8766 \times \omega_g^- + 0.0324 \times N_{NH} - 3.8686$	0.891	0.860	0.883
6	$Log(EC_{50})^{-1} = 24.9910 \times \omega^+ + 64.8970 \times \omega_g^- - 0.0320 \times N_{NH} - 1.5092$	0.733	0.675	0.715
7	$Log(EC_{50})^{-1} = -52.46209 \times \omega + 569.2882 \times \omega_g^+ + 0.6516 \times N_{NH} - 5.5583$	0.901	0.872	0.895

Table 7. Experimental and calculated values of toxicity [Log (EC_{50})$^{-1}$] against D. magna for the model constructed using the data set of 18 CPs

Molecule	Log (EC_{50})$^{-1}$ value (mmol/L)		
	Experimental[a]	Calculated[b]	Residual[c]
2-MCP	0.85	0.87	-0.02
3-MCP	0.91	1.16	-0.25
4-MCP	1.20	1.15	0.05
2,3-DCP	1.50	1.47	0.03
2,4-DCP	1.78	1.47	0.31
2,5-DCP	1.52	1.52	0
2,6DCP	1.24	1.16	0.08
3,4-DCP	1.77	1.7	0.07
3,5-DCP	1.89	1.8	0.09
2,3,4-TCP	1.94	1.93	0.01
2,3,5-TCP	1.94	2.06	-0.12
2,3,6-TCP	1.43	1.67	-0.24
2,4,5-TCP	1.98	1.97	0.01
2,4,6-TCP	1.56	1.63	-0.07
3,4,5-TCP	2.35	2.24	0.11
2,3,4,5-TTP	2.12	2.36	-0.24
2,3,4,6-TTP		2.10[d]	0
2,3,5,6-TTP	2.01	1.98	0.03
PCP	2.54	2.4	0.14

[a]Experimental data as obtained from refs. 43. [b]With ω, ω_g^+ and N_{NH} as descriptors. [c] Difference between experimental and calculated toxicity values. [d] Predicted value using the developed model.

Table 8. Regression models for the toxicity [Log(LC_{50})$^{-1}$] against B. rerio using various descriptors for a training set of 18 CPs

No.	Regression Equations	R^2	R^2_{cv}	R^2_{adj}
1	Log(LC_{50})$^{-1}$ = 0.3567 × N_{NH} − 1.6405	0.659	0.576	0.639
2	Log(LC_{50})$^{-1}$ = 66.8590 × ω − 0.4698 × N_{NH} + 0.3248	0.699	0.628	0.680
3	Log(LC_{50})$^{-1}$ = 569.9761 × ω_g^+ + 0.0091 × N_{NH}	0.908	0.886	0.902
4	Log(LC_{50})$^{-1}$ = 98.1110 × ω_g^- + 0.2460 × N_{NH}	0.717	0.652	0.700
5	Log(LC_{50})$^{-1}$ = − 28.5360 × ω + 620.5343 × ω_g^+ + 0.3311 × N_{NH} − 5.0586	0.912	0.892	0.907
6	Log(LC_{50})$^{-1}$ = 53.5280 × ω + 85.9670 × ω_g^- − 0.4020 × N_{NH} − 0.8538	0.741	0.684	0.726
7	Log(LC_{50})$^{-1}$ = 535.5727 × ω_g^+ + 57.2588 × ω_g^- − 0.0345 × N_{NH} − 4.3907	0.925	0.910	0.922

Table 9. Experimental and Calculated Values of Toxicity [Log (LC$_{50}$)$^{-1}$] against B. rerio for the model constructed using the data set of 18 CPs

Molecule	Log (LC$_{50}$)$^{-1}$ value (mmol/L)		
	Experimental[a]	Calculated[b]	Residual[c]
2-MCP	0.93	0.87	0.06
3-MCP	0.92	1.14	-0.22
4-MCP	1.17	1.09	0.08
2,3-DCP	1.54	1.57	-0.03
2,4-DCP	1.54	1.63	-0.09
2,5-DCP	1.72	1.54	0.18
2,6-DCP	1.35	1.26	0.09
3,4-DCP	1.98	1.67	0.31
3,5-DCP	1.97	2.08	-0.11
2,3,4-TCP	2.01	1.99	0.02
2,3,5-TCP	2.14	2.21	-0.07
2,3,6-TCP	1.42	1.60	-0.18
2,4,5-TCP	2.17	2.09	0.08
2,4,6-TCP	1.89	1.93	-0.04
3,4,5-TCP	2.31	2.29	0.02
2,3,4,5-TTP	2.42	2.43	-0.01
2,3,4,6-TTP		2.54[d]	-
2,3,5,6-TTP	1.81	1.93	-0.12
PCP	2.53	2.40	0.13

[a]Experimental data as obtained from refs. 43 and 44. [b]With ω_g^+, ω_g^- and N$_{NH}$ descriptors. [c] Difference between experimental and calculated toxicity values. [d] Predicted value using the developed model.

Table 10. Regression models for the toxicity [LogIC$_{50}$)$^{-1}$] against Bacillus using various descriptors for a training set of 18 CPs

No.	Regression Equations	R^2	R$^2_{CV}$	R$^2_{adj}$
1	Log(IC$_{50}$)$^{-1}$= 0.5524 × N$_{NH}$ − 4.7884	0.572	0.471	0.544
2	Log(IC$_{50}$)$^{-1}$ = 71.2320 × ω − 0.3282 × N$_{NH}$ − 2.6945	0.587	0.500	0.561
3	Log(IC$_{50}$)$^{-1}$ = 1109.8777 × ω$_g^+$ − 0.1243 × N$_{NH}$ − 9.4016	0.910	0.885	0.903
4	Log(IC$_{50}$)$^{-1}$= 105.8385 × ω$_g^-$ + 0.43303 × N$_{NH}$ − 5.7570	0.594	0.501	0.570
5	Log(IC$_{50}$)$^{-1}$= 1096.5413 × ω$_g^+$ + 22.1961 × ω$_g^-$ − 0.1412 × N$_{NH}$ − 9.5493	0.910	0.887	0.905
6	Log(IC$_{50}$)$^{-1}$ = 56.8190 × ω + 92.9470 × ω$_g^-$ − 0.2548 × N$_{NH}$ − 3.9688	0.605	0.520	0.580
7	Log(IC$_{50}$)$^{-1}$ = −136.5925 × ω + 1351.8836× ω$_g^+$ + 1.4167 × N$_{NH}$ − 14.4227	0.953	0.938	0.949

Table 11. Experimental and Calculated Values of Toxicity [Log (IC$_{50}$)$^{-1}$] against Bacillus for the model constructed using the data set of 18 CPs

Molecule	Log (IC$_{50}$)$^{-1}$ value (mmol/L)		
	Experimental[a]	Calculated[b]	Residual[c]
2-MCP	-0.74	-1.01	0.27
3-MCP	-0.54	-0.31	-0.22
4-MCP	-0.49	-0.35	-0.13
2,3-DCP	0.1	0.13	-0.03
2,4-DCP	0.34	0.11	0.23
2,5-DCP	0.28	0.21	0.07
2,6-DCP	-0.53	-0.63	0.10
3,4-DCP	0.5	0.67	-0.17
3,5-DCP	0.81	0.87	-0.06
2,3,4-TCP	1.18	0.93	0.25
2,3,5-TCP	1.3	1.22	0.08
2,3,6-TCP	0.02	0.30	-0.28
2,4,5-TCP	1.22	1.00	0.22
2,4,6-TCP	-0.08	0.18	-0.26
3,4,5-TCP	1.6	1.67	-0.07
2,3,4,5-TTP	1.76	1.68	0.08
2,3,4,6-TTP		1.04[d]	-
2,3,5,6-TTP	0.63	0.66	-0.03
PCP	1.47	1.50	-0.03

[a]Experimental data as obtained from refs. 45 and 46. [b]With ω, ω_g^+ and N$_{NH}$ as descriptors. [c]Difference between experimental and calculated toxicity values. [d]Predicted value using the developed model.

values. Based on this model, the predicted value of Log (IC$_{50}$)$^{-1}$ toxicity for 2,3,4,6-TTP is found to be 1.04 mmol L^{-1}.

We now compare the performance of our newly proposed QSAR model with earlier reported ecotoxicity study of 18 CPs against *D. magna, B. rerio* and Bacillus (Padmanabhan, Parthasarathi, Subramanian & Chattaraj, 2006). We find that our best proposed three parameter model has maximum coefficient of correlation (R) of 0.949 (R$^2_{CV}$ = 0.872) against *D. magna*, whereas, the earlier reported value for the three parameter model is 0.943 (R$^2_{CV}$ =0.812). Similarly, in case of *B. rerio*, we obtained coefficient of correlation (R) of 0.962 (R$^2_{CV}$ =0.910) for three parameter model, whereas, the earlier reported three parameter model value is 0.963 (R$^2_{CV}$

=0.878). In case of *Bacillus,* the reported three parameter model has coefficient of correlation (R) of 0.959 (R$^2_{CV}$ =0.863), whereas, we report the same to be 0.976 (R$^2_{CV}$ =0.938). It can, therefore, be seen that our newly proposed QSAR model is better than the earlier proposed models. However, it is to be noted carefully, that in the present study, a very simple descriptor, the number of non- hydrogenic atoms (N$_{NH}$) has been utilized as one among the descriptors. By all means, atom counting descriptor is very cheap which does not require any computational resource. Therefore, it can be said, that in comparison to previously reported QSAR models, the presently proposed model is the best, considering it to be, fast and economically cheaper than other models.

CONCLUSION

The utility of net electrophilicity ($\Delta\omega^{\pm}$) as an effective quantum chemical descriptor towards analyzing the structure-toxicity trends for chemical systems is mentioned. A QSAR-based modeling of some aromatic molecules for their ecotoxicity values against various biological species is presented. In the first part of the study, a set of 177 aromatic molecules classified into 97 electron donor and 77 electron acceptor molecules, are studied against *Tetrahymena pyriformis*. It is found that the three parameter QSAR model consisting of electrophilicity index, energy of the molecule and atom counting index is the best-fit protocol for the prediction of toxicity of 177 aromatic molecules. In the second part of the study, 18 chlorophenols are studied against *D. magna, B.rerio* and *Bacillus* wherein, it is found that the best QSAR model is obtained with three parameters consisting of atom counting, group philicity and electrophilicity. The important finding of the study has been in knowing the role of atom counting as a descriptor which is very fast and cheap in comparison to other commonly utilized ones. Thus, it is seen that QSAR modeling of chemical species utilizing conceptual DFT-based descriptors along with atom counting, is a useful technique to correlate physical, chemical, biological, or environmental activities.

ACKNOWLEDGMENT

We thank CSIR, New Delhi for financial support. A.G. thanks Indian Academy of Sciences, Bangalore for Summer Visiting Fellowship, 2009 and A.C. thanks C.T.S, I.I.T. Kharagpur for Visitors' Fellowship.

REFERENCES

Akers, K. S., Sinks, G. D., & Schultz, T. W. (1999). Structure-toxicity relationships for selected halogenated aliphatic chemicals. *Environmental Toxicology and Pharmacology, 7*, 33–39. doi:10.1016/S1382-6689(98)00048-9

Becke, A. D. (1998). Density-functional exchange-energy approximation with correct asymptotic behavior. *Physical Review A., 38*, 3098–3100. doi:10.1103/PhysRevA.38.3098

Chattaraj, P. K. (2009). *Chemical Reactivity Theory: A Density Functional View*. Boca Raton, FL:Taylor & Francis, CRC Press.

Chattaraj, P. K., Chakraborty, A., & Giri, S. (2009). Net electrophilicity. *The Journal of Physical Chemistry A, 113*, 10068. doi:10.1021/jp904674x

Chattaraj, P. K., & Giri, S. (2009). Electrophilicity index within a conceptual DFT framework. *Annu. Rep. Prog. Chem. Sect. C., 105*, 13–39. doi:10.1039/b802832j

Chattaraj, P. K., Maiti, B., & Sarkar, U. (2003). Philicity: A unified treatment of chemical reactivity and selectivity. *The Journal of Physical Chemistry A, 107*, 4973–4975. doi:10.1021/jp034707u

Chattaraj, P. K., Nath, S., & Maiti, B. (2003). Reactivity descriptors. In Tollenaere, J., Bultinck, P., Winter, H. D., & Langenaeker, W. (Eds.), *Computational Medicinal Chemistry for Drug Discovery* (pp. 295–322). New York: Marcel Dekker.

Chattaraj, P. K., & Roy, D. R. (2007). Update 1 of: Electrophilicity index. *Chemical Reviews, 107*, PR46–PR74. doi:10.1021/cr078014b

Chattaraj, P. K., Roy, D. R., Giri, S., Mukherjee, S., Subramanian, V., & Parthasarathi, R. (2007). An atom counting and electrophilicity based QSTR approach. *Journal of Chemical Sciences, 119*, 475–488. doi:10.1007/s12039-007-0061-1

Chattaraj, P. K., Sarkar, U., & Roy, D. R. (2006). Electrophilicity index. *Chemical Reviews, 106*, 2065–2091. doi:10.1021/cr040109f

Chatterjee, S., Price, B., & Hadi, A. S. (1999). *Regression Analysis by Example. Wiley Series in Probability and Statistics* (3rd ed.). New York: John Wiley & Sons.

Chermette, H. (1999). Chemical reactivity indexes in Density Functional Theory. *Journal of Computational Chemistry, 20*, 129–154. doi:10.1002/(SICI)1096-987X(19990115)20:1<129::AID-JCC13>3.0.CO;2-A

Cohen, E., Gamliel, A., & Katan, J. (1988). The fungitoxicity of chlorophenols to the pathogenic fungi.Fusarium oxysporum and Rhizoctonia solani: A structure-activity relationship study. *Pesticide Science, 24*, 139–146. doi:10.1002/ps.2780240205

Cronin, M. T. D., & Schultz, W. (2001). Development of quantitative structure-activity relationships for the toxicity of aromatic compounds to Tetrahymina pyriformis: Comparative assessment of methodologies. *Chemical Research in Toxicology, 14*, 1284–1295. doi:10.1021/tx0155202

Dean-Ross, D., & Rahimi, M. (1995). Toxicity of phenolic compounds to sediment bacteria. *Bulletin of Environmental Contamination and Toxicology, 55*, 245–250. doi:10.1007/BF00203016

Della, G. M., Monaco, P., Pinto, G., Pollio, A., Previtera, L., & Temussi, F. (2001). Phytotoxicity of low-molecular-weight phenols from olive mill wastewaters. *Bulletin of Environmental Contamination and Toxicology, 67*, 352–359. doi:10.1007/s001280132

Devillers, J., & Chambon, P. (1986). Acute toxicity and QSAR of chlorophenols on Daphnia magna. *Bulletin of Environmental Contamination and Toxicology, 37*, 599–605. doi:10.1007/BF01607810

Devillers, J., & Chambon, P. (1986). Toxicité aiguë chlorophénols sur *Daphnia magna* et *Brachydanio rerio. J. Fr. Hydrol., 17*, 111–120. doi:10.1051/water/19861702111

Dimitrov, S. D., Mekenyan, O. G., Sinks, G. D., & Schultz, T. W. (2003). Global modeling of narcotic chemicals: ciliate and fish toxicity. *Journal of Molecular Structure THEOCHEM, 622*, 63–70. doi:10.1016/S0166-1280(02)00618-8

Franke, R. (1984). *Theoretical Drug Design Methods* (p. 115). Amsterdam: Elsevier.

Frisch, M. J., Trucks, G. W., Schlegel, H. B., Scuseria, G. E., Robb, M. A., Cheeseman, J. R., & Zakrzewski, V. G. …Pople, J. A. (1998). *Gaussian 98*, revision A.7. Pittsburg, PA:Gaussian, Inc.

Gao, H., Katzenellenbogen, J. A., Garg, R., & Hansch, C. (1999). Comparative QSAR Analysis of Estrogen Receptor Ligands. *Chemical Reviews, 99*, 723–744. doi:10.1021/cr980018g

Garg, R., Kapur, S., & Hansch, C. (2001). Radical toxicity of phenols: a reference point for obtaining perspective in the formulation of QSAR. *Medicinal Research Reviews, 21*, 73–82. doi:10.1002/1098-1128(200101)21:1<73::AID-MED3>3.0.CO;2-5

Gazquez, J. L., Cedillo, A., & Vela, A. (2007). Electrodonating and electro accepting powers. *The Journal of Physical Chemistry A, 111*, 1966–1970.

Geerlings, P., De Proft, F., & Langenaeker, W. (2003). Conceptual Density Functional Theory. *Chemical Reviews, 103*, 1793–1873. doi:10.1021/cr990029p

Giri, S., Roy, D. R., Bultinck, P., Subramanian, V., & Chattaraj, P. K. (2008). An Atom counting QSPR protocol. *QSAR & Combinatorial Science, 27*, 208–230. doi:10.1002/qsar.200730109

Gupta, A., Chakraborty, A., Giri, S., Subramanian, V., & Chattaraj, P. K. (2010). (in press). Toxicity of halogen, sulfur and chlorinated aromatic compounds: A quantitative-structure-activity-relationship(QSTR). *International Journal of Chemoinformatics and Chemical Engineering.*

Gupta, S. P. (1991). QSAR Studies on Local Anesthetics. *Chemical Reviews, 91,* 1109–1119. doi:10.1021/cr00006a001

Gupta, S. P., Singh, P., & Bindal, M. C. (1983). QSAR Studies on Hallucinogens. *Chemical Reviews, 83,* 633–648. doi:10.1021/cr00058a003

Hansch, C., Hoekman, D., Leo, A., Weininger, D., & Selassie, C. (2002). Chem-Bioinformatics: Comparative QSAR at the Interface between Chemistry and Biology. *Chemical Reviews, 102,* 783–812. doi:10.1021/cr0102009

Hansch, C., Leo, A., & Taft, R. W. (1991). A Survey of Hammett Substituent Constants and Resonance and Field Parameters. *Chemical Reviews, 91,* 165–195. doi:10.1021/cr00002a004

Hansch, C., Maloney, P. P., Fujita, T., & Muir, R. M. (1962). Correlation of Biological Activity of Phenoxyacetic Acids with Hammett Substituent Constants and Partition Coefficients. *Nature, 194,* 178–180. doi:10.1038/194178b0

Hariharan, P. C., & Pople, J. A. (1973). The influence of polarization functions on molecular orbital hydrogenation energies. *Theoretica Chimica Acta, 28,* 213–222. doi:10.1007/BF00533485

Hirshfeld, F. L. (1977). Bonded-atom fragments for describing molecular charge densities. *Theoretica Chimica Acta, 44,* 129–138. doi:10.1007/BF00549096

Karelson, M., Lobanov, V. S., & Katritzky, A. R. (1996). Quantum-Chemical Descriptors in QSAR/QSPR Studies. *Chemical Reviews, 96,* 1027–1043. doi:10.1021/cr950202r

Koopmans, T. A. (1933). Über die Zuordnung von Wellenfunktionen und Eigenwerten zu den Einzelnen Elektronen Eines Atoms. *Physica, 1,* 104. doi:10.1016/S0031-8914(34)90011-2

Leach, A. R., & Gillet, V. J. (2003). *An Introduction to Chemoinformatics.* Dordrecht: Kluwer.

Lee, C., Yang, W., & Parr, R. G. (1988). Local softness and chemical reactivity in the molecules CO, SCN- and H_2CO. *Journal of Molecular Structure THEOCHEM, 163,* 305–313. doi:10.1016/0166-1280(88)80397-X

Lee, C., Yang, W., & Parr, R. G. (1988). Development of the Colle-Salvetti correlation- energy formula into a functional of the electron density. *Physical Review B: Condensed Matter and Materials Physics, 37,* 785–789. doi:10.1103/PhysRevB.37.785

Liu, D., Thomson, K., & Kaiser, K. L. E. (1982). Quantitative structure-toxicity relationship of halogenated phenols on bacteria. *Bulletin of Environmental Contamination and Toxicology, 29,* 130–136. doi:10.1007/BF01606140

Lucic, B., & Trinajstic, N. (1999). Multivariate regression outperforms several robust architectures of neural networks in QSAR modeling. *Journal of Chemical Information and Computer Sciences, 39,* 121–132. doi:10.1021/ci980090f

Maynard, A. T., Huang, M., Rice, W. G., & Covell, D. G. (1998). Reactivity of the HIV-1 nucleocapsid protein p7 zinc finger domains from the perspective of density-functional theory. *Proceedings of the National Academy of Sciences of the United States of America, 95,* 11578–11583. doi:10.1073/pnas.95.20.11578

MATLAB (1999) The Math Works, Inc.:NatickU.S.A.

Padmanabhan, J., Parthasarathi, R., Subramanian, V., & Chattaraj, P. K. (2006). Group philicity and electrophilicity as possible descriptors for modeling ecotoxicity applied to chlorophenols. *Chemical Research in Toxicology, 19*, 356–364. doi:10.1021/tx050322m

Parr, R. G., Donnelly, R. A., Levy, M., & Palke, W. E. (1978). Electronegativity: the density functional viewpoint. *The Journal of Chemical Physics, 68*, 3801–3807. doi:10.1063/1.436185

Parr, R. G., & Pearson, R. G. (1983). Absolute hardness: companion parameter to absolute electronegativity. *Journal of the American Chemical Society, 105*, 7512–7516. doi:10.1021/ja00364a005

Parr, R. G., Szentpaly, L. v., & Liu, S. (1999). Electrophilicity index. *Journal of the American Chemical Society, 121*, 1922–1924. doi:10.1021/ja983494x

Parr, R. G., & Yang, W. (1989). *Density Functional Theory of Atoms and Molecules.* Oxford, UK: Oxford University Press.

Parthasarathi, R., Padmanabhan, J., Elango, M., Subramanian, V., & Chattaraj, P. K. (2004). Intermolecular reactivity through the generalized philicity concept. *Chemical Physics Letters, 394*, 225–230. doi:10.1016/j.cplett.2004.07.002

Parthasarathi, R., Padmanabhan, J., Subramanian, V., Maiti, B., & Chattaraj, P. K. (2003). Chemical reactivity profiles of two selected polychlorinated biphenyls. *The Journal of Physical Chemistry A, 107*, 10346–10352. doi:10.1021/jp035620b

Parthasarathi, R., Padmanabhan, J., Subramanian, V., Sarkar, U., Maiti, B., & Chattaraj, P. K. (2003). Toxicity analysis of benzidine through chemical reactivity and selectivity profiles: A DFT approach. *Internet Electron J. Mol. Des., 2*, 798–813.

Parthasarathi, R., Subramanian, V., Roy, D. R., & Chattaraj, P. K. (2004). Electrophilicity index as a possible descriptor of biological activity. *Bioorganic & Medicinal Chemistry, 12*, 5533–5543. doi:10.1016/j.bmc.2004.08.013

Pearson, R. G. (1997). *Chemical hardness: applications from molecules to solids. Weinheim.* New York: Wiley–VCH.

Penrose, R. (1955). A Generalized inverse for matrices. *Proceedings of the Cambridge Philosophical Society, 51*, 406–413. doi:10.1017/S0305004100030401

Ribo, J. M., & Kaiser, J. L. E. (1983). Effects of selected chemicals to photoluminescent bacteria and their correlations with acute and sublethal effects on other organisms. *Chemosphere, 12*, 1421–1442. doi:10.1016/0045-6535(83)90073-5

Roy, D. R., Giri, S., & Chattaraj, P. K. (2009). Arsenic toxicity: an atom counting and electrophilicity-based protocol. *Molecular Diversity, 13*, 551. doi:10.1007/s11030-009-9133-0

Roy, D. R., Pal, N., Mitra, A., Bultinck, P., Parthasarathi, R., Subramanian, V., & Chattaraj, P. K. (2007). An atom counting strategy towards analyzing the biological activity of sex hormones. *European Journal of Medicinal Chemistry, 42*, 1365–1369. doi:10.1016/j.ejmech.2007.01.028

Roy, D. R., Parthasarathi, R., Maiti, B., Subramanian, V., & Chattaraj, P. K. (2005). Electrophilicity as a possible descriptor of toxicity prediction. *Bioorganic & Medicinal Chemistry, 13*, 3405–3412. doi:10.1016/j.bmc.2005.03.011

Roy, D. R., Parthasarathi, R., Subramanian, V., & Chattaraj, P. K. (2006). An electrophilicity based analysis of toxicity of aromatic compounds towards Tetrahymena Pyriformis. *QSAR & Combinatorial Science, 25*, 114–122. doi:10.1002/qsar.200530146

Roy, D. R., Sarkar, U., Chattaraj, P. K., Mitra, A., Padmanabhan, J., & Parthasarathi, R. (2006). Analyzing toxicity through electrophilicity. *Molecular Diversity, 10*, 119–131. doi:10.1007/s11030-005-9009-x

Schultz, T. W. (1997). *Tetrahymina pyriformis* population growth impairment endpoint: a surrogate for fish lethality. *Toxicology Methods, 7*, 289–309. doi:10.1080/105172397243079

Strotmann, U. J., & Eglsaer, H. (1995). The toxicity of substituted phenols in the nitrification inhibition test and luminescent bacteria test. *Ecotoxicology and Environmental Safety, 30*, 269–273. doi:10.1006/eesa.1995.1030

Verschueren, K. (1996). *Handbook of Environmental Data on Organic Chemicals* (3rd ed.). New York: Van Nostrand Reinhold Company.

Yang, W., & Mortier, W. J. (1986). The use of global and local molecular parameters for the analysis of the gas-phase basicity of amines. *Journal of the American Chemical Society, 108*, 5708–5711. doi:10.1021/ja00279a008

Yang, W., & Parr, R. G. (1984). Density functional approach to the frontier-electron theory of chemical reactivity. *Journal of the American Chemical Society, 106*, 4049–4050. doi:10.1021/ja00326a036

Zeeman, M., Auer, C. M., Clements, R. G., Nabholz, J. V., & Boethling, R. S. (1995). U.S. EPA regulatory perspectives on the use of QSAR for new and existing chemical evaluations. *SAR and QSAR in Environmental Research, 3*, 179–201. doi:10.1080/10629369508234003

ENDNOTE

[1]   DMOL3, Accelrys, Inc., San Diego, California.

Chapter 2
Structural Classification of Complex Molecules by Artificial Intelligence Techniques

Francisco Torrens
Universitat de València, Spain

Gloria Castellano
Universidad Católica de Valencia San Vicente Mártir, Spain

ABSTRACT

Algorithms for classification and taxonomy bases on criteria, e.g., information entropy. The feasibility of replacing a given molecule by similar ones in the composition of a complex drug is studied. Some local anaesthetics currently in use are classified using structural properties. In taxonomy the detailed comparison of the sequences of biomolecules, proteins or nucleic acids, allows the reconstruction of a molecular phylogenetic tree. The method is applied to the classifications of (1) indazolols (against Trichomonas vaginalis), (2) fullerenes and fullerite, (3) living and heat-inactivated lactic acid bacteria against cytokines, (4) phylogenesis of avian birds and 1918 influenza virus, (5) local anaesthetics, (6) transdermal-delivery percutaneous enhancers, (7) quantitative structure–activity relationship of anti-human immunodeficiency virus (HIV) compounds, (8) HIV inhibitors, e.g., thiocarbamates, N-aryloxazolidinone-5-carboxamides and styrylquinolines, (9) antimalarial aryltriazolylhydroxamates, (10) N-aryl-N-(3-aryl-1,2,4-oxadiazol-5-yl) amines against prostate cancer, antimitotic 2-phenylindole-3-carbaldehydes against breast cancer and anti-tubulin agents against gastric cancer with indole ring. The entropy contributions may be studied with the equipartition conjecture. It is not within the scope of our simulation method to replace biological tests of drugs or field data in palaeontology, but such simulation methods can be useful to assert priorities in detailed experimental research. Available experimental and field data should be examined by different classification algorithms to reveal possible features of real biological significance.

DOI: 10.4018/978-1-60960-860-6.ch002

1. INTRODUCTION

Ab initio theoretical calculations, molecular dynamics simulations and docking studies are useful tools for investigating important biological complexes (Da Silva & Carvalho, 2005)(Da Silva, Ponte, Neto & Taft, 2005)(Da Silva, Almeida & Taft, 2004). At least three anti-human immunodeficiency virus type-1 (HIV-1) drugs, for combination therapy, became the standard treatment of acquired immunodeficiency syndrome (AIDS) drugs that have been licensed for clinical use, or are subjected to advanced clinical trials, belong to one of three classes: (1) nucleoside/nucleotide reverse transcriptase inhibitors (NRTIs/NtRTIs) {abacavir (ABC), emitricitabine [(–)FTC], zidovudine (AZT), didanosine (ddI), zalcitabine (ddC), stavudine (d4T), lamivudine (3TC) and tenofovir disoproxil fumarate}, (2) non-nucleoside reverse transcriptase inhibitors (NNRTIs) (emivirine, efavirenz, nevirapine and delavirdine) and (3) protease inhibitors (PIs) (lopinavir, nelfinavir, ritonavir, amprenavir, saquinavir and indinavir) (Da Silva & Taft, 2005) (Da Silva & Taft, 2004)(Arissawa, Taft & Flecman, 2003). Various other events in the HIV replicative cycle can be considered as potential targets for chemotherapeutic intervention: (1) viral entry *via* blockade of viral coreceptors CXCR4 [bicyclam (AMD3100) derivatives] and CCR5 (TAK-799 derivatives), (2) viral adsorption *via* binding to viral envelope glycoprotein gp120 (polysulphates, polysulphonates, polycarboxylates, polyoxometalates, polynucleotides and negatively charged albumins), (3) viral assembly and disassembly *via* NCp7 Zn finger-targeted agents [2,2'-dithiobisbenzamides (DIBAs), azodicarbonamide (ADA)], (4) virus-cell fusion *via* binding to viral envelope glycoprotein gp41 (T-1249), (5) proviral deoxyribonucleic acid (DNA) integration *via* integrase inhibitors (4-aryl-2,4-dioxobutanoic acid derivatives) and (6) viral messenger ribonucleic acid (mRNA) transcription *via* inhibitors of transcription (transactivation) process (flavopiridol, fluoroquinolones) (Kuno, Palangsuntikul & Hannongbua, 2003)(Sharma, Kaushik, Singh, Kumar & Pandey, 2002)(De Clercq, 2002). New NRTIs, NNRTIs and PIs were developed that possess, respectively: (1) improved metabolic characteristics (phosphoramidate and cyclosaligenyl pronucleotides bypassing the first phosphorylation step of NRTIs), (2) increased activity [*second* or *third* generation NNRTIs (TMC-125, DPC-083)] and (3) different, non-peptidic scaffold [cyclic urea (mozenavir), 4-hydroxy-2-pyrone (tripanavir)] (Kasai, Mizushina, Sugawara & Sakaguchi, 2002) (Painter, Andrews & Furman, 2000)(Mlinaric, Kreft, Umek & Strukelj, 2000).

The advent of so many new compounds, other than those that have been formally approved for the treatment of HIV infections, will undoubtedly improve the prognosis of patients with AIDS and AIDS-associated diseases. Nucleoside analogues constitute a family of biological molecules (ddI, d4T, ddC and 3TC), which play an important role in the transcription process of HIV. The normal nucleoside substrates, used by reverse transcriptase (RT) to synthesize DNA, are mimicked by the nucleoside analogues, which lacked a 3'-OH group and, consequently, act as chain terminators when incorporated into DNA by RT. Although the nucleoside analogues show good activity as inhibitors of HIV, their long-term usefulness is limited by toxicities. Resistance and mutation are also problems. The development of better drugs requires a better understanding of how the drugs work, the mechanism of drug resistance and interaction with receptor, and stability of the drugs inside active site. An HIV RT inhibitor ligand was proposed, which indicated highest docking scores and more hydrogen-bond interactions with the residues of RT active site (Da Silva, Carvalho & Taft, 2006).

Garrick *et al.* reviewed the inference of population history by coupling exploratory and model-driven phylogeographic analyses (Garrick, Caccone & Sunnucks, 2010). A simple computerized algorithm, useful for establishing a relation between chemical structures and their biological activities or significance, is proposed and exemplified (Varmuza, 1980)(Benzecri, 1984). The starting point is to use an informational or configurational entropy for pattern recognition purposes. As entropy is weakly discriminating for classification purposes, the more powerful concept of *entropy production* and its *equipartition conjecture* are introduced (Torrens &Castellano, 2006). In earlier publications, the periodic classifications of local anaesthetics (Torrens &Castellano, 2006) (Castellano & Torrens, 2009)(Torrens & Castellano, in press)and HIV inhibitors (Torrens & Castellano, 2009)(Torrens, Castellano, 2009)(Torrens & Castellano, 2010) were analyzed. The aim of the present report is to develop the learning potentialities of the code and, since molecules are more naturally described *via* a varying size structured representation, the study of general approaches to the processing of structured information. Section 2 presents computational method. Section 3 describes classification algorithm. Section 4 exposes the equipartition conjecture of entropy production. Section 5 analyzes learning procedure. Section 6 classifies indazolols against *Trichomonas vaginalis*. Section 7 classifies fullerenes and fullerite. Section 8 classifies lactic acid bacteria by cytokine immunomodulation. Section 9 analyzes the phylogenesis of avian birds and 1918 influenza virus. Section 10 reviews the classification of local anaesthetics. Section 11 classifies transdermal-delivery percutaneous enhancers. Section 12 reviews QSAR modelling of anti-HIV compounds. Sections 13–16 analyze the phylogenesis of α-proteobacteria, vertebrates, mammals, monkeys, apes, hominids, man and extinct species. Sections 17–20 classify HIV inhibitors: thiocarbamates, *N*-aryloxazolidinone-5-carboxamides, styrylquinolines, *etc.* Section 21 groups aryltriazolylhydroxamate antimalarials. Section 22 classifies *N*-aryl-*N*-(3-aryl-1,2,4-oxadiazol-5-yl)amines as potential agents for prostate cancer. Sections 23–24 group 2-phenylindole-3-carbaldehydes against breast cancer and anti-tubulin agents with indole ring against gastric cancer. Section 25 reports perpectives.

2. COMPUTATIONAL METHOD

The key problem in classification studies is to define *similarity indices*, when several criteria of comparison are involved. The first step in quantifying the concept of similarity, for molecules of HIV-1 inhibitors, is to list the most important portions of the molecules. The *vector of properties* $\bar{i} = <i_1, i_2, \dots i_k, \dots>$ should be associated with each inhibitor *i*, whose components correspond to different characteristic groups in the inhibitor molecule, in a hierarchical order according to the expected importance of their pharmacological potency. If the *m-th* portion of the molecule is pharmacologically more significant for the inhibitory effect than the *k-th* portion, then $m < k$. The components i_k are "1" or "0", according to whether a similar portion of rank *k* is present or absent in inhibitor *i*, compared with the reference inhibitor. It is assumed that the *structural elements* of an inhibitor molecule can be *ranked*, according to their contribution to inhibitory activity, in the following order of decreasing importance: number of N atoms > number of O atoms > number of S atoms > number of P atoms > number of halogen atoms. The ddI molecule contains four N, three O, no S, no P and no halogen (X = F, Cl, Br) heteroatoms ($N_4O_3S_0P_0X_0$). Most inhibitors contain no S heteroatom (ddI, ddC, d4T, novel proposed ligand, $N_{3-4}O_3S_0P_0X_0$), while 3TC includes one S heteroatom ($N_3O_3S_1P_0X_0$). In NRTI ddI the molecule contains four N, three O, no S, no P and no halogen ($N_4O_3S_0P_0X_0$, *cf.* Figure 1). Its associated vector is <11111>. The ddI was selected as a *reference* HIV-1 inhibitor because of the good docking scores with receptor RT.

Table 1 contains the vectors associated with 31 HIV-1 inhibitors of various types: NNRTIs, NRTIs, NtRTIs and PIs. Vector <00110> is as-

Figure 1. Molecular structure of an HIV-1 NRTI inhibitor didanosine (ddI) molecule

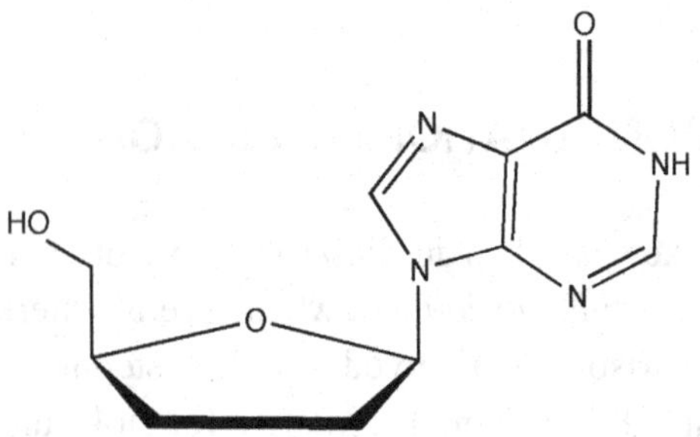

sociated with efavirenz since the molecule contains one N, two O, no S, no P and four halogens. Vector <10111> is associated with nevirapine since there are four N, one O, no S, no P and no halogen. Let us denote by r_{ij} ($0 \leq r_{ij} \leq 1$) the similarity index of two inhibitors associated with the $\bar{i}$ and $\bar{j}$ vectors, respectively. The similitude relation is characterized by a *similarity matrix* $\mathbf{R} = [r_{ij}]$. The similarity index between two inhibitors $\bar{i} = <i_1, i_2, \ldots i_k \ldots>$ and $\bar{j} = <j_1, j_2, \ldots j_k \ldots>$ is defined as:

$$r_{ij} = \sum_k t_k \left(a_k\right)^k \quad (k = 1, 2, \ldots) \tag{1}$$

where $0 \leq a_k \leq 1$ and $t_k = 1$ if $i_k = j_k$, but $t_k = 0$ if $i_k \neq j_k$. The definition assigns a weight $(a_k)^k$ to any property involved in the description of molecule i or j.

3. CLASSIFICATION ALGORITHM

The *grouping algorithm* uses the *stabilized* matrix of similarity, obtained by applying the *max-min composition rule o* defined by:

$$(\mathbf{R}o\mathbf{S})_{ij} = \max_k \left[\min_k \left(r_{ik}, s_{kj} \right) \right] \tag{2}$$

where $\mathbf{R} = [r_{ij}]$ and $\mathbf{S} = [s_{ij}]$ are matrices of the same type, and $(\mathbf{R}o\mathbf{S})_{ij}$ is the (i,j)-*th* element of the matrix $\mathbf{R}o\mathbf{S}$ (Kaufmann, 1975). When apply-

ing the rule iteratively: $\mathbf{R}(n+1) = \mathbf{R}(n) o \mathbf{R}$, there exists an integer n such that: $\mathbf{R}(n) = \mathbf{R}(n+1) = \ldots$ The resulting matrix $\mathbf{R}(n)$ is called the *stabilized similarity matrix*. The importance of stabilization lies in the fact that in the classification process, it will generate a partition into disjoint classes. From now on the stabilized matrix is used and designated by $\mathbf{R}(n) = [r_{ij}(n)]$. The *grouping rule* follows: i and j are assigned to the same class if $r_{ij}(n) \geq b$. The class of i noted $\hat{i}$ is the set of species j that satisfies the rule $r_{ij}(n) \geq b$. The matrix of classes is:

$$\overline{\overline{R}}(n) = \left[\hat{r}_{\hat{i}\hat{j}}\right] = \max_{s,t}\left(r_{st}\right) \quad (s \in \hat{i}, t \in \hat{j}) \tag{3}$$

where s stands for any index of a species belonging to class $\hat{i}$ (similarly for t and $\hat{j}$). Rule (3) means finding the largest similarity index between species of two different classes. In information theory, the *information entropy h* measures the surprise that the source emitting the sequences can give (Shannon, 1948). For a single event occurring with probability p the degree of surprise is proportional to $-\ln p$. Generalizing the result to a random variable X (which can take N possible values $x_1, \ldots, x_N$ with probabilities $p_1, \ldots, p_N$), the average surprise received on learning the value of X is $-\Sigma p_i \ln p_i$. The information entropy associated with the matrix of similarity $\mathbf{R}$ is:

$$h(\mathbf{R}) = -\sum_{i,j} r_{ij} \ln r_{ij} - \sum_{i,j} (1 - r_{ij}) \ln(1 - r_{ij}) \tag{4}$$

Denote by C_b the set of classes and by $\mathbf{R}_b$ the matrix of similarity at the grouping level b. The information entropy satisfies the following properties. (1) $h(\mathbf{R}) = 0$ if $r_{ij} = 0$ or $r_{ij} = 1$. (2) $h(\mathbf{R})$ is maximum if $r_{ij} = 0.5$. (3) $h(\hat{\mathbf{R}}_b) \leq h(\mathbf{R})$ for any b. (4) $h(\hat{\mathbf{R}}_{b_1}) \leq h(\hat{\mathbf{R}}_{b_2})$ if $b_1 < b_2$.

Table 1. Vector properties of human immunodeficiency virus type-1 inhibitors

Non-nucleoside reverse transcriptase inhibitors (NNRTIs)			
1. efavirenz	<00110>	7. R165335 (TMC125)	<00110>
2. nevirapine	<10111>	8. SJ-3366	<01111>
3. delavirdine	<00111>	9. capravirine (AG1549)	<10010>
4. emivirine (MKC-442)	<01111>	10. PNU-142721	<10010>
5. thiocarboxanilide UC-781	<00010>	11. (+)-calanolide A	<00111>
6. DPC 083	<00110>		

Nucleoside reverse transcriptase inhibitors (NRTIs)			
12. didanosine (ddI)	<11111>	17. zidovudine (AZT)	<00111>
13. zalcitabinel (ddC)	<01111>	18. abacavir (ABC)	<00111>
14. stavudine (d4T)	<01111>	19. emtricitabine [(–)-FTC]	<01010>
15. lamivudine (3TC)	<01011>	20. amdoxovir (DAPD)	<01111>
16. novel proposed ligand	<11111>	21.(±)-2'-deoxy-3'-oxa-4'-thiocytidine (dOTC)	<01011>

Nucleotide reverse transcriptase inhibitors (NtRTI)				
22. adefovir dipivoxyl	<00101>	25. d4T aryloxy-phosphoramidate	<00101>	
23. tenofovir disoproxil	<00101>	26.*cyclo*saligenyl d4TMP	<00101>	
24. bis(S-acetyl-2-thioethyl)phosphotriester of 2',3'-dideoxyadenosine [bis(SATE)ddAMP]				<00001>

Protease inhibitors (PIs)			
27. amprenavir	<00011>	30. mozenavir (DMP-450)	<11111>
28. lopinavir	<10111>	31. tipranavir (PNU-140690)	<00010>
29. atazanavir (BMS-232632)	<00111>		

4. THE EQUIPARTITION CONJECTURE OF ENTROPY PRODUCTION

In the classification algorithm, each *hierarchical tree* corresponds to a dependence of entropy on the grouping level, and an *h–b* diagram can be obtained. The Tondeur and Kvaalen *equipartition conjecture of entropy production* is proposed, as a selection criterion among different variants resulting from classification among hierarchical trees. According to the conjecture for a given charge or duty, the best configuration of a flowsheet is the one in which entropy production is most uniformly distributed. One proceeds by analogy using *infor-*

mation entropy instead of thermodynamic entropy. Equipartition implies a linear dependence so that the *equipartition line* is described by:

$$h_{eqp} = h_{max} b \qquad (5)$$

Since the classification is discrete a way of expressing equipartition would be a regular staircase function. The best variant is chosen to be that minimizing the sum of squares of the deviations:

$$SS = \sum_{b_i} (h - h_{eqp})^2 \qquad (6)$$

5. LEARNING PROCEDURE

Learning procedures similar to those encountered in *stochastic methods* are implemented as follows (White, 1989). Consider a given partition into classes as *good* or ideal from practical or empirical observations, which corresponds to a *reference* similarity matrix $\mathbf{S} = [s_{ij}]$ obtained for equal weights $a_1 = a_2 = \ldots = a$ and for an arbitrary number of fictious properties. Consider the same set of species as in the good classification and the actual properties. The similarity degree r_{ij} is then computed with Eq. (1) giving matrix $\mathbf{R}$. The number of properties for $\mathbf{R}$–$\mathbf{S}$ may differ. The learning procedure consists in trying to find classification results for $\mathbf{R}$, as close as possible to the *good* classification. The first weight a_1 is taken constant, and only the following weights a_2, a_3,… are subjected to random variations. A new similarity matrix is obtained using Eq. (1) and the new weights. The distance between the partitions into classes characterized by $\mathbf{R}$–$\mathbf{S}$ is given by:

$$D = -\sum_{ij}\left(1 - r_{ij}\right)\ln\frac{1 - r_{ij}}{1 - s_{ij}} - \sum_{ij} r_{ij}\ln\frac{r_{ij}}{s_{ij}}$$
$$\forall 0 \leq r_{ij}, s_{ij} \leq 1$$

The result of the algorithm is a set of weights allowing adequate classification. The procedure was applied to the synthesis of complex flowsheets using information entropy (Iordache, Corriou, Garrido-Sanchez, Fonteix & Tondeur, 1993).

6. CLASSIFICATION OF INDAZOLOLS: ACTION AGAINST *T. VAGINALIS*

A set of 18 indazolol derivatives were assayed against *Trichomonas vaginalis* (Meneses, Rojas, Sifontes, Lopez & Sariego, 2001)(Marrero-Ponce et al, 2005)(Meneses et al, 2005). The *structural*

substitutions of an indazolol molecule can be *ranked*, according to their contribution to inhibitory activity, as: 5-nitro > 3-hydroxyl > 1-5'-hexenyl (Montero et al, 2005)(Montero-Torres et al, 2006)(Vega, 2006). Reference molecule contains these substitutions; its associated vector is <111> (Marrero-Ponce et al, 2006). All indazolols that showed activity contain a nitro group (–NO_2) at position 5, so it can be hypothetically considered the correspondence of the trichomonacide activity with the presence of –NO_2 in the indazolols (Marrero-Ponce et al, 2008)(Rivera-Borroto, 2009). The dendrogram for indazolols is illustrated in Figure 2.

7. MOLECULAR CLASSIFICATION OF FULLERENES AND FULLERITE

The calculation of the Kekulé structure count K and permanent of adjacency matrix per($\mathbf{A}$) of fullerenes allows the principal components analysis (PCA) of structural parameters and cluster analysis (CA) of fullerenes (Torrens, 2002)(Torrens, 2002). Fullerene K and per($\mathbf{A}$) are related to structural parameters involving the presence of contiguous pentagons p (number of edges common to two pentagons), q (number of vertices common to three pentagons), r (number of pairs of non-adjacent pentagon edges shared between two other pentagons) and, correspondingly, u, v and w for hexagons (Torrens, 2003). Structural parameter PCA and fullerene CA allow classifying them (Torrens, 2003). Linear and nonlinear correlations permit modelling K and per ($\mathbf{A}$) of fullerenes (Torrens, 2003). Structural parameter PCA agrees with CA of fullerenes (Torrens, 2004). A simple linear correlation is a good model for per ($\mathbf{A}$) of fullerenes; $\{q,r,v,w\}$ is redundant information; $\{p,u\}$ contains the essential characters of per($\mathbf{A}$) (Torrens, 2004). Fullerene dendrogram relating to $\{p,q,r,u,v,w,q/p,r/p,v/u,w/u\}$ separates first the 8 units in class 1 (C_{20}-I_h–C_{30}-C_{2v} II, *cf.* Figure 3), class 2 (8 units, C_{32}-D_2–C_{34}-C_s), class 3

Figure 2. Dendrogram for indazolols

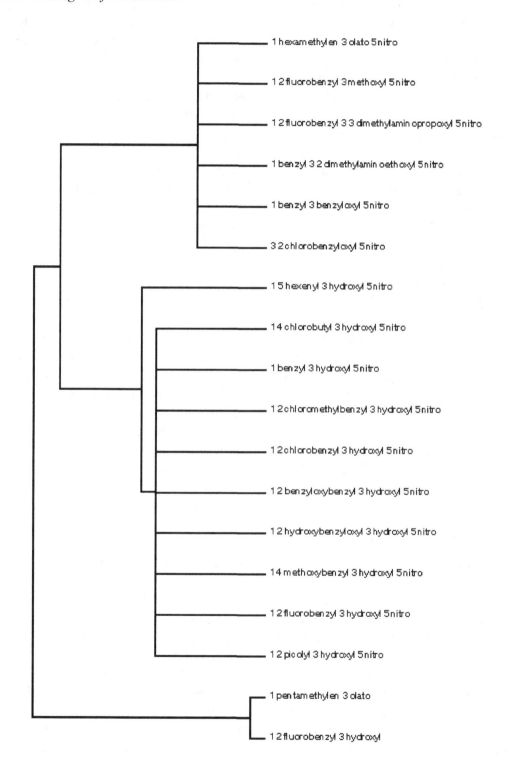

(9 units, C_{36}-D_{6h}–C_{40}-D_{5d} II), class 4 (3 units, C_{40}-T_d–C_{44}-D_{3h}) and class 5 (6 units, C_{60}-I_h–C_{240}-I_h). The classes correspond to PCA and radial tree. For classifying some fullerenes the dendrogram was repeated for smaller sets, resulting their enclosure in new branches attached to C_{28}–D_2 and C_{40}–T_d, respectively (*cf.* Figure 3).

Growth mechanisms of fractal clusters in fullerene solutions are analyzed along with similarity laws determining the thermodynamic characteristics of fullerite crystals (Torrens & Castellano, 2005)(Torrens & Castellano, 2006)(Torrens & Castellano, 2006)(Torrens & Castellano, 2007). A simplified examination of thermodynamic properties in CA can be obtained from hierarchical cluster analysis (HCA) (Torrens & Castellano, 2007)(Torrens & Castellano, 2008)(Torrens & Castellano, 2007)(Torrens & Castello, 2007). The most important result is that in dendrogram Ne (class 1) is separated from Ar, which joins {Kr,Xe} in class 2 (*cf.* Figure 4). Separation of Ne is attributed to well-known quantum effects at low temperatures. Dendrogram is in agreement with partial correlation diagram and radial tree. The Ne is closer to C_{60} than to remaining inert gases. However, result should be taken with care because binary-tree structure is forced by HCA.

8. CLASSIFICATION OF LACTIC ACID BACTERIA

The immune system evolved in its fight against different pathogens (Hooper, Wong, Thelin, Hansson, Falk & Gordon, 2001)(Herias, Hessle, Telemo, Midtvedt, Hanson & Wold, 1999). The system has different levels of action of increasing complexity; it could be modulated by different environmental factors, being diet one of the most important (Cebra, 1999) (Perdigon, Rachid, Budeguer & Valdez, 1994). There is interest in immunonutritional studies, *e.g.*, the functional food called *probiotics* (Link-Amster, Rochat, Saudan, Mignot & Aeschlimann, 1994) (Marteau, Vreses, Cellier & Schrezenmeir, 2001). Probiotics are live

microbial food supplements, which benefit host improving its intestinal microbial balance and which upon ingestion in certain numbers induce health benefits beyond inherent basic nutrition (Isolauri, Juntunen, Rautanen, Sillanaukee & Koivula, 1991) (Malin, Suomalainen, Saxelin & Isolauri, 1996). Yoghurt is a coagulated milk obtained by lactic acid fermentation in the presence of *L. bulgaricus* and *S. thermophilus* (Borchers, Keen &Gershwin, 2002) (Ha, Lee, Zhou, Ustunol & Pestka, 1999). Belief that yoghurt may be beneficial to health is centuries old (Halpern, Vruwink, van de Water, Keen & Gershwin, 1991) (Schiffrin, Rochat, Link-Amster, Aeschlimann & Donnet-Hughes, 1995). An immunostimulatory effect of yoghurt was proposed based on its preventive effect on diseases (Schiffrin, Rochat, Link-Amster, Aeschlimann & Donnet-Hughes, 1995)(Pelto, Isolauri, Lilius, Nuutila & Salminen, 1998). However results were controversial (Matsuzaki, Yamazaki, Hashimoto & Yokokura, 1998) (Takagi, Matsuzaki, Sato, Nomoto, Morotomi & Yokokura, 2001). The number of volunteers on study, strain of bacteria, quantity of intake, analyzed parameters, time of intervention and studies on animal *vs.* humans were different variables conducing finally to a puzzle that might be resolved (Chiang, Sheih, Wang, Liao & Gill, 2000)(Haller, Blum, Bode, Hammes & Schiffrin, 2000). Although some functions of lactic acid bacteria (LAB) can reside in either cytoplasm or cell-wall components (being the heat-inactivated product more effective in the latter), more effects over immune system were demonstrated for the fresh yoghurt than for the heat-inactivated one (Puri, Rattan, Bijlani, Mahapatra & Nath, 1996). The classification of living and heat-inactivated LABs against cytokines was studied (Turchet, Laurenzano, Auboiron & Antoine, 2003)(Tejada-Simon & Pestka, 1999). Eight LABs were classified using the effects (induction, inhibition or no effect) of living and heat-inactivated LABs on the production of nine cytokines (*cf.* Figure 5). The obtained classification (((((((1,4),2),7),6),(3,5)),8) is in agreement with principal component analysis.

Figure 3. Dendrogram for the fullerenes

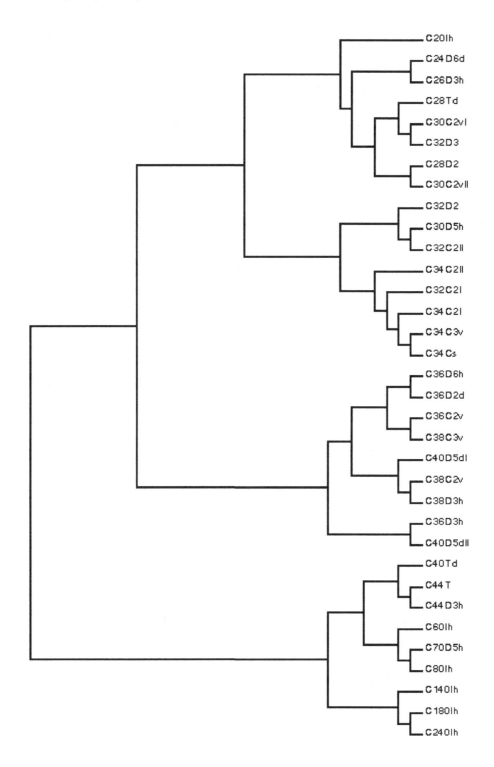

Figure 4. Hierarchical CA dendrogram for properties of inert-gas/C$_{60}$ crystals

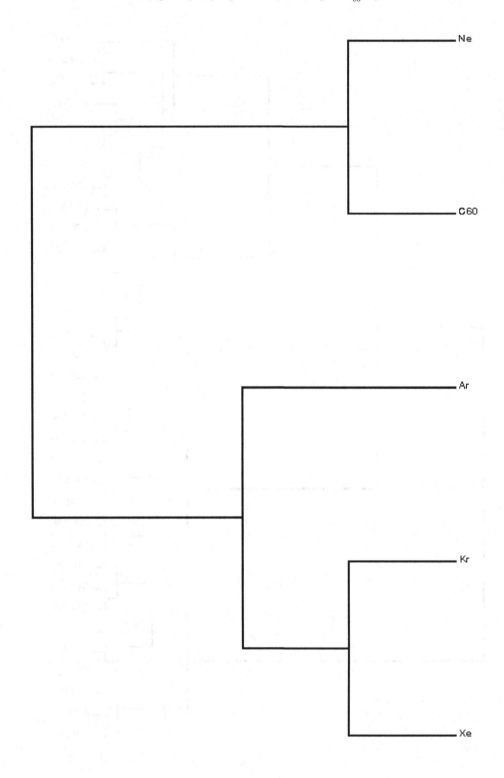

Figure 5. Dendrogram for effects of lactic acid bacteria on production of cytokines

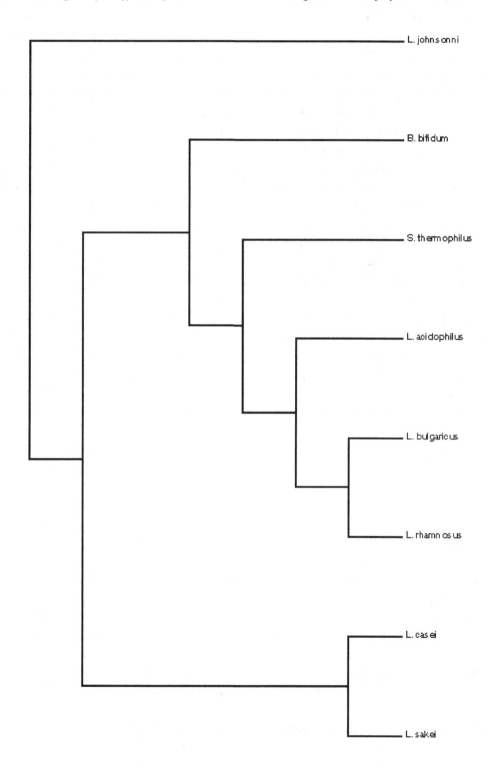

9. PHYLOGENESIS OF AVIAN BIRDS AND 1918 INFLUENZA VIRUS

Lysozyme is an enzyme with 129 residues. The amino-acid compositions of certain avian lysozymes was determined. The amino-acid sequence of hen egg-white lysozyme was annotated (Canfield, 1963). Certain discrepancies exist between the sequence and that reported in (Jolles, Hermann, Niemann & Jolles, 1967) (at residues 40, 41, 42, 46, 48, 58, 65, 66, 92 and 93). Crystallographic analysis (Blake, Mair, North, Phillips & Sarma, 1967) gave results for residues 40, 41, 42, 58, 59, 92 and 93 that are in agreement with the former. Discrepancies at residues 46, 48, 65 and 66 are a difference between Asp or Asn; from the electron density maps it could not be determined whether the residues are amide or free acid. The amino-acid sequences of duck, Japanese quail and turkey egg-white lysozymes were determined (Hermann & Jolles, 1970) (LaRue & Speck, 1969). Amino-acid sequences for human urine and milk lysozymes were determined. Comparative studies of sequences for lysozymes from different origins are interesting from the viewpoint of structure–function relationships (Asp-101 of hen lysozyme, which is known to be implicated at the substrate binding site, is replaced by Gly in turkey lysozyme). The Trp-62 of hen lysozyme, which also plays an important role in substrate binding, is replaced by Tyr in human lysozyme. Differences between avian species sequences that are compared are expressed as percentage of different amino acids in lysozyme. The greater the differences, the farther in time must be separation between species. *Grouping level b* can be identified with *biological time*. Obtained *phylogenetic tree* is represented by scheme: $(1,...,5) \rightarrow (1,4,5)(2,3) \rightarrow (1,5)(2,3)(4) \rightarrow (1)(2,3)(4)(5) \rightarrow (1)(2)(3)(4)(5)$. The scheme is in agreement with data obtained in morphological studies. Optimality criterion SS, associated with different proposals for phylogenetic trees, allows *equipartition conjecture* to be validated or invalidated in phylogenesis. If in the calculation of *entropy* associated with the phylogenetic tree a species is systematically omitted, difference between entropy with and without this species can be considered as a measure of *species entropy*. Such contributions may be studied with equipartiton conjecture. Available experimental and field data should be examined by different classification algorithms to reveal possible features of real biological significance. Scheme (*cf.* Figure 6) is in agreement with data obtained in morphological studies and with the method based on entropy production and the conjecture of equipartiton of production of entropy. Each band of parallel edges indicates a split. The distance between any two taxa x and y corresponds to the sum of weights of all splits that separate x and y.

An arsenal of effective medicines and others in developing phase is available. Research in viral genomes expedites progress (Jones, 1998) (Ellis, 1999) (Root, Kay & Kim. 2001). In the search of the keys of the origin of 1918 virus haemagglutinin (HA), the gene sequences of HA subtype H1 of several strands of influence virus were analyzed (Crosby, 2003)(Reid & Taubenberger, 2003)(Kash et al.,2004). Its phylogenetic tree was built (Tumpey et al, 2005). The samples of 1918 strand are inscribed in that family of influenza virus adapted to man (*cf.* Figure 7) (Taubenberger, Reid, Lourens, Wang, Jin & Fanning, 2005). Distance between 1918 gene H1 and known avian family reflects that it was originated in a strand of avian influenza virus, although it evolved in an unidentified host before emerging in 1918. The Z_inv, a new invariant based on 3DD-curves of DNA sequence, which is simple for calculation and it approximates to the leading eigenvalues of the matrix associated with DNA sequence (Zhang, Luo & Yang, 2007). The utility of the invariant was illustrated on the DNA sequence of 11 species. The Z_inv was used to analyze the phylogenetic relationships for the seven HA (H5N1) sequences of avian influenza virus. Biomacromolecular structural data are maintained by Protein Data Bank (PDB) (Bern-

Figure 6. Dendrogram for distances as different amino acids in lysozyme

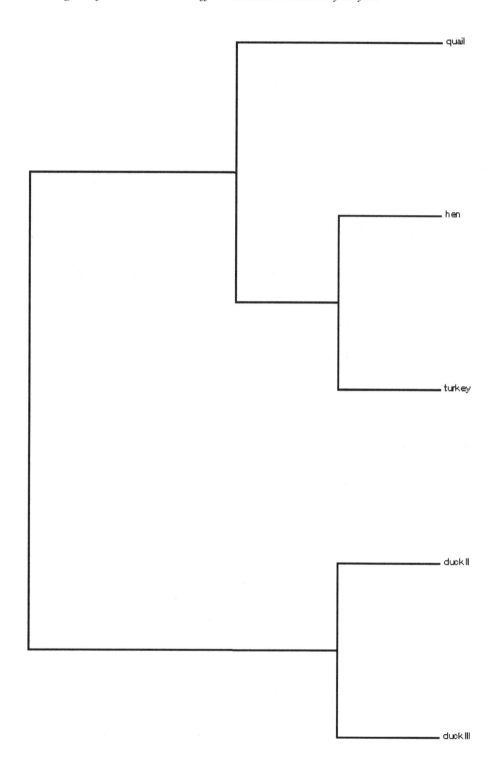

Figure 7. Family dendrogram of influenza

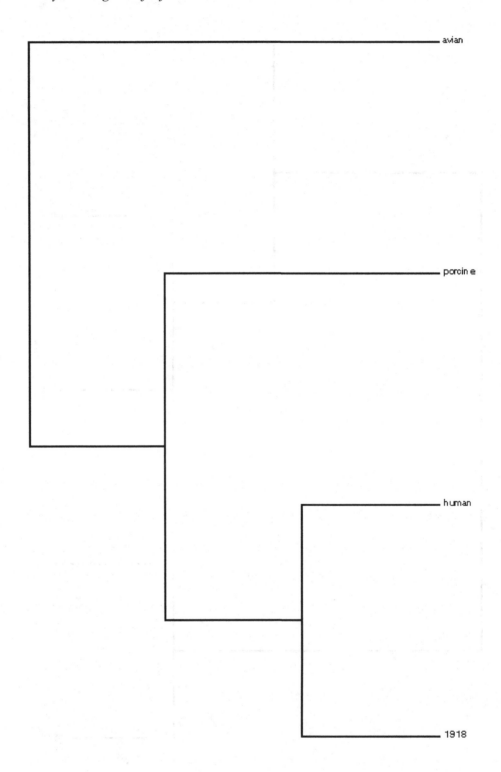

stein, 1977). Classroom applications were described (Torrens, Sanchez-Marin, 1989; Torrens, Sanchez-Perez & Sanchez-Marin, 1989). Three-dimensional (3D) structures can be displayed by program RasMol (Sayle & Milner-White, 1995). Program WPDB compresses PDB structure files into a set of indexed files (Shingyalov & Bourne, 1995; Shingyalov & Bourne, 1997). Program BABEL converts molecular modelling file formats (Walters & Stahl, 1996). Database system RELI-BASE+ analyzes protein-ligand structures in PDB (Hendlich, 1998). Classroom applications of WPDB were described (Tsai, 2001). Successor of RasMol and Chime (MDL, 2007) is Jmol (Claros et al, 2002; Herraezm, 2006; Miro, 2007). Fractals for hybrid orbitals in protein models were proposed (Torrens, Sanchez- Marin &Nebot- Gil, 1998; Torrens, 2000).

10. MOLECULAR CLASSIFICATION OF LOCAL ANAESTHETICS

The classification of 30 local anaesthetics (procaine analogues including phenyl alcohol and ice, *cf.* Figure 8) is in agreement with partial correlation diagrams, *dendrograms* (binary trees), previous results with 27 anaesthetics and earlier publications (Covino, 1972; Covino 1980; Covino, 1986; Corriou, Iordache & Tondeue, 1991). Classification scheme from 1–11 levels is conserved after the addition of S-ropivacaine. S-bupivacaine was compared with racemic bupivacaine (Fawcett et al, 2002). S-ropivacaine is structurally close to bupivacaine; the main difference is that the former is a pure S-(–) enantiomer where the latter is a racemate. Ester and amide local anaesthetics are grouped into different classes; the agents of low potency and short duration are separated from the agents of high–medium potency and long–medium duration. The classification presents lower bias and greater precision, resulting in lower divergence with respect to original distribution. A natural trend is to interchange similar anaesthetics in composi-

tion of complex drugs (Brodin, Nyquist-Mayer & Wadstein, 1984). However mixtures of dissimilar anaesthetics are also used (Friedman, Fogelman, Nouri, Levine & Ashinoff, 1999; Friedman, Mafong, Friedman & Geronemus, 2001; Kuwahara & Skinner, 2001).

11. CLASSIFICATION OF TRANSDERMAL-DELIVERY ENHANCERS

Skin offers an excellent barrier to molecular transport (Diez-Sales, Copovi, Casabo & Herraez, 1991). There was interest in developing systems for controlled delivery of drugs (Diez-Sales, Guzman, Cano, Martin, Sanchez & Herraez, 1991). A suggested technique was to join a specialized patch on skin (Sanchez-Moyano, Seco, Santolaria, Fabra-Campos, Herraez & Martin-Villodre, 1992). Simplest scheme utilized uncoated polymer matrices containing embedded drug (Diez-Sales, López-Castellano, Maiques-Lacer & Herráez-Domínguez, 1993). Pathways form percolating path (Diez-Sales, Perez-Sayas, Martin-Villodre & Herraez-Dominguez, 1993). Pathways are fractal structures (Diez-Sales, Watkinson, Herraez-Dominguez, Javaloyes & Hadgraft, 1996). Several groups developed computational methods for predicting fluxes, *e.g.*, multiple regression methods (Lopez, Morant, Guzman, Borras-Blasco, Diez-Sales & Herraez, 1996). It was reviewed some selective ways for circumventing *stratum corneum* barrier (Lopez, Pellet, Llinares, Diez-Sales, Herraez & Hadgraft, 1997). There was a significant effort directed to finding new drug release systems, in which bioactives contained in a reservoir can be supplied to a host system while controlling the rate and period of delivery (Lopez, Faus, Diez-Sales & Herraez, 1998). Redox chemistry approach was performed to conducting electroactive polymers, for drug delivery and sensing of bioactives. A drug-delivery system consisting of a specialized

Figure 8. Dendrogram for local anaesthetics including physicochemical properties

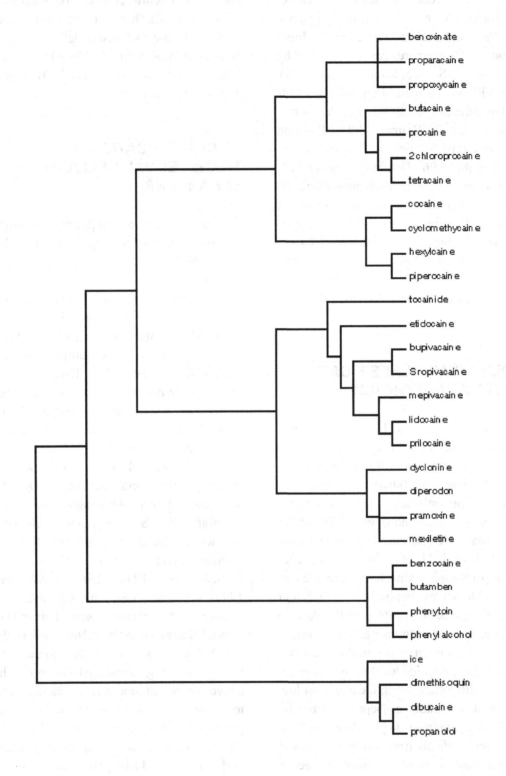

patch joined to the skin was proposed. Fractal dimensions of transdermal-delivery drug models were proposed (Torrens, 2003; Torrens, 2004). It is shown (Figure 9) the molecular classification of transdermal-delivery drug models, percutaneous enhancers of the penetration of anti-cancer drug 5-fluorouracil.

12. QSAR MODELLING OF ANTI-HIV-1 COMPOUNDS

Investigation was performed *via* theoretical approaches, in the field of quantitative structure–activity relationship (QSAR) studies, with a goal of explaining anti-HIV activity, in terms of structural, physicochemical, topological and quantum chemical parameters (Leonard & Roy, 2003). Classical approaches, receptor surface analysis (RSA), molecular shape analysis (MSA) and molecular field analysis (MFA) were performed as 3D-QSARs (Leonard & Roy, 2004). Overall aim was to explore important interaction sites and optimum physicochemical requirements of selected anti-HIV compounds and to develop suitable models of statistical quality with prediction potential, which may help to develop newer compounds with desired activity (Roy & Leonard, 2004). The main aim of a medicinal chemist is to discover novel drugs with greater potency and reduced toxicity, which may be achieved by molecular modification of existing drugs, optimization of various lead compounds, isolation of active constituents from natural sources or syntheses of new series of compounds (Leonard & Roy, 2004). Conventional drug discovery process is costly and time consuming (Roy & Leonard, 2005). Researchers try to highlight novel methods, which reduce time and cost involvement in drug discovery (Roy & Leonard, 2005). The goal of medicinal chemistry is to design and synthesize novel pharmacologically active molecules with reduced toxicity (Roy & Leonard, 2006). The QSARs increased the probability of success and

reduced time and cost in drug discovery (Leonard & Roy, 2006). A rational explanation of drug action was often limited by one's ability to correlate observed physiological effects with a reasonable hypothesis or concept (Leonard & Roy, 2006). Various structural, physicochemical and biological parameters were used to correlate these with biological activity; observed relations were used to predict the activity of a new compound, and the information was exploited to develop newer molecules of optimum activity (Leonard & Roy, 2006). A QSAR of selected classes of anti-HIV ligands was attempt and it was tried to find out the impact of various structural, fragmental, physicochemical and substitutional requirements on binding affinity. Chemometric tools: (1) stepwise regression, (2) multiple linear regression with factor analysis as data preprocessing step for variable selection (FA-MLR), (3) partial least squares with factor analysis as preprocessing step (FA-PLS), (4) multiple linear regression with genetic function approximation (GFA-MLR), (5) genetic partial least squares (G/PLS) and (6) principal component regression analysis (PCRA) were used to identify relation between various descriptors for biological activity. It was performed QSAR of 3-(4-benzylpiperidin-1-yl)-*N*-phenylpropylamine derivatives as potent CCR5 antagonists (*cf.* Figure 10).

13. PHYLOGENETIC ANALYSIS OF A-PROTEOBACTERIA

It was performed a study toward the automatic reconstruction of a highly resolved tree of life, by Dopazo's group (1995) and others (Felsenstein, 1983; 1988a; 1988b). A detailed comparison of the sequences of biomolecules, proteins or nucleic acids allowed for molecular reconstruction. The key argument in molecular phylogeny is the existence of molecular clocks, *i.e.*, a constant rate of change of a given molecule. Various similarity–distance indices can be constructed from primary data. A

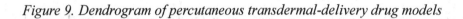

Figure 9. Dendrogram of percutaneous transdermal-delivery drug models

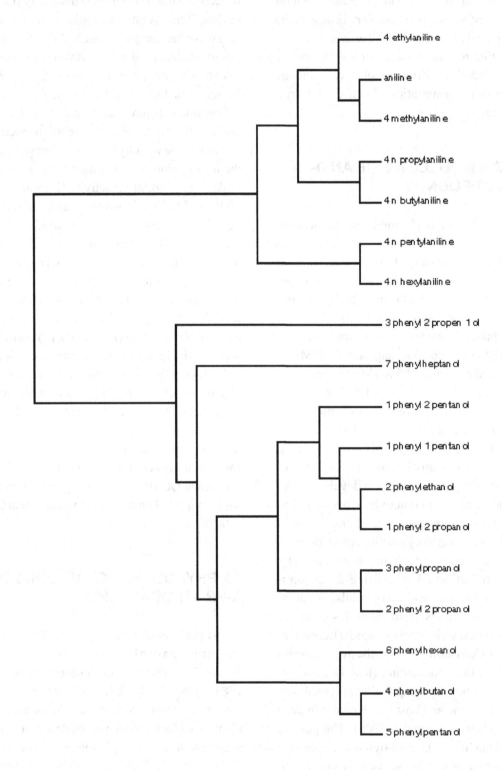

Figure 10. Dendrogram for CCR5 antagonists

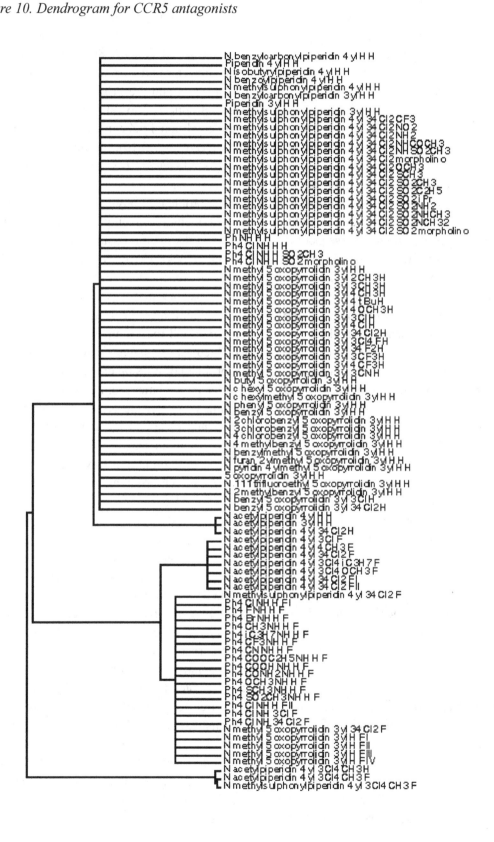

taxonomic distribution of large DNA viruses in the sea was reported (Monier, Claverie & Ogata; 2008). A simple, fast, and accurate method of phylogenomic inference was reported (Wu & Eisen, 2008). An appropriate probe search method to specify groups in higher taxonomic ranks was published (Nakano, Fukuda & Taniguchi; 2009). The cladistic basis for the phylogenetic diversity measure linked evolutionary features to environmental gradients and supported broad applications of microbial ecology's *phylogenetic β-diversity* framework (Faith, Lozupone, Nipperess & Knight; 2009). The importance of protein coding sequences for phylogenetic analysis was recognized (Niraikulam, Hyungdon & Natarajan; 2010). Two new correlation-related distance metrics were proposed to replace the old improper distance metric in the dynamical language approach (Yu et al; 2010). Four genome datasets were employed to evaluate the effects of the replacement from a biological point of view. Both proper distance metrics yielded trees with the same or similar topologies to the ones using the old *distance* and agreed with the tree of life based on 16S (a conserved taxonomic gene) ribosomal (r)RNA in a majority of basic branches. They improved the dynamical language approach for phylogenetic analysis. The phylogeny of 62 α-proteobacteria using the dynamical language approach with chord distance in cases $K = 5$ and 6 are based on all protein sequences (*cf.* Figure 11). The topology of trees obtained by the dynamical language approach with pseudo-distance and piecewise distance in cases $K = 5$ and 6 based on all protein sequences are the same as the one in the figure.

14. PHYLOGENESIS OF VERTEBRATES, MAMMALS AND MONKEYS

The analysis of similarity/dissimilarity of DNA sequences based on a class of 2D graphical representation was reported (Yao; 2008). The analysis of similarities/dissimilarities of DNA sequences was performed based on a novel graphical representation (Yu, Wang & Sun; 2010). The physicochemical properties of amino acids were taken into account and the protein feature sequences were introduced into phylogenetic analysis by using conditional LZ complexity (*cf.* Figure 12) (Zhang & Wang; 2010). The method was applied to the phylogenetic tree of 24 vertebrates and found effectual and feasible.

The problem of phylogenetic inference from datasets including incomplete or uncertain entries is among the most relevant issues in systematic biology (Makarenkov & Lapointe; 2004). A method for reconstructing phylogenetic trees from partial distance matrices is proposed. The new method combines the usage of the four-point condition and the ultrametric inequality with a weighted least-squares approximation to solve the problem of missing entries. It can be applied to infer phylogenies from evolutionary data including some missing or uncertain information, *e.g.*, when observed nucleotide or protein sequences contain gaps or missing entries. In a number of simulations involving incomplete datasets, the proposed method outperformed the well-known Ultrametric and Additive procedures. Generally, the method also outperformed all the other competing approaches including Triangle and Fitch, which is the most popular least-squares method for reconstructing phylogenies. The phylogenetic tree for the ND5 proteins of mammals was based on conditional Lempel-Ziv (LZ) complexity (*cf.* Figure 13). Some interesting theoretical results concerning non-deterministic polynomial-time (NP)-hardness of the ordinary and weighted least-squares fitting of a phylogenetic tree to a partial distance matrix are also established (Chen, Eulenstein & Fernandez-Baca, 2004; Parr, Lee, Campbell & Bederson, 2004; Parr, Lee, Campbell & Bederson, 2004; Gorder, 2005; Hoef-Emden, 2005; Ciccarelli et al, 2006; Stewart, 1993; Li et al, 2001). Six new models to analyze the DNA sequences were constructed

Figure 11. Phylogeny of α-proteobacteria using the dynamical language approach

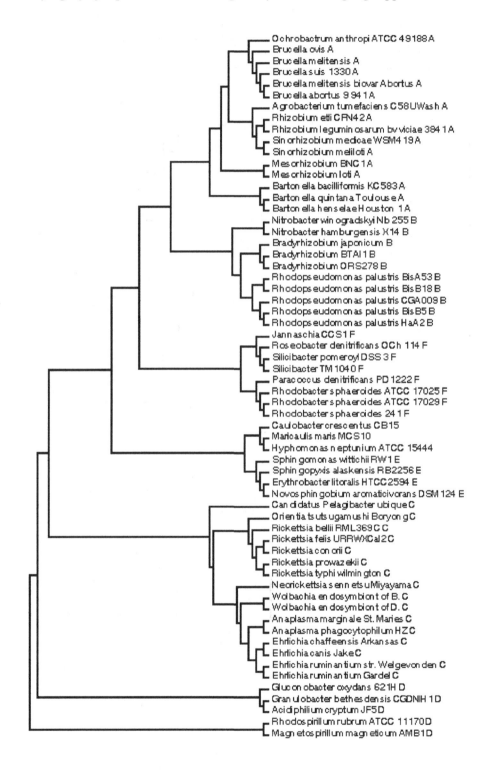

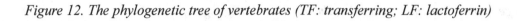

Figure 12. The phylogenetic tree of vertebrates (TF: transferring; LF: lactoferrin)

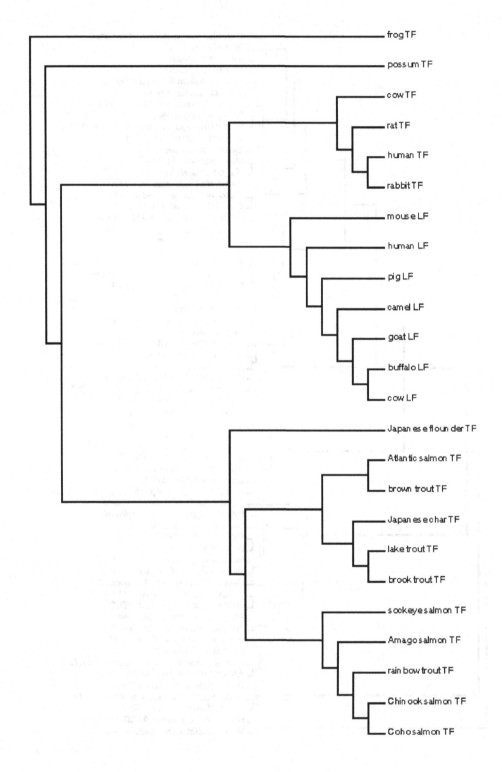

Figure 13. The phylogenetic tree for the ND5 proteins of mammals

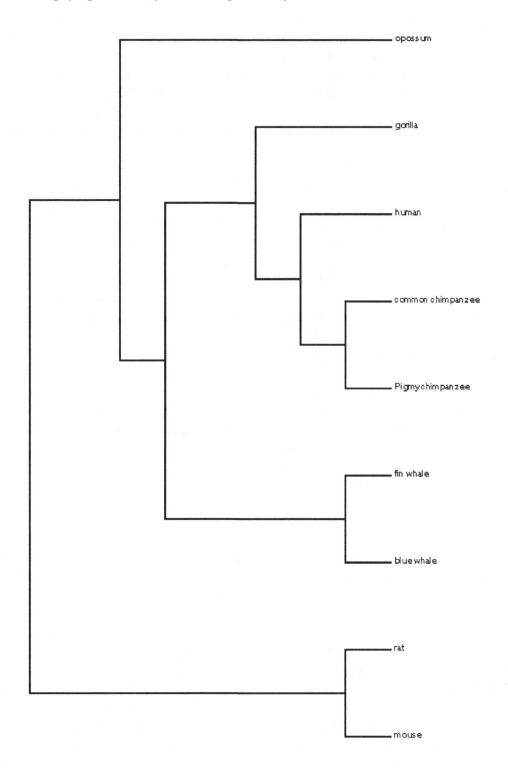

(Dai, Liu, Wang & Vukicevic, 2007). First, a DNA primary sequence was regarded as a random process in *t* and gave three ways to define nucleotides' random distribution functions. Some parameters were extracted from the linear model, and the changes of the nucleotides' distributions were analyzed. In order to facilitate the comparison of DNA sequences, two ways to measure the similarities were proposed. The six models were compared by analyzing the similarities of the presented DNA primary sequences, and the optimal one was selected.

Cartesian coordinates were derived for mathematical denotation of DNA sequence (Liao, Zhu & Liu, 2006). A new method was reported to analyze the similarity based on dual nucleotides of the DNA sequence (Liu, Liao & Zhu, 2009). An improved binary representation of DNA sequences and its applications was published (Chen, Lioa, Xiang & Zhu, 2009). It was proposed a method for constructing phylogenetic trees based on a dissimilarity matrix, in which the smaller an element is, the more similar are the species (Zhu, Liao & Li, 2010). The dissimilarity matrix was translated to a similarity matrix based on proposed rules, which is reflective and symmetric. The transitive closure of the obtained similarity matrix was used to construct a phylogenetic tree of monkeys (*cf.* Figure 14). A novel method for visualizing and analyzing DNA sequences was devised (Wu, Li, Liao & Yeu, 2010). A vertical and horizontal method was proposed for constructing phylogenetic trees (Liao B.,Liao L., Yue, WU & Zhu, 2010).

15. PHYLOGENESIS OF APES, HOMINIDS AND MAN

Several workers have observed that there is an extremely close immunological resemblance between the serum albumins of apes and man (Sarich & Wilson, 1967). The studies with the quantitative microcomplement fixation method confirm the observation. To explain the closeness of the resemblance, previous workers suggested that there has been a slowing down of albumin evolution since the time of divergence of apes and man. Recent evidence, however, indicates that the albumin molecule has evolved at a steady rate. It was suggested that apes and man have a more recent common ancestry than is usually supposed. The calculations lead to the suggestion that, if man and Old World monkeys last shared a common ancestor 30 million years ago (MYA), then man and African apes shared a common ancestor 5 MYA, *i.e.*, in the Pliocene era. The living hominoid primates are Man, the chimpanzees, the Gorilla, the Orangutan and the gibbons (Sibley & Ahlquist, 1984; Cann, Stoneking & Wilson, 1987). Nucleotide sequences of homologous 0.9-kb fragments of mtDNAs, derived from four species of old-world monkeys, one species of new-world monkeys and two species of prosimians, were determined (Hayasaka, Gojobori & Horai, 1988). With the nucleotide sequences and homologous sequences for five species of hominoids, a phylogentic tree for the four groups of primates was constructed. The obtained phylogeny is generally consistent with evolutionary trees constructed in previous studies (*cf.* Figure 15). The results also suggest that the rate of nucleotide substitution for mtDNAs in hominines (human, chimpanzee, gorilla) may have slowed down compared with that for old-world monkeys. The evolutionary feature of mitochondrial genes is similar to one found in nuclear genes.

The cercopithecoids (Old World monkeys) are the sister group of the hominoids (Cavalli, Piazza, Menozzi & Mountain, 1988; Di Rienzo & Wilson, 1991; Torrens, 2000; Shen et al, 2000). The composition of the Hominoidea is not in dispute, but a consensus has not yet been reached concerning the phylogenetic branching pattern and the dating of divergence nodes (*cf.* Figure 16). It was compared the single-copy nuclear DNA sequences of the hominoid genera using DNA–DNA hybridization to produce a complete matrix of Δ-$T_{50}H$

Figure 14. The phylogenic tree of the monkeys

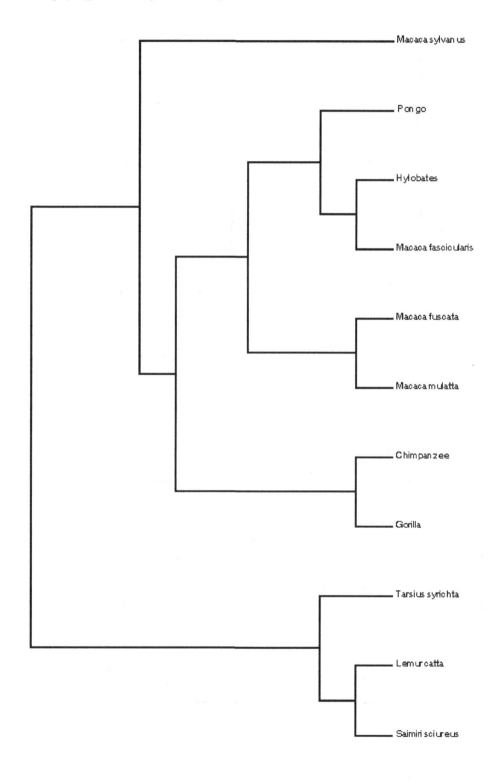

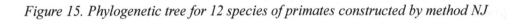

Figure 15. Phylogenetic tree for 12 species of primates constructed by method NJ

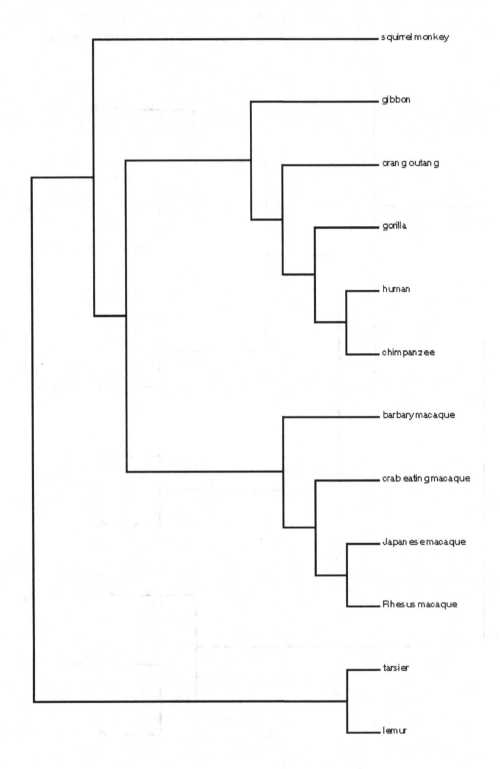

Figure 16. Phylogenetic tree of the apes

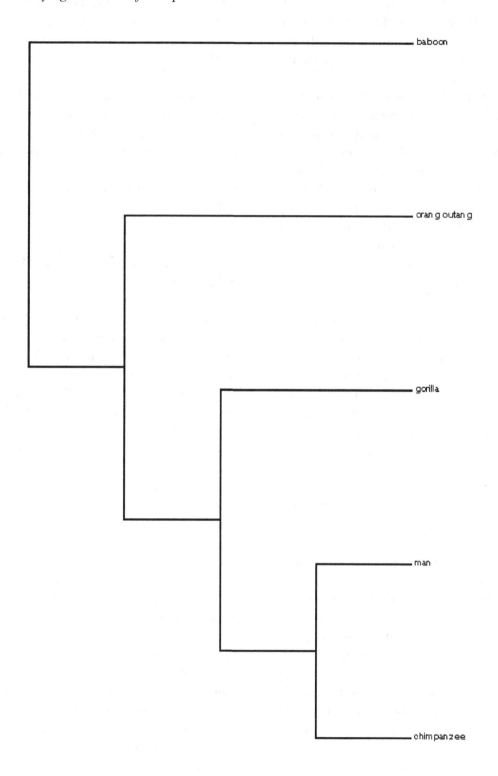

values (Roberts, Eargle, Wright & Luthey-Schulten, 2006). The data showed that the branching sequence of the lineages from oldest to most recent was: Old World monkeys, gibbons, Orangutan, Gorilla, chimpanzees and Man. The calibration of the delta $T_{50}H$ scale in absolute time needs further refinement, but the ranges of the estimates of the datings of the divergence nodes are: Cercopithecoidea, 27–33 MYA; gibbons, 18–22 MYA; Orangutan, 13–16 MYA; Gorilla, 8–10 MYA and chimpanzees–man, 6.3–7.7 MYA.

The analysis of mtDNA was a potent tool in understanding human evolution, owing to characteristics, *e.g.*, high copy number, apparent lack of recombination, high substitution rate and maternal mode of inheritance (Ingman, Kaessmann, Paabo & Gyllensten, 2000). However, almost all studies of human evolution based on mtDNA sequencing were confined to the control region, which constitutes less than 7% of the mitochondrial genome. The studies are complicated by the extreme variation in substitution rate between sites, and the consequence of parallel mutations causing difficulties in the estimation of genetic distance and making phylogenetic inferences questionable. Most comprehensive studies of the human mitochondrial molecule were performed *via* restriction-fragment length polymorphism analysis, providing data that are ill suited to estimations of mutation rate and the timing of evolutionary events. To improve the information obtained from the mitochondrial molecule for studies of human evolution, the global mtDNA diversity in humans was described based on analyses of the complete mtDNA sequence of 53 humans of diverse origins (*cf.* Figure 17). The mtDNA data, in comparison with those of a parallel study of the Xq13.3 region in the same individuals, provide a concurrent view on human evolution with respect to the age of modern humans.

A novel method for phylogenetic analysis of DNA sequence data was proposed (Zhang & Chen, 2008). Comparisons of DNA sequences were reported based on dinucleotide (Chen & Zhang, 2009). A new distance matrix of DNA sequence based on the 3DD-Curves was provided and new similarities/dissimilarities matrix was constructed by using this distance matrix of DNA sequence. As application, a phylogenetic tree for 11 species of primates was constructed (*cf.* Figure 18). The obtained phylogeny is generally consistent with evolutionary trees constructed in previous studies. Three distances for rapid similarity analysis of DNA sequences were proposed (Chen & Zhang, 2009).

16. PHYLOGENESIS OF EXTINCT SPECIES

Two groups of flightless ratite birds existed in New Zealand during the Pleistocene: the kiwis and the moas (Cooper et al, 1992). The latter are now extinct but formerly included 11 species. It has been enzymatically amplified and sequenced *ca.* 400 base pairs of the mitochondrial 12S rRNA gene from bones and soft tissue remains of four species of moas as well as eight other species of ratite birds and a tinamou. Contrary to expectation, the phylogenetic analysis shows that the kiwis are more closely related to Australian and African ratites than to the moas (*cf.* Figure 19). New Zealand probably was colonized twice by ancestors of ratite birds.

The origin and evolution of the genus *Homo* was studied (Foley, 1987; Wood, 1992). DNA was extracted from the Neanderthal-type specimen found in 1856 in western Germany (Krings et al, 1997). By sequencing clones from short overlapping PCR products, a hitherto unknown mitochondrial (mt)DNA sequence was determined. Multiple controls indicate that the sequence is endogenous to the fossil. Sequence comparisons with human mtDNA sequences, and phylogenetic analyses, show that the Neanderthal sequence falls outside the variation of modern humans (*cf.* Figure 20). The age of the common ancestor of

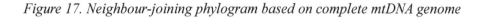

Figure 17. Neighbour-joining phylogram based on complete mtDNA genome

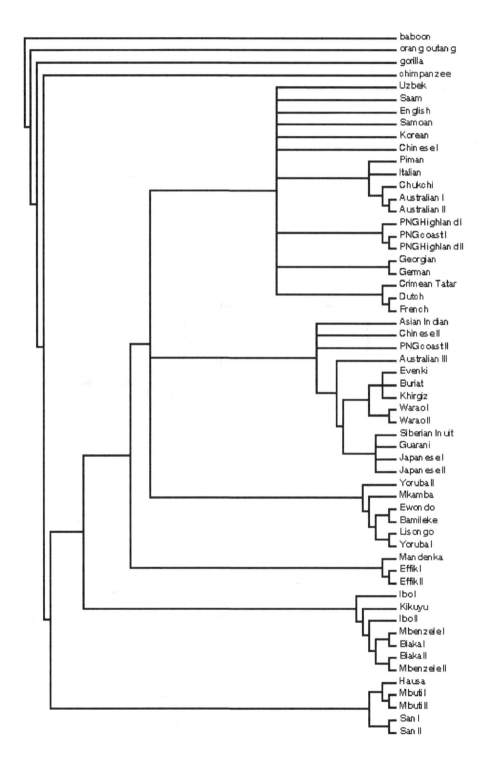

Figure 18. Phylogenetic tree based on 3DD-Curve

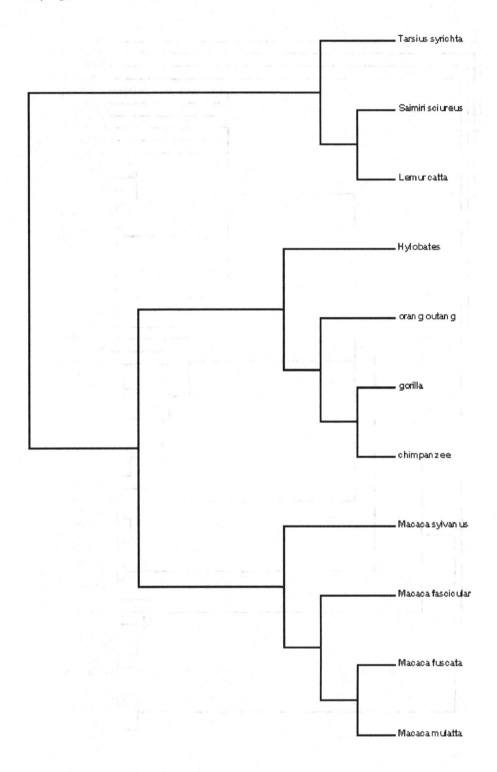

Figure 19. Phylogenetic tree of the flightless ratite birds

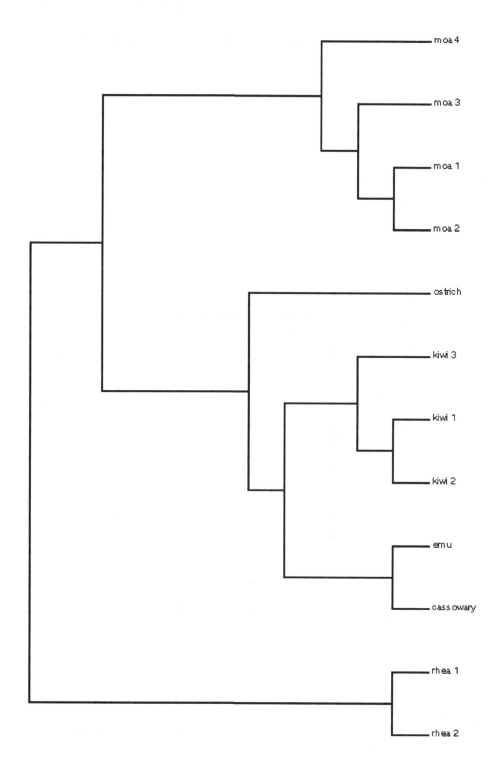

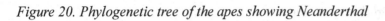

Figure 20. Phylogenetic tree of the apes showing Neanderthal

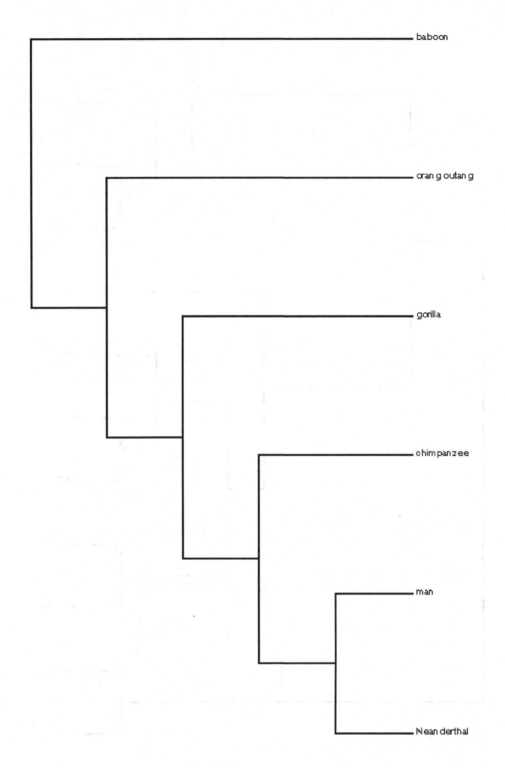

the Neanderthal and modern human mtDNAs is estimated to be four times greater than that of the common ancestor of human mtDNAs, which suggests that Neanderthals went extinct without contributing mtDNA to modern humans.

The expansion of premodern humans into western and eastern Europe *ca.* 40 000 years before the present led to the eventual replacement of the Neanderthals by modern humans *ca.* 28 000 years ago (Ovchinnikov,2000). The second mtDNA analysis of a Neanderthal and the first such analysis on clearly dated Neanderthal remains are reported. The specimen is from one of the eastern-most Neanderthal populations, recovered from Mezmaiskaya Cave in the northern Caucasus. Radiocarbon dating estimated the specimen to be *ca.* 29 000 years old and therefore from one of the latest living Neanderthals. The sequence shows 3.48% divergence from the Feldhofer Neanderthal. Phylogenetic analysis places the two Neanderthals from the Caucasus and western Germany together in a clade that is distinct from modern humans, suggesting that the mtDNA types did not contributed to the modern human mtDNA pool (*cf.* Figure 21). Comparison with modern populations provided no evidence for the multiregional hypothesis of modern human evolution (Aiello & Collard, 2001; Deng et al, 2010). The analysis of ancient DNA raised computational challenges (Prufer, Stenzel, Hofreiter, Paabo, Kelso & Green, 2010).

17. CLASSIFICATION OF HIV VIRUS INHIBITORS

In the present report 31 HIV-1 inhibitors (Table 1) have been studied. Both dendrograms (*cf.* Figure 22) matching to $<i_1,i_2,i_3,i_4,i_5>$ and C_{b_2} separate the same five classes, in agreement with both partial correlation diagrams, binary trees and previous results (Entries 1–3, 12–18, 23, 27, 28). High similarity is found for Entries 2–28 (nevirapine and lopinavir), 3–11–17–18–29 [delavirdine, (+)-calanolide A, AZT, ABC and atazanavir], 12–16–30 (ddI, novel proposed ligand and mozenavir), and 4–8–13–14–20 (emivirine, SJ-3366, ddC, d4T and DAPD). The ddI, novel proposed ligand and mozenavir are grouped into the same class, and emivirine, SJ-3366, ddC, d4T and DAPD. Entries 12–16–30 (ddI, novel proposed ligand and mozenavir) belong to the same class at any grouping level *b*, except at highest level in which each class contains one species.

18. CLASSIFICATION OF ANTI-HIV THIOCARBAMATES

It was studied the molecular classification of thiocarbamates (TCs) as NNRTIs with cytoprotection activity against HIV (*cf.* Figure 23) (Mitra, Roy PP., Kar, Ojha & Roy K.,2010; Torrens & Castellano, 2011). The 62 TCs are classified by structural chemical properties. The analysis includes four regions of structural variations in TCs: position R on the phenyl ring and locations R_{1-2}–$B_{1/2}$. The *structural elements* of a TC can be *ranked* according to inhibitory potency as: $B_{1/2} > R > R_1 > R_2$ substitution. In TC 17, $B_{1/2} = B_1$, R = 4-CH$_3$ and R$_1$ = R$_2$ = H; its associated vector is <1111>, which is selected as a *reference*. In some TCs, $B_{1/2} = B_1$, in some others, $B_{1/2} = B_2$. The analysis is in qualitative agreement with other classification taken as *good* based on *k*-means clustering. A validation is performed with an external property, cytoprotection activity, not used in the development of the classification. The analysis of other properties of TCs would give an insight into classification possible generality.

Figure 21. Phylogenetic relationship of the two Neanderthals and modern humans

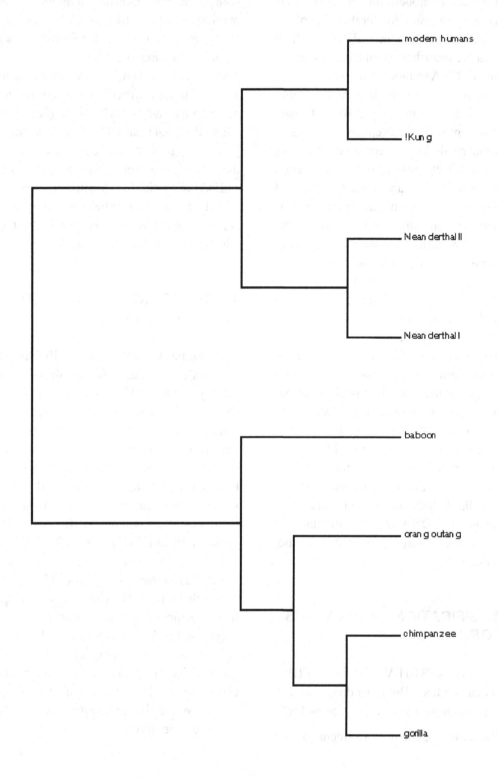

Figure 22. Dendrogram for human immunodeficiency virus type-1 inhibitors

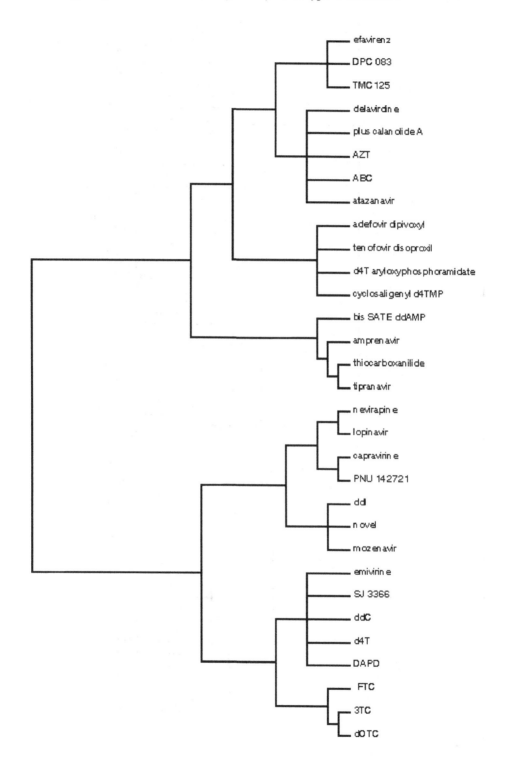

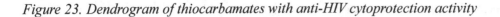

Figure 23. Dendrogram of thiocarbamates with anti-HIV cytoprotection activity

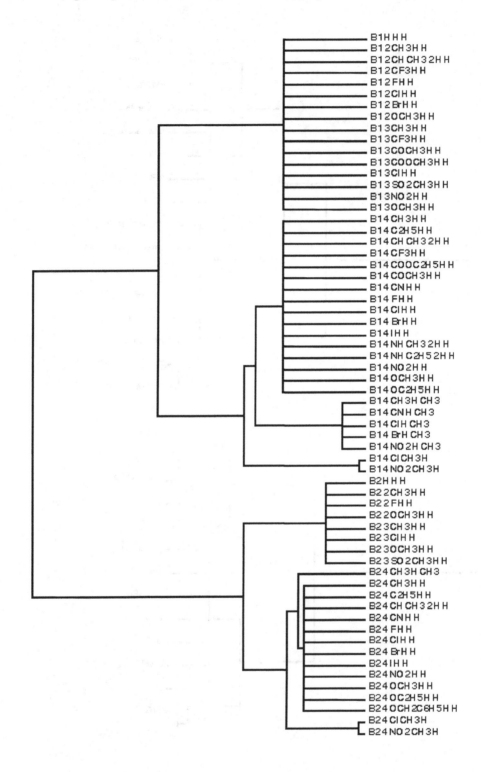

19. CLASSES OF *N*-ARYLOXAZOLIDINONE-5-CARBOXAMIDES

The 38 *N*-aryloxazolidinone-5-carboxamides (NCAs), for HIV PIs, are classified using seven characteristic chemical properties of different portions of molecules (*cf.* Figure 24) (Hadler & Jha, 2010). Several criteria, selected to reduce the analysis to a manageable quantity of NCA structures, refer to structural parameters related to positions $R_{1/2}$ on one phenyl ring, locations R_{3-6} on the other phenyl cycle and site R_7. Many classification algorithms are based on *information entropy*. For sets of moderate size an excessive number of results appear compatible with data and suffer a combinatorial explosion. However, after *equipartition conjecture* one has a selection criterion between different variants resulting from classification between hierarchical trees, according to which the best configuration is the one in which entropy production is most uniformly distributed. The method avoids the problem of others of continuum variables because for the compound with constant <1111111>, null standard deviation always causes a Pearson correlation coefficient of one. The lower-level classification processes show lower entropy.

20. CLASSIFICATION OF ANTI-HIV STYRYLQUINOLINES

The 36 styrylquinolines (SQs) are HIV integrase inhibitors (IIs). On the basis of previous comparative molecular field analysis (CoMFA) of SQs new derivatives were designed. The SQs are classified using four characteristic chemical properties of different portions of their molecules (*cf.* Figure 25) (Leonard & Roy, 2008). The HIV II inhibitory activity data of SQs are studied. The models suggest that the technique could be useful to design potent HIV IIs. Several criteria, selected to reduce analysis to a manageable quantity of SQ structures,

refer to structural parameters related to positions X, Y and Z on phenyl ring and location R on pyridine cycle. Many classification algorithms are based on *information entropy*. For sets of moderate size an excessive number of results appear compatible with data and suffer a combinatorial explosion. However, after the *equipartition conjecture* one has a selection criterion between different variants resulting from classification between hierarchical trees, according to which the best configuration is the one in which the entropy production is most uniformly distributed. The method avoids the problem of others of continuum variables because for the compound with constant <1111>, null standard deviation always causes a Pearson correlation coefficient of one.

21. ARYLTRIAZOLYLHYDROXAMATE ANTIMALARIAL CLASSES

The 35 aryltriazolylhydroxamates (ATHs) presented antimalarial activity (Ojha & Roy, 2010). On the basis of structure–activity relation of ATHs new derivatives were designed. The ATHs were classified using seven characteristic chemical properties of different molecular portions (*cf.* Figure 26). The first feature denotes the number of methylene spacer groups while the last indicates position R on the triazole ring. The antimalarial activity data of ATHs were subjected to study. The number of methylene spacer groups should be optimum (five/six). The technique suggests that the number of methylene groups (between the triazole and hydroxamate moieties) and partial anionic surface areas of the molecules are important parameters for antimalarial activity. The models obtained from the study suggest that the technique could be useful to design potent antimalarial drugs. Several criteria, selected to reduce the analysis to a manageable quantity of ATH structures, refer to the structural parameters related to the number of methylene spacer groups and position R on triazole cycle. Many classifica-

Figure 24. Dendrogram of anti-HIV N-aryloxazolidinone-5-carboxamides

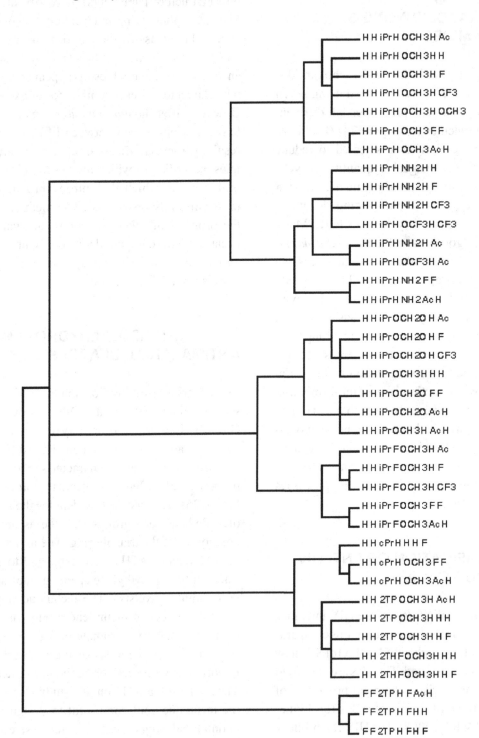

Figure 25. Dendrogram of styrylquinolines with anti-HIV inhibitory activity

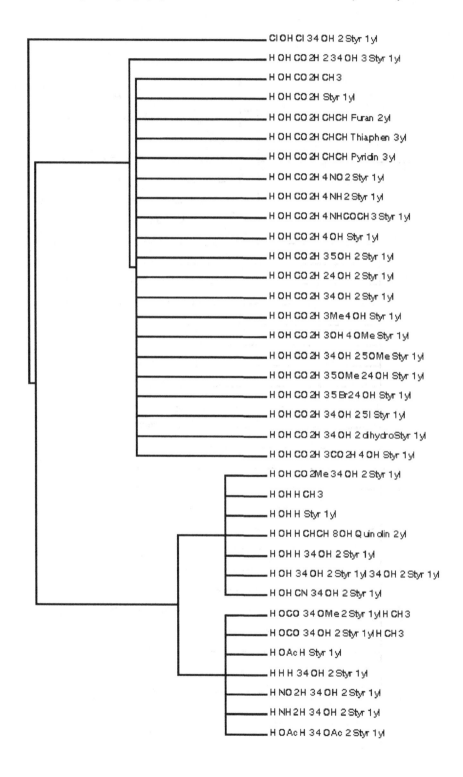

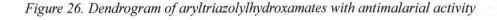

Figure 26. Dendrogram of aryltriazolylhydroxamates with antimalarial activity

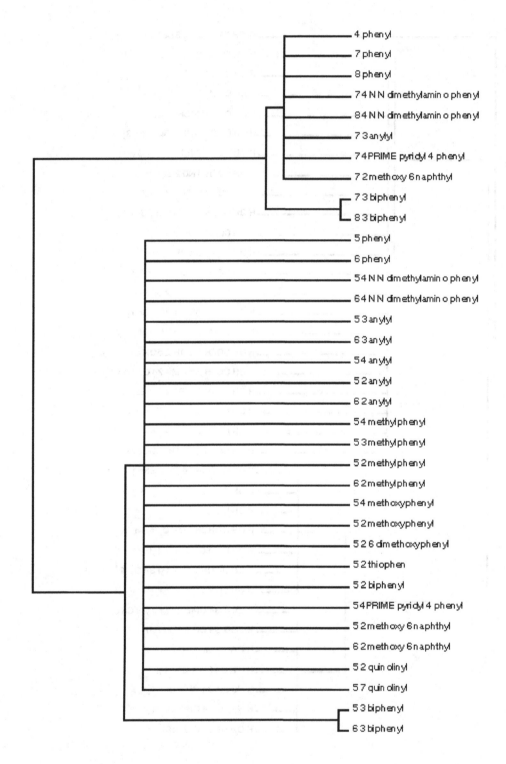

tion algorithms are based on *information entropy*. For sets of moderate size, an excessive number of results appear compatible with the data and suffer a combinatorial explosion. However, after the *equipartition conjecture* one has a selection criterion between different variants resulting from classification between hierarchical trees, according to which the best configuration is the one in which the entropy production is most uniformly distributed. The method avoids the problem of others of continuum variables because for both compounds with constant <11> vector, the null standard deviation always causes a Pearson correlation coefficient of one. The lower-level classification processes show lower entropy.

22. *N*-ARYL-*N*-(3-ARYL-1,2,4-OXADIAZOL-5-YL)AMINE CLASSES

The 26 *N*-aryl-*N*-(3-aryl-1,2,4-oxadiazol-5-yl) amines (NNAs) presented inhibition of human prostate carcinoma cell line DU-145 (Torrens & Castellano, 2009; Krasavin et al., 2010). On the basis of structure–activity relation of NNAs new derivatives were designed. The NNAs were classified using two characteristic chemical properties of different portions of molecules (*cf.* Figure 27). The first feature denotes position R_2 on the amine moiety and the last, location R_1 on the oxadiazole ring. A chemical series of antiproliferative compounds was identified *via* DU-145 high-throughput screening. Medicinal chemistry optimization of two peripheral diversity vectors of the hit, in a hit-targeted library, and testing of the resulting compounds led to structure–activity relation and identification of the *best* pharmacophoric moieties, which were merged into a single compound that exhibits a 200-fold better potency than the original hit. Specific cancer cell cytotoxicity was confirmed for the most potent compounds. The models suggest that the technique could be useful to design potent anti-prostate cancer drugs. Several criteria, selected to reduce the analysis to a manageable quantity of NNA structures, refer to the structural parameters related to position R_2 on the amine moiety and location R_1 on the oxadiazole ring. Many classification algorithms are based on *information entropy*. For sets of moderate size, an excessive number of results appear compatible with the data and suffer a combinatorial explosion. However, after the *equipartition conjecture* one has a selection criterion between different variants resulting from classification between hierarchical trees, according to which the best configuration is the one in which the entropy production is most uniformly distributed. The method avoids the problem of others of continuum variables because for the compound with constant <11> vector, the null standard deviation always causes a Pearson correlation coefficient of one.

23. CLASSIFICATION OF 2-PHENYLINDOLE-3-CARBALDEHYDES

Small molecules, *e.g.*, indoles, are attractive as inhibitors of tubulin polymerization. A number of 2-phenylindole-3-carbaldehydes (PICs) with lipophilic substituents in both aromatic rings was synthesized and evaluated for antitumour activity in MDA-MB231 and MCF-7 breast cancer cells. Some 5-alkylindole derivatives, with a 4-methoxy group in the 2-phenyl ring, strongly inhibited the growth of breast cancer cells with 50% inhibitory concentration (IC_{50}) values of 5–20nM. The action can be rationalized by the cell cycle arrest in G_2/M phase because of the inhibition of tubulin polymerization. Quantitative structure–activity relationship (QSAR) modelling was done on some PICs to find out structural requirements for more active antimitotic agents. It was classified the 33 substituted 2-phenylindole-3-carbaldehydes, inhibitors of MDA-MB231 breast cancer cells (Figure 28) (Halder, Adhikari & Jha, 2009).

Figure 27. Dendrogram of N-aryl-N-(3-aryl-1,2,4-oxadiazol-5-yl)amine inhibitors

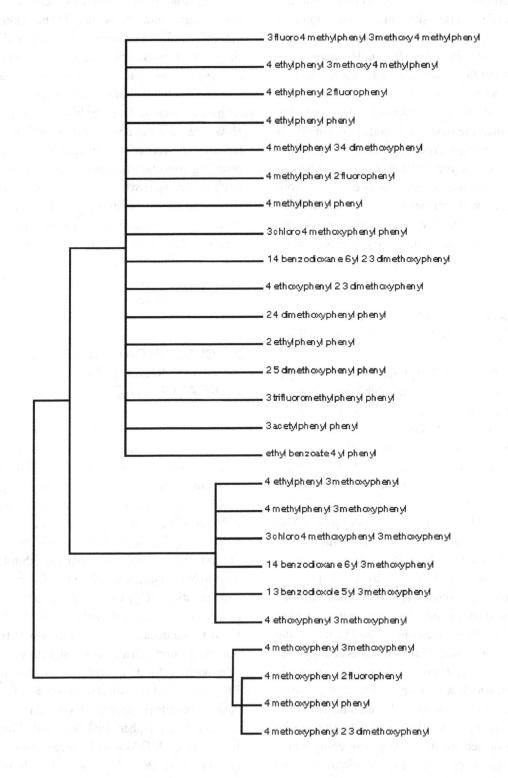

Figure 28. Dendrogram of 2-phenylindole-3-carbaldehydes as antimitotic agents

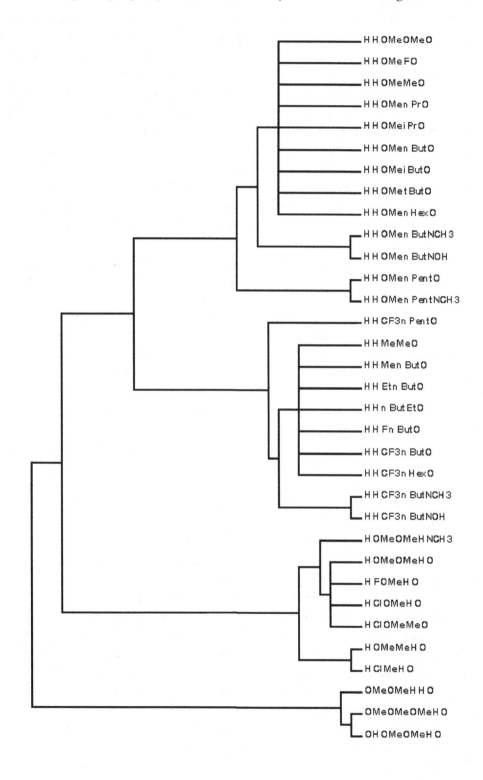

24. CLASSIFICATION OF ANTI-TUBULIN AGENTS WITH INDOLE RING

The IC_{50} values for the inhibition of MKN-45 gastric cancer cells were collected for 59 colchicine-like compounds with indole and trimethoxyphenyl (TMP) rings. The TMP/indole/C=O-bridge inhibitors of MKN-45 gastric cancer cells were classified (*cf.* Figure 29) (Lin, Hsu, Wang, Hsieh & Sun, 2010). Analysis includes seven regions of structural variations in compounds: positions R_{1-4} on the benzo ring, locations R_{5-6} on the pyridine ring and heteroatom X in the indole cycle. Molecular *structural elements* can be *ranked* according to inhibitory activity as $R_1 > R_4 > R_2 > X > R_5 > R_3 > R_6$. In compound 42 $R_1 = R_4 = R_2 = R_5 = H$, $X = N$, $R_3 = OMe$ and $R_6 = CH_3$–OH (<1111111>), which was selected as *reference*. The classification is in agreement with principal component analysis.

25. PERSPECTIVES

Many classification algorithms are based on *information entropy*. For sets of moderate size an excessive number of results appear compatible with data, and the number suffers a combinatorial explosion. However, after the *equipartition conjecture* one has a selection criterion between different variants, resulting from classification between hierarchical trees. According to the conjecture, the best configuration of a flowsheet is the one in which the entropy production is most uniformly distributed. The method avoids the problem of others of continuum variables, because for compounds with the same vector, the null standard deviation causes a Pearson correlation coefficient of one. The lower-level classification processes show lower entropy. If in the calculation of entropy associated with the phylogenetic tree a species is systematically omitted, the difference between the entropy with and without the species can be considered as a measure of the species entropy. The contributions may be studied with the equipartition conjecture. It is not within the scope of our simulation method to replace biological tests of drugs or field data in palaeontology, but such simulation methods can be useful to assert priorities in detailed experimental research. Available experimental and field data should be examined by different classification algorithms to reveal possible features of real biological significance.

Program MolClas is a simple, reliable, efficient and fast procedure for molecular classification, based on the equipartition conjecture of entropy production. It has been written not only to analyze the equipartition conjecture of entropy production, but also to explore the world of molecular classification.

Clusters can form new stable structures, which can be the basis of new solids; they can be used for assembling new materials and be a basis for new technologies. One of the stable cluster structures with close packing is icosahedral, which is realized in various solids and is essential for various processes and interactions in systems with a short-range interaction of atoms. The main problem of large-cluster physics relates to the correspondence with macroscopic particles. Properties of large clusters differ from macroscopic ones. One would expect that a cluster, as a system intermediate between molecules and macroscopic particles, have properties depending on size. A large cluster is an object with specific properties in a wide region of the number of atoms in it. Properties depend on cluster structure. Several criteria were selected to reduce the analysis to a manageable quantity of structures, from the enormous set of fullerene isomers. They refer to the structural parameters related with the presence of contiguous pentagons $\{p,q,r\}$, which destabilize the structures, and hexagons $\{u,v,w\}$. Considering the structure of adjacent hexagons parameters u, v and w are used. A simple linear correlation is a good model for the permanent of the adjacency matrix of fullerenes; $\{q,r,v,w\}$ is redundant information. The $\{p,u\}$

Figure 29. Dendrogram of TMP ring/indole ring/C=O bridge as MKN-45 inhibitors

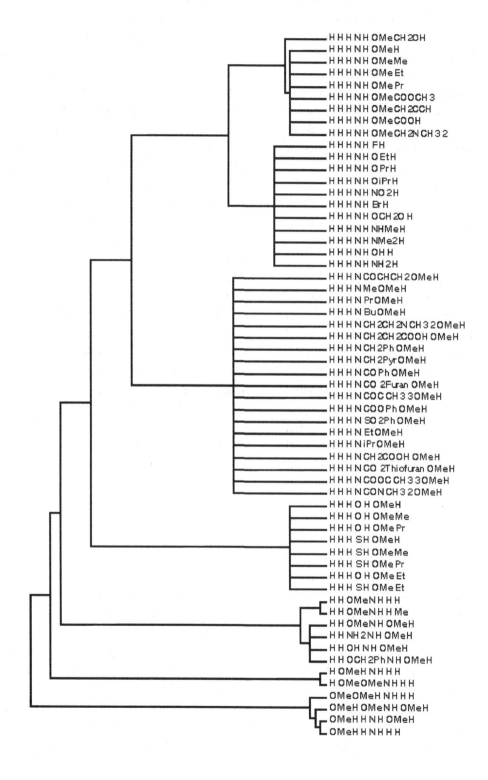

contains the essential characters of the permanent for fullerene structures. The method allowed rapid estimation of the permanent for large fullerenes. Linear methods require that fewer parameters be estimated. A discussion of fullerene aromatic character is problematic because of difficulty in choosing a *benchmark* molecule. Use of planar conjugated molecules as primary references demonstrates a failure to capture the significance of fullerene synthesis, for organic chemistry. If C_{60} is not to be considered aromatic benzene will be condemned to a lonely existence, which makes it a plausible choice as a building block for carbon nanostructures.

In accordance with the similarity laws, the dimensionless Debye temperatures θ_0 for all crystals belonging to the considered class should be close. Temperatures θ_0 are determined *via* similarity relation from experimental–estimated data. Fullerite θ_0 is twice that for inert-gas crystals, which is because of the fact that near the Debye point the crystal is orientationally ordered so that its structure is dissimilar to face-centred cubic. A fullerene molecule, whose thermal rotation is frozen, cannot be considered as a spherical particle. The fulfilment of the similarity laws, which are valuable for particles with spherical interaction potential, would hardly be expected; some contribution to the Debye spectrum of fullerite is made by intramolecular vibrations, which are not considered in formulating similarity laws. If intramolecular–intermolecular vibration frequencies in the Debye temperature range are of the same order, this should be reflected in the Debye frequency.

The detailed comparison of the sequences of enzyme lysozyme allowed for the reconstruction of a molecular phylogenetic tree for birds. Single–complex-linkage perform a binary taxonomy of the parameters that separates avian birds as: $(1,...,5) \rightarrow (1,4,5)(2,3) \rightarrow (1,5)(2,3)(4) \rightarrow (1)(2,3)(4)(5) \rightarrow (1)(2)(3)(4)(5)$.

Topical anaesthetics remain a powerful, new advancement for minimizing pain during cutane-ous procedures. While several new topical anaesthetic agents were released that claim increased efficacy and faster onset, EMLA remains the most widely used topical anaesthetic given its proven efficacy and safety by several clinical trials. As options for practitioner continue to grow the need for studies comparing onset of action, efficacy and safety continues to be of paramount importance. MolClas provides a way to classify the local anaesthtics for difficult cases that are hard to sort *a priori*. EMLA–ice decrease the discomfort associated with needle injection. Although EMLA performs better in pain control, ice has advantages in easy of use, fast action and is less expensive than EMLA. EMLA–ice are good topical anaesthetics each with advantages and disadvantages in clinical use.

The comparison 4-alkylanilines/phenyl alcohols showed that the smaller polar character of the former causes their less negative Gibbs solvation energy and greater hydrophobicity. Both were distinguished by molecular *rugosity*. The correlations point not only to homogeneous molecular structures of phenyl alcohols and 4-alkylanilines, but also to the ability to predict and tailor drug properties. The latter is nontrivial in pharmacology.

Several criteria, selected to reduce the analysis to a manageable quantity of structures from the large set of HIV-1 inhibitors, refer to the structural parameters related with base derivative, *etc*. Good comparison of our classification results, with other taken as *good*, confirm the adequacy of the property vector selected for the molecular structures of HIV-1 inhibitors. Information entropy and principal component analyses permit classifying HIV-1 inhibitors and agree. The HIV-1 inhibitors are grouped into different classes. In general the classical classes of HIV-1 inhibitors are recognized. Inhibitors are classified by structural chemical properties. The *structural elements* of an inhibitor can be *ranked* according to their inhibitory activity as: number of N atoms > number of O atoms > number of S atoms >

number of P atoms > number of halogens. The ddI contains four N atoms, *etc.* ($N_4O_3S_0P_0X_0$, X = F, Cl, Br); its associated vector is <11111>. It was selected as a *reference*. Most inhibitors contain no S atom (ddI, ddC, d4T, novel proposed ligand, $N_{3-4}O_3S_0P_0X_0$), while 3TC includes one S atom ($N_3O_3S_1P_0X_0$). Analysis is in agreement with principal component analysis. It compares well with other classification taken as *good* based on docking, density functional, molecular dynamics, the Rule of Five and absorption, distribution, metabolism, excretion and toxicity. The analysis of the interactions of proposed novel ligand with reverse-transcriptase active site, *via* the Rule of Five, *etc.*, strongly suggests that proposed novel ligand could be a good potential inhibitor for anti-HIV chemotherapy.

It was classified a new group of non-nucleoside reverse transcriptase inhibitor thiocarbamate isosteres of phenethylthiazolylthioureas, with cytoprotection activity against human immunodeficiency virus. Ring-closed compounds bearing *para* substituents on *N*-phenyl ring were potent inhibitors, but maximum potency was reached introducing an additional methyl group at position 4 of framework phthalimide in a *p*-nitro ring-closed molecule. The good comparison of our classification results, with other clustering taken as *good*, confirms the adequacy of cytoprotection activity for thiocarbamate molecular structures. Information entropy permits classifying the compounds and agrees with principal component analyses. Substances are grouped into different classes; the three classical clusters are recognized.

The 38 *N*-aryloxazolidinone-5-carboxamides are classified by structural chemical properties, as human immunodeficiency virus protease inhibitors. Analysis includes seven regions of structural variations in compounds: positions $R_{1/2}$ on one phenyl ring, locations R_{3-6} on the other phenyl cycle and site R_7. Molecular structural elements can be ranked according to inhibitory activity as: $R_3 > R_6 > R_7 > R_4 > R_5 > R_2 > R_1$. In compound 5 $R_3 = R_6 = R_4 = R_2 = H$, $R_7 = iPr$, $R_5 = OCH_3$ and

$R_1 = Ac$ (<1111111>), which was selected as a reference. The classification is in agreement with principal component analysis.

The 36 styrylquinolines are classified by structural chemical properties, as human immunodeficiency virus integrase inhibitors. Analysis includes four regions of structural variations in compounds: positions X, Y and Z on phenyl ring and location R on pyridine cycle. Molecular structural elements can be ranked according to inhibitory activity as: X > Z > Y > R. In compound 15 X = H, Z = OH, Y = CO_2H and R = 2,3,4-$(OH)_3$-Styr-1-yl (<1111>), which was selected as a reference. The classification is in agreement with principal component analysis comparing well with other clustering taken as *good*.

The 35 aryltriazolylhydroxamates with antimalarial activity were classified by structural chemical properties. The analysis includes the number of methylene spacer groups and position R on the triazole cycle. Molecular structural elements can be ranked according to inhibitory activity as: *n* > R. In substance 25 *n* = 6 and R = 3-biphenyl (<11>), which was selected as a reference. The classification is in agreement with principal component analysis comparing well with other clustering taken as *good*.

The 26 *N*-aryl-*N*-(3-aryl-1,2,4-oxadiazol-5-yl) amines were classified as potential therapeutic agents for prostate cancer. There was a clear preference of electron-rich or unsubstituted phenyls in aryl portion R_1 of the molecule, with notorious presence of *meta*-methoxy substituent in 13 active out of 26 compounds for which dose-response curves were obtained. For arylamino fragment R_2 the best activity was observed for substituent *para*-methoxyanilino. Presence of electron-withdrawing or *ortho*-substituents in the arylamino rendered the compounds less active. Structure–activity relations were useful in determining the *activity* chemistry space for future optimization. Substituent *para*-methoxy in arylamino moiety R_2 was combined with substituent *meta*-methoxy in aryl portion R_1. The improved activity of the structure–activity relation compound demonstrated the synergy of effects of the two substituents on the inhibitory potency of the series.

The 33 2-phenylindole-3-carbaldehydes inhibitors of MDA-MB231 breast cancer cells were classified. Analysis includes five regions of structural variations in compounds: positions R_{1-2} on the indole cycle, locations R_{3-4} on the phenyl ring and site R_5 on the carbaldehyde group. Molecular structural elements can be ranked according to inhibitory activity as $R_3 > R_2 > R_4 > R_1 > R_5$. In compound 13 $R_3 = R_2 = H$, $R_4 = OMe$, $R_1 = $ *n*-Pent and $R_5 = O$ (<11111>), which was selected as reference. The classification is in agreement with principal component analysis.

The 59 trimethoxyphenyl/indole/C=O-bridge inhibitors of MKN-45 gastric cancer cells were classified. Analysis includes seven regions of structural variations in compounds: positions R_{1-4} on the benzo ring, locations R_{5-6} on the pyridine ring and heteroatom X in the indole cycle. Molecular structural elements can be ranked according to inhibitory activity as $R_1 > R_4 > R_2 > X > R_5 > R_3 > R_6$. In compound 42 $R_1 = R_4 = R_2 = R_5 = H$, $X = N$, $R_3 = OMe$ and $R_6 = CH_3–OH$ (<1111111>), which was selected as reference. The classification is in agreement with principal component analysis.

ACKNOWLEDGMENT

F. T. belongs to the Institut Universitari de Ciència Molecular and acknowledges financial support from the Spanish Ministerio de Ciencia e Innovación (Project No. BFU2010–19118). G. C. belongs to the Cátedra Energesis de Tecnología Interdisciplinar.

REFERENCES

Aiello, L. C., & Collard, M. (2001). Our newest oldest ancestor? *Nature, 410*, 526–527. doi:10.1038/35069164

Al-Shahrour, F. (2006). BABELOMICS: A systems biology perspective in the functional annotation of genome-scale experiments. *Nucleic Acids Research, 34*, W472–W476. doi:10.1093/nar/gkl172

Al-Shahrour, F., Arbiza, L., Dopazo, H., Huerta, J., Minguez, P., Montaner, D., Dopazo, J. (2007). From genes to functional classes in the study of biological systems. *BMC Bioinformatics*, 8,114-1–17.

Al-Shahrour, F., Díaz-Uriarte, R., & Dopazo, J. (2004). FatiGO: A web tool for finding significant associations of gene ontology terms with groups of genes. *Bioinformatics (Oxford, England), 20*, 578–580. doi:10.1093/bioinformatics/btg455

Al-Shahrour, F., Díaz-Uriarte, R., & Dopazo, J. (2005). Discovering molecular functions significantly related to phenotypes by combining gene expression data and biological information. *Bioinformatics (Oxford, England), 21*, 2988–2993. doi:10.1093/bioinformatics/bti457

Al-Shahrour, F., Minguez, P., Vaquerizas, J. M., Conde, L., & Dopazo, J. (2005). Babelomics: A suite of web-tools for functional annotation and analysis of group of genes in high-throughput experiments. *Nucleic Acids Research, 33*, W460–W464. doi:10.1093/nar/gki456

Alvarez de Andrés, S. (2005). A predictor based on the somatic changes of the BRCA1/2 breast cancer tumors identifies the non-BRCA1/2 tumors with BRCA1 promoter hypermethylation. *Clinical Cancer Research, 11*, 1146–1153.

Aragues, R., Sali, A., Bonet. J., Marti-Renom. M.A,, Oliva, B. (2007). Characterization of protein hubs by inferring interacting motifs from protein interactions. *PLoS Comput Biol,* 3, e178-1–11.

Aranda, M. A., Fraile, A., Dopazo, J., Malpica, J. M., & García-Arenal, F. (1997). Contribution of mutation and RNA recombination to the evolution of a plant pathogenic RNA. *Journal of Molecular Evolution, 44*, 81–88. doi:10.1007/PL00006124

Arbiza, L. (2006). Selective pressures at a codon-level predict deletereous mutations in human disease genes. *Journal of Molecular Biology, 358,* 1390–1404. doi:10.1016/j.jmb.2006.02.067

Arbiza, L., Dopazo, J., Dopazo, H. (2006). Positive selection, relaxation, and acceleration in the evolution of the human and chimp genomes. *PLoS Comp Biol, 2,* e38-1–13.

Arissawa, M., Taft, C. A., & Felcman, J. (2003). Investigation of nucleoside analogs with anti-HIV activity. *International Journal of Quantum Chemistry, 93,* 422–432. doi:10.1002/qua.10580

Avise, J. C., Neigel, J. E., & Arnold, J. (1984). Demopraphic influences on mitochondrial DNA lineage survivorship in animal populations. *Journal of Molecular Evolution, 20,* 99–105. doi:10.1007/BF02257369

Benzecri, J.-P. (1984). *L'analyse des données* (*Vol. 1*). Paris: Dunod.

Bernstein, F. C. (1977). The Protein Data Bank: A computer-based archival file for macromolecular structures. *Journal of Molecular Biology, 112,* 535–542. doi:10.1016/S0022-2836(77)80200-3

Blake, C. C. F., Mair, G. A., North, A. C. T., Phillips, D. C., & Sarma, V. R. (1967). On the conformation of the hen egg-white lysozyme molecule. *Proceedings of the Royal Society of London. Series B. Biological Sciences, 167,* 365–385. doi:10.1098/rspb.1967.0034

Blancourgoiti, B., Sanchez, F., Desanroman, C. P., Dopazo, J., & Ponz, F. (1998). Potato-virus-Y group-C isolates are a homogeneous pathotype but 2 different genetic strains. *The Journal of General Virology, 79,* 2037–2042.

Blancourgoiti, B., Sanchez, F., Dopazo, J., & Ponz, F. (1996). A strain-type clustering of potato-virus-Y based opn the genetic-distance between isolates calculated by RFLP analysis of the amplified coat. *Archives of Virology, 141,* 2425–2442. doi:10.1007/BF01718641

Borchers, A. T., Keen, C. L., & Gershwin, M. E. (2002). The influence of yogurt/*Lactobacillus* on the innate and acquired immune response. *Clinical Reviews in Allergy & Immunology, 22,* 207–230. doi:10.1007/s12016-002-0009-7

Brodin, A., Nyquist-Mayer, A., & Wadstein, T. (1984). Phase diagram and aqueous solubility of the lidocaine–prilocaine binary system. *Journal of Pharmaceutical Sciences, 73,* 481–484. doi:10.1002/jps.2600730413

Calvo, D., Dopazo, J., & Vega, M. A. (1995). Cd36, CLA-1 (Cd36L1), and limpii (Cd36L2) gene family – Cellular-distribution, chromosomal location, and genetic evolution. *Genomics, 25,* 100–106. doi:10.1016/0888-7543(95)80114-2

Canfield, R. E. (1963). The amino acid sequence of egg white lysozyme. *The Journal of Biological Chemistry, 238,* 2698–2707.

Cann, R. L., Stoneking, M., & Wilson, A. C. (1987). Mitochondrial DNA and human evolution. *Nature, 325,* 31–36. doi:10.1038/325031a0

Capriotti, E., Arbiza, L., Casadio, R., Dopazo, J., Dopazo, H., & Marti-Renom, M. A. (2008). The use of estimated evolutionary strength at the codon level improves the prediction of disease related protein mutations in human. *Human Mutation, 29,* 198–204. doi:10.1002/humu.20628

Capriotti, E., & Marti-Renom, M. A. (2008). Computational RNA structure prediction. *Curr Bioinformatics, 3,* 32–45. doi:10.2174/157489308783329823

Cascón, A. (2005). A novel candidate region linked to development of both pheochromocytoma and head/neck paraganglioma. *Genes, Chromosomes & Cancer, 42,* 260–268. doi:10.1002/gcc.20139

Castellano, G., & Torrens, F. (2009). Local anaesthetics classified using chemical structural indicators. *Nereis, 2,* 7–17.

Cavalli Sforza, L. L., Piazza, A., Menozzi, P., & Mountain, J. (1988). Reconstruction of human evolution: Bringing together genetic, archaeological, and linguistic data. *Proceedings of the National Academy of Sciences of the United States of America, 85*, 6002–6006. doi:10.1073/pnas.85.16.6002

Cebra, J. J. (1999). Influences of microbiota on intestinal immune system development. *The American Journal of Clinical Nutrition, 69*, 1046S–1051S.

Chen, D., Eulenstein, O., & Fernández-Baca, D. (2004). Rainbow: A toolbox for phylogenetic supertree construction and analysis. *Bioinformatics (Oxford, England), 20*, 2872–2873. doi:10.1093/bioinformatics/bth313

Chen, W., Liao, B., Xiang, X., & Zhu, W. (2009). An improved binary representation of DNA sequences and its applications. *MATCH Commun Math Comput Chem, 61*, 767–780.

Chen, W., & Zhang, Y. (2009). Comparisons of DNA sequences based on dinucleotide. *MATCH Commun Math Comput Chem, 61*, 533–540.

Chen, W., & Zhang, Y. (2009). Three distances for rapid similarity analysis of DNA sequences. *MATCH Commun Math Comput Chem, 61*, 781–788.

Chiang, B. L., Sheih, Y. H., Wang, L. H., Liao, C. K., & Gill, H. S. (2000). Enhancing immunity by dietary consumption of a probiotic lactic acid bacterium (*Bifidobacterium lactis HN019*): Optimization and definition of cellular immune responses. *European Journal of Clinical Nutrition, 54*, 849–855. doi:10.1038/sj.ejcn.1601093

Ciccarelli, F. D., Doerks, T., von Mering, C., Creevey, C. J., Snel, B., & Bork, P. (2006). Toward automatic reconstruction of a highly resolved tree of life. *Science, 311*, 1283–1287. doi:10.1126/science.1123061

Claros, M. G et al. (2002). *BioROM 2002. Sociedad Española de Bioquímica y Biología Molecular.* Málaga

Claros, M. G. (2003). *BioROM 2003.* Málaga: Sociedad Española de Bioquímica y Biología Molecular–Roche Diagnostics.

Claros, M. G. (2004). *BioROM 2005.* Málaga: Sociedad Española de Bioquímica y Biología Molecular–Universidad Miguel Hernández–Universidad del País Vasco.

Claros, M. G. (2005). *BioROM 2006.* Málaga: Sociedad Española de Bioquímica y Biología Molecular–Pearson Educación.

Claros, M. G. (2006). *BioROM 2007.* Málaga: Sociedad Española de Bioquímica y Biología Molecular–Pearson Educación.

Claros, M. G., Fernández-Fernández, J. M., González-Mañas, J. M., Herráez, Á., Sanz, J. M., & Urdiales, J. L. (2001). *BioROM 1.0 y 1.1.* Málaga: Sociedad Española de Bioquímica y Biología Molecular.

Conde, L. (2004). PupaSNP Finder: A web tool for finding SNPs with putative effect at transcriptional level. *Nucleic Acids Research, 32*, W242–W248. doi:10.1093/nar/gkh438

Conde, L. (2006). PupaSuite: Finding functional SNPs for large-scale genotyping purposes. *Nucleic Acids Research, 34*, W621–W625. doi:10.1093/nar/gkl071

Conde, L., Mateos, Á., Herrero, J., & Dopazo, J. (2003). Improved class prediction in DNA microarray gene expression data by unsupervised reduction of the dimensionality followed by supervised learning with a perceptron. *J VLSI Signal Processing-Syst Signal, Image. Video Technol, 35*, 245–253.

Conde, L., Montaner, D., Burguet-Castell, J., Tárraga, J., Al-Shahrour, F., & Dopazo, J. (2007). Functional profiling and gene expression analysis of chromosomal copy number alterations. *Bioinformation, 1*, 432–435.

Conde, L., Montaner, D., Burguet-Castell, J., Tárraga, J., Medina, I., Al-Shahrour, F., & Dopazo, J. (2007). ISACGH: A web-based environment for the analysis of Array CGH and gene expression which includes functional profiling. *Nucl Acids Res*, 35, W81–W85. Al-Shahrour, F., Minguez, P., Tárraga, J., Medina, I., Alloza, E., Montaner, D., Dopazo, J. (2007). FatiGO+: A functional profiling tool for genomic data. Integration of functional annotation, regulatory motifs and interaction data with microarray experiments. *Nucleic Acids Research, 35*, W91–W96.

Conde, L., Vaquerizas, J. M., Ferrer-Costa, C., Orozco, M., & Dopazo, J. (2005). PupasView: A visual tool for selecting suitable SNPs, with putative pathologic effect in genes, for genotyping purposes. *Nucleic Acids Research, 33*, W501–W505. doi:10.1093/nar/gki476

Conesa, A., & Götz, S. (2008). Blast2GO: A comprehensive suite for functional analysis in plant genomics. *International Journal of Plant Genomics, 2008*, 619832-1–12. doi:10.1155/2008/619832

Cooper, A., Mourer-Chauviré, C., Chambers, G. K., von Haeseler, A., Wilson, A. C., & Pääbo, S. (1992). Independent origins of New Zealand moas and kiwis. *Proceedings of the National Academy of Sciences of the United States of America, 89*, 8741–8744. doi:10.1073/pnas.89.18.8741

Corriou, J. P., Iordache, O., & Tondeur, D. (1991). Classification of biomolecules by information entropy. *Journal de Chimie Physique, 88*, 2645–2652.

Covino, B. G. (1972). Local anesthesia. *The New England Journal of Medicine, 286*, 975–983. doi:10.1056/NEJM197205042861805

Covino, B. G. (1980). Local anesthetic agents for peripheral nerve blocks. *Der Anaesthesist, 29*(7), 33–37.

Covino, B. G. (1986). Pharmacology of local anaesthetic agents. *British Journal of Anaesthesia, 58*, 701–716. doi:10.1093/bja/58.7.701

Crosby, A. W. (2003). *America's forgotten pandemic: The influenza of 1918*. Cambridge, UK: Cambridge University.

Da Silva, C. H. T. P., Almeida, P., & Taft, C. A. (2004). Density functional and docking studies of retinoids for cancer treatment. *Journal of Molecular Modeling, 10*, 38–43. doi:10.1007/s00894-003-0167-4

Da Silva, C. H. T. P., Carvalho, I., & Taft, C. A. (2005). Homology modeling and molecular interaction field studies of α-glucosidases as a guide to structure-based design of novel proposed anti-HIV inhibitors. *Journal of Computer-Aided Molecular Design, 19*, 83–92. doi:10.1007/s10822-005-1486-6

Da Silva, C. H. T. P., Carvalho, I., & Taft, C. A. (2006). Molecular dynamics, docking, density functional, and ADMET studies of HIV-1 reverse transcriptase inhibitors. *Journal of Theoretical and Computational Chemistry, 5*, 579–586. doi:10.1142/S0219633606002441

Da Silva, C. H. T. P., del Ponte, G., Neto, A. F., & Taft, C. A. (2005). Rational design of novel diketoacid-containing ferrocene inhibitors of HIV-1 integrase. *Bioorganic Chemistry, 33*, 274–284. doi:10.1016/j.bioorg.2005.03.001

Da Silva, C. H. T. P., & Taft, C. A. (2004). Computer-aided molecular design of novel glucosidase inhibitors for AIDS treatment. *Journal of Biomolecular Structure & Dynamics, 22*, 59–64.

Da Silva, C. H. T. P., & Taft, C. A. (2005). Molecular dynamics, database screening, density functional and docking studies of novel RAR ligands in cancer chemotherapy. *Biophysical Chemistry*, *117*, 73–77. doi:10.1016/j.bpc.2005.02.006

Dai, Q., Liu, X.-Q., Wang, T.-M., & Vukicevic, D. (2007). Linear regression model of DNA sequences and its application. *Journal of Computational Chemistry*, *28*, 1434–1445. doi:10.1002/jcc.20556

De Clercq, E. (2002). New developments in anti-HIV chemotherapy. *Biochimica et Biophysica Acta*, *1587*, 258–275.

De la Fraga, L. G., Dopazo, J., & Carazo, J. M. (1995). Confidence-limits for resolution estimation in image averaging by random subsampling. *Ultramicroscopy*, *60*, 385–391. doi:10.1016/0304-3991(95)00080-1

Deng, W., Maust, B. S., Nickle, D. C., Learn, G. H., Liu, Y., & Heath, L. (2010). DIVEIN: A web server to analyze phylogenies, sequence divergence, diversity, and informative sites. *BioTechniques*, *48*, 405–408. doi:10.2144/000113370

DeSimone, C., Vesely, R., Negri, R., Bianchi-Salvadori, B., Zanzoglu, S., Cilli, A., & Lucci, L. (1987). Enhancement of immune response of murine Peyer's patches by a diet supplemented with yogurt. *Immunopharmacology and Immunotoxicology*, *9*, 87–100. doi:10.3109/08923978709035203

Di Rienzo, A., & Wilson, A. C. (1991). Branching pattern in the evolutionary three for human mitochondrial DNA. *Proceedings of the National Academy of Sciences of the United States of America*, *88*, 1597–1601. doi:10.1073/pnas.88.5.1597

Díez-Sales, O., Copoví, A., Casabó, V. G., & Herráez, M. (1991). A modelistic approach showing the importance of the stagnant aqueous layers in in vitro diffusion studies, and in vitro-in vivo correlations. *International Journal of Pharmaceutics*, *77*, 1–11. doi:10.1016/0378-5173(91)90295-Y

Díez-Sales, O., Guzmán, D., Cano, D., Martín, A., Sánchez, E., Herráez, M. (1991) A comparative in vitro study of permeability with different synthetic and biological membranes. *Eur J Drug Metab Pharmacokinet* (Spec 3), 441–446.

Díez-Sales, O., López-Castellano, A., Maiques-Lacer, F. J., & Herráez-Domínguez, M. (1993). An in vitro percutaneous absorption study of non-ionic compounds across human skin. *Die Pharmazie*, *48*, 684–686.

Díez-Sales, O., Pérez-Sayas, E., Martín-Villodre, A., & Herráez-Domínguez, M. (1993). The prediction of percutaneous absorption: I. Influence of the dermis on in vitro permeation models. *International Journal of Pharmaceutics*, *100*, 1–7. doi:10.1016/0378-5173(93)90068-Q

Díez-Sales, O., Watkinson, A.C., Herráez-Domínguez, M., & Javaloyes, C., Hadgraf,t J. (1996). A mechanistic investigation of the in vitro human skin permeation enhancing effect of Azone®. *International Journal of Pharmaceutics*, *129*, 33–40. doi:10.1016/0378-5173(95)04237-7

Dopazo, H, Dopazo, J. (2005). Genome-scale evidence of the nematode arthropod clade. *Genome Biol,* *6*, R41-1–10.

Dopazo, H., Santoyo, J., & Dopazo, J. (2004). Phylogenomics and the number of characters required for obtaining an accurate phylogeny of eukaryote model species. *Bioinformatics (Oxford, England)*, *20*, 116–121. doi:10.1093/bioinformatics/bth902

Dopazo, J. (1997). A new index to find regions showing an unexpected variability or conservation in sequence alignments. *Computer Applications in the Biosciences*, *13*, 313–317.

Dopazo, J. (2006). Bioinformatics and cancer: An essential alliance. *Clinical & Translational Oncology*, *8*, 409–415. doi:10.1007/s12094-006-0194-6

Dopazo, J. (2006). Functional interpretation of microarray experiments. *OMICS: A Journal of Integrative Biology, 10*, 398–410. doi:10.1089/omi.2006.10.398

Dopazo, J. (2001). Annotated draft genomic sequence from a *Streptococcus pneumoniae* type 19F clinical isolate. *Microbial Drug Resistance (Larchmont, N.Y.), 7*, 99–125. doi:10.1089/10766290152044995

Dopazo, J., Aloy, P. (2006). Discovery and hypothesis generation through bioinformatics. *Genome Biol, 7*, 307-1–3.

Dopazo, J., & Carazo, J. M. (1997). Phylogenetic reconstruction using an unsupervised growing neural network that adopts the topology of a phylogenetic tree. *Journal of Molecular Evolution, 44*, 226–233. doi:10.1007/PL00006139

Dopazo, J., Zanders, E., Dragoni, I., Amphlett, G., & Falciani, F. (2001). Methods and approaches in the analysis of gene expression data. *Journal of Immunological Methods, 250*, 93–112. doi:10.1016/S0022-1759(01)00307-6

Elena, S., Dopazo, J., de la Peña, M., Flores, R., Diener, T. O., & Moya, A. (2001). Phylogenetic analysis of viroid and viroid-like satellite RNAs from plants: A reassessment. *Journal of Molecular Evolution, 53*, 155–159.

Ellis, R. W. (1999). New technologies for making vaccines. *Vaccine, 17*, 1596–1604. doi:10.1016/S0264-410X(98)00416-2

Escarmis, C., Dopazo, J., Davila, M., Palma, E. L., & Domingo, E. (1995). Large deletions in the 5'-untranslated region of foot-and-mouth-disease virus of serotype-C. *Virus Research, 35*, 155–167. doi:10.1016/0168-1702(94)00091-P

Eswar N, et al. (2007). Comparative protein structure modeling using MODELLER. *Cur. Protocols Prot Sci S50*, 2-9-1–31.

Faith, D. P., Lozupone, C. A., Nipperess, D., & Knight, R. (2009). The cladistic basis for the phylogenetic diversity (PD) measure links evolutionary features to environmental gradients and supports broad applications of microbial ecology's "phylogenetic beta diversity" framework. *International Journal of Molecular Sciences, 10*, 4723–4741. doi:10.3390/ijms10114723

Fawcett, J. P., Kennedy, J. M., Kumar, A., Ledger, R., Kumara, G. M., Patel, M. J., & Zacharias, M. (2002). Comparative efficacy and pharmacokinetics of racemic bupivacaine and S-bupivacaine in third molar surgery. *Journal of Pharmacy & Pharmaceutical Sciences, 5*, 199–204.

Felsenstein, J. (1983). Parsimony in systematics: Biological and statistical issues. *Annual Review of Ecology and Systematics, 14*, 313–333. doi:10.1146/annurev.es.14.110183.001525

Felsenstein, J. (1988). Phylogenies and quantitative characters. *Annual Review of Ecology and Systematics, 19*, 445–471. doi:10.1146/annurev.es.19.110188.002305

Felsenstein, J. (1988). Phylogenies from molecular sequences: Inference and reliability. *Annual Review of Genetics, 22*, 521–565. doi:10.1146/annurev.ge.22.120188.002513

Foley, R. (1987). Hominid species and stone-tool assemblages: How are they related? *Antiquity, 61*, 380–392.

Friedman, P. M., Fogelman, J. P., Nouri, K., Levine, V. J., & Ashinoff, R. (1999). Comparative study of the efficacy of four topical anesthetics. *Dermatologic Surgery, 25*, 950–954. doi:10.1046/j.1524-4725.1999.99138.x

Friedman, P. M., Mafong, E. A., Friedman, E. S., & Geronemus, R. G. (2001). Topical anesthetics update: EMLA and beyond. *Dermatologic Surgery, 27*, 1019–1026. doi:10.1046/j.1524-4725.2001.01855.x

Gabaldón, T. (2005). Evolution of proteins and proteomes: A phylogenetics approach. *Evol. Bioinformatics Online*, *1*, 51–61.

Gabaldón, T. (2006). Computational approaches for the prediction of protein function in the mitochondrion. *American Journal of Physiology. Cell Physiology*, *291*, C1121–C1128. doi:10.1152/ajpcell.00225.2006

Gabaldón, T &Huynen, M.A. (2007). From endosymbiont to host-controlled organelle: The hijacking of mitochondrial protein synthesis and metabolism. *PLoS Comp Biol*, 3, e219-1–10.

Gabaldón, T., Peretó, J., Montero, F., Gil, R., Latorre, A., & Moya, A. (2007). Structural analysis of a hypothetical minimal metabolism. *Philos Trans R Soc B*, *362*, 1751–1762. doi:10.1098/rstb.2007.2067

Gabaldón, T., Snel, B., van Zimmeren, F., Hemrika, W., Tabak, H., Huynen, M.A. (2006). Origin and evolution of the peroxisomal proteome. *Biol Direct,* 1,8-1–14,

Gandía, M. (2007). Transcriptional response of *Citrus aurantifolia* to infection by *Citrus tristeza virus. Virology*, *367*, 298–306. doi:10.1016/j.virol.2007.05.025

Garrick, R. C., Caccone, A., & Sunnucks, P. (2010). Inference of population history by coupling exploratory and model-driven phylogeographic analyses. *International Journal of Molecular Sciences*, *11*, 1190–1227. doi:10.3390/ijms11041190

Goñi, J.R., Vaquerizas, J.M., Dopazo, J., Orozco, M. (2006). Exploring the reasons for the large density of triplex-forming oligonucleotide target sequences in the human regulatory regions. *BMC Genomics,* 7, 63-1–10.

Gorder, P. F. (2005). Computing life's family tree. *Computing in Science & Engineering*, *7*(3), 3–6. doi:10.1109/MCSE.2005.48

Ha, C. L., Lee, J. H., Zhou, H. R., Ustunol, Z., & Pestka, J. J. (1999). Effects of yogurt ingestion on mucosal and systemic cytokine gene expression in the mouse. *Journal of Food Protection*, *62*, 181–188.

Halder, A. K., Adhikari, N., & Jha, T. (2009). Comparative QSAR modelling of 2-phenylindole-3-carbaldehyde derivatives as potential antimitotic agents. *Bioorganic & Medicinal Chemistry Letters*, *19*, 1737–1739. doi:10.1016/j.bmcl.2009.01.081

Halder, A. K., & Jha, T. (2010). Validated predictive QSAR modeling of *N*-aryl-oxazolidinone-5-carboxamides for anti-HIV protease activity. *Bioorganic & Medicinal Chemistry Letters*, *20*, 6082–6087. doi:10.1016/j.bmcl.2010.08.050

Haller, D., Blum, S., Bode, C., Hammes, W. P., & Schiffrin, E. J. (2000). Activation of human peripheral blood mononuclear cells by nonpathogenic bacteria in vitro: Evidence of NK cells as primary targets. *Infection and Immunity*, *68*, 752–759. doi:10.1128/IAI.68.2.752-759.2000

Halpern, G. M., Vruwink, K. G., van de Water, J., Keen, C. L., & Gershwin, M. E. (1991). Influence of long-term yoghurt consumption in young adults. *International Journal of Immunotherapy*, *7*, 205–210.

Hayasaka, K., Gojobori, T., & Horai, S. (1988). Molecular phylogeny and evolution of primate mitochondrial DNA. *Molecular Biology and Evolution*, *5*, 626–644.

Hendlich, M. (1998). Databases for Protein–Ligand Complexes. *Acta Crystallographica. Section D, Biological Crystallography*, *54*, 1178–1182. doi:10.1107/S0907444998007124

Herias, M. V., Hessle, C., Telemo, E., Midtvedt, T., Hanson, L. A., & Wold, A. E. (1999). Immunomodulatory effects of *Lactobacillus plantarum* colonizing the intestine of gnotobiotic rats. *Clinical and Experimental Immunology*, *116*, 283–290. doi:10.1046/j.1365-2249.1999.00891.x

Hermann, J., & Jollès, J. (1970). The primary structure of duck egg-white lysozyme II. *Biochimica et Biophysica Acta, 200,* 178–179.

Hernández P, et al. (2007). Evidence for systems-level molecular mechanisms of tumorigenesis. *BMC Genomics,* 8, 115-1–12.

Herráez, Á. (2006). Biomolecules in the computer: Jmol to the rescue. *Biochemistry and Molecular Biology Education, 34,* 255–261. doi:10.1002/bmb.2006.494034042644

Herrero, J. (2003). GEPAS, a web-based resource for microarray gene expression data analysis. *Nucleic Acids Research, 31,* 3461–3467. doi:10.1093/nar/gkg591

Herrero, J. (2004). New challenges in gene expression data analysis and the extended GEPAS. *Nucleic Acids Research, 32,* W485–W491. doi:10.1093/nar/gkh421

Herrero, J., Díaz-Uriarte, R., & Dopazo, J. (2003). An approach to inferring transcriptional regulation among genes form large-scale expression data. *Comparative and Functional Genomics, 4,* 148–154. doi:10.1002/cfg.237

Herrero, J., Díaz-Uriarte, R., & Dopazo, J. (2003). Gene expression data preprocessing. *Bioinformatics (Oxford, England), 19,* 655–656. doi:10.1093/bioinformatics/btg040

Herrero, J., & Dopazo, J. (2002). Combining hierarchical clustering and self-organizing maps for exploratory analysis of gene expression patterns. *Journal of Proteome Research, 1,* 467–470. doi:10.1021/pr025521v

Herrero, J., Valencia, A., & Dopazo, J. (2001). A hierarchical unsupervised growing neural network for clustering gene expression patterns. *Bioinformatics (Oxford, England), 17,* 126–136. doi:10.1093/bioinformatics/17.2.126

Hillis, D. M., Bull, J. J., White, M. E., Badgett, M. R., & Molineux, I. J. (1992). Experimental phylogenetics: generation of a known phylogeny. *Science, 255,* 589–592. doi:10.1126/science.1736360

Hoef-Emden, K. (2005). Molecular phylogenetic analyses and real-life data. *Computing in Science & Engineering, 7*(3), 86–91. doi:10.1109/MCSE.2005.55

Hoffmann, R., Dopazo, J., Cigudosa, J. C., & Valencia, A. (2005). HCAD, closing the gap between breakpoints and genes. *Nucleic Acids Research, 33,* D511–D513. doi:10.1093/nar/gki061

Hooper, L. V., Wong, M. H., Thelin, A., Hansson, L., Falk, P. G., & Gordon, J. I. (2001). Molecular analysis of commensal host-microbial relationships in the intestine. *Science, 291,* 881–884. doi:10.1126/science.291.5505.881

Huerta-Cepas, J., Bueno, A., Dopazo, J., & Gabaldón, T. (2008). PhylomeDB: A database for complete collections of gene phylogenies. *Nucleic Acids Research, 36,* D491–D496. doi:10.1093/nar/gkm899

Huerta-Cepas, J., Dopazo, H., Dopazo, J., Gabaldón, T. (2007). The human phylome. *Genome Biol,* 8, R109-1–16.

Ingman, M., Kaessmann, H., Pääbo, S., & Gyllensten, U. (2000). Mitochondrial genome variation and the origin of moden humans. *Nature, 408,* 708–713. doi:10.1038/35047064

Iordache, O., Corriou, J. P., Garrido-Sánchez, L., Fonteix, C., & Tondeur, D. (1993). Neural network frames. Application to biochemical kinetic diagnosis. *Computers & Chemical Engineering, 17,* 1101–1113. doi:10.1016/0098-1354(93)80091-Z

Isolauri, E., Juntunen, M., Rautanen, T., Sillanaukee, P., & Koivula, T. (1991). A human *Lactobacillus* strain (*Lactobacillus casei sp. strain GG*) promotes recovery from acute diarrhea in children. *Pediatrics, 88,* 90–97.

Jollès, J., Hermann, J., Niemann, B., & Jollès, P. (1967). Differences between the chemical structures of duck and hen egg-white lysozymes. *European Journal of Biochemistry, 1*, 344–346. doi:10.1111/j.1432-1033.1967.tb00079.x

Jones, P. S. (1998). Strategies for antiviral drug discovery. *Antiviral Chemistry & Chemotherapy, 9*, 283–302.

Kaneda, M., Kato, T., Tominaga, N., Chitani, K., & Narita, K. (1969). The amino acid sequence of quail lysozyme. *Journal of Biochemistry, 66*, 747–749.

Karzynski, M., Mateos, Á., Herrero, J., & Dopazo, J. (2003). Using a genetic algorithm and a perceptron for feature selection and supervised clase learning in DNA microarray data. *Artificial Intelligence Review, 20*, 39–51. doi:10.1023/A:1026032530166

Kasai, N., Mizushina, Y., Sugawara, F., & Sakaguchi, K. (2002). Three-dimensional structural model analysis of the binding site of an inhibitor, nervonic acid, of both DNA polymerase β and HIV-1 reverse transcriptase. *Journal of Biochemistry, 132*, 819–828.

Kash, J. C. (2004). Global host immune response: Pathogenesis and transcriptional profiling of type A influenza viruses expressing the hemagglutinin and neuraminidase genes from the 1918 pandemic virus. *Journal of Virology, 78*, 9499–9511. doi:10.1128/JVI.78.17.9499-9511.2004

Kaufmann, A. (1975). *Introduction à la théorie des sous-ensembles flous, vol. 3 Paris*. Masson.

Krasavin, M., Rufanov, K.A., Sosnov, A.V., Karapetian, R., Godovykh, E., Soldatkina, O., Lavrovsky, Y., Gakh, A.A (2010). Discovery and SAR exploration of *N*-aryl-*N*-(3-aryl-1,2,4-oxadiazol-5-yl)amines as potential therapeutic agents for prostate cancer. *Chem Central J*, 4, 4-1–7.

Krings, M., Stone, A., Schmitz, R. W., Krainitzki, H., Stoneking, M., & Pääbo, S. (1997). Neanderthal DNA sequences and the origin of modern humans. *Cell, 90*, 19–30. doi:10.1016/S0092-8674(00)80310-4

Kuno, M., Palangsuntikul, R., & Hannongbua, S. (2003). Investigation on an orientation and interaction energy of the water molecule in the HIV-1 reverse transcriptase active site by quantum chemical calculations. *Journal of Chemical Information and Computer Sciences, 43*, 1584–1590. doi:10.1021/ci0203850

Kuwahara, R. T., & Skinner, R. B. Jr. (2001). EMLA versus ice as a topical anesthetic. *Dermatologic Surgery, 27*, 495–496. doi:10.1046/j.1524-4725.2001.00343.x

Largo, C. (2006). Identification of overexpressed genes in frequently gained/amplified chromosome regions in multiple myeloma. *Haematologica, 91*, 184–191.

LaRue, J. N., & Speck, J. C. Jr. (1969)... *Federation Proceedings, 28*, 662–662.

Leonard, J. T., & Roy, J. (2008). Exploring molecular shape analysis of styrylquinoline derivatives as HIV-1 integrase inhibitors. *European Journal of Medicinal Chemistry, 43*, 81–92. doi:10.1016/j.ejmech.2007.02.021

Leonard, J. T., & Roy, K. (2003). QSAR modeling of anti-HIV activities of alkenyldiarylmethanes using topological and physicochemical descriptors. *Drug Design and Discovery, 18*, 165–180. doi:10.1080/10559610390484221

Leonard, J. T., & Roy, K. (2004). Classical QSAR modeling of HIV-1 reverse transcriptase inhibitor 2-amino-6-arylsulfonylbenzonitriles and congeners. *QSAR & Combinatorial Science, 23*, 23–35. doi:10.1002/qsar.200330845

Leonard, J. T., & Roy, K. (2004). Classical QSAR modeling of CCR5 receptor binding affinity of substituted benzylpyrazoles. *QSAR & Combinatorial Science, 23*, 387–398. doi:10.1002/qsar.200430871

Leonard, J. T., & Roy, K. (2006). QSAR by LFER model of HIV protease inhibitory data of mannitol derivatives using FA-MLR, PCRA and PLS techniques. *Bioorganic & Medicinal Chemistry, 14*, 1039–1046. doi:10.1016/j.bmc.2005.09.022

Leonard, J. T., & Roy, K. (2006). The HIV entry inhibitors revisited. *Current Medicinal Chemistry, 13*, 911–934. doi:10.2174/092986706776361030

Levin, A. M. (2007). Spatial differentiation in the vegetative mycelium of *Aspergillus niger. Eukaryotic Cell, 6*, 2311–2322. doi:10.1128/EC.00244-07

Li, M., Badger, J. H., Chen, X., Kwong, S., Kearney, P., & Zhang, H. (2001). An information-based sequence distance and its application to whole mitochondrial genome phylogeny. *Bioinformatics (Oxford, England), 17*, 149–154. doi:10.1093/bioinformatics/17.2.149

Liao, B., Liao, L., Yue, G., Wu, R., & Zhu, W. (2010). A vertical and horizontal method for constructing phylogenetic tree. *MATCH Commun Math Comput Chem, 63*, 691–700.

Liao, B., Zhu, W., & Liu, Y. (2006). 3D graphical representation of DNA sequence without degeneracy and its applications in constructing phylogenic tree. *MATCH Commun Math Comput Chem, 56*, 209–216.

Lin, I. H., Hsu, C. C., Wang, S. H., Hsieh, H. P., & Sun, Y. C. (2010). Comparative molecular field analysis of anti-tubulin agents with indole ring binding at the colchicine binding site. *Journal of Theoretical and Computational Chemistry, 9*, 279–291. doi:10.1142/S0219633610005657

Link-Amster, H., Rochat, F., Saudan, K. Y., Mignot, O., & Aeschlimann, J. M. (1994). Modulation of a specific humoral immune response and changes in intestinal flora mediated through fermented milk intake. *FEMS Immunology and Medical Microbiology, 10*, 55–63. doi:10.1111/j.1574-695X.1994.tb00011.x

Liu, Z., Liao, B., & Zhu, W. (2009). A new method to analyze the similarity based on dual nucleotides of the DNA sequence. *MATCH Commun Math Comput Chem, 61*, 541–552.

López, A., Faus, V., Díez-Sales, O., & Herráez, M. (1998). Skin permeation model of phenyl alcohols: Comparison of experimental conditions. *International Journal of Pharmaceutics, 173*, 183–191. doi:10.1016/S0378-5173(98)00231-2

López, A., Morant, M. J., Guzmán, D., Borrás-Blasco, J., Díez-Sales, O., & Herráez, M. (1996). Skin permeation model of phenylalkylcarboxylic homologous acids and their enhancer effect on percutaneous penetration of 5-fluorouracil. *International Journal of Pharmaceutics, 139*, 205–213. doi:10.1016/0378-5173(96)04628-5

López, A., Pellett, M. A., Llinares, F., Díez-Sales, O., Herráez, M., & Hadgraft, J. (1997). The enhancer effect of several phenyl alcohols on percutaneous penetration of 5-fluorouracil. *Pharmaceutical Research, 14*, 681–685. doi:10.1023/A:1012177717336

Makarenkov, V., & Lapointe, F. J. (2004). A weighted least-squares approach for inferring phylogenies from incomplete distance matrices. *Bioinformatics (Oxford, England), 20*, 2113–2121. doi:10.1093/bioinformatics/bth211

Malin, M., Suomalainen, H., Saxelin, M., & Isolauri, E. (1996). Promotion of IgA immune response in patients with Crohn's disease by oral bacteriotherapy with *Lactobacillus GG. Annals of Nutrition & Metabolism, 40*, 137–145. doi:10.1159/000177907

Marrero-Ponce, Y. (2005). A computer-based approach to the rational discovery of new tricho-monacidal drugs by atom-type linear indices. *Current Drug Discovery Technologies, 2,* 245–265. doi:10.2174/157016305775202955

Marrero-Ponce, Y. (2006). Predicting antitricho-monal activity: A computational screening using atom-based bilinear indices and experimental proofs. *Bioorganic & Medicinal Chemistry, 14,* 6502–6524. doi:10.1016/j.bmc.2006.06.016

Marrero-Ponce, Y. (2008). Bond-based linear indices in QSAR: Computational discovery of novel anti-trichomonal compounds. *Journal of Computer-Aided Molecular Design, 22,* 523–540. doi:10.1007/s10822-008-9171-1

Marteau, P.R, de Vrese, M, Cellier, C.J, Schrezen-meir, J. (2001). Protection from gastrointestinal diseases with the use of probiotics. *Am J Clin Nutr, 73*(Supl 2),430S–436S.

Marti-Renom, M. A. (2007). DBAli tools: Mining the protein structural space. *Nucleic Acids Research, 35,* W393–W397. doi:10.1093/nar/gkm236

Marti-Renom, M.A., Rossi, A., Al-Shahrour, F., Davis, F.P., Pieper, U., Dopazo, J., Sali, A. (2007). The AnnoLite and AnnoLyze programs for comparative annotation of protein structures. *BMC Bioinformatics, 8,*S4-1–12.

Martín, M. J., González-Candelas, F., Sobrino, F., & Dopazo, J. (1995). A method for determining the position and size of optimal sequence regions for phylogenetic analysis. *Journal of Molecular Evolution, 41,* 1128–1138. doi:10.1007/BF00173194

Martín, M. J., Herrero, J., Mateos, Á., & Dopazo, J. (2003). Comparing bacterial genomes through conservation profiles. *Genome Research, 15,* 991–998. doi:10.1101/gr.678303

Martín, M. J., Núñez, J. I., Sobrino, F., & Dopazo, J. (1998). A procedure for detecting selection in highly variable viral genomes – Evidence of positive selection in antigenic regions of capsid protein VP1 of foot-and-mouth-disease virus. *Journal of Virological Methods, 74,* 215–221. doi:10.1016/S0166-0934(98)00088-3

Martinez, I., Dopazo, J., & Melero, J. A. (1997). Antigenic structure of the human respiratory syncytial virus G-glycoprotein and relevance of hypermutation events for the generation of antigenic variants. *The Journal of General Virology, 78,* 2419–2429.

Martínez-Delgado, B. (2004). Expression profiling of T-cell lymphomas differentiates peripheral and lymphoblastic lymphomas and defines survival related genes. *Clinical Cancer Research, 10,* 4971–4982. doi:10.1158/1078-0432.CCR-04-0269

Mateos, Á., Dopazo, J., Jansen, R., Tu, Y., Gerstein, M., & Stolovitzky, G. (2002). Systematic learning of gene functional classes from DNA array expression data by using multilayer perceptrons. *Genome Research, 12,* 1703–1715. doi:10.1101/gr.192502

Matsuzaki, T., Yamazaki, R., Hashimoto, S., & Yokokura, T. (1998). The effect of oral feeding of *Lactobacillus casei strain Shirota* on immunoglobulin E production in mice. *Journal of Dairy Science, 81,* 48–53. doi:10.3168/jds.S0022-0302(98)75549-3

MDL. (2007). *Program Chime.* San Leandro, CA: MDL Information Systems.

Medina, I., Montaner, D., Tárraga, J., & Dopazo, J. (2007). Prophet, a web-based tool for class prediction using microarray data. *Bioinformatics (Oxford, England), 23,* 390–391. doi:10.1093/bioinformatics/btl602

Meléndez, B. (2004). Gene expression analysis on chromosomal regions of gain or loss in genetic material detected by comparative genomic hybridization. *Genes, Chromosomes & Cancer, 41*, 353–365. doi:10.1002/gcc.20105

Meneses, A. (2005). A linear discrimination analysis based virtual screening of trichomonacidal lead-like compounds. Outcomes of *in silico* studies supported by experimental results. *Bioorganic & Medicinal Chemistry Letters, 17*, 3838–3843. doi:10.1016/j.bmcl.2005.05.124

Meneses, A., Rojas, L., Sifontes, R. S., López, Y., & Sariego, R. I. (2001). Aplicación de un método alternativo al conteo en cámara de Neubauer para determinar concentración de *Trichomonas vaginalis*. *Revista Cubana de Medicina Tropical, 53*, 180–188.

Mine, R. L. (2006). ERCC4 associated with breast cancer risk: A two-stage case-control study using high-throughput genotyping. *Cancer Research, 66*, 9420–9427. doi:10.1158/0008-5472.CAN-06-1418

Minguez, P., Al-Shahrour, F., Montaner, D., & Dopazo, J. (2007). Functional profiling of microarray experiments using text-mining derived bioentities. *Bioinformatics (Oxford, England), 23*, 3098–3099. doi:10.1093/bioinformatics/btm445

Miró, M. J., Méndez, M. T., Raposo, R., Herráez, Á., Barrero, B., & Palacios, E. (2007). Desarrollo de una asignatura virtual de tercer ciclo como un espacio de enseñanza-aprendizaje que permite la participación activa del alumno. In *III Jornada Campus Virtual UCM* (pp. 304–306). Madrid: Innovación en el Campus Virtual, Metodologías y Herramientas. Complutense.

Mitra, I., Roy, P. P., Kar, S., Ojha, P. K., & Roy, K. (2010). On further application of r_m^2 as a metric for validation of QSAR models. *Journal of Chemometrics, 24*, 22–33. doi:10.1002/cem.1268

Mlinaric, A., Kreft, S., Umek, A., & Strukelj, B. (2000). Screening of selected plant extracts for *in vivo* inhibitory activity on HIV-1 reverse transcriptase (HIV-1 RT). *Die Pharmazie, 55*, 75–77.

Monier, A., Claverie, J.M., Ogata, H. (2008). Taxonomic distribution of large DNA viruses in the sea. *Genome Biol*, 9,R106-1–15.

Montaner, D. (2006). Next station in microarray data analysis: GEPAS. *Nucleic Acids Research, 34*, W486–W491. doi:10.1093/nar/gkl197

Montero, A. (2005). A novel non-stochastic quadratic fingerprints-based approach for the *in silico* discovery of new antitrypanosomal compounds. *Bioorganic & Medicinal Chemistry, 13*, 6264–6275. doi:10.1016/j.bmc.2005.06.049

Montero-Conde, C. (2008). Molecular profiling related to poor prognosis in thyroid carcinoma. Combining gene expression data and biological information. *Oncogene, 27*, 1554–1561. doi:10.1038/sj.onc.1210792

Montero-Torres, A. (2006). Non-stochastic quadratic fingerprints and LDA-based QSAR models in hit and lead generation through virtual screening: Theoretical and experimental assessment of a promising method for the discovery of new antimalarial compounds. *European Journal of Medicinal Chemistry, 41*, 483–493. doi:10.1016/j.ejmech.2005.12.010

Moreno-Bueno, G. (2003). Differential gene expression profile in endometrioid and nonendometrioid endometrial carcinoma: *STK15* is frequently overexpressed and amplified in nonendometrioid carcinomas. *Cancer Research, 63*, 5697–5702.

Nakano, M., Fukuda, K., & Taniguchi, H. (2009). Appropriate probe search method to specify groups in higher taxonomic ranks. *Journal of Basic Microbiology, 49*, 100–108. doi:10.1002/jobm.200800211

Niraikulam, A., Hyungdon, Y., & Natarajan, S. (2010). Protein coding genes for better resolution of phylogenetic analysis. *Res J Biotechnol*, *5*, 74–74.

Nueda, M. J., Conesa, A., Westerhuis, J. A., Hoefsloot, H. C., Smilde, A. K., Talón, M., & Ferrer, A. (2007). Discovering gene expression patterns in time course microarray experiments by ANOVA-SCA. *Bioinformatics (Oxford, England)*, *23*, 1792–1800. doi:10.1093/bioinformatics/btm251

Núñez, J. I. (2001). Identification of optimal regions for phylogenetic studies on VP1 gene of foot-and-mouth disease virus: Analysis of types A and O Argentinean viruses. *Veterinary Research*, *32*, 31–45. doi:10.1051/vetres:2001107

Núñez, J. I., Blanco, E., Hernandez, T., Dopazo, J., & Sobrino, F. (1998). RT-PCR in foot-and-mouth-disease diagnosis. *The Veterinary Quarterly*, *20*, S34–S36.

Núñez, J. I., Blanco, E., Hernandez, T., Gomez-Tejedor, G., Martín, M. J., Dopazo, J., & Sobrino, F. (1998). A RT-PCR assay for the differential-diagnosis of vesicular viral diseases of swine. *Journal of Virological Methods*, *72*, 227–235. doi:10.1016/S0166-0934(98)00032-9

Ojha, P. K., & Roy, K. (2010). Chemometric modelling of antimalarial activity of aryltriazolylhydroxamates. *Molecular Simulation*, *36*, 939–952. doi:10.1080/08927022.2010.492835

Olivares, I., Menendez-Arias, L., Rodriguez-Bernabe, A., Martín, M. J., Dopazo, J., & Lopez-Galindez, C. (1995). Sequence-analysis of HIV-1 vif gene in Spanish isolates. *Virus Genes*, *9*, 283–288. doi:10.1007/BF01702884

Otu, H. H., & Sayood, K. (2003). A new sequence distance measure for phylogenetic tree construction. *Bioinformatics (Oxford, England)*, *19*, 2122–2130. doi:10.1093/bioinformatics/btg295

Ouzounis, C. A., & Valencia, A. (2003). Early bioinformatics: The birth of a discipline–A personal view. *Bioinformatics (Oxford, England)*, *19*, 2176–2190. doi:10.1093/bioinformatics/btg309

Ovchinnikov, I. V., Götherström, A., Romanova, G. P., Kharitonov, V. M., Lidén, K., & Goodwin, W. (2000). Molecular analysis of Neanderthal DNA from the Northern Caucasus. *Nature*, *404*, 490–493. doi:10.1038/35006625

Painter, G. R., Andrews, C. W., & Furman, P. A. (2000). Conformation and local environment of nucleotides bound to HIV type 1 reverse transcriptase (HIV-1 RT) in the ground state. *Nucleosides, Nucleotides & Nucleic Acids*, *19*, 13–29. doi:10.1080/15257770008032994

Palacios, J. (2005). Phenotypic characterization of BRCA1 and BRCA2 tumors based in a tissue microarray study with 37 immunohistochemical markers. *Breast Cancer Research and Treatment*, *90*, 5–14. doi:10.1007/s10549-004-1536-0

Parr, C. S., Lee, B., Campbell, D., & Bederson, B. B. (2004). Visualizations for taxonomic and phylogenetic trees. *Bioinformatics (Oxford, England)*, *20*, 2997–3004. doi:10.1093/bioinformatics/bth345

Pelto, L., Isolauri, E., Lilius, E. M., Nuutila, J., & Salminen, S. (1998). Probiotic bacteria down-regulate the milk-induced inflammatory response in milk-hypersensitive subjects but have an immunostimulatory effect in healthy subjects. *Clinical and Experimental Allergy*, *28*, 1474–1479. doi:10.1046/j.1365-2222.1998.00449.x

Perdigon, G., Rachid, M., de Budeguer, M. V., & Valdez, J. C. (1994). Effect of yogurt feeding on the small and large intestine associated lymphoid cells in mice. *The Journal of Dairy Research*, *61*, 553–562. doi:10.1017/S002202990002848X

Prüfer, K., Stenzel, U., Hofreiter,M., Pääbo, S,. Kelso, J., Green, R.E. (2010). Computational challenges in the analysis of ancient DNA. *Genome Biol,* 11,R47-1–15.

Puri, P., Rattan, A., Bijlani, R. L., Mahapatra, S. C., & Nath, I. (1996). Splenic and intestinal lymphocyte proliferation response in mice fed milk or yogurt and challenged with *Salmonella typhimurium. International Journal of Food Sciences and Nutrition, 47,* 391–398. doi:10.3109/09637489609006952

Quinones-Mateu, M., Holguin, A., Dopazo, J., Najera, I., & Domingo, E. (1996). Point mutant frequencies in the pol gene of human-immunodeficiency-virus type-1 are 2-fold to 3-fold lower than those of env. *AIDS Research and Human Retroviruses, 12,* 1117–1128. doi:10.1089/aid.1996.12.1117

Quinones-Mateu, M. E., Dopazo, J., Este, J. A., Rota, T. R., & Domingo, E. (1995). Molecular characterization of human-immunodeficiency-virus type-1 isolates from Venezuela. *AIDS Research and Human Retroviruses, 11,* 605–616. doi:10.1089/aid.1995.11.605

Rammal, R., Toulouse, G., & Virasoro, M. A. (1986). Ultrametricity for physicists. *Reviews of Modern Physics, 58,* 765–788. doi:10.1103/RevModPhys.58.765

Reid, A. H., & Taubenberger, J. K. (2003). The origin of the 1918 pandemic influenza virus: A continuing enigma. *The Journal of General Virology, 84,* 2285–2292. doi:10.1099/vir.0.19302-0

Reumers, J. (2008). Joint annotation of coding and non-coding single nucleotide polymorphisms and mutations in the 5 SNPeffect and PupaSuite databases. *Nucleic Acids Research, 36,* D825–D829. doi:10.1093/nar/gkm979

Rico, D., Vaquerizas, J.M., Dopazo, H., Boscá, L. (2007). Identification of conserved domains in the promoter regions of nitric oxide synthase 2: Implications for the species-specific transcription and evolutionary differences. *BMC Genomics,* 8, 271-1–10.

Rivera-Borroto, O. M. (2009). Discovery of novel trichomonacidals using LDA-driven QSAR models and bond-based bilinear indices as molecular descriptors. *QSAR & Combinatorial Science, 28,* 9–26. doi:10.1002/qsar.200610165

Roberts, E., Eargle,J., Wright, D., Luthey-Schulten, Z. (2006). MultiSeq: Unifying sequence and structure data for evolutonary analysis. *BMC Bioinformatics, 7,* 382-1–11.

Rodrigo, M. J., & Dopazo, J. (1995). Evolutionary analysis of the picornavirus family. *Journal of Molecular Evolution, 40,* 362–371. doi:10.1007/BF00164022

Rodríguez-Perales, S. (2004). Cloning of a new familial t(3;8) translocation associated with conventional renal cell carcinoma reveals a 5 kb microdeletion and no gene involved in the rearrangement. *Human Molecular Genetics, 13,* 983–990. doi:10.1093/hmg/ddh111

Rojas, J. M., Dopazo, J., Santana, M., Lopez-Galindez, C., & Tabares, E. (1995). Comparative-study of the genetic-variability in thymidine kinase and glycoprotein-B genes of herpes-simplex viruses by the RNase-A mismatch cleavage method. *Virus Research, 35,* 205–214. doi:10.1016/0168-1702(94)00097-V

Root, M. J., Kay, M. S., & Kim, P. S. (2001). Protein design of an HIV-1 entry inhibitor. *Science, 291,* 884–888. doi:10.1126/science.1057453

Roy, K., & Leonard, J. T. (2004). QSAR modeling of HIV-1 reverse transcriptase inhibitor 2-amino-6-arylsulfonylbenzonitriles and congeners using molecular connectivity and E-state parameters. *Bioorganic & Medicinal Chemistry, 12*, 745–754. doi:10.1016/j.bmc.2003.11.009

Roy, K., & Leonard, J. T. (2005). Classical QSAR modeling of anti-HIV 2,3-diaryl-1,3-thiazolidin-4-ones. *QSAR & Combinatorial Science, 24*, 579–592. doi:10.1002/qsar.200430901

Roy, K., & Leonard, J. T. (2005). QSAR by LFER model of cytotoxicity data of anti-HIV 5-phenyl-1-phenylamino-1H-imidazole derivatives using principal component analysis and genetic function approximation. *Bioorganic & Medicinal Chemistry, 13*, 2967–2973. doi:10.1016/j.bmc.2005.02.003

Roy, K., & Leonard, J. T. (2005). QSAR analyses of 3-(4-benzylpiperidin-1-yl)-N-phenyl-propyl-amine derivatives as potent CCR5 antagonists. *Journal of Chemical Information and Modeling, 45*, 1352–1368. doi:10.1021/ci050205x

Roy, K., & Leonard, J. T. (2006). Topological QSAR modeling of cytotoxicity data of anti-HIV 5-phenyl-1-phenylamino-1H-imidazole derivatives using GFA, G/PLS, FA and PCRA techniques. *Indian J Chem Sect A, 45*, 126–137.

Ruiz-Llorente, S.MTC Clinical Group. (2007). Association study of 69 genes in the ret pathway identifies low penetrance loci in sporadic medullary thyroid carcinoma. *Cancer Research, 67*, 9561–9567. doi:10.1158/0008-5472.CAN-07-1638

Ruvolo, M., Disotell, T. R., Allard, M. W., Brown, W. M., & Honeycutt, R. L. (1991). Resolution of the African hominoid trichotomy by use of a mitochondrial gene sequence. *Proceedings of the National Academy of Sciences of the United States of America, 88*, 1570–1574. doi:10.1073/pnas.88.4.1570

Rzhetsky, A., Dopazo, J., Snyder, E., Dangler, C. A., & Ayala, F. J. (1996). Assessing Dissimilarity of genes by comparing their RNase-A mismatch cleavage patterns. *Genetics, 144*, 1975–1983.

Saiz, J. C. (1998). The prognostic relevance of the nonstructural 5A gene interferon sensibility determining region is different in infections with genotype 1B and 3A isolates of hepatitis-C virus. *The Journal of Infectious Diseases, 177*, 839–847.

Sánchez-Moyano, E., Seco, C., Santolaria, A., Fabra-Campos, S., Herráez, M., & Martín-Villodre, M. (1992). Partition behavior of anilines in bulk-phase and high-performance liquid chromatographic systems: Influence on correlation with biological constants. *Journal of Pharmaceutical Sciences, 81*, 720–725. doi:10.1002/jps.2600810727

Sanchez-Palomino, S., Dopazo, J., Olivares, I., Martín, M. J., & Lopez-Galindez, C. (1995). Primary genetic-characterization of HIV-1 isolates from WHO-sponsored vaccine evaluation sites by the RNase-A mismatch method. *Virus Research, 39*, 251–259. doi:10.1016/0168-1702(95)00096-8

Santoyo, J., Vaquerizas, J. M., & Dopazo, J. (2005). Highly specific and accurate selection of siRNAs for high-throughput functional assays. *Bioinformatics (Oxford, England), 21*, 1376–1382. doi:10.1093/bioinformatics/bti196

Sarich, V. M., & Wilson, A. C. (1967). Immunological time scale for hominid evolution. *Science, 158*, 1200–1203. doi:10.1126/science.158.3805.1200

Sayle, R. A., & Milner-White, E. J. (1995). RAS-MOL: Biomolecular graphics for all. *Trends in Biochemical Sciences, 20*, 374–376. doi:10.1016/S0968-0004(00)89080-5

Schiffrin, E. J., Rochat, F., Link-Amster, H., Aeschlimann, J. M., & Donnet-Hughes, A. (1995). Immunomodulation of human blood cells following the ingestion of lactic acid bacteria. *Journal of Dairy Science, 78*, 491–497. doi:10.3168/jds.S0022-0302(95)76659-0

Schluter, A. (2007). PeroxisomeDB: A database for the peroxisomal proteome, functional genomics and disease. *Nucleic Acids Research, 35*, D815–D822. doi:10.1093/nar/gkl935

Shannon, C. E. (1948). A mathematical theory of communication: Part I, discrete noiseless systems. *The Bell System Technical Journal, 27*, 379–423.

Shannon, C. E. (1948). A mathematical theory of communication: Part II, the discrete channel with noise. *The Bell System Technical Journal, 27*, 623–656.

Sharma, B., Kaushik, N., Singh, K., Kumar, S., & Pandey, V. N. (2002). Substitution of conserved hydrodynamic residues in motifs B and C of HIV-1 RT alters the geometry of its catalytic pocket. *Biochemistry, 41*, 15685–15697. doi:10.1021/bi026311z

Shen, P. (2000). Population genetic implications from sequence variation in four Y chromosome genes. *Proceedings of the National Academy of Sciences of the United States of America, 97*, 7354–7359. doi:10.1073/pnas.97.13.7354

Shindyalov, I. N., & Bourne, P. E. (1995). *WPDB* – PC Windows-based interrogation of macromolecular structure. *Journal of Applied Crystallography, 28*, 847–852. doi:10.1107/S0021889895005723

Shindyalov, I. N., & Bourne, P. E. (1997). Protein data representation and query using optimized data decomposition. *CABIOS, 13*, 487–496.

Sibley, C. G., & Ahlquist, J. E. (1984). The phylogeny of the hominoid primates, as indicated by DNA–DNA hybridization. *Journal of Molecular Evolution, 20*, 2–15. doi:10.1007/BF02101980

Sicheritz-Pontén, T., & Andersson, S. G. E. (2001). A phylogenomic approach to microbial evolution. *Nucleic Acids Research, 29*, 545–552. doi:10.1093/nar/29.2.545

Solis-Pereyra, B., Aattouri, N., & Lemonnier, D. (1997). Role of food in the stimulation of cytokine production. *The American Journal of Clinical Nutrition, 66*, 521S–525S.

Stanley, W. A., Fodor, K., Marti-Renom, M. A., Schliebs, W., & Wilmanns, M. (2007). Protein translocation into peroxisomes by ring-shaped import receptors. *FEBS Letters, 581*, 4795–4802. doi:10.1016/j.febslet.2007.09.001

Steel, M. (1992). The complexity of reconstructing trees from qualitative characters and subtrees. *J Classification, 9*, 91–116. doi:10.1007/BF02618470

Stewart, C. B. (1993). The powers and pitfalls of parsimony. *Nature, 361*, 603–607. doi:10.1038/361603a0

Suarez, P., Zardoya, R., Martín, M. J., Prieto, C., Dopazo, J., Solana, A., & Castro, J. M. (1996). Phylogenetic-relationships of European strains of porcine reproductive and respiratory syndrome virus (PRRSV) inferred from DNA-sequences of putative ORF-5 and ORF-7 genes. *Virus Research, 42*, 159–165. doi:10.1016/0168-1702(95)01305-9

Taberner, A., Dopazo, J., & Castanera, P. (1997). Genetic-characterization of populations of a *de-novo* arisen sugar-beet pest, *Aubeonymus-mariaefranciscae* (coleoptera, curculionidae), by Rapd-analysis. *Journal of Molecular Evolution, 45*, 24–31. doi:10.1007/PL00006195

Takagi, A., Matsuzaki, T., Sato, M., Nomoto, K., Morotomi, M., & Yokokura, T. (2001). Enhancement of natural killer cytotoxicity delayed murine carcinogenesis by a probiotic microorganism. *Carcinogenesis, 22*, 599–605. doi:10.1093/carcin/22.4.599

Tamames, J., Clark, D., Herrero, J., Dopazo, J., Blaschke, C., & Fernández, J. M. (2002). Bioinformatics methods for the analysis of expression arrays: Data clustering and information extraction. *Journal of Biotechnology, 98*, 269–283. doi:10.1016/S0168-1656(02)00137-2

Tárraga, J., Medina, I., Arbiza, L., Huerta, J., Gabaldón, T., Dopazo, J., & Dopazo, H. (2007). Phylemon: A suite of web tools for molecular evolution, phylogenetics and phylogenomics. *Nucleic Acids Research*, *35*, W38–W42. doi:10.1093/nar/gkm224

Taubenberger, J. K., Reid, A. H., Lourens, R. M., Wang, R., Jin, G., & Fanning, T. G. (2005). Characterization of the 1918 influenza virus polymerase genes. *Nature*, *437*, 889–893. doi:10.1038/nature04230

Tejada-Simon, M. V., & Pestka, J. J. (1999). Proinflammatory cytokine and nitric oxide induction in murine macrophages by cell wall and cytoplasmic extracts of lactic acid bacteria. *Journal of Food Protection*, *62*, 1435–1444.

Tondeur, D., & Kvaalen, E. (1987). Equipartition of entropy production. An optimality criterion for transfer and separation processes. *Industrial & Engineering Chemistry Fundamentals*, *26*, 50–56.

Torrens, F. (2000). Análisis fractal de la estructura terciaria de las proteínas. *Encuentros en la Biología*, *8*(64), 4–6.

Torrens, F. (2000). Fractal hybrid orbitals in biopolymer chains. *Zh Fiz Khim*, *74*, 125–131.

Torrens, F. (2000). Fractal hybrid orbitals in biopolymer chains. [Engl Transl]. *Russian Journal of Physical Chemistry*, *74*, 115–120.

Torrens, F. (2000). Filogénesis de los simios antropoides. *Encuentros en la Biología*, *8*(60), 3–5.

Torrens, F. (2001). Fractals for hybrid orbitals in protein models. *Complexity Int* 8, torren01-1–13.

Torrens, F. (2001). Fractal hybrid orbitals analysis of tertiary structure of protein molecule. In Lin, S.-K. (Ed.), *Kappe O, Merino P, Marzinzik A, Wennemers H, Wirth T, vanden Eynde J-J* (pp. 1–11). Basel: Synthetic Organic Chemistry V. MDPI.

Torrens, F. (2002). Computing the Kekulé structure count for alternant hydrocarbons. *International Journal of Quantum Chemistry*, *88*, 392–397. doi:10.1002/qua.10176

Torrens, F. (2002). Computing the permanent of the adjacency matrix for fullerenes. *Internet Electron J Mol Des*, *1*, 351–359.

Torrens, F. (2002). Fractal hybrid orbitals analysis of the tertiary structure of protein molecules. *Molecules (Basel, Switzerland)*, *7*, 26–37. doi:10.3390/70100026

Torrens, F. (2003). Principal component analysis of structural parameters for fullerenes. *Internet Electron J Mol Des*, *2*, 96–111.

Torrens, F. (2003). Principal component analysis of new structural parameters for fullerenes. *Internet Electron J Mol Des*, *2*, 546–563.

Torrens, F. (2003). New structural parameters of fullerenes for principal component analysis. *Theoretical Chemistry Accounts*, *110*, 371–376. doi:10.1007/s00214-003-0490-y

Torrens, F. (2003). Fractal dimension of transdermal-delivery drug models. In Mastorakis, N., Er, M. J., & D'Attelis, C. (Eds.), *Non-linear Analysis, Non-linear Systems and Chaos* (pp. 1–6). Athens: WSEAS.

Torrens, F. (2004). Table of periodic properties of fullerenes based on structural parameters. *Journal of Chemical Information and Computer Sciences*, *44*, 60–67. doi:10.1021/ci030029x

Torrens, F. (2004). Table of periodic properties of fullerenes based on structural parameters. *Journal of Molecular Structure THEOCHEM*, *709*, 135–142. doi:10.1016/j.theochem.2003.10.076

Torrens, F. (2004). Fractal dimension of transdermal-delivery drug models. *Lebanese Science Journal*, *5*(1), 61–70.

Torrens, F., & Castellano, G. (2005). Cluster origin of the solubility of single-wall carbon nanotubes. *Computing Letters*, *1*, 331–336. doi:10.1163/157404005776611303

Torrens, F., & Castellano, G. (2006). Periodic classification of local anaesthetics (procaine analogues). *International Journal of Molecular Sciences*, *7*, 12–34. doi:10.3390/i8010012

Torrens, F., & Castellano, G. (2006). Cluster origin of the solubility of single-wall carbon nanotubes. In Maroulis, G. (ed) *Structures and Properties of Clusters: From a few Atoms to Nanoparticles.* (Lecture Series on Computer and Computational Sciences No. 5. Brill, Leiden, pp 187–192).

Torrens, F., & Castellano, G. (2006). Effect of packing on cluster solvation of nanotubes. InBandyopadhyay S, Cahay M (eds), *Nanotechnology VI. Institute of Electrical and Electronics Engineers*, Piscataway (NJ) pp 1–4.

Torrens, F., & Castellano, G. (2007). Cluster origin of the transfer phenomena of single-wall carbon nanotubes. *J Comput Theor Nanosci*, *4*, 588–603.

Torrens, F., & Castellano, G. (2007). Cluster nature of the solvation features of single-wall carbon nanotubes. In Columbus, F. (Ed.), *Progress in Nanotechnology Research* (pp. 1–28). Hauppauge, NY: Nova.

Torrens, F., & Castellano, G. (2007). Effect of packing on the cluster nature of C nanotubes: An information entropy analysis. *Microelectronics Journal*, *38*, 1109–1122. doi:10.1016/j.mejo.2006.04.004

Torrens, F., & Castellano, G. (2007). Asymptotic analysis of coagulation–fragmentation equations of carbon nanotube clusters. *Nanoscale Research Letters*, *2*, 337–349. doi:10.1007/s11671-007-9070-8

Torrens, F., & Castellano, G. (2008). Nuevo diseño y aproximaciones no ortodoxas con nanotubos de carbono. In García-Breijo E, et al.(eds). Workshop on Sensors: A Local Approach. Valencia, Spain: Universidad Politécnica de Valencia, pp. 409-415.

Torrens, F., & Castellano, G. (2009). Periodic classification of human immunodeficiency virus inhibitors. In Sidhu, A. S., Dillon, T., & Bellgard, M. (Eds.), *Biomedical Data Applications*. Berlin: Springer.

Torrens, F., & Castellano, G. (2009). Classification of complex molecules. In Hassanien, A. E., & Abragam, A. (Eds.), *Foundations of Computational Intelligence* (*Vol. 5*, pp. 243–315). Berlin: Springer. doi:10.1007/978-3-642-01536-6_11

Torrens, F., Castellano, G. (2009). Modelling of complex multicellular systems: Tumour–immune cells competition. *Chem Central J 3(Suppl. I)*, 75-1–1.

Torrens, F., & Castellano, G. (2010). Table of periodic properties of human immunodeficiency virus inhibitors. *Int J Comput Intelligence Bioinf Syst Biol*, *1*, 246–273.

Torrens, F., Castellano, G. (2011). Molecular classification of thiocarbamates with cytoprotection activity against human immunodeficiency virus. *Int J Chem Model*, 3(3), 8-1–48

Torrens, F., & Castellano, G. (in press). Information entropy and the table of periodic properties of local anaesthetics. *Int J Chemoinf Chem Eng.*

Torrens, F., Ortí, E., & Sánchez-Marín, J. (1991). Representación de propiedades moleculares en la didáctica de la química. In *Colloquy University Pedagogy. Horsori* (pp. 375–379). Barcelone.

Torrens, F., Sánchez-Marín, J., & Nebot-Gil, I. (1998). Fractals for hybrid orbitals in protein models. In Laxminarayan, S. (Ed.), *Information Technology Applications in Biomedicine* (pp. 1–6). Washington, DC: IEEE.

Torrens, F., Sánchez-Marín, J., & Sánchez-Pérez, E. (1989). Didàctica empírica de la congelació de l'aigua. In Riera, S. (Ed.), *Actes del II Sympòsium sobre l'Ensenyament de les Ciències Naturals. Documents No. 11* (pp. 595–600). Eumo, Vic.

Torrens, F., Sánchez-Marín, J., & Sánchez-Pérez, E. (1989). Estudi interdisciplinari de la congelació de l'aigua. In Riera, S. (Ed.), *Actes del II Sympòsium sobre l'Ensenyament de les Ciències Naturals. Documents No. 11* (pp. 669–669). Eumo, Vic.

Torrens, F., Sánchez-Pérez, E., & Sánchez-Marín, J. (1989). Didáctica empírica de la forma molecular. *Enseñanza de las Ciencias Extra-III Congreso*(1), 267–268.

Tracey, L. (2002). Identification of genes involved in resistance to Interferon-α in cutaneous T-cell lymphoma. *American Journal of Pathology, 161*, 1825–1837. doi:10.1016/S0002-9440(10)64459-8

Trelles, O., Ceron, C., Wang, H. C., Dopazo, J., & Carazo, J. M. (1998). New phylogenetic venues opened by a novel implementation of the DNAml algorithm. *Bioinformatics (Oxford, England), 14*, 544–545. doi:10.1093/bioinformatics/14.6.544

Trelles-Salazar, O., Zapata, E. L., Dopazo, J., Coulson, A. F. W., & Carazo, J. M. (1995). An image-processing approach to dotplots – An X-Window-based program for interactive analysis of dotplots derived from sequence and structural data. *Computer Applications in the Biosciences, 11*, 301–308.

Tsai, C. S. (2001). A computer-assisted tutorial on protein structure. *Journal of Chemical Education, 78*, 837–839. doi:10.1021/ed078p837

Tumpey, T. M. (2005). Characterization of the reconstructed 1918 Spanish influenza pandemic virus. *Science, 310*, 77–79. doi:10.1126/science.1119392

Turchet, P., Laurenzano, M., Auboiron, S., & Antoine, J. M. (2003). Effect of fermented milk containing the probiotic *Lactobacillus casei DN-114001* on winter infections in free-living elderly subjects: A randomised, controlled pilot study. *The Journal of Nutrition, Health & Aging, 7*, 75–77.

Valls, J. (2008). CLEAR-test: Combining inference for differential expression and variability in microarray data analysis. *Journal of Biomedical Informatics, 41*, 33–45. doi:10.1016/j.jbi.2007.05.005

Vaquerizas, J. M. (2005). Gepas an experiment-oriented pipeline for the analysis of microarray gene expression data. *Nucleic Acids Research, 33*, W616–W620. doi:10.1093/nar/gki500

Vaquerizas, J. M., Dopazo, J., & Díaz-Uriarte, R. (2004). DNMAD: Web-based diagnosis and normalization for microarray data. *Bioinformatics (Oxford, England), 20*, 3656–3658. doi:10.1093/bioinformatics/bth401

Varmuza, K. (1980). *Pattern recognition in chemistry*. New York: Springer.

Vega, M. C. (2006). New ligand-based approach for the discovery of antitrypanosomal compounds. *Bioorganic & Medicinal Chemistry Letters, 16*, 1898–1904. doi:10.1016/j.bmcl.2005.12.087

Walters, P., & Stahl, M. (1996). *Program BABEL*. Tucson, AZ: University of Arizona.

Wang, H. C., Dopazo, J., & Carazo, J. M. (1998). Self-organizing tree growing network for classifying amino acids. *Bioinformatics (Oxford, England), 14*, 376–377. doi:10.1093/bioinformatics/14.4.376

Wang, H. C., Dopazo, J., de la Fraga, L. G., Zhu, Y. P., & Carazo, J. M. (1998). Self-organizing tree-growing network for the classification of protein sequences. *Protein Science, 7*, 2613–2622. doi:10.1002/pro.5560071215

Weber, J. (1996). Neutralization serotypes of human-immunodeficiency-virus type-1 field isolates are not predicted by genetic subtype. *Journal of Virology, 70*, 7827–7832.

White, H. (1989)... *AI Expert, 12*, 48–48.

Wood, B. (1992). Origin and evolution of the genus *Homo. Nature, 355*, 783–790. doi:10.1038/355783a0

Wu, R., Li, R., Liao, B., & Yue, G. (2010). A novel method for visualizing and analyzing DNA sequences. *MATCH Commun Math Comput Chem, 63*, 679–690.

Wu. M., Eisen, J.A. (2008). A simple, fast, and accurate method of phylogenomic inference. *Genome Biol, 9*, R151-1–11.

Yao, Y. H., Dai, Q., Nan, X. Y., He, P. A., Nie, Z. M., Zhou, S. P., & Zhang, Y. Z. (2008). Analysis of similarity/dissimilarity of DNA sequences based on a class of 2D graphical representation. *Journal of Computational Chemistry, 29*, 1632–1639. doi:10.1002/jcc.20922

Yu, J. F., Wang, J. H., & Sun, X. (2010). Analysis of similarities/dissimilarities of DNA sequences based on a novel graphical representation. *MATCH Commun Math Comput Chem, 63*, 493–512.

Yu, Z. G., Zhan, X. W., Han, G. S., Wang, R. W., Anh, V., & Chu, K. H. (2010). Proper distance metrics for phylogenetic analysis using complete genomes without sequence alignment. *International Journal of Molecular Sciences, 11*, 1141–1154. doi:10.3390/ijms11031141

Zhang, S., & Wang, T. (2010). Phylogenetic analysis of protein sequences based on conditional LZ complexity. *MATCH Commun Math Comput Chem, 63*, 701–716.

Zhang, X., Luo, J., & Yang, L. (2007). New invariant of DNA sequence based on 3DD-curves and its application on phylogeny. *Journal of Computational Chemistry, 28*, 2342–2346. doi:10.1002/jcc.20760

Zhang, Y., & Chen, W. (2008). A new approach to molecular phylogeny of primate mitochondrial DNA. *MATCH Commun Math Comput Chem, 59*, 625–634.

Zhu, W., Liao, B., & Li, R. (2010). A method for constructing phylogenetic tree based on a dissimilarity matrix. *MATCH Commun Math Comput Chem, 63*, 483–492.

Chapter 3

Nanoparticles:
Towards Predicting Their Toxicity and Physico-Chemical Properties

Bakhtiyor Rasulev
Jackson State University, USA

Danuta Leszczynska
Jackson State University, USA

Jerzy Leszczynski
Jackson State University, USA

ABSTRACT

Nanomaterials are becoming an important component of the modern life and have been the subject of increasing number of investigations involving various areas of natural sciences and technology. However, theoretical modeling of physicochemical and biological activity of these species is still very scarce. The prediction of the properties and activities of 'classical' substances via correlating with molecular descriptors is a well known procedure, i.e. QSAR. In spite of this, the application of QSAR for the nanomaterials is a very complicated task, because of "non-classical" structure of nanomaterials.

Here, the authors show that an application of the QSAR methods for nanomaterials is nevertheless possible and can be useful in predicting their various properties and activities (toxicity). In the chapter briefly explained how the physico-chemical properties can be predicted for nanomaterials. Furthermore, it was also demonstrated how the biological activity, particularly toxicity, can be modeled and predicted for the series of nanoparticles, by applying the quantum-chemical methods in combination with the nano-QSAR.

DOI: 10.4018/978-1-60960-860-6.ch003

INTRODUCTION

During the last three decades there has been a dramatic increase of attention directed towards chemistry and technology of nanoparticles. The search by Google word search engine through publications for the period 1800-2008 indicates an enormous rise in frequency of the use of words "nano" and "nanoparticle" starting from 1980s. So, what is a nanoparticle? Nanoparticles are building blocks for nanotechnology, and are defined as particles (structures) with at least one dimension of less than 100 nm (Buzea et al, 2007). In fact, particles in these size ranges have been used by humankind for thousands of years. However, there has been a recent renaissance in this area because of the technological progress and therefore an ability to synthesize and manipulate such materials (Rotello, 2004). Nanomaterials are being currently used as electronics, optoelectronics, in biomedical, environmental, material and energy related areas, as cosmetics, pharmaceuticals, and catalysts. Nanomaterials exhibit unique physical/chemical properties and impart enhancements to engineered materials, including better magnetic properties, improved electrical activity, and increased optical properties. Because of the potential output of this technology, a worldwide increase in applications and investment in nanotechnology research are on rise (Srivastava et al, 2001; Klabunde, 2001; Feldheim, 2001; Edelstein & Cammarata, 1998). Moreover, the use of nanomaterials in various industries is projected to increase dramatically in the future and as a consequence, contamination of environment by these materials is expected, or at least such possibility cannot be disregarded. In fact, nanotechnology could lead to serious environmental problems. This is because it is still largely unknown how nanoparticles will impact the environment. Besides, there is still a substantial need to comprehensively investigate all physicochemical and then biological properties of nanoparticles to predict their possible impact on environment (Pitkethly, 2004; Oberdörster et al, 2005).

There is a clear need for short-term testing of their potential hazard in order to gain information towards risk assessment related to nanoparticles (Seatona & Donaldson, 2005; Seaton, 2007; Warheit et al, 2007). However, the large number of nanoparticles and the variety of their characteristics including sizes and coatings indicates that the only rational approach that avoids testing every single nanoparticle is to find relationship between physicochemical characteristics of a nanoparticle and its toxicity. For this purpose such approaches as Quantitative Structure-Activity Relationship (QSAR) can be applied (Puzyn et al, 2010; Puzyn et al, 2009). So, this approach can be applied not only to "classical" organic compounds (Kušić et al, 2009; Rasulev et al, 2007; Rasulev et al, 2010; Turabekova et al, 2008), but also for nanoparticles. If a QSAR model is developed then, ideally, toxicity of untested nanoparticle can be predicted on the basis of its physico-chemistry. Actually, there is a strong need to extend the traditional QSAR paradigm to nanoparticles, and some results related to this direction will be shown here.

Unfortunately, up to date, there is very limited information about systematic data on experimentally measured toxic effects for various series of nanoparticles. Only such data can be useful for the QSAR modeling purposes. However, some isolated and limited experiments are published in the last few years (Choi et al, 2008; Lewinski et al, 2008; Franklin et al, 2007; Duffin et al, 2007; Fiorito, 2007; Gill et al, 2007; Powers et al, 2007; Medina et al, 2007; Moore, 2006; Karakoti et al, 2006; Moss & Wong, 2006; Lee & Cho, 2006; Tsuji et al, 2006; Braydich-Stolle et al, 2005; Hussain et al, 2005). The available toxicity data for nanoparticles at this time are mostly *in vitro*, for bacteria cultures (Lewinski, Colvin & Drezek, 2008; Franklin et al, 2007; Duffin et al, 2007; Moss & Wong, 2006; Braydich-Stolle et al, 2005; Hussain et al, 2005). A few studies *in vivo* were published for mammals, particularly for rats or

Figure 1. The schematic representation of the possible pathway of nanoparticles' interaction in living organism and possible responses. In silico modeling can consider tasks showed inside of left ellipse and can effectively solve these tasks.

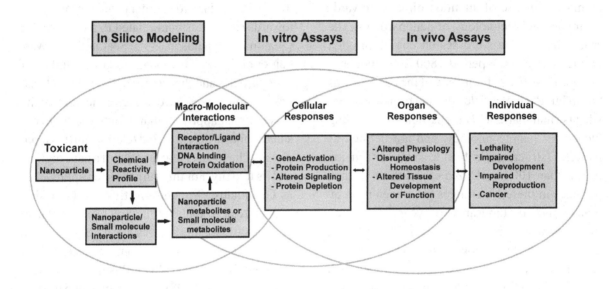

mice (Duffin et al, 2007; Gill et al, 2007; Medina et al, 2007). This limited toxicity information makes difficult the study of structure-toxicity relationship of nanoparticles.

In this chapter we have collected recent results related to our systematical investigations on QSPRs and QSARs of physico-chemical and toxicity endpoints for various kinds of nanoparticles. All these properties were studied by applying different computational approaches, including molecular modeling, and various quantum-mechanical calculations.

NANOPARTICLE INTRINSIC PROPERTIES AND PATHWAYS

Intrinsic properties of nanoparticles make them a very topical object for the development of new materials with unusual and desired properties that could be very small in size. Physicochemical properties that may be important in understanding

the toxic effects of nanomaterials include particle size and size distribution, agglomeration state, shape, crystal structure, chemical composition, surface area, surface chemistry, surface charge, electronic properties (reactivity, interaction energies, etc (Gajewicz, 2011)) and porosity (Edelstein & Cammarata, 1998; Oberdörster et al, 2005). All these properties are important and have to be considered step-by-step in nanoparticle research, separately or if possible in combination.

Figure 1 displays the possible pathways for nanoparticles interactions in living organism (possible responses) and the areas which can be assessed and analyzed by different methods – *in silico*, *in vitro* and *in vivo*. The area which can be assessed theoretically/computationally is labeled as *in silico* modeling (left ellipse). *In silico* modeling approach includes the computational investigation of a nanoparticle itself (structure, various physical and physico-chemical parameters), reactivity and interaction energies with other species (small molecules and large biomolecules).

Figure 2. The representation of the combined use of experimental and modeling methods to predict the properties of nanoparticles

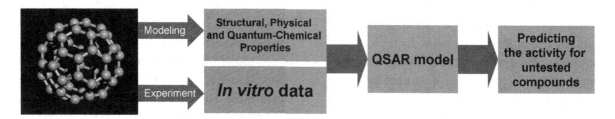

DESCRIPTORS

As it was stated above not only the dose and elemental composition of the nanoparticles define their properties, but also such important features as their surface area, surface characteristics, shape of the particles, tendency to aggregate, and their surface charges. All these features play crucial roles in nanoparticles distribution through the environment, ecosystem and especially, through live organisms, including human body. These factors could contribute towards possible (genetic) toxicity (Fiorito, 2007; Powers, 2007). Modeling the physico-chemical effects could provide information about the factors influencing on aggregation mechanism, distribution in the environment (logP) and interaction pathways.

Therefore, a comprehensive investigation of the basic physicochemical properties of nanoparticles represents a very important step in obtaining clues for the mechanisms of their biological activity and toxicity (Puzyn et al, 2010; Puzyn et al, 2009). For this purpose, the quantum-mechanical *ab initio* methods are very useful, since they allow to model the structural and electronic properties of nanoparticles, such as dipole moment, molecular volume, highest occupied molecular orbital (HOMO), lowest unoccupied molecular orbital (LUMO), HOMO-LUMO energy gap, Fermi energy, band gap, electronic charges, molecular electrostatic potentials, transition energies,

ionization potentials, electron affinity and many other physical properties. These computed properties can then be used as descriptors for the structure-property/activity relationships analysis. Since the nanoparticle systems are very large from quantum chemical point of view it may require the high-performance computational resources or application of some extrapolation techniques to save a computing time. Depending upon the size of the system, the Hartree-Fock (HF) (Slater, 1951), density-functional theory (DFT) (Hohenberg & Kohn, 1964) using different functional, electron correlated approaches such as Moller-Plesset perturbation theory (MP2) (Binkley & Pople, 1975) and coupled cluster (CC) theory (Barlett & Purvis, 1978), along with different basis sets may be utilized. The resolution of identity approximation to electron correlation methods (MP2 and CC) offers an advantage such that these methods (RI-MP2 and RI-CC2) (Weigend et al, 1998; Hattig & Hald, 2002) can be used for larger systems with significant reduction of computation resources. Further, these RI methods provide almost identical results comparing with the corresponding MP2 and CC approaches. The band properties of nanoparticles may be computed using methods based on the periodic boundary conditions; the pseudopotential plane wave density functional can be useful for such calculations.

ENDPOINTS

The unique properties of nanoparticles impel researchers from over the world to develop, synthesize and then assist in production of these unusual compounds in large amounts for further applications. However, not only peculiar properties of nanoparticles require a close attention, but their other characteristics such as solubility, stability, reactivity, toxicity and etc. are also important for their handling. All these properties become extremely important when nanomaterials are produced in large quantities and might affect the environment. For the application in structure-property/activity relationship modeling these properties can be called as endpoints.

For example, one of the most important physicochemical properties of nanomaterials is solubility. Solvent effects may be substantial for the behavior of nanoparticles in environment (Schwarz & Contesu, 1999). Knowledge of solubility of nanoparticles in various solvents can be also useful in manufacturing these species.

Other important endpoints are biological activities, like pharmacological activities and toxicity. Some of the authors found that particle size, hydrophobicity, and protein identity all contribute to nanoparticle–protein association (Cedervall et al, 2007). Particularly, fullerenes are capable of specific interactions with proteins as evidenced by the production of fullerene-specific antibodies (Chen et al, 1998). Fullerenes have been identified as inhibitors of cysteine and serine proteinases (Tokuyama et al, 1993) as well as the protease specific for the human immunodeficiency virus (Friedman et al, 1993; Sijbesma et al, 1993) and are known to interact directly with the virus. For example, the fullerene C_{60} derivatives can interact with the active site of HIV-1 protease (HIVp). The protease specific to the human immunodeficiency virus 1 has been shown to be a viable target for antiviral therapy (Friedman et al, 1998; Marcorin et al, 2000). The active site of this enzyme can be roughly described as an open-ended cylinder,

which is lined almost exclusively by hydrophobic aminoacids. Since the C_{60} molecule has approximately the same radius as the cylinder that defines the active site of the HIVp and since C_{60} (and its derivatives) is primarily hydrophobic, an opportunity therefore exist for a strong hydrophobic interaction between the C_{60} derivative and active site surfaces. This interaction makes the C_{60} derivatives efficient inhibitors of the HIVp. Therefore C_{60} and similar nanoparticles can be interest as good anti-HIV agents.

Toxicity is one of the vital properties of nanoparticles. This property has been investigated by various groups of researchers. Many studies showed much higher toxicity displayed by some of the nanoparticles in comparing to bulk size particles (Puzyn et al, 2009). It is well known, that the metal oxide nanoparticles possess higher toxicity than bulk size particles of the same chemical composition (Puzyn et al, 2010).

The modeling and predictions of these properties (endpoints) are crucial to understand the mechanisms of actions of nanoparticles, decrease the animal use for toxicity experiments, and reduce costs for experiments. Last but not least it allows for quick prediction of the property of interest for new, untested nanoparticles.

RECENT ACHIEVEMENTS IN PREDICTIONS OF THE PHYSICO-CHEMICAL PROPERTIES AND TOXICITY

Solubility

Taking into account that solubility of nanoparticles plays important roles in toxicity expression, in collaboration with various research groups we performed a number of studies related to the structure-solubility relationship for the fullerene in different solvents (Toropov et al, 2007 & 2008) and for carbon nanotubes in water. For the characterization of carbon nanotubes solubility in water the use of chiral vector components had been suggested and this approach was tested for a set of single-walled carbon nanotubes (Toropov et al, 2007).

The data on solubility of the fullerene C_{60} in organic solvents can provide an important information that would be of interest in chemistry and biochemistry. Quantitative structure– solubility relationships approach for this characteristic is not only able to predict numerical data but also it allows evaluating aspect of solubility of fullerene C_{60} as a function of a complex physicochemical phenomenon.

Taking into account an increased number of internet databases that use simplified molecular input line entry system (SMILES) for further analysis of physicochemical parameters and biological activity there is a need to develop SMILES based predictive models (Vidal et al, 2005; Toropova et al, 2005; Toropova et al, 2006; Toropov et al, 2007). The studies will be discussed are aimed to estimate predictive potential of the SMILES based optimal descriptors in QSPR modeling of the fullerene C_{60} solubility in organic solvents as a function of the molecular structure of the solvents represented by the SMILES notation. These studies were published in several publications (Toropov et al, 2007; Toropov et al, 2008; Toropov et al, 2007; Toropov et al, 2009; Petrova et al, 2011; Toropov et al, 2007). The number of solvents used for modeling ranges from 36 (Toropov et al, 2007) to 122 (Toropov et al, 2008; Toropov et al, 2009; Petrova et al, 2011).

It should be noted that for the estimation of the C_{60} solubility in various solvents the information from the structure of solvent was only used and contribution of C_{60} itself was assumed as constant. SMILES notations (http://www.daylight.com, 2008) of organic solvents for these studies (Toropov et al, 2007; Toropov et al, 2008; Toropov et al, 2009; Petrova et al, 2011) have been built with ACD/ChemSketch software (http://www.acdlabs.com). Optimal descriptors have been defined as

$$DCW(SMILES) = \sum_{k=1}^{n} CW(SF_k), \qquad (1)$$

where SF_k is a fragment of SMILES; $CW(SF_k)$ represents correlation weights of the SF_k. Numerical values of the $CW(SF_k)$ have been calculated by Monte Carlo method (Toropov et al, 2005; Toropov et al, 2006; Toropov & Benfenati, 2007). The $CW(SF_k)$ have been iterated continuously to produce as large as possible correlation coefficient between the solubility of fullerene C_{60} and solvents for the training set, i.e. the correlation coefficient is used as the target function for the optimization procedure. As soon as numerical data on the $CW(SFk)$ are obtained the $DCW(SMILES)$ values can be calculated by Eqn (1).

In general, an application of the least squares method yields the following equation:

$$\log S = C_0 + C_1 DCW(SMILES) \qquad (2)$$

After that, the predictive potential of the model calculated with Eqn. (2) can be estimated by utilizing data of organic solvents of the external test set.

In study (Toropov et al, 2007) the obtained models showed a relatively good performance. The final model and statistical characteristics of QSPR for solubility, log (S), (S is expressed as molar fraction) in study (Toropov et al, 2007) are as follows (Figure 3):

$$\log S = -6.6196(\pm 0.0154) + 0.5014(\pm 0.0026) DCW(SMILES) \qquad (3)$$

$n = 92$, $r^2 = 0.8612$, $q^2 = 0.8537$, $s = 0.401$, $F = 558$ (training set),

$n = 30$, $r^2 = 0.8908$, $r2_{pred} = 0.8748$, $s = 0.435$, $F = 228$ (test set)

In the next study of C_{60} solubility (Toropov et al, 2008; Toropov et al, 2008; Toropov et al, 2007) the slightly improved method of optimal descriptors was applied to get better correlations. This

Figure 3. Plot of experimental versus calculated solubility (logS) of fullerene C_{60} for the training set (a) and for the test set (b) according to model (3). Reproduced with permission from Reference (Toropov et al, 2007). Copyright Elsevier, 2007.

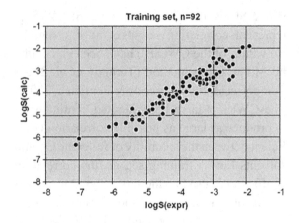

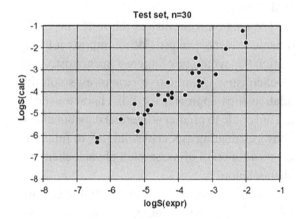

method takes into account combinations of different SMILES attributes.

Here the optimal descriptors are defined as:

$$DCW = CW(Nb) \cdot CW(Ndb) \cdot \prod CW(ss_k)$$
(4)

where Nb is a number of brackets in given SMILES, these are indicated below as '(000', '(001', etc.; Ndb is a number of the double covalent bonds indicated in SMILES by '=', these are indicated below as the '=000', '=001', etc.; ssk represents two SMILES consequent elements in the SMILES strings; and $CW(SA_k)$ is the correlation weight of SMILES attribute of the SA_k, (SA_k = Nb or Ndb or ss_k). $CW(ss_k)$ is a correlation weight of two components' SMILES fragment. The 'Cl', 'Br', 'N+', and 'O-' are SMILES components containing two characters. All other SMILES components contain only one character. The ss_k represents an association of the pairs of SMILES components and can be expressed by the following scheme:

'ABCDE...' = 'AB' + 'BC' + 'CD' + 'DE' +...

or

'CC(N...' = 'CC' + 'C(' + '(N' + ...

In the reviewed study the three splits of data into training and test sets have been examined to estimate the ability of applied approach to give a robust prediction. The following model and statistical data are obtained:

$$\log S = -111.0059(\pm 0.3578) + 104.4283(\pm 0.3482) \, DCW \qquad (5)$$

$n = 92$, $r^2 = 0.9372$, $q^2 = 0.9339$, $s = 0.270$, $F = 1342$ (training set)

$n = 28$, $r^2 = 0.9151$, $r^2_{pred} = 0.9032$, $s = 0.334$, $F = 280$ (test set)

This model represents an improvement over the initial development step as described in (Toropov et al, 2007).

In another study for C_{60} solubility prediction were used optimal descriptors calculated with International Chemical Identifier (InChI) (http://wwmm.ch.cam.ac.uk/inchifaq/, 2011; http://www.warr.com, 2011) to construct one-variable model (Toropov et al, 2009). The following formula has been used to calculate the correlation weights using InChI structure representation:

$$DCW(InChI) = \Sigma W(I_k) \qquad (6)$$

where the I_k is InChI attribute and $W(I_k)$ is the correlation weight for the I_k.

Here, the highest value of correlation weight $W(I_k)$ obtained for the training set is used to calculate the model of fullerene C_{60} solubility:

$$logS = C_0 + C_1 \, DCW(InChI) \qquad (7)$$

The final model obtained by Eqn. (7) in the study could be expressed by:

$$logS = -7.9824(\pm0.1397) + 0.3250(\pm0.0010) \, DCW(InChI) \qquad (8)$$

$n = 92$, $r^2 = 0.9447$, $q^2 = 0.9418$, $s = 0.253$, $SDEP = 0.258$, $F = 1538$ (training set)

$n = 30$, $r^2 = 0.9398$, $r^2_{pred} = 0.9315$, $s = 0.348$, $F = 437$ (test set)

In fact, the optimal descriptors InChI approach is based on groups' contributions. However, the groups which are extracted from the InChI do not have transparent interpretations, which are typical for the Free Wilson (Fouchécourt et al, 2001) scheme, Fujita approach (Gombar & Kapoor), and models based on the semiempirical topological indices (Porto et al, 2008; Castro et al, 2004). However, as it was stated, the lack of simple interpretations of the molecular fragments encoded by InChI attributes can be overridden by getting the reasonable prediction applying described algorithm. Since the InChI attributes (chemical element, connectivity, bonds, charges, etc) have clear genesis it is possible to extract from the model (8) robust heuristic information, which probably is not less important than the groups' contributions. For instance, the InChI-based optimal descriptors may give some clues

for the mechanistic interpretations of fullerene C_{60} solubility (Toropov et al, 2009).

Finally, it can be noted that the described InChI-based model is better than models that are SMILES notations based (Toropov et al, 2007; Toropov et al, 2008; Toropov, et al, 2007; Toropov et al, 2009).

The next model for C_{60} solubility is rather different than all previous and based on quantum-chemical and topological descriptors and was published recently (Petrova et al, 2011). In this study, it was aimed to find a simple, transparent relationship and computationally fast approach, possibly mechanistically interpretable, to predict the solubility of C_{60} in various organic solvents. In the previous studies have been applied the optimal descriptors approach which is effective, but not so transparent and unfortunately, not mechanistically interpretable. The recent approach evaluates predictive potential of the structure-based topological descriptors and quantum-chemical parameters obtained by high level *ab initio* calculations in QSPR modeling of the fullerene C_{60} solubility in organic solvents.

In this study the one of the initial sets of utilized descriptors represents the set of constitutional, topological, and molecular descriptors that were calculated by the *DRAGON* software (Todeschini & Consonni, 2003). Another set represents the quantum-chemical descriptors that have been calculated using Gaussian 03 software (Frisch et al, 2004) by Density Functional Theory (DFT) methodology. Five models were obtained and discussed, from one-variable to five-variable model. The best four-variable model (9) showed the best statistical performance (Figure 4):

$$log\,S = 0.532\,TI2 + 0.698\,X1Sol + 15.694\,FDI - 0.103\,H\text{-}052 - 21.218 \qquad (9)$$

$r^2 = 0.861$, $q^2 = 0.841$, $F = 134.80$, $s = 0.411$

$r^2_{test} = 0.903$, $F = 259.56$, $s = 0.355$

Figure 4. Plot of experimental versus calculated solubility (logS) of fullerene C_{60} for the training set (a) and for the test set (b) according to model (9). Reproduced with permission from Reference (Petrova et al, 2011). Copyright Springer, 2011.

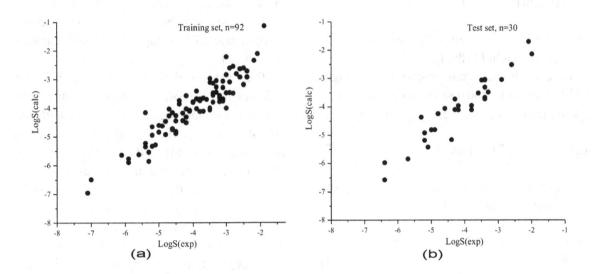

The model includes topological descriptor X1sol, which represents solvation connectivity index (chi-1) that encodes the solvation property of the compound (Todeschini & Consonni, 2000). Briefly, this molecular descriptor is defined in order to model solvation entropy and dispersion interactions in solution (Figure 5). The descriptor relates the characteristic dimension of the molecule to the atomic parameters (quantum number, bond indexes, etc). Next, the TI2 descriptor is topological descriptor, second Mohar index TI2. The Mohar index is derived from Laplacian matrix (Todeschini & Consonni, 2000), which is a distance matrix. As it can be seen from the model (9), the higher value of TI2 descriptor results in the lower solubility of C_{60} in particular solvent. Another important descriptor selected by genetic algorithm is FDI descriptor, which is geometrical descriptor - a folding degree index. The values of the descriptor are defined in a range $0 \leq FDI \leq 1$. This descriptor converges to one for linear molecules (of infinite length) and decreases in accord with the folding degree of the molecule. So, the FDI descriptor can be used as indicator of the degree of departure of a molecule from a strict linearity. FDI contributes positively to the log S value of C_{60} solubility. It indicates that the more linear (less foldings) molecule of the solvent is, the better is solubility of C_{60} in this solvent. The last descriptor, H-052 represents the atom-centered fragments, describing H (hydrogen) attached to C(sp3) with 1X (heteroatom) attached to the next C (Todeschini & Consonni, 2000). The model (9) shows, the higher value of this descriptor relates to the lower solubility of C_{60}.

This study demonstrates that an application of the GA-MLRA technique in combination with quantum-chemical and topological descriptors yields reliable models. The models are quite simple, interpretable, transparent, and statistically comparable to the previously published results (Figure 4). The best performance is accomplished by the four-variable MLRA model with prediction coefficient r^2_{test} = 0.903. The model is comparable with the model published in (Liu et al, 2005) and to the model suggested in the other publications (Toropov et al, 2007; 2008; 2007; 2009).

Figure 5. Fullerene C$_{60}$ inside of periodic box of solvent (ethanol)

One more interesting study which is worth to mention here is prediction of the water solubility and octanol-water partition coefficients for carbon nanotubes (CNT) based on chiral vector (Toropov et al, 2007). Molecules of CNTs contain hundreds or even thousands of atoms. However, because of large number of atoms in structure the application of the "classic" structural descriptors becomes quite problematic. So, there was a need to find a simple parameter for CNT structure-solubility purposes. Best known parameter for the CNT structure is a chiral vector (n, m) (Torrens, 2005). In fact, the components of chiral vector contain information about rolling up graphite layer in CNT. It also known that certain physicochemical behavior of CNTs is correlated with numerical values of chiral vector components. For example, m−n=3k (k is an integer) is known to be a necessary criterion for conductivity in CNT (Ormsby & King, 2004).

In study (Toropov et al, 2007) the multiple linear regression analysis was used to find correlations between chiral vectors of CNTs and solubility (logS), and also for correlations between chiral vector and octanol-water partition coefficient (logP). Two-variable models for the water solubility and octanol-water partition coefficient have been found. Indeed, the obtained models showed a great performance:

$$\log S = -5.1041 - 3.5075n - 3.5941m \qquad (10)$$

$r^2 = 0.9999$, $s = 0.0534$, $F = 126.611$ (training set)

$r^2 = 0.9999$, $s = 0.0933$, $F = 67.456$ (test set)

$$\log P = -3.9193 + 3.7703n - 3.6001m \qquad (11)$$

$r^2 = 0.9991$, $s = 0.364$, $F = 2.927$ (training set)

$r^2 = 0.9996$, $s = 0.287$, $F = 5.928$ (test set)

Moreover, the obtained models are simple and transparent. It was concluded that components of the chiral vectors of CNTs can be used as structural descriptors in QSPR analysis aimed to predict water solubility and octanol water partition coefficient of carbon nanotubes.

Elasticity (Young Modulus)

The physical and mechanical (technological) properties of nanomaterials are also among the priority ones for predicting. Another interesting study in QSPR of nanomaterials provides an example, where an attempt to estimate the ability of a QSPR approach to predict mechanical characteristics of nanomaterials was made. In the study a SMILES-like method was used to predict the elasticity (Young's modulus) of selected nanomaterials (Toropov & Leszczynski, 2006). In this case, authors used technological characteristics to encode nanomaterials, i.e. the SMILES-like nomenclature for a given nanomaterial contains data on atom composition and the technological conditions of its synthesis and is used as basis for calculating optimal descriptors. To be clear, the nomenclature used in this study does not represent standard SMILES, since the function of the nomenclature used here is limited to encoding the available information on the genesis of the nanomaterials as commercial products. In this study the SMILES characteristics reflect detailed (2D, 3D, and even quantum chemical) information on molecular architecture.

The descriptor used for modeling Young's modulus (YM) has been defined as:

$$DCW = \prod_{k=1}^{N} CW(I_k) \qquad (12)$$

where I_k is the component information on the nanostructure (e.g., Al, N, BULK, etc); $CW(I_k)$ is the correlation weight of the component I_k; and N represent the total number of these components in the given nanostructure. Thus, the sequence of components applied to a given nanomaterial such as its code and descriptor calculated with Eq. (12) provides a mathematical function of the code. Using the Monte Carlo method one can calculate the values of the $CW(I_k)$ that yield correlation coefficients between Young's modulus

(YM) and the DCW that are as large as possible for the training set. Then, based on the $CW(I_k)$ values it is possible to compute a YM by least squares method model:

$$YM = C_0 + C_1 DCW \qquad (13)$$

The developed model has the following representation and statistical data:

$$YM = -3720.235 + 3945.175 \, DCW \qquad (14)$$

$$r^2 = 0.9757, s = 18.25, F = 761$$

$$r^2 = 0.8952, r^2_{pred} = 0.8880, s = 34.69, F = 51$$

Interestingly, the information concerning nanomaterials in view of the data used as descriptors (see Table in (Toropov & Leszczynski, 2006)) corresponds to instruction on how to carry out the synthesis of a given substance at manufacturing process. Accordingly, the suggested approach can be used as a tool for estimation of the Young's modulus value for nanomaterials that can be produced under technological conditions which have not been applied before. In other words, the suggested approach can help to save time, money and material resources in search for nanomaterials with required values of Young's modulus. Of course, as it was stated in the study, the accuracy of the prediction will increase with increasing the number of nanomaterials used in the training set.

Finally, it can be noted that totally twenty-nine different nanomaterials characterized by experimental studies were utilized to build a predictive model for module of elasticity.

Toxicity Prediction

The next important step in nanomaterials' investigation and analysis is to find good relationship between structural and/or physical features of nanoparticles and their exhibited toxicity properties.

This it is the most comprehensive task, and for this kind of studies the experimental toxicity data obtained for the considered nanoparticles should be used. Unfortunately, there is still limited information about experimentally measured toxic effects of nanoparticles and it is not systematic. However, some isolated and limited toxicity data are published in the last few years (Duffin et al, 2007; Fiorito, 2007; Gill et al, 2007; Powers et al, 2007; Medina, 2007; Chen, et al, 2006; Moore, 2006; Karakoti, Hench & Seal, 2006; Moss & Wong, 2006; Lee & Cho, 2006; Tsuji et al, 2006; Braydich-Stolle et al, 2005) and due to increasing interest in such data the more similar studies in the near future can be expected. This scarce toxicity information makes difficult the study of structure-toxicity relationship of nanoparticles. Therefore, our group in collaboration with other groups (experimental biology and computational teams) conducted an experimental toxicity evaluation of 17 metal oxides and then used these data to build a nanoparticle-toxicity model, so-called nano-QSAR, to find some important correlations and predict toxicity for new, untested metal oxide nanoparticles (Puzyn et al, 2011).

The *in vitro* toxicity data for investigated nanoparticles on pathogen bacteria cultures (*E.coli*) were used for toxicity evaluation. The initial studies regarding the structure-toxicity relationship analysis of these metal oxides has been initiated. The studied metal oxides include: $ZnO, TiO_2, SnO_2, CuO, La_2O_3, Fe_2O_3, Al_2O_3, Y_2O_3, Bi_2O_3, ZrO_2, SiO_2, In_2O_3, V_2O_3, CoO, NiO, Cr_2O_3$ and Sb_2O_3.

Based on this model and experimental data, the hypothesis was made on the most probable mechanism for the cytotoxicity of these nanoparticles. Utilizing the toxicity data and structural descriptors, a simple but statistically significant ($F = 45.4$, $P = 0.0001$) was developed. The obtained nano-QSAR equation was based on only one descriptor that allows successfully predict the cytotoxicity (EC_{50} - the effective concentration of a compound that brings about a 50% reduction in bacteria viability) of the considered metal oxide nanoparticles:

$$\log(1/EC_{50}) = 2.59 - 0.50\ \Delta H_{Me+} \qquad (15)$$

Interestingly, the descriptor ΔH_{Me+} represents the enthalpy of formation of a gaseous cation having the same oxidation state as that in the metal oxide structure:

$$Me(s) \rightarrow Me^{n+}(g) + n \cdot \bar{e}\Delta H_{Me+} \qquad (16)$$

A complete list of the calculated molecular descriptors and details on the QSAR modeling procedure, including splitting for a training and validation set, data pre-processing, the method of modeling, internal validation, measuring goodness-of-fit and robustness, external validation of predictive ability and applicability domain can be found in the recently published paper (Puzyn et al, 2011).

In fact, the predicted EC_{50} values were calculated using a single descriptor, ΔH_{Me+}. The results indicated that ΔH_{Me+} can be utilized as an efficient descriptor of the chemical stability of metal oxides and, therefore, their cytotoxicity in *E.coli in vitro* tests. Authors noted that during the development of the model, various parameters were tested that were, in some cases, more interpretative than ΔH_{Me+}. The tests included ΔH_L (lattice energy), which describes the dissolution of nanoparticles without oxidation or reduction of the cation, and the electronic properties (energies of HOMO and LUMO) of the oxides, which describe their redox properties. In all these tests, the correlation between the tested descriptors and cytotoxicity was unsatisfactory. It worth to note, the model was built on assumption that all metal oxide nanoparticles from quantum-mechanical point of view within the size range 15-90nm (as in experiments) do not have drastic changes in properties within one type of nanoparticle, for example in electronic properties. It was stated that large, size-dependent change of some electronic

Figure 6. Plot of experimentally determined (observed) versus predicted log values of 1/EC$_{50}$. Squares represent values predicted for the metal oxides from the training set; triangles represent data calculated for metal oxides from the validation sets. Reproduced from Reference (Puzyn et al, 2011). Copyright Nature Publishing Group, 2011.

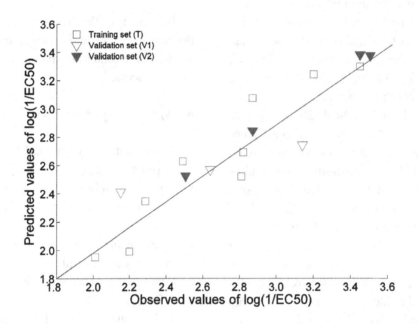

properties (i.e., ionization potential and electron affinity) for metal oxides particles occur below 5 nm (Gajewicz, 2011). Thus, the property value variation with the increasing size of the nanomaterial does not occur until it reaches so-called the saturation point - starting from which the property value does change. Therefore, authors assumed that the property changes between 15 and 90 nm are negligible.

A plot of experimentally determined versus predicted log values of 1/EC$_{50}$ is presented in Figure 6. The straight green line represents a perfect agreement between experimental and calculated values. The model shows a great agreement between the observed toxicity values and those predicted by the nano-QSAR model, for the metal oxides from the training set (squares) and those from the validation sets (triangles). The following statistical results were stated: squared regression coefficient, $r^2 = 0.85$; cross-validated regression coefficient, $q^2_{CV} = 0.77$; externally

validated regression coefficient $q^2_{ext} = 0.83$; root-mean-square error of calibration (RMSEC) = 0.20, of cross-validation (RMSECV) = 0.24, and of external prediction (RMSEP) = 0.19.

In conclusion, based on relatively large number of metal oxide nanoparticles, the discussed study combines experimental testing and computational modeling methodologies to study the cytotoxicity of metal oxide nanoparticles in *E. coli*. This combined study allows developing an interpretative nano-QSAR model that reliably predicts toxicity and provides the foundations for theoretical evaluation of the toxicity of untested nanomaterials, particularly for metal oxide nanoparticles. Importantly, this study resulted in a hypothesis that mechanistically explains differences in toxicity between individual oxides. It is quite obvious that this study can now trigger many new studies in the field of predicting the toxicity and biological activity of various nanoparticles.

One more study recently performed in collaboration with our group where were utilized the same experimental data, but different, SMILES-based optimal descriptors approach (Toropov et al, 2011). This approach also showed a great performance, however, the weak part of optimal descriptors approach is complicated both transparency and mechanistically interpretation of the model.

CONCLUSION

Nanomaterials are becoming an important component of the modern life and have been the subject of increasing number of investigations involving various areas of natural sciences. However, theoretical modeling of physicochemical and biological activity of these species is still very scarce. The prediction of the properties and activities of 'classical' substances via correlating with some molecular descriptors is a well known procedure that generates foundation of the QSAR approaches. In spite of this, the application of these methods for the nanomaterials is a very complicated task, because of "non-classical" structure of nanomaterials and relatively large size of nanospecies from computational point of view. Here we show that an application of the QSAR methods for nanomaterials is nevertheless possible and can be really useful in modeling and predicting their various properties and activities (toxicity). We briefly explained how the physico-chemical properties, such as solubility in various organic solvents, solubility in water, Young modulus and other properties can be predicted for nanomaterials. Furthermore, we also demonstrated how the biological activity, particularly toxicity, can be modeled and predicted for the series of metal oxide nanoparticles, by applying the quantum-chemical methods in combination with the nano-QSAR models.

The research in the field of nanoparticle-property or nanoparticle-activity/toxicity relationships modeling is only in its very early stage. We believe that many cutting-edge developments in predicting of nanomaterials' properties can be expected soon, perhaps generating reliable nano-QSAR methodology within the next 5-10 years.

ACKNOWLEDGMENT

The authors thank for support of the NSF CREST Interdisciplinary Nanotoxicity Center NSF-CREST - Grant # HRD-0833178; NSF-EPSCoR Award #: 362492-190200-01\NSFEPS-0903787; the Department of Defense through the U.S. Army Engineer Research and Development Center, Vicksburg, MS. for generous support through the contracts: High Performance Computational Design of Novel Materials (HPCDNM) - Contract #W912HZ-06-C-0057.

REFERENCES

ACD/Labs. (1996). Retrieved from http://www.acdlabs.com.

Bartlett, R. J., & Purvis, G. D. (1978). Many-body perturbation theory, coupled-pair many-electron theory, and the importance of quadruple excitations for the correlation problem. *International Journal of Quantum Chemistry, 14*(5), 561–581. doi:10.1002/qua.560140504

Binkley, J. S., & Pople, J. A. (1975). Møller–Plesset theory for atomic ground state energies. *International Journal of Quantum Chemistry, 9*(2), 229–236. doi:10.1002/qua.560090204

Braydich-Stolle, L., Hussain, S., Schlager, J. J., & Hofmann, M.-C. (2005). In vitro cytotoxicity of nanoparticles in mammalian germline stem cells. *Toxicological Sciences, 88*(2), 412–419. doi:10.1093/toxsci/kfi256

Buzea, C., Pacheco Blandino, I. I., & Robbie, K. (2007). Nanomaterials and nanoparticles: Sources and Toxicity. *Biointerphases, 2*(4), MR17–MR172. doi:10.1116/1.2815690

Castro, E. A., Torrens, F., Toropov, A. A., Nesterov, I. V., & Nabiev, O. M. (2004). QSAR Modeling Anti-HIV-1 Activities by Optimization of Correlation Weights of Local Graph Invariants. *Molecular Simulation*, *30*, 691–696. doi:10.1080/08927020 412331272449

Cedervall, T., Lynch, I., Lindman, S., Berggard, T., Thulin, E., & Nilsson, H. (2007). Understanding the nanoparticle–protein corona using methods to quantify exchange rates and affinities of proteins for nanoparticles. *Proceedings of the National Academy of Sciences of the United States of America*, *104*(7), 2050–2055. doi:10.1073/ pnas.0608582104

Chen, B.-X., Wilson, S. R., Das, M., Couglin, D. J., & Erlanger, B. F. (1998)... *Proceedings of the National Academy of Sciences of the United States of America*, *95*, 10809–10813. doi:10.1073/ pnas.95.18.10809

Chen, H.-W., Su, S.-F., Chien, C.-T., Lin, W.-H., Yu, S.-L., & Chou, C.-C. (2006). Titanium dioxide nanoparticles induce emphysema-like lung injury in mice. *The FASEB Journal*, *20*(13), 2393–2395. doi:10.1096/fj.06-6485fje

Choi, S.-J., Oh, J.-M., & Choy, J.-H. (2008). Human-related application and nanotoxicology of inorganic particles: complementary aspects. *Journal of Materials Chemistry*, *18*(6), 615–620. doi:10.1039/b711208d

Daylight Chemical Information Systems. (2008). Retrieved from http://www.daylight.com.

Duffin, R., Tran, L., Brown, D., Stone, V., & Donaldson, K. (2007). Proinflammogenic Effects of Low-Toxicity and Metal Nanoparticles In Vivo and In Vitro: Highlighting the Role of Particle Surface Area and Surface Reactivity. *Inhalation Toxicology*, *19*(10), 849–856. doi:10.1080/08958370701479323

Edelstein, A. S., & Cammarata, R. C. (1998). *Nanomaterials: Synthesis, Properties and Applications*. New York: CRC Press.

Feldheim, D. L. (2001). *Metal Nanoparticles: Synthesis, Characterization, and Applications*. New York: CRC Press.

Fiorito, S. (2007). Carbon nanoparticles: benefits and risks for human health. In Zhao, Y., & Nalwa, H. S. (Eds.), *Nanotoxicology, Interactions of Nanomaterials with Biological Systems* (pp. 167–180). New York: American Scientific Publishers.

Fouchécourt, M.-O., Béliveau, M., & Krishnan, K. (2001). Quantitative structure-pharmacokinetic modeling. *The Science of the Total Environment*, *274*, 125–135.

Franklin, N. M., Rogers, N. J., Apte, S. C., Batley, G. E., Gadd, G. E., & Casey, P. S. (2007). Comparative Toxicity of Nanoparticulate ZnO, Bulk ZnO, and $ZnCl_2$ to a Freshwater Microalga (Pseudokirchneriella subcapitata): The Importance of Particle Solubility. *Environmental Science & Technology*, *41*(24), 8484–8490. doi:10.1021/ es071445r

Friedman, S. H., Decamp, D. L., Sijbesma, R. P., Srdanov, G., Wudl, F., & Kenyon, G. L. (1993)... *Journal of the American Chemical Society*, *115*, 6506–6509. doi:10.1021/ja00068a005

Friedman, S. H., Ganapathi, P. S., Rubin, Y., & Kenyon, G. L. (1998). Optimizing the Binding of Fullerene Inhibitors of the HIV-1 Protease through Predicted Increases in Hydrophobic Desolvation. *Journal of Medicinal Chemistry*, *41*(13), 2424–2429. doi:10.1021/jm970689r

Frisch, M. J., Trucks, G. W., Schlegel, H. B., Scuseria, G. E., Robb, M. A., Cheeseman, J. R., et al. (2004). *Gaussian 03, Revision C. 02*. Wallingford, CT: Gaussian, Inc.

Gajewicz, A., Puzyn, T., Rasulev, B., Leszczynska, D., & Leszczynski, J. (2011). Metal Oxide Nanoparticles: Size-Dependence of Quantum-Mechanical Properties. *Nanoscience & Nanotechnology-Asia*, *1*, 53–58. doi:10.2174/2210681211101010053

Gill, S., Lobenberg, R., Ku, T., Azarmi, Sh., Roa, W., & Prenner, E. J. (2007). Nanoparticles: characteristics, mechanisms of action, and toxicity in pulmonary drug delivery - a review. *Journal of Biomedical Nanotechnology*, *3*(2), 107–119. doi:10.1166/jbn.2007.015

Gombar, V. K., & Kapoor, V. K. (1990). Quantitative structure-activity relationship studies: β-adrenergic blocking activity of 1-(2,4-disubstituted phenoxy)-3-aminopropan-2-ols. *European Journal of Medicinal Chemistry*, *25*, 689–695. doi:10.1016/0223-5234(90)90134-O

Hättig, C., & Hald, K. (2002). Implementation of RI-CC2 triplet excitation energies with an application to trans-azobenzene. *Physical Chemistry Chemical Physics*, *4*, 2111–2118. doi:10.1039/b110847f

Hohenberg, P., & Kohn, W. (1964). Inhomogeneous Electron Gas. *Physical Review*, *136*, 864–871. doi:10.1103/PhysRev.136.B864

Hussain, S. M., Hess, K. L., Gearhart, J. M., Geiss, K. T., & Schlager, J. J. (2005). In vitro toxicity of nanoparticles in BRL 3A rat liver cells. *Toxicology In Vitro*, *19*(7), 975–983. doi:10.1016/j.tiv.2005.06.034

Karakoti, A. S., Hench, L. L., & Seal, S. (2006). The potential toxicity of nanomaterials - The role of surfaces. *JOM*, *58*(7), 77–82. doi:10.1007/s11837-006-0147-0

Klabunde, K. J. (2001). *Nanoscale Materials in Chemistry*. New York: John Wiley & Sons, Inc. doi:10.1002/0471220620

Kušić, H., Rasulev, B., Leszczynska, D., Leszczynski, J., & Koprivanac, N. (2009). Prediction of Rate Constants for Radical Degradation of Aromatic Pollutants in Water Matrix: A QSAR Study. *Chemosphere*, *75*, 1128–1134. doi:10.1016/j.chemosphere.2009.01.019

Lee, J.-K., & Cho, M. H. (2006). Toxicity and Tissue Distribution of Magnetic Nanoparticles in Mice. *Toxicological Sciences*, *89*(1), 338–347.

Lewinski, N., Colvin, V., & Drezek, R. (2008). Cytotoxicity of nanoparticles. *Small*, *4*(1), 26–49. doi:10.1002/smll.200700595

Liu, H., Yao, X., Zhang, R., Liu, M., Hu, Z., & Fan, B. (2005). Accurate quantitative structure-property relationship model to predict the solubility of C_{60} in various solvents based on a novel approach using a least-squares support vector machine. *The Journal of Physical Chemistry B*, *109*, 20565–20571. doi:10.1021/jp052223n

Marcorin, G. L., Da Ros, T., Castellano, S., Stefancich, G., Bonin, I., Miertus, S., & Prato, M. (2000). Design and Synthesis of Novel C[60] Fullerene Derivatives as Potential HIV Aspartic Protease Inhibitors. *Organic Letters*, *2*(25), 3955–3958. doi:10.1021/ol000217y

Medina, C., Santos-Martinez, M. J., Radomski, A., Corrigan, O. I., & Radomski, M. W. (2007). Pharmacological and toxicological significance of nanoparticles. *British Journal of Pharmacology*, *150*(5), 552–558. doi:10.1038/sj.bjp.0707130

Moore, M. N. (2006). Do nanoparticles present ecotoxicological risks for the health of the aquatic environment? *Environment International*, *32*(8), 967–976. doi:10.1016/j.envint.2006.06.014

Moss, O. R., & Wong, V. A. (2006). When nanoparticles get in the way: impact of projected area on in vivo and in vitro macrophage function. *Inhalation Toxicology*, *18*(10), 711–716. doi:10.1080/08958370600747770

Oberdörster, G., Oberdörster, E., & Oberdörster, J. (2005). Nanotoxicology: An Emerging Discipline Evolving from Studies of Ultrafine Particles. *Environmental Health Perspectives, 13*(7), 823–839. doi:10.1289/ehp.7339

Ormsby, J. L., & King, B. T. (2004). Clar valence bond representation of π-bonding in carbon nanotubes. *The Journal of Organic Chemistry, 69,* 4287–4291. doi:10.1021/jo035589+

Petrova, T., Rasulev, B. F., Toropov, A. A., Leszczynska, D., & Leszczynski, J. (2011). Improved Model for Fullerene C_{60} Solubility in Organic Solvents Based on Quantum-Chemical and Topological Descriptors. *Journal of Nanoparticle Research, 2011.* doi:.doi:10.1007/s11051-011-0238-x

Pitkethly, M. J. (2004). Nanomaterials – the driving force. *Materials Today, 7*(12), 20–29. doi:10.1016/S1369-7021(04)00627-3

Porto, L. C., Souza, E. S., Da Silva, J. B., Yunes, R. A., & Heinzen, V. E. F. (2008). Semi-empirical topological index: Development of QSPR/QSRR and optimization for alkylbenzenes. *Talanta, 76,* 407–412. doi:10.1016/j.talanta.2008.03.023

Powers, K. W., Palazuelos, M., Moudgil, B. M., & Roberts, S. M. (2007). Characterization of the size, shape, and state of dispersion of nanoparticles for toxicological studies. *Nanotoxicology, 1*(1), 42–51. doi:10.1080/17435390701314902

Puzyn, T., Gajewicz, A., Leszczynska, D., & Leszczynski, J. (2010). Nanomaterials - the Next Great Challenge for QSAR Modelers. In Puzyn, T., Leszczynski, J., & Cronin, M. T. (Eds.), *Recent Advances in QSAR Studies: Methods and Applications. New York.* London, New York: Springer. doi:10.1007/978-1-4020-9783-6_14

Puzyn, T., Leszczynska, D., & Leszczynski, J. (2009). Toward the Development of "Nano-QSARs": Advances and Challenges. *Small, 5,* 2494–2509. doi:10.1002/smll.200900179

Puzyn, T., Rasulev, B., Gajewicz, A., Hu, X., Dasari, T. P., & Michalkova, A. (2011). Using Nano-QSAR to predict the cytotoxicity of metal oxide nanoparticles. *Nature Nanotechnology, 6,* 175–178. doi:10.1038/nnano.2011.10

Rasulev, B. F., Kušic, H., Lesczynska, D., Leszczynski, J., & Koprivanac, N. (2010). QSAR modeling of acute toxicity on mammals for aromatic compounds: the case study using oral LD_{50} for rats. *Journal of Environmental Monitoring, 12*(5), 1037–1044. doi:10.1039/b919489d

Rasulev, B. F., Saidkhodzhaev, A. I., Nazrullaev, S. S., Akhmedkhodzhaeva, K. S., Khushbaktova, Z. A., & Leszczynski, J. (2007). Molecular modeling and QSAR analysis of the estrogenic activity of terpenoids isolated from Ferula plants. *SAR and QSAR in Environmental Research, 18*(7-8), 663–673. doi:10.1080/10629360701428631

Rotello, V. M. (2004). *Nanoparticles: Building Blocks for Nanotechnology* (Lockwood, D. J., Ed.). New York: Springer.

Schwarz, J. A., & Contescu, C. I. (1999). Surfaces of Nanoparticles and Porous Materials. In *Surfactant Science, 78.* New York: CRC Press.

Seaton, A. (2007). Nanotoxicology: Hazard and risk. *NanoBiotechnology, 3,* 316.

Seatona, A., & Donaldson, K. (2005). Nanoscience, nanotoxicology, and the need to think small. *Lancet, 365*(9463), 923–924. doi:10.1016/S0140-6736(05)71061-8

Sijbesma, R., Srdanov, G., Wudl, F., Castoro, J. A., Wilkens, C., & Friedman, S. H. (1993)... *Journal of the American Chemical Society, 115,* 6510–6514. doi:10.1021/ja00068a006

Slater, J. C. (1951). A Simplification of the Hartree-Fock Method. *Physical Review, 81,* 385–390. doi:10.1103/PhysRev.81.385

Srivastava, D., Menon, M., & Cho, K. (2001). Computational Nanotechnology Withcarbon Nanotubes and Fullerenes. *Computing in Science & Engineering, 3*(4), 42–55. doi:10.1109/5992.931903

Todeschini, R., & Consonni, V. (2000). *Handbook of molecular descriptors.* Weinheim: Wiley-VCH.

Todeschini, R., Consonni, V. (2003). *DRAGON software for the calculation of molecular descriptors Version 3.0.*

Tokuyama, H., Yamago, S., Nakamura, E., Shiraki, T., & Suguira, Y. (1993). ... *Journal of the American Chemical Society, 115*, 7918–7923. doi:10.1021/ja00070a064

Toropov, A., Leszczynska, D., & Leszczynski, J. (2007). Predicting water solubility and octanol-water partition coefficient for carbon nanotubes based on the chiral vector. *Computational Biology and Chemistry, 31*, 127–128. doi:10.1016/j.compbiolchem.2007.02.002

Toropov, A., & Leszczynski, J. (2006). A new approach to the characterization of nanomaterials: Predicting Young's modulus by correlation weighting of nanomaterials codes. *Chemical Physics Letters, 433*, 125–129. doi:10.1016/j.cplett.2006.11.010

Toropov, A., Nesmerak, K., Raska, I. Jr, Waisser, K., & Palat, K. (2006). QSPR modeling of the half-wave potentials of benzoxazines by optimal descriptors calculated with the SMILES. *Computational Biology and Chemistry, 30*, 434–437. doi:10.1016/j.compbiolchem.2006.09.003

Toropov, A., Rasulev, B., Leszczynska, D., & Leszczynski, J. (2007). Additive SMILES based optimal descriptors: QSPR modeling of fullerene C_{60} solubility in organic solvents. *Chemical Physics Letters, 444*, 209–214. doi:10.1016/j.cplett.2007.07.024

Toropov, A., Rasulev, B., Leszczynska, D., & Leszczynski, J. (2008). Multiplicative SMILES Based Optimal Descriptors: QSPR Modeling of Fullerene C_{60} Solubility in Organic Solvents. *Chemical Physics Letters, 457*, 332–336. doi:10.1016/j.cplett.2008.04.013

Toropov, A., Toropova, A., Benfenati, E., Leszczynska, D., & Leszczynski, J. (2009). Additive InChI-based optimal descriptors: QSPR modeling of fullerene C_{60} solubility in organic solvents. *Journal of Mathematical Chemistry, 46*(4), 1232–1251. doi:10.1007/s10910-008-9514-0

Toropov, A., Toropova, A., Rasulev, B., Puzyn, T., Hu, X., & Hwang, H.-M. (2011). (in press). QSAR model of toxicity towards E.coli bacteria for nanosized oxides by SMILES-based optimal descriptors. *Chemical Biology & Drug Design.*

Toropov, A. A., & Benfenati, E. (2007). SMILES as an alternative to the graph in QSAR modelling of bee toxicity. *Computational Biology and Chemistry, 31*, 57–60. doi:10.1016/j.compbiolchem.2007.01.003

Toropov, A. A., Leszczynska, D., & Leszczynski, J. (2007). QSPR study on solubility of fullerene C_{60} in organic solvents using optimal descriptors calculated with SMILES. *Chemical Physics Letters, 441*, 119–122. doi:10.1016/j.cplett.2007.04.094

Toropov, A. A., Toropova, A. P., Mukhamedzhanova, D. V., & Gutman, I. (2005). Simplified molecular input line entry system (SMILES) as an alternative for constructing quantitative structure-property relationships (QSPR). *Indian Journal of Chemistry A, 44*, 1545–1552.

Torrens, F. (2005). Partition of solvents and co-solvents of nanotubes: proteins and cyclopyranoses. In Caldwell, G.W., Atta-ur-Rahman, B.A. (Eds.), *Frontiers in Drug Design and Discovery I*, (pp. 231–268). Hilversum, Holland: Springer.

Tsuji, J. S., Maynard, A. D., Howard, P. C., James, J. T., Lam, C.-W., Warheit, D. B., & Santamaria, A. B. (2006). Research Strategies for Safety Evaluation of Nanomaterials, Part IV: Risk Assessment of Nanoparticles. *Toxicological Sciences*, *89*(1), 42–50. doi:10.1093/toxsci/kfi339

Turabekova, M.A., Rasulev, B.F., & Dzhakhangirov, F.N. Salikhov, Sh.I. (2008). *Aconitum* and *Delphinium* alkaloids. "Drug-likeness" descriptors related to toxic mode of action. *Environmental Toxicology and Pharmacology*, *25*, 310–320. doi:10.1016/j.etap.2007.10.035

Unofficial InChI FAQ. University of Cambridge, Cambridge, CB2 1EW (2011). Retrieved from http://wwmm.ch.cam.ac.uk/inchifaq/

Vidal, D., Thormann, M., & Pons, M. (2005). LINGO, an efficient holographic text based method to calculate biophysical properties and intermolecular similarities. *Journal of Chemical Information and Modeling*, *45*(2), 386–393. doi:10.1021/ci0496797

Warheit, D. B., Borm, P. J. A., Hennes, C., & Lademann, J. (2007). Testing Strategies to Establish the Safety of Nanomaterials: Conclusions of an ECETOC Workshop. *Inhalation Toxicology*, *19*(8), 631–643. doi:10.1080/08958370701353080

Weigend, F., Häser, M., Patzelt, H., & Ahlrichs, R. (1998). RI-MP2: optimized auxiliary basis sets and demonstration of efficiency. *Chemical Physics Letters*, *294*(1-3), 143–152. doi:10.1016/S0009-2614(98)00862-8

Wendy Warr & Associates. (2011). Retrieved from http://www.warr.com/

Chapter 4
Active Learning and Mapping:
A Survey and Conception of a New Stochastic Methodology for High Throughput Materials Discovery

Laurent A. Baumes
CSIC-Universidad Politecnica de Valencia, Spain

ABSTRACT

The data mining technology increasingly employed into new industrial processes, which require automatic analysis of data and related results in order to quickly proceed to conclusions. However, for some applications, an absolute automation may not be appropriate. Unlike traditional data mining, contexts deal with voluminous amounts of data, some domains are actually characterized by a scarcity of data, owing to the cost and time involved in conducting simulations or setting up experimental apparatus for data collection. In such domains, it is hence prudent to balance speed through automation and the utility of the generated data. The authors review the active learning methodology, and a new one that aims at generating successively new samples in order to reach an improved final estimation of the entire search space investigated according to the knowledge accumulated iteratively through samples selection and corresponding obtained results, is presented. The methodology is shown to be of great interest for applications such as high throughput material science and especially heterogeneous catalysis where the chemists do not have previous knowledge allowing to direct and to guide the exploration.

DOI: 10.4018/978-1-60960-860-6.ch004

1. INTRODUCTION

Data mining, also called knowledge discovery in databases (Piatetsky-Shapiro & Frawley, 1991;Fayyad, Piatetsky-Shapiro & Smyth, 1996) (KDD) is the efficient discovery of unknown patterns in databases (DBs). The data source can be a formal DB management system, a data warehouse or a traditional file. In recent years, data mining has invoked great attention both in academia and industry. Understanding of field and defining the discovery goals are the leading tasks in the KDD process. It can be distinguished two aims: *i*) *verifications*, where the user hypothesizes and mines the DB to corroborate or disprove the hypothesis; *ii*) *Discovery*, where the objective is to find out new unidentified patterns. Our contribution is concerned by the latter, which can further be either predictive or descriptive. The data mining technology is more and more applied in the production mode, which usually requires automatic analysis of data and related results in order to proceed to conclusions. However, an absolute automation may not be appropriate. Unlike traditional data mining contexts deal with voluminous amounts of data, some domains are actually characterized by a scarcity of data, owing to the cost and time involved in conducting simulations or setting up experimental apparatus for data collection. In such domains, it is hence prudent to balance speed through automation and the utility of the generated data. For these reasons, the human interaction and guidance may lead to better quality output: the need for *active learning* arises.

In many natural learning tasks, knowledge is gained iteratively, by making action, queries, or experiments. Active learning (AL) is concerned with the integration of data collection, design of experiment, and data mining, for making better data exploitation. The learner is not treated as a classical passive recipient of data to be processed. AL can occur due to two extreme cases. *i*) The amount of data available is very large, and therefore a miming algorithm uses a selected data subset rather than the whole available data. *ii*) The researcher has the control of data acquisition, and he has to pay attention on the iterative selection of samples for extracting the greatest benefit from future data treatments. We are concerned by the second situation, which becomes especially crucial when each data point is costly, domain knowledge is imperfect, and theory-driven approaches are inadequate such as for heterogeneous catalysis and material science fields. Active data selection has been investigated in a variety of contexts but as far as we know, this contribution represents the first investigation concerning this chemistry domain.

A catalytic reaction is a chemical reaction in which transformations are accelerated thanks to a substance called catalyst. Basically, starting molecules and intermediates, as soon as they are formed, interact with the catalyst in a specific/discriminating manner. This implies that some transformation steps can be accelerated while other can be kept constant or even slowed down. Catalytic processes constitute the fundamentals of modern chemical industries. Over 90% of the newly introduced chemical processes are catalytic. In the highly developed industrial countries, catalytic processes create about 20% of the Gross Domestic Product. Catalysis is responsible in the manufacture of over $3 trillion in goods and services. We will focus on heterogeneous catalysis which involves the use of catalysts acting in a different phase from the reactants, typically a solid catalyst with liquid and/or gaseous reactants. For further details, the reader is referred to (Ertl, Knozinger & Weitkamp, 1997). During the whole catalytic development, a very large number of features and parameters have to be screened and therefore any detailed and relevant catalyst description remains a challenge. All these parameters generate an extremely high degree of complexity. As a consequence, the entire catalyst development is long (~15 years) and costly. The conventional catalyst development relies essentially on fundamental knowledge and know-how. It implies a complete characterisation of the catalyst in order to establish properties-activity relationship. The main drawback of this approach is to be a very time-consuming process, making and testing one material at a time. Another drawback comes from the relative importance of intuition for the initial choices of development strategy (Jandeleit, Schaefer, Powers, Turner & Weinberg, 1999; Farrusseng, Baumes, Hayaud, Vauthey, 2001; Farruseng, Baumes & Mirodatos, 2003). To overcome these major drawbacks, attempts to shorten this process by using high throughput (HT) technology or experimentation have been reported since about 10-15 years. The HT approach is more pragmatic-oriented. It deals with the screening of collections of samples. However, it may be stressed that relevant parameters are usually unknown and can be hardly directly and individually controlled. In addition, it is in general a combination of factors that provides outstanding properties which are today's required to meet challenging targets. The tools necessary for the combinatorial approach can be classified into two main categories *i*) HT equipments for fast and parallel synthesis and testing of catalysts (Xiang & Takeuchi, 2003; Koinuma &Takeuchi, 2004; Hanak, 2004; Serna, Baumes, Moliner & Corma, 2008; Akporiaye, Dahl, Karlsson, Wendelbo, 1998; Holmgren et al, 2001;Bricker et al, 2004; Pescarmona, Rops, van der Waal, Jansen & Maschmeyer, 2002; Klein, Lehmann, W.; Schmidt & Maier, 1999; Hoffmann, Wolf, SchMth, 1999) and *ii*) computational methods (Montgomery, 1997;Corma, Moliner, Serra, Serna, Díaz-Cabañas & Baumes, 2006;Baumes, Gaudin, Serna, Nicoloyannis & Corma, 2008; Baumes et al, 2009; Baumes, Moliner & Corma, 2006;Caruthers et al, 2003;Todeschini& Consonni, 2000; Rodemerck, Baerns, Holena &Wolf, 2004) and new hardware for time-consuming calculations. (Kruger, Baumes, Lachiche & Collet, 2010; Maitre, Lachiche, Clauss, Baumes, Corma, Collet, 2009; Maitre, Baumes; Lachiche, Collet, Corma, 2009)One should note that algorithms should be adequately selected or created taking into account HT tools

or strategy. (Baumes, Moliner & Corma, 2008; Baumes, Moliner & Corma, 2009; Baumes, Jimenez & Corma, in press) HT experimentation has become an accepted and important strategy in the development of catalysts and materials. (Senkan, 2001; Baumes, Farruseng &Ausfelder, 2004; Gorer, 2004; Sohn, Seo & Park, 2001; Boussie et al, 2003) However, such an approach has more success in the optimization than in the discovery. (Klanner, Farrusseng, Baumes, Lengliz, Mirodatos, Schüth, 2004;Nicolaides, 2005;Klanner, Farrusseng, Baumes, Mirodatos, Schüth, 2003;Farrusseng, Klanner, Baumes, Lengliz, Mirodatos, Schüth, 2005) Despite fast synthesis and testing robots, each catalytic experiment still requires few hours. Here, the learner's most powerful tool is its ability to act, and to gather data. On the other hand, very few recent papers of this domain deal with the strategies called *mapping* that should be used in order to guide a *discovery* study. Mapping develops relationships among properties such as composition, synthesis conditions... while these interactions may be obtained without searching for hits or lead materials. Then, the results of mapping studies can be used as input to guide subsequent screening or optimisation experiments. The purpose of screening experiments is said to identify iteratively, by accumulation of knowledge, hits or small space regions of materials with promising properties. The last manner to guide the chemist, called optimisation, is when experiments are designed to refine material properties. Mapping receives relatively little attention, being too often subsumed under screening. The sampling strategy in HT material science and especially heterogeneous catalysis typically embodies a chemist assessment of where might be a good location to collect data or is derived from the iterative optimization (Wolf, Buyevskaya, Baerns,2000; Buyevskaya, Wolf, Baerns, 2000; Baumes & Collet, 2009; Buyevskaya, Bruckner, Kondratenko, Wolf, Baerns, 2001; Corma, Serra, Chica, 2003; Holena & Baerns, 2003; Serra, Chica, Corma, 2003; Grubert, Kondratenko, Kolf,

Baerns, van Geem, Parton, 2003; Maier et al, 2004; Tchougang, Blansché, Baumes, Lachiche & Collet, 2008; Günter, Jansen, Lucas, Poloni & Beume, 2003; Omata, Umegaki, Watanabe & Yamada, 2003; Paul, Janssens, Joeri, Baron & Jacobs, 2005; Watanabe, Umegaki, Hashimoto, Omata & Yamada, 2004; Cawse, Baerns & Holena, 2004) (principally with evolutionary algorithm) of specific design criteria usually the selectivity or conversion. Homogeneous covering (Bem, Erlandson, Gillespie, Harmon, Schlosser & Vayda, 2003; Cawse & Wroczynski, 2003; Sjöblom, Creaser & Papadakis, 2004; Harmon, 2004) or traditional design of experiment (DoE), (Deming & Morgan, 1993; Montgomery, 1991; Tribus & Sconyi, 1989) which is usually neglected due to the specificity of the different methods and the restrictions imposed by the domain, have been exploited. Otherwise, Simple Random Sampling (SRS) rules the domain. However, SRS should not be underestimated, see (Sammut & Cribb, 1990) for a detailed explanation of SRS robustness.

The general problem considered here is the efficiency of data selection in HT heterogeneous catalysis for a discovery program. Considering such domain, only very fast, *i.e.* qualitative response or relatively noisy information, screening tools should be employed aiming at finding the different "groups" of catalysts outputs. This pre-screening of the search space shall extract information or knowledge from the restricted selected sampling in order to provide guidelines and well defined boundaries for further screenings and optimization. (Serra, Corma, Farrusseng, Baumes, Mirodatos, Flego & Perego, 2003; Baumes, Jouve, Farrusseng, Lengliz, Nicoloyannis, Mirodatos, 2003) The catalytic performances is defined as classes, rank (if exists) is not taken into account since the objective is not the optimization of catalytic outputs. The chemist knowledge is not integrated into the AL methodology but it should permit to define an *a priori* "poorly-previously-explored" parameter space, letting opportunities to surprising or unexpected catalytic results,

especially when considering that HT tools for synthesis and reactivity testing do already restrict much the experimental space. The typical distribution of catalytic outputs usually exhibits unbalanced datasets for which an efficient learning can be hardly carried out.(Baumes, Farruseng, Lengliz & Mirodatos, 2004)Even if the overall recognition rate may be satisfactory, catalysts belonging to rare classes are usually misclassified. On the other hand, the identification of atypical classes is interesting from the point of view of the knowledge gain. Therefore an iterative algorithm is suggested for the characterization of the space structure.(Baumes, 2006)The algorithm should: *i*) Increase the quality of the machine learning (ML) performed at the end of this first exploratory stage. *ii*) Work independently from the choice of the supervised learning system. *iii*) Decrease the misclassification rates of catalysts belonging to small frequency classes of performance. *iv*) Handle both quantitative and qualitative features. *v*) Proceed iteratively while capturing information contained into all previous experiments. *vi*) Integrate inherent constraints such as the *a priori* fixed reactor capacity, *i.e.* the size of the iteratively selected sample to be labelled, and a maximum number of experiments to be conducted, so-called deadline, and *vii*) Be robust considering noisy responses.

The organization of the manuscript is as follow. First, the active learning approaches and the different selection schemes are presented. Then some notations and representations used throughout the text are presented. In the third section, the method and its central criterion are investigated. Section 4 details the creation of the benchmarks, and discusses the great interest of using such testing methodology. Then, in section 5, the method is evaluated on the different benchmarks identified by mathematical functions that exhibit different levels of difficulty. Finally, section 6 will emphasize on quantifying the strength of such a method through statistical analysis and results are thoroughly discussed.

2. ACTIVE LEARNING

Active learning (AL) assumes that the data is provided by a source which is controlled by the researcher. Such control is used for different aims and in different ways. The various fields for which one may wish to use AL are numerous such as *optimization*, where the learner experiments to find a set of inputs that maximize some response variable, for example the response surface methodology (Box & Draper, 1987) which guides hill-climbing through the input space; *adaptive control*, where one must learn a control policy by taking actions. In this field, one may face the complication that the value of a specific action remains unknown until a time delay has occurred; *model selection problem* for driving data collection in order to refine and discriminate a given set of models. For all types of application, the principal AL task is to determine an "optimal" sample selection strategy. Such optimization is defined through a criterion, called *selection scheme*, depending on the user aim. Therefore, considering the model selection problem, the approach can either be motivated by the need to disambiguate among models or to gain the most prediction accuracy from a ML algorithm while requiring the fewest number of labelling.

Before inspecting the different selection schemes proposed earlier and some selected examples from publications, it has to be noted that new samples can either be created by the system or selected from an unlabeled set. The first approach is not investigated here, and considering the domain of application, it remains difficult to generate samples without lack of coherence. Typically a system could produce and ask non existing materials to be labelled. By now, authors who explored this methodology reveal that the protocol often describe "impossible" catalysts such as the following example: prepare by a precipitation process a solid consisting of 30% Ba, 50% Na, and 20% V (oxygen is excluded), using inorganic, non-halide precursors from aqueous solution. Using suitable precursors and finding a precipitation

agent which would precipitate all three metals at the same time is virtually impossible. The second approach is the most common and corresponds to the one we are concerned. Two kinds of selection from an unlabeled set can be distinguished. The pool-based approach allows the selection among an *a priori* restricted set of unlabelled samples while the other one permits to pick up any sample to be labelled from an entire pre-defined search space. Another criterion that should be taken into account when specifying an AL algorithm is the exact role of the ML system. The following cases are discriminated based on the frequency of learning system update. AL which usually starts from a very small number of labelled samples, then iteratively asks for new samples. The selection of new samples may be done in order to update at each new round either the previously obtained model, increasing its performance and accuracy, or a given criterion which remains independent from the learning system allowing a unique use of the ML when the whole selection is achieved. Using the semantic used in *feature selection* domain,(Baumes, Serna &Corma, in press) the first protocol is called a *wrapper* approach while the second one is qualified as *filter*. The advantage of using a wrapper technique is that the selection is optimized considering the learning algorithm that has been previously chosen. However, such choice is not always trivial, and depends on the complexity of the underlying system investigated (which is usually unknown or difficult to be quantified) but also on the complexity of the ML system itself since considering complex algorithms it may be delicate to elaborate the selection scheme. Moreover, for many configurations, such methodology might be intractable.

2.1. Selection Schemes

The primary question of AL is how to choose which points to try next. A simple strategy for sampling is to target locations to reduce our *uncertainty* in modelling, for example by selecting the location that minimizes the posterior generalized variance of a function. The distribution $P(Y/X)$ being unknown, a classical approach consists in approximating P with a large number of samples but then a great number of hypothesis and simplifications have to be done in order to compute the estimated error reduction. For example, using a probabilistic classifier, uncertainty sampling would pick the observation for which the predicted class probabilities yield the greatest entropy. The query by committee utility (Seung, Opper & Sompolinsky, 1992) measures the classification disagreement of a committee of classifiers, choosing an example with high disagreement. Cohn *et al.*(1995) measure the expected reduction in prediction variance of neural networks and other models. Another closely-related solution is to select the most ambiguous sample. *Ambiguity-directed* sampling aims at clarifying the decision-making near the ambiguity. Making the assumption that close elements are similar, the knowledge of one sample should induce the knowledge of the neighbouring. However, ambiguous points are likely to be neighbours. It is therefore important to select ambiguous points spread over the distribution of input variables. Another solutions for choosing these points are to look for "places" where there is no data,(Whitehead, 1991) where it is expected to change the model,(Cohn, Atlas &Ladner,1990) for example, (Juszczak, 2004) relies on measuring the variation in label assignments (of the unlabeled set) between the classifier trained on the training set and the classifiers trained on training set with a single unlabeled object added with all possible labels. Other closely related selection schemes are investigated (Linden & Weber,1993; Schmidhuber & Storck,1993) which respectively aims at choosing points where the system performs poorly, and where it was previously found data that resulted in learning. Other solutions are directly induced by the domain of application, for instance, robot navigation studies. (Thrun &Moller, 1992) In such learning tasks, data-query is neither free

nor of constant cost. Researchers try to integrate the fact that the cost of a query depends on the distance from the current location in state space to the desired query point. On the other hand, such notion of distance is not transferable to the synthesis of materials. Therefore, the next section presents some selected applications and the given solutions proposed in order to better position our approach and underlined its specificities.

2.2. Positioning of the Methodology

An active learner has to efficiently select a set of samples S' in S to be labelled. Nevertheless, it is intractable to compute all possible combinations for S'. The common approach is, then, to select one query sample at each round. Therefore, existing AL approaches such as (Juszczak, & Duin, 2004; Ramakrishnany, Bailey-Kellogg, Tadepalliy, & Pandeyy, 2005) concentrate on the selection of a single element to be labelled. (Ramakrishnany, Bailey-Kellogg, Tadepalliy & Pandeyy, 2005) is an active sampling using entropy-based functions defined over spatial aggregates. This mechanism is applied on numerous 2D functional benchmarks, and for wireless system simulations where the aim is to identify and characterize the nature of the basins of local minima with models of flow classes. However such a solution is not adequate considering our HT approach for which the principal goal is to increase the number of experiments through parallelisation. Moreover, (Cohn, Atlas, & Ladner, 1990) iteratively requires model evaluations such as (Bailey-Kellogg & Ramakrishnan, 2003) where the strategy evaluates models until a high-confidence model is obtained. (Bailey-Kellogg & Ramakrishnan, 2003) employs an AL strategy for model selection problem, and apply their analysis framework to two cases of scientific computing domains. The goal is to empirically characterize problem characteristics (*e.g.* matrix sensitivity) and algorithm performance (*e.g.* convergence) by the data-driven strategy.

Active learning has been applied on relatively new techniques such as Support Vector Machines (SVM).(Brinker, 2003; Tong & Koller, 2001) See (Baumes, Serra, Serna &Corma, 2006; Serra, Baumes, Moliner, Serna &Corma, 2007) for application of SVM in materials science. On the other hand, many of these strategies are meant to be used with specific data mining algorithms (this does not mean that they are wrapper methods). For example, the selection done in (Cohn, Ghahramani, Jordan,Tesauro, Touretzky & Alspector, 1995) is made from a statistical point of view by selecting a new point in order to minimize the estimated variance of its resulting output through an estimate of $P(\tilde{x}, \tilde{y})$, and various assumptions are made considering mixtures of Gaussians, and locally weighted regression, while (Schein, Sandler & Ungar, 2004) develops example selection schemes for a Bayesian logistic regression model in classification settings. Considering only one precise learning system is not desirable for our purpose. First, the choice of the technique is not obvious. Secondly, more than one algorithm or algorithm instance could be employed allowing the use of arcing, boosting, bagging methodologies. Moreover, choosing the learning approach *a posteriori* permits to better handle the complexity of the underlying system investigated by determining an adequate solution. As previously mentioned, our approach should support all kinds of variable type while others are applicable only to continuous output.(Cohn, Ghahramani, Jordan,Tesauro, Touretzky & Alspector, 1995) The technique requires different strong assumptions or simplifications, in order to achieve the minimization of the criterion. In a continuous context, and without differentiable systems, this method is intrinsically limited. For example, considering NN, this approach has many disadvantages: the optimal data selection becomes computationally very expensive and approximate. Moreover, this minimization has to be done for each new example to be potentially integrated in the training set which is very expensive. Similar drawbacks are associated to the maximisation done in (Ramakrishnany, Bailey-Kellogg, Tadepalliy & Pandeyy, 2005).

Pool-based methods (Cohn, Ghahramani, Jordan,Tesauro, Touretzky & Alspector, 1995) take a trained machine learning algorithm and pick the next example from the *a priori* defined pool for labelling according to a measure of expected benefit. (Schein, Sandler, Ungar, 2004) makes the selection of examples with an optimality criteria that describes with some accuracy the expected error induced by a particular training set. (Souvannavong, Mérialdo, Huet, 2004) proposed a partition sampling approach to select a set of ambiguous samples that contain complementary information. Thanks to a clustering technique, they select the most ambiguous element per cluster. They apply this methodology to a video database which is too big and too long to be entirely labelled. The elements are chosen among a pool and therefore the use of a partition algorithm remains reasonable since the pool is finite and tractable. However, in our case, the whole search space is available for labelling.

Other drawbacks have to be noted such as the fact that some studies are noisy-free. For example, (Ramakrishnany, Bailey-Kellogg, Tadepalliy & Pandeyy, 2005) makes the following assumption as most other works on AL: the probability distributions defined by the interpolation model are correct. Despite HT apparatus, one has to bear in mind that the amount of experiments should be in a reasonable range which is usually *a priori* fixed through the time and money associated to a given research contract. On the other hand, (Ramakrishnany, Bailey-Kellogg, Tadepalliy & Pandeyy, 2005) employs the k-nearest neighbours (k-nn with k=8) algorithm with a total number of selected points relatively very high (5% for the initialization and 25% in total) on benchmarks which are all differentiable functions. Considering the total number of combinations possible for materials synthesis, such requirement of data is inaccessible. Moreover, the use of k-*nn* is difficult in a context where the calculation of a distance between catalysts remains tricky due to the qualitative variables such as preparation modes (co-precipitation, impregnation…). It has also to be pointed that some selection schemes such as the maximization of the expected information gain, may select principally extreme solutions. Intuitively, it is expected that gathering data at the location where errors bars on the model are currently the greatest. But the error bars are usually the largest beyond the most extreme points where data have been gathered. Therefore this criterion may lead to gather at the edges of the input space which might be considered as non-ideal. The solution proposed by traditional statistical optimal design (Fedorov, 1972; Chaloner & Verdinelli, 1995) does not meet all the constraints previously underlined. The fundamental objective is hypothesis testing, and an experiment is designed to generate statistically reliable conclusions to specific questions. Therefore, hypothesis must be clearly formulated and experiments are chosen according to the given supposition in order to verify it in a best statistical manner. This strategy is particularly suited to domains that are known sufficiently well that appropriate questions can be formed and models can be pre-defined. In contrast, combinatorial methods are often employed for the express purpose of exploring new and unknown domains.

Although the previously reviewed literature is very valuable and gives theoretical justification of using AL, even without considering the specificities which make them unusable in our case, most of the relevant articles require a degree of statistical sophistication which is beyond the reach of most practitioners of the domain of high throughput materials science. We now present our methodology and empirical results demonstrating the effectiveness of the active mining strategy on synthetic datasets. At the moment, such approach is used in a research program for the discovery of new crystalline materials called zeolites. The strategy is tested against simple random sampling (SRS) on numerous benchmarks with different levels of complexity.

3. THE METHODOLOGY

3.1. Notation

The method is a stochastic group sequential biased sampling which iteratively proposes a sample of the search space noted Ω, and $\omega_p \in \Omega, \left(p \in \left[1..P \right] \right)$ corresponds to an experiment. [Y] is the output set of variables. A process $\wp_{partition}$ is chosen by the user to provide a partition of [Y] in $H \geq 2$ classes noted $C_h, h \in [1..H]$. $\wp_{partition}$ can be a clustering which, in some sense, "discover" classes by itself, by partitioning the examples into clusters, which is a form of unsupervised learning. Note that, once the clusters are found, each cluster can be considered as a "class", see (Senkan, 2001) for an example in the domain of application. [X] is a set of independent variables noted v_i, and x_{i_j} is the value of v_i for the experiment j. Each v_i can be either qualitative or quantitative. If v_i is a given quantitative feature, it is discretized by a process $\wp_{discr}$ providing a set of modalities M_i, with $Card(M_i) = m_i$, $\left(v_i, j \right) = m_{i_j}, j \in \left[1..m_i \right]$ is the modality j of v_i. Whatever the variable, the number of modality m is of arbitrary size. Each cell of a n-dimensional contingency table represents the number of elements that have been observed belonging simultaneously to n given modalities. A so-called "zone" noted s is defined as a set of $1 \leq o \leq n$ modalities.

$$def \left(v_1, \ldots, v_n \right) = \left\{ \left\{ 1..m_{i_1} \right\}, \left\{ 1..m_{i_2} \right\}, \cdots, \left\{ 1..m_{i_n} \right\} \right\},$$
$$s: \quad def \rightarrow \left\{ m_i, - \right\}, \ m_i \in def(v_i)$$

where "–" is the unspecified modality. $o(s)$, called "order", returns the number of defined modalities for s. Let consider a search space partitioned into H classes and N catalysts already evaluated. v_i contains m_i modalities and n^{i_j} corresponds to the amount of experiments with m_{i_j}. The number of experiments belonging to the class h possessing the modality j of the variables v_i is $n_h^{i_j}$. The general notation is summarized in Eq1. A classifier C, $C(.) = \mathcal{C}\left(v_1(.), v_2(.), \cdots, v_n(.)\right)$ is utilized (here C is a NN), which can recognize the class using a list of predictive attributes. The methodology is totally independent from the choice of this ML. It processes as a filter on the sampling in order to enhance the recognition rate by transferring selected catalysts to be synthesized and tested from "stable" search space zones to "unsteady" ones which necessitate more experimental points to be well modelled within the search space.

$$
\begin{array}{c}
\begin{array}{|cccc|c}
\hline
n_1^{i_1} & n_1^{i_2} & \cdots & n_1^{i_{m_i}} & N_1 \\
n_2^{i_1} & \ddots & & n_2^{i_{m_i}} & N_2 \\
\vdots & & \ddots & \vdots & \vdots \\
n_H^{i_1} & n_H^{i_2} & \cdots & n_H^{i_{m_i}} & N_H \\
\hline
\end{array} \Rightarrow \\
n^{i_1} \quad n^{i_2} \quad \cdots \quad n^{i_{m_i}} \quad N
\end{array}
$$

$$
n^{i_j} = \sum_{h=1}^{H} n_h^{i_j}, \quad N_i = \sum_{j=1}^{m_i} n_h^{i_j}, \quad N = \begin{cases} \sum_{h=1}^{H} N_h = \sum_{h=1}^{H} \left(\sum_{j=1}^{m_i} n_h^{i_j} \right) \\ \sum_{j=1}^{m_i} n^{i_j} = \sum_{j=1}^{m_i} \left(\sum_{h=1}^{H} n_h^{i_j} \right) \end{cases}
$$

(1)

3.2. The Mechanism

Importantly, the approach does not need to sample the entire combinatorial space, but only enough so as to be able to identify the structure of classes without forgetting classes obtained only with few experiments. It is thus imperative to focus the sampling at only those locations that are expected to be useful. Such AL does not provide any direct

information but distribution sets can be used to boost the performance of the classifier without requiring a distance measure. A "puzzling" zone is a region of the search space which contains various classes making the recognition or characterization of the structure difficult due to the heterogeneity of the responses. As soon as the emergence of such a confusing region is detected, a natural behaviour may be to select relatively more experiments belonging to the given region in order to better capture the space structure. A better recognition of space zones in which a relatively high dynamism is detected should permit the understanding of the underlying or causal phenomenon and therefore could be used for localizing hit regions. The methodology focuses on irregularity or variability of catalytic responses, *i.e.* the "wavering" behaviour of class distribution. The method transfers the points from potentially stable zones of the landscape to unsteady or indecisive ones. Therefore the following questions must be answered: How is precisely sized the "difficulty" of a space zone? How is balanced the necessity to confirm trends and exploration while bearing in mind that deadline is approaching?

3.3. The Criterion

The calculation of the statistic called χ^2 is used as a measure of how far a sample distribution deviates from a theoretical distribution. This type of calculation is referred to as a measure of Goodness of Fit (GOF). The Chi-square can be used for measuring how the classes are disparate into zones compared to the distribution one gets after the random initialization (k_i points) or the updated one after successive generations. Therefore a given amount of points can be assigned into zones proportionally to the deviation between the overall distribution and observed distributions into zones. Figure 1a shows a given configuration with H=4, N=1000 and v_i (with m_i=5) that splits the root (*i.e.* the overall distribution is on the left

Figure 1. **a)** *Criterion settings, 1ˢᵗ configuration. On the left hand side is represented the entire search space. This given root has been split into 5 leaves where the distributions are given for the last three ones. Each leaf and the root are partitioned into 5 classes. The first class has received 100 elements, and among these 12 belong to the fourth leaf. The Chi-square statistic is given on the right hand side of each leaf in between brackets.* **b)** *Criterion settings, 2ᵈ configuration*

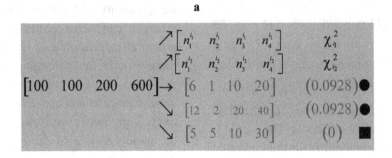

hand side). For equal distributions between the root and a leaf, Chi-square is null ($\chi^2_{l_5}$, ■ in Figure 1a). Chi-square values are equals for two leaves with the same distribution between each other (● in Figure 1a). One would prefer to add a point with the third modality (bottom ●) in order to increase the number of individuals which is relatively low. This is confirmed by the fact that χ^2 is relatively more "reactive" for leaves with smaller populations, see the absolute variations (■ → ● and □ → ○) of two successive χ^2 in Figure 1b.

In order to obtain a significant impact, *i.e.* information gain, by adding a new point it is more interesting to test new catalysts possessing a modality which has been poorly explored (*i.e.* □). Chi-square does not make any difference between leaves that exhibit exactly the same distribution (*i.e.* □ and ■). Therefore n^{i_j} must be minimized

at the same time in order to support relatively empty leaves. Based on the Chi-square behaviour, the criterion is defined by Eq.2.

$$N\left(n^{i_j}+1\right)^{-1} \times \left[\sum_{h=1}^{H} \frac{\left(\dfrac{n_h^{i_j}}{n^{i_j}} - \dfrac{N_h}{N}\right)^2}{N_h} + 1\right] \quad (2)$$

Note that extremely unstable and small zones may have distributions which are very far from the overall distribution. With this criterion, they may attract continuously experiments. However, this may not be due to a natural complex underlying relationship but rather to lack of reproducibility, uncontrolled parameters, noise… Therefore the maximum number of experiments a zone can receive can be bounded by the user. $X^o_{rnd_{k_2}}$ is the

Figure 2. Scheme representing the methodology

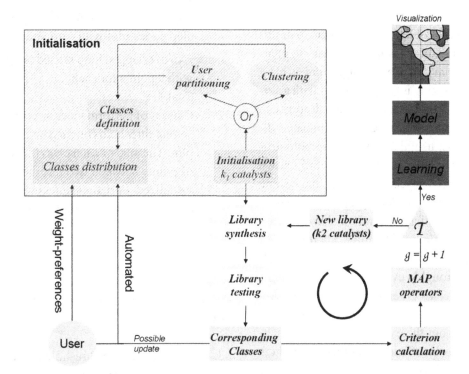

calculated average number of individuals that a zone of order o receives from a SRS of k_2 points. It can be decided a maximum number of points noted $\rho X^o_{rnd_{k_2+k_1}}$, that MAP is authorized to allocate in a zone compared to $X^o_{rnd_{k_2}}$. ρ is a parameter the user has to set. However during our experiments such phenomenon did not appear and thus such parameter is not studied here.

After the distribution zone analysis done after each new selected generation, the algorithm ranks them based on the criterion. Among the whole set of zones, t_s (for tournament size) zones are selected randomly and compete together following the GA-like selection operator called "tournament".(Blickle &Thiele,1995;Thierens,1997)A zone with rank r has $2r \times \left[k_2 \left(k_2 + 1 \right) \right]^{-1}$ of chance to be selected. As the criterion is computed on subsets of modalities (*i.e.* zone of order o), when

a given zone is selected for receiving new points, the modalities that do not belong to s are randomly assigned. Figure 2 is depicting the whole process. The class conception is of great importance since the criterion deeply depends on the root distribution. Enlarging or splitting classes permit an indirect control of the sampling. We recommend to merge uninteresting classes and to split the out of the ordinary ones in order to create relatively unbalanced root distributions. On the other hand, a reasonable balance should be respected otherwise small and interesting classes hidden into large ones will have less chance to be detected. In the experiments presented in next section, o remains fixed and is *a priori* set. For each zone of order o, it is associated the corresponding observed distribution and the related criterion value.

4. TEST CASES

Even if it is impossible to say how many datasets would be sufficient (in whatever sense) to characterize the behaviour of a new algorithm, in most cases, benchmarking is not performed with a sufficient number of different problems. Rarely can the results presented in articles be compared directly. The most useful setup is to use both artificial datasets, whose characteristics are known exactly, and real datasets, which may have some surprising and very irregular properties. Considering the domain of application, real datasets are very costly and time consuming. Therefore, for the first presentation of the new method, its efficiency is thoroughly evaluated with mathematical functions. Two criteria are emphasized: *Reproducibility*. In a majority of cases the information about the exact setup of the benchmarking tests is insufficient for other researchers to exactly reproduce it. *Comparability*. A benchmark is useful if results can directly be compared with results obtained by others for other algorithms. Even if two articles use the same dataset, the results are most often not directly comparable, because either the input/output encoding or the partitioning of training versus test data is not the same or is even undefined. Therefore, the methodology employed for testing the algorithm is fully described. All benchmarks are mathematical functions: $f\left(x_i \in \mathbb{R}\right) \to y \in \mathbb{R}$. For simplicity, $\forall i, x_i \in \left[a \cdots b\right], (a,b) \in \mathbb{R}$ for a given function. A benchmark or test case is used after the three following steps.

1. *n*-dimensions functions are traced onto a first bi-dimensional series plot. $\wp_{discr}$ splits $\left[a \cdots b\right]$ into m_i equal parts ($\forall i, m_i = m$). All the boundaries (*m+1*) are selected as points to be plotted in the series plot. On *x*-axis, an overlapped loop is applied taking into account the selected values of each variable. As example let's consider *Baumes* f_g function (Eq3). Figure 3 shows the associated series plot with *n=6* and $x_i \in \left[-1..1\right]$. An overlapped loop is used on each feature with 9 points for each, *i.e.* 531441 points in total.

2. Classes of performances are constructed by setting thresholds on the *y*-axis of the series plot. The size of each class (*i.e.* the number of points between two thresholds) is easily visualized (horizontal lines in Figure 3). One colour and form is assigned to each class:

$$blue \le 2, 2 < aqua \le 6, 6 < green \le 10, 10 < yellow \le 15, red > 15.$$

Figure 6 gives an example for the placement of points.

3. In between two thresholds, every point is labelled, corresponding to a given class. Figure 4 shows the graph related to Figure 3 and Eq3.

Five different benchmarks, see Figures 5 to 9 (De Jong f_1 and De Jong f_3 (De Jong,(n.d.).), Schwefel f_7 (Whitley, Mathias, Rana, Dzubera,1996), Baumes f_a, and Baumes f_g, see Eq3) have been selected in order to test the algorithm. Among them, some new ones (Baumes f_a and Baumes f_g) have been specially designed in order to trap the method.

$$f_a(x_i) = \left| \tan \left\{ \sum_{i=1}^{n} \left(\sin^2 \left(\left(x_i^2 - 1/2 \right) \middle/ \left(1 + \frac{x_i}{1000} \right)^2 \right) \right) \right\} \right| \qquad 0 \le x_i \le 2$$

$$f_g(x_i) = \sum_{i=1}^{n} \left((n-i+1) \times x_i^2 \right) \qquad -1 \le x_i \le 1$$

$$f_1(x_i) = \sum_{i=1}^{n} x_i^2 \qquad 0 \le x_i \le 6$$

$$f_3(x_i) = A + \sum_{i=1}^{n} \text{int}(x_i) \qquad A = 25 \text{ (option)} \qquad 0 \le x_i \le 3$$

$$f_7(x_i) = nV + \sum_{i=1}^{n} -x_i \times \sin\left(\sqrt{|x_i|}\right) \qquad -500 \le x_i \le 500$$

(3)

Figure 3. Series plot Baumes f_g. The number of variables noted n = 6, and the number of points represented for each feature is 9.

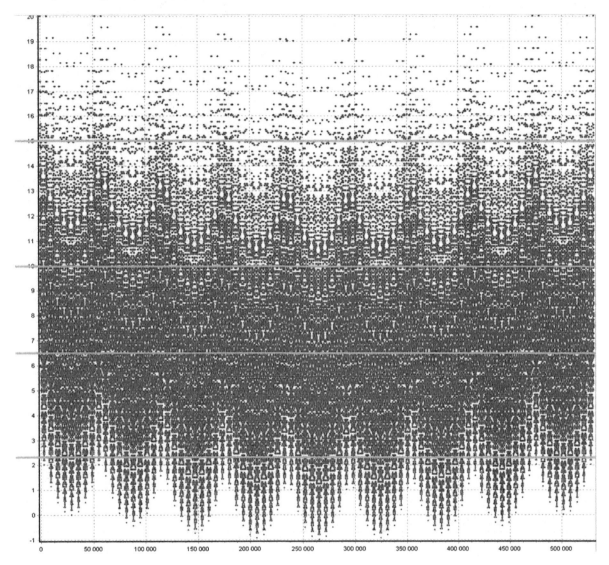

5. RESULTS

5.1. Evaluation Mode 1

Samples and corresponding effects on NN learning are noted for both the proposed methodology and SRS. Dataset are separated into training test and selection test. The use of analytical benchmarks permits the utilization of test sets with an arbitrary amount of cases. In our experiments, small classes are always considered of great interest. For each sample *10000* individuals are randomly chosen as test set. As example, *1500* points have been sampled on De Jong f_1 search space ($9_{var.}/4_{mod.}$), see Table 1. When using our methodology, the number of good individuals (Class A, the smallest) is increased from 4 with SRS (Training + selection A) to 27. Such distribution permits both to increase the overall rate of recognition and the recognition of small classes. For the other bench-

Figure 4. 2D graph for function Baumes f_g (n = 6, 9^{pts}/var)

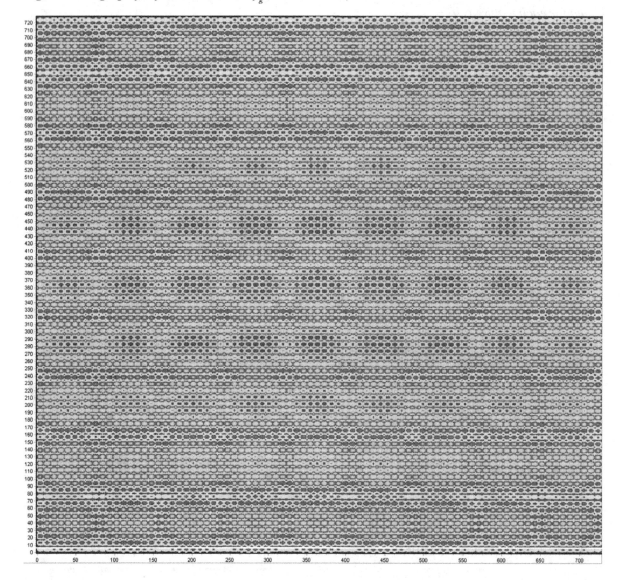

marks, the distributions in the merged training and selection sets are given in Table 2, whereas the distribution in the test sets are shown in Table 3. It can be seen in the respective distributions of every tested benchmarks that small classes received more experiments (the smallest class is greyed), and less experiments belong to the larger one (the largest is in black) as it was expected. Results show clearly that MAP permits a better characterization of small zones than SRS while exploration of the search space is maintained. The

gain of recognition by NN on both the smallest and the largest classes for each benchmark using such active sampling instead of SRS is given in Figure 10. It can be seen that the gains on smallest classes are tremendously increased varying from 18% to an infinite gain (for *Schwefel f_7*, 600 is substituted to the infinite value since assigned to SRS *1* experiment into the smallest zone in order not to obtain a zero division). The loss of recognition rate for the largest classes (if there is) is very low compared to the relatively high gain on small

Figure 5. How multi-dimensional function are represented onto 2D space

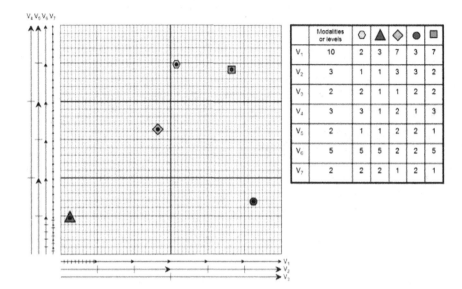

ones. The overall recognition rate being deeply influenced by the relative size of classes does not represent an adequate criterion, however the proposed methodology wins in most of the cases.

5.2. Evaluation Mode 2

As our methodology is not influenced by the choice of the ML applied on selected points, another way to size its influence is to analyze the distribution of points. Therefore if the overall distribution of classes on the whole search space is statistically similar to an SRS, the proposed method does <u>not</u> transfer point from zones to zones. The Chi-square test (Snedecor &Cochran, 1989) is used to test if a sample of data comes from a population with a specific distribution. The Chi-square GoF test is applied to binned data (*i.e.*, data put into classes) and is an alternative to the Anderson-Darling(Stephens,1974) and Kolmogorov-Smirnov(Chakravarti & Roy,1967)GoF tests which are restricted to continuous distributions. We state as a "statistical null hypothesis" noted H_0 something that is the logical opposite of what we believe. Then, using statistical theory, it is expected from the data that H_0 is shown to be

false, and should be rejected. This is called "Reject-Support testing" (RS testing) because rejecting the null hypothesis supports the experimenter's theory. Consequently, before undertaking the experiment, one can be certain that only the *4* possible states summarized in the Table 4 can happen. The Chi-square test statistic follows, approximately, a Chi-square distribution with a degree of freedom (*df*) noted $v=(l-1)(c-1)$ where c is the number of columns and l is the number of rows in the Chi-square table. Therefore, the hypothesis that the data are from a population with the specified distribution is rejected if $\chi^2 > \chi^2_{(\alpha,v)}$ where $\chi^2_{(\alpha,v)}$ is the chi-square percent point function with v *df* and a significance level of α. χ^2_α is the upper critical value from the Chi-square distribution and $\chi^2_{(1-\alpha)}$ is the lower critical value.

Table 5 contains the critical values of the chi-square distribution for the upper tail of the distribution. Therefore statistic tests with v *df* ($v=(l-1)(c-1)=4$) are computed from the data (Table 4). H_0: The_proposed_methdology = SRS, H_1: The_proposed_methdology ≠ SRS is tested. For such an upper one-sided test, one finds the column

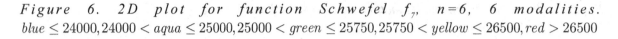

Figure 6. 2D plot for function Schwefel f_7, *n=6, 6 modalities.*
$blue \leq 24000, 24000 < aqua \leq 25000, 25000 < green \leq 25750, 25750 < yellow \leq 26500, red > 26500$

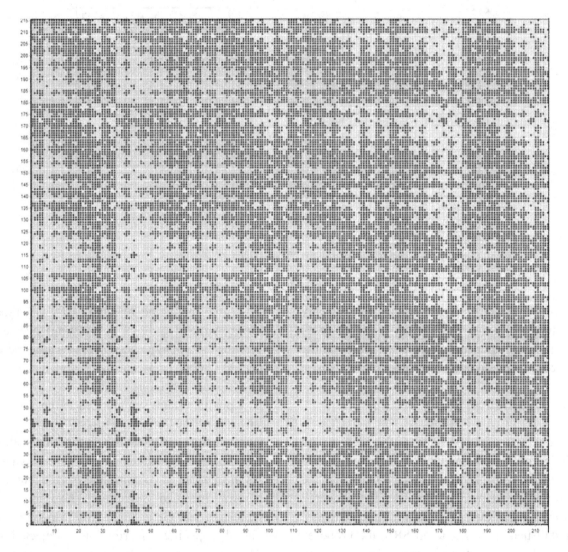

corresponding to α in the upper critical values table and rejects H_0 if the statistic is greater than the tabulated value. The estimation and testing results from contingency tables hold regardless of whether the distribution sample model. Top values in Table 4 are frequencies calculated from Table 1. The Chi-square

$$\chi_v^2 = \sum \left(f_{observed} - f_{theoritical} \right)^2 \times f_{theoritical}^{-1}$$

is noted in red and the critical values at different level are in blue. Yes (Y) or No (N) correspond to answers to the question "is H0 rejected?". Table 5 shows that distributions differ on some cases only. One can note that negative answers are observed on two benchmarks called *Baumes* f_a and *Baumes* f_g (the black cell is discussed later). These benchmarks have been created in order to check the efficiency on extremely difficult problems. However, the analysis of the results in previous section clearly shows that MAP modifies the dis-

Figure 7. 2D plot for function De Jong f_3, n=6, 6 modalities.
$blue \leq 26.5, 26.5 < aqua \leq 27.5, 27.5 < green \leq 28.5, 28.5 < yellow \leq 29.5, red > 29.5$

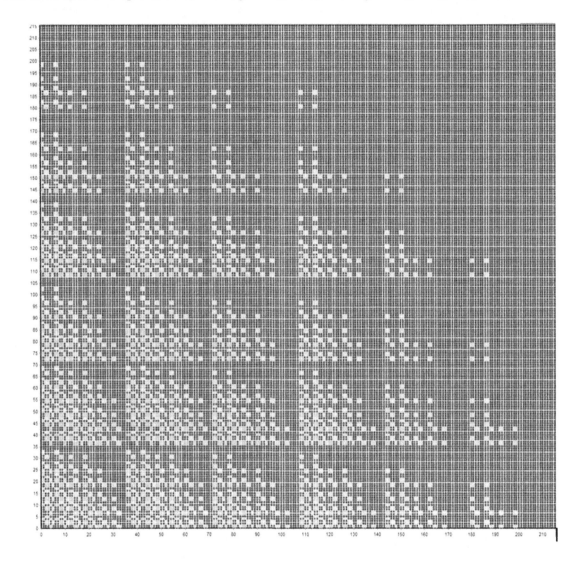

tributions and thus implies improvement of search space characterization through ML. Therefore, we think that the sample size is not large enough in order to discriminate both approaches.

DISCUSSION

It has to be underlined that during all the experiments the root distribution has been calculated after the initialisation. However, the user could *i)*

intentionally not respect the real distribution in order to give weights on selected classes, or *ii)* re-evaluate the root distribution (Eq. 4) using the following notation. The search space partitioned into m_i cells considering only one variable v_i (*i.e.* $Card(M_i) = m_i$), N_i^a represents the total amount of point in the m_i^a cell. "a" is analogous to a strata.

$$\mathcal{M}_i = \left\{m_i^a, m_i^b, \cdots, m_i^{m_i}\right\} \Rightarrow \left|\mathcal{M}_i\right| = m_i, \quad \text{and}$$
$$\forall j, m_i^a \in \omega_j, \left|\Omega\right|/\left|\mathcal{M}_i\right| = N_i^a \Rightarrow \forall a, N_i^a = N_i.$$

The weight of each strata is

Figure 8. 2D plot for function Baumes f_a, *n=9, 4 modalities.* $blue \leq 1, 1 < aqua \leq 2, 2 < green \leq 5, 5 < yellow \leq 15, red > 15$

$\forall a, w_i^a = N_i^a / |\Omega| = 1/|\mathcal{M}_i| = w_i \cdot p_A, p_B, ..., p_K$ are the total proportion of class A (respectively B, ..., K) in the entire population and $p_A^{m_i^a}$ is the proportion of individuals belonging to class A in a. $n^{m_i^a}$ corresponds to the amount of the sampling that possesses m_i^a. $f_i^a = n_i^a / N_i^a$ is the proportion of the sampling for m_i^a and $n_A^{m_i^a}$ corresponds to the amount of sampled individuals in m_i^a that belongs to class A.

$$\tilde{p}_A = \sum_{j=1}^{j=\mathcal{M}_i} w_i^j p_A^{m_i^j} = \sum_{j=1}^{j=\mathcal{M}_i} w_i p_A^{m_i^j} = \frac{\sum_{j=1}^{j=\mathcal{M}_i} p_A^{m_i^j}}{m_i}$$

(4)

Altering the distribution of points in the search space as detected by the evaluation mode 2 is a fact but transferring individuals from stable zones to puzzling ones is different. Therefore new tests have been performed. The overall distribution is split considering a set of modalities or a given

Figure 9. 2D plot for function De Jong f_1, n=9, 4 modalities. blue $\leq$ 30, 30 < aqua $\leq$ 60, 60 < green $\leq$ 90, 90 < yellow $\leq$ 120, red > 120

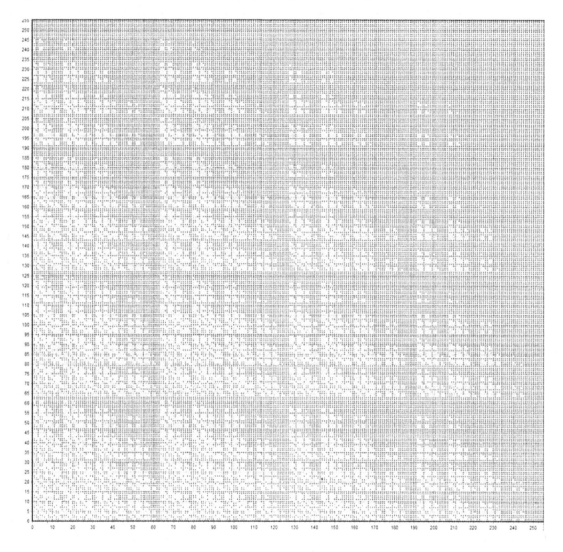

number of variables and a new chi-square GoF is evaluated (Eq5).

$$m_1 \quad n_1^A\left(\bar{E}\left(n_1^A\right)\right) \quad n_1^B\left(\bar{E}\left(n_1^B\right)\right) \quad \cdots \quad \cdots \quad n_1^E\left(\bar{E}\left(n_1^E\right)\right)$$
$$\vdots \qquad \vdots \qquad\qquad \vdots \qquad\qquad\qquad \vdots \qquad \Rightarrow \chi^2 = \sum_{j=1}^{j=i}\sum_{h=A}^{h=E}\frac{\left[n_j^h - \bar{E}\left(n_j^h\right)\right]^2}{\bar{E}\left(n_j^h\right)}$$
$$m_i \quad n_i^A\left(\bar{E}\left(n_i^A\right)\right) \quad n_i^B\left(\bar{E}\left(n_i^B\right)\right) \quad \cdots \quad \cdots \quad n_i^E\left(\bar{E}\left(n_i^E\right)\right)$$

$$(5)$$

If $i=3$ then $v=6$ and the critical value is $\chi^2_{0.5(6)} = 12.5916$. H_0 is accepted when no difference on zones size is observed for the considered variables on a given benchmark and also that H_0 is rejected when a clear difference appears. Tables from these tests are not presented. With "easy" benchmarks, it appears clearly that our methodology acts as it is expected. However, for one case H_0 is accepted, and thus the power of test is quickly discussed. The power testing procedure is set up to give H_0 "the benefit of a doubt" that is, to accept H_0 unless there is strong evidence to support the alternative. Statistical power $(1-\beta)$

Table 1. Training, selection and test sets of De jong f_1 from SRS (upper array) and the new methodology (lower array)

SRS

		Training					Selection					Test			
		A	B	C	D	E	A	B	C	D	E	A	B	C	D	E
A	1	0	0	0	0	1	0	0	0	0	9	4	0	0	0
B	0	47	0	0	0	2	30	10	0	0	51	476	175	0	0
C	0	0	102	0	0	0	8	94	6	0	0	62	1139	111	0
D	0	0	0	231	0	0	0	0	181	12	0	0	143	2509	164
E	0	0	0	0	392	0	0	0	14	361	0	0	0	186	4971

New one

		Training					Selection					Test			
		A	B	C	D	E	A	B	C	D	E	A	B	C	D	E
A	13	0	0	0	0	11	0	0	0	0	20	12	0	0	0
B	0	110	1	0	0	4	75	14	0	0	40	486	93	0	0
C	0	0	178	0	0	0	7	148	11	0	0	44	1242	113	0
D	0	0	0	208	0	0	0	14	206	3	0	0	122	2592	93
E	0	0	0	0	263	0	0	0	3	231	0	0	0	101	5042

should be at least 0.80 to detect a reasonable departure from H_0. The conventions are, of course, much more rigid with respect to α than with respect to β. Factors influencing power in a statistical test include *i*) What kind of statistical test is being performed. Some statistical tests are inherently more powerful than others. *ii*) Sample size. In general, the larger the sample size the larger the power. To ensure a statistical test will have adequate power, one usually must perform special analyses *prior* to running the experiment, to calculate how large the sample size (noted *n*) is required. One could plot power against sample size, under the assumption that the real distribution is known exactly. The user might start with a graph that covers a very wide range of sample sizes, to get a general idea of how the statistical test behaves. The minimum required sample size that permits to start discriminating (significantly with a fixed error rate α) our methodology from SRS is dependent on the search space landscape. Simulations will be investigating in future works. It has to be noted that 1500 points have been selected for each benchmark. However, the search spaces are extremely broad and thus such a

Table 2. Merged training and selection sets after sampling from the proposed appraoch and SRS considering all others benchmarks. In each case 5 classes are present (A to E).

	De Jong F3		Baumes Fa		Baumes Fg		Schwefel F7	
	SRS	New	SRS	New	SRS	New	SRS	New
A	15	58	772	737	58	111	5	25
B	31	123	300	308	397	448	80	180
C	85	196	273	284	592	452	200	320
D	139	213	85	82	402	386	412	402
E	1230	910	70	89	51	103	803	573

Table 3. Distribution of classification by Neural Network in Test depending on the sample (SRS or MAP) for all benchmarks

			De Jong F1					De Jong F3					Baumes Fa					Baumes Fg					Schwefel F7				
			A	B	C	D	E	A	B	C	D	E	A	B	C	D	E	A	B	C	D	E	A	B	C	D	E
Predicted	SRS	A	9	4	0	0	0	32	31	0	0	0	3471	917	642	188	201	248	109	0	0	0	52	36	0	0	0
		B	51	476	175	0	0	73	217	30	0	0	695	469	456	174	125	97	2360	231	0	0	50	3212	223	0	0
		C	0	62	1139	111	0	0	7	517	0	0	756	433	517	130	137	0	362	3488	243	0	0	279	5072	160	0
		D	0	0	143	2509	164	0	0	0	880	4	166	177	157	74	53	0	0	231	2225	103	0	0	155	741	9
		E	0	0	0	186	4971	0	0	0	5	8204	20	11	17	8	6	0	0	0	85	218	0	0	0	11	0
	MAP	A	20	12	0	0	0	105	0	6	0	0	2611	976	862	300	265	275	84	0	0	0	67	45	0	0	0
		B	40	486	93	0	0	0	255	0	0	0	1107	466	377	113	98	70	2481	181	0	0	35	3141	373	0	0
		C	0	44	1242	113	0	0	0	541	0	0	835	351	345	85	98	0	266	3526	175	0	0	341	4800	108	0
		D	0	0	122	2592	93	0	0	0	885	0	290	121	100	51	24	0	0	243	2273	63	0	0	275	789	5
		E	0	0	0	101	5042	0	0	0	0	8208	265	93	105	25	37	0	0	0	105	258	0	0	2	15	4

sample size represents only a very little percentage of the entire research space.

CONCLUSION

This paper develops a targeted sampling mechanism based on a novel, flexible, quantitative analysis of classes' distribution into sub-regions of research spaces. There are several motivations for wanting to alter the selection of samples. In a general sense, we want a learning system to acquire knowledge. In particular, we want the learned knowledge to be as useful as possible, while retaining high performance. If the space of configurations is very large with much irregularity, then it is difficult to adequately sample enough of the space. Adaptive sampling such as our methodology tries to include the most productive samples. Such adaptive sampling allows selecting a criterion over which the samples are chosen. The learned knowledge about the structure is used for biasing the sampling. The results reveal that the proposed sampling strategy makes more judicious use of data points by selecting locations that clarify structural characterization of little represented classes, rather than choosing points that merely improve quality of the global recognition rate. The proposed methodology has been thoroughly presented and tested. As such, this methodology was developed to propose formulations that are relevant to be tested at the very first stage of a HT program when numerous but inherent constraints are taken into account for the discovery of new performing catalysts. Such a methodology is flexible enough to be applied on a broad variety of domains. The main advantages are the following. The number of false negative is highly decreased while the number of true positive is tremendously increased. The approach is totally independent from the classifier and creates more balanced learning sets, permitting both to prevent from over-learning, and to gain higher recognition rates. All previous experiments can

Figure 10. Percentage recognition gain for both the smallest and largest class considering every benchmark when using MAP methodology instead of SRS

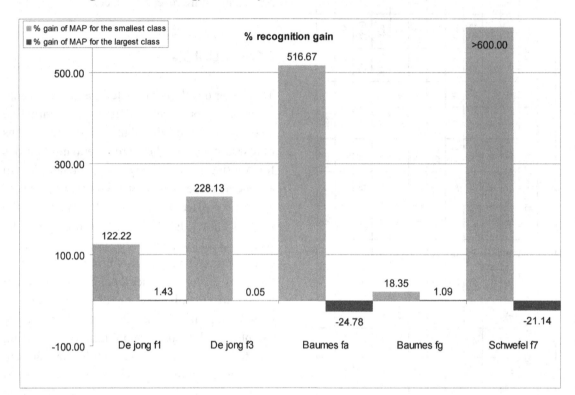

Table 4. Chi-square GOF test

		Baumes fg		De jong f3		De jong f1		Baumes fa		Schwefel f7	
		SRS	MAP	SRS	MAP	SRS	MAP	SRS	MAP	SRS	MAP
		3.86666667	7.4	1	3.86666667	0.53333333	1.86666667	51.4666667	49.1333333	0.33333333	1.66666667
		26.4666667	29.8666667	2.06666667	8.2	5.33333333	12.8	20	20.5333333	5.33333333	12
		39.4666667	30.1333333	5.66666667	13.0666667	14.5333333	23.6666667	18.2	18.9333333	13.3333333	21.3333333
		26.8	25.7333333	9.26666667	14.2	28.3333333	28.5333333	5.66666667	5.46666667	27.4666667	26.8
		3.4	6.86666667	82	60.6666667	51.2666667	33.1333333	4.66666667	5.93333333	53.5333333	38.2
Alpha	Critical value	6.75937209		20.11939707		18.75811101		0.430795216		13.94169525	
0.1	7.779	N		Y		Y		N		Y	
0.5	9.488	N		Y		Y		N		Y	
0.25	11.143	N		Y		Y		N		Y	
0.01	13.277	N		Y		Y		N		Y	
0.001	18.467	N		Y		Y		N		N	

be integrated giving more strength to the method and any type of feature is taken into account. The method is tuneable through the modification of the root distribution.

ACKNOWLEDGMENT

EU Commission FP6 (TOPCOMBI Project) is gratefully acknowledged. We also thank Santiago Jimenez and Diego Bermudez for their collaboration on the hIT$_e$Q platform which integrates all programming codes of the presented methodology.

Table 5. Critical values of the chi-square distribution for the upper tail of the distribution

v	Probability of exceeding the critical value				
	0.10	0.05	0.025	0.01	0.001
1	2.706	3.841	5.024	6.635	10.828
2	4.605	5.991	7.378	9.210	13.816
3	6.251	7.815	9.348	11.345	16.266
4	**7.779**	**9.488**	**11.143**	**13.277**	**18.467**
5	9.236	11.070	12.833	15.086	20.515
6	10.645	12.592	14.449	16.812	22.458
7	12.017	14.067	16.013	18.475	24.322
8	13.362	15.507	17.535	20.090	26.125
9	14.684	16.919	19.023	21.666	27.877
10	15.987	18.307	20.483	23.209	29.588
11	17.275	19.675	21.920	24.725	31.264
12	18.549	21.026	23.337	26.217	32.910
13	19.812	22.362	24.736	27.688	34.528
14	21.064	23.685	26.119	29.141	36.123
15	22.307	24.996	27.488	30.578	37.697
16	23.542	26.296	28.845	32.000	39.252
17	24.769	27.587	30.191	33.409	40.790
18	25.989	28.869	31.526	34.805	42.312
19	27.204	30.144	32.852	36.191	43.820
20	28.412	31.410	34.170	37.566	45.315
21	29.615	32.671	35.479	38.932	46.797
22	30.813	33.924	36.781	40.289	48.268
23	32.007	35.172	38.076	41.638	49.728
24	33.196	36.415	39.364	42.980	51.179
25	34.382	37.652	40.646	44.314	52.620
26	35.563	38.885	41.923	45.642	54.052
27	36.741	40.113	43.195	46.963	55.476
28	37.916	41.337	44.461	48.278	56.892
29	39.087	42.557	45.722	49.588	58.301
30	40.256	43.773	46.979	50.892	59.703
31	41.422	44.985	48.232	52.191	61.098
32	42.585	46.194	49.480	53.486	62.487
33	43.745	47.400	50.725	54.776	63.870
34	44.903	48.602	51.966	56.061	65.247
35	46.059	49.802	53.203	57.342	66.619
36	47.212	50.998	54.437	58.619	67.985
37	48.363	52.192	55.668	59.893	69.347
38	49.513	53.384	56.896	61.162	70.703
39	50.660	54.572	58.120	62.428	72.055
40	51.805	55.758	59.342	63.691	73.402

REFERENCES

Akporiaye, D. E., Dahl, I. M., Karlsson, A., & Wendelbo, R. (1998)... *Angewandte Chemie International Edition, 37*(5), 609–611. doi:10.1002/(SICI)1521-3773(19980316)37:5<609::AID-ANIE609>3.0.CO;2-X

Bailey-Kellogg, N. Ramakrishnan.(2003). *Proc. 17ᵗʰ Int. Workshop on Qualitative Reasoning*, pp. 23-30.\Baumes, L. A. (2006)...*Journal of Combinatorial Chemistry, 8*(3), 304–314. doi:10.1021/cc050130+

Baumes, L. A., Blansché, A., Serna, P., Tchougang, A., Lachiche, N., P. Collet & A. Corma (2009). *Materials and Manufacturing Processes, 24* (3), 282 – 292.

Baumes, L. A., & Collet, P. (2009). [New York: Elsevier.]. *Computational Materials Science, 45*(1), 27–40. doi:10.1016/j.commatsci.2008.03.051

Baumes, L.A., Farruseng, D., Ausfelder, F. (2009). *Catalysis Today*. Special Issue "EuroCombiCat 2009" conference.

Baumes, L. A., Farruseng, D., Lengliz, M., & Mirodatos, C. (2004)... *QSAR & Combinatorial Science, 29*(9), 767–778. doi:10.1002/qsar.200430900

Baumes, L. A., Gaudin, R., Serna, P., Nicoloyannis, N., & Corma, A. (2008)... *Combinatorial Chemistry & High Throughput Screening, 11*(4), 266–282. doi:10.2174/138620708784246068

Baumes, L.A., Jimenez, S., & Corma, A. (in press). *hITeQ: A new workflow-based computing environment for streamlining discovery.* In L.A. Baumes, D. Farruseng, F. Ausfelder (eds). *Application in materials science.* Catalysis Today, Special Issue "EuroCombiCat 2009" Conf.

Baumes, L. A., Jimenez, S., Kruger, F., Maitre, O., Collet, P., & Corma, A. (n.d.). How gaming industry fosters crystal structure prediction? [PCCP]. *Physical Chemistry Chemical Physics.*

Baumes, L. A., Jouve, P., Farrusseng, D., Lengliz, M., Nicoloyannis, N., & Mirodatos, C. (2003). *7ᵗʰ Int. Conf. on Knowledge-Based Intelligent Information & Engineering Systems (KES'2003).* Lecture Notes in AI (LNCS/LNAI series). Sept. 3-5. Univ. of Oxford, UK: Springer-Verlag

Baumes, L.A., Moliner, M., & Corma, A. (2006)... *QSAR & Combinatorial Science, 26*(2), 255–272. doi:10.1002/qsar.200620064

Baumes, L.A., Moliner, M., & Corma, A. (2008)... *CrystEngComm, 10*, 1321–1324. doi:10.1039/b812395k

Baumes, L. A., Moliner, M., & Corma, A. (2009)... *Chemistry (Weinheim an der Bergstrasse, Germany), 15*, 4258–4269. doi:10.1002/chem.200802683

Baumes, L. A., Serna, P., & Corma, A. (in press). Merging traditional and high throughput approaches results in efficient design, synthesis and screening of catalysts for an industrial process. *Applied Catalysis A.*

Baumes, L. A., Serra, J. M., Serna, P., & Corma, A. (2006)...*Journal of Combinatorial Chemistry, 8*(4), 583–596. doi:10.1021/cc050093m

Bem, D. S., Erlandson, E. J., Gillespie, R. D., Harmon, L. A., Schlosser, S. G., & Vayda, A. J. (2003). *Experimental design for combinatorial and high throughput materials development*, 89-107. Hoboken, NJ: Wiley and sons.

Blickle, T., & Thiele, L. (1995). *6ᵗʰ Int. Conf. on Genetic Algorithms.* San Mateo, CA: Morgan Kaufmann.

Boussie, T. R. (2003)... *Journal of the American Chemical Society, 125*, 4306–4317. doi:10.1021/ja020868k

Box, G., & Draper, N. (1987). *Empirical model-building and response surfaces*. New York: John Wiley and Sons.

Bricker, M. L., Sachtler, J. W. A., Gillespie, R. D., McGoneral, C. P., Vega, H., Bem, D. S., & Holmgren, J. S. (2004)... *Applied Surface Science*, *223*(1-3), 109–117. doi:10.1016/S0169-4332(03)00893-6

Brinker, K. (2003). In Proc. of the 20th Int. Conf. on Machine Learning (ICML'03), pp. 59-66.

Buyevskaya, O. V., Bruckner, A., Kondratenko, E. V., Wolf, D., & Baerns, M. (2001)... *Catalysis Today*, *67*, 369–378. doi:10.1016/S0920-5861(01)00329-7

Caruthers, J. M., Lauterbach, J. A., Thomson, K. T., Venkatasubramanian, V., Snively, C. M., & Bhan, A. (2003)... *Journal of Catalysis*, *216*, 98. doi:10.1016/S0021-9517(02)00036-2

Cawse, J. N., Baerns, M., & Holena, M. (2004)... *Journal of Chemical Information and Computer Sciences*, *44*(1), 143–146. doi:10.1021/ci034171+

Cawse, J. N., & Wroczynski, R. (2003). Experimental design for combinatorial and high throughput materials development, 109-127. Hoboken, NJ: Wiley and sons.

Chakravarti, L., & Roy, H. L. (1967). John Wiley and Sons. pp. 392-394.

Chaloner, K., & Verdinelli, I. (1995)... *Statistical Science*, *10*(3), 273–304. doi:10.1214/ss/1177009939

Cohn, D., Atlas, L., & Ladner, R. (1990). *Advances in Neural Information Processing Systems 2*. San Francisco: Morgan Kaufmann.

Cohn, D. A., Ghahramani, Z., & Jordan, M. I. in G. Tesauro, D. Touretzky, J. Alspector, (1995). *Advances in Neural Information Processing Systems 7*. San Francisco: Morgan Kaufmann.

Corma, A., Moliner, M., Serra, J. M., Serna, P., Díaz-Cabañas, M. J., & Baumes, L. A. (2006)... *Chemistry of Materials*, *18*(14), 3287–3296. doi:10.1021/cm060620k

Corma, A., Serra, J. M., & Chica, A. (2002). *Principles and methods for accelerated catalyst design and testing.*

De Jong, K. A. (n.d.). Doctoral dissertation, univ. of Michigan. *Dissertation Abstract International, 36*(10), 5140(B). Univ. of Michigan Microfilms No. 76-9381

Deming, S. N., & Morgan, S. L. (1993). *Experimental design: A chemometric approach* (2nd ed.). Amsterdam: Elsevier Science Publishers B.V.

Derouane, E., Parmon, V., Lemos, F., & Ribeir, F. (2002). *Book Series: NATO SCIENCE SERIES: II: Mathematics, Physics and Chemistry* (*Vol. 69*, pp. 101–124). Dordrecht, Netherlands: Kluwer Academic Publishers.

Derouane, E. G., Parmon, V., Lemos, F., & Ribeiro, F. R. (Eds.). Kluver Academic Publishers: Dordrecht, The Netherlands, pp 153-172.

Ertl, G., Knözinger, H., & Weitkamp, J. (1997). *Handbook of Heterogeneous Catalysis*. New York: Whiley-VCH. doi:10.1002/9783527619474

Farruseng, D., Baumes, L. A., & Mirodatos, C. (2003). Data Management For Combinatorial Heterogeneous Catalysis: Methodology And Development Of Advanced Tools. In Potyrailo, R. A., & Amis, E. J. (Eds.), *High-Throughput Analysis: A Tool for Combinatorial Materials Science* (pp. 551–579). Boston: Kluwer Academic/Plenum Publishers.

Farrusseng, D., Baumes, L. A., Hayaud, C., Vauthey, I., Denton, P., & Mirodatos, C. (2001). Nato series. In E. Derouane (ed). Proc. NATO Advanced Study Institute on Principles and Methods for Accelerated Catalyst Design, Preparation, Testing and Development. Vilamoura, Portugal, 15-28 July 2001. Boston: Kluwer Academic Publisher.

Farrusseng, D., Klanner, C., Baumes, L. A., Lengliz, M., Mirodatos, C., & Schüth, F. (2005)... *QSAR & Combinatorial Science, 24,* 78–93. doi:10.1002/qsar.200420066

Fayyad, U., Piatetsky-Shapiro, G., & Smyth, P. (1996). *From Data Mining to Knowledge Discovery in Databases.*

Fedorov, V. V. (1972). *Theory of optimal experiments.* New York: Acad. Press.

Gorer, A. (2004). U.S. Patent 6.723.678, to Symyx Technologies Inc.

Grubert, G., Kondratenko, E. V., Kolf, S., Baerns, M., van Geem, P., & Parton, R. (2003)... *Catalysis Today, 81,* 337–345. doi:10.1016/S0920-5861(03)00132-9

Hanak, J. J. (2004)... *Applied Surface Science, 223,* 1–8. doi:10.1016/S0169-4332(03)00902-4

Harmon, L. A. (2003)... *Journal of Materials Science, 38,* 4479–4485. doi:10.1023/A:1027325400459

Hoffmann, C., & Wolf, A. & F. SchMth. (1999). *Angew. Chem.* 111, 2971. *Angewandte Chemie International Edition, 38,* 2800. doi:10.1002/(SICI)1521-3773(19990917)38:18<2800::AID-ANIE2800>3.3.CO;2-0

Holena, M., & Baerns, M. (2003)... *Catalysis Today, 81,* 485–494. doi:10.1016/S0920-5861(03)00147-0

Holmgren, J., Bem, D., Bricker, M., Gillespie, R., Lewis, G., & Akporiaye, D. (2001)... *Studies in Surface Science and Catalysis, 135,* 461–470.

Jandeleit, B., Schaefer, D. J., Powers, T. S., Turner, H. W., & Weinberg, W. H. (1999)... *Angewandte Chemie International Edition, 38,* 2494–2532. doi:10.1002/(SICI)1521-3773(19990903)38:17<2494::AID-ANIE2494>3.0.CO;2-#

Juszczak, P., & Duin, R. P. W. (2004). *Proc. 17th Int. Conf. on Pattern Recognition.* IEEE Comp. Soc., Los Alamitos, CA.

Klanner, C., Farrusseng, D., Baumes, L. A., Lengliz, M., Mirodatos, C., & Schüth, F. (2004)... *Angewandte Chemie International Edition, 43*(40), 5347–5349. doi:10.1002/anie.200460731

Klanner, C., Farrusseng, D., Baumes, L. A., Mirodatos, C., & Schüth, F. (2003)... *QSAR & Combinatorial Science, 22,* 729–736. doi:10.1002/qsar.200320003

Klein, J., Lehmann, C. W., Schmidt, H. W., & Maier, W. F. (1999)... *Angewandte Chemie International Edition, 38,* 3369. doi:10.1002/(SICI)1521-3773(19990712)38:13/14<2057::AID-ANIE2057>3.0.CO;2-G

Koinuma, H., & Takeuchi, I. (2004)... *Nature Materials, 3,* 429–438. doi:10.1038/nmat1157

Kruger, F., Baumes, L. A., Lachiche, N., & Collet, P. (2010). In *Lecture Notes in Computer Science,* Publisher Springer Berlin / Heidelberg. Proc. Int. Conf. EvoStar 2010, 7th - 9th April 2010, Istanbul Technical University, Istanbul, Turkey.

Linden, F. Weber.(1993). Proc. 2d Int. Conf. on Simulation of Adaptive Behavior. Cambridge, MA: MIT Press.

Maier, W. F. (2004)... *Polymeric Materials Science and Engineering, 90,* 652–653.

Maitre, O., Baumes, L. A., Lachiche, N., & Collet, P. Corma, A. (2009). *Proc. of the 11th Annual conf. on Genetic and evolutionary computation.* Montreal, Québec, Canada, Session: Track 12: parallel evolutionary systems, 1403-1410. New York: Association for Computing Machinery.

Maitre, O., & Lachiche, N. P., Baumes, L. A., Corma, A. & P. Collet.(2009). In *Lecture Notes in Computer Science,* Publisher Springer Berlin / Heidelberg Vol. 5704/2009 Euro-Par **2009** Parallel Processing, 974-985.

Montgomery, D. C. (1991). *Design and analysis of experiments* (3rd ed.). New York: Wiley.

Montgomery, D. C. (1997). *Design and Analysis of Experiments* (4th ed.). New York: John Wiley & Sons Inc.

Nicolaides, D. (2005)... *QSAR & Combinatorial Science*, 24.

Omata, K., Umegaki, T., Watanabe, Y., & Yamada, M. (2003). [New York: Elsevier Sci. B.V.]. *Studies in Surface Science and Catalysis*, 291–294. doi:10.1016/S0167-2991(03)80217-3

Paul, J. S., Janssens, R., Joeri, J. F. M., Baron, G. V., & Jacobs, P. A. (2005). [ACS.]. *Journal of Combinatorial Chemistry*, 7(3), 407–413. doi:10.1021/cc0500046

Pescarmona, P. P., Rops, J. J. T., van der Waal, J. C., Jansen, J. C., & Maschmeyer, T. (2002)... *J. Mol. Chem. A*, *182-183*, 319–325. doi:10.1016/S1381-1169(01)00494-0

Piatetsky-Shapiro, G., & Frawley, W. (1991). *Knowledge discovery in databases.* Menlo Park, CA: AAAI/MIT Press.

Ramakrishnany, N., Bailey-Kellogg, C., Tadepalliy, S., & Pandeyy, V. N. (2005). *SIAM Int. Conf. on Data Mining, SDM 2005.* Newport Beach, CA, USA.

Rodemerck, U., Baerns, M., Holena, M., & Wolf, D. (2004)... *Applied Surface Science*, *223*, 168. doi:10.1016/S0169-4332(03)00919-X

Sammut, C., & Cribb, J. (1990). *7th Int. Machine Learning Conf.* Austin, TX: Morgan Kaufmann.

Schein, A. I., Sandler, S. T., & Ungar, L. H. (2004). *Univ. of Pennsylvania, Dpt. of Comp. & Information Sci. Tech.* Report No. MS-CIS-04-08.

Schein, A. I., Sandler, S. T., & Ungar, L. H. (2004). *Univ. of Pennsylvania, Dpt. of Comp. & Information Sci. Tech.* Report No. MS-CIS-04-08.

Schmidhuber, J., & Storck, J. (1993). *Tech.* Report, Fakultat fur Informatik. Technische Universitat Munchen.

Senkan, S. (2001)... *Angewandte Chemie International Edition*, *40*(2), 312–329. doi:10.1002/1521-3773(20010119)40:2<312::AID-ANIE312>3.0.CO;2-I

Serna, P., Baumes, L. A., Moliner, M., & Corma, A. (2008)... *Journal of Catalysis*, *1*(258), 25–34. doi:10.1016/j.jcat.2008.05.033

Serra, J. M. (2003)... *Catalysis Today*, *81*(3), 425–436. doi:10.1016/S0920-5861(03)00142-1

Serra, J. M., Baumes, L. A., Moliner, M., Serna, P., & Corma, A. (2007)... *Combinatorial Chemistry & High Throughput Screening*, *10*, 13–24. doi:10.2174/138620707779802779

Serra, J. M., Chica, A. & Corma, A. (2003). *Appl. Catal., A.* 239, 35-42.

Seung, H. S., Opper, M., & Sompolinsky, H. (1992). Proc. of the 5th Annual Workshop on Computational Learning Theory, pp. 287-294.

Sjöblom, J., Creaser, D., & Papadakis, K. (2004). *Proc. 11th Nordic Symposium on Catalysis.* Oulu, Finland

Snedecor, G. W., & Cochran, W. G. (1989). *Iowa State Univ* (8th ed.). Press.

Sohn, K. S., Seo, S. Y., & Park, H. D. (2001)... *Electrochemical and Solid-State Letters*, *4*, H26–H29. doi:10.1149/1.1398560

Souvannavong, F., Mérialdo, B., & Huet, B. (2004). *WIAMIS'04, 5th Int. Workshop on Image Analysis for Multimedia Interactive Services.* Inst. Sup. Técnico, Lisboa, Portugal. Apr. 21-23.

Stephens, M. A. (1974)... *Journal of the American Statistical Association*, *69*, 730–737. doi:10.2307/2286009

Tchougang, A., Blansché, A., Baumes, L. A., Lachiche, N., & Collet, P. (2008). *Lecture Notes in Computer Science 599-609, Volume 5199*. In Rudolph, G., Jansen, T., Lucas, S. M., Poloni, C. & Beume, N. (eds). *Parallel Problem Solving from Nature – PPSN X*. Berlin: Springer.

Thrun, S., & Moller, K. (1992). *Advances in Neural Information Processing Systems 4*. San Francisco: Morgan Kaufmann.

Todeschini, R., & Consonni, V. (2000). *Handbook of Molecular Descriptors*. Weinheim, Germany: Wiley-VCH.

Tong, S., & Koller, D. (2001)... *Journal of Machine Learning Research, 2*, 45–66. doi:10.1162/153244302760185243

Tribus, M., & Sconyi, G. (1989). An alternative view of the Taguchi approach. *Quality Progress, 22*, 46–48.

Watanabe, Y., Umegaki, T., Hashimoto, M., Omata, K., & Yamada, M. (2004). [New York: Elsevier Sci. B.V.]. *Catalysis Today, 89*(4), 455–464. doi:10.1016/j.cattod.2004.02.001

Whitehead, S. (1991). *A study of cooperative mechanisms for reinforcement learning. TR-365, Dpt. of comp. sci.* Rochester, NY: Rochester Univ.

Whitley, D., Mathias, K., Rana, S., & Dzubera, J. (1996)... *Artificial Intelligence, 85*(1-2), 245–276. doi:10.1016/0004-3702(95)00124-7

Wolf, D.; Buyevskaya, O. V.; Baerns, M. (2000). *Appl. Catal. A*, 63-77.

Xiang, X. D., & Takeuchi, I. (2003). *Combinatorial Materials Science*. New York: Dekker. doi:10.1201/9780203912737

Chapter 5
Molecular Similarity:
Combining Neural Networks and Knn Methods

Abdelmalek Amine
Tahar Moulay University & Djillali Liabes University, Algeria

Zakaria Elberrichi
Djillali Liabes University, Algeria

Michel Simonet
Joseph Fourier University, France

Ali Rahmouni
Tahar Moulay University, Algeria

ABSTRACT

In order to identify new molecules susceptible to become medicines, the pharmaceutical research has more and more resort to new technologies to synthesize big number of molecules simultaneously and to test their actions on given therapeutic target. This data can be exploited to construct the models permitting to predict the properties of molecules not yet tested, even not yet synthesized. Such predictive models are very important because they make it possible to suggest the synthesis of new molecules, and to eliminate very early in the the molecule's search process the molecules whose properties would prevent their use as medicine. The authors call it virtual sifting. It is within this framework that research by similarity is registered. It is a practical approach to identify molecules candidates (to become medicines) from the data bases or the virtual chemical libraries by comparing the compounds two by two. Many statistical models and learning tools have been developed to correlate the molecule's structure with their chemical, physical or biological properties. The large majority of these methods start by transforming each molecule in a vector of great dimension (using molecular descriptors), then use a learning algorithm on these vectorial descriptions. The objective of this chapter is to study molecular similarity using a particular type of neural networks: the Kohonen networks (also called "SOM" Self- Organizing Maps), applying the nearest neighbor algorithm to the projection of the molecules (coordinates) in the constructed MAP.

DOI: 10.4018/978-1-60960-860-6.ch005

INTRODUCTION

Research by molecular similarity is nowadays a very important tool in various process of conception of products having particular properties such as medicines (van de Waterbeemd & Gifford, 2003). This tool is one of the virtual sifting methods that permits to reach the searched molecule in a very short time and to lower the costs of these processes.

The virtual sifting methods developed profit from the availability of both the increasing computer's powerfulness and the sophisticated algorithms.

The method compares some features called descriptors of the molecule studied with those of molecules of one or several data bases (Mozziconacci, 2003; Willett, 1998). This operation permits the elimination of an important number of molecules that doesn't present the sought properties. The experimental tests will only be done on a reduced number of molecules that research by similarity would have given like potential candidates.

Many statistical models and learning tools can correlate the structures of the molecules with their chemical, physical or biological properties (Mahé & Vert, 2007). The vast majority of these methods represents the molecules by vectors of high dimension whose components are the molecular descriptors. They use an algorithm combined to a chosen measure to determine the molecules having descriptors close to those of the studied molecule.

Among these methods we can mention the linear models as the linear regression and the multiple linear regression, and the nonlinear models as the artificial neuron networks, the genetic algorithms and the SVM (support vector machine) (Mahé & Vert, 2007).

In this chapter we use a particular type of neural networks; the Kohonen networks known also SOM (Self Organizing Maps). This type of networks permits to reduce the dimensionality of the molecule's representation and to classify the molecules by groups of similar molecules. The nearest neighbor algorithm is applied then on the bidimensional map generated after the first phase to search for the molecules most similar to a given molecule.

After this introduction, section 2 presents some general notions on the similarity and the molecular similarity in particular. Some methods are described there as well as similarity measures and distance. Section 3 presents the principles of similarity based on descriptors. Section 4 is dedicated to molecular descriptors. Section 5 introduces artificial neuron networks and nearest neighbor methods applied in the used approach. Section 6 presents the tests of the developed application. Some results are presented there. A conclusion will put an end to this chapter.

SIMILARITY

Functions of similarity are used in many fields, in particular in Data Analysis, Form Recognitions, Symbolic Machine Learning, and Cognitive Sciences.

In a general way, a function of similarity is defined in a universe U that can be modelled using a quadruplet: *(Ld, Ls, T, FS)*.

- *Ld* is the language of representation used to describe the data.
- *Ls* is the language of representation of the similarities.
- *T* is a set of knowledge that we possess on the studied universe.
- *FS* is the binary function of similarity, such as: *FS: Ld x Ld → Ls*

When, the function of similarity has for object to quantify the resemblances between the data, the Ls language corresponds to the set of the values in the interval [0...1] or in the R+ set and we will speak then of similarity measurement (Bisson, 2000).

Most works concerning the similarity measures have as base the mathematical concept of distance (the inverse notion of similarity) which was well studied in DA (Mahé & Vert, 2007; Bisson, 2000).

It is defined in the following way: let Ω the set of the individuals of the studied domain a metric D which is a function of $\Omega X \Omega$ in $R+$, $\forall a, b, c \in \Omega$.

1. $D(a, a) = 0$ (property of minimality)
2. $D(a, b) = D(b, a)$ (property of symmetry)

When the function D verifies the properties 1 and 2, it is called index of dissimilarity (or more simply a dissimilarity).

The other properties are also interesting:

3. $D(a, b) = 0 \Rightarrow a = b$ (property of identity)
4. $D(a, c) \leq D(a, b) + D(b, c)$ (triangular inequality)
5. $D(a, c) \leq Max [D(a, b), D(b, c)]$

If the function D verifies the properties 1, 2 and 3 we speak of a distance index. If this index also verifies the property 4 we call it a distance and if it also verifies the property 5 it is called a ultrametric distance. In addition, when the function D verifies properties 1, 2 and 4 we speak of a variation (a gap), and when it verifies properties 1, 2 and 5 we speak of a variation ultrametric. Let us underline finally that the passage from the dissimilarity index D to the dual concept of similarity index of, noted **s** is easy. If we call **Smax** the similarity of an element with itself, it is sufficient to pose: $D(a, b) = |Smax-s(a, b)|$.

Molecular Similarity

The approaches for molecular similarity are based on the principle of the similarity of the properties according to which molecules of close structures possess similar physicochemical and biological properties (Monev, 2004; Johnson & Maggiora, 1990). A research by similarity is carried out by comparing a reference molecule with a molecular dataset. Many methods of similarity were developed, and a large variety of approaches have been experimented. Obviously, it would be impossible to present them all. All these methods deal conceptually with two independent aspects:

*   how to represent the molecules
*   how to calculate the similarity

Similarity Methods Based on Superposition of Graphs

A large class of the superposition methods tries to trace a molecule on others. In 2D representation, it comes down to treat the molecules A and B as graphs and to find the correspondence between the atoms in molecule A and the atoms in the molecule B (Sheridan & Kearsley, 2002). In 3D representation, it comes down to find the best superposition of the molecules as being 3D objects (with or without taking into account flexibility) (Sheridan & Kearsley, 2002). The superposition can be based on the atoms or on the fields (including the form) surrounding these atoms. The similarity would take account of the overlapping between the fields of A and the fields of B.

Similarity Methods Based on Superposition of the Spectra and the Histograms

Another class of methods determines from the structures, one or more spectra or histograms and then compares the overlapping of these spectra or histograms (Sheridan & Kearsley, 2002).

Similarity Methods Based on Descriptors

The third and most famous class of methods represents a molecule like a set of numbers or descriptors, such as a molecule can be considered as a point in a multidimensional space of descriptors (Sheridan & Kearsley, 2002). The disadvantage of these methods compared to the superposition methods, is that the equivalence between the molecule parts is lost, but the advantage is that the calculation is much simpler. A subclass of these methods uses a set of numbers where each number is a property of the molecule (for example the molecular mass, the logP, the index of Kier, the dipole moment, the BCUT parameters,...) (Mozziconacci, 2003 ; Willett, 1998).

The similarity between two molecules is an inverse function of the distance between them in the space of the descriptors. Our approach belongs to this class.

Principle of Similarity Based on Descriptors

A molecule is characterized by structural descriptors. An index of similarity is evaluated between every compound of the base and the molecule of reference. This index is a quantitative measure which makes it possible to classify the molecules according to their structural resemblance to the known active molecule. The molecules classified among the first have the greatest probability of having the same properties as the molecule of reference (Willett, 1998). The numerous methodologies (of this class) that have been developed to estimate the molecular similarity differ from the point of view the descriptors and/or the metric used. Various structural descriptors can be used to characterize the molecules in this kind of approach. The quantification of the similarity by a distance between the pairs of molecules is the most classically used. Among these metrics, we find the indices of Tanimoto, Cosine, Dice, the Euclidean distances and Hamming...

To evaluate the similarity between 2 molecules A and B, it is necessary to define a descriptive diagram common to all molecules first, whatever their size, type of atoms, type of links. The automatic generation of descriptors (Qsar) will make it possible for example to retain as descriptive diagram of each molecule Logp, Dipole moment, Ehomo,......

Each molecule is thus represented in a multi-dimensional space by a vector including the value of each descriptor (Willett, 1998; Monev, 2004).

A molecule A can, therefore, be described by means of a vector X_A of n attributes such as:

$$\mathbf{X_A} = \{x_{1A},\ x_{2A},\ x_{3A},...,\ x_{jA},...,\ x_{nA}\}$$

where, x_{jA} is the value of the ith attribute of the molecule A.

The values of the attributes can be real numbers (quantitative), or binary (dichotomic), indicating the absence (0) or the presence (1) of certain properties of the molecule.

The attributes can be a set of n topological indices or calculated physicochemical properties, or the state "on/off" of each of the n bits in the "fingerprint" representation of the molecule (Monev, 2004; Willett, 1998; Kearsley et al., 1996).

Some indices are distance measures, or dissimilarities between objects and have a zero value (0) for identical objects, whereas others measure directly the similarity and have the maximum value for identical objects.

The choice of a suitable index is fundamental, because all ulterior analysis will be done on the matrix of association which results from it.

Descriptors

The molecular descriptors constitute a mode of representation of the molecules properties. They make it possible to compare them and to position them in the chemical space. The descriptors are thus at the base of the quantitative structure-activity relation techniques (or property) (QSAR or QSPR) and of the similarity studies. The molecular descriptors are the result of mathematical or logical procedures that transforms the chemical information, coded in a symbolic representation of the molecule, in a usable number. They can also be the experimental result of measurement standardized on these molecules (Willett, 1998; Bender at al., 2004). These descriptors must be applicable to all molecules according to a precise evaluation procedure. It puts therefore aside the experimentally measured descriptors. Indeed, they can be used only when one sample of each molecule is available, in particular those whose activity is to predict (Todeschini & Consonni, 2000). A great number of molecular descriptors were developed until now. For example, the software Dragon (Todeschin et al., 2005) only makes it possible to calculate more than 1664 whereas the software AdriannaCode (Schwab & Gasteiger, 2006) makes it possible to calculate more than 1200 of them. They are based on various concepts such as the graph theory, the information theory, those of molecular modelling, and chemical reactivity or those connected to the physical properties. Nevertheless, the existing descriptors are still imperfect. It is even one of the factors limiting the QSAR methods. The molecular descriptors are made to convey information on the chemical structure of the molecule. Nevertheless, a descriptor and even a set of descriptors, evidently encode only a certain part of the necessary information to describe the structural complexity of a molecule or one of its physicochemical or biological properties (Willett, 1998; Bender at al., 2004).

We can classify the different types of descriptors in four categories according to their dimensionnality which conditions mainly their use (Mozziconacci, 2003; Willett, 1998; Mahé & Vert, 2007).

- *The descriptors (0D)* These are descriptors independent of the molecular geometry such as the number of atoms, the number of links, the molecular mass, the sums of the atomic properties, etc. (Todeschini & Consonni, 2000).
- *The descriptors (1D)* These are descriptors that encode physico-chemical properties (steric, electronic and lipophilic) of the molecules which play an important role in

the phenomena of fixing of the ligands to their target and of transport. Among these, we find for example the coefficient of partition octanol-water (logP), the volume of van der Waals and the refraction index. The energy of the orbital HOMO and LUMO, the heat of formation, the potential of ionization and the dipole moment of the molecules are quantum descriptors classically used (Mozziconacci, 2003; Willett, 1998; Todeschini & Consonni, 2000). It should be noted that among these descriptors, there are those which can be calculated and those which can be measured.

- *Bi-dimensional descriptors (2D)* The bi-dimensional descriptors are directly derived from the molecular graphs, i.e. the way in which the atoms are bound. They encode the topology of the molecule therefore. We consider the molecule only in its planar form while being interested only in its developed chemical formula. The idea is to analyze the substructures found in the molecule (Mozziconacci, 2003; Willett, 1998; Todeschini & Consonni, 2000). In this category, we distinguish among others:
  - The topological indices that are calculated from the molecular connectivity and encode information such as the number of atoms, the presence of heteroatoms, the ramification and the cycles of the molecule or the orders of link.
  - The pairs of atoms, the topological torsions and the projections of atomic properties along the molecular graph.
  - The binary descriptors 2D (*substructure keys* and *hashed fingerprints*) that encode the presence or the absence of structural fragments predefined or not.
- *Three-dimensional descriptors (3D)* The three-dimensional descriptors are evaluated on the basis of the coordinate 3D of

the molecule. They depend logically on its considered conformation. A conformational research is therefore necessary to define the descriptors which encode the global characteristics of the molecule.

COMBINING NEURAL NETWORKS AND KNN METHODS

To implement a research by similarity consists in the first place in choosing a way of characterizing the structures of the molecules, i.e. defining a certain number of descriptors conveying this information. Secondly, it is also necessary to choose a measure of similarity. And lastly it is necessary to define a model of prediction that we will develop starting from the descriptors and the chosen metric.

Choice of the Descriptors

In the used approach, the description of molecules was made in two stages:

- The generation of descriptors
- The adaptation of data

For the representation of molecules, we used the software AdrianaCode (Schwab & Gasteiger, 2006) for the descriptors generation. However, the produced data are not directly exploitable, for this reason we achieved an application (FORMFILE) which converted the data generated by Adriana-Code into a format adapted for our software.

Choice of the Metric

Two molecules A and B are, therefore, described by means of the vectors X_A and X_B of n attributes (descriptors) such as:

$$X_A = \{x_{1A}, x_{2A}, x_{3A}, ..., x_{jA}, ..., x_{nA}\}$$

$$X_B = \{x_{1B}, x_{2B}, x_{3B}, ..., x_{jB}, ..., x_{nB}\}$$

Our objective being to describe the proximities between molecules, in other words, the comparison of molecules; we need to measure the similarity, it is then a question of measuring a distance separating the molecules A and B described by their vectors X_A and X_B. If two molecules are separated by a short distance then they resemble each other.

The data (descriptors) which we handle are real values (quantitative), of this fact the measurement of distance most appropriate to this kind of approach is the Euclidean distance.

If we suppose that the molecules A and B are described by the vector X_A and X_B, The Euclidean distance is calculated in the following way:

$$D(X_A, X_B) = \left(\sum_{j=1}^{n} (x_{jA} - x_{jB})^2\right)^{1/2}$$

There is also the weighted Euclidean distance definite as follows:

$$D(X_A, X_B) = \left(\sum_{j=1}^{n} m_j (x_{jA} - x_{jB})^2\right)^{1/2}$$

where the coefficients m_j, strictly positive, ponders the influence of the jth descriptor. The way in which the descriptors are pondered is quite crucial so that the taken measure is relevant. However, this weighting is not always easy to carry out, in particular if there is not "an expert of the field" able to provide it. In general m_j is equal to 1.

Choice of the Methods

Many algorithms are appropriate for the implementation of a research by similarity. We adopted, in our approach, a connexionnist method: the Kohonen network (Self Organized Maps) (Kohonen, 1982) in order to tempt to regroup the similar molecules and to reduce the dimensionality of the input space without losing information. Indeed, this method makes it possible to represent the data by preserving the topology, thus close data (in the entry space) will have close representations in the exit space and thus will be classified in the same class or close classes. Our goal being to search for the most similar molecules to a given molecule, we apply the algorithm of the nearest neighbors compared to the projection of this molecule (its coordinates) in the MAP constructed after the learning phase.

The Kohonen Network for the Reduction and the Regrouping

The input data, which are N-dimensional vectors, are projected on a two-dimensional map of nodes, or neurons, which are self-organized according to the definition of the vicinity in the network of Kohonen. We have a set (data base) of N molecules, in which each molecule is described by a vector X_I of n descriptors x_{jI} (quantitative variables with real values).

Molecule *I*: $X_I = \{x_{1I}, x_{2I}, x_{3I}, ..., x_{jI}, ..., x_{nI}\}$

The data are arranged in a table (matrix) X of N lines and n columns.

Our model is a Kohonen network: a two-dimensional grid of p by p neurons Ni. Our network is constituted:

- of an entry layer: any molecule to be classified is represented by a multidimensional vector (the vector of entry). To each molecule is affected a neuron representing the class center.

- of an exit layer (or layer of competition). The neurons of this layer enter in competition to be activated, only one neuron is activated (winner-takes-*all neuron*) following the competition.

The lines of the X table are the entries of the SOM algorithm. Each neuron N_i is represented in space R^p by its vector of weight W_i (or *vector code*) of size equal to that of the space of entry:

$$W_i = (w_{i1}, w_{i2}, ..., w_{ij,...}, w_{in}),$$

The weights w_{ij} are generated randomly.

Moreover, each neuron is connected to each dimension of the entry space. The input vectors as well as the weight vectors are normalized.

We present to the map an input vector. We calculate the distance between the presented vector:

$$X_I = \{x_{1I}, x_{2I}, x_{3I}, ..., x_{jI}, ..., x_{nI}\},$$

and the weight vector of each neuron:

$$W_i = (w_{i1}, w_{i2}, ..., w_{ij,...}, w_{in})$$

The distance considered here is the Euclidean distance.

We choose the neuron whose D_i is the smallest; the weights of this neuron will be actualized:

$$w_{ij} = w_{ij} + \alpha.[\, x_{jI} - w_{ij}\,]$$

α is the learning coefficient included in the interval [0,1], it decrease with time.

After the training phase, each neuron N_i, then each entry is classified: the input X_I belongs to the class Ni if and only if the weight W_i is the closest among all the weights.

The vectors X_I of n dimensions will be projected on a two-dimensional map, we will thus have the dimensionality of the input vectors reduced to 2 without any loss of information.

Search of Similar Molecules: Knn Method

Let:

- Our bidimensional previously determined map containing projected information of the input space.

- Set A of N points (neurons) of this map.
- Number $K \leq N$.

Considering a point X located in this space, not belonging necessarily to A, our problem consists in determining which are the k points of A closest to X within the meaning of a certain measure of distance, usually the Euclidean distance.

We speak then about finding a neighbourhood of size k around the point X.

The algorithm of research of the neighborhood of X consists in passing through the set of the N points of A and to look if the point is nearer or no that one of the nearest neighbors already selected, and if so, to insert it.

RESULTS AND DISCUSSIONS

We developed our application on Pentium (2,66 GHz / 256 Mo) with the C++ language (C++ Builder 6.0).

This application has for main missions:

- The reduction of the dimensionality of a set of molecules described by a significant number of descriptors.
- The regrouping of the similar molecules.
- The research of the similar molecules to a given molecule according to the used descriptors.

The application has three parts: the "training" part, the "seeks the similar molecules of the data base used" part and the "seeks molecules similar to a given molecule" part.

We used a data base with the format Structure Date file (SDF) containing 1000 molecules downloaded from http://chembank.broad.harvard.ed.

In our simulation we used 2D descriptors: *2DMol_Weight* (Molecular weight), *2DMol_HAcc* (Number of hydrogen bonding acceptors), *2DMol_HDon* (Number of hydrogen bonding donors), *2DMol_Polariz* (Mean molecular polarizability),

2DMol_TPSA (Topological polar surface area), generated by software AdrianaCode. The Kohonen map size is 10x10; each element of the map represents a neuron with a vector of 5 elements. A training of 100 iterations is made.

Our testing base consists of 10 molecules, and we research the 5 (*5-nn*) more similar molecules with each molecule of the testing base classified from the most similar to the least similar. It should be noted that the choice of the descriptors and that of the number of similar molecules was justified by no criterion, but only to test our application (see Table 1).

Molecules of the testing base

- $C_{22}H_{35}NO_2$ [(+)-himbacine]
- $C_{11}H_{15}N_4O_7P$ [(1s)-1(9-deazahypoxanthin-9yl)1,4-dideoxy-1,4-imino-d-ribitol-5-phosphate],
- $C_{20}H_{24}N_4O_2$ [+/-methyl 4-(aminoiminomethyl)-beta-[3- inh (aminoimino)phenyl]benzene pentanoate]
- $C_6H_{13}NO_4$ [1-deoxynorjrimycin]
- $C_{23}H_{30}O_5$ [17-phenyl-trinor-prostaglandin E2]
- $C_9H_{13}N_3O_4$ [2-Deoxycytidine]
- $C_{29}H_{26}N_2O_3$ [4-[(4,4-dimethyl-1,2,3,4-tetrahydro-[1,2']binapthalenyl-7-carbonyl)-amino]-benzoic acid]
- $C_{17}H_{17}BrN_4O$ [9-bromo-phenazine-1-carboxylic acid (2-dimethylamino-ethyl)-amide] C2H6O [Alcohol]
- $C_8H_9NO_5$ [Amoxicillin/clavulanate]

Now, it is a question to evaluate the obtained results by our approach, for that, it would be necessary to make a comparison with results obtained with other methods with the same used parameters. But we don't have at our disposal such results.

For this reason we will make manual calculations on some samples, compare them with the calculation carried out by our software then draw conclusions on the degree of performance of our

Table 1. Similar molecules (5) to the molecule of testing base

Molecule (formula, name)	Similar Molecules (5) (formula et name)
$C_{22}H_{35}NO_2$ (+)-himbacine	1 - $C_{21}H_{21}ClN_2O$ →[1-(2-CHLOROPHENYL)-N-METHYL-N-(1-METHYLPROPYL)-3-ISOQUINOLINE CARBOXAMIDE] 2 - $C_{22}H_{27}N_3O$ →[6-NOR-6-ALLYLLYSERGIC ACID DIETHYLAMIDE D] 3 - $C_{22}H_{40}O_2$ →[7,7-dimethyleicosadienoic acid] 4 - $C_{23}H_{42}O$ →[3-Hydroxy-14-methyldocosa-(4E)-en-1-yne] 5 - $C_{16}H_{22}Cl_2O_3$ →[2,4-dichlorophenoxyacetic acid, isooctyl ester]
- $C_{11}H_{15}N_4O_7P$ - (1s)-1(9-deazahypoxanthin-9yl)1,4-dideoxy-1,4-imino-d-ribitol-5-phosphate	1 - $C_{10}H_{14}N_5O_7P$ →[adenosine phosphate] 2 - $C_{10}H_{14}N_5O_7P$ →[3'-azido-3'-deoxythymidine-5'-monophosphate] 3 - $C_9H_{13}N_2O_{10}P$ →[1-(5'-phospho-beta-d-ribofuranosyl)barbituric acid] 4 - $C_{11}H_{17}N_2O_8P$ →[[3-hydroxy-2-mehtyl-5-phosphonooxymethyl-pyridin-4-ylmethyl]-serine] 5- $C_6H_8F_3N_3O_7P_2$ →[4-amino-2-trifluoromethyl-5-hydroxymehtylpyrimidine pyrophosphate]
- $C_{20}H_{24}N_4O_2$ - +/-methyl 4-(aminoiminomethyl)-beta-[3- inh (aminoimino)phenyl]benzene pentanoate	1 - $C_{17}H_{11}NO_8$ →[9-hydroxy aristolochic acid] 2 - $C_{16}H_{18}N_3O_4S$- →[ampicillin] 3 - $C_{13}H_{14}O_8P_2$ →[4-phosphonooxy-phenyl-methyl-[4-phosphonooxy]benzen] 4 - $C_{16}H_{19}N_3O_5S$ →[amoxicillin] 5 - $C_{18}H_{30}O_6$ →[2,3-di-northromboxane B2]
- $C_6H_{13}NO_4$ - 1-deoxynorjrimycin	1 - $C_6H_{13}NO_4$ →[2(r),5(r)-bix(hydroxymethyl)-3(r),4(r)-dihydroxypyrrolidine] 2 - $C_6H_{13}NO_4$ →[1,'-DIDEOXY-1,4-IMINO-D-MANNITOL] 3 - $C_6H_{10}O_5$ →[3-hydroxy-3-mehtyl-glutaric acid] 4 - $C_6H_{12}O_5$ →[2-deoxyglucose] 5 - $C_6H_{12}O_5$ →[2,5-Anhydro-D-mannitol]
- $C_{23}H_{30}O_5$ - 17-phenyl-trinor-prostaglandin E2	1 - $C_{22}H_{36}O_5$ →[16,16-dimethylprostaglandin E2] 2 - $C_{19}H_{21}NO_5S$ →[2-ETHOXYCARBONYLMETHYL-(TOLUENE-4-SULFONYL)-AMINO-BENZOIC ACID METHYL ESTER] 3 - $C_{21}H_{27}N_5O_2$ →[[phenylalaninyl-prolinyl]-[2-(pyridine-4-ylamino)-ethyl]-amine] 4 - $C_{22}H_{34}O_6$ →[9-DEOXYFORSKOLIN] 5 - $C_{19}H_{22}N_2O_4S$ →[[4-(4-phenyl-piperidin-1-yl)-benzenesulfonylamino]-acetic acid]
- $C_9H_{13}N_3O_4$ - 2-Deoxycytidine	1 - $C_{10}H_{14}O_6$ →[4,7-dioxosebacic acid] 2 - $C_8H_9N_5O_3$ →[5,6-cyclic-tetrahydropteridine] 3 - $C_{10}H_{11}N_5O_2$ →[2'-hydroxy, 3'-ketocyclopent-4'-enyladenine] 4 - $C_8H_{11}N_5O_3$ →[acyclovir] 5 - $C_8H_{11}N_5O_3$ →[Acycloguanosine]
- $C_{29}H_{26}N_2O_3$ - 4-[(4,4-dimethyl-1,2,3,4-tetrahy-dro-[1,2']binapthalenyl-7-carbonyl)-amino]-benzoic acid	1 - $C_{27}H_{23}N_5O_2$ →[(20s)-19,20,22,23-tetrahydro-19-oxo-5h,21h-18,20-ethano-12,14-etheno-6,10-methenobenz[d]imidazo[4,3-l][1,6,9,13]oxatriazacyclonoadecosine-9-carbonitrile] 2 - $C_{27}H_{28}N_6O$ →[2'-(4-ethoxyphenyl)-5-(4-methyl-1-piperazinyl)-2,5'-bi-benzimidazole] 3 - $C_{20}H_{20}Cl_2N_4O_2S$ →[5-(3,5-dichlorophenyl)thio-4-isopropyl-1-(pyridin-4-yl-methyl)-1h-imidazol-2-yl-methylcarbamate] 4 - $C_{16}H_{11}BrF_3N_3O_2S$ →[1-phenylsulfonamide-3-trifluoromethyl-5-parabromophenylpyrazole] 5 - $C_{26}H_{21}N_5O_2$ →[(20s)-19,20,21,22-tetrahydro-19-oxo-5h-18,20-ethano-12,14-etheno-6,10-metheno-18h-benz[d]imidazo[4,3-k][1,6,9,12]oxatriaza-cyclooctadecosine-9-carbonitrile]
- $C_{17}H_{17}BrN_4O$ - 9-bromo-phenazine-1-carboxylic acid (2-dimethylamino-ethyl)-amide	1 - $C_{22}H_{26}O_5$ →[(+)-Calanolide A] 2 - $C_{22}H_{24}O_5$ →[12-Oxocalanolide A] 3 - $C_{22}H_{28}O_5$ →[(-)-7,8-Dihydrocalanolide B] 4 - $C_{22}H_{26}O_5$ →[7,8-Dihydro-12-oxo-calanolide B] 5 - $C_{13}H_{18}Br_2N_2O$ →[ambroxol]
- C_2H_6O - Alcohol	1 - $C_2H_8N_2$ →[1,2-dimethylhydrazine hydrochloride] 2 - $C_2H_5N_O$ →[acetamide] 3 - C_2H_6OS →[2-mercaptoethanol] 4 - $C_4H_6N_2$ →[1-methylimidazole] 5 - $C_3H_6N_2$ →[3-aminopropionitrile]
$C_8H_9NO_5$ Amoxicillin/clavulanate	1 - $C_9H_{10}O_5$ →[(+/-)-Vanillylmandelic acid] 2 - $C_7H_5ClN_2O_3$ →[aklomide] 3 - $C_6H_{11}ClO_5$ →[2-Chloro-2-deoxy-D-glucose] 4 - $C_{10}H_{10}N_4O$ →[5-Amino-1-phenyl-4-pyrazolecarboxamide] 5 - $C_{10}H_{13}NO_3$ →[alpha-Methyl-DL-m-tyrosine]

Table 2. The descriptors values for the molecule (+) - himbacine and of the similar molecules

	Molecule	Weight	TPSA	MPolariz	HDon	HAcc
	$C_{22}H_{35}NO_2$	**345.519**	**29.54**	**39.93**	**0**	**3**
1	$C_{21}H_{21}ClN_2O$	352.857	33.2	42.244	0	3
2	$C_{22}H_{27}N_3O$	349.469	39.34	42.919	1	4
3	$C_{22}H_{40}O_2$	336.552	37.3	41.483	1	2
4	$C_{23}H_{42}O$	334.579	20.23	42.32	1	1
5	$C_{16}H_{22}Cl_2O_3$	333.249	35.53	34	0	3

The Euclidean distance between the molecule (+)- *himbacine* and each similar molecule:
D1=8,5203544 D2=11,0714326 D3=12,0431099 D4=14,7333567 D5=14,8861647

application. To compare the various molecules with their similar we use the Euclidean distance.

The molecules are represented by their empirical formulas.

We use as a sample the following molecules with their similes determined by our application:

- *(+)-himbacine* ($C_{22}H_{35}NO_2$) (see Table 2)
- *(1s)-1(9-deazahypoxanthin-9yl)1,4-dideoxy-1,4-imino-d-ribitol-5-phosphate* ($C_{11}H_{15}N_4O_7P$) (see Table 3)
- *+/-methyl 4-(aminoiminomethyl)-beta-[3-inh (aminoimino)phenyl]benzene pentanoate (*$C_{20}H_{24}N_4O_2$*) (see Table 4)

Thus the molecules of the tables are classified from the "most similar" to the least "more similar" respectively according to order 1, 2, 3, 4, 5.

That corresponds to the calculation carried out automatically by our software.

CONCLUSION AND FUTURE WORKS

In this chapter we tempted to study research by molecular similarity. Often little information is necessary to make such a research.

This research rests on the principle according to which close molecular structure implies close physical, chemical or biological properties. We considered an approach based on the SOM as model and the Knn algorithm, using the Euclidian distance as a metric to achieve an application of research by similarity. The choice of the descriptors that we used in our simulation has been motivated by no criteria but only to test our software. We got satisfactory results. However it is to note that, the

Table 3. The descriptors values for the molecule (1s)-1(9-deazahypoxanthin-9yl)1,4-dideoxy-1,4-imino-d-ribitol-5-phosphate and for the similar molecules

	Molecule	Weight	TPSA	MPolariz	HDon	HAcc
	$C_{11}H_{15}N_4O_7P$	**346.233**	**176.5**	**29.869**	**7**	**11**
1	$C_{10}H_{14}N_5O_7P$	347.221	174.16	28.249	3	12
2	$C_{10}H_{14}N_5O_7P$	347.221	186.07	29.294	6	12
3	$C_9H_{13}N_2O_{10}P$	340.181	182.93	25.337	5	12
4	$C_{11}H_{17}N_2O_8P$	336.235	169.44	28.556	6	10
5	$C_6H_8F_3N_3O_7P_2$	353.086	165.09	22.199	5	10

D1=5,1064805 D2=9,7412354 D3=10,1740172 D4=12,3906243 D5=15,5235501

Table 4. The descriptors values for the molecule +/-methyl4-(aminoiminomethyl)-beta-[3-nhaminoimino) phenyl]benzenepentanoate and for the similar molecules

	Molécule	Weight	TPSA	MPolariz	HDon	HAcc
	$C_{20}H_{24}N_4O_2$	352.43	126.04	40.319	6	6
1	$C_{17}H_{11}NO_8$	357.271	131.04	34.953	2	9
2	$C_{16}H_{18}N_3O_4S-$	348.398	115.23	34.981	3	7
3	$C_{13}H_{14}O_8P_2$	360.193	133.52	30.875	4	8
4	$C_{16}H_{19}N_3O_5S$	365.405	132.96	36.073	5	8
5	$C_{18}H_{30}O_6$	342.427	115.06	35.558	4	6

D1=10,1108474 D2=13,0998995 D3=14,6083436 D4=15,4682106 D5=15,7253785

results are very dependent of the descriptors and the used metrics. Numerous ways remain open for the improvement of this application. First, we consider using other metrics and descriptors, and to compare the different gotten results. In a second phase and in the setting of Data Mining, we wish to extend our model to heterogeneous data base.

REFERENCES

Bender, A., Mussa, H. Y., & Glen, R. C. (2004). Molecular similarity searching using atom environments, information-based feature selection, and a naïve bayesian classifier. *Journal of Chemical Information and Computer Sciences*, *44*(1), 170–178. doi:10.1021/ci034207y

Bisson, G. (2000). *La similarité: une notion symbolique/numérique. Apprentissage symbolique-numérique* (*Vol. 2*, pp. 169–201). Eds Moulet, Brito. Editions Cépadues.

Downs, G. M., Willett, P., & Fisanick, W. (1994). Similarity Searching and Clustering of Chemical-Structure Databases Using Molecular Property Data. *Journal of Chemical Information and Computer Sciences*, *34*, 1094–1102. doi:10.1021/ci00021a011

Johnson, M. A., & Maggiora, G. M. (1990). *Concepts and Applications of Molecular Similarity*. New York: John Wiley & Sons.

Kearsley, S. K., Sallamack, S., Fluder, E. M., Andose, J. D., Mosley, R. T., & Sheridan, R. P. (1996). Chemical Similarity Using Physicochemical Property Descriptors. *Journal of Chemical Information and Computer Sciences*, *36*, 118–127. doi:10.1021/ci950274j

Kohonen, T. (1982). Self-organized formation of topologically correct feature maps. *Biological Cybernetics*, *43*, 59–69. doi:10.1007/BF00337288

Legendre, P., & Legendre, L. (1998). *Numerical ecology*. Amsterdam: Second English Edition, Elsevier.

Mahé, P., & Vert, J. P. (2007). *Virtual screening with support vector machines and structure kernels* (Technical report HAL-00166188), Paris: Ecole des Mines de Paris, Centre de Bioinformatique.

Monev, V. (2004). Introduction to Similarity Searching in Chemistry. *Match-Communications in Mathematical and in Computer Chemistry*, *51*, 7–38.

Mozziconacci, J. C (2003). *Développement et application de méthodes de drug design: Combinaison des approches de docking-scoring et de QSAR*. Unpublished doctoral dissertation, Orleans University, Orleans.

Schwab, C. H., & Gasteiger, J. (2006). *Adriana-Code software version 2.0*. Germany: Molecular Networks GmbH Computerchemie.

Sheridan, R. P., & Kearsley, S. K. (2002). Why do we need so many chemical similarity search methods? *Drug Discovery Today, 7*(17), 903–911. doi:10.1016/S1359-6446(02)02411-X

Todeschin, R., Consonni, V., Mauri, A., & Pavan, M. (2005). Dragon software version 5.3, Milano, Italy.

Todeschini, R., & Consonni, V. (2000). *Handbook of Molecular Descriptors*. New York: Wiley-VCH 11, pp. 667.

van de Waterbeemd, H., & Gifford, E. (2003). ADMET in silico modelling: towards prediction paradise? *Journal of Chemical Information and Computer Sciences, 2*(3), 192–204.

Willett, P. (1998). Chemical Similarity Searching. *Journal of Chemical Information and Computer Sciences, 38*, 983–996. doi:10.1021/ci9800211

Chapter 6

A QSAR/QSPR Study with Graph–Theoretical Indices Based on a New Type of Vertex Degree

Lionello Pogliani
Università della Calabria, Italy

ABSTRACT

Valence molecular connectivity indices are indices based on the concept of valence delta, δ^v, that can be derived from general chemical graphs or chemical pseudographs. A general graph or pseudograph is a graph with multiple edges and loops and it can be used to encode, through the valence delta, chemical entities like the sigma-, pi- and non-bonding n-electrons. Two other graph-theoretical concepts that can also be derived from chemical pseudographs are the intrinsic (I) and the electrotopological state (E) values that are the main tools used to define the valence delta of the pseudoconnectivity indices, $\psi_{I,S}$. Complete graphs can, instead, be used to encode, through a new type of valence delta, the core electrons of any type of atoms in a molecule. The connectivity indices either valence connectivity or pseudoconnectivity indices are the starting point to develop, by the aid of a dual procedure, the dual connectivity indices, i.e., the dual connectivity, valence connectivity and pseudoconnectivity indices. The dual indices show the interesting property that not only some of them can assume negative values but also that they can cover a wide range of numerical values. Graph concepts can also be used to deal with the problem of the hydrogen contribution in hydrogen depleted chemical graphs, which are the normal type of graphs used in chemistry. For this purpose a perturbation parameter can be introduced into the definition of the valence delta that allows to differentiates among compounds with similar hydrogen-suppressed chemical

DOI: 10.4018/978-1-60960-860-6.ch006

graphs but different number of hydrogen atoms, like CH_3F and BH_2F. The new definition of the central parameter of the molecular connectivity theory, the valence delta, consent to define of a completely new set of connectivity indices, which can be distinguished by their configuration and that can advantageously be used to model different properties and activities of compounds.

INTRODUCTION

The many new types of molecular connectivity indices (Pogliani, 2000, 2002, 2004, 2005, 2006, 2007, 2009, 2010; Garcia-Domenech et al. 2008), which will be discussed and used for model purposes in this paper are defined by a family of formally similar algorithms, first formulated by Randić (Randić, 1975) and then developed into a general theory, known as the molecular connectivity (MC) theory, by Kier and Hall (Kier & Hall, 1986, 1999). This theory has, since then, been enriched and discussed in many ways (Pogliani, 2000; Garcia-Domenech, et al., 2008; Trinajstić, 1992; Devillers & Balaban, 1999, Todeschini & Consonni, 2000; Diudea, 2000; Estrada, 2001; Li & Gutman, 2006). The central parameter of the molecular connectivity theory is the valence delta number, δ^v, which, in the hands of Pogliani, has undergone a major transformation (Pogliani, 2000-2010; Garcia-Domenech, et al. 2008). This graph-theoretical number, shown in eq. (1) actually encodes not only the *sigma-*, *pi-* and non-bonding *n*-electrons but also the core electrons and the contribution of the suppressed hydrogen atoms,

$$\delta^v = \frac{(q + f_\delta^n)\delta^v(ps)}{(pr + 1)} \qquad (1)$$

Parameter $\delta^v(ps)$ is the vertex degree number of an atom in a pseudograph. Parameter q equals 1 or p; parameter $p \cdot r$ equals the sum of all vertex degrees in a complete graph, and it equals twice the number of its connections. Notice that parameter q has fixed values and it is not used as an optimizing parameter, something like Randić's variable index (Randić & Basak, 2001). The fact that $q =$

1 or p has the consequence that four possible sets of molecular connectivity indices can be obtained and they are: for $q = 1$ and $p = odd$ (1, 3, 5,..) a K_p-(p-odd) set of indices is obtained, for $q = 1$ and $p =$ sequential (1, 2, 3, …) a K_p-(p-seq) set is obtained, for $q = p$ and $p = odd$ a K_p-(pp-odd) set is obtained, and for $q = p$ and $p = seq$ a K_p-(pp-seq) set of indices is obtained. The rationale of this distinction resides in the fact that in many cases MC indices derived with p odd-valued show a superior model quality. Perturbation parameter f_δ takes care of the suppressed hydrogen atoms in a chemical graph or pseudograph, and is defined in the following way

$$f_\delta = [\delta^v_m(ps) - \delta^v(ps)]/\delta^v_m(ps) = 1 - \delta^v(ps)/\delta^v_m(ps) = n_H/\delta^v_m(ps) \qquad (2)$$

Here, $\delta^v_m(ps)$ is the maximal $\delta^v(ps)$ value a heteroatom can have in a chemical HS-pseudograph when all bonded hydrogens are substituted by heteroatoms, and n_H equals the number of hydrogen atoms normally bonded to any heteroatom (C inclusive).

For completely substituted carbons (or heteroatoms): $n_H = 0$, $f_\delta = 0$ [as: $\delta^v_m(ps) = \delta^v(ps)$], while for alkanes δ and δ^v are now related as, $\delta^v(ps) = \delta$ and $\delta^v = (1 + f_\delta^n)\delta$ (in this case $p = 1$). Only for quaternary carbons (with $f_\delta = 0$) $\delta^v = \delta$ is obtained. Exponent n can have different values, and even negative values to allow for a strong perturbation value. The higher the value of n the lower the perturbation and for very high values ($n \geq 50$) the perturbation is practically zero. The reader should notice that the hydrogen perturbation allows to differentiate among p- and $\delta^v(ps)$-similar atoms, which differ in the number of bonded hydrogen atoms as in the case of the HS chemical pseudographs plus complete graphs of LiF, BeHF, BH_2F, and CH_3F.

For every n value a specific set of constant molecular connectivity index values is obtained, and this allows to check the amount of hydrogen perturbation, which is responsible for the best model. This parameter is not used as a variable parameter (even if it could) and this means that the number of molecular connectivity indices can be quite large as each set depends now on the values of q, p and n. These three values determine what could be defined a configuration of the molecular connectivity indices: $K_p(p$-odd/seq; pp-$odd/seq)/f_\delta^n$.

Chemical Graphs, Pseudographs and Complete Graphs

Let us now spend two words about graphs, pseudographs (or general graphs) and complete graphs (Kier & Hall, 1986, 1999; Trinajstić, 1992; Devillers & Balaban, 1999, Todeschini & Consonni, 2000; Diudea, 2000; Estrada, 2001; Li & Gutman, 2006). Those interested in the history of chemical graph theory should consult Randić & Trinastić, 1994. A *graph G* can informally be seen as a set of vertices together with a set of edges (connections) that connect these vertices. The *degree of a vertex* in a graph is the number of edges that occur with it. The degree of a vertex ($= \delta$) known also as its valence, is the central concept of the molecular connectivity theory, which is the chemical counterpart of graph theory and it is based on the concept of *chemical graph* (also, *molecular graph, structural graphs, constitutional graphs*). A *chemical graph* is a graph where atoms and bonds are represented by vertices and simple edges respectively. As some mathematicians reserve the term *simple graph* for a graph with no multiple edges and loops, this type of chemical graphs can then be called *simple chemical grahs*. Double bonds and lone-pair electrons can, instead, only be fitted by chemical pseudographs or general graphs which allow multiple bonds and lone-pair

electrons. A *pseudograph* (or general graph) may contain *multiple edges* between pairs of vertices and *self-connections* (or loops), which are edges from a vertex to itself. A *chemical pseudograph* is a general graph with either simple, multiple, or self-connecting edges. The degree of a vertex in a chemical pseudograph, $\delta^v(ps)$, its valence, is the number of edges and self-connections that occur with it (loops contribute twice to its valence). The valence delta number, δ^v, which for simple K_1 vertices (see next paragraph) equals $\delta^v(ps)$, is the main tool not only of the valence molecular connectivity indices, but also of the newly defined pseudoconnectivity indices and, together with δ, is also the main tool of the dual connectivity and pseudoconnectivity indices.

A *complete graph*, K_p, of order p, is a graph where every pair of vertices is adjacent. A complete graph is always r-regular, i.e., it has all of its vertices with the same degree r, where with $r = p - 1$. The contrary is not true, for instance, pure (non-branched) cyclic graphs are regular but they are not complete. A *chemical complete graph* is a complete graph whose vertices encode core electrons of atoms in a molecule. The vertices of simple graphs can thus be considered K_1 graphs. A *null K_0 graph* has also been defined (Harary & Read, 1977) and it is a complete graph with no edges and vertices, which has a negative regularity, $r = -1$. The null graphs may be used to encode the depleted hydrogen atoms, and in this case a hydrogen-suppressed (HS) simple chemical graph is a set of K_0 and K_1 complete graphs and a set of edges connecting the K_1 graphs. For second-row K_1 ($p = 1$, $q = 1$) vertices: $\delta^v = (1 + f_\delta^n)\delta^v(ps)$, and for the HS chemical graph of alkanes (more generally for sp^3 carbon atoms) $\delta^v(ps) = \delta$ holds, which for completely substituted sp^3 carbon atoms simplifies into $\delta^v = \delta$.

In Figure 1, from top to bottom, are: a generic simple HS chemical graph with four K_1 vertices, the chemical pseudograph, with K_1 vertices, of 1, 2 difluoroethylene, the HS chemical pseudograph, with K_1 (carbon) and K_3 (Cl) vertices, of

Figure 1. From top to bottom: a HS simple chemical graph with four K_1 vertices, the HS chemical pseudograph with K_1 of 1, 2 difluoroethylene, the HS chemical pseudograph with K_1 and K_3 of 1, 2-dichoro ethylene, and the HS chemical pseudograph with K_1 and K_5 of 1, 2 dibromoethylene

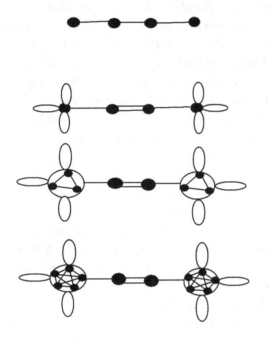

Molecular Connectivity Indices

Before getting into the details of the molecular connectivity indices it should be reminded that two new molecular connectivity indices were introduced by the author (Pogliani, 1992, 2000), the sum-delta and the valence sum-delta index: $D = \Sigma_i \delta_i$ and $D^v = \Sigma_i \delta^v_i$. In the present study only eight types of molecular connectivity indices will be used, four non-valence indices and four valence indices, which are formally similar. The four MC non-valence indices, which can be derived from a simple HS graph are: the *sum*-delta, the *zeroth*-order ($^0\chi$), the *first*-order ($^1\chi$), and the *total*-order (χ_t) molecular connectivity indices (this last index was introduced by Needham et al., 1988),

$$D = \Sigma_i \delta_i \tag{3}$$

$$^0\chi = \Sigma_i (\delta_i)^{-0.5} \tag{4}$$

$$^1\chi = \Sigma (\delta_i \delta_j)^{-0.5} \tag{5}$$

$$\chi_t = (\Pi \delta_i)^{-0.5} \tag{6}$$

1, 2-dichoroethylene, and the HS chemical pseudograph, with K_1 (carbon) and K_5 (Br) vertices, of 1, 2 dibromo-ethylene. Core electrons have here been encoded with odd complete graphs ($p = 1, 3, 5, 7...$). The circle around the complete graphs is just a frame, and has no meaning. The δ values for the vertices of the HS simple chemical graph of Figure 1(top) and the δ^v values for the vertices of second, third and fourth HS chemical pseudographs plus complete graphs in this same figure (with f^1_δ) are shown in Table 1 for the different configurations of complete graphs. In Table 2 are the f^n_δ values for $n = 50, 5, 1, 0.5, -0.5$, and -1 for hydrogenated carbon, nitrogen and oxygen atoms, which are encoded with a K_1 type of vertex.

Replacing δ with δ^v in Eqs. 3-6 the corresponding four valence MC indices, which can be derived from HS general graphs or pseudograph, are obtained: D^v, $^0\chi^v$, $^1\chi^v$, and χ^v_t. Sums and products in Eqs. 3, 4, and 6 stretch over all vertices of the chemical graph, while the sum in Eq. 5 stretches over all single ij connections of a chemical graph (i.e., σ bonds). The valence MC indices (χ^v), even if they are formally similar to the non-valence indices, they encode a different electronic information and give rise to different values. The choice to use only eight molecular connectivity indices is done with the intent to avoid a huge combinatorial problem at the moment of the choice of the multilinear descriptor, as these are not the only type of indices that will be defined and used in the present study. It should be reminded that with multilinear relationships,

Table 1. δ (top graph) and δ^v values for C, F, Cl, and Br of Figure 1 throughout the four types of core electrons, for f_δ^n with n = 1 (C: n_H = 1; F, Cl, and Br: n_H = 0)

Configurations	C	F	Cl	Br
δ -Simple graph (top)	2	1	1	1
δ^v- K_p-(p-odd)	3.75	7	1	0.3333
δ^v- K_p-(p-seq)	3.75	7	2.333	1
δ^v- K_p-(pp-odd)	3.75	7	3	1.667
δ^v- K_p-(pp-seq)	3.75	7	4.667	3

Table 2. The f_δ^n values for n = 50, 5, 1, 0.5, - 0.5, and -1 for hydrogenated C, N, and O

Groups/n	50	5	1	0.5	-0.5	-1
≡ CH	0	0.001	0.25	0.5	2.00	4
= CH$_2$	0	0.031	0.50	0.71	1.41	2
- CH$_3$	0	0.237	0.75	0.87	1.15	1.333
- OH	0	0.0001	0.17	0.41	2.45	6
= NH	0	0.0003	0.20	0.45	2.24	5
- NH$_2$	0	0.010	0.4	0.63	1.58	2.5

the number of combinations to be tested to find an optimal descriptor for a specific activity or property can increases dramatically with increasing number of indices.

Molecular Pseudoconnectivity Indices

The pseudoconnectivity indices, denoted by ψ, are centered on the concept of pseudograph, which is used to derive the valence delta values, δ^v, the basic parameter of this type of indices. The set of valence molecular connectivity indices, $\{\chi^v\}$, are also based on pseudographs but for historical reasons they have other names. These indices are related to the valence delta, δ^v, through the following *I*-State (ψ_I subset) and *S*-State (ψ_E subset) indices (Kier & Hall, 1999),

$$I = (\delta^v +1) / \delta, \quad S = I + \Sigma\Delta I, \text{ with } \Delta I = (I_i - I_j) / r_{ij}^2 \tag{7}$$

Here, r_{ij} counts the atoms in the minimum path length separating two atoms *i* and *j*, which equals the graph distance, $d_{ij} + 1$. Factor $\Sigma\Delta I$ incorporates information about the influence of the molecular environment. Here are the definitions of some of them, and the reader can notice the formal similarity with the corresponding molecular connectivity χ indices,

$$^S\psi_I = \Sigma\, I_i \tag{8}$$

$$^0\psi_I = \Sigma\, (I_i)^{-0.5} \tag{9}$$

$$^1\psi_I = \Sigma(I_i I_j)^{-0.5} \tag{10}$$

$$^T\psi_I = (\Pi I_i)^{-0.5} \tag{11}$$

Replacing I_i with S_i the corresponding ψ_E subset is obtained: $\{^S\psi_E, ^0\psi_E, ^1\psi_E, ^T\psi_E\}$. Superscripts *S* means sum (this index is formally similar to index *D*) and superscript *T* means total (historical reasons are behind the definition of χ_t), while the other sub- and superscripts follow the established denomination for the χ indices. The $\Sigma\Delta I$ parameter can give rise to negative S values for atoms bonded to highly electronegative groups. To avoid imaginary ψ_E values (due to $S < 0$) all S values should be rescaled. For instance, if in a class of compounds there are carbon atoms with negative S values (because they are bonded to electronegative atoms) it can be advantageous to rescale the S values of all atoms of all compounds in such a way that the carbon atom in CF_4, which has a $S(C) = - 5.5$, becomes positive by adding a constant amount to it. The rescaling procedure should be done with the intent to avoid either too small or too large S values and in this case it has a minor influence on the quality of the modeling (Garcia-Domenech et al., 2008). One of the results of the I_S concept as developed by Kier and Hall implies that $\Sigma_i S_i = \Sigma_i I_i$, with the consequence that $^S\psi_I = {}^S\psi_E$. Nevertheless, the rescaling procedure brings about, in most cases, that $^S\psi_I \neq {}^S\psi_E$.

Higher-order χ indices have been defined by Kier and Hall (Kier & Hall, 1986), and the proposed general algorithm (eq. 12) for (nearly) all of them can also be used to define a general algorithm for the ψ indices, shown in eq. (13)

$$^k\chi_T = \sum_{j=1}^{k_n t}\left(\prod_{i \in S_j}\delta_i\right)^{-1/2} \rightarrow \quad ^k\psi_{IT} = \sum_{j=1}^{k_n t}\left(\prod_{i \in S_j}I_i\right)^{-1/2}$$

$$(12 \rightarrow 13)$$

Substitution of δ with δ^v and of I with S in eq. 12 allow to obtain the corresponding χ^v and ψ_E values. Here, S_j represents the j_{th} sub-structure of order k and type T, $^k n_t$ is the total number of subgraphs of order k and type T that can be identified in the molecular structure. Types used are path (p), cluster (c) and path-cluster (pc). A sub-graph of type p is formed by a *path*; a sub-graph of type c is formed by a *star*, while a pc sub-graph can be defined as every *tree* which is not a *path* nor a *star* (for more details see introductory concepts). Nevertheless this algorithm is unable not only to define the sum delta index but also the following dual indices.

The Dual Molecular Connectivity Indices

The dual of a Boolean expression is obtained by interchanging sums and products and interchanging zeros and ones, where zero is the identity element for sums and one is the identity element of products. In Boolean algebra $x + 0 = x$ and $x \cdot 1 = x$, are dual operations, and they define the identity laws. Two kinds of dual connectivity and pseudoconnectivity indices have been developed, the original dual (subscript d) and the soft dual indices (subscript s) (Pogliani, 2002, 2010; Garcia-Domenech, 2008). The dual indices used in the present study are,

$$^0\chi_d = (- 0.5)^N\Pi_i(\delta_i) \tag{14}$$

$$^0\psi_{Id} = (- 0.5)^N\Pi_i(I_i) \tag{15}$$

$$^1\chi_d = (- 0.5)^{(N + \mu - 1)}\Pi(\delta_i + \delta_j) \tag{16}$$

$$^1\psi_{Id} = (- 0.5)^{(N + \mu - 1)}\Pi (I_i + I_j) \tag{17}$$

$$^1\chi_s = \Pi(\delta_i + \delta_j)^{-0.5} \tag{18}$$

$$^1\psi_{Is} = \Pi (I_i + I_j)^{-0.5} \tag{19}$$

Replacing δ with δ^v in Eqs. (14), (16), and (18) the corresponding dual valence MC indices ($\chi^v_{d,s}$) are obtained. Replacing, instead, I with S in Eqs. (15), (17), and (19) the corresponding dual $\psi_{Ed,s}$ are obtained. The extension of these definitions to all other types of connectivity and pseudoconnectivity indices is straightforward. Parameter μ in eqs. (16) and (17) is the cyclomatic number (Trinajstić, 1992), which obeys the relationship: $\mu = q - N + 1$, where q is the number of edges, and N the number of vertices. This number indicates the number of cycles of a chemical graph and it is equal to the minimal number of edges necessary to be removed in order to convert the (poly)-cyclic graph to the related acyclic graph. For acyclic molecules (in graph theory represented as trees) $\mu = 0$, for monocyclic compounds $\mu = 1$ and for bicyclic compounds $\mu = 2$.

It should be noticed that the dual indices, $^0\chi_d$ and $^0\chi^v_d$, $^1\chi_d$ and $^1\chi^v_d$, as well as $^0\psi_{Id}$ and $^0\psi_{Ed}$, $^1\psi_{Id}$ and $^1\psi_{Ed}$ can give rise, depending on the number of atoms of a molecule (N) to negative values. Furthermore, $^1\chi^v_d$ but especially the rescaled $^1\psi_{Ed}$ index can give rise to quite large positive and negative values even for small compounds, which is an interesting feature for modeling purposes.

The reader may have noticed how starting with a set four MC indices, obtained from simple chemical graphs, using rather similar algorithms we have obtained a set of twenty-eight indices, which are shown in Eqs (20) and (21)

$$\{\chi\} = \{D, \, ^0\chi, \, ^0\chi_d, \, ^1\chi, \, ^1\chi_d, \, ^1\chi_s, \, \chi_t, \, D^v, \, ^0\chi^v, \, ^0\chi^v_d, \, ^1\chi^v, \, ^1\chi^v_d, \, ^1\chi^v_s, \, \chi^v_t\} \tag{20}$$

$$\{\psi\} = \{^S\psi_I, \, ^0\psi_I, \, ^0\psi_{Id}, \, ^1\psi_I, \, ^1\psi_{Id}, \, ^1\psi_{Is}, \, ^T\psi_I, \, ^S\psi_E, \, ^0\psi_E, \, ^0\psi_{Ed}, \, ^1\psi_E, \, ^1\psi_{Ed}, \, ^1\psi_{Es}, \, ^T\psi_E\} \tag{21}$$

Before closing this section on dual indices, let us notice that with special classes of compounds degeneracy among dual and non-dual indices may arise (Pogliani, 2002, 2010; Garcia-Domenech, 2008), and this happens with isomeric classes of compounds, i.e, classes whose compounds can be represented by graphs with the same number of vertices and edges, and with metal halides, whose deceptively simple graphs can be represented as two connected points: •—•.

Of all the statistical methods used to validate QSAR/QSPR studies the most important are the of the leave-one-out method with its q^2 parameter, and the use of a training and an evaluation set. The prediction coefficient for the leave-one out method is $q^2 = (SD - PRESS) / SD$, where $SD = \Sigma(y_i - \langle y \rangle)^2$ is the squared deviation of the observed value from their mean, and $PRESS = \Sigma(y_i - y_{iloo})^2$, where y_{iloo} is a predicted value of the studied property where the prediction has been made by the leave-one-out method. Another important statistical validation method is the observed vs. calculated plot and the residual plot. About the importance of plots in model studies the reader is referred to Pogliani & Julian-Ortiz, 2004, 2005; Besalu et al., 2006, 2007, 2009, 2010.

QSAR and QSPR Model of Two Different Classes of Compounds

Two sets of properties belonging to two different classes of compounds will here be modeled with the given indices. The first one concerns the partition coefficient (Log$P$) of twenty-five halocompounds in different media and the second one is a set of four properties of a highly heterogeneous class of compounds for which two new indices will be introduced.

Partition Coefficients in Different Media of Halogenated Organic Compounds

The partition coefficients of twenty-five halogenated compounds in six different media are collected in Table 3, they are taken from ref. Cargas et al., 1988 (Pogliani, 2006, 2010; Garcia-Domenech et al., 2008). Practically this is the model of six different properties of a class of compounds. Here, the K_p-$(p\text{-}odd)$ description for the core electrons shows the best model quality. Three new indices are hare used: $D_F = \Sigma_i \delta_F$, $D_{Cl} = \Sigma_i \delta_{Cl}$, and $D_{Br} = \Sigma_i \delta_{Br}$, for F, Cl, and Br atoms, respectively. They practically count the number of halogen atoms in a molecule.

Table 4 shows the r - s - q^2 values for $f_\delta^2 \neq 0$ for the complete case and for leave-10-out (those with * and + in Table 3), i.e., working with a training set of fifteen compounds. For the training choice the best descriptor for the saline, blood and liver case is $^{f2}\{^0\chi, \, ^0\psi_I, \, D_F, \, D_{Cl}\}^{po}$. Superscripts on the left and right side of a combination means the type of configuration, for instance, superscript $f2$ means that the (δ^v-based) valence MC indices

Table 3. The liquid and rat tissue air partition coefficient, LogP, in different media at 37° C, for twenty-five halocompounds

Molecule	Saline	OliveOil	Blood	Liver	Muscle	Fat
CH_3Cl	- 0.056	0.933	0.393	0.540	- 0.013	1.130
*CH_2Cl_2	0.775	2.117	1.288	1.152	0.899	2.079
+$CHCl_3$	0.529	2.604	1.318	1.324	1.143	2.307
CCl_4	- 0.456	2.573	0.655	1.152	0.657	2.555
$CH_2=CHCl$	- 0.367	1.387	0.225	0.204	0.342	1.301
$CCl_2=CH_2$	- 0.456	1.808	0.699	0.645	0.312	1.836
*$CHCl=CHCl(cis)$	0.512	2.444	1.334	1.185	0.785	2.356
+$CHCl=CHCl(tr)$	0.149	2.250	0.981	0.952	0.547	2.170
$CCl_2=CHCl$	- 0.081	2.743	1.340	1.435	1.004	2.744
$CCl_2=CCl_2$	- 0.102	3.329	1.276	1.847	1.301	3.214
CH_3-CH_2Cl	0.037	1.590	0.611	0.558	0.508	1.587
*$CHCl_2-CH_3$	0.389	2.270	1.049	1.033	0.709	2.215
+CH_2Cl-CH_2Cl	1.057	2.563	1.483	1.553	1.369	2.537
CCl_3-CH_3	- 0.125	2.470	0.760	0.934	0.498	2.420
$CHCl_2-CH_2Cl$	1.124	3.249	1.763	1.863	1.360	3.158
$CHCl_2-CHCl_2$	1.369	3.803	2.152	2.292	2.004	3.576
*CCl_3-CH_2Cl	0.548	3.429	1.620	1.945	1.597	3.332
+CH_2F_2	0.117	0.678	0.204	0.439	0.158	0.155
CH_2FCl	0.489	1.348	0.706	0.537	0.391	1.188
CH_2BrCl	0.937	2.558	1.618	1.465	1.045	2.512
CH_2Br_2	1.158	2.981	1.870	1.833	1.607	2.899
*$CF_3-CHClBr$	- 0.301	2.297	0.721	0.882	0.649	2.260
+$CH_2=CHBr$	- 0.357	1.748	0.607	0.522	0.354	1.692
CH_2Br-CH_2Cl	0.950	2.755	1.722	1.631	1.405	2.982
CF_3-CH_2Cl	- 0.377	1.380	0.104	0.265	0.090	1.326

* + Left out compounds in two different leave-out methods.

Table 4. The $F / r^2 / s$ values for the $N = 15$ and the $F / r^2 / s / q^2$ values for $N = 25$ due to $\{^{f2}\{^0\chi, \,^0\psi_P, \, D_P, \, D_{Cl}\}^{po}$

f_δ^2	Saline	Blood	Liver	Oil	Muscle	Fat
$N = 15$	9.1/0.785/0.4	25/0.910/0.2	48/0.951/0.2	96/0.974/0.1$_5$	29/0.922/0.2	281/0.992/0.1
$N = 25$	19/0.789/0.3/ 0.689	53/0.914/0.2/ 0.873	81/0.941/0.1$_5$/ 0.902	219/0.978/0.1/ 0.964	48/0.904/0.2/ 0.862	283/0.982/0.1 0.968

have been obtained with the f_δ^2 hydrogen pertur- bation, while superscript *p-odd* on the right means that these indices have been obtained with the $K_p(p\text{-}odd)$ representation for the core electrons where p = odd and q = 1 (i.e., $K_p(p\text{-}odd) / f_\delta^2$ configuration).

Figure 2 shows the obs. vs. calc. *LopP* plot and the corresponding residual plot (they are in scale) of eighty training points plus twenty exter- nal validated points (five left-out points for Log*P* in every media, with asterisk in Table 3).

The calculated points have been obtained with the following correlations vectors for indices $^{f2}\{^0\chi, {}^0\psi_P, D_F, D_{Cl}\}^{po}$. Here, in parenthesis are the utilities (the ratio between the regression coefficient and its error, c_i/s_i).

$C(\text{Bl})$ = [- 2.81203 (8.2), 3.15516 (9.9), 0.74932 (4.7), 0.10050 (1.2), 1.68496 (5.8)]

$C(\text{Liv})$ = [- 2.66129 (8.7), 2.99186 (11), 0.77664 (5.5), 0.19568 (2.7), 1.47851 (5.7)]

$C(\text{Oil})$ = [- 2.08605 (8.3), 2.85394 (12), 0.37152 (3.2), 0.03685 (0.6), 1.37054 (6.5)]

$C(\text{Fat})$ = [- 1.78911 (8.6), 2.66236 (14), 0.14340 (1.5), - 0.07069 (1.4), 1.05050 (6.0)]

Four Properties of a Class of Organic Compounds

Table 5 shows the values of four properties, which have been modeled not only by the aid of molecular connectivity, pseudoconnectivity and dual indices but also by the aid of the molar mass and of the same experimental properties in a kind of semi-empirical description (Pogliani, 2010, JCC, 2010/2011 MATCH). The observed vs. calculated plots and the residual plots have been calculated with the correlation vector C of the given descriptor, where in parenthesis are the errors of the regression parameters (not the utilities!). The model of these four properties needs the help of two new indices: $\Delta = \Sigma_{EA} n_{EA}$ and $\Sigma = \Sigma_{EA} <S_{EA}>$. The first index encodes the number of electronegative atoms (n_{EA}), while the

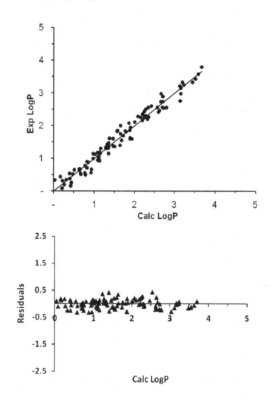

Figure 2. Model of eighty training plus twenty evaluated points of LogP in four different media (Blood, Liver, Oil, and Muscle), with combination $^{f2}\{^0\chi, {}^0\psi_P, D_P, D_{Cl}\}^{po}$

Σ index encodes the sum of the *S*-State index for the electronegative atoms: *N, O, F, Cl, Br* ($<S_{EA}>$ is the average value for a specific type of atom).

Boiling Points, T_b.
The model of this property needs also the help of an *ad hoc* AH^b 0-1 parameter to take care of the hydrogen bonding (Pogliani, 2010). The value of this ad hoc parameter is shown in parenthesis throughout the T_b column of Table 5, only when it differs from zero.

The ad hoc parameter AH^b. The model of T_b has twelve outliers, which with a descriptor with no AH^b deviate from the experimental values by 10% or even more, and they are: SO_2 (41%), DMSO (22%), dimethylether (23%), EthylenCarbonate

Table 5. Four properties of organic solvents inclusive of their molar mass, M (g·mol⁻¹): T_b, boiling points (K, in parenthesis AH^b values); RI, refractive index (20°C); d, density (at 20°C±5°C relative to water at 4°C, g/cc); ε, dielectric constant

Solvents	M	T_b	RI	d	ε
(°)Acetone	58.1	329	1.359	0.791	20.7
(°)Acetonitrile	41.05	355 (1)	1.344	0.786	37.5
Benzene	78.1	353	1.501	0.84	2.3
Benzonitrile	103.1	461	1.528	1.010	25.2
1-Butanol	74.1	391 (1)	1.399	0.810	17.1
(°)2-Butanone	72.1	353	1.379	0.805	18.5
Butyl Acetate	116.2	398	1.394	0.882	5.0
CS$_2$	76.1	319	1.627	1.266	2.6
CCl$_4$	153.8	350	1.460	1.594	2.2
Cl-Benzene	112.6	405	1.524	1.107	5.6
1Cl-Butane	92.6	351	1.4024	0.886	7.4
CHCl$_3$	119.4	334	1.446	1.492	4.8
Cyclohexane	84.2	354	1.426	0.779	2.0
(°)Cyclopentane	70.1	323	1.400	0.751	2.0
1,2-diCl-Benzene	147.0	453	1.551	1.306	9.9
1,2-diCl-Ethane	98.95	356	1.444	1.256	10.4
diCl-Methane	84.9	313	1.424	1.325	9.1
N,N-diM-Acetamide	87.1	438 (1)	1.438	0.937	37.8
N,N-diM-Formamide	73.1	426 (1)	1.431	0.944	36.7
1,4-Dioxane	88.1	374	1.422	1.034	2.2
Ether	74.1	308	1.353	0.708	4.3
Ethyl acetate	88.1	350	1.372	0.902	6.0
(°)Ethyl alcohol	46.1	351 (1)	1.360	0.785	24.3
Heptane	100.2	371	1.387	0.684	1.9
Hexane	86.2	342	1.375	0.659	1.9
2-Methoxyethanol	76.1	398 (1)	1.402	0.965	16.0
(°)Methyl alcohol	32.0	338 (1)	1.329	0.791	32.7
(°)2-Methylbutane	72.15	303	1.354	0.620	1.8
4-Me-2-Pentanone	100.2	391	1.396	0.800	13.1
2-Me-1-Propanol	74.1	381 (1)	1.396	0.803	17.7
2-Me-2-Propanol	74.1	356 (1)	1.387	0.786	10.9
DMSO	78.1	462 (2)	1.479	1.101	46.7
(°)Nitromethane	61.0	374	1.382	1.127	35.9
1-Octanol	130.2	469 (1)	1.429	0.827	10.3
(°)Pentane	72.15	309	1.358	0.626	1.8
3-Pentanone	86.1	375	1.392	0.853	17.0
(°)1-Propanol	60.1	370 (1)	1.384	0.804	20.1

continued on following page

Table 5. Continued

Solvents	M	T_b	RI	d	ε
(°)2-Propanol	60.1	356 *(1)*	1.377	0.785	18.3
Pyridine	79.1	388	1.510	0.978	12.3
tetraCl-Ethylene	165.8	394	1.506	1.623	2.3
(°)tetra-Hydrofuran	72.1	340	1.407	0.886	7.6
Toluene	92.1	384	1.496	0.867	2.4
1,1,2triCl,triFEthane	187.4	321	1.358	1.575	2.4
2,2,4-triMe-Pentane	114.2	372	1.391	0.692	1.9
o-Xylene	106.2	417	1.505	0.870	2.6
p-Xylene	106.2	411	1.495	0.866	2.3
(°)Acetic acid	60.05	391 *(1)*	1.372	1.049	6.15
Decaline	138.2	465	1.476	0.879	2.2
diBr-Methane	173.8	370	2.497	1.542	7.8
1,2-diCl-Ethylen(Z)	96.9	334	1.449	1.284	9.2
(°)1,2-diCl-Ethylen(E)	96.9	321	1.446	1.255	2.1
1,1-diCl-Ethylen	96.9	305	1.425	1.213	4.7
Dimethoxymethane	76.1	315	1.356	0.866	2.7
(°)Dimethylether	46.1	249 *(-0.5)*			5.0
Ethylen Carbonate	88.1	511 *(2)*	1.425	1.321	89.6
(°)Formamide	45.0	484 *(2)*	1.448	1.133	109
(°)Methylchloride	50.5	249 *(-0.5)*	1.339	0.916	12.6
Morpholine	87.1	402 *(1)*	1.457	1.005	7.3
Quinoline	129.2	510	1.629	1.098	9.0
(°)SO$_2$	64.1	263 *(-1)*		1.434	17.6
2,2-tetraCl-Ethane	167.8	419	1.487	1.578	8.2
tetraMe-Urea	116.2	450	1.449	0.969	23.1
triCl-Ethylen	131.4	360	1.480	1.476	3.4

(°) left-out compounds to build the training set.

(23%), Formamide (19%), and methychloride (15%), and four 10% outliers: N,N-diMe-Acetamide, N,N-diMe-Formamide, Nitromethane, and Acetonitrile. The aim of this *ad hoc* parameter is to fill the void due to the lack of detailed quantitative information about hydrogen bonds, steric, dipolar, and van der Waals interactions. Many compounds have -OH, -NH or -NH$_2$ groups which can undergo hydrogen bonding. Moreover, DMSO and SO$_2$ are rather small molecules (as well as CH$_3$-Cl and diMe-Ether) but while DMSO has a relatively high boiling point, SO$_2$, CH$_3$-Cl and diMe-Ether have a quite low boiling point. DMSO has a rather high ε values, the other three compounds, instead, show rather low ε values. Also Formamide, N,N-diMe-Acetamide, N,N-diMe-Formamide, Nitromethane, and Acetonitrile have rather high ε values. These considerations suggest to use the following set of AH^b values: for compounds with a −OH and −NH groups, a AH^b = 1 is used, for EthylenCarbonate, instead, a AH^b = 2 is used. This compound not only can undergo hydrogen bond but has three oxygen atoms and a double bond and its ε value is quite consistent.

For the small molecule Formamide with a $-NH_2$ group, a O group and with high ε value a $AH^b = 2$ is used, while for Acetonitrile, Nitromethane, N,N-diMe-Acetamide and N,N-diMe-Formamide a $AH^b = 1$ is used. For DMSO a $AH^b = 2$ is used, for SO_2 a $AH^b = -1$ is used, and for CH_3-Cl and diMe-Ether a $AH^b = -0.5$ is used. For all other compounds a $AH^b = 0$ is used. The values of this *ad hoc* parameter are shown in parenthesis in Table 5 throughout the T_b column.

The best semiempirical description belongs to the $K_p(pp\text{-}odd) / f_\delta^{50}$ configuration,

$$f^{50}\{\varepsilon, AH^b, M, D, {}^1\psi_E, \Sigma\}^{pp\text{-}odd}: N = 63, r^2 = 0.951,$$
$$s = 13, q^2 = 0.933, F = 181$$
$$C = [0.88\,(0.1), 44.1\,(4.2), 0.68\,(0.07), 26.1\,(1.9),$$
$$-295\,(31), 2.27\,(0.6), 195.2\,(7)]$$

This same descriptor shows for the training set (with no (°) items of Table 5) the following statistics: $N = 45$, $r^2 = 0.939$, $s = 14$, $q^2 = 0.802$, $F = 97$. It should be noticed that the dielectric constant is the only experimental parameter that can here be used, as it has $N = 63$. Among the six indices of the descriptor only ${}^1\psi_E$ and Σ are configuration-dependent. Figure 3 shows the quite good exp./calc. plot together with the corresponding residual plot.

The rather strong correlation, $r(D, {}^1\psi_E) = 0.97$, between the two indices should not worry too much, as explained by some authors (Mihalić et al., 1992; Peterangelo & Seybold, 2004). Nevertheless, a conceptually easy orthogonalization procedure can always be performed on the given indices (Randić, 1991).

Refractive Index, RI.

The full combinatorial technique finds the following seven-index descriptor, where the only experimental parameter that contributes to the description is the molar mass M, and where the four indices, χ_t^v, ${}^0\psi_p$, and ${}^1\psi_{Is}$ belong to the $K_p(p\text{-}odd) / f_\delta^5$ configuration,

Figure 3. The Exp./Calc. plot of T_b together with its residual plot (bottom)

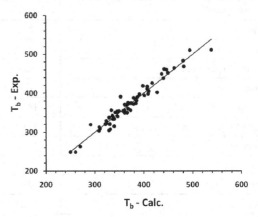

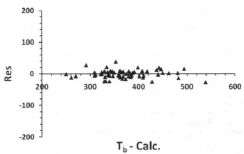

$$f^5\{M, D, {}^1\chi_s, \chi_t^v, {}^0\psi_p, {}^1\psi_{Is}, \Delta\}^{p\text{-}odd}: N = 61, r^2 = 0.944,$$
$$s = 0.04, q^2 = 0.915, F = 129$$
$$C = [0.0019\,(0.0006), 0.054\,(0.006), 0.88\,(0.1_5),$$
$$0.82\,(0.05), -0.17\,(0.02), -2.73\,(0.3), -0.043$$
$$(0.01), 1.41\,(0.03)]$$

The training test with the same descriptor (no items (°) in Table 5) shows the following results: $N = 45$, $r^2 = 0.957$), $s = 0.04$, $q^2 = 0.878$, $F = 117$. In Figure 4 are shown the exp./calc. and residual plots, which exhibit some clustering of the data around value 1.4. Such clustering of data should be avoided whenever possible (Eriksson et al., 2000). A rather strong but not excessively worrying correlation exists between two indices: $r(D, {}^0\psi_p) = 0.97$.

Figure 4. The Exp./Calc. plot of RI together with its residual plot (bottom)

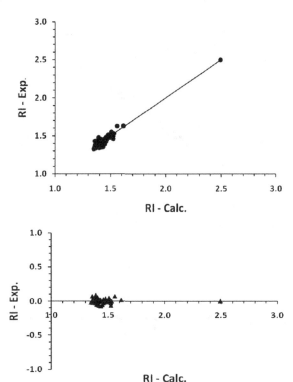

Density, d.

The model is here possible only thanks to composite indices that are the ratio of molecular connectivity indices and the molar mass.

No empirical parameters are here needed to improve the model quality. The descriptor belonging to the $K_p(pp\text{-}odd)/f_\delta^{50}$ configuration (for two composite indices only: $^S\psi_I/M$ and $^0\psi_E/M$) is,

$$^{f50}\{D/M, {}^S\psi_I/M, {}^0\psi_E/M, \Delta\}^{pp\text{-}odd}: N = 62, r^2 = 0.975,$$
$$s = 0.04, q^2 = 0.969, F = 556$$
$$C = [10.9\,(0.5), 1.72\,(0.2), -109\,(4.5), 0.05\,(0.01),$$
$$1.79\,(0.04)]$$

The training set with no (°) items has the following statistics: $N = 45$, $r^2 = 0.969$, $s = 0.05$, $q^2 = 0.960$, $F = 310$. Figure 5 displays the exp./calc. density plot and the residual plot.

Dielectric Constant, ε.

Without the strong outlier ethylencarbonate the full combinatorial search technique finds a quite good semi-empirical descriptor with eight indices. Here only the last five indices belong to the $K_p(p\text{-}odd)/f_\delta^{-0.5}$ configuration,

$$^{f\text{-}0.5}\{T_b, {}^0\chi, {}^1\chi, D^v, \chi_t^v, {}^0\psi_{Id}, {}^0\psi_E, {}^1\psi_E\}^{p\text{-}odd}: N = 62,$$
$$r^2 = 0.914, s = 5.2, q^2 = 0.835, F = 70$$

The following more compact semiempirical combination (no Ethylencarbonate) achieves a more interesting model, whose obs./calc. plot and residual plot are shown in Figure 6,

$$^{f8}\{T_b, {}^0\psi_E, T_{\Sigma M}\}^{p\text{-}odd}: N = 62, r^2 = 0.916, s = 4.9,$$
$$q^2 = 0.902, F = 210$$
$$C = [0.11\,(0.02), -8.22\,(1.5), 25.4\,(1.8), -19.9$$
$$(4.8)]$$

Figure 5. The Exp./Calc. plot of the density, d, together with its residual plot (bottom)

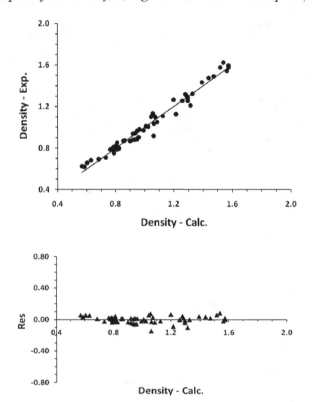

With this last descirptor the training set with no (°) compounds of Table 5 and no ethylencarbonate shows the following statistics: $N = 44$, $r^2 = 0.883$, $s = 3.7$, $q^2 = 0.846$, $F = 100$.

The composite $T_{\Sigma/M}$ term, found by trial-and-error Procedure (Pogliani, 2000), is contributed by an index and by the molar mass in the following way: $T_{\Sigma/M} = \Sigma^3/M^{1.7}$. Here both Σ and $^0\psi_E$ are $K_p(p\text{-}odd) / f_\delta^8$ configuration-dependent. Notice that the $T_{\Sigma/M}$ term encodes the information about the the molar mass but also about the overall E-State index of the electronegative atoms, i.e., it reflects the charge distribution due to these atoms, normalized to the molar mass.

CONCLUSION

The present QSAR/QSPR study with graph-theoretical centered on a vertex degree based on simple, general (or pseudograph), and complete graphs has shown the ability of the, connectivity, pseudoconnectivity and dual indices to achieve a quite good model of activities (*LogP*) in six different media and of four properties of two different and highly heterogeneous classes of compounds. The possibility to derive indices belonging to different configurations together with the introduction of pseudoconnectivity and dual indices, but also of some electrotopological indices widens the set of molecular connectivity indices to such an extent that they can cover a huge range of values from very small and negative values to very high and positive values. It has also been also shown how advantageous is

Figure 6. The Exp./Calc. plot of ε together with its residual plot (bottom)

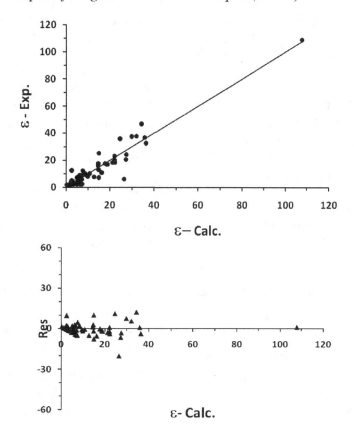

the use of experimental parameters, such as the molar mass and other experimental properties, for the derivation of semi-empirical descriptors with improved descriptive quality.

Before closing let us remind other important graph-theoretical contributions to chemistry such as the recent reviews on aromaticity (Randić, 2003; Balaban et al., 2005, 2005), and the use of graph-theoretical concepts to outline a metalanguage for thermodynamics (Pogliani, 2008, 2011).

REFERENCES

Balaban, A. T., Oniciu, D. C., & Katrizky, A. R. (2004). Aromaticity as a Cornerstone of Heterocyclic Chemistry. *Chemical Reviews, 104*, 2777–2812. doi:10.1021/cr0306790

Besalu, E. de Julian.Ortiz, J.V., Pogliani, L. (2010). On Plopts QSAR/QSPR Methodologies. In M. Putz (Ed.) *Quantum Frontiers of Atoms and Molecules in Physics, Chemistry, and Biology* (pp. 581-598). New York: Nova Publishing Inc.

Besalu, E., de Julian-Ortiz, J. V., Iglesias, M., & Pogliani, L. (2006). An Overlooked Property of Plot Methods. *Journal of Mathematical Chemistry, 39*, 475–484. doi:10.1007/s10910-005-9035-z

Besalu, E., de Julian-Ortiz, J. V., & Pogliani, L. (2006). Some Plots Are not that Equivalent. *MATCH Communications in Mathematical and Computer Chemistry, 55*, 281–286.

Besalu, E., de Julian.Ortiz, J. V., & Pogliani, L. (2007). Trends and Plot Methods in MLR Studies. *Journal of Chemical Information and Modeling, 47*, 751–760. doi:10.1021/ci6004959

Besalu, E., de Julian.Ortiz, J. V., & Pogliani, L. (2010). Ordinary and Orthogonal Regressions in QSAR/QSPR and Chemistry-Related Studies. *MATCH Communications in Mathematical and Computer Chemistry, 63*, 573–583.

Cargas, M. L., & Seybold, P.G., Andersen. (1988). M. E. Modeling the tissue solubilities and metabolic rate constant (V_{max}) of halogenated compounds. *Toxicology Letters, 43*, 235–256. doi:10.1016/0378-4274(88)90031-8

Devillers, J., & Balaban, A. T. (1999). *Topological Indices and Related Descriptors in QSAR/QSPR*. Amsterdam: Gordon and Breach.

Diudea, M. V. (Ed.). (2000). *Studies by Molecular Descriptors*. New York: Nova Science Publishing.

Eriksson, L., Johansson, E., Muller, M., & Wold, S. J. (2000). On the Selection of Training Set in Environmental QSAR when Compounds are Clustered. *Chemometrics, 14*, 599–616. doi:10.1002/1099-128X(200009/12)14:5/6<599::AID-CEM619>3.0.CO;2-8

Estrada, E. (2001). Recent advances on the role of topological indices in drug discovery research. *Current Medicinal Chemistry, 8*, 1573–1588.

García-Domenech, R., Gálvez, J., de Julián-Ortiz, J. V., & Pogliani, L. (2008). Some New Trends in Chemical Graph Theory. *Chemical Reviews, 108*, 1127–1169. doi:10.1021/cr0780006

Harary, F., & Read, R. (1977). *Proc.Graphs and Combinatorics Conference*. New York: George Washington University, Springer. Cited in, Barrow, J.D. (2000). *The Book of Nothing* (p.155). New York: Vintage Books.

Kier, L. B., & Hall, L. H. (1986). *Molecular Connectivity in Structure-Activity Analysis*. New York: Wiley.

Kier, L. B., & Hall, L. H. (1999). *Molecular Structure Description. The Electrotopological State*. New York: Academic Press.

Li, X., & Gutman, I. (2006). *Mathematical Aspects of Randić-Type Molecular Structure Descriptors. MCM 7*. Kragujevac: University of Kragujevac Press.

Mihalić, Z., Nikolić, S., & Trinajstić, N. (1992). Comparative study of molecular descriptors derived from the distance matrix. *Journal of Chemical Information and Computer Sciences, 32*, 28–37. doi:10.1021/ci00005a005

Needham, D. E., Wei, I.-C., & Seybold, P. G. (1988). Molecular modeling of the physical properties of the alkanes. *Journal of the American Chemical Society, 110*, 4186–4194. doi:10.1021/ja00221a015

Peterangelo, S. C., & Seybold, P. G. (2004). Synergistic Interactions among QSAR Descriptors. *International Journal of Quantum Chemistry, 96*, 1–9. doi:10.1002/qua.10591

Pogliani, L. (1992). Molecular Connectivity Model for Determination of Isoelectric Point of Amino Acids. *Journal of Pharmaceutical Sciences, 81*, 334–336. doi:10.1002/jps.2600810407

Pogliani, L. (2000). From Molecular Connectivity Indices to Molecular Connectivity Terms. Recent Trends in Graph Theoretical Descriptors. *Chemical Reviews, 100*, 3827–3858. doi:10.1021/cr0004456

Pogliani, L. (2002). Topics in Molecular Modeling: Dual Indices, Quality of Modeling and Missing Information, Truncation. *THEOCHEM, 581*, 87–109. doi:10.1016/S0166-1280(01)00746-1

Pogliani, L. (2004). Encoding the Core Electrons with Graph Concepts. *Journal of Chemical Information and Computer Sciences, 44*, 42–49. doi:10.1021/ci0341262

Pogliani, L. (2005). A Natural Graph-Theoretical Model for the Partition and Kinetic Coefficients. *New Journal of Chemistry, 29*, 1082–1088. doi:10.1039/b506091p

Pogliani, L. (2005). Model of Physical Properties of Halides with Complete Graph based Indices. *International Journal of Quantum Chemistry, 102*, 38–52. doi:10.1002/qua.20295

Pogliani, L. (2006). The Hydrogen Perturbation in Molecular Connectivity Computations. *Journal of Computational Chemistry, 27*, 869–882. doi:10.1002/jcc.20375

Pogliani, L. (2007). Implementing the Molecular connectivity theory, a Basic Tool in Modeling Drugs. *Journal of Pharmaceutical Sciences, 96*, 1856–1871. doi:10.1002/jps.20862

Pogliani, L. (2008). Graphs and Thermodynamics. *Journal of Mathematical Chemistry, 46*, 15–23. doi:10.1007/s10910-008-9452-x

Pogliani, L. (2010). Model of Twelve Properties of a Set of Organic Solvents with Graph-Theoretical and/or Experimental Parameters. *Journal of Computational Chemistry, 31*, 295–307.

Pogliani, L. (2010). Novel Molecular Connectivity Indices: Pseudoconnectivity, Dual, *cis-trans* Indices and Indices based on a New Valence Delta. In Gutman, I., & Furtula, B. (Eds.), *Novel Molecular Structure Descriptors - Theory and Applications I, MCM 8* (pp. 39–72). Kragujevac: University of Kragujevac Press.

Pogliani, L. (2010/2011). Two QSPR Methodologies, The Random, and The Super-Descriptors, *MATCH Commununications in Mathematical and Computer Chemistry*, in print.

Pogliani, L. (2011). The E and S Thermodynamic Directed Graphs. *International Journal of Chemical Modeling* (special issue for Eduardo Castro's anniversary), in print.

Pogliani, L., & de Julian-Ortiz, J. V. (2004). Plot Methods in Quantitative Structure-Property Studies. *Chemical Physics Letters, 393*, 327–330. doi:10.1016/j.cplett.2004.06.066

Pogliani, L., & de Julián-Ortiz, J. V. (2005). Residual plots and the quality of a model. *MATCH Communications in Mathematical and Computer Chemistry, 53*, 175–180.

Randić, M. (1975). On characterization of molecular branching. *Journal of the American Chemical Society, 97*, 6609–6615. doi:10.1021/ja00856a001

Randić, M. (1991). Resolution of ambiguities in Structure-Property studies by use of orthogonal descriptors. *Journal of Chemical Information and Computer Sciences, 31*, 311–320. doi:10.1021/ci00002a018

Randić, M. (1991). Orthogonal molecular descriptors. *New Journal of Chemistry, 15*, 517–525.

Randić, M. (2003). Aromaticity of polyciclic conjugated hydrocarbons. *Chemical Reviews, 103*, 3449–3605. doi:10.1021/cr9903656

Randić, M., & Basak, S. C. (2001). On use of the variable connectivity index $^1\chi^f$ in QSAR: toxicity of aliphatic ethers. *Journal of Chemical Information and Computer Sciences, 41*, 614–618. doi:10.1021/ci000114u

Randić, M., & Trinajstić, N. (1994). Notes on some less known early contributions to chemical graph theory. *Croatica Chemica Acta, 67*, 1–35.

Todeschini, R., & Consonni, V. (2000). *The Handbook of Molecular Descriptors*. Weinheim, Germany: Wiley-VCH.

Trinajstić, N. (1992). *Chemical graph theory* (2nd ed.). Boca Raton, FL: CRC Press.

Chapter 7
Logistic vs. W–Lambert Information in Modeling Enzyme Kinetics at Quantum Level

Mihai V. Putz
West University of Timişoara, Romania

Ana-Maria Putz
Timisoara Institute of Chemistry of Romanian Academy, Romania

ABSTRACT

The logistic temporal solution of the generalized Michaelis-Menten kinetics is employed to provide a quantum basis for the tunneling time and energy evaluations of Brownian enzymic reactions. The mono-substrate and mixed inhibition cases are treated and the associated quantum diagrams of the reaction mechanisms are depicted in terms of intermediate enzyme complexes. The methodology is suited for practically controlling of the enzymic activity throughout absorption spectroscopy.

INTRODUCTION

Although in the first century from their discover the enzymes were mainly studied for elucidation of their kinetics (Schnell & Maini, 2003), emphasising on how their structure is changed with the chemical modifications of functional groups (Hirs, 1967), or for experiencing the "forced

DOI: 10.4018/978-1-60960-860-6.ch007

evolution" (Rigby, Burleigh, & Hartley, 1974), in current years the focus was on controlling them towards biotechnological roles through the knowledge based methods such as the site-directed mutagenesis (Graham et al., 1994; Tyagi et al., 2005) or gene-shuffling techniques (Stemmer, 1994). However, aiming to create a better enzyme, with improved specificity near the "catalytic perfection" (Albery & Knowles, 1976), raises the intrinsic difficulty to rationalize a general model for its activity since the relatively poor level of comprehension about the enzyme machinery (Nixon, Ostermeier, & Benkovic, 1998). As such, deviations from classical behaviour were reported for enzymes yeast alcohol dehydrogenase (Cha, Murray, & Klinman, 1989), bovine serum amine oxidase (Grant & Klinman, 1989), monoamine oxidase (Jonsson, Edmondson, & Klinman, 1994), glucose oxidation (Kohen, Jonsson, & Klinman, 1997), or for enzyme lipoxygenase (Jonsson et al., 1996), in which it was shown that H-transfer is catalysed by quantum tunneling process. These, and other experimental (Bahnson & Klinman, 1995) and computational (Bala et al., 1996; Hwang & Warshel, 1996; Alper et al., 2001; Astumian et al., 1989; Ross et al., 2003) indications of conformational fluctuations during protein dynamics, suggested the attractive hypothesis that quantum tunneling and the enzyme catalysis are inter-correlated (Ringe & Petsko, 1999; Sutcliffe & Scrutton, 2000).

The solvent dynamics, i.e. the in vitro and in vivo conditions, and "natural breathing", i.e. the quantum fluctuations in the active site, of the enzyme molecule need to be counted in a more complete picture of enzymic catalysis. However, the quantum (fluctuating) nature of the enzymic reactions can be visualised by combining the relationship between the catalytic rate (k_{cat}) and temperature (T) (DeVault & Chance, 1966) with that between the reaction rate and the turnover number or the effective time of reaction (Δt) via Heisenberg relation

$$\frac{1}{k_{cat}} \propto \Delta t \cong \frac{\hbar}{\Delta E_{tunnelling}} = \frac{\hbar}{k_B T} \qquad (1)$$

were $\hbar$ and k_B stand for the reduced Planck and Boltzmann constants, respectively. Of course, in relation (1) the equivalence between quantum statistics and quantum mechanics was physically assumed when equating the thermal and quantum (tunneling) energies, $k_B T$ and ΔE, respec-

tively (Kleinert, Pelster, & Putz, 2002). Nevertheless, relation (1) is the basis of rethinking upon the static character of the energetic barrier, recalling the so called steady state approximation, usually assumed in describing enzymic catalysis (Laidler, 1955), within the transition state theory (TST) (Glasstone, Laidler, & Eyring, 1941).

Basically, when applied to enzymic reactions the recent developments suggest that the "textbook" TST is, at least in some situations, necessarily flawed. This because TST primarily treat the enzymes as being only particle-like entities, completely ignoring their electronic and protonic constitution when mediate chemical information-transfer when act on substrate. On contrary, as electrical insulators the proteins can transfer their electrons only by means of wave-like properties or tunneling processes. However, while electron transfer occurs at large distances, up to ca. 25Å, the same tunneling probability may be achieved by the protium (C – H group) at the distance of 0.58Å, the specific range for enzyme-substrate binding site. Such picture is sustained also by the electrostatic complementary of the catalytic site hypothesis, first suggested by Pauling (Pauling, 1946), and then refined by Marcus theory of electron transfer in chemical reactions (Marcus, 1993), stating that the dynamic fluctuations of the environment develop the driving force for that chemical reactions proceed.

Actually, the wave-particle duality of matter allows designing new pathway from reactants (enzyme E and substrate S) to products (enzyme and product P) in a Brownian enzymic reaction (Brown, 1902)

$$E + S \leftrightarrow ES \xrightarrow{\ delay\ } EP \to E + P \qquad (2)$$

by means of passing through the barrier between the ground states of enzyme-substrate (ES) and enzyme-product (EP) complexes, employing the wave-like manifestation, instead of passing over it, as the TST predict for the particle-like manifestation of enzymes, see Figure 1. In this context, the thermal activation is realized on the basis of vibrational enhancement, at its turn sustained by quantum fluctuations of the enzyme-binding substrate active site, followed by the tunneling effect. As a result, an increase in the catalytic efficiency is produced.

This quantum analysis was systematised within the vibrationally enhanced ground-state tunneling theory (VEGST) [(Bruno & Bialek, 1992), experimentally verified on reactions catalysed by the bacterial enzyme methylamine dehydrogenase (Basran, Sutcliffe, & Scrutton, 1999), despite some limitations for those enzyme in which the tunneling process acts so close to the saddle point of energy surface so that reactants passes over barrier before to penetrate it (Truhlar & Gordon, 1990).

Within this framework, the quest of analytical recovering of the tunneling effect is in the current work envisaged through generalizing the classical enzyme kinetics. The present strategy relies on employing the progress curves of the substrate to provide the fluctuation time, and consequently the needed tunneling energy, that assures the intrinsic motor of the enzyme catalyzed reactions. The degree with which the present venture produces a viable conceptual and computational basis to address the quantum control of the enzyme activity is discussed in various catalytic circumstances.

THE THEORETICAL MODEL

W-Lambert Enzyme Kinetics

Traditionally, the baseline mechanism of the enzyme kinetics was initially proposed by Henri (1901), followed by Michaelis and Menten (1913), assuming that when an enzyme acts upon a sub-

Figure 1. Reaction coordinate representation for a Brownian enzyme-catalyzed reaction (2) while molecular vibrations of the reactive substrate and enzyme-substrate complex are superimposed on the energy profile for the reaction. Tunneling of the vibrational states of active site of substrate becomes most favourable within the enzyme-substrate complex (ES) leading with the penetration of the enzyme-product complex (EP) curve below the classical transition state at the saddle-point of the potential energy profile.

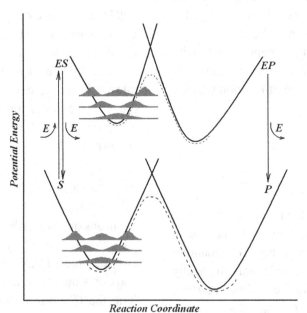

strate the complex ES is formed which in turn is converted into a product and enzyme (Rubinow, 1975; Cantor & Schimmel, 1980; Murray, 1990; Voet & Voet, 1995; Copeland, 2000; Ross, Schreiber, & Vlad, 2006)

$$E + S \underset{k_{-1}}{\overset{k_1}{\rightleftharpoons}} ES \xrightarrow{k_2} E + P \tag{3}$$

That is, the *EP* intermediate enzyme complex of the Brownian reaction (2) was hidden within the *ES* complex. Such simplification leads to the somehow forced idea that *ES* itself undergo to transition state *ES**, on which, afterwards, the differential TS stabilization had to be accounted in order to assure the reaction barrier lowering (Kędzierski et al., 2004). In fact, the stabilization of the *ES* complex, through his associated (thermally) activated state *ES**, was analytically solved by considering the so called quasi-steady-state-approximation (QSSA) by imposing the extreme condition $d[ES] / dt \approx 0$ be fulfilled (Segel & Slemrod, 1989). From kinetic point of view, such phase can be attained when the initial concentration of substrate molecule is in great excess of the free enzyme concentration, i.e. $[S]_0 = \varepsilon^{-1}[E]_0$, $10^{-7} < \varepsilon < 10^{-2}$. From the present quantum-mechanically perspective, this condition assures the proper time necessary the quantum tunneling from *ES* to *EP* be produced, according with the generalized mechanism in Figure 1.

However, being the *EP* state absorbed in the *ES* one in the mechanism (3) also the allied kinetics, the so called Michaelis-Menten kinetics (Michaelis & Menten, 1913; Cantor & Schimmel, 1980; Voet & Voet, 1995; Copeland, 2000)

$$-\left(\frac{d[S]}{dt}\right)^{MM} = \frac{V_{max}[S]}{K_M + [S]} \tag{4}$$

with maximum velocity of the uptake and the Michaelis constants parameters, $V_{max} = k_2[E]_0, K_M = \left(k_{-1} + k_2\right)/k_1$, respec-

tively, despite having included the QSSA, it virtually suffers from incompleteness regarding the considering the formation of the enzyme-product complex. Nevertheless, we have to mention that distributed differential delay mechanisms in enzyme-substrate reactions were studied (Hinch & Schnell, 2004), however, with the conclusion that multiple intermediate complexes may be equivalent to a distributed delay system without complexes. In other terms, even the Michaelis-Menten equation (3) may be further simplified, and reduced to

$$E + S \xrightarrow{delay} P + E \tag{5}$$

the price results in even more delay for the $S \rightarrow P$ conversion. This picture can be regard as the natural hierarchy from the quantum effects to the semiclassical and classical approximations. In other words, as more equivalence is considered in enzyme mechanism as the classical degree of analysis will increase.

With all these consideration the Michaelis-Menten mechanism (3) may be considered as a semiclassical one between the quantum Brownian (2) and the classical resumed (5) one. It may, however, serve as the most useful basis of the actual developments.

Firstly, we have to quote that, despite the challenging task of integration of the differential rate equation (4) in an explicitly manner, a rather accurate analysis of the progress curves of the enzyme-catalyzed reactions have been produced with numerical integration procedures (Huang & Niemann, 1951; Jennings & Niemann, 1953; Jennings & Niemann, 1955; Duggleby & Morrison, 1977; Duggleby & Morrison, 1978; Duggleby & Morrison, 1979; Duggleby, 1986; Duggleby & Wood, 1989; Boeker, 1984; Boeker, 1985; Boeker, 1987; Varón et al., 1997; Yago et al., 2006; Yeow et al., 2004] until the discovery of the closed-form solution (Schnell & Mendoza, 1997; Schnell & Mendoza, 2000a; Schnell & Mendoza, 2000b;)

by the aid of W-Lambert function. The so called W-Lambert enzyme kinetics can be revealed by the direct time integration of the Michaelis-Menten equation (4) leading with the intermediate form

$$-tV_{max} = K_M \ln[S] - K_M \ln[S]_0 + [S] - [S]_0$$

(6)

Now, although solved with ingenious numerical schemes, the equation (6), due to its transcendent nature, was not analytically explicated until Schnell and Mendoza recognized its similitude with the basic definition of the W-Lambert function $W(x)$ (Corless et al., 1996)

$$W(x)e^{W(x)} = x \ , \ x \geq -1/e$$

(7)

By appropriate, however straight, rearrangement of equation (7) until the form (6) is reached the substrate W-Lambert solution (8) easily followed

$$[S](t)^W =$$
$$K_M W\left(\frac{[E]_0}{\varepsilon K_M} \exp\left(\frac{[E]_0}{\varepsilon K_M}\right) \exp\left(-\frac{tV_{max}}{K_M}\right)\right)$$

(8)

nevertheless in an closed form, i.e. with an implicit dependency on time. This can be easily see while trying to solve (7) for $W(x)$. At the first step one gets

$$W(x) = \ln\left(x / W(x)\right)$$

(9)

while through successive repeating of the procedure it arrives at the infinite continuous fraction

$$W(x) =$$
$$\ln\frac{x}{\ln\left(W(x)\right)} = \ln\frac{x}{\ln\dfrac{x}{\ln\left(W(x)\right)}} = \ldots = \ln\frac{x}{\ln\dfrac{x}{\ln\dfrac{x}{\ln\dfrac{x}{\ln\dfrac{x}{\ddots}}}}}$$

(10)

In other words, W-Lambert solution (8) has no finite closed form solution. About W-function worth mentioning that bears Lambert name due to the quotation of Euler (1779), being then only in the second half of the XX century reloaded (Corless et al., 1996; Wright, 1959; Fritsch, Shafer, & Crowley, 1973; Barry et al., 2000; Barry, Culligan-Hensley, & Barry, 1995). It surprisingly lead with appropriate modelling of natural complex systems, among which application to water movement in soil (Barry et al., 1993), enzyme-substrate reactions (Goudar, Sonnad, & Duggleby, 1999), population growth (Corless et al., 1996), disease spreading (Corless et al., 1996), or herbivore-plant coexistence (Hambäck, 1998), are just a few of them with biological impact.

Logistic Enzyme Kinetics

Since it is well understood that the W-Lambert solution (8) have no analytical expression, despite progress curves can be analyzed numerically to any desired degree of precision (Goudar, Sonnad, & Duggleby, 1999; Duggleby, 2001; Câteau & Tanaka, 2002; Goudar et al., 2004), the Michaelis-Menten equation (4) may be still solved by further generalization into what we may call the logistic enzyme kinetics, with the working form (Putz, Lacrămă, & Ostafe, 2006; Putz & Lacrămă, 2007; Putz, Lacrămă, & Ostafe, 2007; Lacrămă, Putz, & Ostafe, 2008; Putz, 2011)

$$-\left(\frac{d[S]}{dt}\right)^{Log} = V_{max}\left(1 - e^{-\frac{[S]}{K_M}}\right)$$

(11)

The advancement of introducing this new enzymic kinetics can be proved in two steps. Once is simply revealed since it recovers the Michaelis-Menten equation (3) as first order approximation

$$-\left(\frac{d[S]}{dt}\right)^{Log} \overset{[S]\to 0}{\cong} V_{\max}\left(1-\frac{1}{1+\dfrac{[S]}{K_M}}\right) = -\left(\frac{d[S]}{dt}\right)^{MM}$$

(12)

at the end of enzymatic reactions, i.e. when the substrate depletion is almost complete. This means that for the intermediate kinetic phase, i.e. when QSSA applies, we assured a richer internal kinetics of the intermediate *ES* complex. Beside this, the direct integration of the logistic rate equation (11) furnishes a complete analytical solution

$$[S](t)^{Log} =$$
$$K_M \ln\left(1+\left(\exp\left(\frac{[E]_0}{\varepsilon K_M}\right)-1\right)\exp\left(-\frac{V_{\max}}{K_M}t\right)\right)$$

(13)

Going to emphasize on logistics vs. W-Lambert enzyme kinetics difference one may firstly note that, despite having no published tables of $W(x)$ numerical evaluations give rises to the plot depicted in Figure 2-(a) from where we see that it can be divided in three branches, from which only the so called principal ones, W_0^+ and W_0^-, are relevant for enzyme kinetics since the maximum velocity and Michaelis-Menten constants in (8) are either both positive or negative (Hayes, 2005) through furnishing values of *W*-function greater than −1.

Most notably, albeit the W-function departs considerably from the elementary logarithm, see Figure 2-(a), once the enzymatic W-solution (8) is transformed in the associated logistical one (13) one, through the generalized ansatz

$$f_1 W\left(f_2 \exp^{f_2}\exp^{-f_3 t}\right) \to f_1 \ln\left(1+\left(\exp^{f_2}-1\right)\exp^{-f_3 t}\right)$$

(14)

their progress curves becomes both similar and approaching each other, see Figure 2-(b), from where the main text idea to consider their difference in simulating the quantum fluctuations of the substrate progress curve. On mathematical side, the spread use of the W-function had lead with the debates on whether it will be the next elementary function is considered (Hayes, 2005). In some sense it is considered as "the simplest example of the root of an exponential polynomial...the next simplest class of functions after polynomials" (Corless & Jeffrey, 2002). However, on this matter worth meditating in the future whether the enzymatic type of correspondence (14) may add new insight on the issue of the possible replacement of the W-function (and of exponential polynomials) by elementary functions.

For the reason that the substrate logistic solution (13) lies enough closely to above the W-Lambert counterpart, for many enzymatic circumstances, see below, we may consider it as the substrate-binding-enzyme solution which is counting of the $ES \to EP$ intra-conversion. Formally, if we associate W-Lambert $[S](t)^W$ solution with the Michaelis-Menten kinetics (3), i.e. involving *ES* as the intermediate complex only, and the logistic $[S](t)^{Log}$ solution with the Brownian kinetics (2), involving both *ES* and *EP* as intermediate complexes, we may expect that their difference will generate the tunneling effects, in terms of time and energy, assisting the quantum fluctuations of *ES* that transforms it in *EP*. Nevertheless, this difference has to be employed on a physical background so that the quantum control of the enzymic reactions is assured. Next section will reveal such procedure.

Quantum Enzyme Catalysis

Searching for suitable markers to screen the new biomaterials for adverse effects in cell and tissues (e.g. overt toxicity causing cell death around an implant, chronic inflammatory reactions due to the neoplastic changes, or undergoing degradation

Figure 2. (a) Representation of the branches of W-Lambert function, $W_0^+(x)$, $W_0^-(x)$, and $W_{-1}(x)$, and of the logarithm function, respectively. (b) Comparison between W-Lambert (thin line) and logistic (dashed line) kinetics, according with the left and right sides of transformation (14), respectively, together with their difference (thick line) on an arbitrary temporal scale.

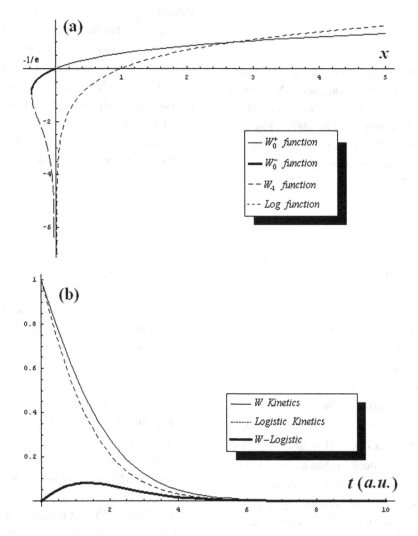

of the material in vivo) the enzymes' activity has been found to be the most reliable because their catalytic properties are sensitively affected by exposure to a biomaterial. Accordingly, the biophysical chemistry analysis of cell fractions from tissue culture experiments by the enzyme-linked immunoassays (ELISAs) or spectrophotometry techniques provides exact quantisation of the released enzymes as an accurate measure of cell membrane integrity and cell viability (Willams, 1986; Allen & Rushton, 1994).

In this respect, we can make use of the unique feature of absorption spectroscopy as an experimental controlling tool since the substrate time dependent concentration, which entirely follow the course of an enzymatic reaction, can be related with the absorbance of the substrate molecules (at a particular wavelength) through the adapted Beer-Lambert law (Cantor & Schimmel, 1980)

$$A_S(t) = a_M l[S](t) \tag{15}$$

where l is the path length of the sample traversed by the light beam while a_M stands for the molar absorptivity as an intrinsic constant of the substrate molecule. However, considering the free substrate absorption

$$A_0 = a_M l[S]_0 \tag{16}$$

we can deal, for convenience, with the normal absorptivity of the substrate defined

$$a_S(t) = \frac{A_S(t)}{A_0} = \frac{[S](t)}{[S]_0} \tag{17}$$

At this point we can employ the associate absorbance progress curves for substrate (or for the product) when the W-Lambert or logistic solutions (8) or (13) are implemented, respectively. The starting point consists in writing of the normal absorbance for the product in the same way as for the substrate (17)

$$a_P(t) = \frac{A_P(t)}{A_0} = \frac{[P](t)}{[S]_0} \tag{18}$$

Then, the link with the substrate concentration is made through combining the free substrate and enzyme conservation equations

$$[S]_0 = [S](t) + [ES](t) + [P](t) \tag{19}$$

$$[E]_0 = [E](t) + [ES](t) \tag{20}$$

with the Michaelis-Menten constant viewed as the dynamic dissociation constant

$$K_M = \frac{[E](t)[S](t)}{[ES](t)} \tag{21}$$

of the first part of the reaction (3) (Cantor & Schimmel, 1980; Voet & Voet, 1995).

With appropriate substitutions of relations (19)-(21) in (18) the normal absorption curve for product takes the expression

$$a_P(t) =$$
$$1 - a_S(t) - \frac{\varepsilon[S](t)}{[S](t) + K_M}, \ 10^{-7} < \varepsilon \equiv \frac{[E]_0}{[S]_0} < 10^{-2} \tag{22}$$

While the parameter ε fixes the in vivo to in vitro regimes as it decreases to zero the product's normal absorbance can be approximated as

$$a_P(t) \cong 1 - a_S(t) \tag{23}$$

this way providing the quasi-equivalence of the absorption differences

$$\Delta a(t) = a_S^W(t) - a_S^{Log}(t) \cong a_P^{Log}(t) - a_P^W(t) \tag{24}$$

when the W-Lambert and logistic expressions in substrate calculation is employed.

Next, for making an idea on how the enzyme-substrate and enzyme-product complexes information are encoded within the W-Lambert and logistic time dependent substrate solutions, in Figure 3 their associated absorbance curves together with the absorption differences of (24) for a trial enzymatic reaction are simulated. At first sight, as expected, there are no significant differences between the W-Lambert and logistical plots of normal absorption of substrate depletion and product formation in various enzymic environment, from the in vitro, when $\varepsilon \in (10^{-6}, \ 10^{-4})$, to the in vivo conditions, when $\varepsilon \geq 10^{-2}$. As a note, there is observed that as the in vivo conditions are approached, substrate catalysis begins earlier, with an increase in the actual time of the enzymatic reaction by which the substrate becomes the product.

Figure 3. The first two rows show the normal absorptions for substrate (continuous curves) and product (dashed curves) concentrations of the enzyme-catalyzed reaction without inhibition, based on the logistical temporal approximation, and on the W-Lambert temporal solution, respectively; the third row depicts the difference between W-Lambert and logistical counterpart for substrate or product normal absorption progress curves; on the columns, the plots are presented for the enzyme/substrate ratio ε taking the in vitro and almost the in vivo values, from 10^{-6} to 10^{-4} and equal or greater than 10^{-2}, respectively; the employed kinetic parameters are the maximum velocity of enzyme reaction $V_{max}=10^{-4}M\cdot s^{-1}$ and the Michaelis constant $K_M=2\cdot10^{-4}M$, while the total enzyme concentration is set at $[E]_0=10^{-6}M$; the time infinite range has been mapped onto the interval $(0,1)$ with the aid of the exponential time scale $\tau=1-1/\ln(t+e)$, being expressed in arbitrary units (a.u.) (Putz & Lacrămă, 2007).

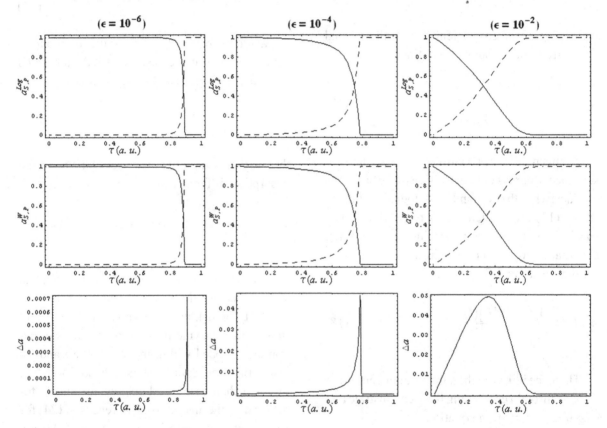

Nevertheless, when about the absorbance differences a clear signal over the time interval of the enzymatic reaction in the third row of Figure 3 is detected. This stands as the computational proof that considering the logistic kinetics and its substrate solution the difference respecting the classical Michaelis-Menten one is transposed at the spectroscopic level in small (however important for tunneling) difference of substrate or product concentration that is engaged or emerged, respectively, throughout of the energetic barrier of the enzyme-transition state complex, see Figure 4-(a), leading with consequent activation of whole reaction.

Worth noting that the product's difference in (24), namely $\Delta a(t) \cong a_P^{Log}(t) - a_P^{W}(t)$, , gives the best visualisation of how the logistic solution comprise the difference information over W-

Figure 4. (a) Illustration of the tunneling process and energy between the intermediate complexes ES and EP across the enzyme-transition state complex. (b) Diagram of the energy levels of the Brownian enzyme-catalyzed reaction $E+S \leftrightarrow ES \rightarrow EP \rightarrow E+P$ by means of the intermediate enzyme-complexes, $\left| ES \right\rangle$ and $\left| EP \right\rangle$, separated by the tunneling energy of reaction ΔE^{00}. All the reactants, enzyme (E), substrate (S), and product (P), and the intermediate molecular complexes (ES, EP) are depicted by their symbolic representations. The arrows in the diagrams indicate the final direction of the reactions they refer to.

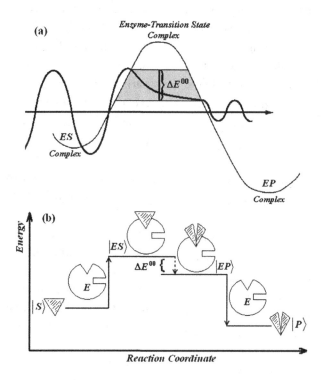

Lambert counterpart solution, that information that characterizes the *EP* complex against the *ES* in the course of transition-state stabilization through tunneling.

Putted different, given that we can define the effective time of reaction as the width at the half height of the recorded signal $\Delta a(t)$, the difference absorption (24) provides the predicted effective time of reaction Δt and the turnover number – the catalytic rate, as estimated from the first part of the chain relation (1). As well, the estimate of the tunneling energy ΔE^{00}, which makes the enzymic reaction proceeding according with the Brownian mechanism of (2) and Figure

1, also follows from the Heisenberg relation in (1).

This way, we faced with two new perspectives of enzymic kinetics.

Firstly, we showed that the quantum fluctuation and tunneling may be simulated when among the Michaelis-Menten also the logistic kinetics and its solution is considered, a feature confirmed by applying the Beer-Lambert law of absorption spectroscopy. Such picture is in accordance with the observed enhanced rate of the vibrationally states of *ES* by means of quantum tunneling when considered within the Brownian mechanism (2) and Figure 1.

Secondly, we have the opportunity to design new energy diagrammatic representation of the enzyme catalysis at the quantum level. For that worth noting that, as a catalyst, enzyme molecule is found at the end of reaction unaffected respecting its initial free status. This characteristic permits assimilating enzyme with the "photon role" in quantum absorption and emission processes. Then, we can consider the molecular ground states of all involved species and representing them with the associate eigen-energies while the eigen-states will be appropriately symbolised, within Dirac notation, as $|S\rangle$, $|ES\rangle$, $|EP\rangle$, and $|P\rangle$ for the free substrate, enzyme-substrate complex, enzyme-product complex, and free product, respectively.

With these, and taking account of quantum tunneling process and energy, in Figure 4-(b) the resulted quantum enzymic diagram of the Brownian mechanism (2) is depicted. Such diagrams are qualitatively different by the ordinary thermodynamic ones (Copeland, 2000) having the advantage of considering all TS information in tunneling energies, thus providing a clear overlook of the course of enzyme reaction and of associate mechanism.

From the experimental point of view, the present algorithm may prescribe the quantum control of the enzymatic activity through absorption, while the computational simulation may indicate the time range of the type spectroscopy to be used, from pressure and temperature jumps to the electron paramagnetic resonance and electric field jumps, depending on the output of the tunneling times fixing the fast-reaction ranges (Cantor & Schimmel, 1980).

The actual model can also be extended to the cases when different types and degrees of enzymatic inhibition are considered leading with important effects of biological regulations as will be in next exposed.

APPLICATION TO MIXED INHIBITION

The developed theory of allosteric regulation (from Greek: *allos*, other + *stereos*, space) prescribes that, within a cooperative interaction, the binding of one ligand (substrate) at a specific site is influenced by the binding of another ligand (inhibitor) at a different or allosteric site on the protein (or enzyme). However, actually, such behaviour is generalized at the level of organism and cellular regulation in which the cell converts the comparison of the proteins with organisms needs into metabolic process. It follows that the proteins and gene expression are far from being the endpoint but a bridge from where the process of editing RNA transcripts begins, altering and maintaining the genome, over and over again by signalling other cells or bio-inspired nano-implants (Goodman, Bellato, & Khidr, 2005; Hartwell, 2005). In this process of cell differentiation, proliferation, and programming, the receptors (substrates and inhibitors) and enzymes play the role of molecular messengers. Therefore, studying the effects of the inhibitors on the enzymatic reactions, here at the theoretical level, should be most valuable for the forefront of biomedical researches.

Figure 5 displays the main types of allosteric interactions involving enzymes. Main point of the presented scheme is introduction into the reaction a further ligand called inhibitor, *I*, which interacts with enzyme *E* leading to form *EI* while the *ES* complex also interacts with I giving the intermediate complex *ESI*. The discrimination on the degree with which the favourite formation is that of the complex *EI* rather than that of *ESI* one fixes the type of inhibition.

The *competitive inhibition*, quantified by the parameter $\alpha = \left([E] + [EI]\right) / [E]$, appears when the inhibitor has a molecular structure analogue to that of the substrate and binds with the enzyme on this complementarity ground. Typical examples are the anti-metabolites, e.g. the sulphanilamide as the competitive antagonist of the para-amino-

Figure 5. Symbolic representation of the competitive and uncompetitive inhibitions acting through the inhibitor (I) on the enzyme (E) or on enzyme-substrate complex (ES), being quantified by parameters α and α' respectively, adjacent to the baseline Michaelis-Menten reaction E+S↔ES→E+P (Putz & Lacrămă, 2007)

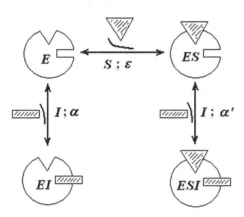

benzoic acid (known as the H-vitamin), which display bacterio-static effects due to the blocking of microorganisms growth and multiplication. On the other way, when the inhibitor is acting upon the enzyme-substrate complex the *uncompetitive inhibition* type, quantified by the parameter $\alpha' = ([ES] + [ESI]) / [ES]$, regulates the enzymatic catalysis. This situation is specific to the in vivo occasions when, for instance, the adenosine three phosphatase inhibitor blocks the enzymes of glycol so controlling the energetic release in cell. However, mixed inhibitions can also appear since both competitive and uncompetitive inhibitions take place in the course of complex biosynthesis.

With these, the basic Michaelis-Menten equation (4) is reconsidered with the kinetic parameters of the mono-substrate reactions (2) and (3) become $V_{\max}^{mixed} = (1 / \alpha') V_{\max}^{mono}$ and $K_M^{mixed} = (\alpha / \alpha') / K_M^{mono}$, for the maximum velocity of reaction and the Michaelis-Menten constant, respectively (Voet & Voet, 1995).

In these conditions, the actual working forms for the W-Lambert and logistic substrate solutions can be immediately generalized from the expressions (8) and (13) to be:

$$[S](t)^W =$$
$$\frac{\alpha}{\alpha'} K_M W \left(\frac{\alpha'[E]_0}{\alpha \varepsilon K_M} \exp \left(\frac{\alpha'[E]_0}{\alpha \varepsilon K_M} \right) \exp \left(-\frac{t V_{\max}}{\alpha K_M} \right) \right)$$
(25)

$$[S]^{Log}(t) =$$
$$\frac{\alpha}{\alpha'} K_M \ln \left(1 + \left(\exp \left(\frac{\alpha'[E]_0}{\alpha \varepsilon K_M} \right) - 1 \right) \exp \left(-\frac{V_{\max}}{\alpha K_M} t \right) \right)$$
(26)

Actually, the quantum enzyme mechanisms of the mixed reactions from Figure 5 are driven by the tunneling times and energies prescribed by the difference between the absorptions induced by the solutions (25) and (26). This picture represents the natural generalization of the Brownian enzyme reaction (2) to include the allosteric effects.

Going to simulate the quantum fluctuations appeared in mixed enzyme catalysis of Figure 5 the absorption difference curves (24) are computed, in various in vitro-to-in vivo mixed inhibition combinations, with the results in Figure 6 displayed.

By comparing the plots of the Figure 6 with those corresponding to the no inhibition case (00) of Figure 3, the hierarchy of the tunneling times for competitive (α0), uncompetitive (0α'), and mixed (αα') Brownian reactions is worked out:

$$\Delta \tau^{0\alpha'} < \Delta \tau^{\alpha \alpha'} < \Delta \tau^{00} < \Delta \tau^{\alpha 0}, \varepsilon \in \left(10^{-6}, 10^{-4} \right)$$
(27)

$$\Delta \tau^{\alpha 0} < \Delta \tau^{\alpha \alpha'} < \Delta \tau^{00} < \Delta \tau^{0\alpha'}, \varepsilon \geq 10^{-2}$$
(28)

Figure 6. Differences between W-Lambert and logistical counterparts for substrate or product normal absorption progress curves; on the columns, the plots are presented for the enzyme/substrate ratio ε taking the in vitro and almost the in vivo values, from 10⁻⁶ to 10⁻⁴ and equal or greater than 10⁻², respectively; on rows different competitive and uncompetitive inhibition combinations quantified by the α and α' parameters, taking the values equal with 1 and 20, are respectively considered; the employed kinetic parameters and temporal scales are the same as used in Figure 3(Putz & Lacrămă, 2007)

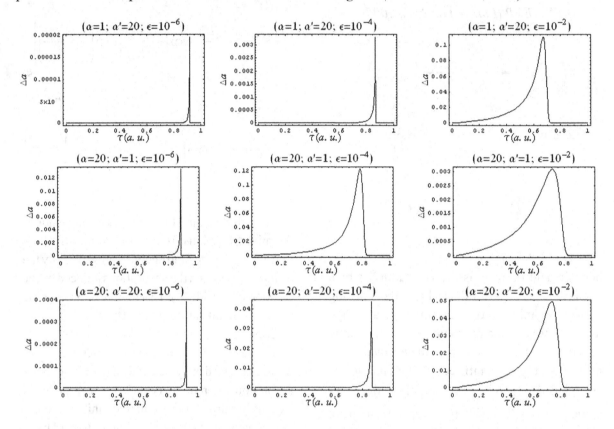

for the in vitro and in vivo environments, respectively, while for the tunneling energies for the associated enzyme-transition state complexes the pecking orders of (27) and(28) are reversed:

$$\Delta E^{0\alpha'} > \Delta E^{\alpha\alpha'} > \Delta E^{00} > \Delta E^{\alpha 0}, \varepsilon \in \left(10^{-6}, 10^{-4}\right)$$
(29)

$$\Delta E^{\alpha 0} > \Delta E^{\alpha\alpha'} > \Delta E^{00} > \Delta E^{0\alpha'}, \varepsilon \geq 10^{-2}$$
(30)

due to the spectroscopic Heisenberg relation in (1).

With these results, we may build the quantum diagrams for the considered types of enzymic reactions by employing the following conceptual-computational algorithm. Firstly, as already considered in treating the mono-substrate case without inhibition, two general rules are considered:

1. the enzyme assume the "photon role", as before, since as a catalysis enters and outs unaffected, i.e. caring the same amount of energy in and out of the reaction;

2. all other involved molecular complexes, including intermediates, are considered in their ground state and represented by their Dirac-ket vector $|\bullet\rangle$;

while for the particular in vivo-in vitro competitive-uncompetitive cases the next particular rules apply:

3. the non inhibited transition state $\left| ES \right\rangle$ is always placed between inhibited intermediary complexes, $\left| EI \right\rangle$ and $\left| ESI \right\rangle$, as conceptually revealed from the Figure 7;

4. the energy of inhibitor state $\left| I \right\rangle$ is presumably higher in vivo than in vitro, as compared with the energy level of substrate $\left| S \right\rangle$, due to the crowding of the in vivo environment;

5. competitive inhibition is firstly considered, due to the direct attack on the enzyme;

6. consequently, the states $\left| EI \right\rangle$ and $\left| ES \right\rangle$ are coexisting and undergo quantum combination in a mixed new intermediary state $\left| EI \right\rangle \otimes \left| ES \right\rangle$;

7. the uncompetitive inhibited state $\left| ESI \right\rangle$ is obtained from the state $\left| ES \right\rangle$ so that the (iii) rule above is complied with;

8. when both competitive $\left| EI \right\rangle \otimes \left| ES \right\rangle$ and uncompetitive $\left| ESI \right\rangle$ states are present, they further combine and the new mixed intermediary quantum $\left| EI \right\rangle \otimes \left| ES \right\rangle \otimes \left| ESI \right\rangle$ state arises, which always has to lay above the $\left| ES \right\rangle$ one;

9. all new inhibited intermediary states decay on the same $\left| EP \right\rangle$ state as in the case of no-inhibition (00);

10. it follows that the energetic differences as compared with the no-inhibition case are due to the tunneling induced by the inhibited transition states which regulate the delayed times of mixed catalysis.

These rules can be phenomenologically visualised in diagrams of Figure 7, in full agreement with the computational tunneling energies of equations (29) and (30) for the in vitro and in vivo Brownian enzymic reactions, respectively.

An interesting fact is that the no-inhibition case always lies between mixed and some particular case of inhibition, without being at the end sides of the energetic chains of (29) and (30), as should roughly be presumed. Another observation regards the fact that the competitive and uncompetitive inhibitions change their dominant role in passing from the in vitro to the in vivo circumstances.

While the in vitro cases are regulated by the uncompetitive fast reactions in which the transition state is tunnelled with a considerable energetic stabilization decay until the competitive slow catalysis with a small energetic width of tunneling of the enzyme-transition states – see relations (27) and (29), within the in vivo cases the order of times and energetic widths tunneling is vice versa for inhibition regulation situations – see the relations (28) and (30).

The present general discussion may serve for practical estimates of temporal scales of tunneling when controlling the enzymatic activity (with inhibition) at the spectroscopic level. It can also be extended in the line of quantum computation of the conditional probability of the altered heritable gene expression from the product formation by delays in proteomic and enzymic interactions. However, this field of investigation is just opening now and requires much synergetic work to asses the future quantum theory of enzymic reactions.

CONCLUSION

From the discovery of the quantum principles and the elucidation subsequent limitation of knowledge through measurements no molecular science that attempts be analytical is not complete until acquires a certain degree of quantum comprehension. While standard enzymology was based on studying how the enzymes facilitates the passage

Figure 7. Quantum in vitro (a) and in vivo (b) energetic diagrams of the generalized Brownian enzyme-catalyzed reaction E+S↔ES→EP→E+P in the presence of the inhibitor (I) acting competitively on the enzyme (E), uncompetitively on enzyme-substrate complex (ES), or by mixed competition on both the enzyme and enzyme-substrate (the thin lines of mechanisms), in relation with the no inhibition case (the thick lined mechanism), providing the tunneling time of specific reaction and the associated tunneling energies of formed enzyme-transition state complexes, $\Delta E^{\alpha 0}$, $\Delta E^{0\alpha}$, $\Delta E^{\alpha\alpha'}$, and ΔE^{00}, respectively. The arrows in the diagrams indicate the final direction of the reactions they refer to (Putz & Lacrămă, 2007)

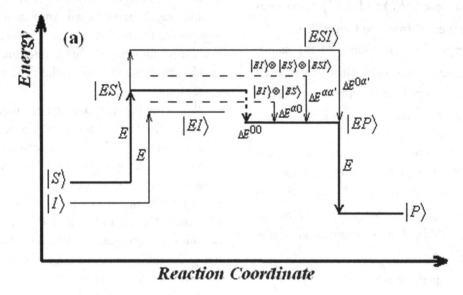

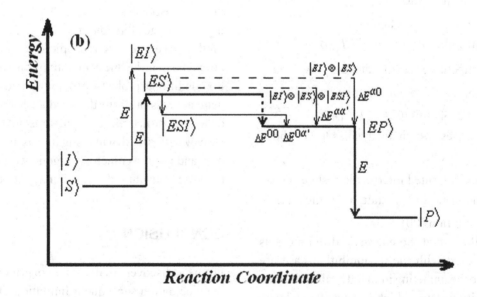

of a reaction over a static potential-energy barrier, with the new millennium mankind exploitation of the biological catalyst the quantum tunneling and the quantum fluctuation effects of the protein dynamics provides the alternative hypothesis that the enzyme activation is produced through rather than over the enzyme transition state.

In this context, the present work proposes a way of simulating the quantum fluctuation by supplementing the basic Michaelis-Menten kinetic and of its temporal W-Lambert solution with its logistical extension and solution. Beside the fact that the proposed logistic kinetics furnishes an analytical exact temporal solution for the substrate depletion it provides also the way of computing the tunneling time and energy for a given enzymic reactions. It leaves also with the possibility of drawing of a quantum diagram for the concerned enzymic mechanism.

That is, once the classical Michaelis-Menten is solved until its W-Lambert closed form the associate logistical temporal solution can be immediately draw by a simple correspondence rule, see (14). The conceptual richness of the actual approach resides on the fact that the Michaelis-Menten kinetics was proved be recovered in the first order expansion of the logistical one respecting the substrate depletion. Such behaviour supports the further assumption that the Brownian mechanism may be modelled by logistical temporal solution while the Michaelis-Menten by the W-Lambert temporal closed form. Nevertheless, considering the molecular picture of the involved reactants, the difference between the two substrate temporal solutions provides also the computation basis from extracting the temporal range of tunneling throughout their absorbance progress curves. Then, the involving of the Heisenberg spectroscopic relation gives out also the tunneling energies. With all these the quantum diagram for the studied enzyme mechanism is revealed, in which the enzyme plays the "photonic" role

that activates the whole reaction and drives the combined intermediate complexes.

The present algorithm was explored on the mono-substrate enzymic catalysis and extended for the inhibition mixed cases, both for the in vitro and in vivo environments. It can be further applied on more complex enzyme and proteomic combinations and suitable linked with real experimental data following the same line of analysis since the recursive feature of the presented algorithm and the close connection with the enzymatic activity through the spectroscopic absorption method.

ACKNOWLEDGMENT

This work appears in the framework of the research project <Quantification of The Chemical Bond Within Orthogonal Spaces of Reactivity. Applications on Molecules of Bio-, Eco- and Pharmaco- Logical Interest>, Code CNCS-UEFISCDI (former CNCSIS-UEFISCSU) TE16/2010-2011/ PN II-RU-TE-2009-1.

REFERENCES

Albery, W. J., & Knowles, J. R. (1976). Evolution of enzyme function and the development of the catalytic efficiency. *Biochem.*, *15*, 5631–5640. doi:10.1021/bi00670a032

Allen, M. J., & Rushton, N. (1994). Use of the CytoTOX 96(TM) assay in routine biocompatibility testing in vitro. *Promega Notes Magazine*, *45*, 7–10.

Alper, K. O., Singla, M., Stone, J. L., & Bagdassarian, C. K. (2001). Correlated conformational fluctuations during enzymatic catalysis: Implications for catalytic rate enhancement. *Protein Science*, *10*, 1319–1330. doi:10.1110/ps.220101

Astumian, R. D., Chock, P. B., Tsong, T. Y., & Westerhoff, H. V. (1989). Effects of oscillations and energy-driven fluctuations on the dynamics of enzyme catalysis and free-energy transduction. *Physical Review A.*, *39*, 6416–6435. doi:10.1103/PhysRevA.39.6416

Bahnson, B. J., & Klinman, J. P. (1995). Hydrogen tunneling in enzyme catalysis. *Methods in Enzymology*, *249*, 373–397. doi:10.1016/0076-6879(95)49042-6

Bala, P., Grochowski, P., Lesyng, B., & McCammon, J. A. (1996). Quantum-classical molecular dynamics simulation of proton transfer processes in molecular complexes and in enzymes. *Journal of Physical Chemistry*, *100*, 2535–2545. doi:10.1021/jp952642s

Barry, D. A., Culligan-Hensley, P. J., & Barry, S. J. (1995). Real values of the W-function. *Assoc. Comput. Machinery Trans. Math. Software*, *21*, 161–171. doi:10.1145/203082.203084

Barry, D. A., Parlange, J.-Y., Li, L., Prommer, H., Cunningham, C. J., & Stagnitti, F. (2000). Analytical approximations for real values of Lambert W-function. *Mathematics and Computers in Simulation*, *53*, 95–103. doi:10.1016/S0378-4754(00)00172-5

Barry, D. A., Parlange, J.-Y., Sander, G. C., & Sivaplan, M. (1993). A class of exact solutions for Richards' equation. *Journal of Hydrology (Amsterdam)*, *142*, 29–46. doi:10.1016/0022-1694(93)90003-R

Basran, J., Sutcliffe, M. J., & Scrutton, N. S. (1999). Enzymatic H-transfer requires vibration-driven extreme tunneling. *Bichem.*, *38*, 3218–3222. doi:10.1021/bi982719d

Boeker, E. A. (1984). Integrated rate equations for enzyme-catalyzed first-order and second-order reactions. *The Biochemical Journal*, *223*, 15–22.

Boeker, E. A. (1985). Integrated rate equations for irreversible enzyme-catalysed first-order and second-order reactions. *The Biochemical Journal*, *226*, 29–35.

Boeker, E. A. (1987). Analytical methods for fitting integrated rate equations. A discontinuous assay. *The Biochemical Journal*, *245*, 67–74.

Brown, A. J. (1902). Enzyme Action. *Journal of the Chemical Society Transactions*, *81*, 373–388. doi:10.1039/ct9028100373

Bruno, W. J., & Bialek, W. (1992). Vibrationally enhanced tunneling as a mechanism for enzymatic hydrogen transfer. *Biophysical Journal*, *63*, 689–699. doi:10.1016/S0006-3495(92)81654-5

Cantor, C. R., & Schimmel, P. R. (1980). *Biophysical Chemistry. Part III: The Behavior of Biological Macromolecules*. San Francisco: Freeman & Co.

Câteau, H., & Tanaka, S. (2002). Kinetic analysis of multisite phosphorylation using analytic solutions to Michaelis-Menten equation. *Journal of Theoretical Biology*, *217*, 1–14. doi:10.1006/jtbi.2002.3024

Cha, Y., Murray, C. J., & Klinman, J. P. (1989). Hydrogen tunneling in enzyme reaction. *Science*, *143*, 1325–1330. doi:10.1126/science.2646716

Copeland, R. A. (2000). *Enzymes*. New York: Wiley-VCH. doi:10.1002/0471220639

Corless, R. M., Gonnet, G. H., Hare, D. E. G., Jeffrey, D. J., & Knuth, D. E. (1996). On the Lambert W function. *Advances in Computational Mathematics*, *5*, 329–359. doi:10.1007/BF02124750

Corless, R. M., & Jeffrey, D. J. (2002). The right ω function. In Calmet, J., Benhamou, B., Caprotti, O., Henocque, L., & Sorge, V. (Eds.), *Artificial Intelligence, Automated Reasoning, and Symbolic Computation* (pp. 76–89). Berlin: Springer. doi:10.1007/3-540-45470-5_10

DeVault, D., & Chance, B. (1966). Studies of photosynthesis using a pulsed laser. I. Temperature dependence of cytochrome oxidation rate in chromatium. Evidence for tunneling. *Biophysical Journal, 6*, 825–847. doi:10.1016/S0006-3495(66)86698-5

Duggleby, R. G. (1986). Progress-curve analysis in enzyme kinetics. Numerical solution of integrated rate equations. *The Biochemical Journal, 235*, 613–615.

Duggleby, R. G. (2001). Quantitative analysis of the time courses of enzyme-catalyzed reactions. *Methods (San Diego, Calif.), 24*, 168–174. doi:10.1006/meth.2001.1177

Duggleby, R. G., & Morrison, J. F. (1977). The analysis of progress curves for enzyme-catalysed reactions by non-linear regression. *Biochimica et Biophysica Acta, 481*, 297–312.

Duggleby, R. G., & Morrison, J. F. (1978). Progress curve analysis in enzyme kinetics: model discrimination and parameter estimation. *Biochimica et Biophysica Acta, 526*, 398–409.

Duggleby, R. G., & Morrison, J. F. (1979). The use of steady-state rate equations to analyse progress curve data. *Biochimica et Biophysica Acta, 568*, 357–362.

Duggleby, R. G., & Wood, C. (1989). Analysis of progress curves for enzyme-catalysed reactions. Automatic construction of computer programs for fitting integrated equations. *The Biochemical Journal, 258*, 397–402.

Euler, L. (1779). *De serie Lambertina plurimisque eius insignibus proprietatibus.* 1921 reprinted at B.G. Teubner, Leipzig and Berlin in *Opera Omnia*, series 1, *6*, 350-369.

Fritsch, F. N., Shafer, R. E., & Crowley, W. P. (1973). Algorithm 443: solution of the transcendental equation $we^w = x$. *Communications of the ACM, 16*, 123–124. doi:10.1145/361952.361970

Glasstone, S., Laidler, K. J., & Eyring, H. (1941). *The theory of the rate processes.* New York: McGraw-Hill.

Goodman, A. F., Bellato, C. M., & Khidr, L. (2005). The uncertain future for central dogma. *Scientist (Philadelphia, Pa.), 19*, 20–21.

Goudar, C. T., Harris, S. K., McInerney, M. J., & Suflita, J. M. (2004). Progress curve analysis for enzyme and microbial kinetic reactions using explicit solutions based on the Lambert W function. *Journal of Microbiological Methods, 59*, 317–326. doi:10.1016/j.mimet.2004.06.013

Goudar, C. T., Sonnad, J. R., & Duggleby, R. G. (1999). Parameter estimation using a direct solution of the integrated Michaelis-Menten equation. *Biochimica et Biophysica Acta, 1429*, 377–383. doi:10.1016/S0167-4838(98)00247-7

Graham, L. D., Haggett, K. D., Hayes, P. J., Schober, P. A., Jennings, P. A., & Whittaker, R. G. (1994). A new library of alpha-lytic protease S1 mutants generated by combinatorial random substitution. *Biochemistry and Molecular Biology International, 32*, 831–839.

Grant, K. L., & Klinman, J. P. (1989). Evidence that protium and deuterium undergo significant tuneling in the reaction catalyzed by bovine serum amine oxidase. *Biochem., 28*, 6597–6605. doi:10.1021/bi00442a010

Hambäck, P. A. (1998). Seasonality, optimal foraging, and prey coexistence. *American Naturalist, 152*, 881–895. doi:10.1086/286215

Hartwell, L. (2005). How to build a cancer sensor system. *Scientist (Philadelphia, Pa.), 19*, 18–19.

Hayes, B. (2005). Why W? *American Scientist, 93*, 104–108.

Henri, V. (1901). Über das gesetz der wirkung des invertins. *Zeitschrift für Physikalische Chemie, 39*, 194–216.

Hinch, R., & Schnell, S. (2004). Mechanism equivalence in enzyme-substrate reactions: distributed differential delay in enzyme kinetics. *Journal of Mathematical Chemistry, 35,* 253–264. doi:10.1023/B:JOMC.0000033258.42803.60

Hirs, C. H. W. (1967). *Methods Enzymol. 11 (Enzyme Structure).* New York: Academic Press.

Huang, H. Y., & Niemann, C. (1951). The Kinetics of the α-Chymotrypsin Catalyzed Hydrolysis of Acetyl- and Nicotinyl-L-tryptophanamide in Aqueous Solutions at 25° and *p*H 7.9. *Journal of the American Chemical Society, 73,* 1541–1548. doi:10.1021/ja01148a040

Hwang, J.-K., & Warshel, A. (1996). How important are quantum mechanical nuclear motion in enzyme catalysis? *Journal of the American Chemical Society, 118,* 11745–11751. doi:10.1021/ja962007f

Jennings, R. R., & Niemann, C. (1953). The Kinetics of the α-Chymotrypsin Catalyzed Hydrolysis of Acetyl-L-hexahydrophenylalaninamide in Aqueous Solutions at 25° and pH 7.9. *Journal of the American Chemical Society, 75,* 4687–4692. doi:10.1021/ja01115a020

Jennings, R. R., & Niemann, C. (1955). The Evaluation of the Kinetic Constants of Enzyme-catalyzed Reactions by Procedures Based upon Integrated Rate Equations. *Journal of the American Chemical Society, 77,* 5432–5433. doi:10.1021/ja01625a077

Jonsson, T., Edmondson, D. E., & Klinman, J. P. (1994). Hydrogen tunneling in the flavoenzyme monoamine oxidase B. *Biochem., 33,* 14871–14878. doi:10.1021/bi00253a026

Jonsson, T., Glickman, M. H., Sun, S., & Klinman, J. P. (1996). Experimental evidence for extensive tunneling of hydrogen in the lipoxygenase reaction: implication for enzyme catalysis. *Journal of the American Chemical Society, 118,* 10319–10320. doi:10.1021/ja961827p

Kędzierski, P., Wielgus, P., Sikora, A., Sokalski, W. A., & Leszczyński, J. (2004). Visualization of the differential transition state stabilization within the active site environment. *International Journal of Molecular Sciences, 5,* 186–195. doi:10.3390/i5040186

Kleinert, H., Pelster, A., & Putz, M.V. (2002). Variational perturbation theory for Markov processes. *Phys. Rev. E, 65,* 066128/1-7.

Kohen, A., Jonsson, T., & Klinman, J. P. (1997). Effects of protein glycosylation on catalysis: changes in hydrogen tunneling and enthalpy of activation in the glucose oxidase reaction. *Biochem., 36,* 2603–2611. doi:10.1021/bi962492r

Lacrămă, A.-M., Putz, M. V., & Ostafe, V. (2008). Designing a Spectral Structure-Activity Ecotoxico-Logistical Battery. In Putz, M. V. (Ed.), *Advances in Quantum Chemical Bonding Structures* (pp. 389–419). Kerala, India: Transworld Research Network.

Laidler, K. J. (1955). Theory of transient phase in kinetics, with special reference to enzyme systems. *Canadian Journal of Chemistry, 33,* 1614–1624. doi:10.1139/v55-195

Marcus, R.A., Electron-transfer reactions in chemistry- theory and experiment (Nobel lecture). (1993). *Angew. Chem. Int. Ed.,32,* 1111-1121. doi:10.1002/anie.199311113

Michaelis, L., & Menten, M. L. (1913). Die kinetik der invertinwirkung. *Biochemische Zeitschrift, 49,* 333–369.

Murray, J. D. (1990). *Mathematical Biology.* Berlin: Springer Verlag.

Nixon, A. E., Ostermeier, M., & Benkovic, S. J. (1998). Hybrid enzymes: manipulating enzyme design. *Trends in Biotechnology, 16,* 258–264. doi:10.1016/S0167-7799(98)01204-9

Pauling, L. (1946). Molecular architecture and biological reactions. *Chemical and Engineering News*, *24*, 1375–1377. doi:10.1021/cen-v024n010.p1375

Putz, M. V. (2011). On reducible character of Haldane-Radić enzyme kinetics to conventional and logistic michaelis-menten models. *Molecules (Basel, Switzerland)*, *16*, 3128–3145. doi:10.3390/molecules16043128

Putz, M. V., & Lacrămă, A.-M. (2007). Enzymatic control of the bio-inspired nanomaterials at the spectroscopic level. *Journal of Optoelectronics and Advanced Materials*, *9*, 2529–2534.

Putz, M. V., Lacrămă, A.-M., & Ostafe, V. (2006). Full analytic progress curves of the enzymic reactions in vitro. *International Journal of Molecular Sciences*, *7*, 469–484. doi:10.3390/i7110469

Putz, M. V., Lacrămă, A.-M., & Ostafe, V. (2007). Introducing logistic enzyme kinetics. *Journal of Optoelectronics and Advanced Materials*, *9*, 2910–2916.

Rigby, P. W. J., Burleigh, B. D., & Hartley, B. S. (1974). Gene duplication in experimental enzyme evolution. *Nature*, *251*, 200–204. doi:10.1038/251200a0

Ringe, D., & Petsko, G. A. (1999). Quantum enzymology: Tunnel vision. *Nature*, *399*, 417–418. doi:10.1038/20819

Ross, G., Loverix, S., De Proft, F., Wyns, L., & Geerlings, P. (2003). A computational and conceptual DFT study of the reactivity of anionic compounds: implications for enzymatic catalysis. *The Journal of Physical Chemistry A*, *107*, 6828–6836. doi:10.1021/jp034376l

Ross, J., Schreiber, I., & Vlad, M. O. (2006). *Determination of Complex Reaction Mechanisms: Analysis of Chemical, Biological and Genetic Networks*. Oxford, UK: Oxford University Press.

Rubinow, S. I. (1975). *Introduction to Mathematical Biology*. New York: Wiley.

Schnell, S., & Maini, P. K. (2003). A Century of enzyme kinetics: reliability of the K_M and v_{max} estimates. *Comments on Theoretical Biology*, *8*, 169–187. doi:10.1080/08948550302453

Schnell, S., & Mendoza, C. (1997). Closed form solution for time-dependent enzyme kinetics. *Journal of Theoretical Biology*, *187*, 207–212. doi:10.1006/jtbi.1997.0425

Schnell, S., & Mendoza, C. (2000). Enzyme kinetics of multiple alternative substrates. *Journal of Mathematical Chemistry*, *27*, 155–170. doi:10.1023/A:1019139423811

Schnell, S., & Mendoza, C. (2000). Time-dependent closed form solution for fully competitive enzyme reactions. *Bulletin of Mathematical Biology*, *62*, 321–336. doi:10.1006/bulm.1999.0156

Segel, L. A., & Slemrod, M. (1989). The quasy-steady-state assumption: a case study in perturbation. *SIAM Review*, *31*, 446–477. doi:10.1137/1031091

Stemmer, W. P. C. (1994). Rapid evolution of a protein in vitro by DNA shuffling. *Nature*, *370*, 389–391. doi:10.1038/370389a0

Sutcliffe, M., & Scrutton, N. (2000). Enzymology takes a quantum leap forward. *Philosophical Transactions of the Royal Society of London. Series A: Mathematical and Physical Sciences*, *358*, 367–386. doi:10.1098/rsta.2000.0536

Truhlar, D. G., & Gordon, M. S. (1990). From force-fields to dynamics – classical and quantal paths. *Science*, *249*, 491–498. doi:10.1126/science.249.4968.491

Tyagi, R., Lee, Y.-T., Guddat, L. W., & Duggleby, R. G. (2005). Probing the mechanism of the bifunctional enzyme ketol-acid reductoisomerase by site-directed mutagenesis of the active site. *The FEBS Journal*, *272*, 593–602. doi:10.1111/j.1742-4658.2004.04506.x

Varón, R., Sevilla, F. G., García-Moreno, M., García-Cánovas, F., Peyro, R., & Duggleby, R. G. (1997). Computer program for the equations describing the steady state of enzyme reactions. *Computer Applications in the Biosciences, 13*, 159–167.

Voet, D., & Voet, J. G. (1995). *Biochemistry* (2nd ed.). New York: John Wiley and Sons, Inc.

Williams, D. F. (Ed.). (1986). *Techniques of Biocompatibility Testing* (*Vol. II*). Boca Raton, FL: CRC Press.

Wright, E. M. (1959). Solution of the equation $z\exp(z)=a$. *Proc. R. Soc. Edinburgh A, 65*, 193–203.

Yago, J. M., Sevilla, F. G., de Solo, C. G., Duggleby, R. G., & Varón, R. (2006). A Windows program for the derivation of steady-state equations in enzyme systems. *Applied Mathematics and Computation, 181*, 837–852. doi:10.1016/j.amc.2006.02.016

Yeow, Y. L., Pokethitiyook, P., Cheah, M. Y., Dang, H. D. T., & Law, C. K. P. (2004). An alternative way of analyzing the progress curves of enzyme-catalyzed reactions. *Biochemical Engineering Journal, 21*, 1–10. doi:10.1016/j.bej.2004.04.009

Chapter 8
Advances in Relevant Descriptor Selection

Željko Debeljak
University of Zagreb, Croatia

Marica Medić-Šarić
University of Zagreb, Croatia

ABSTRACT

During the last few decades the number of available molecular descriptors has grown exponentially. A reduced set of descriptors, containing only relevant descriptors, enables better understanding of the interaction between the molecule and some biological entity and in turn, it enables more reliable molecular modeling and chemical database mining. As a consequence, many new off-line and on-line descriptor selection methods have emerged. Overview of the most important feature selection methods, their advantages, disadvantages and applications in SAR and QSAR is given.

INTRODUCTION

Numerous facts about chemical and biological entities are generated on a daily basis. However, it is hard to find a small set of consistent, non-redundant, quantitative rules that represent a chemical or life science theory which enables deduction of many chemical or biological phenomena. At this moment most researchers in these scientific fields are focused on a search for reliable descriptors and models of the selected phenomena that constitute only a tiny fraction of the specific field. Researchers are especially interested in such descriptors which provide important information about different entities. Widely applicable descriptors or measures that carry a piece of useful information about different entities are critical prerequisites for the development of theories that can integrate different locally applicable models. From purely academic standpoint, the selection of descriptors and their evaluation through modeling, therefore, represents an attempt to rationalize the

DOI: 10.4018/978-1-60960-860-6.ch008

phenomenon and put it in a wider context. From the practical standpoint, modeling and development of reliable theories provides means for better control of chemical and life science phenomena.

The search for reliable models represents the essence of structure-activity relationship (SAR) and quantitative structure-activity relationship (QSAR). Reliable SAR/QSAR models enable rational drug design as well as the prediction of toxicity and other molecular properties. Model development and reliability here, as in all other cases, heavily depends on the descriptor selection. Chemical database mining based on relevant descriptors aimed at drug candidates' identification represents yet another important application of the relevant descriptor selection. In short, a lack of knowledge about the descriptor impact makes the rational approach to the molecular modeling and mining impossible.

The history of descriptor selection is as old as the SAR/QSAR modeling. One of the earliest attempts to establish QSAR was made by C. Hansch (1963). Even these early QSAR modeling attempts involved off-line descriptor selection. The basic idea was to put interactions between molecules and biological entities in the context of thermodynamics and quantum chemistry. Hansch and colleagues derived suitable descriptors from thermodynamical quantities and adjusted them for the QSAR applications. Since the number of available descriptors was not so high, there was no need for on-line descriptor selection. Models were simply built from the pool of all available descriptors. These attempts are unique in a way since they represent early attempts of unsupervised off-line descriptor selection. The relative success of these models confirmed original premise that biological phenomena could be, at least partially explained by established theories such as thermodynamics. The need for descriptors that carry useful information about different molecules gave an impulse to the development of new theories like the chemical graph theory (Trinajstić, 1992).

BACKGROUND

During the last few decades the number of available molecular descriptors became substantially larger. In most situations this number is practically infinite. Without previous detailed knowledge about the phenomenon at hand, it is difficult to conduct the unsupervised off-line descriptor selection that is theoretically justified. Modern QSAR studies, therefore, frequently include thousands of descriptors generated for a few dozens of molecules. From the statistical point of view, the estimation of QSAR model parameters is highly unreliable or impossible in the described settings. Even the application of the machine learning approaches to the model development leads to serious problems. So-called "curse of dimensionality" (Guyon, 2003), caused by a large number of descriptors and their possible interactions, makes model development intractable. Even if obtained models pass the external validation criteria, their interpretation is blurred by numerous descriptors of unknown relevance. This property makes the rational molecular design or data base mining a very complex task.

"Curse of dimensionality" that emerges in many scientific fields provoked the development of methods for the relevant feature selection. These can be divided roughly in two large groups: off-line and on-line methods of descriptor selection. The members of the first group, which are known as "filters", are independent of predictive QSAR model development, while members of the second group i.e. "wrappers" are coupled to the predictive model development tools. While the first group can be further divided in two subsets, unsupervised and supervised methods, the members of the second group are always supervised learning methods. Finally, some methods for predictive QSAR model development allow *post hoc* determination of descriptor relevance. Overview of different methods for relevant descriptor selection is given in the following text.

UNSUPERVISED OFF-LINE METHODS

There are situations when the number of selected molecules is relatively small or when one is only trying to interpret results of structural biology experiments. In such situations the selection of relevant descriptors represents the problem of its own i.e. the problem which is independent of the quantitative predictor development. These experimental settings imply a lack of reliable measurements of the specific response. In this case the problem of relevant descriptor selection belongs to a group of unsupervised learning methods. The same situation could happen even during the QSAR development if one wants to make rational descriptors selection before he starts the predictor development. The selection of descriptors for chemical data base mining may also rely on this approach.

It is always possible to apply the principles of thermodynamics and quantum chemistry to explain biological phenomena. Good examples of successfully used descriptors for such purpose are logP and partial atomic charges (Todeschini, 2002). However, the selection of theoretical variables or, more frequently, their derivatives that carry information about the problem at hand should be made cautiously. All possible interactions between a molecule and the biological entity could be hardly recognized. For example, logP is frequently used for the prediction of absorption of orally taken drugs. However, there are many situations when drugs are absorbed by active transport and logP can not explain high bioavailability of such drugs. Moreover, ionization could make a significant impact on bioavailability. If unrecognized, it also alleviates the value of logP. Without the knowledge about the molecular properties and corresponding interactions, off-line selection could be misleading. On the other hand, quantum chemical descriptors and their derivatives suffer from some methodological limitations, too. First of all, the level of approximation determines

the value of such descriptors. It is well-known that semi-empirical calculations and quantities obtained this way provide relatively reliable description of covalent structures (Stewart, 1991). However, most interactions between molecules and biological entities are based on van der Waals interactions. Even the density-functional theory (DFT) of *in vacuo* molecules can not describe many molecules in reliable fashion. Water molecules should be invoked even for the reliable DFT descriptions of simple molecules like γ-aminobutiric acid (Crittenden, 2005). This level of theory along with the molecular clusters puts huge burden on the computational resources. Problems with quantum chemical descriptors do not end up here. Derivation of interpretable descriptors like partial atomic charges can be done by at least three different methods which provide different results. *Ad hoc* selection of the method of calculation is always questionable. Therefore a lack of biological information as well as methodological problems put important limitations on the unsupervised off-line descriptor selection approach. However, numerous examples of successful application of some descriptors for the interpretation of interactions of molecules with biological entities confirm their value (Todeschini, 2002). In situations when these descriptors can not explain problems at hand, theoretical alternatives like ligand-receptor docking experiments or biochemical experiments should be considered. In situations when the structural biology information about the target or ligand-receptor complex is available, rational off-line descriptor selection is easier task. Even when such information is available, the rational off-line selection of descriptors based on the structural biology information is not a straightforward process.

An unsupervised approach to off-line selection of descriptors intended for predictive QSAR development is the least biased approach. But the rational unsupervised off-line selection requires a detailed knowledge about the problem that is not available all the time. In most situations one of the tasks in front of the modeler is to extract such knowledge in a form of critical biological determinants i.e. descriptors relevant for the given phenomenon. Therefore, the narrow unsupervised off-line descriptor selection is less frequently used today as a part of the QSAR development which leaves the problem with bias and overly optimistic predictions still open.

SUPERVISED OFF-LINE METHODS

This group of methods represents theoretically founded methods for descriptor selection that allow fast computations. Moreover, the number of molecules needed for the descriptor selection based on these methods is relatively low. Therefore these methods are well suited for usual SAR analyses. However, precautionary measures should be taken since small number of molecules could lead to chance correlations and unreliable conclusions.

The analysis of variance (ANOVA) and corresponding nonparametric alternatives, linear discriminant analysis (LDA) and logistic regression are well established statistical methods that can be used as "filters". These methods were devised for the detection of differences between the analyzed sets of objects. The use of these methods for the selection of relevant descriptors relies on the following rationale: if two sets of molecules, for example biologically active and inactive analogues, are well differentiated by a selected descriptor, then it is reasonable to conclude that the given descriptor is really a relevant one. Their multivariate counterparts, like LDA or multiple factors ANOVA can be also used for the selection of relevant descriptor subsets and even descriptor interactions but these methods are classified as *post hoc* methods since they are closely related to the predictive model development. Although frequently used single factor ANOVA and univariate logistic regression suffer from few disadvantages: they are univariate approaches

that rely on binary response variables. However, these methods offer a simple and straightforward graphical interpretation of the results applicable to common SAR tasks. Hence their popularity.

Another popular approach to the off-line descriptor selection relies on the analysis of correlation matrices. However, this approach suffers from many shortcomings. First of all, there is no theoretical foundation for this approach. In nonlinear multivariate modeling case, the use of datasets containing highly correlated descriptors may lead to models with improved predictive performance, in comparison to models developed for the datasets from which correlated descriptors have been eliminated. The next important problem with this approach is the use of biological variables i.e. response variables for the off-line descriptor elimination. If one uses the correlation of a certain descriptor with the response variable as the exclusion or inclusion criterion, he can not use the same set for appropriate predictor validation. In the opposite case, the result is overly optimistic prediction.

Somewhat better unsupervised off-line approach to the "curse of dimensionality" problem is based on the principal component analysis (PCA). In short, this approach transforms the original descriptor space in the set of orthogonal components. A small number of principal components, in most instances 2-3 of them, is used for the cluster analysis of analyzed molecules. Although relationships between molecules can be visualized this way, and the likelihood of the establishment of predictive models is increased, the information about the descriptors relevance is lost. This problem is common in SAR and QSAR. Even many frequently used supervised methods of prediction like partial least squares regression or support vector machines (SVM) suffer from this disadvantage.

During the last few decades, new off-line supervised feature selection methods have emerged. Among the theoretically founded methods appropriate for the SAR and the structural model interpretation purposes cluster significance analysis (Cronin, 1996), RELIEF algorithm (Sun, 2008) and mutual information feature selection (MIFS) (Venkatraman, 2004) should be mentioned. The first two methods are appropriate for the analysis of the datasets with the discrete response variable, while the MIFS algorithm can handle problems with continuous response variable.

If the selected descriptor set is optimal in terms of classification performance, distances between the members of the class of molecules of interest should be small in comparison to distances between the members of different classes or members of classes that are of no interest. This premise along with forward selection represents the basis of the CSA algorithm for the selection of relevant descriptor subset (Cronin, 1996). This approach is intuitive as is the RELIEF approach. The RELIEF algorithm relies on similar premise but, instead of the optimal descriptor subset, this algorithm provides descriptor weights (Sun, 2008). Descriptors with the highest weights are considered to be the relevant ones. The important difference between the two methods is related to the relevant descriptor combinations. RELIEF allows linear combinations of relevant descriptors, while CSA provides descriptor subsets that can not be combined in general. This is a consequence of different merit functions. In the CSA case, the merit function includes non-additive statistic, while the RELIEF relies on geometric distances per each dimension/descriptor which are additive. The selection of descriptor subsets in CSA case in addition requires subset formation algorithm like the forward descriptor search algorithm and a large number of calculations per each selection step. This algorithm is therefore quite demanding in terms of computational resources, while RELIEF is less demanding and consequently faster.

Among given algorithms, MIFS is the only multivariate alternative that can handle continuous response variables. This algorithm tries to maximize the mutual information among descriptors and the response variable (Venkatraman, 2004).

The calculation of this function requires the calculation of joint or conditional probability density functions of the selected descriptor subsets and the response variable. In order to do so it is necessary to estimate corresponding distributions. Finally, the use of search algorithm, like forward selection or branch and bound algorithm, is an unavoidable part of MIFS. It is clear that this algorithm is quite demanding in terms of computational resources. However, its utility in QSAR and related fields has been proven (Venkatraman, 2004).

SUPERVISED ON-LINE METHODS

Filters could be coupled with predictive algorithms like partial least squares regression, artificial neural networks (ANN), SVM, kth nearest neighbors etc and obtained hybrids are called "wrappers" (Kohavi, 1997). Besides descriptor selection, they enable supervised predictive modeling i.e. they are suitable for the QSAR analysis under usual conditions. The main disadvantage of wrappers is the need for large datasets. Namely, training of filters wrapped in a predictive training loop requires more training examples in addition to the set used for the sole predictive tool training and/or validation. The development of wrappers, therefore, requires three data subsets: training, validation and the test set. This requirement is reflected in the demands for large datasets and in the slow computation. It should be also noted that the large datasets are available in toxicology but they are less frequently available in pharmacological activity modeling. On the other hand, wrappers offer response predictions. By inclusion of the external test set, the quality of these predictions could be computationally validated. Models that pass the validation criteria provide additional reliability to the selected descriptors which is the most important advantage of wrappers.

Besides filters that can be used as standalone tools, descriptor selection tools that are exclusively used as wrappers should be mentioned. The most popular feature selection approaches from this group which have been used for hybridization with appropriate predictors are evolutionary algorithms (EA). Among those genetic algorithms (GA) are the most frequently used variants since their hybrids with mentioned predictive tools show very good predictive performance (Chiu, 2003). These algorithms are heuristics that rely on specific evolutionary principles (Haupt, 1998). The first principle is the survival of the fittest individuals. Many models are generated per each generation but only the best performing models survive. The second principle is the mutation. Mutation i.e. random generation of some model parameters, like randomly chosen descriptors, is used as a driving force for generation of offspring. In comparison to other EA GA include the third principle: breeding of the best performing individuals. Besides EA and GA, simulated annealing (SA) should be mentioned since corresponding hybrids also provide good predictive performance. SA is a general purpose optimization algorithm and as such SA could be used as a stand alone predictive tool. However, SA has been used as a variable selection tool more frequently in QSAR (Olof, 2005). A slow search over the descriptor space driven by small stochastic steps forms the basis of the algorithm. Both, steps towards states characterized by worse and better fitness are allowed as opposed to so-called greedy optimization algorithms. This property leads to the increased chance of finding global optimum, but it also puts a large computational burden that can become huge in case of a large number of deep local minima.

The search for globally optimal set of descriptors is a very complex task that can be rarely achieved. EA, GA and SA in most instances provide sub-optimal solutions in terms of relevant descriptor selection. Among given algorithms, SA offers greatest chances for finding a global optimum but at the expense of long computations. Moreover, its use frequently requires a great deal of expertise. Branch and bound algorithm is a global search method that also offers this goal, but it is rarely used in chemometrics.

Some predictor development methods include feature selection as their inseparable part. This property is very appealing since it represents predictive modeling based on model interpretability. Decision trees (DT) and inductive logic programming (ILP) belong to this class of supervised online methods. These two related approaches rely on the premise given in the previous section. Namely, descriptors that detect differences among classes are good candidates for relevant descriptors. Predictive performance of this approach is further improved by a process known as the recursive partitioning that includes the sequential combination of two or more descriptors and formation of DT. Obtained model interpretation is simple and straightforward. However, in comparison to the state-of-the-art predictive model, the development tools predictive performance of these methods is only moderate. It has been shown that the DT ensembles provide better performances and they largely replaced DT themselves (Breiman, 2001).

POST HOC METHODS

Post hoc approaches to the descriptor selection depend on the characteristics of underlying predictive models. Therefore, these approaches are divided in accordance with the classification of predictive model development tools. The most important predictor classes in this regard are the artificial neural networks (ANN) and random forests (RF). *Post hoc* descriptor selection methods have few advantages over already mentioned approaches. First of all, they rely on validated models. Besides, they are off-line methods which means that they do not put a large computational burden. Still, they are not as fast as filters since they require predictive model development and validation.

Early representatives of this class of descriptor selection algorithms are so-called pruning algorithms. They have been developed for ANN and DT. Either nodes, branches or connections are pruned from these structures based on the appropriate fitness function. Node pruning represents the way of relevant descriptor selection, while the connection pruning provides information about the relevant descriptor interactions and their relationship with the response variable. Although on-line versions of the pruning algorithms also exist off-line, *post hoc* pruning methods are more frequently used (Poppi, 1998). The basic idea on which these algorithms rely is that either tree or neural network structure complexity reduction could result in the predictive performance improvement. Therefore these algorithms use some structure complexity measures and they combine them with the predictive performance measures. The bases for the search of optimal structures are frequently optimization algorithms that use Hessian matrices like the Levenberg-Marquardt algorithm. This is the case with the frequently used optimal brain damage and optimal brain surgeon algorithms (Poppi, 1998). The downside of pruning algorithms is related to predictive tools for which they have been developed. Both, ANN and DT enable the development of models with moderate predictive performance. Therefore these methods have been largely replaced by corresponding ensembles, at least in QSAR applications since ANN ensembles and RF generally provide better predictive performance (Debeljak, 2005; Breiman, 2001).

One of the latest *post hoc* algorithms is implemented in the RF algorithm. RF is a powerful predictive model development tool which represents an ensemble of DT (Breiman, 2001; Svetnik, 2003). Unfortunately, ensemble formation leads to the loss of the descriptor relevance information that is inherent to DT but ensures better predictive performance. The importance of descriptors in RF is revealed by so-called "out of the bag" (OOB) estimation conducted in a *post hoc* manner. OOB term is related to objects, in our case molecules that have not been used for predictor training. The influence of the random permutation of descriptor values on the predictions for OOB samples is used as the relevance measure. Descriptors in which randomization does not cause the decrease in accuracy are considered to be irrelevant. This approach enables descriptor ranking by relevance.

Although a term "descriptor relevance" seems to be self-explanatory, it should be placed in the model development context. Models as a concept imply their limited scope. Different sets of relevant descriptors will be selected depending on the molecular subset which the model describes adequately. Even the validated models provide different sets of relevant descriptors for the same data sets depending on the applied predictive model development method (Debeljak, 2005). Moreover, stochastic methods like RF or EA/ANN hybrids could provide different relevant descriptors depending on the random seed value that has been applied. Descriptor relevance obviously depends on the descriptor selection method. This problem leads to the next question: which descriptors are truly relevant? Without the appropriate laboratory experiments, which are frequently unavailable unequivocal answer to this question, could not be given. The fact that different models describe different molecular subsets provides the rationale for the relevant descriptor aggregation. Besides, variations of relevant descriptor subsets' composition could be caused by the random effects. Finally, analyzed biological phenomenon could be composed of two or more separate events which are described by different models. These facts also justify descriptor aggregation. The simplest implementation of the relevant descriptor aggregation idea relies on descriptor ranking according to the frequency of descriptor occurrence among different relevant subsets (Debeljak, 2007).

Small changes of relevant descriptor subsets composition cause significant predictive performance deterioration. An example for this statement is related to the EA/ANN hybrids. By switching only one input neuron i.e. replacement of only one relevant descriptor by other descriptor inevitably leads to the loss of predictive performance of trained ANN. Even the training of new network rarely provides results that are comparable to predictive performance of the original network (Debeljak, 2005). This example shows the importance of descriptor interactions and the relevant descriptor subset stability. Ensemble methods like EA/ANN ensembles enable generation of large number of predictors accompanied by a large number of relevant descriptor subsets. The search for descriptor subsets with the highest frequency could also eliminate random effects. Even the unique descriptor subsets that appear to be relevant for different molecular subsets could be found (Debeljak, 2005). In such case model interpretability is far less complex while the model itself looks more convincing.

FUTURE RESEARCH DIRECTIONS

The number of available molecular descriptors is growing steadily. Some of the described methods, like EA/ANN or SA hybrids can hardly cope with thousands of descriptors that are available for the model development. A question that described experimental settings raise is how many molecules are needed for the development of reliable models? Both problems could be solved by PCA/GA hybrids (Hemmateenejad, 2003). GA could be used for the selection of relevant principle components among the highly ranked candidates which in turn enable reliable predictive model development. Although both problems, descriptor set dimensionality and the lack of large data sets are solved this way, descriptor relevance is blurred. Extraction of this information from the selected principle components represents a problem that yet remains to be solved.

Next important problem is the nonlinear dependence between descriptors and the response variable which makes nonlinear predictive models

less useful. Local approach based on gradients that tackles the problem has been recently published (Carlsson, 2009). Still, this approach is not yet widely used and less complex solutions are expected. Another even more important problem is the problem of the relevant descriptor interactions. Without the knowledge of the relationship between descriptors and the response relevant descriptor selection could be hardly used for practical purposes like rational drug design. This is the downside of all *post hoc* methods, as well as univariate approaches. ANN provide the most useful information in this respect among given alternatives. In most instances feed-forward networks which can not capture complex interactions like feedback loops are used. Bayesian networks (Burden, 2000) offer different types of connections among neurons along with different types of pruning, while dynamic Bayesian networks even offer the building of models with feedback loops. The predictive performance of these networks remains to be evaluated by wider QSAR community. If such networks can provide good predictive performances, their ability to give an insight into relevant descriptor interactions is certainly an advantage.

CONCLUSION

Whichever method for descriptor selection is applied, the result is a model of the relationship between selected molecules and some response variable. Unfortunately many developed models do not reflect true relationships i.e. they are unreliable. Model reliability could be gained through sound theoretical background of the descriptor selection process and through the empirical evaluation of the obtained model. Descriptor selection tools rooted in theory are fast but suffer from described limitations like univariate and/or linear relationships modeling. Heuristics and metaheuristics more frequently provide good predictive performance but they require large data sets and they are computationally demanding. If the theoretically founded descriptor selection or ranking is incorporated in the predictive model development and external validation, the obtained model interpretation gains more credibility. This credibility can be enhanced further by a predictor ensemble formation and a descriptor subset stability analysis. Described principles form the basis for the modern descriptor selection and model interpretation.

This overview is not an exhaustive one since new methods for the relevant descriptor selection, especially different heuristics, emerge very quickly. Many existing algorithms have not been thoroughly evaluated in SAR and QSAR although their evaluation in related fields like bioinformatics or analytical chemistry gave promising results. The aim of this overview was to provide the most frequently used descriptor selection tools along with corresponding criteria for their evaluation. Model validation, exhaustive vs. partial descriptor space search, computational requirements, descriptor interactions and model interpretability are issues of critical importance for the successful relevant descriptor selection.

REFERENCES

Breiman, L. (2001). Random Forests. *Machine Learning*, *45*, 5–32. doi:10.1023/A:1010933404324

Burden, F. R., Ford, M. G., Whitley, D. C., & Winkler, D. A. (2000). Use of automatic relevance determination in QSAR studies using Bayesian neural networks. *Journal of Chemical Information and Computer Sciences*, *40*(6), 1423–1430. doi:10.1021/ci000450a

Carlsson, L., Ahlberg Helgee, E., & Boyer, S. (2009). Interpretation of nonlinear QSAR models applied to Ames mutagenicity data. *Journal of Chemical Information and Modeling*, *49*(11), 2551–2558. doi:10.1021/ci9002206

Chiu, T.-L., & So, S.-S. (2003). Genetic neural networks for functional approximation. *QSAR & Combinatorial Science*, *22*(5), 519–526. doi:10.1002/qsar.200310004

Crittenden, D. L., Chebib, M., & Jordan, M. J. (2005). Stabilization of zwitterions in solution: GABA analogues. *The Journal of Physical Chemistry A*, *109*(18), 4195–4201. doi:10.1021/jp050320a

Cronin, M. T. D. (1996). The use of cluster significance analysis to identify asymmetric QSAR data sets in toxicology. An example with eye irritation data. *SAR and QSAR in Environmental Research*, *5*(3), 167–175. doi:10.1080/10629369608032987

Debeljak, Ž., Marohnić, V., Srečnik, G., & Medić-Šarić, M. (2005). Novel approach to evolutionary neural network based descriptor selection and QSAR model development. *Journal of Computer-Aided Molecular Design*, *19*, 835–855. doi:10.1007/s10822-005-9022-2

Debeljak, Ž., Škrbo, A., Jasprica, I., Mornar, A., Plečko, V., Banjanac, M., & Medić-Šarić, M. (2007). QSAR study of antimicrobial activity of some 3-nitrocoumarins and related compounds. *Journal of Chemical Information and Modeling*, *47*, 918–926. doi:10.1021/ci600473z

Guyon, I., & Elisseeff, A. (2003). An introduction to variable and feature selection. *Journal of Machine Learning Research*, *3*, 1157–1182. doi:10.1162/153244303322753616

Hansch, C., Muir, R. M., Fujita, T., Maloney, P. P., Geiger, F., & Streich, M. (1963). The correlation of biological activity of plant growth regulators and chloromycetin derivatives with Hammett constants and partition coefficients. *Journal of the American Chemical Society*, *85*(18), 2817–2824. doi:10.1021/ja00901a033

Haupt, R. L., & Haupt, S. E. (1998). *Practical genetic algorithms*. New York: John Wiley & Sons, Inc.

Hemmateenejad, B., Akhond, M., Miri, R., & Shamsipur, M. (2003). Genetic algorithm applied to the selection of factors in principal component-artificial neural networks: application to QSAR study of calcium channel antagonist activity of 1,4-dihydropyridines (Nifedipine Analogous). *Journal of Chemical Information and Computer Sciences, 43*(4), 1328–1334. doi:10.1021/ci025661p

Kohavi, R., & John, G: H. (1997). Wrappers for feature subset selection. *Artificial Intelligence Journal, 97*(1-2), 273–324. doi:10.1016/S0004-3702(97)00043-X

Ling. *Journal of Chemical Information and Computer Sciences, 43*, 1947–1958.

Oloff, S., Mailman, R. B., & Tropsha, A. (2005). Application of validated QSAR models of D1 dopaminergic antagonists for database mining. *Journal of Medicinal Chemistry, 48*(23), 7322–7332. doi:10.1021/jm049116m

Poppi, R. J., & Massart, D. L. (1998). The optimal brain surgeon for pruning neural network architecture applied to multivariate calibration. *Analytica Chimica Acta, 375*, 187–195. doi:10.1016/S0003-2670(98)00462-0

Stewart, J. J. P. (1990). Semiempirical molecular orbital methods. In Lipkowitz, K. B., & Boyd, D. B. (Eds.), *Reviews in Computational Chemistry* (*Vol. 1*, pp. 45–81). New York: VCH Publishers. doi:10.1002/9780470125786.ch2

Sun, Y., & Wu, D. (2008). A RELIEF based feature extraction algorithm, In M. J. Zaki, K. Wang, C. Apte, & H. Park (Eds.), *8th SIAM International Conference on Data Mining* (pp. 188–195). Philadelphia, PA: SIAM.

Svetnik, V., Liaw, A., Tong, C., Culberson, J. C., Sheridan, R. P., & Feuston, B. P. (2003) Random Forest: A classification and regression tool for compound classification and QSAR mode

Todeschini, R., & Consonni, V. (2002). *Handbook of molecular descriptors*. Weinstein, Germany: Wiley-VCH.

Trinajstić, N. (1992). *Chemical graph theory*. Boca Raton, FL: CRC Press.

Venkatraman, V., Rowland Dalby, A., & Rong Yang, Z. (2004). Evaluation of mutual information and genetic programming for feature selection in QSAR. *Journal of Chemical Information and Computer Sciences, 44*(5), 1686–1692. doi:10.1021/ci049933v

Chapter 9
Analytical Solution of Cubic Autocatalytic Reaction–Diffusion Equations:
Homotopy Pertuburation Approach

D. Shanthi
Madura College, India

L. Rajendran
Madura College, India

ABSTRACT

The system is considered here with two chemical species, the reactant a and autocatalyst b. The Gray-Scott model of cubic-autocatalysis with linear decay is coupled with diffusion and considered in a one-dimensional reactor (a reactor-diffusion cell). Steady-state and non steady- state concentration profiles of the reactant and autocatalyst in Gray-Scott model are obtained using He's Homotopy pertuburation method for small values parameters. A satisfactory agreement with analytical and numerical results are noted.

INTRODUCTION

It is the purpose of this paper to present the approximate analytical and numerical solution of cubic autocatalytic reaction-diffusion equations. There is a great deal of interest in chemical reactions which exhibit oscillatory solutions. These

DOI: 10.4018/978-1-60960-860-6.ch009

oscillations occur due to feedback in the system either chemical feedback such as autocatalysis or temperature feedback due to non-isothermal reaction. Two well-studied examples of reactions exhibiting oscillatory solutions are the isothermal Belousov-Zhabotinsky reaction and Sal'nikov thermokinetic oscillator. However simple a chemical scheme we are seeking, it must have at least two independent variables, if it is to represent oscillations. Although a single independent variable can lead to multiple stationary states, and hence to 'ignitions' and 'extinctions', oscillatory behaviour requires a richer soil than multi stability. The simplest polynomial necessary is a cubic, and cubic autocatalysis as a source of multi stability in an isothermal open system was clearly, although briefly, expounded by Zel'dovich & Zysin in 1941. Accordingly the chemist wishing to invoke autocatalysis to explain oscillations should first look for the simplest manner of decoupling any stoichiometric connection between reactant and catalyst concentrations. If the autocatalysis by the product B has the form $A+B \rightarrow 2B$ or $A+2B \rightarrow 3B$, then adding the reaction $B \rightarrow C$ is sufficient for this task. This simply means the catalyst has a finite lifetime, its activity here decaying in a first-order way. These are the reactions constituting the 'autocatalator.'

The Gray-Scott scheme, which represents cubic-autocatalysis with linear catalyst decay, has been much considered, because of its decay, has been much considered, because of its multiple steady-state responses and oscillatory solutions. See Gray (1988) and Gray & Scott (1990) for reviews and descriptions of much of this work. The scheme is $A+2B \rightarrow 3B$, rate $= \beta ab^2$, $B \rightarrow C$, rate $= \beta \gamma b$, where the concentrations of the reactant and autocatalyst a and b, respectively. The parameters β and γ are rate constants. The catalyst is not stable, but undergoes a simple linear decay to a product C. This allows a much wider variety of behavior in the system than does the cubic reaction alone. This system of equations has been considered by Kay & Scott (1988) numerically. Recently Marchant (2002) obtained the steady-state solutions for the cubic-autocatalytic reaction with linear decay in a reaction-diffusion cell using semi-analytical method. However, to the best of our knowledge there was no analytical result corresponding to the steady-state concentration of reactant and auto-catalyst for all positive values of parameters have reported. The purpose of this communication is to

derive the approximate analytical expressions for the concentrations of the reactant and autocatalyst for steady and non steady state, using Homotopy perturbation method and Laplace transformation.

Formulation of the Problem and Analysis

The simplest forms of autocatalytic reactions may be expressed by the prototype reaction-steps: $A+mB \rightarrow (m+1)B$. The stoichiometry of these reactions are $A \rightarrow B$, but the reaction rate depends differently on the concentration of the product species B (rate $= \alpha[A][B]^n$, $n = 1,2$). We will refer the case as cubic autocatalysis if $n = 2$. In autocatalysis $A+2B \rightarrow 3B$, the rate $= \beta ab^2$ and in catalyst decay $B \rightarrow C$, the rate $= \beta \gamma b$. For cubic autocatalytic reaction ($n = 2$) the mass balance equation in non-dimensional form are as follows.

$$\frac{\partial^2 a}{\partial x^2} - \beta \, a \, b^2 = 0 \tag{1}$$

$$\frac{\partial^2 b}{\partial x^2} + \beta \, a \, b^2 - \beta \, \gamma \, b = 0 \tag{2}$$

where a and b denotes the concentration of reactant and autocatalyst. The first and second term of Eqs. (1) and (2) represent the diffusion arrival and autocatalytic reaction terms. The third term in the Eq. (2) represent catalyst decay term. The boundary conditions are

$$\frac{\partial a}{\partial x} = 0, \quad \frac{\partial b}{\partial x} = 0 \text{ at } x = 0, \tag{3}$$

$$a = 1, \, b = c_0 \text{ at } x = 1. \tag{4}$$

The reactor has permeable boundary at $x = 1$. The system is characterized by three non-dimensional parameters c_0, β and γ. The ratio of the auto-catalyst and reactant concentrations in the reservoir are c_0 The parameter β is a measure of the importance of the reaction terms, compared with diffusion, while γ is a measure of the importance of autocatalyst decay, compared with the cubic-reaction. The simplest way to adjust the non-dimensional parameters experimentally is by changing the reservoir concentrations. Other possibilities for varying the non-dimensional parameters include changing the diffusivity of the system or the length of the reactor. The diffusivity could be changed by adjusting the temperature or by the addition of inactive salts. See Scott (1987) for a fuller discussion of these possibilities. The steady-state solutions are found by stepping forward in time until the solution is stationary. Normally the initial condition used for the steady-state solution found for the value of β; hence only a moderate amount of calculation is needed to generate a complete steady-state solutions.

Solution of the Steady: State Problem Using Homotopy Perturbation Method

Recently many authors have applied the HPM (Ghori, Ahmed, and.Siddiqui (2007), Ozis and Yildirim, (2007), Cai., Wu and Li (2006) and Ariel (2010)) to various problems and demonstrated the efficiency of the HPM for handling non-linear structures.. This method is a combination of homotopy in topology and classic perturbation techniques. Huan He (1999) have used the HPM to solve the Lighthill equation, the Duffing equation and the Blasius equation.The idea has been used to solve non-linear boundary value problems, integral equations. The authors Odibat and Momani, (2007) and Chowdhury and Hashim (2007) have used the HPM to solve Klein-Gordon and Sine-Gordon equations, Emden-Fowler type equations respectively and also many other problems. This wide variety of applications shows the power of the HPM to solve functional equations The HPM is unique in its applicability, accuracy and efficiency. The HPM uses the imbedding

parameter p as a small parameter and only a few iterations are needed to search for an asymptotic solution. By solving the Eqs.(1) and (2) using of Homotopy Perturbation method (see Appendix A), the concentration of reactant a and autocatalyst b can be obtained.

$$
a = 1 + \frac{\beta\, c_0^{\,2}}{4 \cosh^2 \sqrt{\beta\,\gamma}} \left[\frac{\cosh 2\sqrt{\beta\,\gamma} x}{2\beta\,\gamma} - \frac{\cosh 2\sqrt{\beta\,\gamma}}{2\beta\,\gamma} + x^2 - 1 \right]
$$
(5)

$$
b = \frac{c_0 \cosh\sqrt{\beta\,\gamma} x}{\cosh\sqrt{\beta\,\gamma}} + \frac{c_0^{\,2}\cosh\sqrt{\beta\,\gamma}\; x}{4\gamma\cosh^3\sqrt{\beta\,\gamma}} \left[\frac{2\cosh 2\sqrt{\beta\,\gamma}}{3} - 2 \right] - \frac{c_0^{\,2}}{4\gamma\cosh^2\sqrt{\beta\,\gamma}} \left[\frac{2\cosh 2\sqrt{\beta\,\gamma}\; x}{3} - 2 \right]
$$
(6)

Solution of Non-Steady State Problem Using Laplace Transformation

In the case of non-steady state, equations (1) and (2) are expressed in the following format:

$$
\frac{\partial a}{\partial t} = \frac{\partial^2 a}{\partial x^2} - \beta\, a\, b^2
$$
(7)

$$
\frac{\partial b}{\partial t} = \frac{\partial^2 b}{\partial x^2} + \beta a b^2 - \beta\,\gamma\, b
$$
(8)

Now the initial and boundary conditions are represented as follows.

$$
\frac{\partial a}{\partial x} = 0, \quad \frac{\partial b}{\partial x} = 0 \text{ when x=0}
$$
(9)

$$
a = 1, \quad b = c_0 \text{ when } x = 1, \; t = 0
$$
(10)

Here in the eq.(7), we can replace $ab^2 \approx ac_0^{\,2}$ (since the initial concentration of $b = c_0$) and in the eq.(8) we can replace $ab^2 \approx bc_0$ (since the initial concentration of $a=1, b=c_0$). By applying Laplace transform technique to the partial differential Eqs. (7) and (8) and using the boundary condition Eq. (9) and Eq. (10), we get the following transformed differential equations in Laplace plane.

$$s\bar{a} - 1 = \frac{\partial^2 \bar{a}}{\partial x^2} - \beta \, c_0^2 \, \bar{a}, \tag{11}$$

$$s\bar{b} - c_0 = \frac{\partial^2 \bar{b}}{\partial b^2} + (\beta \, c_0 - \beta \, \gamma) \, \bar{b}, \tag{12}$$

Now the boundary conditions become

$$x = 0, \quad \frac{\partial \bar{a}}{\partial x} = 0 \text{ and } \frac{\partial \bar{b}}{\partial x} = 0 \tag{13}$$

$$x = 1, \quad \bar{a} = \frac{1}{s} \text{ and } \bar{b} = \frac{c_0}{s} \tag{14}$$

where s is the Laplace variable and an over bar indicates a Laplace-transformed quantity.

Solving the Eqs. (11) and (12) by using the boundary conditions (13) and (14), we can obtain the concentrations which is as follows:

$$\bar{a} = \frac{1}{s} \frac{\cosh(x\sqrt{\beta c_0^2 + s})}{\cosh(\sqrt{\beta c_0^2 + s})} -$$

$$\frac{\cosh(x\sqrt{\beta c_0^2 + s})}{(s + \beta c_0^2)\cosh(\sqrt{\beta c_0^2 + s})} + \tag{15}$$

$$\frac{1}{(s + \beta c_0^2)}$$

$$\bar{b} = \frac{c_0 \cosh(x\sqrt{\beta\gamma - \beta c_0 + s})}{s \cosh(\sqrt{\beta\gamma - \beta c_0 + s})} -$$

$$\frac{c_0 \cosh(x\sqrt{\beta\gamma - \beta c_0 + s})}{(s + \beta\gamma - \beta c_0)\cosh(\sqrt{\beta\gamma - \beta c_0 + s})} +$$

$$\frac{c_0}{(s + \beta\gamma - \beta c_0)} \tag{16}$$

Using residue theorem, we can obtain the approximate solution of Eqs. (11) and (12) (see Appendix-D), which is as follows:

$$a(x,t) = \frac{\cosh(x\sqrt{\beta c_0^2})}{\cosh(\sqrt{\beta c_0^2})} +$$
$$\pi\sum_{n=0}^{\infty}(-1)^n \left\{ \frac{(2n+1)\cos(((2n+1)/2)\pi x)}{((2n+1)^2\pi^2/4) + \beta c_0^2} \right\} \exp\left[-\left\{((2n+1)^2\pi^2/4) + \beta c_0^2\right\}t\right] -$$
$$\pi\sum_{n=0}^{\infty}(-1)^n \left\{ \frac{\cos(((2n+1)/2)\pi x)}{((2n+1)\pi/4)} \right\} \exp\left[-\left\{((2n+1)^2\pi^2/4) + \beta c_0^2\right\}t\right] \tag{17}$$

$$b(x,t) = \frac{c_0 \cosh(x\sqrt{\beta\gamma - \beta c_0})}{\cosh(\sqrt{\beta\gamma - \beta c_0})} -$$
$$\pi\sum_{n=0}^{\infty}(-1)^n \left\{ \frac{\cos(((2n+1)/2)\pi x)}{((2n+1)\pi/4)} \right\} c_0\exp\left[\left\{(-(2n+1)^2\pi^2/4) - \beta\gamma + \beta c_0\right\}t\right] +$$
$$\pi\sum_{n=0}^{\infty}(-1)^n \left\{ \frac{(2n+1)\cos(((2n+1)/2)\pi x)}{((2n+1)^2\pi^2/4) + \beta\gamma - \beta c_0} \right\} c_0\exp\left[\left\{(-(2n+1)^2\pi^2/4) - \beta\gamma + \beta c_0\right\}t\right] \tag{18}$$

Numerical Simulation

The non-linear differential Eqs.(1) and (2) are also solved by numerical methods. The function bvp4c in Scilab Software which is a function of solving two-point boundary value problems (BVP) for ordinary differential equations. The numerical solution is compared with Homotopy perturbation method and gives a satisfactory result. The Scilab program is also given in Appendix C.

Discussion for Steady State

Eqs. (5) and (6) are the approximate analytical expression of concentration of the reactant and auto-catalyst for small values of parameters β and γ. Tables 1 to 10 (Appendix D) indicate the concentration of the reactant and auto-catalyst, evaluated using Eqs. (5) and (6) together with the simulation result calculated using Scilab program. The average relative difference between, analytical result and numerical result is less than 2% for small values of parameters β, γ and c_0. From these tables it is inferred that, the values of the concentration of the auto-catalyst is approximately equal to c0 (ratio of the auto-catalyst and reactant concentration in the reservoir) for all small values of rate constants β and γ. Also the value of concentration of the reactant a is equal to 1 for all values of rate constant.

Discussion for Non-Steady State

Eqs. (17) and (18) are the approximate analytical expression of concentration of the reactant and auto-catalyst for small values of parameters β and γ. In Figures 1-6 (Appendix D), the dimensionless concentration of the reactant a and auto-catalyst b for various values of parameters β, γ and c_0 are reported and satisfactory agreement with the simulation results (Scilab program) is noticed. From these figures it is inferred that the values of the concentration of the reactant and auto-catalyst are increases when time increases for all small values of rate constants β and γ.

CONCLUSION

In this work, the coupled system of time independent and dependent differential equations for cubic autocatalytic reaction-diffusion equations has been formulated and solved analytically using the HPM. We have presented the analytical solution of system of coupled reaction-diffusion problem. Moreover, we have also presented an approximate analytical expression for the non-steady state concentration profiles. The extension

of the procedure to well-stirred reactor (CSTR) models seems possible [6].

REFERENCES

Ariel, P. D. (2010). Homotopy perturbation method and natural convection flow of a third grade fluid through a circular tube. *Nonlinear. Sci. Lett, 1*, 43–52.

Biazar, J., & Ghazvini, H. (2009). He's homotopy-perturbation method for solving systems of Volterra integral equations. *Chaos, Solitons, and Fractals, 39*, 770. doi:10.1016/j.chaos.2007.01.108

Cai, X. C., Wu, W. Y., & Li, M. S. (2006). Approximate period solution for a kind of nonlinear oscillator by He's perturbation method. *Int. J. Nonlinear. Sci. Numer. Simulation, 7*(1), 109–117. doi:10.1515/IJNSNS.2006.7.1.109

Chowdhury, M. S. H., & Hashim, I. (2007). Solutions of time- dependent Emden-Fowler type equations by homotopy- perturbation method. *Physics Letters. [Part A], 368*, 305–313. doi:10.1016/j.physleta.2007.04.020

Ghasemi, M., Tavassoli Kajani, M., & Babolian, E. (2007). Numerical solutions of nonlinear Volterra-Fredholm integral equations by using homotopy- perturbation method. *Applied Mathematics and Computation, 188*, 446–449. doi:10.1016/j.amc.2006.10.015

Ghori, Q. K., Ahmed, M., & Siddiqui, A. M. (2007). Application of homotopy perturbation method to squeezing flow of a Newtonian fluid. *Int. J. Nonlinear Sci. Numer. Simulat., 8*(2), 179–184. doi:10.1515/IJNSNS.2007.8.2.179

Golbabai, A., & Keramati, B. (2008). Modified homotopy- perturbation method for solving Fredholm integral equations. *Chaos, Solitons, and Fractals, 37*, 1528. doi:10.1016/j.chaos.2006.10.037

Gray, P. (1988). Instabilities and oscillations in chemical reactions in closed and open systems. *Proceedings of the Royal Society of London, 415,* 1–34. doi:10.1098/rspa.1988.0001

He, J. H. (1999). Homotopy perturbation technique. *Comput. Math. Appl. Mech. Eng., 178,* 257–262. doi:10.1016/S0045-7825(99)00018-3

He, J. H. (2003). Homotopy perturbation method: A new nonlinear analyticaltechnique. *Applied Mathematics and Computation, 135,* 73–79. doi:10.1016/S0096-3003(01)00312-5

He, J. H. (2003). A simple perturbation approach to Blasius equation. *Applied Mathematics and Computation, 140,* 217–222. doi:10.1016/S0096-3003(02)00189-3

He, J. H. (2006). Homotopy-perturbation method for solving boundary value problems. *Physics Letters. [Part A], 350,* 87–88. doi:10.1016/j.physleta.2005.10.005

He, J. H. (2006). Some asymptotic methods for strongly nonlinear equations. *International Journal of Modern Physics B, 20*(10), 1141–1199. doi:10.1142/S0217979206033796

Marchant, T. R. (2002). Cubic autocatalytic reaction–diffusion equations: semi-analytical solutions. *Proceedings of the Royal Society of London. Series A, 458,* 873–888. doi:10.1098/rspa.2001.0899

Meena, A., & Rajendran, L. (2010). Mathematical modeling of amperometric and potentiometric biosensors and systems of non-linear equations - homotopy- perturbation method. *Journal of Electroanalytical Chemistry, 644,* 50–59. doi:10.1016/j.jelechem.2010.03.027

Odibat, Z., & Momani, S. (2007). A reliable treatment of homotopy- perturbation method for Klein-Gordon equations. *Physics Letters. [Part A], 365,* 351–357. doi:10.1016/j.physleta.2007.01.064

Ozis, T., & Yildirim, A. (2007). A comparative study of He's homotopy- perturbation method for determining frequency-amplitude relation of a nonlinear oscillator with discontinuities. *Int. J. Nonlinear Sci. Numer. Simulation, 8*(2), 243–248. doi:10.1515/IJNSNS.2007.8.2.243

APPENDIX A

BASIC CONCEPTS OF THE HPM

The HPM method has overcome the limitations of traditional perturbation methods. It can take full advantage of the traditional perturbation techniques, so a considerable deal of research has been conducted to apply the homotopy technique to solve various strong non-linear equations. To explain this method, let us consider the following function:

$$D_o(u) - f(r) = 0, \qquad r \in \Omega \tag{A1}$$

with the boundary conditions of

$$B_o(u, \frac{\partial u}{\partial n}) = 0, \qquad r \in \Gamma \tag{A2}$$

where D_o is a general differential operator, B_o is a boundary operator, $f(r)$ is a known analytical function and Γ is the boundary of the domain Ω. Generally speaking, the operator D_o can be divided into a linear part L and a nonlinear part N. Eq. (A1) can therefore be written as

$$L(u) + N(u) - f(r) = 0 \tag{A3}$$

By the homotopy technique, we construct a homotopy $v(r, p) : \Omega \times [0,1] \to \Re$ that satisfies

$$H(v, p) = (1 - p)[L(v) - L(u_0)] + p[D_o(v) - f(r)] = 0. \tag{A4}$$

$$H(v, p) = L(v) - L(u_0) + pL(u_0) + p[N(v) - f(r)] = 0. \tag{A5}$$

where $p \in [0,1]$ is an embedding parameter, and u_0 is an initial approximation of Eq. (A1) that satisfies the boundary conditions. From Eqs. (A4) and (A5), we have

$$H(v, 0) = L(v) - L(u_0) = 0 \tag{A6}$$

$$H(v, 1) = D_o(v) - f(r) = 0. \tag{A7}$$

When $p=0$, Eq. (A4) and Eq. (A5) become linear equations. When $p=1$, they become non-linear equations. The process of changing p from zero to unity is that of $L(v) - L(u_0) = 0$ to $D_o(v) - f(r) = 0$. We first use the embedding parameter p as a "small parameter" and assume that the solutions of Eqs. (A4) and (A5) can be written as a power series in p:

$$v = v_0 + pv_1 + p^2 v_2 + \dots \dots \tag{A8}$$

Setting $p=1$ results in the approximate solution of Eq. (A1):

$$u = \lim_{p \to 1} v = v_0 + v_1 + v_2 + \dots \tag{A9}$$

This is the basic idea of the HPM.

APPENDIX B

APPROXIMATE ANALYTICAL SOLUTIONS OF THE EQUATIONS (1) AND (2) USING HOMOTOPY PERTURBATION METHOD.

In this Appendix, we indicate how Eqs. (5) and (6) in this paper are derived. In order, to determine the solution of Eqs. (1) and (2), initially we construct a Homotopy as follows:

$$(1-p) \left[\frac{\partial^2 a}{\partial x^2} \right] + p \left[\frac{\partial^2 a}{\partial x^2} - \beta \, ab^2 \right] = 0 \tag{B1}$$

$$(1-p) \left[\frac{\partial^2 b}{\partial x^2} - \beta \, \gamma \, b \right] + p \left[\frac{\partial^2 b}{\partial x^2} + \beta \, a \, b^2 - \beta \, \gamma \, b \right] = 0 \tag{B2}$$

and the initial approximations are as follows:

$$x = 1 : \quad a = 1 , b = c_0 \tag{B3a}$$

$$x = 0 : \frac{\partial a}{\partial x} = 0, \frac{\partial b}{\partial x} = 0 \tag{B3b}$$

The approximate solutions of (B1) and (B2) are

$$a = a_0 + pa_1 + p^2 a_2 + p^3 a_3 + \dots \dots \tag{B4}$$

and

$$b = b_0 + pb_1 + p^2 b_2 + p^3 b_3 + \dots \dots \tag{B5}$$

Substituting Eqs. (B4) and (B5) into Eqs. (B1) and (B2) and comparing the coefficients of like powers of p

$$p^0 : \quad \frac{\partial^2 a_0}{\partial x^2} = 0 \tag{B6}$$

and

$$p^1 : \quad \frac{\partial^2 a_1}{\partial x^2} - \beta\, a_0 b_0^{\,2} = 0 \tag{B7}$$

$$p^0 : \quad \frac{\partial^2 b_0}{\partial x^2} - \beta\, \gamma\, b_0 = 0 \tag{B8}$$

and

$$p^1 : \quad \frac{\partial^2 b_1}{\partial x^2} + \beta\, a_0 b_0^{\,2} - \beta\, \gamma\, b_1 = 0 \tag{B9}$$

Solving the equations (B6) to (B9), and using the boundary conditions (B3a) and (B3b), we can find the following results

$$a_0(x) = 1 \tag{B10}$$

and

$$a_1(x) = \frac{\beta\, c_0^{\,2}}{4\cosh^2\sqrt{\beta\,\gamma}} \left[\frac{\cosh 2\sqrt{\beta\,\gamma}x}{2\beta\,\gamma} - \frac{\cosh 2\sqrt{\beta\,\gamma}}{2\beta\,\gamma} + x^2 - 1 \right] \tag{B11}$$

$$b_0(x) = \frac{c_0 \cosh\sqrt{\beta\,\gamma}x}{\cosh\sqrt{\beta\,\gamma}} \tag{B12}$$

and

$$b_1(x) = \frac{c_0^{\,2}\cosh\sqrt{\beta\,\gamma}\,x}{4\gamma\cosh^3\sqrt{\beta\,\gamma}}\left[\frac{2\cosh 2\sqrt{\beta\,\gamma}}{3} - 2\right] - \frac{c_0^{\,2}}{4\gamma\cosh^2\sqrt{\beta\,\gamma}}\left[\frac{2\cosh 2\sqrt{\beta\,\gamma}\,x}{3} - 2\right] \tag{B13}$$

According to the HPM, we can conclude that

$$a(x) = \lim_{p \to 1} a(x) = a_0 + a_1 \qquad (B14)$$

$$b(x) = \lim_{p \to 1} b(x) = b_0 + b_1 \qquad (B15)$$

After putting Eqs. (B10) and (B11) into Eq. (B14) and Eqs. (B12) and (B13) into Eq. (B15), the final results can be described in Eqs. (5) and (6) in the text.

APPENDIX C

SCILAB PROGRAM TO FIND THE NUMERICAL SOLUTION OF EQS. (1) AND (2)

```
function pdex4
m = 0;
x = linspace(0,1);
t = linspace(0,1000);
sol = pdepe(m,@pdex4pde,@pdex4ic,@pdex4bc,x,t);
a1 = sol(:,:,1);
b2 = sol(:,:,2);
 % A solution profile can also be illuminating.
figure
plot(x,u1(end,:))
 % A solution profile can also be illuminating.
figure
plot(x,u2(end,:))
 % --------------------------------------------------------------
function [c,f,s] = pdex4pde(x,t,u,DuDx)
c = [1; 1];
f = [1; 1].* DuDx;
β =0.1;
F=-β *a(1)*b(2)^2;
r=0.5;
F1=β *a(1)*b(2)^2-β * γ *b(2);
s = [F; F1];
 % --------------------------------------------------------------
function u0 = pdex4ic(x);
u0 = [1; 0.1;
 % --------------------------------------------------------------
function [pl,ql,pr,qr] = pdex4bc(xl,ul,xr,ur,t)
pl = [0; 0];
```

```
ql = [1; 1];
pr = [ur(1)-1; ur(2)-0.1];
qr = [0; 0];
```

APPENDIX D

$$y(\tau) = \frac{1}{2\pi i} \int\limits_{c-i\infty}^{c+i\infty} \exp[s\tau]\bar{y}(s)ds = \frac{1}{2\pi i} \oint\limits_{c} \exp[s\tau]\bar{y}(s)ds \tag{D1}$$

$$\oint\limits_{c} F(z)dz = 2\pi i \sum_{n} \mathrm{Re}\, s[F(z)]_{z=z_n} \tag{D2}$$

$$y(\tau) = \sum_{n} \mathrm{Re}\, s[\exp[s\tau]\bar{y}(s)]_{s=s_n} \tag{D3}$$

From the theory of complex variables we can show that the residue of a function $F(z)$ at a simple pole at $z=a$ is given by:

$$\mathrm{Re}\, s[F(z)]_{z=a} = \mathop{Lim}\limits_{z \to a}\{(z-a)F(z)\} \tag{D4}$$

Hence in order to invert Eq. (D5), we need to evaluate $\mathrm{Re}\, s[\cosh(\sqrt{\beta c_0^2 + s}\, x)\,/\, s\cosh(\sqrt{\beta c_0^2 + s})$ at the poles. Now the poles are obtained from $s\cosh(\sqrt{\beta c_0^2 + s}) = 0$. Hence there is a simple pole at $s=0$ and there are infinitely many poles given by the solution of the equation $\cosh(\sqrt{\beta c_0^2 + s_n}) = 0$ and so $s_n = -\frac{1}{4}(2n+1)^2 \pi^2 - \beta c_0^2$ with $n=0,1,2\ldots$. Hence we note that:

$$a(x,s) =$$

$$\mathrm{Re}\, s\left[\frac{\cosh(x\sqrt{\beta c_0^2 + s})}{s\cosh(\sqrt{\beta c_0^2 + s})}\right]_{s=0} + \mathrm{Re}\, s\left[\frac{\cosh(x\sqrt{\beta c_0^2 + s})}{s\cosh(\sqrt{\beta c_0^2 + s})}\right]_{s=s_n} =$$

$$\mathop{Lim}\limits_{s \to 0}(s-0)\left\{\exp(sT)\frac{\cosh(x\sqrt{\beta c_0^2 + s})}{s\cosh(\sqrt{\beta c_0^2 + s})}\right\} + \mathop{Lim}\limits_{s \to s_n}(s-s_n)\left\{\exp(sT)\frac{\cosh(x\sqrt{\beta c_0^2 + s})}{s\cosh(\sqrt{\beta c_0^2 + s})}\right\} \tag{D5}$$

The first residue in Eq. (B5) is given by

$$\mathrm{Re}\,s\left[\frac{\cosh(x\sqrt{\beta c_0^{\,2}+s})}{s\cosh(\sqrt{\beta c_0^{\,2}+s})}\right]_{s=0}=$$

$$\underset{s\to 0}{Lim}\left\{\exp(sT)\frac{\cosh(x\sqrt{\beta c_0^{\,2}+s})}{\cosh(\sqrt{\beta c_0^{\,2}+s})}\right\}=\frac{\cosh(x\sqrt{\beta c_0^{\,2}})}{\cosh(\sqrt{\beta c_0^{\,2}})}$$

(D6)

The second residue in Eq. (D5) can be evaluated as follows. It is established that if $F(z)$ can be expressed as $F(z)=f(z)/g(z)$, where the functions f and g are analytic at $s=s_n$ and $g(s_n)=0$ while $g'(s_n)=0$ and $f(s_n)\neq 0$.

Then $\mathrm{Re}\,s[F(z)]_{s=s_n}=\sum_{n=0}^{\infty}\dfrac{f(s_n)}{g'(s_n)}\exp[s_n\tau]$ Hence we can show that:

$$\underset{s\to s_n}{Lt}\ e^{st}\frac{\cosh(x\sqrt{\beta c_0^{\,2}+s})}{\dfrac{d}{ds}\cosh(\sqrt{\beta c_0^{\,2}+s})}=$$

$$\underset{s\to s_n}{Lt}\ e^{st}\frac{\cosh(x\sqrt{\beta c_0^{\,2}+s})(2\sqrt{\beta c_0^{\,2}+s})}{s_n\sinh(\sqrt{\beta c_0^{\,2}+s})}=$$

(D7)

$$\frac{2(n+1/2)\pi i e^{((-(n+1/2)^2\pi^2-\beta c_0^{\,2})t)}\cosh((n+1/2)\pi i x)}{(-(n+1/2)^2\pi^2-\beta c_0^{\,2})\sinh((n+1/2)\pi i)},$$

$$n=0,\ 1,\ 2......$$

Using $\cosh(i\theta)=\cos(\theta)$ and $\sinh(i\theta)=i\sin(\theta)$

$$\underset{s\to s_n}{Lt}\ e^{st}\frac{\cosh(x\sqrt{\beta c_0^{\,2}+s})}{\cosh(\sqrt{\beta c_0^{\,2}+s})}=$$

$$2\pi\sum_{n=0}^{\infty}(-1)^n\left\{\frac{(n+1/2)\cos\left[(n+1/2)\pi x\right]}{(n+1/2)^2\pi^2+\beta c_0^{\,2}}\right\}\exp\left[-\left\{(n+1/2)^2\pi^2+\beta c_0^{\,2}\right\}T\right]$$

(D8)

Similarly we can take the inverse Laplace transform to Eqs. (16).

Table 1. Comparison of normalized steady-state reactant concentration of a using Eq. (6) and the simulation results for various values of c_0=0.1, β=1 and γ=0.05

x	Numerical solution	This work (Analytical solution) Eq. (6)	% of deviation between Numerical and Analytical solution
0.00	0.9948	0.9952	0.040193
0.10	0.9949	0.9952	0.030145
0.20	0.995	0.9953	0.030142
0.30	0.9953	0.9956	0.030133
0.40	0.9957	0.9959	0.020082
0.50	0.9961	0.9964	0.030108
0.60	0.9967	0.9969	0.020062
0.70	0.9974	0.9975	0.010025
0.80	0.9982	0.9983	0.010017
0.90	0.9991	0.9991	0
1.00	1	1	0
Average deviation			0.020082

Table 2. Comparison of normalized steady-state autocatalyst concentration of b using Eq. (7) and the simulation results for various values of c_0=0.1, β=1 and γ=0.05

x	Numerical solution	This work (Analytical solution) Eq. (7)	% of deviation between Numerical and Analytical solution
0.00	0.1026	0.1023	-0.29326
0.10	0.1026	0.1022	-0.39139
0.20	0.1025	0.1021	-0.39177
0.30	0.1024	0.1020	-0.39216
0.40	0.1022	0.1018	-0.39293
0.50	0.102	0.1016	-0.3937
0.60	0.1017	0.1014	-0.29586
0.70	0.1013	0.1011	-0.19782
0.80	0.1009	0.1007	-0.19861
0.90	0.1005	0.1003	-0.1994
1.00	0.1000	0.1000	0
Average deviation			-0.28608

Table 3. Comparison of normalized steady-state reactant concentration of a using Eq. (6) and the simulation results for various values of c_0=0.1, β=3 and γ=0.08

x	Numerical solution	This work (Analytical solution) Eq. (6)	% of deviation between Numerical and Analytical solution
0.00	0.9844	0.9876	0.324018
0.10	0.9845	0.9877	0.323985
0.20	0.9850	0.9880	0.303644
0.30	0.9858	0.9886	0.283229
0.40	0.9869	0.9895	0.262759
0.50	0.9884	0.9906	0.222088
0.60	0.9901	0.9920	0.191532
0.70	0.9922	0.9936	0.140902
0.80	0.9946	0.9955	0.090407
0.90	0.9973	0.9977	0.040092
1.00	1	1	0
Average deviation			0.198423

Table 4. Comparison of normalized steady-state autocatalyst concentration of b using Eq. (7) and the simulation results for various values of c_0=0.1, β=3 and γ=0.09

x	Numerical solution	This work (Analytical solution) Eq. (7)	% of deviation between Numerical and Analytical solution
0.00	0.1033	0.1004	-2.88845
0.10	0.1033	0.1004	-2.88845
0.20	0.1032	0.10036	-2.82981
0.30	0.1030	0.100365	-2.62542
0.40	0.1028	0.100366	-2.42512
0.50	0.1024	0.100360	-2.03268
0.60	0.1021	0.100341	-1.75302
0.70	0.1016	0.100303	-1.29308
0.80	0.1011	0.100238	-0.85995
0.90	0.1006	0.100135	-0.46437
1.00	0.1	0.1	0
Average deviation			-1.82367

Table 5. Comparison of normalized steady-state reactant concentration of a using Eq. (6) and the simulation results for various values of $c_0=0.2$, $\beta=1$ and $\gamma=0.2$

x	Numerical solution	This work (Analytical solution) Eq. (6)	% of deviation between Numerical and Analytical solution
0.00	0.9804	0.9830	0.264496
0.10	0.9806	0.98312	0.256327
0.20	0.9812	0.98363	0.247044
0.30	0.9822	0.98447	0.230581
0.40	0.9836	0.98566	0.208997
0.50	0.9854	0.98779	0.241954
0.60	0.9876	0.98908	0.149634
0.70	0.9902	0.99133	0.113988
0.80	0.9932	0.99395	0.075457
0.90	0.9966	0.99695	0.035107
1.00	1	1	0
Average deviation			0.16578

Table 6. Comparison of normalized steady-state autocatalyst concentration of b using Eq. (7) and the simulation results for various values of $c_0=0.2$, $\beta=1$ and $\gamma=0.2$

x	Numerical solution	This work (Analytical solution) Eq. (7)	% of deviation between Numerical and Analytical solution
0.00	0.1996	0.1973	-1.16574
0.10	0.1996	0.197297	-1.16728
0.20	0.1997	0.19739	-1.17027
0.30	0.1977	0.19755	-0.07593
0.40	0.1977	0.19778	0.040449
0.50	0.1977	0.19806	0.181763
0.60	0.1998	0.19839	-0.71072
0.70	0.1998	0.19876	-0.52324
0.80	0.1999	0.19916	-0.37156
0.90	0.1999	0.19960	-0.1503
1.00	0.2	0.2	0
Average deviation			-0.4648

Table 7. Comparison of normalized steady-state reactant concentration of a using Eq. (6) and the simulation results for various values of $c_0=1$, $\beta=0.5$ and $\gamma=0.08$

x	Numerical solution	This work (Analytical solution) Eq. (6)	% of deviation between Numerical and Analytical solution
0.00	0.7190	0.7581	5.157631
0.10	0.7219	0.7606	5.088088
0.20	0.7306	0.7679	4.857403
0.30	0.7351	0.7802	5.780569
0.40	0.7653	0.7974	4.025583
0.50	0.7913	0.8195	3.441123
0.60	0.8231	0.8466	2.775809
0.70	0.8605	0.8782	2.015486
0.80	0.9035	0.9157	1.332314
0.90	0.9519	0.9578	0.615995
1.00	1	1	0
Average deviation			3.19

Table 8. Comparison of normalized steady-state autocatalyst concentration of b using Eq. (7) and the simulation results for various values of $c_0=1$, $\beta=0.5$ and $\gamma=0.08$

x	Numerical solution	This work (Analytical solution) Eq. (7)	% of deviation between Numerical and Analytical solution
0.00	1.257	1.218	-3.20197
0.10	1.254	1.216	-3.125
0.20	1.246	1.209	-3.06038
0.30	1.233	1.198	-2.92154
0.40	1.214	1.183	-2.62046
0.50	1.191	1.163	-2.40757
0.60	1.162	1.139	-2.01932
0.70	1.128	1.110	-1.62162
0.80	1.088	1.076	-1.11524
0.90	1.044	1.038	-0.57803
1.00	1	1	0
Average deviation			-2.06101

Table 9. Comparison of normalized steady-state reactant concentration of a using Eq. (6) and the simulation results for various values of $c_0=2$, $\beta=0.1$ and $\gamma=0.02$

x	Numerical solution	This work (Analytical solution) Eq. (6)	% of deviation between Numerical and Analytical solution
0.00	0.8048	0.8003	-0.56229
0.10	0.8067	0.8024	-0.53589
0.20	0.8127	0.8085	-0.51948
0.30	0.8226	0.8187	-0.47636
0.40	0.8364	0.8329	-0.42022
0.50	0.8543	0.8512	-0.36419
0.60	0.8761	0.8736	-0.28617
0.70	0.9020	0.9001	-0.21109
0.80	0.9319	0.9367	0.512437
0.90	0.9659	0.9653	-0.06216
1.00	1	1	0
Average deviation			-0.26595

Table 10. Comparison of normalized steady-state autocatalyst concentration of b using Eq. (7) and the simulation results for various values of $c_0=2$, $\beta=0.1$ and $\gamma=0.02$

x	Numerical solution	This work (Analytical solution) Eq. (7)	% of deviation between Numerical and Analytical solution
0.00	2.193	2.198	0.22748
0.10	2.191	2.195	0.182232
0.20	2.185	2.189	0.182732
0.30	2.175	2.179	0.18357
0.40	2.162	2.165	0.138568
0.50	2.144	2.147	0.13973
0.60	2.123	2.125	0.094118
0.70	2.097	2.099	0.095283
0.80	2.067	2.069	0.096665
0.90	2.034	2.034	0
1.00	2	2	0
Average deviation			0.121853

Figure 1. Non steady-state reactant concentration a profiles calculated using Eq. (17). The parameters are $c_0 = 0.1$ and $\beta = 1$

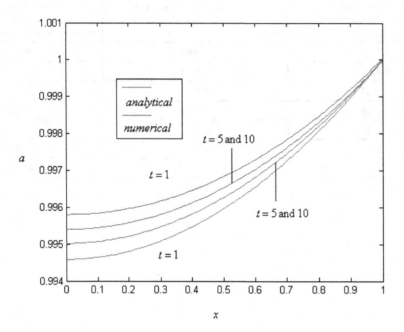

Figure 2. Non steady-state autocatalyst concentration b profiles calculated using Eq.(18). The parameters are $c_0 = 0.1$, $\beta = 1$ and $\gamma = 0.2$

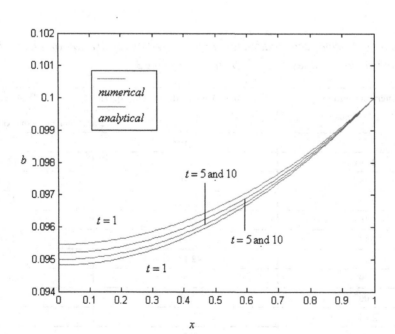

Figure 3. Non steady-state reactant concentration a profiles calculated using Eq. (17). The parameters are $c_0 = 2$ and $\beta = 0.1$

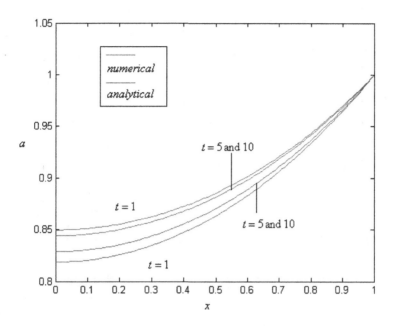

Figure 4. Non steady-state autocatalyst concentration b profiles calculated using Eq.(18). The parameters are $c_0 = 2$, $\beta = 0.1$ and $\gamma = 3$

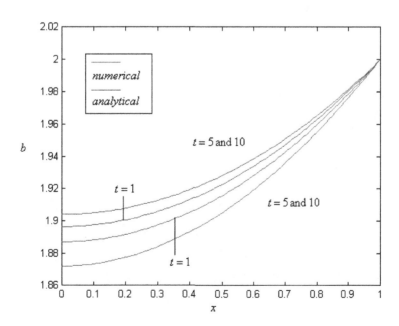

Figure 5. Non steady-state reactant concentration a profiles calculated using Eq. (17). The parameters are $c_0 = 5$ *and* $\beta = 0.1$

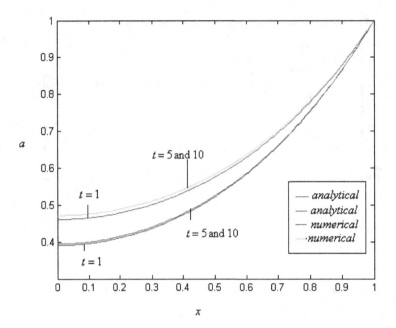

Figure 6. Non steady-state autocatalyst concentration b profiles calculated using Eq.(18). The parameters are $c_0 = 5$ *,* $\beta = 0.1$ *and* $\gamma = 6$

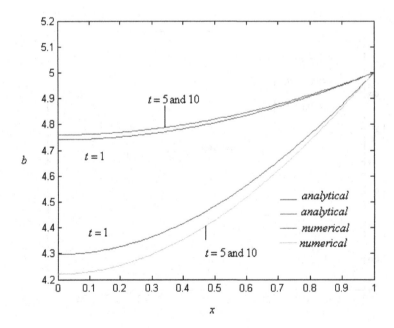

Chapter 10
On Applications of Macromolecular QSAR Theory

Pablo R. Duchowicz
INIFTA, CCT La Plata-CONICET, Argentina

Eduardo A. Castro
INIFTA, CCT La Plata-CONICET, Argentina

ABSTRACT

Present chapter reviews the application of Quantitative Structure-Activity Relationships for the treatment of molecules involving thousands of atoms, such as proteins, nucleic acids (DNA, RNA), or polysaccharides. This is a new developing area of interest in Chemoinformatics, and it is expected to have a growing number of applications during the forthcoming years. Among the several points to be addressed during the modeling of macromolecules, the most important one appears to be the accurate representation of the chemical structure through numerical descriptors. It has to be noticed that descriptors based on optimized three-dimensional geometry are difficult to specify, and it is also a drawback the fact that the experimental geometry is not available. However, different experts in the field have been generalizing the employment of classical types of topological descriptors in macromolecular systems.

INTRODUCTION

During last decades, the Quantitative Structure-Activity Relationships (QSAR) (Hansch, 1995; Kubinyi, 2008) Theory has played an important role in many research areas, such as Medicinal Chemistry, enabling to prevent time consuming and costs associated to experiments. Since the pioneer studies performed by Hansch and Fujita in 1964 (Hansch, 1964), the QSAR formalism has been extensively applied to the study of different biological activities of interest, so the development of the theory is encouraged (Duchowicz, 2008; Duchowicz, 2009a; Duchowicz, 2009b; Goodarzi, 2009; Puzyn, 2009; Selassie, 2002).

DOI: 10.4018/978-1-60960-860-6.ch010

The basis of QSAR relies on the main hypothesis that the biological activity manifested by a chemical compound completely results from its own molecular structure. It is an approach that has a thermodynamical resemblance, in the sense that QSAR is only interested on the initial and final states (molecular structure and final activity, respectively), but does not offer specific details on the usually complex mechanism/path of action involved. However, it is possible to get insight on the underlying mechanism by means of the predicted activity.

In the realms of the theory, the molecular structure is translated into the so-called molecular descriptors, describing some relevant feature of the compounds, with mathematical formulae obtained from Chemical Graph Theory, Information Theory, Quantum Mechanics, Markov Chains Theory, etc. There exist more than a thousand available descriptors in the literature (Diudea, 2001; Katritzky, 1995; Todeschini, 2009; Trinajstic, 1992), and many of these molecular descriptors are topological indices (TIs) or invariants obtained from the molecular graph, whose vertices are atoms weighted with different physicochemical properties (mass, polarity, electronegativity, charge) (Katritzky, 1993).

Even though the relationship between the structure and the activity remains unknown for a given dataset, the QSAR technique has been based on statistically determined linear or nonlinear models relating the chemical behavior of compounds with descriptors, in order to find out useful parallelisms. Altogether, QSAR studies are effected by various factors from which the most important are: (a) the selection of molecular descriptors that should include maximum information of structures and minimum colinearity between them; (b) the use of suitable modeling methods; (c) the number of descriptors to be included in the model; (d) the composition of the training and test sets; and (e) the employment of validation techniques to verify the predictive performance of the developed models. Feature (descriptor) selection has been an active research area in Pattern Recognition, Statistics and Data Mining communities, and its main objective is to select a subset of input variables by eliminating features with little or no predictive information (Guyon, 2003).

In the early 1990´s there has been a great explosion in the proposal of new TIs, and a huge number of TIs have been derived for small-sized molecules that many of them result redundant and their structural information content overlaps with that of others (González-Díaz, 2007d). In addition, most TIs are obtained via vector-matrix-vector procedures (Estrada, 2001). However, the perspective is different for Macromolecular Science, as classical TIs and the more elaborated topographic indices (TPGIs) have never-explored applications on this field. Present chapter reviews such applications performed by different authors during last years.

BACKGROUND

There is a constant need to have an accurate description of the molecular structure, as the characterization of the underlying connectivity of a system enables one to introduce mathematical tools for studying the properties of macromolecules through the QSAR Theory (González-Díaz, 2008b; González-Díaz, 2009). It is possible to extend the classical QSAR applications beyond the study of small-sized molecules. In a chemical graph, each node represents one part of a complex system and the edges represent geometrical or functional relationships between these parts. At the macromolecular scale, such node may be an aminoacid or a protein. A molecular graph can be numerically described using various classic TIs, such as the Wiener index, Zagreb indices, Harary numbers, Randic connectivity indices, valence connectivity indices, Marrero-Ponce quadratic or linear forms, Balaban index, Broto-Moreau autocorrelation, and graph TIs for Markov matrices reported by González-Díaz et al. (2005a)

Among the advantages of using TIs for protein representation appear: a) fast estimation of RNA secondary structure from a sequence; b) simple representation of RNA as graphs susceptible to matrix manipulation; c) easy of computation of TIs.

Different graph representations can be used in order to enumerate macromolecular structures (González-Díaz, 2008b). The Bond-Atom Graph (BAG) approach identifies atoms with graph nodes and chemical bonds with graph edges, thus generating very large graphs which can be employed in complex network theory to treat RNA secondary structures. Other RNA graphs identify vertices or edges with RNA secondary topologies, and the approach is called Secondary Topology Graphs (STG) which follow different predetermined rules (Gan, 2003). The Nucleotide or Amino acid Adjacency Networks (NAANs) graph representation identifies each node with a nucleotide or amino acid and each edge with nucleotide-nucleotide or amino acid-amino acid adjacency relationships due to binding by covalent bonding, hydrogen bonding or another kind of relationship. The appropriate selection of a given structural representation is strongly dependent on the problem under study.

QSAR ON DNA, RNA AND PROTEIN SEQUENCES

There is an increasing use of TIs to study proteins or DNA/RNA sequence-function relationships (Aguero-Chapin, 2008), and classic TIs can be expanded to study protein sequences. The work of Ramos de Armas et al. (2004a) reports the generalization of Markovian entropies and stochastic spectral moments to predict biological properties of polypeptide chains. Furthermore, the Amino Acid Sequence Autocorrelations (AASA) represent new TIs that are based on the well-known Broto-Moreau 2D-Autocorrelation descriptors, also employed for the analysis of wild-type and mutant lysozymes (Caballero, 2006), and for

studying the conformational stability of gene V proteins (Fernández, 2007). Among the examples of TIs without analogues for small-scale molecules appear the sequence-order-coupling numbers introduced by Chou, which have proven very useful for the prediction of membrane-type proteins (Chou, 2005; Chou, 2007), nucleic acid binding proteins (Cai, 2003), enzyme classes (Cai, 2005), protein quaternary structure (Chou, 2003) and protein sub-cellular locations (Chou, 2006).

Various recent publications describe the definition and calculation of new RNA TIs for NAANs, which can be identified as RNA secondary structure stochastic spectral moments (Gonzalez-Diaz, 2005), entropies and potentials (González-Díaz, 2006a) in analogy to those derived on small-sized molecules. Coupling numbers can also be extended to RNA secondary structures, and so a study describes a QSAR for the prediction of activity in ACOs (1-aminocyclopropane-1-carboxylic acid oxidases) proteins, having a 97.8% accuracy in a ten-fold cross-validation (González-Díaz, 2007a). Another study reports the prediction of a new sequence of ACO protein from *Psidium guajaba* with a QSAR model based on entropy type TIs (Gonzalez-Diaz, 2005). Such types of TIs are also used to distinguish mycobacterial protein synthesis promoters from random sequences, resulting in a relevant QSAR that does not rely on sequence alignments (González-Díaz, 2007b; González-Díaz, 2006a; Kalate, 2003). Also, it is proposed the use of quantum chemical descriptors and weighted structural descriptors, closely related to Randic TIs and Balaban distance indices as a distinctive characteristic of each RNA structure (Galindo, 2006).

In contrast to RNA, there are very few realistic and natural representations for DNA and protein sequences that can be transformed into NAANs (González-Díaz, 2008b). Various researchers have developed artificial but effective representations of DNA and proteins. Many TIs have been reviewed in detail for NAAN-type representations of DNA sequences (Liao, 2005; Liao, 2006; Nandy, 1994;

Nandy, 1996; Nandy, 2006; Randic, 2001). In addition, the 2D-level has been surmounted by the construction of 3D (Randic, 2000), 4D (Randic, 2003), and 6D level (Liao, 2004) NAANs for DNA primary sequences.

QUANTITATIVE STRUCTURE-BINDING-RELATIONSHIPS

Methods from QSAR Theory which relate to protein-drug or RNA-drug interactions are referred as Quantitative Structure-Binding Relationships (QSBR) studies, as they involve a hybrid of QSAR with 3D-topographic indices (TPGIs) and Molecular Docking procedures (Chalk, 2004) for describing the drug-target complex (Deng, 2004). The prediction of the binding affinity is a critical component of computer-aided drug design.

A novel TPGI derived on the basis of the computational geometry of protein-ligand interfaces and atomic electronegativities is used in a QSBR study of 264 diverse protein-ligand complexes with known binding constants (Zhang, 2006). Another QSBR analysis involves the study of steroid-DB3 antibody binding affinities with a proposed TPGI as protein folding degree index, calculated from the eigenvalues of a matrix that is obtained by introducing the cosines of the polypeptide chain dihedral angles in the main diagonal of the Adjacency matrix (Estrada, 2003). It is also important to predict protein function from structure, and different methods are proposed that are capable of assigning protein function in the absence of sequence similarity (Dobson, 2005; Han, 2006).

The use of TIs in RNA-drug interaction problems remains under development. For instance, a QSAR model is established (González-Díaz, 2003a) to predict local binding affinity constants of the antibiotic Paromomycin with specific nucleotides at the packaging region of the RNA present in type-1 HIV. The TIs describing the local drug-nucleic acid complexes in a linear regression model are called the Markov chain vibration entropies of the drug-RNA complex, and could result important in the discovery of new anti-HIV compounds or in the elucidation of their mode of action. Other kind of TIs applied to model this system involve stochastic spectral moments of the drug-RNA complex (González-Díaz, 2003b), and topological linear and quadratic indices of the RNA NAANs (Marrero-Ponce, 2004b; Marrero Ponce, 2005).

FUTURE RESEARCH DIRECTIONS

In many situations the biological activity under investigation is highly dependent on the spatial arrangement of the protein, and detailed X-ray descriptions (x, y, z crystal cartesian coordinates) for protein amino acids are difficult to obtain. However, it is possible to get more quickly useful 3D structural information of close contact amino acid pairs from Nuclear Magnetic Resonance (NMR) data (Navarro, 2002; Navarro, 2004). In this way, it is possible to translate the protein as a NAAN type graph, with vertices being amino acids and edges expressing the pair-wise closeness of these amino acids.

From the respective graph matrix representation, one can calculate pseudo-spatial TIs for proteins. As it is known, the advantage of using pseudo 3D-CIs is that they have fast calculation times because they are based only on NANNs constructed from sequence connectivity and partial 3D information such as atom proximity due to hydrogen bonding, disulfide bridges or salt bridge (González-Díaz, 2007c; González-Díaz, 2005d). The use of this strategy allows introducing protein Markov entropies (Ramos de Armas, 2004b) and stochastic spectral moments (González-Díaz, 2005d), protein TIs based on linear (Marrero-Ponce, 2005) and quadratic (Marrero-Ponce, 2004a) algebraic forms, and TIs of pseudo-electrostatic potentials (González-Díaz, 2005c). The previous TIs can easily be extended to detailed structural TPGIs (González-Díaz, 2005b; González-Díaz, 2006b; Saiz-Urra, 2005).

Another comparative study shows the different degrees of accuracy obtained in the classification of stable/non-stable proteins using TIs of variable complexity (González-Díaz, 2007c). Furthermore, an application of the pseudo 3D-CIs mentioned above is performed for characterizing the protein surface, which finds importance for example in establishing a model that predicts the probability with which various viral capsid proteins of one strain of human rhinovirus (HRV) bind to each of two possible receptors (González-Díaz, 2008b).

It is possible to translate the information contained by mass spectra (MS) into chemical graphs, in order to build different TIs and link them to the disease/health situation of a clinical patient. Blood proteome mass spectra represent a potential tool for the early detection of diseases through the employment of modeling techniques (González-Díaz, 2008b), as every cell in the body leaves a record of its physiological state in the products it sheds to the blood, either as waste or as signals to neighboring cells. The use of TIs may help to capture not only linear but non-linear relationships between the regions in the MS. The application of this approach requires finding the best graphs and TIs that lead to the best results. For instance, Nandy's DNA graph (Nandy, 1996), Randic's Shining-Star (Randic, 2007) and Square-Spiral graphs (Randic, 2005) are employed to represent human serum-plasma-proteome MS for healthy and prostate cancer patients (González-Díaz, 2008a). These graphs have been previously applied to DNA and protein sequences.

CONCLUSION

The study of drug interaction with biomolecules is a very important area of research and constitutes a significant step toward rational drug design. Present review covers various interesting applications of topological descriptors in macromolecular QSAR studies, which find crucial importance for

describing proteins, DNA, RNA, or polysaccharides in term of their associated biological activities. This is a new promising research field that will remain under development during the forthcoming years, as the three-dimensional macromolecular structure is usually unknown. In addition, the graph-based approaches allow the rapid collection, annotation, retrieval, comparison and mining of chemical structures within large databases. As the QSAR Theory is well-established for small-sized molecules, the mathematical procedures to be implemented in the macromolecular scale are essentially the same ones, and so many novel applications of the theory can be expanded to this relatively unexplored field. In other words, once the macromolecular chemical structure is properly quantified, there are available several alternative mathematical tools for establishing predictive QSAR models for a given purpose.

ACKNOWLEDGMENT

We thank to the Consejo Nacional de Investigaciones Científicas y Técnicas (CONICET) and the Universidad Nacional de La Plata for supporting this work.

REFERENCES

Aguero-Chapin, G., Antunes, A., Ubeira, F. M., Chou, K.-C., & González-Díaz, H. (2008). Comparative Study of Topological Indices of Macro/Supramolecular RNA Complex Networks. *Journal of Chemical Information and Modeling, 48*, 2265–2277. doi:10.1021/ci8001809

Caballero, J., Fernandez, L., Abreu, J. I., & Fernandez, M. (2006). Amino acid sequence autocorrelation vectors and ensembles of Bayesian-regularized genetic neural networks for prediction of conformational stability of human lysozyme mutants. *Journal of Chemical Information and Modeling, 46*, 1255–1268. doi:10.1021/ci050507z

Cai, Y. D., & Chou, K. C. (2005). Predicting enzyme subclass by functional domain composition and pseudo amino acid composition. *Journal of Proteome Research, 4,* 967–971. doi:10.1021/pr0500399

Cai, Y. D., & Lin, S. L. (2003). Support vector machines for predicting rRNA-, RNA-, and DNA-binding proteins from amino acid sequence. *Biochimica et Biophysica Acta, 1648,* 127–133.

Chalk, A. J., Worth, C. L., Overington, J. P., & Chan, A. W. (2004). PDBLIG: classification of small molecular protein binding in the Protein Data Bank. *Journal of Medicinal Chemistry, 47,* 3807–3816. doi:10.1021/jm040804f

Chou, K. C., & Cai, Y. D. (2003). Predicting protein quaternary structure by pseudo amino acid composition. *Proteins, 53,* 282–289. doi:10.1002/prot.10500

Chou, K. C., & Cai, Y. D. (2005). Prediction of membrane protein types by incorporating amphipathic effects. *Journal of Chemical Information and Modeling, 45,* 407–413. doi:10.1021/ci049686v

Chou, K. C., & Shen, H. B. (2006). Predicting protein subcellular location by fusing multiple classifiers. *Journal of Cellular Biochemistry, 99,* 517–527. doi:10.1002/jcb.20879

Chou, K. C., & Shen, H. B. (2007). MemType-2L: A web server for predicting membrane proteins and their types by incorporating evolution information through Pse-PSSM. *Biochemical and Biophysical Research Communications, 360,* 339–345. doi:10.1016/j.bbrc.2007.06.027

Deng, W., Breneman, C., & Embrechts, M. J. (2004). Predicting protein-ligand binding affinities using novel geometrical descriptors and machine-learning methods. *Journal of Chemical Information and Computer Sciences, 44,* 699–703. doi:10.1021/ci034246+

Diudea, M. V. E. (2001). *QSPR/QSAR Studies by Molecular Descriptors.* New York: Nova Science Publishers.

Dobson, P. D., & Doig, A. J. (2005). Predicting enzyme class from protein structure without alignments. *Journal of Molecular Biology, 345,* 187–199. doi:10.1016/j.jmb.2004.10.024

Duchowicz, P. R., & Castro, E. A. (2008). Partial Order Theory Applied to QSPR-QSAR Studies. In Brueggemann, R. (Ed.), *Combinatorial Chemistry and High Throughput Screening (special issue)* (pp. 783–793). New York: Bentham Science Publishers.

Duchowicz, P. R., & Castro, E. A. (2009a). Application of the Fuzzy Logic Theory to QSAR/QSPR Studies. In Putz, M. (Ed.), *Quantum Frontiers of Atoms and Molecules in Physics, Chemistry and Biology.* Cairo, Egypt: Hindawi Publishing Corp.

Duchowicz, P. R., Fernández, F. M., & Castro, E. A. (2009b). The Employment of Orthogonalization Methods in QSPR-QSAR Studies. In Pandalai, S. G., & Castro, E. A. (Eds.), *QSPR-QSAR Studies on Desired Properties for Drug Design.* New York: Research Signpost/Transworld Research Network.

Estrada, E. (2001). Generalization of topological indices. *Chemical Physics Letters, 336,* 248–252. doi:10.1016/S0009-2614(01)00127-0

Estrada, E. (2003). Application of a novel graph-theoretic folding degree index to the study of steroid-DB3 antibody binding affinity. *Computational Biology and Chemistry, 27,* 305–313. doi:10.1016/S1476-9271(02)00078-6

Fernández, L., Caballero, J., Abreu, J. I., & Fernández, M. (2007). Amino acid sequence autocorrelation vectors and Bayesian regularized genetic neural networks for modeling protein conformational stability: Gene V protein mutants. *Proteins, 67,* 834–852. doi:10.1002/prot.21349

Galindo, J. F., Bermudez, C. I., & Daza, E. E. (2006). tRNA structure from a graph and quantum theoretical perspective. *Journal of Theoretical Biology, 240,* 574–582. doi:10.1016/j.jtbi.2005.10.017

Gan, H. H., Pasquali, S., & Schlick, T. (2003). Exploring the repertoire of RNA secondary motifs using graph theory; implications for RNA design. *Nucleic Acids Research, 31,* 2926–2943. doi:10.1093/nar/gkg365

González-Díaz, H., Agüero-Chapin, G., Varona, J., Molina, R., Delogu, G., & Santana, L. (2007a). 2D-RNA-coupling numbers: A new computational chemistry approach to link secondary structure topology with biological function. *Journal of Computational Chemistry, 28,* 1049–1056. doi:10.1002/jcc.20576

González-Díaz, H., Aguero-Chapin, G., Varona-Santos, J., Molina, R., de la Riva, G., & Uriarte, E. (2005). 2D RNA-QSAR: assigning ACC oxidase family membership with stochastic molecular descriptors; isolation and prediction of a sequence from Psidium guajava L. *Bioorganic & Medicinal Chemistry Letters, 15,* 2932–2937. doi:10.1016/j.bmcl.2005.03.017

González-Díaz, H., Cruz-Monteagudo, M., Vina, D., Santana, L., Uriarte, E., & De Clercq, E. (2005a). QSAR for anti-RNA-virus activity, synthesis, and assay of anti-RSV carbonucleosides given a unified representation of spectral moments, quadratic, and topologic indices. *Bioorganic & Medicinal Chemistry Letters, 15,* 1651–1657. doi:10.1016/j.bmcl.2005.01.047

González-Díaz, H., de Armas, R. R., & Molina, R. (2003a). Markovian negentropies in bioinformatics. 1. A picture of footprints after the interaction of the HIV-1 Psi-RNA packaging region with drugs. *Bioinformatics (Oxford, England), 19,* 2079–2087. doi:10.1093/bioinformatics/btg285

González-Díaz, H., de Armas, R. R., & Molina, R. (2003b). Vibrational Markovian modelling of footprints after the interaction of antibiotics with the packaging region of HIV type 1. *Bulletin of Mathematical Biology, 65,* 991–1002. doi:10.1016/S0092-8240(03)00064-8

González-Díaz, H., Ferino, G., Podda, G., & Uriarte, E. (2008a). Discriminating prostate cancer patients from control group with connectivity indices. *ECSOC, 12,* 1–10.

González-Díaz, H., González-Díaz, Y., Santana, L., Ubeira, F. M., & Uriarte, E. (2008b). Proteomics, networks and connectivity indices. *Proteomics, 8,* 750–778. doi:10.1002/pmic.200700638

González-Díaz, H., Molina, R., & Uriarte, E. (2005b). Recognition of stable protein mutants with 3D stochastic average electrostatic potentials. *FEBS Letters, 579,* 4297–4301. doi:10.1016/j.febslet.2005.06.065

González-Díaz, H., Pérez-Bello, A., Cruz-Monteagudo, M., González-Díaz, Y., Santana, L., & Uriarte, E. (2007b). Chemometrics for QSAR with Low Sequence Homology: Mycobacterial Promoter Sequences Recognition with 2D-RNA Entropies. *Chemometrics and Intelligent Laboratory Systems, 85,* 20–26. doi:10.1016/j.chemolab.2006.03.005

González-Díaz, H., Perez-Bello, A., Uriarte, E., & González-Díaz, Y. (2006a). QSAR study for mycobacterial promoters with low sequence homology. *Bioorganic & Medicinal Chemistry Letters, 16,* 547–553. doi:10.1016/j.bmcl.2005.10.057

González-Díaz, H., Pérez-Castillo, Y., Podda, G., & Uriarte, E. (2007c). Computational chemistry comparison of stable/nonstable protein mutants classification models based on 3D and topological indices. *Journal of Computational Chemistry, 28,* 1990–1995. doi:10.1002/jcc.20700

González-Díaz, H., Prado-Prado, F., Pérez-Montoto, L. G., Duardo-Sánchez, A., & López-Díaz, A. (2009). QSAR Models for Proteins of Parasitic Organisms, Plants and Human Guests: Theory, Applications, Legal Protection, Taxes, and Regulatory Issues. *Current Proteomics, 6,* 214–227. doi:10.2174/157016409789973789

González-Díaz, H., Sanchez-González, A., & González-Díaz, Y. (2006b). 3D-QSAR study for DNA cleavage proteins with a potential anti-tumor ATCUN-like motif. *Journal of Inorganic Biochemistry, 100,* 1290–1297. doi:10.1016/j.jinorgbio.2006.02.019

González-Díaz, H., & Uriarte, E. (2005c). Proteins QSAR with Markov average electrostatic potentials. *Bioorganic & Medicinal Chemistry Letters, 15,* 5088–5094. doi:10.1016/j.bmcl.2005.07.056

González-Díaz, H., Uriarte, E., & Ramos de Armas, R. (2005d). Predicting stability of Arc repressor mutants with protein stochastic moments. *Bioorganic & Medicinal Chemistry, 13,* 323–331. doi:10.1016/j.bmc.2004.10.024

González-Díaz, H., Vilar, S., Santana, L., & Uriarte, E. (2007d). Medicinal Chemistry and Bioinformatics-Current Trends in Drugs Discovery with Networks Topological Indices. *Current Topics in Medicinal Chemistry, 7,* 1015–1029. doi:10.2174/156802607780906771

Goodarzi, M., Duchowicz, P. R., Wu, C. H., Fernández, F. M., & Castro, E. A. (2009). New Hybrid Genetic Based Support Vector Regression as QSAR Approach for Analyzing Flavonoids-GABA(A) Complexes. *Journal of Chemical Information and Modeling, 49,* 1475–1485. doi:10.1021/ci900075f

Guyon, I., & Elisseeff, A. (2003). An Introduction to Variable and Feature Selection. *Journal of Machine Learning Research, 3,* 1157–1182. doi:10.1162/153244303322753616

Han, L., Cui, J., Lin, H., Ji, Z., Cao, Z., Li, Y., & Chen, Y. (2006). Recent progresses in the application of machine learning approach for predicting protein functional class independent of sequence similarity. *Proteomics, 6,* 4023–4037. doi:10.1002/pmic.200500938

Hansch, C., & Fujita, T. (1964). Q-σ-π Analysis. A Method for the Correlation of Biological Activity and Chemical Structure. *Journal of the American Chemical Society, 86,* 1616–1626. doi:10.1021/ja01062a035

Hansch, C., & Leo, A. (1995). *Exploring QSAR. Fundamentals and Applications in Chemistry and Biology.* Washington, D. C.: American Chemical Society.

Kalate, R. N., Tambe, S. S., & Kulkarni, B. D. (2003). Artificial neural networks for prediction of mycobacterial promoter sequences. *Computational Biology and Chemistry, 27,* 555–564. doi:10.1016/j.compbiolchem.2003.09.004

Katritzky, A. R., & Goordeva, E. V. (1993). Traditional Topological Indices vs. Electronic, Geometrical, and Combined Molecular Descriptors in QSAR/QSPR Research. *Journal of Chemical Information and Computer Sciences, 33,* 835–857. doi:10.1021/ci00016a005

Katritzky, A. R., Lobanov, V. S., & Karelson, M. (1995). QSPR: the correlation and quantitative prediction of chemical and physical properties from structure. *Chemical Society Reviews, 24,* 279–287. doi:10.1039/cs9952400279

Kubinyi, H. (2008). *QSAR: Hansch Analysis and Related Approaches.* New York: Wiley-Interscience.

Liao, B., & Ding, K. (2005). Graphical approach to analyzing DNA sequences. *Journal of Computational Chemistry, 26,* 1519–1523. doi:10.1002/jcc.20287

Liao, B., & Wang, T. M. (2004). Analysis of similarity/dissimilarity of DNA sequences based on nonoverlapping triplets of nucleotide bases. *Journal of Chemical Information and Computer Sciences, 44*, 1666–1670. doi:10.1021/ci034271f

Liao, B., Xiang, X., & Zhu, W. (2006). Coronavirus phylogeny based on 2D graphical representation of DNA sequence. *Journal of Computational Chemistry, 27*, 1196–1202. doi:10.1002/jcc.20439

Marrero Ponce, Y., Castillo Garit, J. A., & Nodarse, D. (2005). Linear indices of the 'macromolecular graph's nucleotides adjacency matrix' as a promising approach for bioinformatics studies. Part 1: prediction of paromomycin's affinity constant with HIV-1 psi-RNA packaging region. *Bioorganic & Medicinal Chemistry, 13*, 3397–3404. doi:10.1016/j.bmc.2005.03.010

Marrero-Ponce, Y., Medina-Marrero, R., Castillo-Garit, J. A., Romero-Zaldivar, V., Torrens, F., & Castro, E. A. (2005). Protein linear indices of the 'macromolecular pseudograph alpha-carbon atom adjacency matrix' in bioinformatics. Part 1: prediction of protein stability effects of a complete set of alanine substitutions in Arc repressor. *Bioorganic & Medicinal Chemistry, 13*, 3003–3015. doi:10.1016/j.bmc.2005.01.062

Marrero-Ponce, Y., Medina-Marrero, R., Castro, E. A., Ramos de Armas, R., González, H., Romero, V., & Torrens, F. (2004a). Protein quadratic indices of the "macromolecular pseudograph's a-carbon atom adjacency Matrix". 1. prediction of Arc repressor alanine-mutant's stability. *Molecules (Basel, Switzerland), 9*, 1124–1147. doi:10.3390/91201124

Marrero-Ponce, Y., Nodarse, D., González-Díaz, H., Ramos de Armas, R., Romero-Zaldivar, V., Torrens, F., & Castro, E. A. (2004b). Nucleic acid quadratic indices of the "macromolecular graph's nucleotides adjacency matrix" modeling of footprints after the interaction of paromomycin with the HIV-1 C-RNA packaging region. *International Journal of Molecular Sciences, 5*, 276–293. doi:10.3390/i5110276

Nandy, A. (1994). Recent investigations into global characteristics of long DNA sequences. *Indian Journal of Biochemistry & Biophysics, 31*, 149–155.

Nandy, A. (1996). Two-dimensional graphical representation of DNA sequences and intron-exon discrimination in intronrich sequences. *Computer Applications in the Biosciences, 12*, 55–62.

Nandy, A., Harle, M., & Basak, S. C. (2006). Mathematical descriptors of DNA sequences: Development and applications. *ARKIVOC, 9*, 211–238.

Navarro, E., Fenude, E., & Celda, B. (2002). Solution structure of a D,L-alternating oligonorleucine as a model of doublestranded antiparallel beta-helix. *Biopolymers, 64*, 198–209. doi:10.1002/bip.10172

Navarro, E., Fenude, E., & Celda, B. (2004). Conformational and structural analysis of the equilibrium between single- and double-strand beta-helix of a D,L-alternating oligonorleucine. *Biopolymers, 73*, 229–241. doi:10.1002/bip.10549

Puzyn, T., Leszczynski, J., & Cronin, M. T. (2009). *Recent Advances in QSAR Studies: Methods and Applications*. New York: Springer.

Ramos de Armas, R., González-Díaz, H., Molina, R., Pérez-Gonzalez, M., & Uriarte, E. (2004a). Stochastic-based descriptors studying peptides biological properties: Modeling the bitter tasting threshold of dipeptides. *Bioorganic & Medicinal Chemistry, 12,* 4815–4822. doi:10.1016/j. bmc.2004.07.017

Ramos de Armas, R., González-Díaz, H., Molina, R., & Uriarte, E. (2004b). Markovian Backbone Negentropies: Molecular descriptors for protein research. I. Predicting protein stability in Arc repressor mutants. *Proteins, 56,* 715–723. doi:10.1002/prot.20159

Randic, M., & Balaban, A. T. (2003). On a four-dimensional representation of DNA primary sequences. *Journal of Chemical Information and Computer Sciences, 43,* 532–539. doi:10.1021/ci020051a

Randic, M., Guo, X., & Basak, S. C. (2001). On the characterization of DNA primary sequences by triplet of nucleic acid bases. *Journal of Chemical Information and Computer Sciences, 41,* 619–626. doi:10.1021/ci000120q

Randic, M., Lers, N., Plavsic, D., Basak, S., & Balaban, A. T. (2005). Four-color map representation of DNA or RNA sequences and their numerical characterization. *Chemical Physics Letters, 407,* 205–208. doi:10.1016/j.cplett.2005.03.086

Randic, M., Vracko, M., Nandy, A., & Basak, S. C. (2000). On 3-D graphical representation of DNA primary sequences and their numerical characterization. *Journal of Chemical Information and Computer Sciences, 40,* 1235–1244. doi:10.1021/ci000034q

Randic, M., Zupan, J., & Vikic-Topic, D. (2007). On representation of proteins by star-like graphs. *Journal of Molecular Graphics & Modelling, 26,* 290–305. doi:10.1016/j.jmgm.2006.12.006

Saiz-Urra, L., González-Díaz, H., & Uriarte, E. (2005). Proteins Markovian 3D-QSAR with spherically-truncated average electrostatic potentials. *Bioorganic & Medicinal Chemistry, 13,* 3641–3647. doi:10.1016/j.bmc.2005.03.041

Selassie, C. D., Mekapati, S. B., & Verma, D. P. (2002). QSAR: Then and Now. *Current Topics in Medicinal Chemistry, 2,* 1357–1379. doi:10.2174/1568026023392823

Todeschini, R., & Consonni, V. (2009). *Molecular Descriptors for Chemoinformatics.* Weinheim: Wiley-VCH.

Trinajstic, N. (1992). *Chemical Graph Theory.* Boca Raton, FL: CRC Press.

Zhang, S., Golbraikh, A., & Tropsha, A. (2006). Development of quantitative structure-binding affinity relationship models based on novel geometrical chemical descriptors of the protein-ligand interfaces. *Journal of Medicinal Chemistry, 49,* 2713–2724. doi:10.1021/jm050260x

Chapter 11

Virtual Screening:
An Emergent, Key Methodology for Drug Development in an Emergent Continent– A Bridge Towards Patentability

Alan Talevi
CCT La Plata CONICET, Argentina

Eduardo A. Castro
INIFTA, CCT La Plata CONICET, Argentina

Luis E. Bruno-Blanch
CCT La Plata CONICET, Argentina

ABSTRACT

The universe of known organic chemical compounds has grown exponentially during the last 50 years, which greatly increases the probability of finding chemotherapeutic agents which interact selectively with any given molecular target. Traditional systematic pharmacological screening of available drug-like compounds has, however, can not keep the pace with the uninterrupted growth of the chemical space. The last 20 years have thus witnessed the emergence of novel high throughput screening technologies conceived to explore the vast chemical universe in an efficient manner, among them, virtual or in silico screening.

In this chapter, the authors analyze virtual screening advantages and the classification of virtual screening approaches. They also discuss the current and potential importance of virtual screening for drug development in Latin America. Finally, they present a brief overview on virtual screening perspectives.

DOI: 10.4018/978-1-60960-860-6.ch011

INTRODUCTION

The advances in Organic Chemistry and in technologies related to chemical synthesis have resulted in a tremendous increase in the rate of development of new chemical entities. The number of known chemical compounds has been growing exponentially during the last four decades. In 2009, the Chemical Abstract Service (http://www.cas.org), a subsidiary of the American Chemical Society responsible for the most comprehensive collection of disclosed chemical substance information in the world (from both patent and journal literature), announced the record of its 50 millionth substance. The 40 millionth compound had been registered just nine months before. In contrast, the 10 millionth chemical was not registered until 1990. Pubchem Substance (http://pubchem.ncbi.nlm.nih.gov), a chemical database oriented to small chemical compounds, includes to the day more than 17 million records of substances.

This is a promising scenario for the pharmaceutical sector: in this virtual infinite universe of chemicals it is highly probable to find compounds that selectively interact with any given molecular target of interest. Nevertheless, as Kubinyi has once and again described, the drug discovery process is, in this background, quite equivalent to the proverbial search for a needle in a haystack (Kubinyi, 2002; the reader may also see Profesor Kubinyi's website and conferences therein, http://www.kubinyi.de/). Exploring this vast chemical space in an exhaustive manner (through systematic pharmacological screening of all known chemical entities against all possible biological targets) is no longer feasible (nor rational) in terms of time and resources that ought to be invested. Instead, Medicinal Chemists have developed alternative approaches to explore the haystack in a cost and time-efficient manner. *High Throughput Screening* (HTS), for example, merges microarrays and robotics to test small samples of a series of compounds against a wide range of in vitro tests (Pereira & Williams, 2007). Instead of asking a researcher to carefully analyze each element of the haystack until the unique properties of the needle are revealed to the experienced eye, HTS replaces (to some extent) the human ingredient by automated technologies relying on robotics, controlling software and sensitive detectors. On the other hand there is Virtual Screening (VS): a heterogenic set of computational techniques to explore digital representations of chemical entities recorded in chemical databases, in order to indentify potential candidates gathering an array of structural constrains or requisites that are somehow linked to certain biological and/or chemical properties. The use of VS has been progressively increasing since the first campaigns in the early 1990s, as illustrated in Figure 1.

In this chapter we will analyze the advantages and types of VS and we will discuss the opportunities linked to the use of this approach in Latin America, related to potential patenting of research and development (R&D) on new drugs and possible collaborations between the academic and the industrial sectors. We will also include a short section on perspectives of VS.

BACKGROUND

Advantages of Virtual Screening

Among the advantages of VS one might mention:

- **Time-efficiency**. Today, the fastest approaches can today easily handle a collection of several millions of chemical structure in a few weeks period (Muegge & Oloffa, 2006). The ever-growing processor speed of computers may allow attaining this time-efficiency when more complex approaches are involved, in the near future.
- **Cost-efficiency**. Once a lab has acquired (or developed in-house) a chemical database and the necessary hardware and software to apply a given methodology, the

Figure 1. Frequency of appearance of the expression "virtual screening" in article titles or keywords (considering both original articles and reviews) in well-know scientific literature browsers Scirus (public access, http://www.scirus.com) and Scopus (access under subscription). The expansion in the use of VS techniques can be clearly observed.

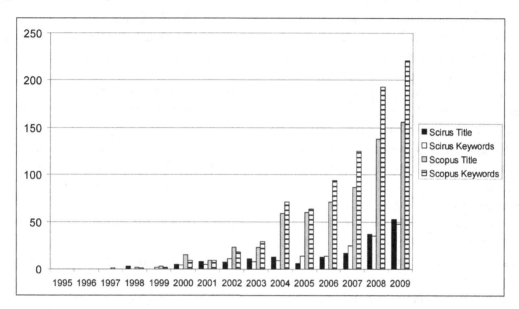

cost of the VS campaign is just the time that the process demands to the specialized human resources assigned to the project. One should bear in mind that there do exist public chemical databases such as ZINC or Pubchem (Irwin & Shoichet, 2005; Baykoucheva, 2007) and that free applications to assist in VS campaigns may also be obtained (e.g., PowerMV from the National Institute of Statistical Sciences is a free resource that allows for similarity searches on chemical databases (Liu, Feng, & Young, 2005); similarity searches are also possible –online- through Pubchem itself (Hur, 2008). More complex, specific applications usually require acquisition of permanent or temporary licenses. Regarding hardware, most applications run smoothly in a modern personal computer. VS can help optimizing expenditure on *in vitro*, pre-clinical and clinical testing on a rational basis, early avoiding the experi-

mental testing and development of those compounds with low *a priori* probability of gathering the desired pharmacological and pharmacokinetic profile. Of course one has to consider, among the costs associated to a VS experiment, the expenditure on synthesis or acquisition of the selected hits and their pharmacological testing. However, the balance between sensitivity and specificity is user-defined and context dependent (Triballeau, Acher, Brabet, Pin, & Bertrand, 2005). In a background of limited resources to invest in acquisition and testing of compounds a researcher might choose to minimize the number of false positives at the expense of sacrificing potential novel scaffolds; on the contrary, when resources abound one might admit a higher degree of failure at pharmacological testing in order to obtain a wider range of chemotypes among the hits.

- **Theoretical nature.** In HTS, (very small) samples of the compounds to be tested have to be acquired or synthesized. VS does not require samples of the database compounds previously to the screening, and even hypothetic structures can be considered in the database. Pharmacological testing (either *in vitro* or *in vivo*) follows a selection of potential candidates on a rational basis. This advantage has pushed the development of integrated VS and HTS campaigns (Gong, Fang, Peng, Liu, & Du, 2010; Bajorath, 2002; Edwards et al., 2005).

- **Second uses.** Off-label medication use, i.e. the clinical application of drugs for indications other than those evaluated and approved by public regulatory organisms, is widespread in many areas of Medicine (Pandolfini & Bonati, 2005; Pickar, Vinik, & Bartko, 2008; Levêque, Michallat, Schaller, & Ranc, 2005). Recently, on the other hand, much attention has been given to *drug repurposing* or *drug reprofiling*, i.e. finding (and eventually patenting, through a *Swiss-type* claim) a new use for an existing drug or molecule, a practice that can provide a fast and low-risk return on investment (note that many drugs approved for indications different from those originally researched, such as sildenafil or finasteride, have became major blockbusters) (Verma et al., 2005; Carley, 2005; Carley, 2005; Tobinick, 2009). In other words, it exists plenty empirical and systematic evidence of the potential therapeutic and economic benefits of finding new indications for known drugs. VS can serve as a tool to assist researching on second uses from a rational and systematic perspective, by prioritizing pharmacological testing of VS hits already used for treatment of other

conditions unrelated to the therapeutic target of the VS campaign.

- **Bioethics.** Bioethical considerations urge researchers to replace and reduce the use of animal models as much as possible by early application of *in silico* and *in vitro* experiments (Claude, 2009).

Classification of Virtual Screening Methods

The most basic classification scheme of VS approaches splits the different methodologies in target and ligand-based techniques.

Structure-Based Virtual Screening

Target- (or structure-) based methodologies may be applied whenever the tertiary or quaternary structure of the molecular target of interest (usually a protein) is available through X rays crystallography, NMR, or homology modeling efforts. Structure-based VS implies docking of each of the compounds in the screened database (in one or more conformations) to the binding site of the molecular target, simulating molecular recognition events (see and example in Figure 2).

Most available protein structures correspond to water-soluble proteins, due to the intrinsic difficulties linked to obtaining membrane/transmembrane proteins such as ionic channels, multidrug resistance transporters, etc. (Seddon, Curnow, & Booth, 2004; Lin & Guidotti, 2009; Macher & Yen, 2007; Caffrey, 2003). Membrane proteins are usually present in low levels at biological membranes; thus, they can not be readily obtained in sufficient amounts from their native environment and they must be over-expressed. A major difficulty for the over-expression of membrane proteins in vectors such as *E. coli* is the aggregation of the protein in the cytoplasm of the host cell and the absence of post-translational modifications in bacterial hosts. Secondly, membrane

Figure 2. Screenshot of docking of bencylsulfamide to carbonic anhdrase, isoenzime II

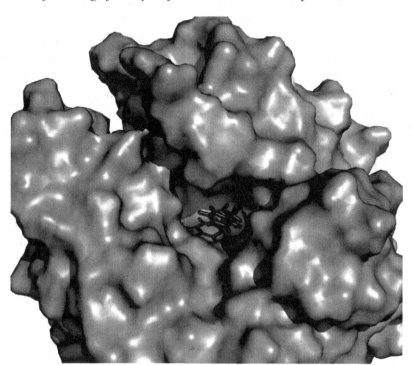

proteins are embedded in a lipid, dynamic and complex bilayer, which limits the application of standard biophysical techniques to determine their structure. Finally, membrane proteins are generally non-soluble in aqueous solution, and they require special synthetic systems (e.g. detergents) for *in vitro* work. The limitations to characterize membrane proteins and the fact that about 30% of the human genome is estimated to codify membrane proteins (Terstappen & Reggiani, 2001) (which are potential therapeutic targets) explain the importance of ligand-based techniques when the structure of the molecular target is not available.

Ligand-Based Virtual Screening

Among the VS ligand-based methodologies we propose three sub-categories: pharmacophore-based approaches, descriptor-based approaches and similarity-based approaches.

A pharmacophore is a molecular framework that carries the essential features required for a drug's biological activity, or, according to IUPAC's definition, an ensemble of steric and electronic features that is necessary to ensure the optimal supramolecular interactions with a specific biological target and to trigger (or block) its biological response (Wermuth, Ganellin, Lindberg, & Mitscher, 1998). Many good recent reviews on pharmacophore-based VS have been published (Gao, Yang, & Zhu, 2010; Sun, 2008; Yang, 2010). Pharmacophore generation is usually performed by extracting common features from 3D molecular structures of known ligands (the training or calibration set). The central issues when building and applying pharmacophore hypothesis are: handling conformational flexibility and conducting molecular alignment (superimposition) (Yang, 2010). Detailed analysis of these challenges is out of the scope of this chapter. Nevertheless, three strategies have been considered to cope with molecular flexibility: a) building the pharmacophore hypothesis from one or more rigid, active ligands; b) pre-enumerating and saving multiple, plausible conformations of the training set and the screened database compounds or; c) carrying the conformational analysis during the pharmacophore modeling process (on the fly approach). The conformational sampling can be performed through different approaches: systematic conformational analysis, genetic algorithms, Monte Carlo algorithms and others. Regarding molecular alignment, it can essentially be conducted through either point-based approaches (in which distances between atoms or chemical feature points are minimized) or through property-based approaches (which use molecular field descriptors –usually represented through Gaussian functions- to generate the alignment) (Wolber, Seidel, Bendix, & Langer, 2008; Lemmen & Lengauer, 2000). Predefining anchor points may well be a problem when structurally dissimilar ligands are considered. It jumps out from the previous description that pharmacophore-based VS can be very time consuming when applied to large chemical databases with flexible molecules. Combined VS approaches integrating screening filters in increasing order of complexity have been proposed to overcome this limitation (see *Future research directions* section for more detail).

Descriptor-based approaches rely on numerical representations of different aspects of molecular structure, called molecular descriptors. Statistical approaches are applied to find meaningful correlations between a dependent variable (the modeled property or activity of a training set of compounds) and one or more molecular descriptors. These relationships are known as Quantitive Structure-Activity/Property Relationships (QSAR, QSPR). When the scope of the modeling effort is to apply the resulting QSAR model in a VS campaign, two essential requisites are to assure the molecular diversity of the training set (during the modeling process) and to perform a careful applicability domain assessment (during the screening of the chemical database). Once

again, the reader is referred to the *Future research directions* section for some notes on applicability domain. Descriptors can be either of high dimensionality (3D descriptors) or low dimensionality (0D-2D descriptors). The use of 3D descriptors requires previous conformational analysis of the compounds from both the training set and the chemical database (to assure sampling of representative, low-energy conformations or at least to perform the computations on a single, probable conformer); in some cases, the alignment issue is also present (e.g. in the CoMFA approach). An alternative to solve the flexibility and alignment problems is the use of low dimensional descriptors, from constitutional, 0D descriptors (derived from the chemical formula, such as the molecular weight or the number of atoms of a given chemical element that are present in the compound) to 2D descriptors (e.g. topological descriptors). A recent review from the group of molecular topology from the Valencia University shows that the application of topological descriptors has been successful in the search of drugs from diverse therapeutic categories, among them antivirals, antibiotics, anticancer agents, hypoglucemics and many others (García-Doménech, Gálvez, de Julián Ortiz, & Pogliani, 2008).

At last, the medicinal chemist may resort to similarity-based VS when a very limited number of know ligands of the chosen molecular target are known and thus there is no training set to derive meaningful QSAR models from (Willet, 2006). The most basic similarity measurement involves a quantitative comparison of two molecules. The comparison is usually based on contrasting bitstrings derived from the molecules being compared: binary sequences in which every bit indicates the presence or absence of a given structural feature. The features encrypted in the bitstring may be of 2D or 3D nature. As Willet (2006) describes, a similarity measure comprises three components: the system used to characterize the pair of molecules that are being compared; a weighting scheme to assign different degrees of

Figure 3. An example of similarity comparison

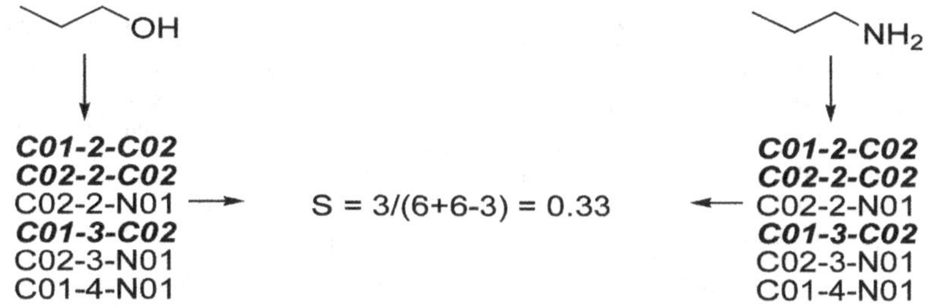

importance to the different patterns involved in the comparison and; an algorithm used to quantify the degree of relatedness between the two bitstrings derived from both molecules (i.e. a similarity coefficient, the most frequently used coefficient being Tanimoto similarity coefficient). The features most commonly compared are 2D substructures, defined as a subgraph of the graph associated to a chemical structure, labeled or colored in a manner that reflects the nature of the atoms and bonds comprised in the parental molecule (Merlot, Domine, Cleva, & Church, 2003). An example of 2D substructure used in similarity comparison are Carhart's atom pairs, defined as:

(atom 1 description) – (separation) – (atom 2 description)

where description of the atoms includes the atom type (chemical element) plus the number of π electrons it bears plus the number of non-hydrogen atoms bonded to it, and separation stands for the number of atoms involved in the atom pair (including atom 1 and atom 2) or, what is the same, the topological distance between atom 1 and atom 2 plus one. Figure 3 presents a similarity comparison between two simple structures, n-propanol and n-propylamine. Tanimoto similarity coefficient in its binary form is used for assessment of similarity:

$$S_{A,B} = \frac{c}{a + b - c} \qquad (1)$$

where a is the number of features (types of Carhart atom pairs) present in compound A (let us say, n-propanol), b is the number of features present in compound B (let us say n-propylamine) and c is the number of common features.

During the last 15 years increasing attention has been given to 3D substructure systems (the reader is referred to the pioneering work of Good & Kuntz (1995), Mason et al. (1999) and Mason & Cheney (1999). 3D substructures used in the context of similarity searching have been mostly based on the idea of capturing classical pharmacophore features such as hydrophobic and aromatic moieties, hydrogen bond donor and acceptor groups, groups with formal negative and positive charges and others (e.g. chirality centers). 3D fingerprints (encrypt information of pairs, triplets or quartets of such pharmacophore elements, using different distance ranges between these features.

It is worth mentioning that recent systematic comparisons of the performance (in terms of both bare enrichment factor and scaffold hopping) through VS simulations across different molecular targets has shown that, surprisingly, simpler approaches (e.g. 2D similarity) can outperform more complex methodologies (docking and 3D similarity) in terms of enrichment factor, thought pharmacophore fingerprints and structure-based VS seem to be superior in terms of scaffold hopping (Good, Hermsmeier, & Jindle, 2004; Zhang & Muegge, 2006). This supports the in parallel combined use of 2D ligand-based approaches and 3D ligand-based or structure-based methodolo-

Table 1. Pros and cons of the different VS approaches

VS Approach	Advantages	Disadvantages
Structure-based	Allows visualization and understanding of ligand-target interactions. Scaffold hopping.	Requires NMR or X rays structure of the molecular target (or, at least, a homolog protein). Difficulties to solve membrane proteins structures.
Pharmacophore-based	Considers optic isomers. It can be applied when there are few known-ligands, especially if one of them is not flexible. Good scaffold hopping.	High computational cost. Flexibility and alignment-related issues.
3D Descriptor-based	In the case of grid-based methods, easy interpretation. It can take into account optic isomers. In the case of alignment independent 3D methodologies, alignment is not an issue.	Flexibility and alignment issues (the latter only when grid-based, alignment-dependent methodologies such as CoMFA are used). A diverse sets of known ligands is required.
2D Descriptor-based	Low computational cost. Conformation-independent and alignment-independent.	Difficulties with optic isomers. The (physicochemical) meaning of some 2D descriptors is difficult to interpret. A diverse sets of known ligands is required.
2D Similarity-based	Only one known ligand required. Low computational cost. High enrichment factors. Conformation and alignment- independent.	Difficulties with optic isomers. Low scaffold hopping.

gies, as we will discuss later. Table 1 presents a comparative synthesis of the advantages and disadvantages of the different VS approaches discussed here.

VIRTUAL SCREENING IN LATIN AMERICA: ACHIEVEMENTS AND POTENTIALITIES

Issues

Even though filling science to market gap (i.e. commercializing university research by transforming basic and applied research into industrial, technology-oriented innovations) is a universal problem (Shibata, Kajikawa, & Sakata, 2010; Hellman, 2007; Rasmussen, 2008; Curry, 2008), it is an especially important issue in Latin America, where most of the R&D expenditure is funded by government and executed by government R&D institutes and universities (see Brazil, Argentina and Mexico data in the Organization for Economic Co-operation and Development's Main Science and Technology Indicators 2010/1 edition and Science, Technology and Industry Scoreboard

2007. In contrast, in developed countries (e.g. the United States or Japan) most of the R&D expenditure is financed by industry. In Argentina, for example, 67.5% of R&D expenditure are financed by government, while in US and Japan 67.3 and 78.2%, in that order, are financed by industry. The important gap between Latin American countries and developed countries regarding patent application can be visualized in Figure 4.

It has been point out that patenting scientific discoveries encourages the scientific community to push their discoveries out to industry (Hellman, 2007). It has been proved, also (through analysis of references to non-patent literature in patent applications), that some patent classes are more dependent on the progress of scientific knowledge than others, among them biotechnology, pharmaceuticals, fine organic chemistry and information and communication technologies (Organization for Economic Co-operation and Development, 2007; European Commission, 2002; Jaffe & Trajyenberg, 2002; Webb, Dernis, Harhoff, & Hoisl, 2005). Therefore, promoting patenting of scientific inventions linked to the patent classes that depend heavily on scientific knowledge (e.g. pharmaceuticals) seems as a necessary activity in

Figure 4. Number of patent applications to the US Patent and Trademark Office, by country. The graph was build from the Organization for Economic Co-operation and Development (OECD) compendium of patent statistics 2008 (available in http://www.oecd.org). Note the significant gap between Latin American countries and developed countries. Note that scale on the y-axis is logarithmic.

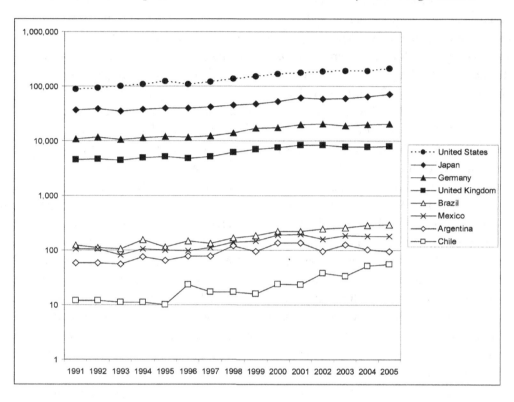

a region characterized by a very high participation of governments in R&D funding. Nevertheless, introducing a new drug into the market demands about 800 million dollars and 12 years (mainly due to the clinical phases of the development) (Dimasi, Hansen, & Grabowsky, 2003) and local industry seems reluctant to invest in such risky, expensive activity. Little exploration has thus been given to drug development in Latin America besides the work in the academia and public research facilities, which rarely makes it to the market in our region. Note that only 20 out of 1393 new drugs introduced in the world pharmaceutical market between 1975 and 1999 correspond to chemotherapeutic entities meant for the treatment of tropical diseases (Trouiller et al., 2002).

Solutions and Recommendations

We believe the use of VS to rationally guide drug repurposing (finding second uses of known drugs) is a clever strategy to promote drug patenting in our continent, through Swiss-type claims (use of substance X in the manufacture of a medicament for the treatment of condition Y), and attend urgent therapeutic needs in our continent and other developing regions. Since known drugs are well characterized in terms of their pharmacokinetic and toxicological profile, finding second uses of known drugs would also mean a significant saving in the clinical phases of drug development, allowing participation of Latin America in a market that rises to more than 600,000 million dollars a year (European Federation of Pharmaceutical Industries and Associations, 2007).

Currently, most of the efforts for drug development based on VS in Latin America come from the research groups of Bruno-Blanch and collaborators (La Plata, Argentina) (Prieto, Talevi, & Bruno-Blanch, 2006; Talevi, Bellera, Castro, Bruno-Blanch, 2006; Talevi, Sella-Cravero, Castro, & Bruno-Blanch, 2007; Talevi, Bellera, Castro, & Bruno-Blanch, 2007; Bellera, Talevi, & Bruno-Blanch, 2007; Gavernet, Talevi, Castro, & Bruno-Blanch, 2008), da Silva and collaborators (Sao Paulo, Brazil) (da Silva et al., 2008; Braun et al., 2008, da Silva et al., 2010; Hage-Melim, da Silva, Semighini, Taft, & Sampaio, 2009) and, fundamentally, Las Villas (Cuba) research group (Castillo-Garit et al., 2010; Casañola-Martin et al., 2008; Casañola-Martin et al., 2007; Montero-Torres et al., 2006; Marrero-Ponce et al., 2005; Meneses-Marcel et al., 2005), although other groups are emerging fast, especially in Brazil and Mexico (the list of citations is not exhaustive and serves only for guiding purposes). As an example of drug reprofiling, it is worth highlighting that Talevi et al. have identified the anticonvulsant activity in the MES test of widely-used preservatives propylparaben and methylparaben (Talevi, Bellera, Castro, & Bruno-Blanch, 2007). We would also like to underline the integrated approach taken by da Silva and coworkers (da Silva et al., 2008; Braun et al., 2008) and the fact that many of the VS campaigns from Latin America are oriented to the discovery of novel therapeutic agents for the treatment of endemic, poverty-related health conditions, such as Chagas disease, tuberculosis and malaria (Prieto, Talevi, & Bruno-Blanch, 2006; Casañola-Martin et al., 2007; Castillo-Garit et al., 2010; Montero-Torres et al., 2006; Prado-Prado, González-Díaz, de la Vega, Ubeira, & Chou, 2008; Malvezzi et al., 2008; Freitas et al., 2009; da Rocha Pita et al., 2009; Segura-Cabrera & Rodríguez Pérez, 2008).

FUTURE RESEARCH DIRECTIONS

In the last five years, several articles have reported the used of combined VS strategies, which integrated either 2D and 3D ligand-based VS approaches or ligand-based and structure-based methodologies in a single VS campaign. The combination of techniques can be cascade-like (in series) or in parallel. In series approaches used computationally inexpensive approaches (e.g. similarity-based VS) at the beginning of the VS cycle, pruning the list of potential candidates to a manageable number that can be analyzed through more costly methodologies, from the computational point of view. When different approaches are integrated through in parallel schemes, the general idea is to take advantage of the higher enrichment obtained through low-dimensionality VS and the high scaffold hopping observed in the case of 3D ligand-based or target-based methodologies. A vast review on this matter was recently published by Talevi, Gavernet & Bruno-Blanch (2009).

Another issue that has recently raised much interest is applicability domain assessment, i.e. determining what region of the chemical space is a given training set representative of, or, in other words, to quantify how much reliable the prediction on a VS hit is. Different methods have been proposed to define the applicability domain of a model, among them the classical descriptor-range method (strictly valid when the training set compounds are uniformly distributed in the chemical space), geometrical approaches, distance-based techniques and probability density distribution methods (Jaworska, Nokolova-Jeliazkova, & Aldenberg, 2005). This last approach includes parametric and non-parametric methods: parametric methods assume that the distribution of the data fits a standard distributions such as Gaussian or Poisson distributions, while non-parametric methods make no assumptions about data distribution and reflects the actual distribution, identifying empty sub-regions inside the boundaries of the region of the chemical space defined by the training set, with no need to define any reference points. Similarity-based approaches have also been explored (e.g. the count of the number of neighbors with similarity above a given threshold in the training set, the count of well-predicted neighbors, the similarity to the n-nearest neighbors from the training set, etc) (Sheridan, Feuston, Maiorov, & Kearsley, 2004; Dragos, Gilles, & Alexandre, 2009).

Finally, from the observation that most drug development projects used to fail because of distribution and toxicity-related problems (see Figure 5) (Schuster, Laggner, & Langer, 2005), in the last 15 years we have witnessed the development and application of high-throughput screening technologies (*in vitro* and *in silico*) aimed to discard candidates with unfavorable absorption, distribution, metabolism, excretion and toxicity properties (ADME/T) at the very early phases of development (lead discovery) (Khakar, 2010; Hop et al., 2008; Van de Waterbeemd, 2005). The advent of in vitro ADME-HTS provided a large amount ADME quality data that fueled the development of *in silico* models. Current challenge is to develop global (rather than local) accurate models to ultimately replace the in vitro experimental counterparts.

CONCLUSION

VS is a modern, efficient tool for the exploration of the increasingly vast chemical space of known small organic molecules in search for new lead compounds. Its application in Latin America has not been fully explored yet, though more and more groups in the region are beginning to realize its huge potential and producing their first VS-based drug discoveries. Among the Latin American groups with the greatest experience on this topic the innovative and prolific work of the group of Marrero-Ponce and coworkers (Cuba) deserves to be highlighted. The potential VS-guided discovery of second uses of known drugs represents a great opportunity in a region characterized by high investment on R&D from the public sector, low investment from private enterprises, neglected diseases such as Chagas disease and few international patent applications. The discovery of second uses could trigger an increase of pharmaceutical patent applications through Swiss-type claims. Many of the current VS projects aim to locally develop therapeutic answers to orphan diseases that provide low economic incentives to the international pharmaceutical companies. Eventually, public efforts towards drug discovery should be accompanied by strong "push" policies from the government and the high education institutions to establish bonds with the private sector, disclose

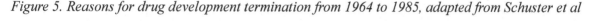

Figure 5. Reasons for drug development termination from 1964 to 1985, adapted from Schuster et al

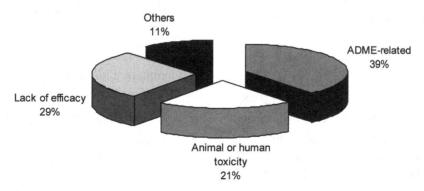

research outcomes and locate and commercialize the scientific developments from academia.

Current hot topics related to VS include research on applicability domain assessment (a critical issue if one remembers that, from a limited training set, millions of compounds from chemical repositories are analyzed and predicted), integrating global ADME/T filters and combining VS approaches of different level of complexity.

ACKNOWLEDGMENT

The authors would like to thank CONICET and National University of La Plata. A. Talevi would like to thank TWAS for the travel grant to assist to TWAS/BioVisionAlexandria.NXT 2010 and BioVisionAlexandria 2010 Conference; which were very inspiring for his contributions to the present chapter.

REFERENCES

Bajorath, J. (2002). Integration of virtual and high-throughput screening. *Nature Reviews. Drug Discovery*, *1*(11), 882–894. doi:10.1038/nrd941

Baykoucheva, S. (2007). A new era in chemical information: PubChem, DiscoveryGate, and chemistry central. *Online (Wilton, Connecticut)*, *31*(5), 16–20.

Bellera, C. L., Talevi, A., & Bruno-Blanch, L. E. (2007). Aplicación de Análisis Lineal Discriminante en la Búsqueda de Drogas Antiepileptogénica. *Latin American Journal of Pharmacy*, *26*(2), 244–252.

Braun, G. H., Jorge, D. M., Ramos, H. P., Alves, R. M., da Silva, V. B., & Giuliatti, S. (2008). Molecular dynamics, flexible docking, virtual screening, ADMET predictions, and molecular interaction field studies to design novel potential MAO-B inhibitors. *Journal of Biomolecular Structure & Dynamics*, *25*(4), 347–355.

Caffrey, M. (2003). Membrane protein crystallization. *Journal of Structural Biology*, *142*(1), 108–132. doi:10.1016/S1047-8477(03)00043-1

Carley, D. W. (2005). Drug repurposing: Identify, develop and commercialize new uses for existing or abandoned drugs. Part I. *IDrugs*, *8*(4), 306–309.

Carley, D. W. (2005). Drug repurposing: Identify, develop and commercialize new uses for existing or abandoned drugs. Part II. *IDrugs*, *8*(4), 310–313.

Casañola-Martin, G. M., Marrero-Ponce, Y., Khan, M. T. H., Ather, A., Sultan, S., Torrens, F., & Rotondo, R. (2007). TOMOCOMD-CARDD descriptors-based virtual screening of tyrosinase inhibitors. Evaluation of different classification model combinations using bond-based linear indices. *Bioorganic & Medicinal Chemistry*, *15*(3), 1483–1503. doi:10.1016/j.bmc.2006.10.067

Casañola-Martín, G. M., Marrero-Ponce, Y., Tareq Hassan Khan, M., Torrens, F., Pérez-Giménez, F., & Rescigno, A. (2008). Atom- and bond-based 2D TOMOCOMD-CARDD approach and ligand-based virtual screening for the drug discovery of new tyrosinase inhibitors. *Journal of Biomolecular Screening*, *13*(10), 1014–1024. doi:10.1177/1087057108326078

Castillo-Garit, J. A., Vega, M. C., Rolon, M., Marrero-Ponce, Y., Kouznetsov, V. V., & Torres, D. F. A. (2010). Computational Discovery of novel trypanosomicidal drug-like Chemicals by using bond-based non-stochastic and stochastic quadratic maps and linear discriminant analysis. *European Journal of Pharmaceutical Sciences*, *39*(1-3), 30–36. doi:10.1016/j.ejps.2009.10.007

Claude, N. (2009). Reducing the use of laboratory animals. *Bulletin de l'Académie Nationale de Médicine*, *193*(8), 1767–1772.

Curry, S. H. (2008). Translational science: past, present and future. *BioTechniques*, *44*(2), 2–8. doi:10.2144/000112749

Da Rocha Pita, S. S., Cirino, J. J. V., de Alencastro, R. B., Castro, H. C., Rodrigues, C. R., & Albuquerque, M. G. (2009). Molecular docking of a series of peptidomimetics in the trypanothione binding site of *T. cruzi* Trypanothione Reductase. *Journal of Molecular Graphics & Modelling*, *28*(4), 330–335. doi:10.1016/j.jmgm.2009.08.011

Da Silva, C. H. T. de P., da Silva, V. B., Resende, J., Rodrigues, P. F., Bononi, F. C., Benevenuto, C. G., & Taft, C. A. (2010). Computer-aided drug design and ADMET predictions for identification and evaluation of novel potential farnasyltransferase inhibitors in cancer therapy. *Journal of Molecular Graphics & Modelling, 28*(6), 513–523. doi:10.1016/j.jmgm.2009.11.011

Da Silva, V. B., Kawano, D. F., Gomes, A. S., Carvalho, I., Taft, C. A., & da Silva, C. H. T. de P. (2008). Molecular dynamics, density functional, ADMET predictions, virtual screening, and molecular interaction field studies for identification and evaluation of novel potential CDK2 inhibitors in cancer therapy. *The Journal of Physical Chemistry A, 112*(38), 8902–8910. doi:10.1021/jp8011969

Dimasi, J. A., Hansen, R. W., & Grabowsky, H. G. (2003). The price of innovation: new estimates of drug development costs. *Journal of Health Economics, 22*(2), 151–185. doi:10.1016/S0167-6296(02)00126-1

Dragos, H., Gilles, M., & Alexandre, V. (2009). Predicting the predictability: a unified approach to the applicability domain problem of QSAR models. *Journal of Chemical Information and Modeling, 49*(7), 1762–1776. doi:10.1021/ci9000579

Edwards, B. S., Bologa, C., Young, S. M., Balakin, K. V., Prossnitz, E. R., & Savchuck, N. P. (2005). Integration of virtual screening with high-throughput flow cytometry to identify novel small molecule formylpeptide receptor antagonists. *Molecular Pharmacology, 68*(5), 1301–1310. doi:10.1124/mol.105.014068

European Commission. Linking science to technology bibliographic references in patents (2002). *DG Research project report.*

European Federation of Pharmaceutical Industries and Associations (2007). *The pharmaceutical industry in figures.*

Freitas, R. F., Prokopczyk, I. M., Zottis, A., Oliva, G., Andricopulo, A. D., & Trevisan, M. T. S. (2009). Discovery of novel Trypanosoma cruzi glyceraldehyde-3-phosphate deshydrogenase inhibitors. *Bioorganic & Medicinal Chemistry, 17*(6), 2476–2482. doi:10.1016/j.bmc.2009.01.079

Gao, Q., Yang, L., & Zhu, Y. (2010). Pharmacophore based drug design approach as a practical process in drug discovery. *Current Computer-aided Drug Design, 6*(1), 37–49. doi:10.2174/157340910790980151

García-Doménech, R., Gálvez, J., de Julián Ortiz, J. V., & Pogliani, I. (2008). Some new trends in chemical graph theory. *Chemical Reviews, 108*(3), 1127–1169. doi:10.1021/cr0780006

Gavernet, L., Talevi, A., Castro, E. A., & Bruno-Blanch, L. E. (2008). A combined virtual screening 2D and 3D QSAR methodology for the selection of new anticonvulsant candidates from a natural products library. *QSAR & Combinatorial Science, 27*(9), 1120–1129. doi:10.1002/qsar.200730055

Gong, L. L., Fang, L. H., Peng, J. H., Liu, A. L., & Du, G. H. (2010). Integration of virtual screening with high-throughput screening for the identification of novel Rho-kinase I inhibitors. *Journal of Biotechnology, 145*(3), 295–303. doi:10.1016/j.jbiotec.2009.12.003

Good, A. C., Hermsmeier, M. A., & Hindle, S. A. (2004). Measuring CAMD technique performance: a virtual screening case study in the design of validation experiments. *Journal of Computer-Aided Molecular Design, 18*(7-9), 529–536. doi:10.1007/s10822-004-4067-1

Good, A. C., & Kuntz, I. D. (1995). Investigating the extension of pairwise distance pharmacophore measures to triplet-based descriptors. *Journal of Computer-Aided Molecular Design, 9*(4), 373–379. doi:10.1007/BF00125178

Hage-Melim, L. I. da S., da Silva, C. H. T de P., Semighini, E. P., Taft, C. A., & Sampaio, S. V.Computer-aided drug design of novel PLA2 inhibitor candidates for treatment of snakebite. *Journal of Biomolecular Structure & Dynamics, 27*(1), 27–36.

Hellmann, T. (2007). The role of patents for bridging the science to market gap. *Journal of Economic Behavior & Organization, 63*(4), 624–647. doi:10.1016/j.jebo.2006.05.013

Hop, C. E. (2008). High throughput ADME screening: practical considerations, impact on the portfolio and enabler of in silico ADME models. *Current Drug Metabolism, 9*(9), 847–853. doi:10.2174/138920008786485092

Hur, J., & Wild, D. J.(n.d.). PubChemSR: A search and retrieval tool for PubChem. *Chemistry Central Journal, 2*, 11.

Irwin, J. J., & Shoichet, B. K. (2005). Zinc – A free database of commercially available compounds for virtual screening. *Journal of Chemical Information and Modeling, 45*(1), 177–182. doi:10.1021/ci049714+

Jaffe, A., & Trajtenberg, M. (2002). *Patents, citations and innovations: A window on the knowledge economy*. Cambridge, MA: MIT Press.

Jaworska, J., Nikolova-Jeliazkova, N., & Aldenberg, T. (2005). QSAR applicability domain estimation by projection of the training set in descriptor space: a review. *Alternative to Laboratoy Animals: ATLA, 33*(5), 445–459.

Khakar, P. S. (2010). Two-dimensional (2D) in silico models for absorption, distribution, metabolism, excretion and toxicity (ADME/T) in drug discovery. *Current Topics in Medicinal Chemistry, 10*(1), 116–126. doi:10.2174/156802610790232224

Kubinyi, H. (2002). The design of combinatorial libraries. *Drug Discovery Today, 7*(9), 503–504. doi:10.1016/S1359-6446(02)02274-2

Lemmen, C., & Lengauer, T. (2000). Computational methods for the structural alignment of molecules. *Journal of Computer-Aided Molecular Design, 14*(3), 215–232. doi:10.1023/A:1008194019144

Levêque, D., Michallat, A. C., Schaller, C., & Ranc, M. (2005). Off label drug use in adult patients treated by anticancer chemotherapy. *Bulletin du Cancer, 92*(5), 498–500.

Lin, S. H., & Guidotti, G. (2009). Chapter 35. Purification of membrane proteins. *Methods in Enzymology, 463*, 619–629. doi:10.1016/S0076-6879(09)63035-4

Liu, K., Feng, J., & Young, S. S. (2005). PowerMV: A software environment for molecular viewing, descriptor generation, data analysis and hit evaluation. *Journal of Chemical Information and Modeling, 45*(2), 515–522. doi:10.1021/ci049847v

Macher, B. A., & Yen, T. Y. (2007). Proteins at membrane surfaces – a review of approaches. *Molecular BioSystems, 3*(10), 705–713. doi:10.1039/b708581h

Malvezzi, A., de Rezende, L., Izidoro, M. A., Cezari, M. H. S., Juliano, L., & Amaral, A. T. d. (2008). Uncovering false positives on a virtual screening search for cruzain inhibitors. *Bioorganic & Medicinal Chemistry Letters, 18*(1), 350–354. doi:10.1016/j.bmcl.2007.10.068

Marrero-Ponce, Y., et al.. (n.d.). Atom, atom-type and total molecular linear indices as a promising approach for bioorganic and medicinal chemistry: theoretical and experimental assessment of a novel method for virtual screening and rational design of new lead anthelmintic. *Bioorganic and Medicinal Chemistry, 13*(4), 1005-1020.

Mason, J. S., & Cheney, D. L. (1999). Ligand-receptor 3-D similarity studies using multiple 4-point pharmacophores. *Pacific Symposium on Biocomputing, 4*, 456-467.

Mason, J. S., Morize, I., Menard, P. R., Cheney, D. L., Hulne, C. C., & Labaudinieres, R. F. (1999). New 4-Point Pharmacophore Method for Molecular Similarity and Diversity Applications: Overview of the Method and Applications, Including a Novel Approach to the Design of Combinatorial Libraries Containing Privileged Substructures. *Journal of Medicinal Chemistry, 42*(17), 3251–3264. doi:10.1021/jm9806998

Meneses-Marcel, A., Marrero-Ponce, Y., Machado-Tugores, Y., Montero-Torres, A., Pereira, D. M., & Escario, J. A. (2005). A linear discrimination analysis virtual screening of trichomonacidal lead-like compounds: outcomes of in silico studies supported by experimental results. *Bioorganic & Medicinal Chemistry, 15*(17), 3838–3843. doi:10.1016/j.bmcl.2005.05.124

Merlot, C., Domine, D., Cleva, C., & Church, D. J. (2003). Chemical substructures in drug discovery. *Drug Discovery Today, 8*(13), 594–602. doi:10.1016/S1359-6446(03)02740-5

Montero-Torres, A., García-Sánchez, R. N., Marrero-Ponce, Y., Machado-Tugores, Y., Nogal-Ruiz, J. J., & Martínez-Fernández, A. R. (2006). Non-stochastic quadratic fingerprints and LDA-based QSAR models in hit and lead generation through virtual screening: theoretical and experimental assessment of a promising method for the discovery of new antimalarial compounds. *European Journal of Medicinal Chemistry, 41*(4), 483–493. doi:10.1016/j.ejmech.2005.12.010

Muegge, I., & Oloffa, S. (2006). Advances in virtual screening. *Drug Discovery Today. Technologies, 3*(4), 405–411. doi:10.1016/j.ddtec.2006.12.002

Organization for Economic Co-operation and Development (2007). *OECD Science*, Technology and Industry Scoreboard 2007.

Organization for Economic Co-operation and Development (2010). *Main Science and Technology Indicators (MSTI): 2010/1 edition.*

Pandolfini, C., & Bonati, M. (2005). A literature review on off-label drug use in children. *European Journal of Pediatrics, 164*(9), 552–558. doi:10.1007/s00431-005-1698-8

Pereira, D. A., & Williams, J. A. (2007). Origin and evolution of high throughput screening. *British Journal of Pharmacology, 152*(1), 53–61. doi:10.1038/sj.bjp.0707373

Pickar, D., Vinik, J., & Bartko, J. J. (2008). Pharmacotherapy of schizophrenic patients: preponderance of off-label drug use. *PLoS ONE, 3*(9), e3150. doi:10.1371/journal.pone.0003150

Prado-Prado, F. J., González-Díaz, H., de la Vega, O. M., Ubeira, F. M., & Chou, K. C. (2008). Unified QSAR approach to antimicrobials. Part 3: first multi-tasking QSAR model for input-coded prediction, structural back-projection, and complex networks clustering of antiprotozoal compounds. *Bioorganic & Medicinal Chemistry, 16*(11), 5871–5880. doi:10.1016/j.bmc.2008.04.068

Prieto, J. J., Talevi, A., & Bruno-Blanch, L. E. (2006). Application of linear discriminant analysis in the virtual screening of trypanothione reductase inhibitors and redox cycling agents. *Molecular Diversity, 10*(3), 361–375. doi:10.1007/s11030-006-9044-2

Rasmussen, E. (2008). Government instruments to support the commercialization of university research: Lessons from Canada. *Technovation, 28*(8), 506–517. doi:10.1016/j.technovation.2007.12.002

Schuster, D., Laggner, C., & Langer, T. (2005). Why drugs fail – A study on side effects of new chemical entities. *Current Pharmaceutical Design, 11*(27), 3545–3559. doi:10.2174/138161205774414510

Seddon, A. M., Curnow, P., & Booth, P. J. (2004). Membrane proteins, lipids and detergents: not just soap opera. *Biochimica et Biophysica Acta, 1666*(1-2), 105–117. doi:10.1016/j.bbamem.2004.04.011

Segura-Cabrera, A., & Rodriguez-Perez, M. A. (2008). Structure-based prediction of Mycobacterium tuberculosis shikimate kinase inhibitors by high-throughput virtual screening. *Bioorganic & Medicinal Chemistry Letters, 18*(11), 3152–3157. doi:10.1016/j.bmcl.2008.05.003

Sheridan, R. P., Feuston, B. P., Maiorov, V. N., & Kearsley, S. K. (2004). Similarity to molecules in the training set is a good discriminator for prediction accuracy in QSAR. *Journal of Chemical Information and Computer Sciences, 44*(6), 1912–1928. doi:10.1021/ci049782w

Shibata, N., Kajikawa, Y., & Sakata, I. (2010). Extracting the commercialization gap between science and technology – Case study of a solar cell. *Technological Forecasting and Social Change, 77*(7), 1146–1155. doi:10.1016/j.techfore.2010.03.008

Sun, H. (2008). Pharmacophore-based virtual screening. *Current Medicinal Chemistry, 15*(10), 1018–1024. doi:10.2174/092986708784049630

Talevi, A., Bellera, C. L., Castro, E. A., & Bruno-Blanch, L. E. (2006). Application of molecular topology in descriptor-based virtual screening for the discovery of new anticonvulsant agents. *Drugs of the Future, 31*(Suppl. A), 188.

Talevi, A., Bellera, C. L., Castro, E. A., & Bruno-Blanch, L. E. (2007). A successful virtual screening application: Prediction of anticonvulsant activity in the MES test of widely used pharmaceutical and food preservatives methylparaben and propylparaben. *Journal of Computer-Aided Molecular Design, 21*(9), 527–538. doi:10.1007/s10822-007-9136-9

Talevi, A., Gavernet, L., & Bruno-Blanch, L. E. (2009). Combined virtual screening strategies. *Current Computer-aided Drug Design, 5*(1), 23–37. doi:10.2174/157340909787580854

Talevi, A., Sella-Cravero, M., Castro, E. A., & Bruno-Blanch, L. E. (2007). Discovery of Anticonvulsant Activity of Abietic Acid through Application of Linear Discriminant Analysis. *Bioorganic & Medicinal Chemistry Letters, 17*(6), 1684–1690. doi:10.1016/j.bmcl.2006.12.098

Terstappen, G. C., & Reggiani, A. (2001). *In silico* research in drug discovery. *Trends in Pharmacological Sciences, 22*(1), 23–26. doi:10.1016/S0165-6147(00)01584-4

Tobinick, E. L. (2009). The value of drug repositioning in the current pharmaceutical market. *Drug News & Perspectives, 22*(2), 119–125. doi:10.1358/dnp.2009.22.2.1343228

Triballeau, N., Acher, F., Brabet, I., Pin, P., & Bertrand, H. O. Virtual screening workflow development guided by the "Receiver Operating Characteristic" Curve approach. Application to high-throughput docking on metabotropic glutamate receptor subtype 4. *Journal of Medicinal Chemistry, 48*(7), 2534–2547. doi:10.1021/jm049092j

Trouiller, P., Olliaro, P., Torreele, E., Orbinski, J., Laing, R., & Ford, N. (2002). Drug development for neglected diseases: a deficient market and a public-health policy failure. *Lancet, 359*(9324), 2188–2194. doi:10.1016/S0140-6736(02)09096-7

Van de Waterbeemd, H. (2005). From in vivo to in vitro/in silico ADME: progress and challenges. *Expert Opinion on Drug Metabolism & Toxicology*, *1*(1), 1–4. doi:10.1517/17425255.1.1.1

Verma, U., Sharma, R., Gupta, P., Kapoor, V., Bano, G., & Swahney, B. (2005). New uses for old drugs: Novel therapeutic options. *Indian Journal of Pharmacology*, *37*(5), 279–287. doi:10.4103/0253-7613.16850

Webb, C., Dernis, H., Harhoff, D., & Hoisl, K. (2005). Analyzing European and International Patent Citations – A set of EPO patent database building blocks. *STI Working Paper 2005/9*, OECD, Paris.

Wermuth, C. G., Ganellin, C. R., Lindberg, P., & Mitscher, L. A. (1998). Glossary if terms used in medicinal chemistry (IUPAC Recommendations 1997). *Annual Reports in Medicinal Chemistry*, *33*, 385–395. doi:10.1016/S0065-7743(08)61101-X

Willet, P. (2006). Similarity-based virtual screening using 2D fingerprints. *Drug Discovery Today*, *11*(23-24), 1046–1053. doi:10.1016/j.drudis.2006.10.005

Wolber, G., Seidel, T., Bendix, F., & Langer, T. (2008). Molecule-pharmacophore superpositioning and pattern matching in computational drug design. *Drug Discovery Today*, *13*(1-2), 23–29. doi:10.1016/j.drudis.2007.09.007

Yang, S. Y. (2010). Pharmacophore modeling and applications in drug discovery: challenges and recent advances. *Drug Discovery Today*, *15*(11-12), 444–450. doi:10.1016/j.drudis.2010.03.013

Zhang, O., & Muegge, I. (2006). Scaffold hopping through virtual screening using 2D and 3D similarity descriptors: ranking, voting, and consensus scoring. *Journal of Medicinal Chemistry*, *49*(5), 1536–1548. doi:10.1021/jm050468i

Chapter 12

Synthesis, Properties, and Applications of Special Substrates Coated by Titanium Dioxide Nanostructured Thin Films via Sol–Gel Process

Hamid Dadvar
University of Guilan, Iran

Farhad E. Ghodsi
University of Guilan, Iran

Saeed Dadvar
Isfahan University of Technology, Iran

ABSTRACT

In this chapter, the sol-gel made titanium dioxide nanostructured thin films deposited on special substrates such as glasses, mica, steels, textiles, fibers, and other organic/inorganic substrates were reviewed. Through this review, several distinctive properties such as optical, electrical, photocatalytic, morphological, and mechanical properties of TiO_2 nanostructured thin films were described. Also, a wide range of practical application of TiO_2 nanostructured thin films such as dye-sensitised solar cells, optical coatings, humidity and gas sensors, selfcleaning, dielectric, and antibacterial surfaces were discussed in details. Dip and spin coating techniques were demonstrated as suitable methods for deposition of thin films. It has been shown that properties of such films can be affected by type of coating technique, stabilizer, precursor material, solvents, pH and viscosity of precursor solution, aging, and etc. Finally, Successive Interference Fringes Method (SIFM) was presented as a simple method for the determination of optical constants and thickness of TiO_2 thin films from single transmission measurements.

DOI: 10.4018/978-1-60960-860-6.ch012

Table 1. Physical, optical, and electrical properties of four different spatial configurations of TiO$_2$ (Bally, 1999)

Properties	Anatase	Rutile	Brookite	Srilankite
Configuration	Tetragonal	Tetragonal	Orthorhombic	Orthorhombic
Density (g/cm^3)	3.89	4.25	4.12	4.37
Refraction Index*,**	n_{per}(to c axis)=2.55 n_{par}(to c axis)=2.48	n_{per}(to c axis)=2.60 n_{par}(to c axis)=2.89	n_{par}(to a or b axis)=2.57 n_{par}(to c axis)=2.69	--- ---
Dielectric Constant*	k_{per}(to c axis)=31 k_{par}(to c axis)=48	k_{per}(to c axis)=89 k_{par}(to c axis)=173	78 78	--- ---
Band Gap (eV)	$E_{g(per)}$(to c axis, direct)=3.42 $E_{g(par)}$(to c axis, indirect)=3.46	$E_{g(per)}$(to c axis, direct)=3.04 $E_{g(par)}$(to c axis, indirect)=3.05	3.14 3.14	--- ---
Electron Mobility (10^{-4} m^2/Vs)	As a Crystal=15-550 As a Thin Film=0.1-4	As a Crystal=0.1-10 As a Thin Film=0.1	--- ---	--- ---

* 'per' = 'perpendicular' and 'par' = 'parallel'

** Measured at λ = 600 nm.

INTRODUCTION

'Nanostructures' or 'nanomaterials' as wide groups of nanoscale materials with unrivaled properties, are the most well-known substances used in solid state physics as well as other basic sciences. Currently, a lot of nanomaterials such as nanoparticles, -powders, -tubes, and -wires have been discovered. Among these nanomaterials, 'nanoparticles' have been received a growing interest in the most of scientific projects especially those based on solid state physics (Ramsden, 2005).

Nanoparticles can be classified into three categories: conductors, semiconductors, and insulators. From the standpoints of practical applications, metal oxide based semiconductor nanoparticles are recently finding increasing attention particularly in solid state physics. For instance, smooth or rough surfaces like glasses and textiles, respectively, can be coated using these nanoparticles by several methods to attain novel properties with effective specifications (Battiston, Gerbasi, Porchia, & Marigo, 1994; Brinker & Harrington, 1981; Leinen, Fernández, Espinós, Belderrain, & González-Elipe, 1994; Löbl, Huppertz, & Mergel, 1994; Martin, Rousselot, Savall, & Palmino,

1996). Among huge variety of nanosized metal oxide semiconductor particles such as ZrO$_2$, ZnSe, CdS, SnO$_2$, Al$_2$O$_3$, MgO, ZnO, and TiO$_2$, titanium dioxide (TiO$_2$) nanoparticles with high refractive index, high dielectric constant, excellent physical and chemical stability, and wide band gap are the best inorganic metal oxides capable to provide inconceivable properties. Basically, four crystalline spatial configurations have been suggested for nanosized TiO$_2$ particles: anatase, rutile, brookite, and srilankite. However, rutile phase with refractive index about 2.7 at a wavelength of 500 nm is thermodynamically stable in high temperatures than the other crystalline phases. The main properties of these structures are summarized in Table 1 (Ye, Liu, Tang, & Zhai, 2007). Studies show that tetragonal rutile and anatase structures are highly ordered in comparison with orthorhombic structure of brookite and srilankite. Figure 1 shows spatial configurations suggested for rutile and anatase structures of the nanosized TiO$_2$ particles (Bally, 1999).

Optical behavior (Ghodsi, Tepehan, & Tepehan, 2008b), dye-sensitivity (Sung & Kim, 2007), dielectric activity (W. Yang & Wolden, 2006), selfcleaning and photocatalytic effects (Euvana-

Figure 1. Spatial configurations suggested for (a) anatase and (b) rutile structures of the nanosized TiO_2 particles (Bally, 1999)

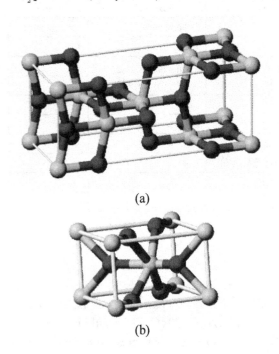

(a)

(b)

nont, Junin, Inpor, Limthongkul, & Thanachayanont, 2008; Fretwell & Douglas, 2001; Perera et al., 2004; Tavares et al., 2007) are major properties that have been raised from coated substrates using nanosized TiO_2 particles. Preparation of nanostructured thin films containing nanoparticles using deposition methods is one of the most applicable techniques has been discovered for coating of different substrates such as glasses, mica, steels, textiles, fibers, and other organic/inorganic substrates (Abidi, Hequet, Tarimala, & Dai, 2007; Barati & Faghihi Sani, 2009; Battiston et al., 1994; Ben Amor, Baud, Jacquet, & Pichon, 1998; Bozzi, Yuranova, Guasaquillo, Laub, & Kiwi, 2005; Gupta, Jassal, & Agrawal, 2008; Hong, Li, Zheng, & Zou, 2006; Jing et al., 2003; Li, Qiu, & Yang, 2009; Medina-Valtierra, Sánchez-Cárdenas, Frausto-Reyes, & Calixto, 2006; Nasr-Esfahani & Habibi, 2009; Paez & Matoušek, 2004; Pucher et al., 2007; Tavares et al., 2007; Tsaneva et al., 2008; Veronovski, Rudolf, Sfiligoj Smole,

Kreže, & Geršak, 2009; Watanabe et al., 1999; Wu et al., 2009; Xin, Daoud, & Kong, 2004). Several deposition methods such as electron-beam evaporation (Habibi, Talebian, & Choi, 2007), ion-beam assisted deposition (C. Yang, Fan, Xi, Chen, & Li, 2008), DC and RF reactive magnetron sputtering (Ben Amor et al., 1998), chemical vapor deposition with/without plasma treatments (Sun et al., 2008), and sol-gel (Barati & Faghihi Sani, 2009; Beganskienė, Šakirzanovas, Melninkaitis, Sirutkaitis, & Kareiva, 2006; Brinker & Harrington, 1981; Chrysicopoulou, Davazoglou, Trapalis, & Kordas, 1998; Daoud & Xin, 2004; Dimitriev, Ivanova, & Iordanova, 2008; Dislich & Hinz, 1982; Falaras & Xagas, 2002; Fretwell & Douglas, 2001; Ghodsi, Tepehan, & Tepehan, 2006; Guang-Lei, Hong-Bo, & Jian-Da, 2005; Hamid & Rahman, 2003; Hasan, Haseeb, Saidur, & Masjuki, 2008; Hemissi & Amardjia-Adnani, 2007; Jiménez González & Gelover Santiago, 2007; Jing et al., 2003; Mahltig, Fiedler, & Böttcher, 2004; Medina-Valtierra et al., 2006; Nasr-Esfahani & Habibi, 2009; Paez & Matoušek, 2004; Pourmand & Taghavinia, 2008; Sankar & Gopchandran, 2009; Sasani Ghamsari & Bahramian, 2008; Suciu et al., 2009; Viana, Mohallem, Nascimento, & Mohallem, 2006; Wang, Helmersson, & Käll, 2002; Wen, Gao, & Shen, 2001; Wetchakun & Phanichphant, 2008; Yoon, Noh, Kwon, & Muhammed, 2006; Yu, Zhao, & Zhao, 2001; Yu et al., 2002; Yuan, Zhang, Li, & Li, 2007; Zainal, Lee, Hussein, & Kassim, 2004; Zarycka, Ilczuk, & Czekaj, 2003; Zulkarnain & Yong, 2005) have been mentioned in literatures for the preparation of nanostructured TiO_2 thin films. Among them, sol-gel is the most favorite one because of notable advantages such as relatively low temperature steps, chemical homogeneity, and a more uniform phase distribution, particularly in the case of multicomponent systems (Ghodsi, Tepehan, & Tepehan, 1999; Ghodsi, Tepehan, & Tepehan, 2008a; Zhang, Chen, Yu, Chen, & Yin, 2006). As sol-gel method has already been widely used to produce various kinds of functional thin films on substrates, there is no good collection of different works done by several researchers; so this chapter is aimed to review synthesis, properties and major applications of nanostructured TiO_2 thin film coated substrates via sol-gel method according to the recent academic works in details up to 2010. Preparation of dip-coating solutions, sol-gel synthesis and deposition methods, properties of TiO_2 nanostructured thin films, practical applications of TiO_2 nanostructured thin films, and Optical Constants Determination of TiO_2 Nanostructured Thin Films using SIFM are the most important issues which are discussed in this review.

PREPARATION OF DIP-COATING SOLUTIONS

During the last few decades, there have been increasing interest on utilization of new precursor compounds such as titanium isopropoxide (Ahn, Kim, Kim, & Hahn, 2003; Chen, Zhang, Zhu, Chen, & Xu, 2006; Ergün, KarslioǦlu, Yilmaz, & Üner, 2007; Euvananont, Junin et al., 2008; Jiménez González & Gelover Santiago, 2007; Liau & Chiang, 2007; Medina-Valtierra et al., 2006; Miki, Nishizawa, Suzuki, & Kato, 2004; Suciu et al., 2009; Yoon et al., 2006; Yu et al., 2002), titanium butoxide (Falaras & Xagas, 2002; Kozłowska, Łukowiak, Szczurek, Dudek, & Maruszewski, 2005; Yao & Wanghe, 2006), tetrabutyl titanate (Barati & Faghihi Sani, 2009; Ming-Fang, Shan, Xin-Man, & Yan-Zhi, 2006; Yu et al., 2001), titanium chloride (Jahromi, Taghdisian, Afshar, & Tasharrofi, 2009), titanium fluoride (Pourmand & Taghavinia, 2008), isopropyl titanate (Hamid & Rahman, 2003; Viana et al., 2006; Zainal et al., 2004; Zulkarnain & Yong, 2005), titanium tetraethoxide (Chrysicopoulou et al., 1998), and oxotitanate derivatives (Jiang et al., 2009), for synthesis of titanium dioxide ultra thin films via sol-gel process. There are a lot of parameters such as type of primary precursor, solvent, stabilizer, catalyst, pH, and hydrolyze

condition concern with the preparation of dip-coating solutions which play an important role in the preparation of TiO_2 dip-coating solutions. Apart from precursor material, solvents as a second component are usually common organic alcohols such as ethanol (Barati & Faghihi Sani, 2009; Chrysicopoulou et al., 1998; Ergün et al., 2007; Falaras & Xagas, 2002; Hamid & Rahman, 2003; Jahromi et al., 2009; Jiménez González & Gelover Santiago, 2007; Medina-Valtierra et al., 2006; Yao & Wanghe, 2006; Yu et al., 2001; Yu et al., 2002; Zainal et al., 2004; Zulkarnain & Yong, 2005), isopropanol (Euvananont, Junin et al., 2008; Miki et al., 2004), isopropyl (Ahn et al., 2003; Yoon et al., 2006), butanol (Kozłowska et al., 2005), and n-propyl (Chen et al., 2006) which brought a suitable reaction bath for the preparation of dip-coating solutions. Stabilizers such as acetyl acetone (Barati & Faghihi Sani, 2009; Chen et al., 2006; Euvananont, Junin et al., 2008; Kozłowska et al., 2005; Ming-Fang et al., 2006), diethanolamine (Yao & Wanghe, 2006; Yu et al., 2001; Zulkarnain & Yong, 2005), triethanolamine (Yu et al., 2002), and polyethylene glycol (Miki et al., 2004; Zulkarnain & Yong, 2005) and have a sensitive role during the preparation process. Furthermore, acidity or basicity of the main precursor solution is important as well as other factors. Acids such as acetic acid (Ergün et al., 2007; Euvananont, Junin et al., 2008; Hamid & Rahman, 2003; Ponce et al., 2009), hydrochloric acid (Ahn et al., 2003; Falaras & Xagas, 2002; Jiménez González & Gelover Santiago, 2007; Pourmand & Taghavinia, 2008; Viana et al., 2006), and nitric acid (Chrysicopoulou et al., 1998; Jahromi et al., 2009; Medina-Valtierra et al., 2006; Miki et al., 2004; Ming-Fang et al., 2006; Yoon et al., 2006; Zainal et al., 2004) or bases such as ammonia (Jiang et al., 2009) are conventional pH regulators used to control the hydrolysis reactions by adjusting the pH level which result in high quality thin films with desired properties. In addition, it should be noted that stirring, temperature, and time considerably affect the homogeneity and quality of resultant precursor solution. Further details are summarized hereinafter regarding some preparation methods of dip-coating solutions using typical precursors and other components mentioned above.

Euvananont et al. (2008) provided precursor solution using titanium isopropoxide. At the first, titanium isopropoxide was dissolved in isopropanol under stirring at room temperature for 30 min. Secondly, acetyl acetone was added and the solution stirred again for less than 30 min. Finally, by addition of acetic acid as an initiating agent of isopropanol hydrolysis, the final transparent yellow precursor solution was prepared. Miki et al. (2004) used the same precursor solution but there is a little difference in kind and proportion of reagents. Firstly, isopropanol solution containing certain amount of titanium isopropoxide was poured into a mixed solution of distilled water and polyethylene glycol under stirring condition. Afterwards, dip-coating solution was prepared by addition of nitric acid to the resultant suspension and heating the mixture at 80°C under strong stirring.

Chen et al. (2006) provided sol-gel precursor solution using two step method. Firstly, acetyl acetone and titanium isopropoxide were dissolved in n-propyl alcohol (*Solution A*). Secondly, deionized water and n-propyl alcohol was also mixed together (*Solution B*). Finally, sol-gel dip-coating solution was made by addition of *Solution B* to *Solution A* dropwise under stirring and aging over 12 hours.

Medina-Valtierra et al. (2006) suggested different method for the preparation of dip-coating solution. Firstly, titanium isopropoxide was dissolved in ethanol under stirring for 1 hour. Then, a micellar solution was prepared dissolving cetyltrimethyl ammonium bromide in ethanol followed by 30 min under stirring. Subsequently, alcoholic solution of titanium isopropoxide was added to the micellar solution dropwise and stirred again for further 30 min. Finally, similar to the last method, dip-coating solution was prepared by addition of nitric acid and ethanol to induce

hydrolysis in the resultant suspension. Titanium isopropoxide, acetic acid, and 2-propanol (as a non-ionic surfactant) was applied to provide the precursor solution by Ponce et al. (2009). These ingredients mixed together and then, water was added dropwise under stirring. At the end, dip-coating solution was afforded by aging obtained solution through 24 hours. Liau et al. (2007) applied novel process to make precursor solution. In this procedure, dip-coating solution was produced by mixing titanium isopropoxide with H_2O_2 and together with alcohol at 75°C for 6 hours. Ahn et al. (2003) made the main precursor solution using titanium isopropoxide as a primary precursor in a single step. For this purpose, final sol-gel solution was provided by adding a mixture of HCl and isopropyl alcohol to a mixture of titanium isopropoxide and isopropyl alcohol under continuous agitation in nitrogen atmosphere at room temperature. Yoon et al. (2006) mixed titanium isopropoxide and isopropyl alcohol to prepare precursor solution of sol-gel process. Dip-coating solution was provided by stirring the mixture for 10 min and then, addition of water and nitric acid under stirring again at 80°C for 8 hours.

Ergün et al. (2007) handled an inverse method for the preparation of precursor solution. Water, ethanol, and acetic acid were mixed together first, and then, titanium isopropoxide was moderately added to the well-mixed solution and stirred for 16 hours. Before using the precursor solution, the process was completed by refrigerating the solution for three days at 4°C.

Jiménez González et al. (2007) prepared sol-gel precursor solution in a different way using titanium isopropoxide. For this purpose, titanium isopropoxide was placed into a ball bicker and ethanol added slowly. A mixture of ethanol, H_2O, and HCl was appended to the last solution in order to catalyze the hydrolysis process of titanium isopropoxide. Finally after 24 hours, a yellowish transparent dipping solution was prepared for the sol-gel process. In another method, Suciu et al. (2009) intermingled titanium isopropoxide, acetyl acetone, H_2O, and 1-butanol in order to make primary precursor solution. Subsequently, by addition of Tween 80 as a typical surfactant and 1-butanol as a solvent to the last solution under rigorous stirring at room temperature, homogeneous dip-coating solution was prepared. In another suggested procedure used by Yu et al. (2002), titanium isopropoxide and triethanolamine were firstly dissolved in absolute ethanol under stirring vigorously for 1 hour at room temperature. A mixture of water and ethanol was then added dropwise to the last solution under stirring. Subsequently, the precursor solution was formed through complete hydrolysis of resultant alkoxide solution under further stirring for 2 hours at room temperature. These researchers also prepared dip-coating solution through a different way. In this method, Triton X-100 as a surfactant and water were firstly dissolved in cyclohexane and stirred vigorously for 30 min at room temperature. Finally, resultant dip-coating solution was made by addition of titanium isopropoxide to the reaction mixture under stirring for further 2 hours at the same condition.

In another alternative method introduced by Pourmand et al. (2008), dip-coating solution was provided through one step preparation procedure by gradually addition of titanium fluoride as primary precursor in deionized water containing HCl and NH_4OH under stirring for 10 min at room temperature.

Viana et al. (2006) mixed isopropyl titanate as a precursor, isopropanol as an organic solvent, and HCl as a catalyst together. The resultant alcoholic solution was then maintained under agitation process for 1 hour at room temperature, and finally allowed to reach a desired value of viscosity during further 4 hours at the same condition.

Zainal et al. (2004) prepared the main precursor solution by addition of concentrated nitric acid to water, followed by isopropyl titanate in ethanol. Finally, mixture was stirred for 5-6 days to provide a thick fully hydrolyzed solution for dip-coating process. In a simple method, Hamid et al. (2003)

added isopropyl titanate to a mixture of glacial acetic acid and ethanol under stirring for 1 hour at room temperature. In another method, Zulkarnain et al. (2005) dissolved firstly polyethelene glycol in ethanol as a solvent. Subsequently, the clear and transparent dip-coating solution was prepared by adding diethanolamine, isopropyl titanate, and water to the resultant alcoholic solution under stirring for several hours at room temperature.

Barati et al. (2009) prepared sol-gel precursor solution using tetrabutyl titanate as a primary precursor. At first, ethanol and ethyl acetone acetate, and tetrabutyl titanate were mixed together under continuous stirring for 8 hours at room temperature. Through the first 1 hour, deionized water was also carefully added to the mixture for hydrolysis. Finally, dip-coating solution was made by maintaining the resultant solution over 24 hours in order to complete the hydrolysis process. Yu et al. (2001) provided dip-coating solution using the same precursor. In this method, tetrabutyl titanate and diethanolamine were dissolved in ethanol under stirring vigorously for 2 hours at room temperature. Later, mixture of water and ethanol was added dropwise to the last solution under stirring. At last, precursor solution was prepared by aging the resultant solution over 2 hours at room temperature to complete the hydrolysis reaction.

Dip-coating solution was prepared through a different procedure by Ming-Fang et al. (2006). In this way, certain amounts of tetrabutyl titanate and acetyl acetone were mixed together and ethanol was poured subsequently under rigorous stirring over 1 hour at room temperature. Afterward, distilled water and nitric acid were added under stirring into the above solution. The resultant alkoxide solution was further mixed with carbamide/chloroethylamine solution for 1 hour and maintained at room temperature for hydrolysis completion. Pomoni et al. (2005) also made their sol-gel precursor solutions approximately similar to mentioned above procedure but without any further mingling with mixture of carbamide/chloroethylamine solution.

Jahromi et al. (2009) prepared dip-coating solution using titanium chloride, ethanol, and nitric acid through a high temperature process. At the first, deionized water was added to titanium chloride as precursor. Subsequently, an exact amount of nitric acid was added to aqueous solution of titanium chloride under stirring for about 7 hours at room temperature. Finally, a stable dip-coating solution was prepared by maintaining the resultant alkoxide solution for 24 hours at 80°C.

Chrysicopoulou et al. (1998) prepared dip-coating solution by dissolving titanium tetraethoxide as a precursor, in ethanol as a solvent, following addition of nitric acid, and then distilled water. At the end, final precursor solution was formed by stirring obtained solution for 2 hours at room temperature.

Falaras et al. (2002) applied mixture solvents for the preparation of dipping solution. Firstly, titanium butoxide as a primary precursor was added dropwise in ethanol/isopropanol mixture solvents under vigorous stirring condition. Subsequently, a homogeneous semitransparent dipping solution was formed by addition of HCl as a catalyst. Finally, clear dip-coating solution was prepared by allowing the resultant mixture to peptize for 12 hours.

Yao et al. (2006) prepared precursor solution of sol-gel process using titanium butoxide as primary precursor. Firstly, titanium butoxide and diethanolamine were dissolved in ethanol under stirring for 1 hour. Then deionized water and ethanol were mixed together and added dropwise to the above solution under vigorous stirring. Finally, the obtained solution was then stirred for 1 hour to form a uniform, transparent, and yellowish dip-coating solution. The procedure proposed by Kozłowska et al. (2005) contained titanium butoxide as precursor, butanol, and acetyl acetone. These reagents were mixed together and sonicated for about 1 hour. Subsequently, distilled water was added to the resultant solution and mixing continued for further 30 min. Finally, precursor solution was formed by aging the last solution for 24 hours at

room temperature. Karwasz et al. (2005) followed the same method for the preparation of sol-gel solution as well.

Jiang et al. (2009) made sol-gel dip-coating solution using an aqueous solution of two different precursors, namely, ammonium bis(oxalate)oxotitanate and titanium oxide sulfate. These primary precursors were mixed with aqueous solution of ammonia under vigorous stirring. Subsequently, the resulting precipitates were centrifuged and washed repeatedly with water to remove $C_2O_4^{2-}$, SO_4^{2-}, and ammonia. The precipitates were then dissolved in aqueous solution of H_2O_2 at 5°C. As the acidic, orange solution aged approximately through 24 hours at 5°C, raising the pH slowly, the color changed from orange to yellow. Finally, dip-coating solution with alkali pH was provided by adding aqueous solution of ammonia to last yellow solution under vigorous stirring. The final dip-coating solution is yellow-green and persistent during 48-72 hours at 5°C.

SOL-GEL SYNTHESIS AND DEPOSITION METHODS

Metal alkoxides are derivatives of alcohols which are usually easily so handy and inexpensive organic compounds, and are extremely weak as acids, easily removable via hydrolysis and thermal treatment, leaving high purity hydrated oxides. These make metal alkoxides the most common nominees as dip-coating sol-gel precursors. Sol-gel technique as a versatile tool for the creation of transparent metal oxide thin films that adhere well to various substrates, has been became an innovative procedure during the recent years (Chun et al., 2009).

Principally, there are two major steps for the sol-gel process; hydrolysis and condensation that theoretically can be represented as following reaction equations (Equations (1) and (2), respectively) where M is a metal species and R is an organic group. These two stages result in an oxide network in the gel form upon drying treatments (Medina-Valtierra et al., 2006).

$$M - OR + H_2O \rightarrow M - OH + RO \qquad (1)$$

$$M - OH + HO - M \rightarrow M - OM + H_2O \qquad (2)$$

Practically, there are various methods for deposition of nanosized TiO_2 nanoparticles on different substrates such as glass, mica, steels, textiles, and other organic/inorganic substrates (Abidi et al., 2007; Barati & Faghihi Sani, 2009; Battiston et al., 1994; Ben Amor et al., 1998; Bozzi et al., 2005; Gupta et al., 2008; Hong et al., 2006; Jing et al., 2003; Li et al., 2009; Medina-Valtierra et al., 2006; Nasr-Esfahani & Habibi, 2009; Paez & Matoušek, 2004; Pucher et al., 2007; Tavares et al., 2007; Tsaneva et al., 2008; Veronovski et al., 2009; Watanabe et al., 1999; Wu et al., 2009; Xin et al., 2004). Among these, dip- and spin-coating are the most frequently used methods especially for planar substrates. There are some distinctions between these methods. Although spin-coating process leads to denser films possibly because of the higher evaporation rates, however, dip-coating is favorable procedure to study structure of nanostructured thin film coated substrates. In the latter method, a substrate was immersed into a precursor solution allowing perfect coverage of the substrate. Then, the coated substrate was extruded through a controlled rate till the substrate covered uniformly by the precursor solution. At last, the coated substrate was dried very fast in the atmosphere resulting in an oxide network in the gel form. Figure 2 depicts schematically these two major types of sol-gel methods (Hamid & Rahman, 2003; Sakka, 2005).

Paez et al. (2004) dipped glass substrates using transparent nanosized TiO_2 thin films. After washing the glass substrates with deionized water, deposition process was done using TiO_2 precursor solution. Subsequently, samples dried for 2 hours at 80°C and then, the process continued by tempering dried samples for 1 hour at 550°C through an air flow and finished by cooling with the ramp of 20°C/min. Chrysicopoulou et al. (1998) suggested such a coating procedure for glass substrates using uniform amorphous gel layers based on sol-gel process. In this procedure, layers of nanosized titanium oxide particles were layered on

Figure 2. Typical (a) dip-coating and (b) spin-coating methods for sol-gel process (Sakka, 2005)

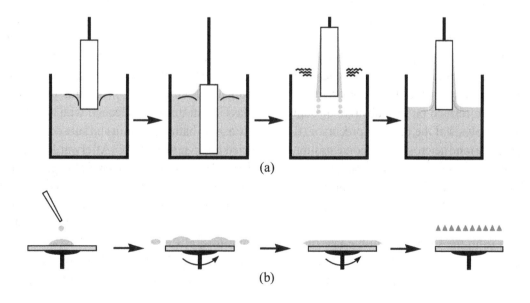

both sides of glass substrate with constant thickness controlled via speed of the withdrawal from the precursor solution. After dip-coating process, coated substrates sintered at 400°C for 30 min, leading to oxide thin film nanostructures.

A systematic procedure that is of great potential for the sol-gel based synthesis and deposition methods proposed by Ahn et al. (2003). In this method, after thoroughly rinsing and washing of glass substrates using acetone solvent and deionized water, respectively, dipping was done on substrates withdrawing of 80 mm/min. The coated glasses were subsequently dried for 30 min at 100°C. Dipping and drying were repeated three cycles at the same condition. Finally, the substrates was subjected to slow heating at a rate of 5°C/min to a desired temperature from 400 to 1000°C and then holding at that temperature typically for 1 hour. As results demonstrated, the thickness of TiO_2 nanostructured thin films deposited on glass substrates reached about 200 nm after three times dipping and drying processes.

Pourmand et al. (2008) were the only researchers studied mica substrates coated using nanosized titanium dioxide particles via dip-coating method. First of all, as done by Ahn et al. (2003), mica substrates carefully cleaned by treating ultrasonically with detergent and then acetone, and rinsed with deionized water. For further assurance of removing all the organic residues, substrates were subsequently put in a furnace for 1 hour at 500°C. In a typical sol-gel procedure, dip-coating of cleaned substrates were done in an already prepared precursor solution and TiO_2 nanostructured thin films were formed on the substrate through stepwise hydrolysis of the primary precursor (titanium fluoride) and heterogeneous condensation. As performed by researchers above said, Viana et al. (2006) also cleaned the glass substrates using the same reagents. Then, the substrates were immersed vertically into the precursor solution and withdrawn from the solution with the rate of 60 mm/min, which is the necessary velocity to happen the hydrolysis and condensation of the gel

coatings, simultaneously. Subsequently, coated substrates were dried in air for 30 min and thermally treated for 10 min at specific temperatures from 100 to 400°C. At the end, titanium dioxide nanostructured thin films formed on the both sides of the glass substrates through rapid hydrolysis and polycondensating processes. Schulze et al. (2005) described an interesting method for the deposition of TiO_2 nanostructured thin films on glass substrates. In this procedure, the glass substrates were washed by immersion for 12 hours in a solution of H_2SO_4 and H_2O_2. Subsequently, the obtained substrates were immersed in a solution of water, NH_3, and H_2O_2 for 10 min followed by rinsing with deionized water. Afterward, the rinsed substrates were treated with poly(ethylenimine) solution for 5 min. After pretreatment processes, the pretreated glass substrates were dipped in a precursor solution for 5 min, washed for 1 min with deionized water, and finally dried under N_2 gas atmosphere. Hemissi et al. (2007) also introduced the same method for the deposition of TiO_2 nanostructured thin films on glass substrates via sol-gel process. For this purpose, through a simple process, the substrates were immersed in precursor solution withdrawing of 80 mm/min and then dried for 15 min at 100°C. At the end, titanium dioxide nanostructured thin films were formed by annealing the obtained substrates for 20 min at 400°C. In an innovative procedure, Indium Tin Oxide (ITO) glass substrates as the conducting supporting materials for titanium dioxide were coated using TiO_2 nanostructured thin films by Zulkarnain et al. (2005). For this purpose, ITO glass substrates were cleaned with acetone in an ultrasonic bath for 15 min and subsequently, were dried for 15 min at 100°C. Afterward, cleaned and dried ITO glass substrates were dipped in precursor solution and left to dry at room temperature. Finally, the coated substrates were sintered for 5 min at 100°C and annealed for 2 hours at 400°C. Jahromi et al. (2009) also suggested a novel procedure for the deposition of TiO_2 thin films on soda lime glass substrates. The glass substrates firstly were washed with detergent and oxidant solution composed of H_2SO_4 and H_2O_2 as auxiliaries for the effective adhesion of thin films to substrates, for 30 min and then rinsed with deionized water. The substrates were subsequently treated with a basic solution of NaOH in certain time and temperature and afterward, the obtained substrates were washed anew with deionized water and dried. After pretreatment processes, the pretreated substrates were immersed in precursor solution for 10 min at room temperature and TiO_2 nanostructured thin films were deposited. Finally, after drying the substrates for 1 hour at room temperature, the nanosized TiO_2 particles were immobilized onto the substrates through calcination treatment for 3 hours at 550°C.

In another method, Barati et al. (2009) immobilized TiO_2 nanoparticles on the stainless steel substrates through sol-gel mechanism. After sanding with the stainless steel substrates with emery papers, and then polishing with aluminum oxide powder, the substrates were cleaned by ethanol and acetone. Subsequently, the obtained substrates were immersed in TiO_2 precursor solution at room temperature. After drying in air flow, the resultant substrates were heated in an oven at 150°C for 30 min. Finally, the substrates were subjected to slow heating at a rate of 5°C/min to a desired temperature from 350 to 550°C to remove all organic residuals. As a result of this study, crack defects might be formed on obtained thin films due to removal of organic solvents used in preparation of precursor solution previously; so for the prevention of these defects, the coated substrates should be dried in a solvent bath containing ethanol solution to decrease the rate of solvent removal from thin films. Li et al. (2009) also immobilized TiO_2 nanoparticles-embedded thin films on the stainless steel substrates. The substrates were cleaned in dry ethanol and methyl ketone using an ultrasonic cleaner, and were dried for 6 hours at 300°C. Subsequently, TiO_2 nanostructured thin films were prepared by dip-coating the substrates into precursor solutions withdrawing of 30 mm/

min for 30 second. Finally, the obtained substrates were sintered in air flow at a rate of 1°C/min to a desired temperature from 700 to 900°C to form TiO_2 nanostructured thin films. Aluminum substrates were coated using TiO_2 precursor solution through sol-gel method by Chen et al. (2006). In this method, the substrates firstly were cleaned in sodium hydroxide solution and distilled water. Subsequently, the obtained substrates merged in precursor solution and thin films were coated on them by dipping method. Finally, a single layer of TiO_2 thin film was loaded on the substrates through calcination for 2 hours at 450°C.

PROPERTIES OF TIO$_2$ NANOSTRUCTURED THIN FILMS

TiO_2 nanostructured thin films efficiently deposited on special substrates can be investigated from the standpoint of morphological, mechanical, optical, electrical, and photocatalytic properties. As mentioned before, sol-gel prepared titanium dioxide nanoparticle as an important inorganic functional material is suitable especially for thin film applications. Several researchers (Barati & Faghihi Sani, 2009; Chen et al., 2006; Chrysicopoulou et al., 1998; Euvananont, Doungratsamee, Junin, Tippo, & Thanachayanont, 2008; Hasan et al., 2008; Hemissi & Amardjia-Adnani, 2007; Kościelska, Murawski, & Wicikowski, 2005; Paez & Matoušek, 2004; Sankar & Gopchandran, 2009; Wetchakun & Phanichphant, 2008; Yu et al., 2002) have characterized major properties of thin films immobilized on various substrates. However, some issues of these major properties are discussed in details hereinafter.

Morphological Properties

Scanning Electron Microscopy (SEM), Transmission Electron Microscopy (TEM), X-ray Diffraction (XRD), and Atomic Force Microscopy (AFM) are the most common characterizing

Figure 3. Typical AFM photograph of TiO$_2$ nanostructured thin films immobilized on glass substrates (Yu et al., 2002)

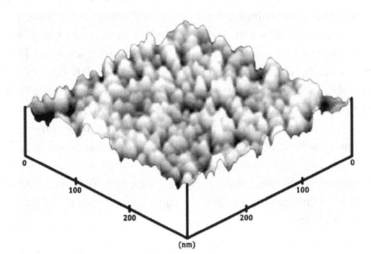

instruments which used to describe morphological and structural properties of TiO$_2$ nanostructured thin films immobilized on different substrates. Yu et al. (2002) revealed that the surface morphology and roughness of obtained TiO$_2$ nanostructured thin films have a granular form and composed of spherical particles of about 80 nm in diameter. As indicated in Figure 3, resultant TiO$_2$ nanostructured thin film is rough and has a larger surface area for absorbing UV radiation.

In another study, Barati et al. (2009) verified some realities raised from optical images. In a typical experiment, they investigated the behavior of TiO$_2$ nanostructured thin film over different drying conditions provided. The results revealed that there are some visible cracks on TiO$_2$ nanostructured thin film created after drying through an air flow at 150°C due to high rapid removal of solvent (Figure 4a). Hence, in order to prevent crack formation and achieve a uniform TiO$_2$ nanostructured thin film, the dipped glass substrate should be dried in the solvent bath, especially in ethanol bath, to reduce the rate of solvent removal (Figure 4b).

Morphological properties of TiO$_2$ nanostructured thin films deposited on aluminum substrates

have been investigated over AFM micrographs by Chen et al. (2006). This study demonstrated that specific surface area of TiO$_2$ nanostructured thin film immobilized on aluminum substrate were decreased after six cycles of dip-coating process due to the change of surface particles (in both shape and size). Sankar et al. (2009) also studied morphological properties of TiO$_2$ nanostructured thin films deposited on quartz plates from different point of view. They demonstrated that as the temperature increase from room temperature to 900°C, the crystallite size increases along with more keen edged grains. SEM studies also clearly showed that the average grain size increases with increase in sintering temperature (Figure 5).

Hasan et al. (2008) presented different results concerned with the surface morphology of TiO$_2$ nanostructured thin films immobilized on glass substrates. All deposited TiO$_2$ thin films exhibited smooth surface with uniform particles. The surface morphology also revealed that the nanocrystalline TiO$_2$ particles combine together to make denser films significantly as the temperatures increased. Results showed that the annealing treatment up to 500°C doesn't impart any sig-

Figure 4. Optical images of thin films deposited on glass substrates after drying: (a) through an air flow at 150°C, (b) at controlled conditions (ethanol bath) (Barati & Faghihi Sani, 2009)

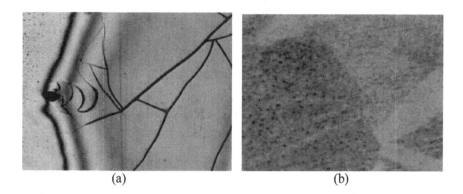

(a)   (b)

nificant change in structure. At temperatures of 600°C the particles get larger but the basic structure remains unchanged. The films were mainly made of spherical particles. It was observed that the surfaces of the films exhibited a certain degree of roughness and the film came rougher when the annealing temperature increases. These researchers also investigated the issue from another viewpoint via XRD patterns. Figure 6 illustrates XRD patterns of the TiO_2 nanostructured thin films at different annealing temperatures. It was also found that all the films were polycrystalline having anatase phase. However, deposited thin films annealed at 300°C, 400°C, and 500°C exhibited characteristic peaks of anatase crystal plane (101), (200), and (211) because of high

enough kinetic energy of the impinging particle to initiate the crystallization. Considerably, for the sample sintered at 600°C, other characteristic peaks of anatase crystal plane (204) and (220) appeared, but the intensity of these peaks is very weak. Overall, it should be noted that the intensities of these peaks of few anatase planes increased slightly with the increase of annealing temperature. Kościelska et al. (2005), Jahromi et al. (2009), and Euvananont et al. (2008) also proved the above observations by XRD studies and obtained the same characteristic peaks of anatase crystal plane for the deposited TiO_2 nanostructured thin films.

Paez et al. (2004) measured thickness of solgel prepared TiO_2 nanostructured thin films de-

Figure 5. SEM images of TiO_2 nanostructured thin films deposited on quartz plates at (a) room temperature and annealed at (b) 700, and (c) 900°C (Sankar & Gopchandran, 2009)

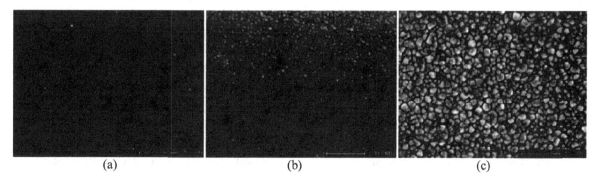

(a)   (b)   (c)

Figure 6. XRD patterns of TiO₂ nanostructured thin films deposited on glass substrates at (a) room temperature and annealed at (b) 300°C, (c) 400°C, (d) 500°C, and (e) 600°C (Hasan et al., 2008)

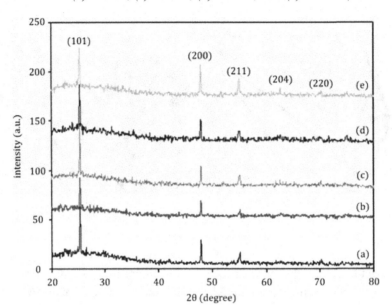

posited on glass substrates. Glass substrates were dipped for one, two, and three times in the precursor solution and thickness values of 88, 106, and 201 nm were obtained, respectively. According to the results, the layer consisting of one film wasn't smooth and has a lot of aggregates on its surface. However, the layer consisting of two films yielded completely smooth surface, whereas the layer consisting of three films revealed wrinkle surface morphology. Figure 7 clearly depicts SEM image of glass substrate dipped three times in the precursor solution.

Mechanical Properties

Mechanical properties of nanostructured titanium dioxide thin films in turn have a lot of significance in comparison with other properties. However there are few studies specially related to the nanostructured undoped TiO₂ thin films. One of the most popular tests which are employed to evaluate the mechanical properties of thin layers is the indentation technique. In this technique, displacement and applied load on nanostructured

thin films continuously records in an ultra-low range (lower than 1 mN). In an specific studies, Kościelska et al. (2005) investigated the mechanical properties of nitrided TiO₂ thin films. For this purpose, hardness and Young's modulus were calculated from the displacement dependence of the indenter load at the depth of 30 nm. Typical load and displacement resolutions were 75 nN and 0.04 nm, respectively. To ensure the results, approximately, 10 indents were acted on each film and the mean values of hardness and modulus were calculated. Liu et al. (2003) also reported the results raised from indentation experiments on Au-TiO₂ nanostructured thin films, but they did indentation tests through a different condition. Load and displacement resolutions were 1 μN and 0.1 nm, respectively. Also, for the calculation of hardness and Young's modulus, peak load of 2mN and maximum penetration depth of 100 nm were used. Hardness and Young's modulus mean values of these assays are summarized in Table 2. As results showed, the hardness and elastic modulus increased as the calcination temperature increased from 400 to 600°C. Calcination at a

Figure 7. SEM image of glass substrate dipped three times in the precursor solution (Paez & Matoušek, 2004)

certain high temperature (500°C) reduced the size of the particles, which in turn improved the mechanical properties of thin films. It should be noted that higher temperatures maybe show an adverse effect on the mechanical properties of thin films, likely, due to the growth of TiO_2 crystallites.

Optical Properties

TiO_2 nanostructured thin films are extensively used in optical devices, because of their good transmittance in the visible region, high refractive index and chemical stability. Several optical methods can be used to study optical properties such as

Table 2. Hardness and Young's modulus of Au-TiO$_2$ films on glass at various calcination temperatures (Liu et al., 2003)

Sintering Temperature (°C)	Hardness (GPa)	Young's modulus (GPa)
400	4.97	86.3
500	6.48	90.2
600	6.45	89.9

reflectance, transmittance, refractive index, and extinction coefficient of thin films. Also, advanced optical analysis such as Raman and infrared spectroscopy can be used to investigate the change of light polarization inside atomic structure of thin film (Gnyba, Kozanecki, & Wierzba, 2005).

Donets et al. (2009) determined refractive index and thickness of TiO_2 nanostructured thin films using reflecto- and ellipsometric methods. According to these methods they found 116 nm for thickness mean value and 1.8 for refractive index approximately. Hemissi et al. (2007) calculated refractive index, dielectric constant, thickness, and the third order optical nonlinear susceptibility of the deposited TiO_2 nanostructured thin film using transmittance spectrum data. Behavior of refractive index in the long wavelength region was fairly smooth but increased rapidly towards shorter wavelengths. The refractive index was estimated about 2.28. The extinction coefficient decreased gradually to have in view short wavelength. These researchers showed that the calculated extinction coefficient values actually contain total optical losses because of both absorption and scattering phenomena. However, low value of extinction coefficient in visible and infrared region indicated a smoothness surface of TiO_2 nanostructured thin film. The optical band and thickness were estimated to be 2.79 eV and 270 nm, respectively. The dielectric constant was estimated to be 5.20. Also, calculated third order nonlinear susceptibility of TiO_2 nanostructured thin film showed that it is raised by increasing photon energy. The third order nonlinear susceptibility was estimated about 0.021×10^{-10} esu using Wagner model.

Electrical Properties

TiO_2 nanostructured thin films have wide forbidden band gap, thus electrical properties of pure TiO_2 thin film are so weak and in more cases, it is really an insulator material. To enhance conductivity or resistivity of TiO_2 nanostructured thin films, they have to be synthesized using doped TiO_2 precursor solutions (Kurakula, 2007). There are many researches published surveying electrical properties of TiO_2 nanostructured thin films (Bally, 1999; Kościelska et al., 2005; Kurakula, 2007; Lin, Uchino, Kozuka, & Yoko, 1997; Sankar & Gopchandran, 2009). In a research work, Lin et al. (1997) prepared transparent semiconductive n- and p-type TiO_2 nanostructured thin films using co-doping of Ru and Ta (Nb) and co-doping of Co and Nb (Sb), respectively. They showed that solar light can be absorbed by n- and p-type TiO_2 nanostructured thin films, respectively. Therefore, they concluded that these films can convert solar light to electrical energy easily; i.e. they can be used to fabricate solar cells which produce electrical energy via absorbing solar light. Sankar et al. (2009) studied electrical resistance and transport behavior of excess charge carriers in TiO_2 nanostructured thin films. Results showed that electrical properties increased with annealing temperature. Ahmad et al. (2010) also explained affect of annealing temperature on electrical properties of TiO_2 nanostructured thin films using Current-Voltage analysis.

Photocatalytic Properties

Titanium dioxide semiconductors can act as a photocatalyst due to their filled valence and empty conduction bands. The energy difference between the lowest energy level of the conduction band and the highest energy level of the valence band is the so-called band gap energy. As mentioned already, TiO_2 is a semiconductor with band gap energy of 3.2 eV. When TiO_2 nanoparticles are exposed to energy photons of 3.2 eV with a wavelength of 388 nm, the band gap exceeds and an electron promotes from the valence to the conduction band (Duzhko, Timoshenko, Koch, & Dittrich, 2001; Yoon et al., 2006).

Naturally, TiO_2 nanoparticles are super-hydrophilic photocatalyst, and can decompose inorganic substances through photocatalysis reactions. Special substrates coated by TiO_2 semiconducting material show unrivaled behavior against any dirt on them due to photocatalytic activity of titanium dioxide. This means that the dirt on this modified substrate can be easily washed away by some water, keeping the substrate clean for long times. Originally, two mechanisms should be considered; Firstly, a super-hydrophilic surface has a higher affinity to water than to inorganic dirt. Secondly, ultraviolet illumination of TiO_2 leads to the formation of a photogenerated hole-electron pair that reacts with oxygen and water in the environment to generate potential cleaning agents on the modified substrate. The radical species (•OH, •OOH) decompose large organic molecules to smaller fragments. The combination of photocatalysis and super-hydrophilicity allows dirt to be swept away with water (Benedix, Dehn, Quaas, & Orgass, 2000).

Watanabe et al. (1999) investigated photocatalytic properties of glass substrates coated using nanostructured TiO_2 thin films. In this study, the photocatalytic activities of the coated substrates were evaluated by dye decomposition. For this purpose, the coated substrates were soaked in aqueous solution of methylene blue, and then irradiated by UV to examine decomposition rate of the dye by measuring the absorbance value. As results showed, the substrates coated using anatase form of polycrystalline TiO_2 nanostructured thin films exhibit high dye decomposition, and neither of the rutile form of single crystalline TiO_2 nanostructured thin films showed photocatalytic decomposability at all during 1 hour of light exposure. In another investigation performed by Yu et al. (2001) and also Yoon et al. (2006) but through a little different description, TiO_2 films were dipped in aqueous methyl orange together with air bubbling and UV irradiation. The concentration of methyl orange, which was decolorized, was determined by transmission spectrophotometer. The photocatalytic decolorization of methyl orange is pseudo-first-order reaction (Equation (3)).

$$ln\ (C_0/C) = k.t \qquad (3)$$

where k is the apparent reaction rate constant, C_0 and C are the initial concentration and the reaction concentration of methyl orange, respectively. The results of this research exhibit that there is a strong dependence between apparent rate constants and thickness of TiO_2 nanostructured thin films. As expected, it is found that the rate constant increases with increasing film thickness and approach a limiting value at thick film. The former is attributed to the increase in amount of titanium dioxide to participate in the photocatalytic reaction. The latter mainly results from the following two factors: (a) aggregation of TiO_2 particles in the interior region of thick films which underwent a long term heat treatment, causing a decrease in the number of surface active sites, and (b) increase in opacity and light scattering of TiO_2 thick films, leading to a decrease in the passage of irradiation through the film. Also, when TiO_2 nanostructured thin films are calcinated at 500°C, the apparent rate constants increase with increasing calcination time, reach a maximum at the calcination time of 60 min and then decrease by further calcination. The occurrence of a maximum in the rate constant of TiO_2 nanostructured thin films at 500°C for 60 min is likely due to charge recombination between the photogenerated electrons and holes. This process is often a major limiting factor of photocatalytic activity of TiO_2 nanostructured thin films as it impedes charge transfer at the semiconductor-electrolyte interface. It is also found that the calcination temperature affects the photocatalytic activity of the as-prepared TiO_2 nanostructured thin films. The photocatalytic activity of TiO_2 nanostructured thin films is enhanced with the increase of the calcination temperature, being ascribed to the crystalline transformation of TiO_2 nanostructured thin films from amorphous to anatase phase. As mentioned before, the photocatalytic activity of anatase is higher than that of amorphous and rutile TiO_2. Thus, the photocatalytic activity of TiO_2 films at 500°C shows the maximum.

PRACTICAL APPLICATIONS OF TiO_2 NANOSTRUCTURED THIN FILMS

Special substrates coated by TiO_2 nanostructured thin films created based on nanotechnology have versatile applications in micro- and nanosystems devices, such as sensors, selfcleaning surfaces, dye-sensitized solar cells, dielectric surfaces, and antibacterial surfaces due to their drastic reactivity, high refractive index, chemical stability, and excellent optical, electrical, and photocatalytic properties. Hereinafter, there are brief descriptions about major practical applications of special substrates coated by TiO_2 nanostructured thin films were introduced recently by several researchers (Ahn et al., 2003; Banerjee, Gopal, Muraleedharan, Tyagi, & Raj, 2006; Benedix et al., 2000; Bozzi et al., 2005; Damchan, Sikong, Kooptarnond, & Niyomwas, 2008; Daoud & Xin, 2004; Euvananont, Doungratsamee et al., 2008; Euvananont, Junin et al., 2008; Grätzel, 2003; Gupta et al., 2008; Hua, Cheuk, Wei-ning, Chen, & Chang-fa, 2007; Jakubik, 2006; Jiang et al.,

2009; Lao et al., 2005; Mardare & Rusu, 2004; Ming-Fang et al., 2006; Ponce et al., 2009; Trah, Franz, & Marek, 1999; Veronovski et al., 2009; Wegner, Barborini, Piseri, & Milani, 2006; Wei, 2010; Wu et al., 2009; Yu et al., 2002).

Sensors

A sensor is a device that measures physical/chemical quantity and converts it into a signal which can be read by a detector, and exactly, it is a device which receives and responds to a stimulus. Here, the term "stimulus" means a property or a quantity that needs to be converted into electrical form. Hence, sensor can be defined as a device which receives a signal and converts it into electrical form which can be further used for electronic devices. A sensor differs from a transducer in the way that a transducer converts one form of energy into other form whereas a sensor converts the received signal into electrical form only (Trah et al., 1999).

Today, various precise sensors can be manufactured based on nanotechnology. In most cases, a microsensor reaches a significantly higher speed and sensitivity using special nanomaterials compared with macroscopic approaches. Ceramic based sensors are used quite extensively to monitor oxygen, combustible gases, and humidity among other parameters. As an example, in order to reduce exhaust pollution, automobile manufacturers use devices which are sensitive to the oxygen fugacity in the exhaust stream. There are efforts underway to try using TiO_2 based resistive sensors instead of ZrO_2 one. Recently, ZrO_2 based resistive sensors are being replaced TiO_2 based ones. Researchers indicated that oxygen sensors based on TiO_2 nanostructured thin films have fast responses and rapid gas permeability. As discussed latter, sol-gel is a process which can be easily used to form thin layers on a special substrate to make a resistive sensor with high sensitivity and preferential porosity. The resultant thin films have high surface area and are useful for O_2 gas

sensing. TiO_2 nanostructured thin films are well known material in sensor technology and have been applied for measuring many gases including O_2, CO, NO_2, water vapor and hydrocarbon gases. Also, the use of nanoscale particles was observed to be critical in order to achieve high sensitivity. A great sensitivity to H_2 and ethanol has been found for undoped anatase form of TiO_2 nanostructured thin films at 400°C, whereas Sr, Tb and Y-doped thin films were barely sensitive to those gases (Wegner et al., 2006). Ponce et al. (2009) reported gas sensor application of anatase form of undoped-TiO_2 nanostructured thin film. As-prepared thin films have a porous structure, being composed of small particles in the range of 20-40 nm. In this research work, impedance spectroscopy technique was used in order to evaluate the electrical behavior of the samples under different atmospheres and temperatures. The sensors based on undoped-TiO_2 nanostructured thin films exhibited a good response time, with the electrical resistance being almost constant after approximately 120 second. The film also exhibited a very strong increase in resistance (almost three orders of magnitude) when air was introduced in the test condition. Jakubik et al. (2006) studied another type of sensors so-called surface acoustic wave gas sensors and compared different gases with them. Surface acoustic wave gas sensors are very attractive because of their remarkable sensitivity due to changes of the boundary conditions of the propagating wave, introduced by the interaction of active material with specific gas molecules. This unusual sensitivity results from the simple fact that most of the wave energy is concentrated near the crystal surface within one or two wavelengths. Consequently, the surface wave is in its first approximation highly sensitive to any changes of the physical or chemical properties of the nanostructured thin active film previously placed on the crystal surface. Gas sensors based on TiO_2 nanostructured thin films are particularly attractive as reducing structures since their response is affected to a lesser extent by humidity of the environment, than the conventional based gas sensors. The interaction temperatures were from 30 to 400°C and the structure was tested towards H_2S, H_2 and NH_3 gases.

Selfcleaning Surfaces

Selfcleaning applications using semiconducting powders or thin films have become a subject of increasing interest especially in the last 10 years. The selfcleaning property has been known to be a mutual effect between photocatalysis and hydrophilicity. The photocatalysis property helps decompose the organic substances that come into contact with the surface and thus prevent them from building up. The hydrophilicity makes the cleaning more effective as the water spread over the surface rather than remaining as droplets which helps collect the dirt better, makes the surface dry faster, and moreover, prevents the undesirable water streaking or spotting on the surface. In practice, surface cleaning of building materials like tiles, facades and glass panes causes considerable trouble, high consumption of energy and chemical detergents and, consequently, high costs (Damchan et al., 2008). To realize selfcleaning material surfaces there are two principal ways: the development of so-called super hydrophobic or super-hydrophilic surfaces. The wetting of a solid with water, where air is the surrounding medium, is dependent on the relation between the interfacial tensions (water/air, water/solid and solid/air). The ratio between these tensions determines the contact angle θ between water droplets on a given surface. A contact angle of 0° means complete wetting, and a contact angle of 180° corresponds to complete non-wetting. Hydrophobic surfaces with low wettability and contact angles of about 180° are known for a long time. The higher this angle the lower is the value of the adhesion work. Decreasing of the contact angle leads to enlarged values of the adhesion work (hydrophilic surfaces). By transferring the microstructure of selected plant surfaces to practical materials, super-hydrophobic surfaces could be developed. The water repellency of plant surfaces has been known for many years. That water-repellent surfaces also indicate selfcleaning properties has been completely overlooked. Recently, some of scientists investigated and proved the correlation between the microstructure, wettability, and contaminants in detail using lotus leaves. This was called the Lotus effect because it can be demonstrated beautifully with the great leaves of the Lotus plant. The micro rough surfaces show contact angles higher than 130°. That means, the adhesion of water, as well as particles is extremely reduced. Water which contacts such surfaces will be immediately contracted to droplets. The particles of contaminants adhere to the droplet surfaces and are removed from the rough surface when the droplets roll off (Benedix et al., 2000). Cleaning procedures based on low contact angles are known since the discovery of soap. Generally, detergents reduce the surface tension of water and the contact angle will lowered. Another very interesting possibility to cause low contact angles without detergents is the use of active thin films on the material surface. For the preparation of these thin layers mainly photocatalytic active metal oxides or sulfides have been applied. In the last years, substrates coated by TiO_2 nanostructured thin films are of increasing interest. If a substrate coated by anatase form of TiO_2 nanostructured thin film is exposed to UV light, very low contact angles are obtained (lower than 1°). These modified substrates have the unique property of attracting rather than repelling water (super-hydrophilicity). The water lies flat on the surface in sheets instead of forming droplets. If the illumination is stopped, the super-hydrophilic behavior of the TiO_2 surface is retained for approximately two days. Furthermore, UV illumination of titanium dioxide leads to the formation of powerful agents with the ability to oxidize and decompose many types of bacteria, organic and inorganic materials (Benedix et al., 2000). Euvananont et al. (2008) prepared TiO_2 nanostructured thin film coated soda lime glasses with self cleaning properties. As mentioned before, typically, hydrophilicity and photocatalytic activity of the TiO_2 nanostructured thin films were evaluated by measuring the contact angle of water on the modified substrate and the photocatalytic decolorization of aqueous solution of methylene blue, respectively. Results indicated that the super-hydrophilicity of substrates coated by TiO_2 nanostructured thin films were due to un-doped anatase TiO_2. Also, it should be noted that an increase in number of dipping times was found to increase the photocatalytic activity. Moreover, the best selfcleaning properties were obtained by dip-coating of TiO_2 precursor solution three times on soda lime glass substrates.

Veronovski et al. (2009) evaluated selfcleaning properties of Lyocell fabric substrate coated by TiO_2 nanostructured thin films via sol-gel method. The results of the selfcleaning test, which was based on the photocatalytic degradation of such an organic dye solution dropped on the surface of fabric substrate, indicate the high degradation capability under UV irradiation. These researchers also examined composite form of TiO_2 nanostructured thin films along with nanosized SiO_2 particles and gained excellent selfcleaning results. Figure 8 clearly depicts SEM images of Lyocell fibres coated by nanosized TiO_2 particles via sol-gel process. Similarly, Bozzi et al. (2005) also prepared cotton fabric substrates with selfcleaning properties through sol-gel process nearly with the same conditions. Wu et al. (2009) used sol-gel process through a facile approach to produce selfcleaning cotton fabric substrates. They deduced that cotton fabric substrates coated using TiO_2 nanostructured thin films possessed the ability to decompose dyes upon UV irradiation. Approximately, 60% of methyl orange was reduced on modified fabric substrates after 3 h UV irradiation. The mechanism of organic decomposition over TiO_2 particles under UV irradiation is well known as that highly oxidative radicals are generated on the TiO_2 surface. As shown in SEM images (images not mentioned here), the adherence of TiO_2 thin films to the cot-

ton fabric substrates is strong and can't be broken easily. Here, a question can be raised as how is the interactions between TiO_2 thin film and cotton fabric substrate? These researchers demonstrated that there are naturally great affinity of TiO_2 toward hydroxyl and carbonyl groups. As it can be seen from the structure of macromolecular chains of cellulose, there is a large number of hydroxyl and carbonyl groups exist on the surface of the cotton fabrics, so they can provide active sites for coordination with nanosized TiO_2 particles.

Gupta et al. (2008) deduced that the rate of dye stain degradation on cotton fabric substrates coated by TiO_2 nanostructured thin films was faster in first 12 h of UV irradiation. Also, they found that with the increase in concentration of TiO_2 nanoparticles, i.e. thickness of TiO_2 thin films, the rate of discoloration increases marginally. Particle size of TiO_2 nanoparticles was reported approximately lower than 10 nm. These researchers also expressed the same mechanism according to Wu et al. (2009) statements for the selfcleaning effect of TiO_2 coated cotton fabric substrates.

Dye-Sensitized Solar Cells

Dye-sensitized solar cells provide a functional authoritative concept to present day p-n junction photovoltaic devices. Dye-sensitized solar cells based on wide band gap nanocrystalline semiconductor oxides have been intensively studied and developed during the 90s and the present decade, since their discovery in 1991. These devices were conceived as an environmentally friendly and economically viable alternative to conventional inorganic devices, based on solid state p-n junctions. Dye-sensitized solar cells differ from conventional semiconductor devices (p-n junction), since in these photoelectrochemical devices the function of light absorption and the transport occur separately (Grätzel, 2003).

Many companies and institutions have been engaged in research and development to address

Figure 8. SEM images of (a) uncoated Lyocell fibres and (b) coated using nanosized TiO$_2$ particles via sol-gel process (Veronovski et al., 2009)

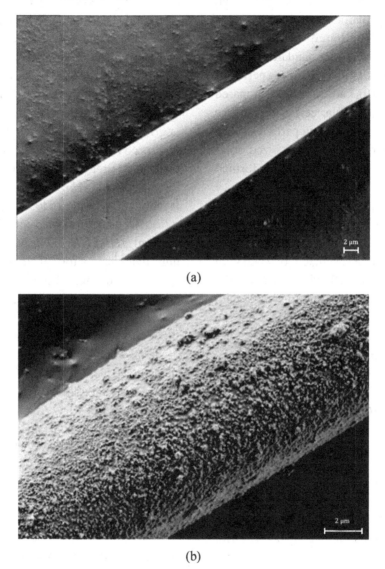

(a)

(b)

practical solutions to remaining challenges for practical applications of the dye-sensitized solar cells technology. The dye-sensitized solar cells differ from conventional semiconductor devices in that they separate the function of light absorption from charge carrier transport. Dye sensitizer absorbs the incident sunlight and exploits the light energy to induce vectorial electron transfer reaction. The weakest point of the present dye-sensitized solar cells is the limited long term

stability of the liquid junction devices with high conversion efficiency. Possible desorption of loosely attached dyes, and photodegradation in the desorbed state as well as corrosion of the Pt counter electrode have been suggested as some of the critical factors limiting the long term performance of the devices, specially at elevated temperature. In order to match specifications required for practical outdoors applications, light soaking and thermal stability tests performed under realistic conditions have been carried out. Best result in sealed laboratory devices have been obtained using non-volatile electrolytes based on ionic liquids, whose initial top efficiency (η=8.3%) remains almost invariable after standard aging test at 80°C and light soaking at 65°C, over a period of 1000 hours (Wei, 2010). Lao et al. (2005) prepared a typical dye-sensitized solar cell using anatase nanocrystalline TiO_2 with a mean particle size of 10 nm. High-performance dye-sensitized solar cell with nanocrystalline TiO_2 electrode formed from the hydrolysis of $TiCl_4$ was achieved. Its I and V values reached 21.62 mA/cm^2 and 727.9 mV, respectively, and the photovoltaic conversion efficiency reached 9.13%, which is 7.5% higher than those of dye-sensitized solar cell with TiO_2 made from titanium alkoxides. They are the highest values obtained from the solar cells with nanocrystalline TiO_2 electrode formed from the hydrolysis of $TiCl_4$. Also, the film can be thinner than the conventional TiO_2 electrode, which means less TiO_2 is needed for one device.

Dielectric Surfaces

TiO_2 nanocrystalline particles have high dielectric constant and can be used in microelectronic devices such as capacitors. Also, high stability of TiO_2 nanostructured thin films in severe conditions and elevated temperatures make them attractive transparent metal oxide semiconductor thin film for enormous microelectronic applications (Euvananont, Doungratsamee et al., 2008). Jiang et al. (2009) found that multilayer dielectric stacks exhibit high reflectivity due to constructive interference between light rays reflected from layers with alternating high and low refractive indices that are each one quarter- wavelength thick. This device is also known as a distributed Bragg reflector, and exhibits high reflectivity over a wide range (Stop Band) when the alternating layers have a large index contrast. If two distributed Bragg reflectors are separated by a spacer with a thickness of an integer number of half wavelengths,

then the whole device exhibits a narrow region of high transmission (low reflectivity) within the stop band. This narrow-band filter is also known as a Fabry-Perot cavity or an optical micro cavity when the separation is only a few half wavelengths. The standard designation for a multilayer dielectric stack of quarter-wavelength high (*H*) and low (*L*) index materials deposited on a glass (*g*) substrate is *g(HL)ma*, where *m* is the number of bilayers and *a* refers to the air above the last layer. The distributed Bragg reflectors described here are of the form *g(HL)mHa*, where the extra high-index layer on top is designed to increase the maximum reflectivity. The fabricated optical microcavity has the form *g(HL)2HH(LH)2a*, where the two interior high-index layers form a single half-wavelength spacer, often referred to as the defect layer. In another study, Mardare et al. (2004) evaluated dielectric properties of TiO_2 nanostructured thin films on $ITO/TiO_2/Au$ substrate at width region of signal frequencies. They found that electrical capacitance increases by doping with Nb and Ce. This increase alludes to increase of the dielectric constant of thin film. At the frequency of 100 Hz, the dielectric constant increases from 83.6 for the undoped sample, to 179 by doping with Ce, and to 108 by doping with Fe. However, Nb dopants determine a large increase of the dielectric constant, till 371, which is very important in fabricating capacitors.

Antibacterial Surfaces

There are many researches which revealed the antibacterial properties of TiO_2 nanostructured thin films. In an investigation performed by Banerjee et al. (2006), bacterial colony persisted on unanodized substrates even after the substrates were exposed to UV irradiation. No bacteria persisted on the anodized substrates after exposure to UV irradiation. Researches indicate that TiO_2 nanoparticles don't have any bactericidal activity in dark conditions. Yu et al. (2002) inserted an amount of *Escherichia coli* cell suspension with appropriate colony forming unit (CFU) onto glass substrate coated by TiO_2 nanostructured thin films. The glass was illuminated by a long wavelength UV lamp positioned above the glass. An amount of aliquots of serially diluted suspensions were placed on duplicate LB agar plates at 10 min intervals. The plates were then incubated at 37°C for 24 hours and the numbers of colonies on the plates were counted. For the strain of *Escherichia coli DH5α* at the cell concentration of 10^4, 10^5, and 10^6 $CFUml^{-1}$, the survival percentage of the cell on the two types of TiO_2-coated glass reached near-zero levels after 50 min irradiation. For the cell concentration of 10^6 $CFUml^{-1}$, the bacterial survival percentage ranged from 80 to 100% for the first 30 min, which then dropped to 30% at 40 min and finally reached <10% at 50 min of UV irradiation. A similar trend appeared at cell concentrations of 10^5 $CFUml^{-1}$. However, the bacterial survival percentage only stayed high for the first 20 min, after which it started to drop. It reached 40% and <10% at 30 and 40 min of UV irradiation, respectively. The bactericidal process was virtually completed after 50 min. For even lower cell concentrations of 10^4 $CFUml^{-1}$, the cell numbers started to drop at the beginning and reached <10% after 30 min of UV illumination. From the above results, it can be concluded that the time for inactivating the cell number of *Escherichia coli DH5α* depends on the initial cell concentration. The higher the initial cell concentration, the longer it takes to lower the survival percentage of *Escherichia coli DH5α*. In a solution with high initial cell concentration, the cells are packed closely and only a small percentage of the cells would be in contact with the TiO_2 film surface. It isn't surprising that only a small portion of the cells are killed in the initial stage of irradiation. Moreover, the dead cells can't diffuse away easily from TiO_2 nanostructured thin film surface and they stayed in contact with the film surface. The chance for the living cells to come in contact with the film surface would be lowered. Therefore, the amount of living cells relative to the dead cells

is high for the first 20 min in the high initial cell concentration setup. As time goes on, this shielding effect would decrease gradually. The survival percentage starts to drop at about 40-50 min as more bacterial cells can come in contact with the film surface and be degraded by the oxidizing species. For lower initial cell concentrations, there are only a limited number of bacterial cells on the film surface. Therefore, the dead cells would not affect the killing of the other living cells, and the survival percentage drops gradually according to the time of UV irradiation. Wu et al. (2009) tested the antibacterial activity of cotton fabrics coated by TiO_2 nanostructured thin films by comparing the growth of the bacteria in the liquid and solid Luria-Bertani Medium (LBM). It was obviously observed that the growth of bacteria was inhibited significantly on cotton fabrics coated by TiO_2 nanostructured thin films in the both incubation. These researchers attributed antibacterial effect of TiO_2 coated cotton fabrics to the destruction of the bacteria cell wall and membrane by the reactive oxygen species on surface of TiO_2 nanoparticles. Hua et al. (2007) evaluated the antibacterial activity of cotton fabric substrates coated using TiO_2 nanoparticles against *Escherichia coli* and *Bacillus subtilis*. As the amount of TiO_2 nanoparticles increases, the active ingredients produced from the photocatalytic process increase, hence contributing to the antibacterial performance. Results represented that modified cotton fabric substrates has stronger effect on *Escherichia coli* than on *Bacillus subtilis*. The reason may attribute to the cell wall difference between the two distant bacteria, in which *Escherichia coli* has thinner and slack cell walls, while *Bacillus subtilis* has thicker and denser cell wall. This order of precedence appears to be reasonable if it is assumed that the primary step in the photocatalytic decomposition consists of attacks by the anion radicals on the cell wall, leading to the formation of punctures and finally death of cell. Daoud et al. (2004) and Gupta et al. (2008) also reached similar results by studying the antibacterial activity of sol-gel TiO_2

coated cotton fabric substrates using *Klebsiella pneumoniae* gram negative bacteria.

OPTICAL CONSTANTS AND THICKNESS DETERMINATION OF TIO$_2$ NANOSTRUCTURED THIN FILMS BY SIFM

Sol-gel made titanium dioxide based thin films have been extensively studied due to their importance in the industry (Ivanova, Harizanova, & Surtchev, 2002). Apart from this, they have shown interesting optical behavior in a wide variety of optical and optoelectronic devices. Usually a detailed knowledge of optical properties (especially refractive index and thickness) of such films is required to understand the behavior of these devices. Numerous methods have been developed for determination of optical properties of thin films. These methods can be divided in three groups (Poelman & Frederic, 2003). The first group is based on at least two different optical measurements. In this method, the combinations of the transmission and reflectance measurements are used to determination of optical constants (Djurisic, Fritz, & Leo, 1999). The second is a wavelength-dependent refractive index or dispersion relation, which assumes a specific empirical-dispersion equation for the wavelength-dependent refractive index (Jenkins & White, 1981). Virtual measurement as a second variable is the third group. In this method, envelopes around the transmission maxima and transmission minima are constructed and considered as continuous spectra versus wavelength, T$_{max}$ (λ) and T$_{max}$ (λ), respectively (Ghodsi, Tepehan, & Tepehan, 1997; Swanepoel, 1983).

In this section, a simple method (Ghodsi, 2005) will be presented to obtain the optical constants and thickness of a weakly absorbing TiO$_2$ thin films deposited on transparent substrate by using Successive Interference Fringes Method (SIFM)

without any envelopes around the transmission maxima and transmission minima.

Assuming a homogenous, isotropic weakly absorbing thin film with uniform thickness d and complex refractive index, $n_f = n_{f-} ik_f$ is deposited onto a transparent finite substrate. Where n_f is the real part of complex refractive index and k_f the imaginary part of complex refractive index that related to the absorption coefficient of the film. All of film and substrate system are surrounded by air with a refractive index of one. The situation for a weakly absorbing thin film deposited on transparent substrate shown in Figure 9. The refractive index and absorption coefficient of substrate is n_s and α_s, respectively. Since the substrate is transparent, then α_s becomes zero.

The optical transmission (Figure 10), T of a thin absorbing uniform film deposited onto a finite transparent substrate can be given by the following equations (in the case: $k_f^2 \ll n_f^2$) (Swanepoel, 1983):

$$T = \frac{Ax}{B - Cx \cos \varphi + Dx^2} \tag{4}$$

where

$$A = 16 n_s n_f^2 \tag{5a}$$

$$B = \left(n_f + 1\right)^3 \left(n_f + n_s^2\right) \tag{5b}$$

$$C = \left(n_f^2 - 1\right)\left(n_f^2 - n_s^2\right) \tag{5c}$$

$$D = \left(n_f - 1\right)^3 \left(n_f - n_s^2\right) \tag{5d}$$

$$\varphi = 4\pi n_f d / \lambda \tag{5e}$$

$$x = exp\left(-\alpha_f d\right) \tag{5f}$$

Figure 9. Transmission of a light beam through a system of absorbing film on a finite transparent substrate

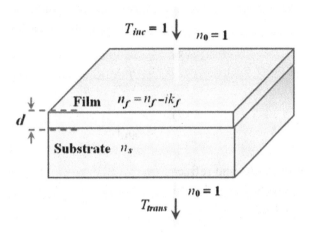

$$\alpha_f = 4\pi k_f / \lambda \qquad (5g)$$

The wavelengths of the successive transmission extremes of the interference fringes can be given by the well-known equation:

$$2n_f d = m\lambda \qquad (6)$$

where m is the interference order number of extreme. The maxima and minima of the transmission correspond to integer and half integer values of m, respectively.

Assuming the ith interference order number is m_i. Therefore, for the ith extreme and its two adjacent extremes, equation (6) can be written as follows:

Figure 10. Transmission spectra in the visible and near-infrared wavelength range of a typical TiO$_2$ thin film deposited onto a transparent substrate

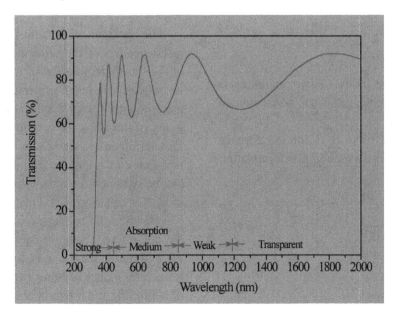

$$2n_{f,i-1}d = \left(m_i - \frac{1}{2}\right)\lambda_{i-1} \tag{7}$$

$$2n_{f,i}d = m_i\lambda_i \tag{8}$$

$$2n_{f,i+1}d = \left(m_i + \frac{1}{2}\right)\lambda_{i+1} \tag{9}$$

Two relations between thickness and refractive index of the film and wavelength yields on substituting equations (7) and (8) into equation (9):

$$d = \frac{\lambda_{i-1}\lambda_i}{4\left(n_{f,i}\lambda_{i-1} - n_{f,i-1}\lambda_i\right)} \tag{10}$$

$$d = \frac{\lambda_i\lambda_{i+1}}{4\left(n_{f,i+1}\lambda_i - n_{f,i}\lambda_{i+1}\right)} \tag{11}$$

Because of uniformity of the film thickness, both (10) and (11) equations must be equal. Thus, a film thickness and interference order number independent relationship for refractive index of ith extreme is obtained:

$$n_{f,i} = \left(\frac{\lambda_i}{2\lambda_{i-1}}\right)n_{f,i-1} + \left(\frac{\lambda_i}{2\lambda_{i+1}}\right)n_{f,i+1} \tag{12}$$

If the refractive index of two extremes is known, other refractive index can be calculated from equation (9).

If we put $\cos\varphi = \pm 1$ (-1 for interference minima and $+1$ for interference maxima) equation (4) then becomes:

$$T_{\substack{max \\ min}} = \frac{Ax}{B \mp Cx + Dx^2} \tag{13}$$

Assuming that, in the transparent region $\alpha_f \approx 0$ or $x \approx 1$, the extremes of the interference fringes can be written as follows:

$$T_{max} = \frac{2n_s}{n_s^2 + 1} \tag{14}$$

and

$$T_{min} = \frac{4n_f^2 n_s}{n_f^4 + n_f^2\left(n_s^2 + 1\right) + n_s^2} \tag{15}$$

or

$$n_s = \frac{1}{T_{max}} + \left(\frac{1}{T_{max}^2} - 1\right)^{\frac{1}{2}} \tag{16}$$

and

$$n_f = \left[\frac{2n_s}{T_{min}} - \frac{n_s^2 + 1}{2} + \left[\left(\frac{2n_s}{T_{min}} - \frac{n_s^2 + 1}{2}\right)^2 - n_s^2\right]^{\frac{1}{2}}\right]^{\frac{1}{2}} \tag{17}$$

The maxima of the interference fringes are just dependent on the substrate's refractive index in the transparent region of the spectrum. Thus, the refractive index of substrate can be calculated using equation (16). In this region, the refractive index of the films for two adjacent minima can be determined by using equation (17). The refractive index of middle maximum of two minima can be obtained on substituting these refractive indices in equation (12). Thus, for three different wavelengths the refractive indices of extremes are determined. Solving equation (12) for $(i + 1)^{th}$ extreme, it can be used for determination of refractive indices of other extremes for the case of negligible and medium absorption region:

$$n_{f,i+1} = \left(\frac{2\lambda_{i+1}}{\lambda_i}\right) n_{f,i} + \left(\frac{\lambda_{i+1}}{\lambda_{i-1}}\right) n_{f,i-1} \qquad (18)$$

Once the refractive indices of all extremes are known, the thickness of the film can be calculated using equation (10) or (11) dependent of which extreme is selected. For the ith interference fringe, all the constants in equation (8) are known and the ith interference order number m_i can be obtained. In fact, the interference order numbers of adjacent extremes are consecutive integers and half integers for the maxima and minima of the spectrum respectively. The order number m_i is rounded appropriately if it is necessary. The average value of thickness is obtained. Then the refractive index of each extreme is recalculated using equation (8). Figure 11 shows the wavelength dependence of refractive index for a 400 nm TiO_2 thin film deposited on glass substrate.

In this step, the corresponding absorption coefficients for the region of weak and medium absorption can be calculated. Substituting equation (13) into (5f) and solving for the absorption coefficient yields:

$$\alpha_f \left(T_{\substack{max \\ min}}\right) = -\frac{1}{d} \times ln \left\{ \frac{F_{\substack{max \\ min}} - \left[F_{\substack{max \\ min}}^2 - \left(n_f^2 - 1\right)^3 \left(n_f^2 - n_s^4\right) \right]^{\frac{1}{2}}}{\left(n_f - 1\right)^3 \left(n_f - n_s^2\right)} \right\} \qquad (19)$$

where

$$F_{\substack{max \\ min}} = \frac{8n_f^2 n_s}{T_{\substack{max \\ min}}} \pm \left(n_f^2 - 1\right)\left(n_f^2 - n_s^2\right) \qquad (20)$$

The optical absorption coeeficient of TiO_2 thin films determined by using equations (19) and (20) is depicted in Figure 12.

In the strong absorption region, the interference fringes disappear. In this region, the values of refractive index can be estimated by extrapolating the values of refractive index determind in the transparent, weak and medium absorbing regions of spectrum. For very large values of absorption cooefficient (or $x \ll 1$) the interference effects are ignored and equation (4) can be written as:

Figure 11. Wavelength-dependence of refractive index of a 400 nm TiO_2 thin film

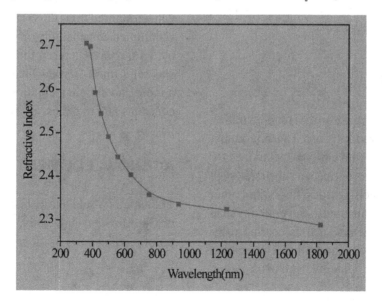

Figure 12. Spectral dependence of absorption coefficients of 400 nm TiO₂ thin films

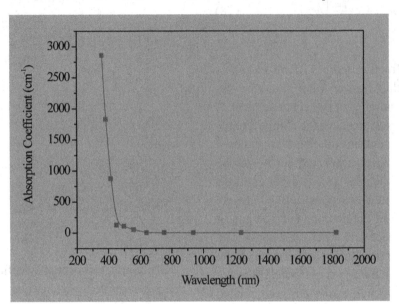

$$T \approx Ax / B \qquad (21)$$

or

$$x \approx \frac{\left(n_f + 1\right)^3 \left(n_f + n_s^2\right)}{16 n_s\, n_f^2}\, T \qquad (22)$$

Now x is known in the strong absorption region. The absorption coefficient in this region can be calculated from equation (5f).

CONCLUSION

The sol-gel process is a useful tool for preparation of TiO_2 nanostructured thin films. The dip and spin coating become two conventional techniques for deposition of the films on special substrates such as glasses, mica, steels, textiles, fibers, and other organic/inorganic substrates. Several physical and chemical parameters such as coating techniques, drying condition, annealing temperature, stabilizer, precursor material, solvents, aging, the pH and viscosity of precursor solution, and etc influence the electrical, optical, mechanical, and other physical/chemical properties of TiO_2 nanostructured thin films. The TiO_2 nanostructured thin film is an insulator with wide band gap energy and relatively high refractive index. However, its band gap decreases by co-doping of some transition metals such as Ru and Ta. The coated substrates reveal high dye decomposition by using anatase form of polycrystalline TiO_2 nanostructured thin films. The growth of bacteria is inhibited considerably on cotton fabrics coated by TiO_2 nanostructured thin films in the liquid and solid Luria-Bertani Medium. Also, SIFM is a rapid and simple technique to estimate optical constants and thickness of TiO_2 thin films.

ACKNOWLEDGMENT

The authors would like to thank Mr. Peiman Azimi at Bu Ali Sina University, Hamedan, Iran, for proof reading parts of the manuscript.

REFERENCES

Abidi, N., Hequet, E., Tarimala, S., & Dai, L. L. (2007). Cotton fabric surface modification for improved UV radiation protection using sol-gel process. *Journal of Applied Polymer Science, 104,* 111–117. doi:10.1002/app.24572

Ahmad, M. K., Halid, M. L. M., Rasheid, N. A., Ahmed, A. Z., Abdullah, S., & Rusop, M. (2010). Effect of annealing temperatures on surface morphology and electrical properties of titanium dioxide thin films prepared by sol-gel method. *Journal of Sustainable Energy & Environment, 1,* 17–20.

Ahn, Y. U., Kim, E. J., Kim, H. T., & Hahn, S. H. (2003). Variation of structural and optical properties of sol-gel TiO_2 thin films with catalyst concentration and calcination temperature. *Materials Letters, 57,* 4660–4666. doi:10.1016/S0167-577X(03)00380-X

Bally, A. (1999). *Electronic properties of nanocrystaline titanium dioxide thin films.* Lausanne: École Polytechnique Fédérale de Lausanne.

Banerjee, S., Gopal, J., Muraleedharan, P., Tyagi, A. K., & Raj, B. (2006). Physics and chemistry of photocatalytic titanium dioxide: visualization of bactericidal activity using atomic force microscopy. *Current Science, 90*(10), 1378–1383.

Barati, N., & Faghihi Sani, M. A. (2009). Coating of titania nanoparticles on stainless steel using an alkoxide precursor. *Progress in Color. Colorants and Coatings, 2,* 71–78.

Battiston, G. A., Gerbasi, R., Porchia, M., & Marigo, A. (1994). Influence of substrate on structural properties of TiO_2 thin films obtained via MOCVD. *Thin Solid Films, 239,* 186–191. doi:10.1016/0040-6090(94)90849-4

Beganskienė, A., Šakirzanovas, S., Melninkaitis, A., Sirutkaitis, V., & Kareiva, A. (2006). Sol-gel derived optical coating with controlled parameters. *Materials Science, 12*(4), 283–286.

Ben Amor, S., Baud, G., Jacquet, M., & Pichon, N. (1998). Photoprotective titania coatings on PET substrates. *Surface and Coatings Technology, 102,* 63–72. doi:10.1016/S0257-8972(97)00558-6

Benedix, R., Dehn, F., Quaas, J., & Orgass, M. (2000). Application of titanium dioxide photocatalysis to create self-cleaning building materials. *Leipzig Annual Civil Engineering Report, 5*(157).

Bozzi, A., Yuranova, T., Guasaquillo, I., Laub, D., & Kiwi, J. (2005). Self-cleaning of modified cotton textiles by TiO_2 at low temperatures under daylight irradiation. *Journal of Photochemistry and Photobiology A Chemistry, 174,* 156–164. doi:10.1016/j.jphotochem.2005.03.019

Brinker, C. J., & Harrington, M. S. (1981). Sol-gel derived antireflective coatings for silicon. *Solar Energy Materials, 5,* 159–172. doi:10.1016/0165-1633(81)90027-7

Chen, S. Z., Zhang, P. Y., Zhu, W. P., Chen, L., & Xu, S. M. (2006). Deactivation of TiO_2 photocatalytic films loaded on aluminium: XPS and AFM analyses. *Applied Surface Science, 252,* 7532–7538. doi:10.1016/j.apsusc.2005.09.023

Chrysicopoulou, P., Davazoglou, D., Trapalis, C., & Kordas, G. (1998). Optical properties of very thin (<100 nm) sol-gel TiO_2 films. *Thin Solid Films, 323,* 188–193. doi:10.1016/S0040-6090(97)01018-3

Chun, H. Y., Park, S. S., You, S. H., Kang, G. H., Bae, W. T., & Kim, K. W. (2009). Preparation of a transparent hydrophilic TiO_2 thin film photocatalyst. *Journal of Ceramic Processing Research, 10*(2), 219–223.

Damchan, J., Sikong, L., Kooptarnond, K., & Niyomwas, S. (2008). Contact angle of glass substrate coated with TiO_2/SiO_2 thin film. *Journal of Natural Sciences, 7*(1), 19.

Daoud, W. A., & Xin, J. H. (2004). Low temperature sol-gel processed photocatalytic titania coating. *Journal of Sol-Gel Science and Technology, 29*, 25–29. doi:10.1023/B:JSST.0000016134.19752. b4

Dimitriev, Y., Ivanova, Y., & Iordanova, R. (2008). History of sol-gel science and technology [review]. *Journal of the University of Chemical Technology and Metallurgy, 43*(2), 181–192.

Dislich, H., & Hinz, P. (1982). History and principles of the sol-gel process, and some new multicomponent oxide coatings. *Journal of Non-Crystalline Solids, 48*, 11–16. doi:10.1016/0022-3093(82)90242-3

Djurisic, A. B., Fritz, T., & Leo, K. (1999). Determination of optical constants of thin absorbing films from normal incidence reflectance and transmittance measurements. *Optics Communications, 166*, 35–42. doi:10.1016/S0030-4018(99)00246-1

Donets, V. V., Melnichenko, L. Y., Shaykevich, I. A., & Lomakina, O. V. (2009). Determination of refractive index dispersion and thickness of thin antireflection films TiO_2 and Si_3N_4 on surfaces of silicon photoelectric converters. *Journal of Semiconductor Physics. Quantum Electronics & Optoelectronics, 12*, 162–164.

Duzhko, V., Timoshenko, V. Y., Koch, F., & Dittrich, T. (2001). Photovoltage in nanocrystalline porous TiO_2. *Physical Review B: Condensed Matter and Materials Physics, 64*, 1–7. doi:10.1103/PhysRevB.64.075204

Ergün, O., KarslioĞlu, O., Yilmaz, A., & Üner, D. (2007). Preparation and characterization of ordered TiO_2 photocatalysts: films and mesoporous structures. *Turkish Journal of Chemistry, 31*, 501–508.

Euvananont, C., Doungratsamee, J., Junin, C., Tippo, T., & Thanachayanont, C. (2008). Microstructures of dip-coated TiO_2 thin film capacitor. *Journal of Microscopy Society of Thailand, 22*, 34–36.

Euvananont, C., Junin, C., Inpor, K., Limthongkul, P., & Thanachayanont, C. (2008). TiO_2 optical coating layers for self-cleaning applications. *Ceramics International, 34*, 1067–1071. doi:10.1016/j.ceramint.2007.09.043

Falaras, P., & Xagas, A. P. (2002). Roughness and fractality of nanostructured TiO_2 films prepared via sol-gel technique. *Journal of Materials Science, 37*, 3855–3860. doi:10.1023/A:1019686902277

Fretwell, R., & Douglas, P. (2001). An active, robust and transparent nanocrystalline anatase TiO_2 thin film-preparation, characterization and the kinetics of photodegradation of model pollutants. *Journal of Photochemistry and Photobiology A Chemistry, 143*, 229–240. doi:10.1016/S1010-6030(01)00526-3

Ghodsi, F. E. (2005). Determination of the optical constants and thickness of semitransparent thin films using successive interference fringes of transmission spectra. *Surface Review and Letters, 12*(3), 1–7. doi:10.1142/S0218625X05007256

Ghodsi, F. E., Tepehan, F. Z., & Tepehan, G. G. (1997). Optical properties of Ta_2O_5 thin films deposited using the spin coating process. *Thin Solid Films, 295*, 11–15. doi:10.1016/S0040-6090(96)09509-0

Ghodsi, F. E., Tepehan, F. Z., & Tepehan, G. G. (1999). Optical and electrochromic properties of sol-gel made CeO_2-TiO_2 thin films. *Electrochimica Acta, 44*, 3127–3136. doi:10.1016/S0013-4686(99)00030-4

Ghodsi, F. E., Tepehan, F. Z., & Tepehan, G. G. (2006). Atomic force microscopy and spectroscopy studies of annealed Ce/Ti/Zr mixed oxide thin films prepared by sol-gel process. *Surface Science, 600*, 4361–4364. doi:10.1016/j.susc.2006.02.078

Ghodsi, F. E., Tepehan, F. Z., & Tepehan, G. G. (2008a). Electrochromic properties of heat-treated thin films of CeO$_2$-TiO$_2$-ZrO$_2$ prepared by sol-gel route. *Solar Energy Materials and Solar Cells, 92*, 234–239. doi:10.1016/j.solmat.2007.02.026

Ghodsi, F. E., Tepehan, F. Z., & Tepehan, G. G. (2008b). Optical and structural properties of sol-gel made Ce/Ti/Zr mixed oxide thin films as transparent counter electrode for electrochromic devices. *Optical Materials, 31*, 63–67. doi:10.1016/j.optmat.2008.01.014

Gnyba, M., Kozanecki, M., & Wierzba, P. (2005). Spectroscopic studies of sol-gel derived thin-film structures for integrated optics. *Journal of Molecular and Quantum Acoustics, 26*, 81–89.

Grätzel, M. (2003). Dye-sensitized solar cells. *Journal of Photochemistry and Photobiology C, Photochemistry Reviews, 4*, 145–153. doi:10.1016/S1389-5567(03)00026-1

Guang-Lei, T., Hong-Bo, H., & Jian-Da, S. (2005). Effect of microstructure of TiO$_2$ thin films on optical band gap energy. *Chemical Physics Letters, 22*(7), 1787–1789. doi:10.1088/0256-307X/22/7/062

Gupta, K. K., Jassal, M., & Agrawal, A. K. (2008). Sol-gel derived titanium dioxide finishing of cotton fabric for self-cleaning. *Indian Journal of Fiber & Textile Research, 33*, 443–450.

Habibi, M. H., Talebian, N., & Choi, J. H. (2007). The effect of annealing on photocatalytic properties of nanostructured titanium dioxide thin films. *Dyes and Pigments, 73*, 103–110. doi:10.1016/j.dyepig.2005.10.016

Hamid, M. A., & Rahman, I. A. (2003). Preparation of titanium dioxide (TiO$_2$) thin films by sol-gel dip coating method. *Malaysian Journal of Chemistry, 5*(1), 86–91.

Hasan, M. M., Haseeb, A. S. M. A., Saidur, R., & Masjuki, H. H. (2008). Effects of annealing treatment on optical properties of anatase TiO$_2$ thin films. *International Journal of Chemical and Biomolecular Engineering, 1*(2), 93–97.

Hemissi, M., & Amardjia-Adnani, H. (2007). Optical and structural properties of titanium oxide thin films prepared by sol-gel method. *Digest Journal of Nanomaterials and Biostructures, 2*(4), 299–305.

Hong, Y., Li, D., Zheng, J., & Zou, G. (2006). Sol-gel growth of titania from electrospun polyacrylonitrile nanofibres. *Nanotechnology, 17*, 1986–1993. doi:10.1088/0957-4484/17/8/032

Hua, D., Cheuk, K., Wei-ning, Z., Chen, W., & Chang-fa, X. (2007). Low temperature preparation of nano TiO$_2$ and its application as antibacterial agents. *Transactions of Nonferrous Metals Society of China, 17*, 700–703.

Ivanova, T., Harizanova, A., & Surtchev, M. (2002). Formation and investigation of sol-gel TiO$_2$-V$_2$O$_5$ system. *Materials Letters, 55*, 327–333. doi:10.1016/S0167-577X(02)00387-7

Jahromi, H. S., Taghdisian, H., Afshar, S., & Tasharrofi, S. (2009). Effects of pH and polyethylene glycol on surface morphology of TiO$_2$ thin film. *Surface and Coatings Technology, 203*, 1991–1996. doi:10.1016/j.surfcoat.2009.01.034

Jakubik, W. P. (2006). Investigations of thin film of titanium dioxide (TiO$_2$) in a surface acoustic wave gas sensor system. *Molecular and Quantum Acoustics, 27*, 133–139.

Jenkins, F. A., & White, H. E. (1981). *Fundamentals of optics. Ackland*. McGraw-Hill.

Jiang, K., Zakutayev, A., Stowers, J., Anderson, M. D., Tate, J., & McIntyre, D. H. (2009). Low-temperature, solution processing of TiO₂ thin films and fabrication of multilayer dielectric optical elements. *Solid State Sciences*, *11*, 1692–1699. doi:10.1016/j.solidstatesciences.2009.05.026

Jiménez González, A. E., & Gelover Santiago, S. (2007). Structural and optoelectronic characterization of TiO₂ films prepared using the sol-gel technique. *Semiconductor Science and Technology*, *22*, 709–716. doi:10.1088/0268-1242/22/7/006

Jing, C., Zhao, X., Han, J., Zhu, K., Liu, A., & Tao, H. (2003). A new method of fabricating internally sol-gel coated capillary tubes. *Surface and Coatings Technology*, *162*, 228–233. doi:10.1016/S0257-8972(02)00568-6

Karwasz, G. P., Miotello, A., Zomer, E., Brusa, R. S., Kościelska, B., & Armellini, C. (2005). Structural studies of titanium oxide multilayers. *Acta Physica Polonica A*, *107*(6), 977–982.

Kościelska, B., Murawski, L., & Wicikowski, L. (2005). Electrical and mechanical properties of nitrided sol-gel derived TiO₂ and SiO₂-TiO₂ films. *Materials Science-Poland*, *23*(1), 93–100.

Kozłowska, K., Łukowiak, A., Szczurek, A., Dudek, K., & Maruszewski, K. (2005). Sol-gel coatings for electrical gas sensors. *Optica Applicata*, *XXXV*(4), 783–790.

Kurakula, S. R. (2007). *Studies on the electrical properties of titanium dioxide thin film dielectrics for microelectronic applications*. Bangalore: Indian Institute of Science.

Lao, C., Chuai, Y., Su, L., Liu, X., Huang, L., & Cheng, H. (2005). Mix-solvent-thermal method for the synthesis of anatase nanocrystalline titaniumdioxide used in dye-sensitized solar cell. *Solar Energy Materials and Solar Cells*, *85*, 457–465. doi:10.1016/j.solmat.2004.10.002

Leinen, D., Fernández, L. A., Espinós, J. P., Belderrain, T. R., & González-Elipe, A. R. (1994). Ion beam induced chemical vapor deposition for the preparation of thin film oxides. *Thin Solid Films*, *241*, 198–201. doi:10.1016/0040-6090(94)90425-1

Li, Z., Qiu, N., & Yang, G. (2009). Effects of synthesis parameters on the microstructure and phase structure of porous 316L stainless steel supported TiO₂ membranes. *Journal of Membrane Science*, *326*, 533–538. doi:10.1016/j.memsci.2008.10.035

Liau, L. C. K., & Chiang, P. I. (2007). Multiple nano-TiO₂ layers to prevent dye/nano-TiO₂ from photodegradation under a UV-exposure environment. *Applied Surface Science*, *253*, 3982–3986. doi:10.1016/j.apsusc.2006.08.031

Lin, H., Uchino, T., Kozuka, H., & Yoko, T. (1997). Electrical properties of transparent doped titania films by sol-gel method. *ICR Annual Report*, *4*, 22–23.

Liu, W. m., Chen, Y. x., Kou, G. T., Xu, T., & Sun, D. C. (2003). Characterization and mechanical/tribological properties of nano Au-TiO₂ composite thin films prepared by a sol–gel process. *Wear*, *254*, 994–1000. doi:10.1016/S0043-1648(03)00305-3

Löbl, P., Huppertz, M., & Mergel, D. (1994). Nucleation and growth in TiO₂ films prepared by sputtering and evaporation. *Thin Solid Films*, *251*, 72–79. doi:10.1016/0040-6090(94)90843-5

Mahltig, B., Fiedler, D., & Böttcher, H. (2004). Antimicrobial sol-gel coatings. *Journal of Sol-Gel Science and Technology*, *32*, 219–222. doi:10.1007/s10971-004-5791-7

Mardare, D., & Rusu, G. I. (2004). Comparison of the dielectric properties for doped and undoped TiO₂ thin films. *Journal of Optoelectronics and Advanced Materials*, *6*(1), 333–336.

Martin, N., Rousselot, C., Savall, C., & Palmino, F. (1996). Characterizations of titanium oxide films prepared by radio frequency magnetron sputtering. *Thin Solid Films, 287*, 154–163. doi:10.1016/S0040-6090(96)08782-2

Medina-Valtierra, J., Sánchez-Cárdenas, M., Frausto-Reyes, C., & Calixto, S. (2006). Formation of smooth and rough TiO_2 thin films on fiberglass by sol-gel method. *Journal of the Mexican Chemical Society, 50*(1), 8–1.

Miki, T., Nishizawa, K., Suzuki, K., & Kato, K. (2004). Preparation of thick TiO_2 film with large surface area using aqueous sol with poly(ethylene glycol). *Journal of Materials Science, 39*, 699–701. doi:10.1023/B:JMSC.0000011535.89376.93

Ming-Fang, X., Shan, L., Xin-Man, C., & Yan-Zhi, P. (2006). Studies on characteristics of nanostructure of N-TiO_2 thin films and photo-bactericidal action. *Journal of Zhejiang University. Science. B., 7*(7), 586–590. doi:10.1631/jzus.2006.B0586

Nasr-Esfahani, M., & Habibi, M. H. (2009). A comparative study on physicochemical properties and photocatalytic behavior of two different nanostructure composite TiO_2 films coated on glass substrate. *Desalination and Water Treatment, 3*, 64–72. doi:10.5004/dwt.2009.441

Paez, L. R., & Matoušek, J. (2004). Properties of sol-gel TiO_2 layers on glass substrate. *Ceramics-Silikáty, 48*(2), 66–71.

Perera, V. P. S., Jayaweera, P. V. V., Pitigala, P. K. D. D. P., Bandaranayake, P. K. M., Hastings, G., & Perera, A. G. U. (2004). Construction of a photovoltaic device by deposition of thin films of the conducting polymer polythiocyanogen. *Synthetic Metals, 143*, 283–287. doi:10.1016/j.synthmet.2003.12.018

Poelman, D., & Frederic, S. P. (2003). Methods for the determination of the optical constants of thin films from single transmission measurements. *Journal of Physics. D, Applied Physics, 36*, 1850–1857. doi:10.1088/0022-3727/36/15/316

Pomoni, K., Vomvas, A., & Trapalis, C. (2005). Transient photoconductivity of nanocrystalline TiO_2 sol-gel thin films. *Thin Solid Films, 479*, 160–165. doi:10.1016/j.tsf.2004.12.005

Ponce, M. A., Parra, R., Savu, R., Joanni, E., Bueno, P. R., & Cilense, M. (2009). Impedance spectroscopy analysis of TiO_2 thin film gas sensors obtained from water-based anatase colloids. *Sensors and Actuators. B, Chemical, 139*, 447–452. doi:10.1016/j.snb.2009.03.066

Pourmand, M., & Taghavinia, N. (2008). TiO_2 nanostructured films on mica using liquid phase deposition. *Materials Chemistry and Physics, 107*, 449–455. doi:10.1016/j.matchemphys.2007.08.011

Pucher, P., Benmami, M., Azouani, R., Krammer, G., Chhor, K., & Bocquet, J. F. (2007). Nano-TiO_2 sols immobilized on porous silica as new efficient photocatalyst. *Applied Catalysis A, General, 332*, 297–303. doi:10.1016/j.apcata.2007.08.031

Ramsden, J. J. (2005). What is nanotechnology? *Nanotechnology Perceptions, 1*, 3–17.

Sakka, S. (2005). *Handbook of sol-gel science and technology*. Boston: Kluwer Academic Publishers.

Sankar, S., & Gopchandran, K. G. (2009). Effect of annealing on the structural, electrical and optical properties of nanostructured TiO_2 thin films. *Crystal Research and Technology, 44*(9), 989–994. doi:10.1002/crat.200900073

Sasani Ghamsari, M., & Bahramian, A. R. (2008). High transparent sol-gel derived nanostructured TiO_2 thin film. *Materials Letters, 62*, 361–364. doi:10.1016/j.matlet.2007.05.053

Schulze, K., & Kirstein, S. (2005). Layer-by-layer deposition of TiO$_2$ nanoparticles. *Applied Surface Science, 246,* 415–419. doi:10.1016/j. apsusc.2004.11.064

Suciu, R. C., Indrea, E., Silipas, T. D., Dreve, S., Rosu, M. C., & Popescu, V. (2009). TiO$_2$ thin films prepared by sol-gel method. *Journal of Physics: Conference Series, 182,* 1–4. doi:10.1088/1742-6596/182/1/012080

Sun, H., Wang, C., Pang, S., Li, X., Tao, Y., & Tang, H. (2008). Photocatalytic TiO$_2$ films prepared by chemical vapor deposition at atmosphere pressure. *Journal of Non-Crystalline Solids, 354,* 1440–1443. doi:10.1016/j.jnoncrysol.2007.01.108

Sung, Y. M., & Kim, H. J. (2007). Sputter deposition and surface treatment of TiO$_2$ films for dye-sensitized solar cells using reactive RF plasma. *Thin Solid Films, 515,* 4996–4999. doi:10.1016/j. tsf.2006.10.079

Swanepoel, R. (1983). Determination of the thickness and optical constants of amorphous silicon. *Journal of Physics. E, Scientific Instruments, 16,* 1214–1222. doi:10.1088/0022-3735/16/12/023

Tavares, C. J., Vieira, J., Rebouta, L., Hungerford, G., Coutinho, P., & Teixeira, V. (2007). Reactive sputtering deposition of photocatalytic TiO$_2$ thin films on glass substrates. *Materials Science and Engineering B, 138,* 139–143. doi:10.1016/j. mseb.2005.11.043

Trah, H.-P., Franz, J., & Marek, J. (1999). Physics of semiconductor sensores. *Advances in Solid State Physics, 39,* 25–36. doi:10.1007/BFb0107462

Tsaneva, G., Kozhukharov, V., Kozhukharov, S., Ivanova, M., Gerwann, J., & Schem, M. (2008). Functional nanocomposite coatings for corrosion protection of aluminum alloy and steel. *Journal of the University of Chemical Technology and Metallurgy, 43*(2), 231–238.

Veronovski, N., Rudolf, A., Sfiligoj Smole, M., Kreže, T., & Geršak, J. (2009). Self-cleaning and handle properties of TiO$_2$-modified textiles. *Fibers and Polymers, 10*(4), 551–556. doi:10.1007/s12221-009-0551-5

Viana, M. M., Mohallem, T. D. S., Nascimento, G. L. T., & Mohallem, N. D. S. (2006). Nanocrystalline titanium oxide thin films prepared by sol-gel process. *Brazilian Journal of Physics, 36*(3B), 1081–1083. doi:10.1590/S0103-97332006000600075

Wang, Z., Helmersson, U., & Käll, P. O. (2002). Optical properties of anatase TiO$_2$ thin films prepared by aqueous sol-gel process at low temperature. *Thin Solid Films, 405,* 50–54. doi:10.1016/S0040-6090(01)01767-9

Watanabe, T., Nakajima, A., Wang, R., Minabe, M., Koizumi, S., & Fujishima, A. (1999). Photocatalytic activity and photoinduced hydrophilicity of titanium dioxide coated glass. *Thin Solid Films, 351,* 260–263. doi:10.1016/S0040-6090(99)00205-9

Wegner, K., Barborini, E., Piseri, P., & Milani, P. (2006). Gas-phase synthesis of nanostructured particulate films. *Journal of KONA Powder and Particle, 24,* 54–64.

Wei, D. (2010). Dye Sensitized Solar Cells. *International Journal of Molecular Sciences, 11,* 1103–1113. doi:10.3390/ijms11031103

Wen, T., Gao, J., & Shen, J. (2001). Preparation and characterization of TiO$_2$ thin films by the sol-gel process. *Journal of Materials Science, 36,* 5923–5926. doi:10.1023/A:1012989012840

Wetchakun, N., & Phanichphant, S. (2008). Effect of temperature on the degree of anatase-rutile transformation in titanium dioxide nanoparticles synthesized by the modified sol-gel method. *Current Applied Physics, 8,* 343–346. doi:10.1016/j. cap.2007.10.028

Wu, D., Long, M., Zhou, J., Cai, W., Zhu, X., & Chen, C. (2009). Synthesis and characterization of self-cleaning cotton fabrics modified by TiO_2 through a facile approach. *Surface and Coatings Technology, 203,* 3728–3733. doi:10.1016/j.surfcoat.2009.06.008

Xin, J. H., Daoud, W. A., & Kong, Y. Y. (2004). A new approach to UV-blocking treatment for cotton fabrics. *Textile Research Journal, 74*(2), 97–100. doi:10.1177/004051750407400202

Yang, C., Fan, H., Xi, Y., Chen, J., & Li, Z. (2008). Effects of depositing temperatures on structure and optical properties of TiO_2 film deposited by ion beam assisted electron beam evaporation. *Applied Surface Science, 254,* 2685–2689. doi:10.1016/j.apsusc.2007.10.006

Yang, W., & Wolden, C. A. (2006). Plasma-enhanced chemical vapor deposition of TiO_2 thin films for dielectric applications. *Thin Solid Films, 515,* 1708–1713. doi:10.1016/j.tsf.2006.06.010

Yao, F., & Wanghe, C. (2006). Preparation of transparent TiO2 nanocrystalline film for UV sensor. *Chinese Science Bulletin, 51*(14), 1657–1661. doi:10.1007/s11434-006-2022-3

Ye, Q., Liu, P. Y., Tang, Z. F., & Zhai, L. (2007). Hydrophilic properties of nano-TiO_2 thin films deposited by RF magnetron sputtering. *Vacuum, 81,* 627–631. doi:10.1016/j.vacuum.2006.09.001

Yoon, K. H., Noh, J. S., Kwon, C. H., & Muhammed, M. (2006). Photocatalytic behavior of TiO_2 thin films prepared by sol-gel process. *Materials Chemistry and Physics, 95,* 79–83. doi:10.1016/j.matchemphys.2005.06.001

Yu, J., Zhao, X., & Zhao, Q. (2001). Photocatalytic activity of nanometer TiO_2 thin films prepared by the sol-gel method. *Materials Chemistry and Physics, 69,* 25–29. doi:10.1016/S0254-0584(00)00291-1

Yu, J. C., Tang, H. Y., Yu, J., Chan, H. C., Zhang, L., & Xie, Y. (2002). Bactericidal and photocatalytic activities of TiO_2 thin films prepared by sol-gel and reverse micelle methods. *Journal of Photochemistry and Photobiology A Chemistry, 153,* 211–219. doi:10.1016/S1010-6030(02)00275-7

Yuan, Z., Zhang, J., Li, B., & Li, J. (2007). Effect of metal ion dopants on photochemical properties of anatase TiO_2 films synthesized by a modified sol-gel method. *Thin Solid Films, 515,* 7091–7095. doi:10.1016/j.tsf.2007.02.101

Zainal, Z., Lee, C. Y., Hussein, M. Z., & Kassim, A. (2004). Photoelectrochemical properties of sol-gel derived TiO_2 thin films in aqueous sodium oxalate solution. *Materials Science-Poland, 22*(2), 99–110.

Zarycka, A., Ilczuk, J., & Czekaj, D. (2003). Application of the sol-gel method to deposition of thin films. *Materials Science, 21*(4), 439–443.

Zhang, W., Chen, Y., Yu, S., Chen, S., & Yin, Y. (2006). Preparation, characterization and photocatalytic activity of in situ Fe-doped TiO_2 thin films. *Thin Solid Films, 496*(2), 273–280. doi:10.1016/j.tsf.2005.08.352

Zulkarnain, Z., & Yong, L. C. (2005). Properties of sol-gel derived TiO_2 thin films prepared with different dip-coating layers. *Materials Science (Medžiagotyra), 11*(2), 97–100.

Chapter 13

Electrostatic Potential at Nuclei:
An Accurate Reactivity Descriptor for Organic Compounds

Sonia Ilieva
University of Sofia, Bulgaria

Boris Galabov
University of Sofia, Bulgaria

ABSTRACT

The chapter surveys mostly original work of the authors on the application of the electrostatic potential at nuclei (EPN) as a reactivity index in quantifying hydrogen bonding as well as different reactions of organic compounds. The EPN index was defined and introduced by E. B. Wilson (1962). However, it was first applied as a reactivity index much later in works from our laboratory (Bobadova-Parvanova & Galabov, 1998; Galabov & Bobadova-Parvanova, 1999; Dimitrova, Ilieva, & Galabov, 2002; Cheshmedzhieva, Ilieva, Hadjieva, Trayanova, & Galabov, 2009; Galabov, Cheshmedzhieva, Ilieva, & Hadjieva, 2004; Galabov, Ileiva, & Schaefer, 2006; Galabov, Nikolova, Wilke, Schaefer, & Allen, 2008; Galabov, Ilieva, Hadjieva, Atanasov, & Schaefer, 2008; Koleva, Galabov, Wu, Schaefer, & Schleyer, 2009).

Numerous applications showed that the EPN index, an accurate quantum mechanical quantity, predicts with remarkable accuracy the energy shifts accompanying hydrogen bonding. The theoretically evaluated EPN descriptor correlates also excellently with experimental and theoretically evaluated kinetic parameters for a number of important organic reactions. Based on these findings an efficient computational approach for the evaluation of substituent constants was developed.

DOI: 10.4018/978-1-60960-860-6.ch013

INTRODUCTION

In the report "Opportunities in Chemistry: Today and Tomorrow" (known as the "Pimentel Report") published in 1985 as the result of a study of the National Academy of Sciences of the United States "to survey the chemical science" under the chairmanship of George C. Pimentel, priority was recommended to five research frontiers. The first was "Understanding Chemical Reactivity: … to apply the full power of modern instrumental techniques and chemical theory to the clarification of factors that control the rates of reaction and to the development of new synthetic pathways for chemical change". For organic chemistry, the quantitative characterization of reactivity is of key conceptual importance. It underlines the link between properties of reactants and their behavior in chemical interactions and supports the understanding of organic chemistry as a fully quantitative science. Since the pioneering works of Hammett (1937; 1938), the interpretation of organic reactivities has been in the focus of numerous studies. Quantum chemistry has open new perspectives in understanding the factors governing chemical reactivity (Carey & Sanders, 2000; Fukui, 1975; Klopman, 1974; Parr & Yang, 1989; Streitwieser, 1961). In recent times, the introduction of reactivity indices, defined in the framework of density functional theory, has contributed greatly in understanding the factors governing the rates of chemical reactions (Chattaraj, 2009; Pearson, 1997; Sen & Jorgersen, 1993; Toro-Labbe, 2006). In spite of the impressive progress, achieving a quantitative accord between theoretical predictions and experimental kinetic rates is still a challenging task. It is, therefore, paramount to characterize chemical reactivity by analyzing the correspondence between theory and experiment.

In this chapter we describe the application of the electrostatic potential at nuclei, a non-approximate quantum mechanical quantity, in quantifying reactivity of molecules for intermolecular interac-

tions (hydrogen bonding) and several reactions of organic compounds. Comparisons with alternative approaches for reactivity predictions is made for all studied processes

Parallel to EPN we will also summarize results from the application of alternative theoretically derived reactivity indices, variously defined atomic charges, and the Parr electrophilicity index (ω) (Parr, Szentpály, & Liu, 1999), in a comparative approach. In the first section we present results on the application of EPN and atomic charges in quantifying reactivity of several series of molecules for processes of hydrogen bonding. In the second section we discuss chemical reactivities in several important organic reactions. The third part shows the successful application of the electrostatic potential at nuclei in quantitatively predicting substituent constants for aromatic systems.

BACKGROUND

An important theoretical quantity employed in analyzing chemical reactivity is the molecular electrostatic potential (MEP) (Scrocco & Tomasi, 1973; Politzer & Truhlar, 1981; Murray & Politzer, 1988; Murray, Lans, Brinck, & Politzer, 1991; Tomasi, Bonaccorsi, & Cammi, 1990; Gadre, Kulkarni, & Srivastava, 1992; Murray & Sen, 1996; Naray-Szabo & Ferenczy, 1995; Suresh & Gadre, 1997; Suresh & Gadre, 2007). Minima and maxima of the surface MEP have been widely used in studying the structural factors determining the relative rates of various intermolecular interactions. Extensive surveys on the subject are available (Scrocco & Tomasi, 1973; Murray & Politzer, 1988; Murray & Sen, 1996; Naray-Szabo & Ferenczy, 1995; Politzer & Truhlar, 1981; Tomasi, Bonaccorsi, & Cammi, 1990). The great advantage of MEP over alternative theoretical approaches in analyzing reactivity is the fact that no additional approximations are introduced in deriving MEP. Thus, maps of MEP, typically at the Van der Waals surface of the molecule, have been successfully employed in determining the intramolecular factors governing reactivity (Scrocco & Tomasi, 1973; Murray & Politzer, 1988; Murray, Lans, Brinck, & Politzer, 1991; Gadre, Kulkarni, & Srivastava, 1992; Murray & Sen, 1996; Naray-Szabo & Ferenczy, 1995; Politzer & Truhlar, 1981; Suresh & Gadre, 1997; Suresh & Gadre, 2007; Tomasi, Bonaccorsi, & Cammi, 1990). MEP is defined as follows (in atomic units, bold font denotes vector quantities) (Politzer & Truhlar, 1981):

$$V(\boldsymbol{r}) = \sum_{A} \frac{Z_A}{\left|\boldsymbol{R}_A - \boldsymbol{r}\right|} - \int \frac{\rho(\boldsymbol{r}')}{\left|\boldsymbol{r}' - \boldsymbol{r}\right|} d\boldsymbol{r}' \qquad (1)$$

In this equation Z_A is the charge on nucleus A with radius-vector $\boldsymbol{R}_A$, $\rho(\boldsymbol{r})$ is the electronic density function of the respective molecule as obtained from ab initio calculations and $\boldsymbol{r}'$ is a dummy integration variable.

Eq. 1 shows that MEP depends on the distribution of the electric charges in the molecule: the positive charges of the nuclei and the electron density $\rho(\boldsymbol{r})$. A shortcoming of MEP in characterizing the electronic factors governing reactivity is that its extremal values (minima and maxima) are not necessarily situated at particular functional groups or at atomic positions in the molecule, where chemical interactions take place. Thus, regiospecificity of reactions cannot be usually analyzed reliably. These shortcomings of MEP are greatly overcome when a theoretical derivative of MEP, the electrostatic potential at nuclei (EPN), is used instead. In the present chapter we describe the application of the electrostatic potential at nuclei (EPN) in quantifying the reactivity of organic molecules for processes of hydrogen bonding and in various reactions of organic compounds. The EPN index was defined and introduced by E. B. Wilson (1962). However, it was first applied

as a reactivity index much later in the works of Galabov and coauthors (Bobadova-Parvanova & Galabov, 1998; Galabov & Bobadova-Parvanova, 1999; Dimitrova, Ilieva, & Galabov, 2002; Galabov, Cheshmedzhieva, Ilieva, & Hadjieva, 2004; Galabov, Ileiva, & Schaefer, 2006; Galabov, Nikolova, Wilke, Schaefer, & Allen, 2008; Galabov, Ilieva, Hadjieva, Atanasov, & Schaefer, 2008; Cheshmedzhieva, Ilieva, Hadjieva, Trayanova, & Galabov, 2009; Koleva, Galabov, Wu, Schaefer, & Schleyer, 2009). Further studies in other laboratories (Alia & Edwards, 2005; Alia & Edwards, 2007; Cedillo, Contreras, Galvan, Aizman, Andres, & Safont, 2007; Karpfen & Kryachko, 2005; Novakovic, Bogdanovic, Fraisse, Ghermani, Bouhmaida, & Spasojevic-de Bire, 2007; Novakovic, Fraisse, Bogdanovic, & Spasojevic-de Bire, 2007; Sadlej-Sosnowska, 2007; Sadlej-Sosnowska & Murlowska, 2008; Zheng, Wong, & Li, 2004; Zheng, Wong, & Tian, 2005) have emphasized the usefulness of this proposed reactivity index.

Politzer (Politzer & Truhlar, 1981) has employed Eq. 2 to define the electrostatic potential at a particular nucleus (Y) positioned at $\boldsymbol{R}_Y$, in which the singular term $\boldsymbol{R}_A = \boldsymbol{R}_Y$ has been excluded:

$$V_Y \equiv V(\boldsymbol{R}_Y) = \sum_{A \neq Y} \frac{Z_A}{\left|\boldsymbol{R}_Y - \boldsymbol{R}_A\right|} - \int \frac{\rho(\boldsymbol{r})}{\left|\boldsymbol{R}_Y - \boldsymbol{r}\right|} d\boldsymbol{r}$$

$$(2)$$

Unlike atomic charges, which depend strongly on their definition and additional approximations, inherent in their evaluation, the electrostatic potential at nuclei values V_Y reflect the variations of electron densities rigorously. Because of the factor $1/r$ (Eq. 2) the dominant contribution to V_Y comes from the local densities around the respective atomic sites. More negative V_Y values indicate greater electron densities.

EPN AS A REACTIVITY INDEX FOR PROCESSES OF HYDROGEN BONDING

Hydrogen bonding (HB) is a process of paramount importance for chemistry, physics and biology. Thus, characterizing the ability of molecules to participate in the formation of hydrogen bonds as proton acceptors or proton donors has long been of prime importance (Bader, 1990; Besler, Merz, & Kollman, 1990; Breneman & Wiberg, 1990; Kamlet, Abboud, Abraham, & Taft, 1983; Kamlet, Doherty, Abboud, Abraham, & Taft, 1986; Kollman, McKelvey, Johansson, & Rothenberg, 1975; Mulliken, 1955; Reed, Curtiss, & Weinhold, 1988). Quantifying the HB donor and acceptor properties of different sites in a molecule is of special importance in QSAR and QSPR studies, since the process is one of the principal mechanisms in ligand – bioreceptor interactions.

Important experimental reactivity parameters are the solvatochromic hydrogen bond donor terms α and hydrogen bond acceptor terms β (Kamlet, Abboud, Abraham, & Taft, 1983; Kamlet, Doherty, Abboud, Abraham, & Taft, 1986). These quantities are derived from spectroscopic data. Abraham et al. (Abraham, Duce, Prior, Barrat, Morris, & Taylor, 1989) developed scales of solute hydrogen-bonded acidity ($\log K_\alpha$) and solute *hydrogen-bond* basisity ($\log K_\beta$), using tetrachloromethane as solvent. The proton donor abilities have been determined against N-methylpyrrolidinone as a common acceptor. The proton accepting abilities have been measured against 4-nitrophenole as a common donor. The hydrogen bonding equilibrium constants scales have been created for application of medicinal chemistry and drug design. Later Abraham and co-authors (Abraham, Berthelot, Laurence, & Taylor, 1998) defined additional parameters α_2^H and β_2^H. There are several scales of hydrogen bonding accepting power (hydrogen bonding basicity) intended to quantify the solute-solvent interactions (Abboud & Notario, 1999).

Numerous attempts have been made to replace the experimental hydrogen bonding parameters with theoretical descriptors (Gancia, Montana, & Manallack, 2001). Minima and maxima in the molecular surface electrostatic potential have been shown to predict satisfactorily the hydrogen bonding ability of a number of molecules (Murray & Politzer, 1992). The respective values correlate very well with the solvatochromic parameters α and β (Murray & Politzer, 1992; Murray, Brinck, Grice, & Politzer, 1992) as well as with the Abraham's solute scales of relative acidities (α_2^H) and basicities (β_2^H) (Murray & Politzer, 1992). Applying the CoMFA technique on a set of heterocycles with nitrogen as the hydrogen bond acceptors, Kenny (1994) emphasized that the gradient of the electrostatic potential can be a useful predictor of hydrogen bond basicity. The hydrogen bonding equilibrium constants $\log K_\alpha$ and $\log K_\beta$ have been shown to correlate well with quantum mechanically calculated properties such as atomic superdelocalizabilty and self-polarizability of the atoms involved (Gancia, Montana, & Manallack, 2001).

In this section we survey the results from the application of the electrostatic potential at nuclei as a descriptor of proton-donor and proton-accepting abilities of individual atom in molecules. In all of these studies the EPN index was determined by applying electronic structure methods. The results obtained provide a compelling evidence for the remarkable accuracy of EPN as a local reactivity index for hydrogen bonding.

Characterizing Proton Accepting Properties of Functional Groups

Proton accepting ability of carbonyl and nitrile groups. HF/6-31+G(d,p) and MP2/6-31+G(d,p) ab initio computations were applied for estimating the binding energies and properties of isolated molecules and their complexes with hydrogen fluoride (Bobadova-Parvanova & Galabov, 1998; Dimitrova, Ilieva, & Galabov, 2002; Galabov & Bobadova-Parvanova, 1999). Aliphatic carbonyl and nitrile compounds of the type R-CHO and R-CN, where R= -H, -OH, -SH, -OCH$_3$, -NH$_2$, -NO$_2$, -CN, -F, -Cl, -CH$_3$ and CF$_3$ were studied.

The estimated energies of hydrogen-bond formation were corrected for zero-point vibrational energy, basis-set superposition error (BSSE) and fragment relaxation energy contributions.

The completely corrected energy represents the sum of uncorrected energy and all corrections:

$$\Delta E^{cor} = \Delta E + \Delta E^{zpe} + \Delta E^{bsse} + \Delta E^{rel} \tag{3}$$

In Eq. 3 the different terms are:

ΔE is the uncorrected energy of hydrogen-bond formation estimated as a difference between the energy of fully optimized structures of the complex and monomers.

$$\Delta E = E_{R-CHO\cdots HF} - \left(E_{R-CHO} + E_{HF} \right) \tag{4}$$

ΔE^{zpe} is the zero-point vibrational energy correction calculated as:

$$\Delta E^{zpe} = k \left[E^{zpe}_{R-CHO\cdots HF} - \left(E^{zpe}_{R-CHO} + E^{zpe}_{HF} \right) \right] \tag{5}$$

where k is a scaling factor, depending on the quality of the method/basis set used. For B3LYP/6-31G(d,p) calculations the scaling factor for the zero-point vibrational energy is $k = 0.9804$. In many cases the scaling factor can be omitted.

ΔE^{bsse} is a correction for basis-set superposition error (BSSE) calculated according the method of Boys & Bernardi (1970):

$$\Delta E^{bsse} = \left(E_{R-CHO} + E_{HF} \right) - \left(E^{gc}_{R-CHO\{HF\}} + E^{gc}_{HF\{R-CHO\}} \right) \tag{6}$$

In this expression, $E_{R-C\equiv C-H\{NH_3\}}$ is the energy of the acetylenic monomer in the respective complex geometry using the full basis set of the complex.

ΔE^{rel}, the fragment relaxation energy, is the energy necessary for distorting the equilibrium geometry of the isolated monomer toward the "flexed" geometry in the respective molecular complex.

$$\Delta E^{rel} = E^{rel}_{R-CHO} + E^{rel}_{HF} \tag{7}$$

$$E^{rel}_{R-CHO} = E^{gc}_{R-CHO} - E_{R-CHO} \tag{8}$$

$$E^{rel}_{HF} = E^{gc}_{HF} - E_{HF} \tag{9}$$

E^{gc}_{R-CHO} and E^{gc}_{HF} are the energies of R-CHO and HF from single point calculations with the geometry of the hydrogen-bonded complex. In effect the fragment relaxation energy term represent a correction to the BSSE term.

The optimized structures of the hydrogen-bonded complexes for acetaldehyde and acetonitrile are shown in Figure 1.

The attention is focused on complexes formed at the carbonyl and nitrile groups binding sites. It should be mentioned that the magnitude of the BSSE corrections at the MP2/6-31+G(d,p) level of theory are higher than the respective values at the HF/6-31+G(d,p) level. This is an evidence that the inclusion of electron correlation results in increasing the BSSE correction. Attempt to rationalize the reactivity of the two series of molecules in terms of theoretically calculated Mulliken (1955), CHELPG (Breneman & Wiberg, 1990) and MK (Besler, Merz, & Kollman, 1990) atomic charges did not produce positive results.

The molecular electrostatic potential at the sites of the proton accepting atoms (EPN) offers an excellent opportunity to discuss the reactivity of isolated molecules from the series studied.

Figure 1. Hydrogen bonded complexes of acetaldehyde and acetonitrile with HF

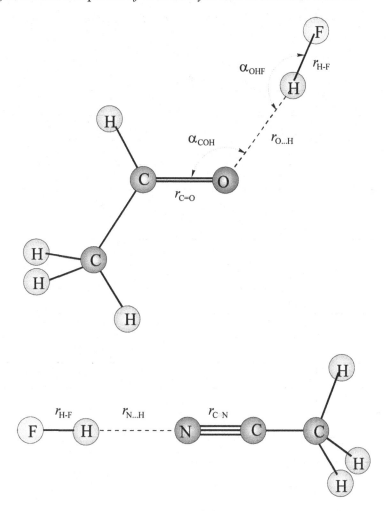

Minima in the molecular surface electrostatic potential (Murray & Politzer, 1991) as well as values of the electrostatic potential at selected points in the vicinities of the binding atoms (Kollman, McKelvey, Johansson, & Rothenberg, 1975) have been used to explain the ability of molecules to form hydrogen bonds. Here we select a simply defined and easily accessible quantity to express the electrostatic driving force for the complexation process: the atomic potentials at the binding atoms. These quantities are obtained as a standard option of the Gaussian and other quantum chemistry programs. In the Gaussian software package the electrostatic potential at nuclei (EPN) is calculated most easily by employing the *pop=chelpg* com-

mand. The computed values for the electrostatic potentials at the sites of the carbonyl oxygen (V_O) and nitrile nitrogen (V_N) atoms are given in Table 1. The statistical analysis reveals that the binding energies for the two series of complexes are linearly related with the respective atomic potentials V_O and V_N. The respective linear regression correlation coefficients are r = 0.981 for the carbonyl compounds, and r = 0.988 for the aliphatic nitrile compounds. Interestingly, the dependence between changes in the binding energy $\Delta E'$ ($\Delta E' = \Delta E^{R\text{-}CN} - \Delta E^{H\text{-}CN}$ and $\Delta E' = \Delta E^{R\text{-}CHO} - \Delta E^{HCHO}$) and the similarly defined ΔV ($\Delta V = \Delta V^{R\text{-}CN} - \Delta V^{H\text{-}CN}$ and $\Delta V = \Delta V^{R\text{-}CHO} - \Delta V^{H\text{-}CHO}$) values fall into the same linear regression equation for the two series

Table 1. HF/6-31+G(d,p) ab initio calculated energy of hydrogen-bond formation $\Delta E'$ and the variations of molecular electrostatic potential ΔV at the nitrile nitrogen and at the carbonyl oxygen in the isolated molecules

Molecule	$\Delta E'$ [kcal/mol]	ΔV [volts]
HCHO	0	0
HOCHO	-0.4711	-0.3238
HSCHO	0.1193	0.1306
CH_3OCHO	-1.1027	-0.6014
NH_2CHO	-2.5627	-1.2735
NO_2CHO	3.1980	2.0327
NCCHO	2.1024	1.3089
FCHO	1.4016	0.5959
ClCHO	1.6707	0.9116
CH_3CHO	-1.1482	-0.4708
CF_3CHO	1.7486	1.0830
HCN	0	0
HOCN	-1.1721	-0.4898
HSCN	-0.4575	-0.1225
CH_3OCN	-1.7699	-0.7919
NH_2CN	-1.9408	-0.8953
NO_2CN	2.5303	1.7034
NCCN	2.1114	1.3905
FCN	0.3593	0.2912
ClCN	0.1959	0.2286
CH_3CN	-1.4268	-0.7510
CF3CN	1.4149	0.9442

of compounds (r = 0.992). The plot is shown in Figure 2 for all 22 compounds from the carbonyl and nitrile series.

The results clearly show that the molecular electrostatic potentials at the sites of the proton accepting atoms can be used as reactivity descriptor for the respective molecular sites.

(HCN)$_n$ hydrogen-bonded clusters. In this section we present briefly the principal results from the computational study on the applicability of the electrostatic potential in analyzing the co-operative effects in longer hydrogen bonded associates of the type (HCN)$_n$, n = 2-7 (Galabov & Bobadova-Parvanova, 2000). It is known that HCN molecules

Figure 2. Dependence between variations of energy of hydrogen-bond formation ($\Delta E'$) and molecular electrostatic potential (ΔV)

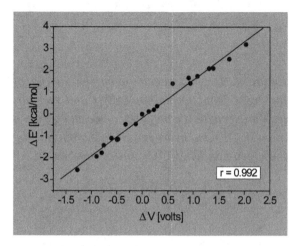

form linear hydrogen-bonded clusters in all phases (Nesbitt, 1988). Ab initio MO results of King & Weinhold (1995) have revealed that the co-operative effects in $(HCN)_n$ are essentially non-linear and can be rationalized in terms of $\pi_N \rightarrow \sigma^*_{CH}$ "charge transfer" nature of hydrogen bonding. More recently Sokolov (1997) demonstrated that the non-linear effects can be explained with a simple model including Coulomb interaction of the effective atomic charges, inductive action of these charges on the neighboring chemical bonds and

the exchange repulsion of the atoms. As was shown in the previous part, the molecular electrostatic potential at atomic sites can quantitatively predict the variations of the energy of hydrogen bond formation. It was of interest, therefore, to see whether such easily obtainable, accurately defined, and simple molecular quantity can adequately explain the nonlinear co-operative effects of (HCN)$_n$ clusters and serve as a reactivity index in describing the formation of hydrogen bonded clusters. The properties of hydrogen-bonded $(HCN)_n$ associates for n = 2-7 were calculated at HF/6-31+G(d) level of theory. The choice of this basis set allows full comparison with the results of King and Weinhold [38]. Harmonic vibrational frequencies (at the same level of theory) confirmed that the located structures correspond to minima having no imaginary frequencies. The HF/6-31+G(d) ab initio calculated molecular electrostatic potentials at the end nitrogen $V_N^{(n)}$ and hydrogen $V_H^{(n)}$ atom for the hydrogen-bonded $(HCN)_n$ clusters studied are presented in Table 2. These quantities are also defined in Figure 3. As mentioned above, the absolute values of the energy of formation of the last hydrogen bond increase non-linearly with increased cluster size and tend asymptotically to a given value. It can be seen from Table 2 that the absolute values of the molecular electrostatic potential at the end nitrogen

Table 2. HF/6-31+G(d) ab initio calculated corrected energy of hydrogen bond formation (ΔE^{COR}, in kcal/mol) and molecular electrostatic potential at the end nitrogen atom $V_N^{(n)}$ (in volts) for the hydrogen bonded (HCN)$_n$ clusters studied

n	ΔE^{COR}	$V_N^{(n)}$	$V_H^{(n)}$
1		-498.5944	-26.0114
2	-3.347	-499.2312	-26.0114
3	-4.365	-499.4461	-25.3910
4	-4.706	-499.5441	-25.1760
5	-4.853	-499.5985	-25.0753
6	-4.920	-499.6312	-25.0236
7	-4.947	-499.6529	-24.9882

Figure 3. Structure of hydrogen-bonded (HCN)$_n$ clusters studied and definition of geometrical parameters and molecular electrostatic potentials ($V_N^{(n-1)}$; $V_H^{(n-1)}$)

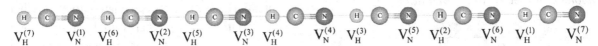

$V_H^{(7)}$ $V_N^{(1)}$ $V_H^{(6)}$ $V_N^{(2)}$ $V_H^{(5)}$ $V_N^{(3)}$ $V_H^{(4)}$ $V_N^{(4)}$ $V_H^{(3)}$ $V_N^{(5)}$ $V_H^{(2)}$ $V_N^{(6)}$ $V_H^{(1)}$ $V_N^{(7)}$

atom ($|V_N^{(n)}|$) also increase non-linearly with n. On the contrary, the absolute values of molecular electrostatic potential at the end hydrogen atom ($|V_N^{(n)}|$) decrease non-linearly with increased n. It can also be noted that the higher is $|V_N^{(n)}|$, the smaller is $|V_H^{(n)}|$ and there is a perfect linear correlation between these two quantities ($r = 0.99997$). Figure 4 represents the dependence between $\Delta E^{(n)}$ and $V_N^{(n-1)}$; $V_H^{(n-1)}$.

The relation found clearly shows that EPN can adequately describe the co-operative effects in hydrogen bonding. When n is small, with increasing the cluster size the electrostatic potential at the end nitrogen atom becomes more negative. Consequently, the participation of the atom in the formation of a new hydrogen bond becomes more favorable. For higher n there is a gradual saturation, $V_N^{(n)}$ becomes approximately constant value and consequently the energies of all new formed hydrogen bonds become approximately equal. It was interesting to also study the dependence between $\Delta E^{(n)}$ and the molecular electrostatic potential at the other atom participating in hydrogen bond formation: the end hydrogen atom of each cluster. In the light of the fact mentioned above that there is perfect relation between $V_N^{(n)}$ and $V_H^{(n)}$, a linear dependence can be expected. Indeed, as can be seen from Figure 4, there is an excellent correlation between $\Delta E^{(n)}$ and $V_H^{(n-1)}$.

As expected, the trends of changes of the molecular electrostatic potentials of nitrogen and hydrogen atom are opposite reflecting the different role of the two atoms in the process of hydrogen bonding. The more negative the electrostatic potential of the electron donating atom is, the

Figure 4. Dependence between the energy of hydrogen bond formation ($\Delta E^{(n)}$) and the molecular electrostatic potential at the end nitrogen atom ($V_N^{(n-1)}$) and hydrogen ($V_H^{(n-1)}$) atoms for the hydrogen-bonded (HCN)$_n$ clusters studied, n=2-7

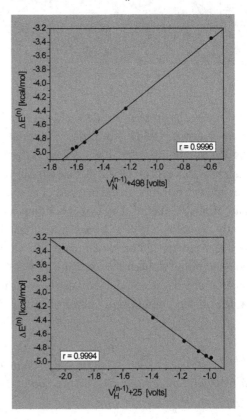

higher is its ability to form hydrogen bonds. On the contrary, the less negative the electrostatic potential of the electron accepting atom is, the higher is its ability to form a hydrogen bond.

Reactivity descriptors for the hydrogen bonding ability of pyridine bases. Hydrogen bonding is a fundamental factor for protein folding and the stabilization of DNA and RNA macromolecules.

Hydrogen bond formation is also found to be a key element in many ligand-receptor interactions determining the activity of drugs and other biologically active molecules. The quantitative characterization of the reactivity of particular molecular sites, both proton donating and proton accepting, is therefore of considerable importance for structure-activity analysis. The discovery of appropriate descriptors for the hydrogen bonding process is a theme of numerous studies generalized by Dearden et al. (Dearden & Ghafourian, 1999). QSAR and QSPR studies employ a number of different experimental and theoretically evaluated hydrogen bonding descriptors (Gancia, Montana, & Manallack, 2001; Kireev, Raevsky, & Fetisov, 1993).

Computations aimed at establishing dependences between the experimental hydrogen bond basicity parameters β and theoretically determined electronic structure parameters for a series of twelve substituted pyridine bases were carried out (Dimitrova, Ilieva, & Galabov, 2004). Water was used as model proton donor. Experimental β constants for these systems have been reported by Kamlet et al. (Kamlet, Abboud, Abraham, & Taft, 1983). The simultaneous application of experimental and theoretical reactivity parameters and their possible interdependences are of particular interest since experimental solvatochromic parameters are available for a limited numbers of molecules. This is a considerable limitation for their wider application.

The hydrogen bond between a set of pyridines and water has been found to be of lone-pair...H-O and not π...H-O type [59]. The theoretically evaluated binding energies of the hydrogen bonded complexes of the present series are listed in Table 3. Theoretically estimated Mulliken (1955), CHELPG charges (Breneman & Wiberg, 1990) and NBO atomic charges (Reed, Curtiss, & Weinhold, 1988), EPN values and the experimental β constants are also given in Table 3.

In principle, atomic charges are considered suitable hydrogen bonding descriptors since these quantities are expected to characterize the Coulombic attraction forces behind the process. The different methods for evaluation of atomic charges are, however, necessarily approximate. Thus, the actual electrostatic forces involved in the process may be better characterized by the electrostatic potential at atomic sites, which is an accurately defined quantum mechanical quantity. From the data in Table 3 it is seen that none of the considered charges provides a satisfactory description of the reactivity of the different studied proton acceptors sites. An excellent linear dependence between binding energy and EPN values is, however, obtained. The plot is illustrated in Figure 5. These results show that EPN values at the site of the basic nitrogen provide a basis for quantifying the reactivity of the studied molecules as proton acceptors in hydrogen bonding.

The two quantities, the basicity constants β (Kamlet, Abboud, Abraham, & Taft, 1983) and the electrostatic potential at nuclei characterize quantitatively the variations of the binding energy of hydrogen-bonded complexes of a series of pyridines and pyrimidine. The results prompted us to assess the direct link between these parameters. The dependence is illustrated in Figure 6

It is indeed plausible to find that a purely experimental quantity – the solvatochromic basicity constants β - correlates well with the theoretically derived EPN values. Such a good interrelation is quite significant. It shows that it is possible to use alternatively these two quantities as reactivity descriptors. The EPN values are, however, easily determined for an arbitrary molecule, while the number of available basicity constants is quite limited.

Characterizing Proton Donating Properties of Functional Groups

Complexes of monosubstituted acetylene derivatives with ammonia. In this section the results

Table 3. B3LYP/6-31G(d,p) ab initio calculated values of atomic charges (in units of electron) at the nitrogen atom in pyridines and pyrimidine, Q_N, derived via different procedures (Mulliken, CHELPG, NBO) and electrostatic potential V_N (in volts)

Molecule	ΔE^{cor}	$Q_N^{Mulliken}$	Q_N^{CHELPG}	Q_N^{NBO}	V_N	β
Pyridine	-3.0044	-0.4283	-0.6005	-0.4502	-499.7237	0.64
2n-Buthylpyridine	-3.2626	-0.4751	-0.5818	-0.4650	-499.9114	0.66
2,4-Dimethylpyridine	-3.5420	-0.4788	-0.6251	-0.4684	-500.0693	0.74
2,6-Dimethylpyridine	-3.4223	-0.5175	-0.6456	-0.4743	-500.1291	0.76
2,4,6-Trimethylpyridine	-3.6606	-0.5239	-0.6629	-0.4805	-500.2597	0.78
3-Bromopyridine	-2.4141	-0.4247		-0.4310	-499.2801	0.51
3-Methylpyridine	-3.0939	-0.4312	-0.5627	-0.4458	-499.8216	0.68
3,5-Dichloropyridine	-2.0728	-0.4185	-0.5753	-0.4179	-498.8638	0.42
4-Methylpyridine	-3.2061	-0.4342	-0.6049	-0.4569	-499.8733	0.67
4-Methoxypyridine	-3.3925	-0.4411	-0.6298	-0.4738	-499.9931	0.72
4-N,N-(dimethylamino)pyridine	-3.8713	-0.4511	-0.6191	-0.4878	-500.3904	0.87
Pyrimidine	-2.5425	-0.4002	-0.7132	-0.4744	-499.3264	0.48
3-Fluoropyridine	-2.6373	-0.4254	-0.5440	-0.4336	-499.3699	
3,4-Dimethylpyridine	-3.3478	-0.4369	-0.5855	-0.4516	-499.9631	
3-Chloropyridine	-2.6145	-0.4227	-0.5802	-0.4335	-499.2693	
Pyrazine	-2.2663	-0.3970	-0.4248	-0.4168	-499.0461	
4-Acetylpyridine	-2.6306	-0.4392	-0.5864	-0.4502	-499.3727	
2-Chloropyridine	-2.3301	-0.4133	-0.5452	-0.4496	-499.1876	
2-Fluoropyridine	-2.7789	-0.4566	-0.5990	-0.4851	-499.3863	
Correlation with ΔE^{cor} (correlation coefficient)		0.717	0.492	0.744	0.992	-0.983

from a computational study (Dimitrova, Ilieva, & Galabov, 2002) on the applicability of several types of molecular structure descriptors associated with the electric charge distribution to rationalize the reactivity of a series of monosubstituted acetylene derivatives towards to the process of hydrogen bond formation with ammonia as a model proton acceptor are presented. The results described illustrate the effect of changes in structure of the proton donor molecules on the energy profile of the interaction in the case of monosubstituted acetylene derivatives with general formula R-C≡C-H, where R = H, F, Cl, CH_3, CH_2F, CHF_2, CF_3, CH_2Cl, $CHCl_2$, CCl_3, CN, H-C≡C, F-C≡C, Cl-C≡C. Ammonia is used as a model proton acceptor in the respective hydrogen bonded complexes. The selected series of molecules and their complexes offer also an opportunity to analyze the reactivity of C-H acidic systems. Density functional theory at B3LYP/6-31G(d,p) level was applied in calculating the optimized geometries and vibrational frequencies for the isolated acetylenic derivatives and their hydrogen-bonded complexes with ammonia.

The calculated fully corrected energy of hydrogen bond formation (ΔE^{COR}) for the com-

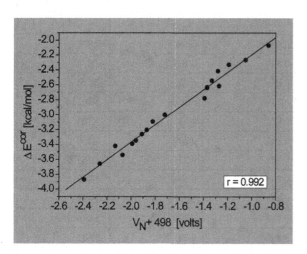

Figure 5. Dependence between energy of hydrogen-bond formation (ΔE^{cor}) and the electrostatic potential at the nitrogen atom in the molecules of pyridine/pyrimidine (V_N)

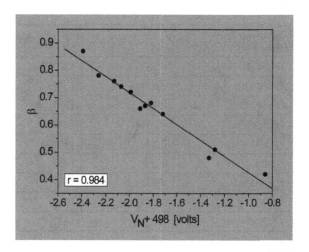

Figure 6. Dependence between basicity constant β and the electrostatic potential at the nitrogen atom in pyridine and pyrimidine derivatives (V_H)

plexes of monosubstituted acetylenes and diacetylenes with ammonia are given in Table 4. Electric charge properties - Mulliken, CHELPG, MK, and AIM atomic charges - of the isolated acetylene derivatives were theoretically determined in order to describe the reactivity of the molecules studied with respect the process of hydrogen bonding with ammonia. The electrostatic potential values at the site of the C-H hydrogen were also theoretically estimated. The computed values are given in Table 5.

All of these quantities were plotted against the calculated binding energies. The partial atomic charges at the binding site of the substituted acetylene derivatives are expected to describe the reactivity of the molecules towards formation of hydrogen bonded complexes with ammonia. The results obtained can be summarized as follows: (1) The Mulliken charges do not correlate well with the variation of binding energy (linear regression correlation coefficient r = 0.750); (2) The electrostatic potential related atomic charges CHELPG and MK do not provide also a quantitative description of the ability of the acetylenic

compounds to form a hydrogen bond with ammonia. The respective linear regression coefficients are r = 0.087 for CHELPG charges and r = 0.142 for MK charges; (3) A satisfactory description of the hydrogen bonding ability of the acetylenic derivatives is provided by the AIM atomic charges of Bader (1990), r = 0.963.

It was of interest, in view of the results for several series of molecules, to study the applicability of the atomic electrostatic potential as descriptor of the hydrogen bonding ability of proton donor molecules such as the studied series of acetylene derivatives. An excellent linear link, as shown in Figure 7, is found between the electrostatic potential at the acetylenic hydrogen and the binding energy.

It should be underlined that in the literature the molecular surface electrostatic potential (MSEP) has been mostly employed in describing hydrogen bonding (Murray, Brinck, Grice, & Politzer, 1992; Murray & Politzer, 1991; Murray & Sen, 1996). The results discussed above underline the applicability of the electrostatic potential at nuclei as a reactivity index describing in quan-

Table 4. B3LYP/6-31G(d,p) ab initio calculated non-corrected energy of hydrogen-bond formation (ΔE), zero-point vibrational energy correction (ΔE^{ZPE}), BSSE correction (ΔE^{BSSE}), relaxation correction (ΔE^{REL}) and totally corrected energy (ΔE^{COR}) for the substituted acetylene derivatives. All values are in kcal/mol

Acetylenic monomer	ΔE	ΔE^{ZPE}	ΔE^{BSSE}	ΔE^{REL}	ΔE^{COR}
H-C≡C-H	-5.287	1.402	0.896	0.111	-2.878
F-C≡C-H	-5.529	1.397	0.891	0.163	-3.078
Cl-C≡C-H	-5.882	1.352	0.873	0.141	-3.516
H₃C-C≡C-H	-4.354	1.243	0.838	0.111	-2.162
FH₂C-C≡C-H	-5.549	1.310	0.829	0.147	-3.263
F₂HC-C≡C-H	-6.501	1.359	0.803	0.209	-4.130
F₃C-C≡C-H	-7.240	1.417	0.825	0.233	-4.765
ClH₂C-C≡C-H	-5.754	1.331	0.802	0.169	-3.452
Cl₂HC-C≡C-H	-6.797	1.377	0.757	0.235	-4.428
Cl₃C-C≡C-H	-7.425	1.397	0.712	0.270	-5.046
NC-C≡C-H	-8.190	1.516	0.769	0.243	-5.662
H-C≡C-C≡C-H	-6.049	1.393	0.820	0.157	-3.679
F-C≡C-C≡C-H	-5.862	1.337	0.820	0.153	-3.552
Cl-C≡C-C≡C-H	-6.127	1.393	0.820	0.155	-3.759

titative terms the ability of proton donor molecules to form hydrogen bonds.

As is well known several different factors, besides electrostatic forces, contribute to hydrogen bonding. According to Morokuma et al. (Kitaura & Morokuma, 1976; Morokuma, 1971; Umeyama & Morokuma, 1977) the following terms contribute to the binding energy: electrostatic interaction, polarization interaction, exchange repulsion, and charge transfer of electron delocalization interaction. It was, therefore, of considerable interest to explain why such perfect linear relationship between binding energy and electrostatic potential at nuclei was found. The treatment of this problem is presented later in the present part.

Complexes of ammonia with C-H, N-H and O-H proton donor. Hydrogen bonded complexes of ammonia with 16 proton donor molecules with C-H, N-H and O-H bonds as proton donor sites were studied (Dimitrova, Ilieva & Galabov, 2003) by density functional theory computations

at B3LYP/6-31G(d,p) level. The proton donor molecules are:

C-H proton donors: $H_2C=CH_2$, $H_3C-C\equiv C-H$, $H_2C=CH-C\equiv C-H$, HCN

N-H proton donors: CH_3NH_2, $(CH_3)_2NH$, $C\equiv N^+-H$, $C_6H_5NH_2$, Cytosine, $HCONHCH_3$

O-H proton donors: CH_3OH, C_2H_5OH, C_3H_7OH, C_6H_5OH, HCOOH, CH_3COOH

Dependences between binding energy and a number of local structural, spectroscopic and electric charge parameters associated with the sites of the hydrogen bond formation were analyzed. The principal focus of interest was the applicability of local electric charge parameters, such as partial atomic charges and electrostatic potential at nuclei, in quantifying the reactivity of monomer proton donor molecules for the process of hydrogen bonding.

Table 5. B3LYP/6-31G(d,p) ab initio calculated values of atomic charges (in electrons) at the acetylenic hydrogen atom in isolated molecules Q_H, derived via different procedures (Mulliken, CHELPG, MK and AIM) and molecular electrostatic potential V_H (in atomic units)

Acetylenic monomer	$Q_H^{Mulliken}$	Q_H^{CHELPG}	Q_H^{MK}	Q_H^{AIM}	V_H
H-C≡C-H	0.1487	0.2372	0.2664	0.1257	-28.4196
F-C≡C-H	0.1534	0.2939	0.3202	0.1403	-28.2781
Cl-C≡C-H	0.1604	0.2623	0.2678	0.1387	-28.1611
H$_3$C-C≡C-H	0.1477	0.2706	0.3154	0.1139	-28.8305
FH$_2$C-C≡C-H	0.1647	0.2638	0.3037	0.1306	-28.2890
F$_2$HC-C≡C-H	0.1776	0.2611	0.2959	0.1429	-27.8835
F$_3$C-C≡C-H	0.1887	0.2602	0.2941	0.1524	-27.5760
ClH$_2$C-C≡C-H	0.1676	0.2739	0.3131	0.1335	-28.2019
Cl$_2$HC-C≡C-H	0.1809	0.2816	0.3136	0.1468	-27.7856
Cl$_3$C-C≡C-H	0.1904	0.2926	0.3087	0.1565	-27.4917
NC-C≡C-H	0.2095	0.2576	0.2789	0.1666	-27.1706
H-C≡C-C≡C-H	0.2004	0.2622	0.2892	0.1417	-28.0958
F-C≡C-C≡C-H	0.1956	0.2788	0.2994	0.1385	-28.1665
Cl-C≡C-C≡C-H	0.2029	0.2646	0.2789	0.1424	-28.0522
Correlation with ΔE^{cor} (correlation coefficient)	**0.750**	**0.087**	**0.142**	**0.963**	**0.996**

As already underlined the electrostatic interactions have a key role in hydrogen bond formation. It is expected that the partial atomic charges would characterise the reactivity of the respective sites in the molecules toward the complexation process. It was of interest, therefore, to assess the applicability of several types of theoretical partial atomic charges as reactivity descriptors for hydrogen bonding. It should be noted that the descriptors refer to properties of the monomer molecules. Mulliken partial charges, the electrostatic potential derived CHELPG and MK charges, and AIM charges were determined. The results are presented in Table 6.

The four types of partial atomic charges at the binding site of the isolated molecules were plotted against the calculated binding energies. The results obtained can be summarized as follows:

Figure 7. Dependence between energy of hydrogen-bond formation (ΔE^{COR}) and the molecular electrostatic potential at the acetylenic hydrogen atoms in isolated molecules (V_H)

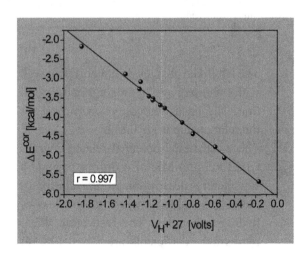

Table 6. B3LYP/6-31G(d,p) ab initio calculated values of energy of hydrogen-bond formation ΔE^{cor} (in kcal/mol) and atomic charges (in units of electron) at the hydrogen atom in monomer molecules, Q_H, derived via different procedures (Mulliken, CHELPG, MK and AIM) and electrostatic potential V_H (in volts)

Molecule	ΔE^{cor}	$Q_H^{Mulliken}$	Q_H^{CHELPG}	Q_H^{MK}	Q_H^{AIM}	V_H
$H_2C=CH_2$	-0.3512	0.1012	0.1236	0.1449	0.0004	-30.3897
$H_3C-C\equiv C-H$	-2.1626	0.1477	0.2706	0.3154	0.1139	-28.8305
$H_2C=CH-C\equiv C-H$	-2.7314	0.1603	0.2683	0.2829	0.1247	-28.5529
HCN	-6.2516	0.2089	0.1886	0.2063	0.1849	-26.7379
CH_3NH_2	-1.9113	0.2361	0.3389	0.3438	0.3466	-29.3502
$(CH_3)_2NH$	-2.2884	0.2363	0.3428	0.3452	0.3352	-29.3584
$C^-\equiv N^+-H$	-9.6368	0.3014	0.2578	0.2726	0.5308	-25.4808
$C_6H_5NH_2$	-3.9420	0.2547	0.3367	0.3366	0.3837	-28.3570
Cytosine	-5.8351	0.2697	0.3831	0.3800	-	-27.4590
$HCONHCH_3$	-5.5804	0.2586	0.2807	0.2697	-	-27.6413
CH_3OH	-5.6923	0.3014	0.3876	0.3883	0.5698	-27.6168
C_2H_5OH	-5.6649	0.3040	0.3750	0.3743	0.5613	-27.6549
C_3H_7OH	-5.7341	0.3039	0.3982	0.4009	0.5619	-27.6495
C_6H_5OH	-7.8935	0.3160	0.4058	0.4098	0.5821	-26.6291
HCOOH	-10.2826	0.3238	0.4208	0.4248	0.6026	-25.8808
CH_3COOH	-10.0186	0.3220	0.4050	0.4011	0.6015	-26.2508
Correlation with ΔE^{cor} (correlation coefficient)	0.812	0.498	0.478	0.779	0.973	

1. The Mulliken charges do not correlate well with the energy of hydrogen-bond formation. The linear regression coefficient for the relationship is r = 0.812.

2. The electrostatic-potential-related charges CHELPG and MK also do not provide a satisfactory description of the ability of molecules studied towards the process of hydrogen bonding. The respective linear regression coefficients are r = 0.498 for CHELPG charges and r = 0.478 for MK charges.

3. The charges obtained by AIM method also are not well correlated with the binding energies. The respective linear regression coefficient is r = 0.779.

In a previous study on complexes of mono-substituted acetylene derivatives with ammonia it was shown that among these four types of partial atomic charges the Bader's AIM charges

Figure 8. Dependence between energy of hydrogen-bond formation (ΔE^{cor}) and the electrostatic potential at the hydrogen atom in C–H, N–H and O–H binding sites of monomer molecules (V_H). V_Y (volts) = 27. 2113961 V_Y (a.u.)

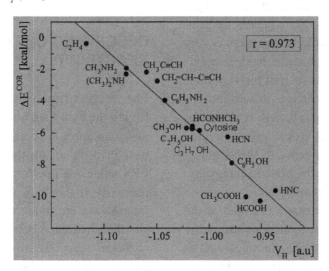

provide a satisfactory characterization of the binding ability of the respective acetylene derivatives. In the present series of molecules with different types of proton donor sites, however, none of the tested partial atomic charges provided satisfactory description of the binding ability of the molecules studied. The plot between ΔE^{cor} and V_H is shown in Figure 8.

It is gratifying to find that a very good linear dependence between the two quantities is established. The result indicates that the EPN values are applicable in characterising the proton donor abilities of molecular sites having different environment of the hydrogen atom. It may be concluded that these quantities have wider application as reactivity descriptors for molecules with differing proton donor sites.

THEORETICAL EXPLANATION: A MOROKUMA ANALYSIS

In the previous sections it was demonstrated that the electrostatic potential at the atoms partici-

pating in hydrogen bonding can be successfully employed as a reactivity descriptor reflecting the ability of isolated molecules to form hydrogen bonds. According to the energy decomposition analysis (EDA) of Morokuma et al. (Kitaura & Morokuma, 1976; Morokuma, 1971; Umeyama & Morokuma, 1977) the binding energy of the interacting system can be decomposed into the following components:

$$\Delta E = ES + PL + EX + CT + MIX \qquad (10)$$

ES is the electrostatic interaction term reflecting the interaction between the undistorted electron distribution of the two monomers. PL, the polarization interaction term, accounts for the effect of the polarization of the electron distribution in the two monomers. EX is the exchange repulsion term, accounting for the short-range repulsion due to the overlap of charge densities of the two interacting molecules. CT is the charge transfer of electron delocalization interaction term. Finally, MIX is a coupling term, accounting for higher order interactions. These energy decomposition terms were evaluated by the EDA procedure implemented in the GAMESS program package.

The highest contribution to the total energy comes from the electrostatic interaction and the exchange repulsion terms. Nevertheless, the principal question that needs to be answered is why the electrostatic potential at the binding atoms in the monomers predicts so well the variations in binding energy upon changes in substitutions in the series of molecules studied. It should be underlined that the EDA procedure provided clear and convincing evidence to the origin of the dependence between the binding energy and the electrostatic potential at niclei.

We plotted the electrostatic potential at the site of the acidic acetylenic hydrogens against the different energy decomposition terms as well as the total energy. The dependences obtained are shown in Figure 9.

Very good linear relations are found between the variations of V_H and the values for the ES, PL, EX and CT terms (Eq. (10)). It is seen that these energy terms change in phase with each other with high correlation coefficients. Thus, the electrostatic potential at the acetylenic hydrogen atom basically correlates linearly not only with the electrostatic energy term (ES) but also with the three other energy terms. Much poorer link is found between V_H and the changes in the higher order coupling term (MIX). However, the MIX term makes small contributions to the total binding energy in the range of 1.5–4.7%. In general, the changes in the MIX energy term in the studied series of molecules cannot influence the overall dependence between V_H and total binding energy. Thus, the application of the EDA procedure of Morokuma et al. (Kitaura & Morokuma, 1976; Morokuma, 1971; Umeyama & Morokuma, 1977) provided clear theoretical explanation for the linear relationships between electrostatic potential at the binding atom and the energy of hydrogen bond formation. These results substantiate the usefulness of the electrostatic potential at nuclei as reactivity descriptor for the process of hydrogen bonding.

DESCRIBING CHEMICAL REACTIVITY

The success of applying the EPN index in quantifying the hydrogen bonding abilities of proton donor and proton acceptor molecules prompted us to investigate how the theoretically evaluated EPN values will perform in analyzing chemical reactivity. It should be underlined that chemical interactions are much more complex phenomena than hydrogen bonding. In many cases the chemical reactions involve several steps. The electrostatic potential at nuclei is usually evaluated for the isolated reactants and can be employed with confidence for processes, in which the first stage is rate-controlling. It is certainly possible to evaluate the changes in EPN along the entire reaction path. Such examples are discussed later in the present chapter. Still, such computations are usually complicated. Other limitations arise from the definition of EPN (Eq. 2). One cannot expect good correlation between the EPN values and kinetic data for series of molecules, where the structural variations are in the immediate vicinity of the reaction center. Nevertheless, applications to numerous organic reactions show that the EPN index can serve as an excellent local reactivity index. As already emphasized, its evaluation does not involve additional approximations to the molecular wave function and is an accurate quantum mechanical value within the level of theory employed.

In this section we present results illustrating the utility of EPN in characterizing reactivity of molecules in several important organic reactions. The application of several alternative reactivity indices is discussed in a comparative context.

Figure 9. Dependence between energy terms **ES, PL, EX, CT, MIX** *and the molecular electrostatic potential at the acetylenic hydrogen atoms in isolated molecules* $\left(V_H\right)$

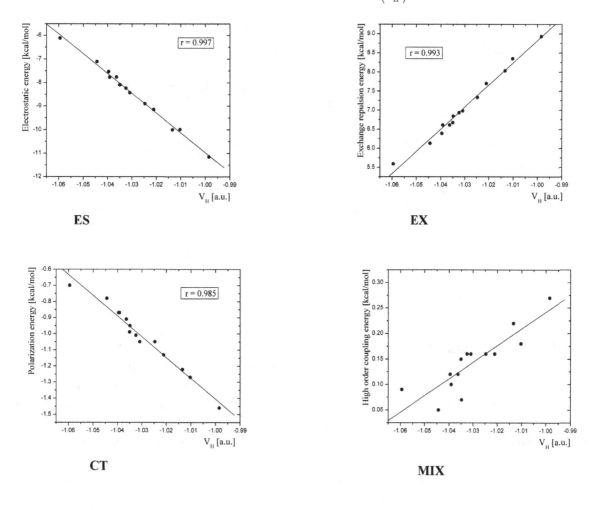

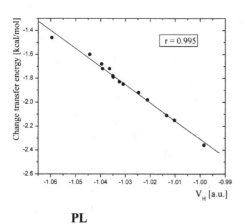

PL

Figure 10. Energy diagram for the alkaline hydrolysis of acetanilide in water solution

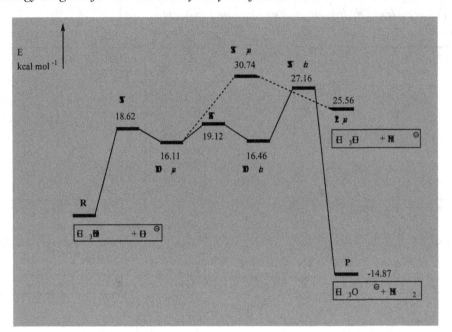

Alkaline Hydrolysis of Amides

The amide hydrolysis has been the subject of numerous experimental (Bender, 1960; Brown, Bennet & Slebocka-Tilk, 1992; Eriksson, 1968; Young, Pazhanisamy & Schowen, 1984) and theoretical studies (Chalmet, Harb & Ruiz-Lopez, 2001; Hori, Kamimura, Ando, Mizumura & Ihara, 1988; Lopez, Mujika, Blackburn & Karplus, 2003; Xiong & Zhan, 2006) because it is regarded as a model process for the cleavage of peptide bonds. In our combined kinetic and computational study (Cheshmedzhieva, Ilieva, Hadjieva & Galabov, 2009) we showed that the rate of the alkaline hydrolysis of three secondary amides - N-methylbenzamide, N-methylacetamide and acetanilide – is governed by the second stage of the reaction. This stage involves the breakdown of the initially formed tetrahedral intermediate to products. The computational and kinetic results provided a detailed picture of the variations of the free energy barriers for the reactions of the three amides studied.

RHF/6-31+G(d), B3LYP/6-31++G(d,p), and QCISD/6-31++G(d,p) quantum mechanical computations were carried out in studying the mechanism of alkaline hydrolysis of acetanilide. The computations showed that in both gas phase and water solution the rate-determining stage of the reaction is the breakdown of the tetrahedral intermediate. The decomposition of the tetrahedral intermediate is shown to be a concerted process involving cleavage of the C–N bond and simultaneous proton transfer. No evidence is found for the formation of a dianion intermediate along the reaction pathway. The theoretical computations reveal that the energy profile of the reaction is quite different in gas phase and in solution. All stationary points in water have higher energy than the reactants (Figure 10). The reaction is exothermic in both gas phase and solution.

The rate constants (at 25 ^{0}C) for the alkaline hydrolysis of a series of seven acetanilide derivatives were experimentally determined (Cheshmedzhieva, Ilieva, Hadjieva & Galabov, 2009; Galabov, Cheshmedzhieva, Ilieva & Hadjieva, 2004). The series included the parent com-

Table 7. Theoretical reactivity indices from B3LYP/6-31+G(d,p) computations and Hammett constants for acetanilide and p-substituted derivatives

Substituent	q_C MPA	q_C NBO	ω	V_C [volts] Reactant	V_N [volts] Reactant	V_N [volts] TS2	Hammett σ constants	ln k
H	0.7285	0.6782	1.11	-397.8279	-497.6719	-504.2979	0.000	-11.856
CH$_3$	0.7453	0.6767	1.04	-397.9068	-497.7427	-504.4367	-0.170	-11.934
OCH$_3$	0.7926	0.6747	0.94	-397.9476	-497.7672	-504.3904	-0.268	-11.863
NH$_2$	0.7361	0.6725	0.87	-398.0565	-497.8733	-504.6190	-0.660	-13.044
COCH$_3$	0.7958	0.6818	1.91	-397.5286	-497.3454	-503.1823	0.502	-9.880
CHO	0.7556	0.6829	2.10	-397.4252	-497.2311	-503.0761	0.420	-8.734
NO$_2$	0.7492	0.6847	2.86	-397.2265	-497.0080	-502.1836	0.778	-7.285
Correlation coefficient	**0.173**	**0.952**	**0.985**	**0.990**	**0.993**	**0.986**	**0.947**	

pound of acetanilide and the following para substituted derivatives: CH$_3$, OCH$_3$, NH$_2$, CHO, COCH$_3$, NO$_2$. The obtained kinetic data were then correlated with the theoretically estimated reactivity indices: Mulliken and NBO atomic charges, the Parr electrophilicity index (ω), and the electrostatic potential at the carbon and nitrogen atoms of the reaction center (V_C, V_N). The respective values for these electronic parameters are given in Table 7.

Table 7 contains also the usual Hammett constants for the substituents. In the bottom row of the table are shown the linear regression correlation coefficients (r) for the dependences between the experimental ln k values and the respective reactivity parameters. It is seen that the Mulliken charges (q_C MPA) do not correlate linearly with the ln **k** values. A better correlation, though far from satisfactory, is obtained when the NBO charges (q_C NBO) on the carbonyl carbon are applied. The global electrophilicity index ω provides very good predictions for the relative reaction rates. The electrophilicity index is evaluated from theoretical data using the relations:

$$\omega = \frac{\mu^2}{2\eta} \tag{11}$$

$$\mu = -\left(I + A\right)/2 \tag{12}$$

$$\eta = \left(I - A\right)/2 \tag{13}$$

The dependence between the electrostatic potential at the carbonyl carbon atom (V_C) and ln k is characterized by the highest correlation coefficient (r = 0.990).

The variations of the electrostatic potential values as well as the NBO charges at the electrophilic center reflect clearly the influence of polar groups at the para position in the aromatic ring. The increased partial positive charge at the carbonyl carbon under the influence of electron withdrawing substituents favors the interaction between the two reactants. Inversely, electron donating substituents, such as CH$_3$, OCH$_3$ and NH$_2$, lead to increased electron density at the site of the electrophilic center, thus hampering its interaction with the electronegative hydroxide ion.

The rate-limiting stage of the reaction studied (Cheshmedzhieva, Ilieva, Hadjieva & Galabov, 2009) is associated with the second transition state (TS2). This stage involves simultaneous breaking of the amide C-N bond and the transfer of a proton to the emerging amine anion. The significantly increased negative charge at the amide nitrogen

Figure 11. Plot of ln k vs. the electrostatic potential at the nitrogen atom (V_N) for the alkaline hydrolysis of the series of acetanilides studied

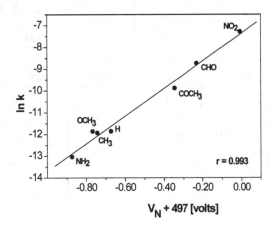

in TS2 reflects in the lower values of V_N in TS2 compared to reactants seen in Table 2. The nascent negative charge at the nitrogen atom can be stabilized by electron delocalisation toward the aromatic ring. This process is strongly favoured by electron withdrawing substituents, such as CHO, $COCH_3$ and NO_2 groups. It is, therefore, not surprising that acetanilides containing these substituents react much faster than the unsubstituted acetanilide or derivatives with electron donating groups. The linear dependences between rate constants and the electrostatic potential at the nitrogen atom in both reactants and transition state are characterized by high correlation coefficients. The plot between ln k and V_N in reactants is illustrated in Figure 11.

The excellent correlations between the electrostatic potential at nuclei and ln k values are not surprising. This index has two characteristics that are behind its successful applications in describing the chemical reactivity: (1) It is a *local* index, characterizing the reactivity of atoms in particular reaction center in molecules; (2) No further assumptions or approximations with respect to the wave function considered are introduced. Thus the electrostatic potential at nuclei reflects accurately fine variations in the electron density at particular atomic sites caused by structural changes.

Aminolysis of Esters

The quality of reactivity predictions coming from alternative theoretical approaches as well as experimental reactivity constants is examined in the case of the ester aminolysis process. The ester aminolysis plays a crucial role in the generation of amide functional groups in proteins and peptides. The biological process has received much attention in experimental and computational works (Barta, Dorner & Polacek, 2001; Fersht, 1999; Rangelov, Vayssilov, Yomtova & Petkov, 2005). The ester aminolysis is also an important reaction in organic chemistry and has been the subject on numerous kinetic (Bruice & Benkovic, 1966; Castro, Ruiz, Salinas & Santos, 1999; Jencks, 1969; Um, Kim, Park, Fujio & Tsuno, 2004) and theoretical studies (Adalstensson & Bruice, 1998; Kim, Li, Lee, Sohn, Chun & Lee, 2000; O'Hair & Androutsopoulos, 2000; Yang & Drueckhammer, 2000; Zipse, Wang & Houk, 1996). The derivatives and reaction studied are presented in Scheme 1.

The barrier heights for the rate determining stage of the aminolysis of 16 phenyl acetate derivatives were predicted employing density functional theory at the B3LYP/6-31+G(d,p) level (Galabov, Ilieva, Hadjieva, Atanasov & Schaefer, 2008). Computational study (Ilieva, Galabov, Musaev, Morokuma & Schaefer, 2003) shows that under a general base catalysis the most favored pathway for the reaction is an addition/elimination stepwise mechanism involving two transition states. If general base catalysis is not involved results for the parent compound of phenylacetate predict distinctly lower barrier for the concerted mechanism. Thus both mechanistic pathways for the reaction are explored. The theoretical activation energies are rationalized in terms of global and local reactivity indices derived from density functional theory. The theoretical quantities are summarized in Table 8.

Scheme 1.

R—⬡—OCOCH₃ + R'NH2 ⟶ CH₃CONHR' + R—⬡—OH

R = H, CH₃, C(CH₃)₃, OH, OCH₃, NH₂, NHCH₃,
F, Cl, CCH, CN, CH₂F, CHF₂, CF₃, NO₂, NO

Both Mulliken and NBO charges predict qualitatively well (Table 8) the reactivity of the phenyl esters in the aminolysis reaction. The correlation of the theoretical activation energies with the q_C(NBO) values is, as expected, slightly better ($r = 0.965$ for the stepwise pathway and 0.971 for the concerted mechanism). Most importantly, both of these methods show that electron-withdrawing substituents in the aromatic ring increase the partial positive charge at the carbonyl carbon thus facilitating the attack by the nucleophile. Electron-donating substitients have the opposite effect. It should be emphasized that the atomic charges are model dependent quantities. Definitive information regarding the electron density variations at the reaction center is provided by the electrostatic potential at nuclei. The V_C values obtained (Table 8) clearly show that the electron

Table 8. Theoretically Evaluated Barrier Heights for the Stepwise and Concerted Mechanisms of the Aminolysis of para Substituted Phenyl Acetates and Reactivity Descriptors

R	ΔE_{TSI} [kcal/mol]	ΔE_{CTS} [kcal/mol]	σ	ω [eV]	q_C [e] (Mulliken)	q_C [e] (NBO)	V_C [volts]
H	42.19	32.33	0	0.0284	0.472842	0.8140	-397.0823
CH₃	42.58	32.96	-0.170	0.0286	0.469286	0.8135	-397.1530
C(CH₃)₃	42.58	32.93	-0.200	0.0285	0.446169	0.8135	-397.1612
OH	42.83	33.04	-0.370	0.0283	0.454127	0.8133	-397.1449
OCH₃	42.98	33.35	-0.268	0.0284	0.463674	0.8130	-397.1966
NH₂	43.24	34.18	-0.660	0.0247	0.453770	0.8131	-397.2809
NHCH₃	43.41	34.44	-0.592	0.0255	0.455569	0.8126	-397.3326
F	41.96	31.57	0.060	0.0332	0.469911	0.8151	-396.9462
Cl	41.54	30.80	0.227	0.0322	0.493098	0.8145	-396.8918
CCH	41.38	30.48	0.230	0.0351	0.485823	0.8143	-396.9354
CN	40.04	27.76	0.660	0.0444	0.510167	0.8159	-396.6034
CH₂F	41.40	30.76	0.110	0.0342	0.469181	0.8145	-396.9245
CHF₂	41.34	30.29	0.320	0.0385	0.490435	0.8149	-396.8537
CF₃	40.55	28.97	0.540	0.0404	0.495201	0.8156	-396.7285
NO₂	39.43	26.17	0.778	0.0620	0.525401	0.8179	-396.5109
NO	39.30	25.86	0.910	0.0609	0.544451	0.8173	-396.5462
Correlation coefficient r	*with* ΔE_{TSI}		0.982	0.940	0.942	0.965	0.991
	with ΔE_{CTS}	0.976	0.959	0.953	0.971	0.989

density at the carbon atom is increased under the influence of electron-donating substituents (increased negative value of V_C) such as OH, OCH_3 and NH_2, and significantly lowered by the effect of electron-withdrawing groups (CN, CF_3, NO_2, NO). Excellent linear dependence between barrier heights and EPN values (V_C) at the carbonyl carbon in the monomer esters are obtained for both possible mechanisms of the process. The dependences between ΔE and V_C are illustrated in Figure 12.

Experimental kinetic studies (Galabov, Ilieva, Hadjieva, Atanasov & Schaefer, 2008) were carried out for the n-butylaminolysis of seven p-substituted phenyl acetates in acetonitrile. Thus the predictive power of the theoretically evaluated reactivity indices was assessed by direct comparison with experimental results.

Pseudo-first order kinetics of the reaction of seven p-substituted phenyl acetates at 25°C was followed by IR spectroscopy. The clear separation between the carbonyl group bands in the reactant esters and the amide products provides a basis for the kinetic measurements (Figure 13). Experiments were carried for seven compounds with substituent R = H, CH_3, $C(CH_3)_3$, OCH_3, Cl, CF_3, NO_2. As can be seen, the series includes the parent compound as well as three electron-donating and three electron-withdrawing groups. Thus the derivatives selected are expected to reflect alternative polar influences of the para substituents. An example of the pseudo-first order kinetics for the n-butylaminolysis of phenyl acetate is illustrated in Figure 13.

The obtained ln **k** values are plotted against four reactivity indices: the NBO atomic charges at the carbonyl carbon atom, the global electrophilicity index (ω), the experimental Hammett constants (σ), and the electrostatic potential at the carbonyl carbon atom (V_C) in the reactant phenyl acetates. These plots obtained are illustrated in Figure 14.

The NBO charges provide a good description of the experimentally established reactivities of

Figure 12. The plots between barrier heights for stepwise and concerted pathways of the aminolysis of phenyl acetates and the electrostatic potential at the carbonyl carbon atom of reactant esters

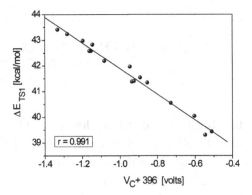

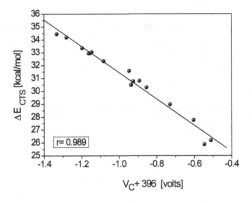

Figure 13. Kinetics of the n-butylaminolysis of phenyl acetate in acetonitrile at 25⁰C as followed by FTIR spectroscopy. The ordinate axis is in absorbance units

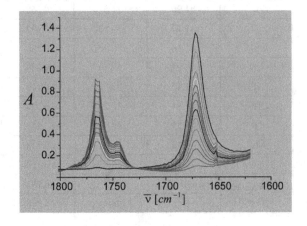

Figure 14. Plots between ln k values for the n-butylaminolysis of phenyl acetates and NBO charges at the carbonyl carbon atom, global electrophilicity index (ω) for the reactant esters, Hammett σ$_p$ constants, and the electrostatic potential at the carbonyl carbon atom (V$_C$) for the reactant phenyl acetates

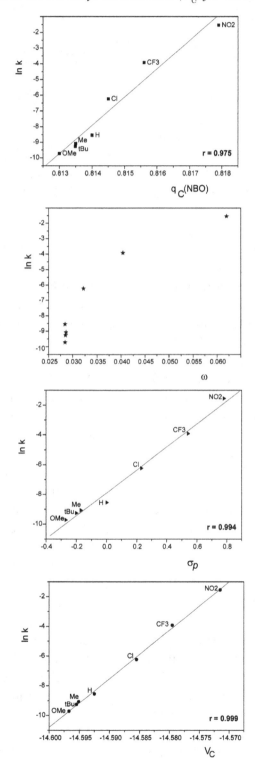

Scheme 2. Series of S_N2 reactions for analysis of the benzylic effect; R = H, CH$_3$, OH, OCH$_3$, NH$_2$, F, Cl, CN, NO$_2$, COF, CCH

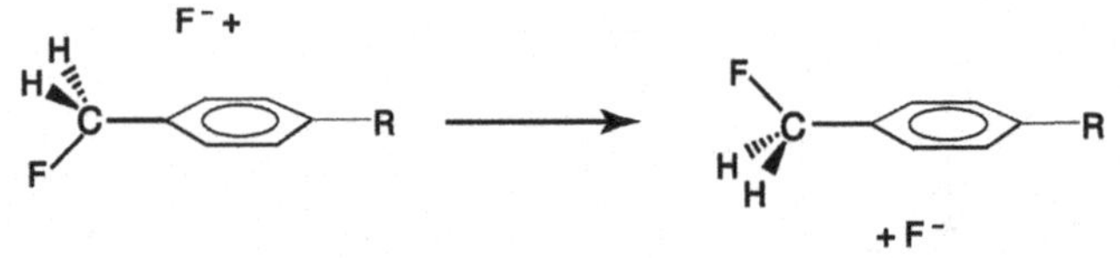

the compounds from the series studied (Figure 14). The electrophilicity index, however, only qualitatively describes the trend of rate constant variations (Figure 14). As already discussed, the result can be attributed to the global nature of the index. As expected, the experimentally determined Hammett substituent constants correlate very well with the observed rate constants (Figure 14).

In harmony with the theoretical results discussed in the previous part the best prediction of reactivity is provided by the EPN values at the carbonyl carbon in the reactant phenyl acetates. Figure 14 illustrates the plot between ln **k** and V$_C$. The respective correlation coefficient is r = 0.999. It is indeed somewhat surprising to obtain such perfect theoretical predictions of the experimental reactivities.

In general, these results support the following conclusions: (1) contemporary electronic structure methods provide reactivity descriptors that can be employed to predict with a good accuracy the rates of chemical reactions; (2) the atomic electrostatic potential is a reliable local reactivity index.

S$_N$2 Identity Exchange Reaction of Benzyl Halides

The S$_N$2 identity exchange reactions of the fluoride ion with benzyl fluoride and ten para-substituted derivatives (RC$_6$H$_4$CH$_2$F, R = CH$_3$, OH, OCH$_3$, NH$_2$, F, Cl, CCH, CN, COF, NO$_2$) have been investigated by both rigorous *ab initio* methods and carefully calibrated density functional theory. Groundbreaking focal point computations were

executed for the C$_6$H$_5$CH$_2$F + F$^-$ and C$_6$H$_5$CH$_2$Cl + Cl$^-$ S$_N$2 reactions at the highest possible levels of electronic structure theory, employing complete basis set (CBS) extrapolations of aug-cc-pVXZ (X = 2-5) Hartree-Fock and MP2 energies, and including higher-order electron correlation via CCSD/aug-cc-pVQZ and CCSD(T)/aug-cc-pVTZ coupled cluster wave functions.

Benzylic effect is confirmed and quantified by a series of massive MP2 and coupled cluster computations to ascertain reliable S$_N$2 barriers for the C$_6$H$_5$CH$_2$F + F$^-$ and C$_6$H$_5$CH$_2$Cl + Cl$^-$ archetypes (Galabov, Nikolova, Wilke, Schaefer & Allen, 2008). Subsequently, B3LYP density functional theory is used to analyze the factors governing S$_N$2 fluoride identity exchange reactions within the series of p-substituted benzyl fluorides shown in Scheme 2. The distant variations of structure with respect to the reaction center in these derivatives, as well as the absence of specific steric influences, is intended to reveal the intrinsic features of the S$_N$2 benzylic effect and thus contribute to the understanding of S$_N$2 reactivity in general.

The key energetic quantities (E^w, $E*$, E^b, Scheme 3) for S$_N$2 identity exchange in benzyl fluoride and benzyl chloride are compared with analogous data for CH$_3$F and CH$_3$Cl in Table 9. The focal point E^b computations for the chloride reactions are in excellent accord with the activation energies derived from Fourier transform ion cyclotron resonance (C$_6$H$_5$CH$_2$Cl + Cl$^-$, +0.2 kcal mol^{-1}) (Wladkowski, Wilbur & Brauman, 1994) and Flowing Afterglow-SIFT-Drift (CH$_3$Cl + Cl$^-$, 1±1 kcal mol^{-1}) (Barlow, Van Doren & Bierbaum,

Table 9. Comparison of complexation energies (E^w), central activation barriers (E^*), and net activation barriers (E^b) (in kcal mol^{-1}) for the S_N2 identity exchange reactions of methyl vs. benzyl fluoride and methyl vs. benzyl chloride. All quantities include zero-point vibrational energy (ZPVE) (reproduced from ref. 37, with permission)

Method	E^w	E^*	E^b
$CH_3Cl + Cl^-$			
B3LYP/DZP++[a]	−9.71	8.38	−1.31
FPA[a]	−11.03	12.88	+1.85
Expt.			+1±1[b]
$C_6H_5CH_2Cl + Cl^-$			
B3LYP/DZP++	−12.13	10.02	−2.11
FPA	−14.78	15.02	+0.24
Expt.			+0.2[c]

[a] (Gonzales, Allen & Schaefer, 2005). [b] (Barlow, Van Doren & Bierbaum, 1988). [c] (Wladkowski, Wilbur & Brauman, 1994).

Scheme 3. Energy profile of S_N2 identity exchange reactions of benzyl derivatives

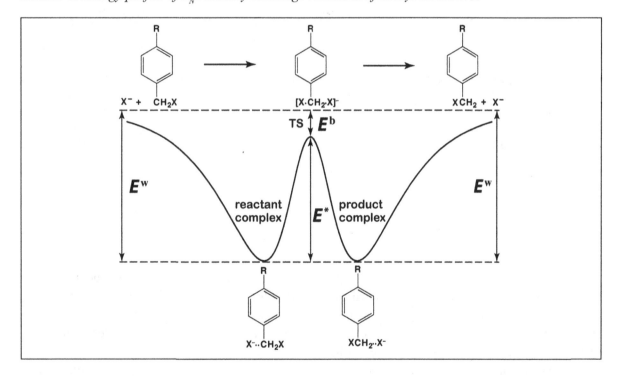

1988) rate measurements. The focal point analysis definitively confirms the intrinsic benzylic effect, showing that substitution of an aromatic ring at the central carbon lowers the S_N2 net barriers of the methyl fluoride and methyl chloride reactions by 3.8 and 1.6 kcal mol^{-1}, respectively.

Such changes in nearly thermoneutral activation barriers can indeed dramatically accelerate chemical reactions.

Different hypotheses have been put forward to explain the greater S_N2 reactivity of benzylic compounds, as discussed above. The computed

Figure 15. NBO atomic charges and electrostatic potential on the central carbon (V_C, in volts) for benzyl chloride (BzCl), methyl chloride (MeCl), their reactant ion-molecule complexes, and respective transition states for S_N2 identity exchange (B3LYP/DZP++ method). For ease of interpretation, the values shown in brackets around the aromatic ring are sums of NBO charges on the carbon atoms and the attached hydrogens.

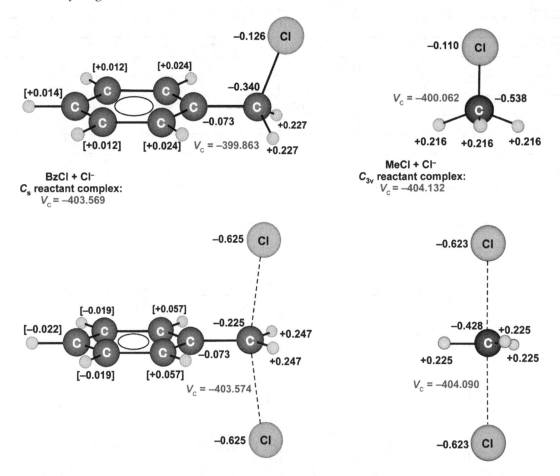

NBO atomic charges for the $C_6H_5CH_2F$, CH_3F, $C_6H_5CH_2Cl$, and CH_3Cl reactions have been examined to elucidate the benzylic effect, as presented in Figure 15. The analysis of the variation of the EPN values at the reaction center – the methylene carbon – reveals that in the benzylic system the V_C value is higher than in the respective methyl chloride. This indicates lower electron density of the reaction center, which favors the attack by the nucleophilic Cl^- anion. The NBO analysis reveals that only 4% of the excess negative charge brought by Cl^- is delocalized in the aromatic ring. Thus, the classic textbook explanation for the benzylic effect, which refers to the stabilization of the transition state via electron delocalization in the ring, is evidently, not confirmed.

To investigate the consequences of chemical structure variations on S_N2 reactivity in benzylic systems, a representative series of derivatives (Scheme 1) containing both electron-donating and electron-withdrawing substituents has been selected. Para-substitution has been chosen in all of these derivatives to eliminate proximity effects on the reaction center.

In Table 10, S_N2 net activation barriers are compiled alongside V_C values in the reactant and transition state for the series of benzylic derivatives. A striking linear dependence, with correlation coefficient $r = 0.994$, exists between V_C(reactant) and E^b, as illustrated in the top panel of Figure 16. Thus, the reactivity of the benzyl fluorides toward S_N2 identity exchange with fluoride ion is predicted very well by the pre-existing V_C values in the reactants. The bottom panel of Figure 16 reveals an even better linear correlation between the transition-state electrostatic potential $[V_C(TS)]$ and the net barriers E^b. In essence, a strong structure-reactivity relationship is established in two steps: the net S_N2 barrier is largely determined by electrostatic effects in the transition state that are embedded in $V_C(TS)$, and in turn the $V_C(TS)$ values are closely correlated with the corresponding V_C potentials in the reactants.

Finally, V_C potentials cannot be replaced simplistically by NBO charges as a satisfactory index of intrinsic S_N2 reactivity in these systems. For the p-substituted benzyl fluoride reactants, the NBO charge at the reaction-center carbon (q_C) lies in too narrow a range ($+0.0805e$ to $+0.0842e$) to contain much information about the eventual barrier, and the plot of E^b vs. q_C is scattered. Apparently, q_C in isolation is not a sufficiently sensitive measure of the regional electrostatics that influence the S_N2 reactions.

EPN in Evaluating Substituent Constants

An efficient and accurate computational approach for the evaluation of σ^0 substituent constants for substituted benzene systems is established (Galabov, Ileiva, & Schaefer, 2006). It is based on the excellent linear correlation between the experimental reactivity constants and the theoretical electrostatic potential values (EPN) at the carbon atoms in para and meta positions.

Figure 16. Relationship between the net S_N2 activation barrier (E^b) and the reaction-center electrostatic potential (V_C) for the substituted benzyl fluorides of Scheme 1. In the top and bottom panels, V_C is computed for the central carbon atom in the isolated reactant and the S_N2 transition state (TS), respectively. Data for [top, bottom] linear fits: y-intercept = [−32.45(94), −124.5(27)], slope = [−19.66(76), −18.80(44)], linear regression coefficient (r) = [0.994, 0.998].

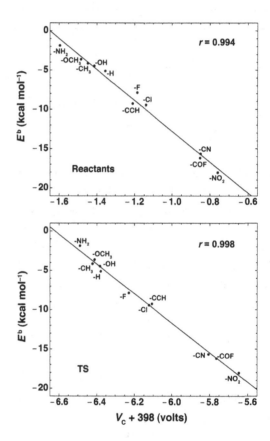

Density functional theory computations at the B3LYP/6-311+G(2d,2p) and BPW91/6-311G(d,p) levels were carried out for a series of fifteen monosubstituted benzene derivatives to study dependences between electronic structure parameters and experimental reactivity constants. The molecules treated are given in Table 11. The electronic parameters evaluated are as follows: the

307

Table 10. B3LYP/DZP++ net activation barriers (E^b) and electrostatic potentials (V_C) at the reaction-center carbon atom of reactants and transition states (TS) for the S_N2 identity exchange reactions of benzyl fluorides

Substituent	E^b (kcal mol^{-1})	V_C(reactant)+398 (volts)	V_C(TS)+398 (volts)
-H	−5.11	−1.354	−6.379
p-CH$_3$	−4.15	−1.448	−6.423
p-OH	−4.46	−1.414	−6.383
p-OCH$_3$	−3.63	−1.484	−6.412
p-NH$_2$	−1.87	−1.596	−6.489
p-F	−7.87	−1.186	−6.229
p-Cl	−9.43	−1.140	−6.123
p-CN	−15.66	−0.849	−5.806
p-NO$_2$	−18.04	−0.759	−5.646
p-COF	−16.20	−0.852	−5.764
p-CCH	−9.26	−1.210	−6.107

electrostatic potential values for the carbon and hydrogen atoms, the NBO charges at the same atoms, and the mean dipole moment derivatives or GAPT atomic charge for the hydrogen atom of the para C-H bonds. The results from the B3LYP/6-311+G(2d,2p) computations involving the C-H bond in the para position to the substituents are presented in Table 11. The last columns contain the σ^0 constants (Exner, 1978) introduced by Van Bekkum et al. (Van Bekkum, Verkade, & Wepster, 1959) and Taft (1960). The σ^0 constants are defined to reflect the isolated effect of individual substituents unperturbed by possible resonance interactions with a second substituent.

The best correlations are found for the relationships between the theoretically estimated electrostatic potential at the carbon and hydrogen atoms and the respective σ^0 constants. The correlations between substituent constants, the natural charges at the carbon and hydrogen atoms, and the GAPT charges at the hydrogen atoms of the para C-H bond reveal that overall linearity between the theoretical and experimental quantities exists.

It is certainly of interest to plot simultaneously the electrostatic potential values for both para and meta C-H bonds. The following linear regression was obtained:

$$V_C = 1.181 \; \sigma^0 - 1.088 \qquad (14)$$

$n = 29, r = 0.995, s = 0.030$

This relationship is illustrated in Figure 17. The quality of the linear dependence between the σ^0 substituent constants and the theoretically estimated EPN values for the carbon atom in the para and meta positions of the aromatic ring indicates that the relationship found offers a useful computational approach for the evaluation of reactivity constants.

It should be underlined that σ^0 constants are determined from solution kinetic and chemical equilibrium studies (Van Bekkum, Verkade, & Wepster, 1959; Taft, 1960). It is, therefore, quite surprising to find such a nearly perfect linear correlation between these experimental quantities and the theoretical EPN values obtained without consideration of the solvent effect. To analyze the influence of solvent, computations employing the SCIPCM method were carried out. Full geometry

Table 11. Experimental reactivity constants and theoretical parameters for the meta and para C-H bond in mono-substituted benzenes from B3LYP/6-311+G(2d,2p) computations

	$V_C$para [volts]	$V_C$meta [volts]	q_C^{para} (NBO) [e]	q_H^{para} (GAPT) [e]	σ_m^0	σ_p^0
-H	-402.0669	-402.0669	-0.20356	0.03175	0	0
-CH$_3$	-402.2067	-402.1545	-0.20983	0.03074	-0.07	-0.12
-OCH$_3$	-402.2903	-402.0976	-0.23644	0.03398	0.06	-0.13
-NH$_2$	-402.4484	-402.2038	-0.24596	0.03180	-0.09	-0.33
-F	-401.8663	-401.6903	-0.22005	0.03981	0.33	0.20
-Cl	-401.7651	-401.6685	-0.20709	0.03920	0.38	0.24
-CN	-401.2843	-401.3262	-0.17764	0.04388	0.65	0.71
-CHO	-401.4720	-401.5915	-0.17035	0.03989	0.41	0.47
-NO$_2$^{e}	-401.1654	-401.2250	-0.16875	0.04689	0.71	0.81
-COOH	-401.5950	-401.7028	-0.17417	0.03842	0.35	0.44
-COF	-401.2851	-401.4027	-0.16534	0.04318	0.55	0.70
-COCl	-401.2535	-401.3765	-0.16212	0.04313	0.53	0.69
-CCH	-401.8190	-401.8323	-0.19381	0.03590	0.20	0.22
-CHF$_2$	-401.7126	-401.7153	-0.19185	0.03745	0.32	0.35
-CF$_3$	-401.4998	-401.5164	-0.18302	0.04090	0.46	0.53
r (with σ_m^0)		**0.994**				
r (with σ_p^0)	**0.997**		**0.921**	**0.937**		

Figure 17. Dependence between the theoretical electrostatic potential at the meta- and para-carbon atoms in mono-substituted benzenes and the σ^0 constants

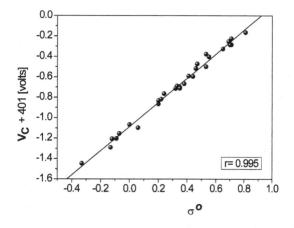

optimization for the molecules studied at the B3LYP/6-311+G(2d,2p) level of theory was performed. Theoretical computations to assess the influence of water solvent using the SCIPCM method showed that the solvent enhances the overall effect of polar substituents by about 30% (Galabov, Ileiva, & Schaefer, 2006). The results obtained indicate also that the relative values of the σ^0 constants are predominantly determined by intramolecular influences.

Thus, the established excellent correlation between the $\sigma_m{}^o$ and $\sigma_p{}^o$ constants and EPN values for the respective carbon positions (V_C) provides a method for determining substituent constants in arbitrary arenes, including polysubstituted and polynuclear aromatic derivatives. Unlike atomic charges, which depend strongly on their definition and additional approximations, inherent in their evaluation, the electrostatic potential at nuclei values V_Y reflect the variations of electron densities rigorously. The dominant contribution to V_Y comes from the local densities around the respective atomic sites. More negative V_Y values indicate greater electron densities.

FUTURE RESEARCH DIRECTIONS

The results surveyed clearly indicate the wide applicability of the electrostatic potential at nuclei as an accurate local reactivity descriptor for chemical interactions. The research along these directions can be extended to cover interactions and processes of great biological relevance. These may include the characterization of hydrogen bonding ability of different atomic sites in biological molecules, the interaction between various ligands (potential medicines) with bioreceptors and many others. The properties of various nanosystems may also be described in quantitative terms using the non-approximate electrostatic potential at nuclei as a local reactivity index. It should certainly be recognized that EPN is not a universally applicable reactivity descriptor. Considering its definition (Eq. 2) it is clear that EPN may strongly be influenced by the electronic densities at close neighboring atoms. In such cases its principal advantage as a local index will not be valid. Nevertheless, for a great number of chemical and biological interactions where the variations in structure are at some distance from the reaction center, EPN may successfully be employed as a reliable descriptor of the variations in electronic structure at a given functional group. The results surveyed in the present chapter provide a compelling evidence in this respect.

CONCLUSION

The results surveyed in this chapter as well as data obtained in other laboratories clearly show that the electrostatic potential at nuclei is an accurate descriptor of the reactivity of local atomic sites in a molecule. The specific limitation for its successful application is the requirement that the structural variations for a given reaction series are not in the immediate vicinity of the functional group considered. EPN provides a powerful theoretical approach to predict and analyze reactivities for variety of charge-controlled chemical interactions. Theoretically estimated barrier height and interaction energies or experimental kinetic parameters are predicted with remarkable accuracy with the aid of the electrostatic potential of nuclei data. Considerable advantage of EPN is that its values are easily determined and procedures for its evaluation are implemented in most quantum chemistry software packages.

The applications of EPN as a reactivity index, first introduced 12 years ago, demonstrate the great power of contemporary quantum mechanical computations in characterizing molecular properties and chemical interactions with impressive accuracy.

REFERENCES

Abboud, J.-L. M., & Notario, R. (1999). Critical compilation of scales of solvent parameters. Part I. Pure, non-hydrogen bond donor solvents. *Pure and Applied Chemistry*, *71*(4), 645–718. doi:10.1351/pac199971040645

Abraham, M. H., Berthelot, M., Laurence, C. H., & Taylor, P. J. (1998). Analysis of hydrogen-bond complexation constants in 1,1,1-trichloroethane: the α_2^H and β_2^H relationship. *Journal of the Chemical Society, Perkin Transactions 2: Physical Organic Chemistry*, *1*, 187–191. doi:10.1039/a702326j

Abraham, M. H., Duce, P. P., Prior, D. V., Barrat, D. G., Morris, J. J., & Taylor, P. J. J. (1989). Hydrogen bonding. Part 9. Solute proton donor and proton acceptor scales for use in drug design. *Journal of the Chemical Society, Perkin Transactions 2: Physical Organic Chemistry*, *10*, 1355–1375. doi:10.1039/p29890001355

Adalstensson, H., & Bruice, T. C. (1998). What is the mechanism of catalysis of ester aminolysis by weak amine bases? Comparison of experimental studies and theoretical investigation of the aminolysis of substituted phenyl esters of quinoline-6- and -8-carboxylic acids. *Journal of the American Chemical Society*, *120*(14), 3440–3447. doi:10.1021/ja972162+

Alia, J. M., & Edwards, H. G. (2005). Vibrational spectroscopic properties of hydrogen bonded acetonitrile studied by DFT. *The Journal of Physical Chemistry A*, *109*(35), 7977–7987. doi:10.1021/jp051892y

Alia, J. M., & Edwards, H. G. (2007). Vibrational dynamics of hydrogen-bonded HCN complexes with OH and NH acids: Computational DFT systematic study. *International Journal of Quantum Chemistry*, *107*(5), 1170–1180. doi:10.1002/qua.21235

Bader, R. F. W. (1990). *Atoms in molecules: A quantum theory*. Oxford, UK: Oxford University Press.

Barlow, S. E., Van Doren, J. M., & Bierbaum, V. M. (1988). The gas phase displacement reaction of chloride ion with methyl chloride as a function of kinetic energy. *Journal of the American Chemical Society*, *110*(21), 7240–7242. doi:10.1021/ja00229a064

Barta, A., Dorner, S., & Polacek, N. (2001). Mechanism of ribosomal peptide bond formation. *Science*, *291*, 203a–204. doi:10.1126/science.291.5502.203a

Bender, M. L. (1960). Mechanisms of catalysis of nucleophilic reactions of carboxylic acid derivatives. *Chemical Reviews*, *60*(1), 53–113. doi:10.1021/cr60203a005

Besler, B. H., Merz, K. M., & Kollman, P. A. (1990). Atomic charges derived from semiempirical methods. *Journal of Computational Chemistry*, *11*(4), 431–439. doi:10.1002/jcc.540110404

Bobadova-Parvanova, P., & Galabov, B. (1998). Ab initio molecular-orbital study of hydrogen-bonded complexes of carbonyl aliphatic compounds and hydrogen fluoride. *The Journal of Physical Chemistry A*, *102*(10), 1815–1819. doi:10.1021/jp9710852

Boys, S. F., & Bernardi, F. (1970). The calculation of small molecular interactions by differences of separate total energies - some procedures with reduced errors. *Molecular Physics*, *19*(4), 553–566. doi:10.1080/00268977000101561

Breneman, C. M., & Wiberg, K. B. (1990). Determining atom-centered monopoles from molecular electrostatic potentials. The need for high sampling density in formamide conformational analysis. *Journal of Computational Chemistry*, *11*(3), 361–373. doi:10.1002/jcc.540110311

Brown, R. S., Bennet, A. J., & Slebocka-Tilk, H. (1992). Recent perspectives concerning the mechanism of H3O+- and hydroxide-promoted amide hydrolysis. *Accounts of Chemical Research, 25*(11), 481–488. doi:10.1021/ar00023a001

Bruice, T. C., & Benkovic, S. J. (1966). *Bioorganic mechanisms*. New York: W.A. Benjamin Inc.

Carey, F. A., & Sanders, R. J. (2000). *Advanced organic chemistry Part A, Structure and mechanisms*. New York: Springer.

Castro, E. A., Ruiz, M. G., Salinas, S., & Santos, J. G. (1999). Kinetics and mechanism of the aminolysis of phenyl and 4-nitrophenyl chloroformates in aqueous solution. *The Journal of Organic Chemistry, 64*(13), 4817–4820. doi:10.1021/jo990146k

Cedillo, A., Contreras, R., Galvan, M., Aizman, A., Andres, J., & Safont, V. S. (2007). Nucleophilicity index from perturbed electrostatic potentials. *The Journal of Physical Chemistry A, 111*(12), 2442–2447. doi:10.1021/jp068459o

Chalmet, S., Harb, W., & Ruiz-Lopez, M. F. (2001). Computer simulation of amide bond formation in aqueous solution. *The Journal of Physical Chemistry A, 105*(51), 11574–11581. doi:10.1021/jp0135656

Chattaraj, P. K. (Ed.). (2009). *Chemical reactivity theory. A density functional view*. Boca Raton, FL: CRS Press. doi:10.1201/9781420065442

Cheshmedzhieva, D., Ilieva, S., Hadjieva, B., & Galabov, B. (2009). The mechanism of alkaline hydrolysis of amides: a comparative computational and experimental study of the hydrolysis of N-methylacetamide, N-methylbenzamide, and acetanilide. *Journal of Physical Organic Chemistry, 22*(6), 619–631. doi:10.1002/poc.1492

Cheshmedzhieva, D., Ilieva, S., Hadjieva, B., Trayanova, T., & Galabov, B. (2009). Reactivity of acetanilides in the alkaline hydrolysis reaction: Theory vs. experiment. *Molecular Physics, 107*(8), 1187–1192. doi:10.1080/00268970902799890

Dearden, J. C., & Ghafourian, T. (1999). Hydrogen bonding parameters for QSAR: Comparison of indicator variables, hydrogen bond counts, molecular orbital and other parameters. *Journal of Chemical Information and Computer Sciences, 39*, 231–235. doi:10.1021/ci980065+

Dimitrova, M., Ilieva, S., & Galabov, B. (2004). Reactivity descriptors for the hydrogen bonding ability of pyridine bases. *SAR and QSAR in Environmental Research, 15*(4), 311–319. doi:10.1080/1062936041000172491

Dimitrova, V., Ilieva, S., & Galabov, B. (2002). Electrostatic potential at atomic sites as a reactivity descriptor for hydrogen bonding. Complexes of monosubstituted acetylenes and ammonia. *The Journal of Physical Chemistry A, 106*(48), 11801–11805. doi:10.1021/jp026203m

Dimitrova, V., Ilieva, S., & Galabov, B. (2003). Electrostatic potential at nuclei as a reactivity index in hydrogen bond formation. Complexes of ammonia with C–H, N–H and O–H proton donor molecules. *Journal of Molecular Structure THEOCHEM, 637*(1), 73–80. doi:10.1016/S0166-1280(03)00402-0

Eriksson, S. O. (1968). Hydrolysis of anilides. IV. Hydroxylaminolysis, hydrazinolysis, and general acid-catalysed alkaline hydrolysis of trifluoroacetanilide. *Acta Chemica Scandinavica, 22*, 892–906. doi:10.3891/acta.chem.scand.22-0892

Exner, O. (1978). *Correlation Analysis in Chemistry* (Chapman, N. B., & Shorter, J., Eds.). London: Plenum.

Fersht, A. (1999). *Structure and mechanism in protein science*. New York: W.H. Freeman and Company.

Fukui, K. (1975). *Theory of orientation and stereoselection. Reactivity and structure concepts in organic chemistry* (*Vol. 2*). Berlin: Springer.

Gadre, S. R., Kulkarni, S. A., & Srivastava, I. H. (1992). Molecular electrostatic potentials: A topographical study. *The Journal of Chemical Physics*, *96*(7), 5253–5260. doi:10.1063/1.462710

Galabov, B., & Bobadova-Parvanova, P. (1999). Molecular electrostatic potential as reactivity index in hydrogen bonding: Ab initio molecular orbital study of complexes of nitrile and carbonyl compounds with hydrogen fluoride. *The Journal of Physical Chemistry A*, *103*(34), 6793–6799. doi:10.1021/jp984313g

Galabov, B., & Bobadova-Parvanova, P. (2000). Molecular electrostatic potential as reactivity index in hydrogen bond formation: an HF/6-31+G(d) study of hydrogen-bonded $(HCN)_n$ clusters, n=2,3,4,5,6,7. *Journal of Molecular Structure*, *550*, 93–98. doi:10.1016/S0022-2860(00)00383-5

Galabov, B., Cheshmedzhieva, D., Ilieva, S., & Hadjieva, B. (2004). Computational study of the reactivity of N-phenylacetamides in the alkaline hydrolysis reaction. *The Journal of Physical Chemistry A*, *108*(51), 11457–11462. doi:10.1021/jp046199+

Galabov, B., Ileiva, S., & Schaefer, H. F. (2006). An efficient computational approach for the evaluation of substituent constants. *The Journal of Organic Chemistry*, *71*(17), 6382–6387. doi:10.1021/jo0605288

Galabov, B., Ilieva, S., Hadjieva, B., Atanasov, Y., & Schaefer, H. F. (2008). Predicting reactivities of organic molecules. theoretical and experimental studies on the aminolysis of phenyl acetates. *The Journal of Physical Chemistry A*, *112*(29), 6700–6707. doi:10.1021/jp8007514

Galabov, B., Nikolova, V., Wilke, J. J., Schaefer, H. F., & Allen, W. D. (2008). Origin of the S_N2 benzylic effect. *Journal of the American Chemical Society*, *130*(30), 9887–9896. doi:10.1021/ja802246y

Gancia, E., Montana, J. G., & Manallack, D. T. (2001). Theoretical hydrogen bonding parameters for drug design. *Journal of Molecular Graphics & Modelling*, *19*(3-4), 349–362. doi:10.1016/S1093-3263(00)00084-X

Gonzales, J. M., Allen, W. D., & Schaefer, H. F. (2005). Model identity S_N2 reactions $CH_3X + X^-$ (X = F, Cl, CN, OH, SH, NH_2, PH_2): Marcus theory analyzed. *The Journal of Physical Chemistry A*, *109*(46), 10613–10628. doi:10.1021/jp054734f

Hammett, L. P. (1937). The effect of structure upon the reactions of organic compounds. Benzene derivatives. *Journal of the American Chemical Society*, *59*(1), 96–103. doi:10.1021/ja01280a022

Hammett, L. P. (1938). Linear free energy relationships in rate and equilibria phenomena. *Transactions of the Faraday Society*, *34*, 156–165. doi:10.1039/tf9383400156

Hori, K., Kamimura, A., Ando, K., Mizumura, M., & Ihara, Y. (1988). *Ab initio* molecular orbital study on the mechanism of amide hydrolysis dependent on leaving groups. *Tetrahedron*, *53*(12), 4317–4330. doi:10.1016/S0040-4020(97)00158-0

Ilieva, S., Galabov, B., Musaev, D. G., Morokuma, K., & Schaefer, H. F. (2003). Computational study of the aminolysis of esters. The reaction of methylformate with ammonia. *The Journal of Organic Chemistry*, *68*(4), 1496–1502. doi:10.1021/jo0263723

Jencks, W. P. (1969). *Catalysis in chemistry and enzymology*. New York: McGraw Hill.

Kamlet, M. J., Abboud, J. L. M., Abraham, M. H., & Taft, R. W. (1983). Linear solvation energy relationships. 23. A comprehensive collection of the solvatochromic parameters. pi.*. alpha., and. beta., and some methods for simplifying the generalized solvatochromic equation. *The Journal of Organic Chemistry*, *48*(17), 2877–2887. doi:10.1021/jo00165a018

Kamlet, M. J., Doherty, R. M., Abboud, J. L. M., Abraham, M. H., & Taft, R. W. (1986). Linear solvation energy relationships. 36. Molecular properties governing solubilities of organic nonelectrolytes in water. *Journal of Pharmaceutical Sciences*, *75*, 338–349. doi:10.1002/jps.2600750405

Karpfen, A., & Kryachko, E. S. (2005). Strongly blue-shifted C–H stretches: Interaction of formaldehyde with hydrogen fluoride clusters. *The Journal of Physical Chemistry A*, *109*(39), 8930–8937. doi:10.1021/jp050408o

Kenny, P. W. (1994). Prediction of hydrogen basicity from computed molecular electrostatic properties: Implications for Comparative Molecular Field Analysis. *Journal of the Chemical Society, Perkin Transactions 2: Physical Organic Chemistry*, *2*, 199–202. doi:10.1039/p29940000199

Kim, C. K., Li, H. G., Lee, H. W., Sohn, C. K., Chun, Y. I., & Lee, I. (2000). Ab initio study of the X^- + RCOY displacement reactions with R = H, CH_3 and X, Y = Cl, Br. *The Journal of Physical Chemistry A*, *104*(17), 4069–4076. doi:10.1021/jp994238p

King, B. F., & Weinhold, F. (1995). Structure and spectroscopy of $(HCN)_n$ clusters: Cooperative and electronic delocalization effects in C–H···N hydrogen bonding. *The Journal of Chemical Physics*, *103*(1), 333–347. doi:10.1063/1.469645

Kireev, D. B., Raevsky, O. A., & Fetisov, V. I. (1993). QSAR H-bonding descriptors. In Wermuth, C. G. (Ed.), *Trends in QSAR and molecular modelling 92*. Leiden: ESCOM.

Kitaura, K., & Morokuma, K. (1976). A new energy decomposition scheme for molecular interactions within the Hartree-Fock approximation. *International Journal of Quantum Chemistry*, *10*(2), 325–340. doi:10.1002/qua.560100211

Klopman, G. (Ed.). (1974). *Chemical reactivity and reaction paths*. New York: Wiley.

Koleva, G., Galabov, B., Wu, I. J., Schaefer, H. F., & Schleyer, P. V. R. (2009). Electrophile affinity: A reactivity measure for aromatic substitution. *Journal of the American Chemical Society*, *131*(41), 14722–14727. doi:10.1021/ja902194y

Kollman, P., McKelvey, J., Johansson, A., & Rothenberg, S. (1975). Theoretical studies of hydrogen-bonded dimers. Complexes involving HF, H2O, NH3, CH1, H2S, PH3, HCN, HNC, HCP, CH2NH, H2CS, H2CO, CH4, CF3,H, C2H2, C2H4, C6H6, F- and H3O+. *Journal of the American Chemical Society*, *97*(5), 955–965. doi:10.1021/ja00838a001

Lopez, X., Mujika, J. I., Blackburn, G. M., & Karplus, M. (2003). Alkaline hydrolysis of amide bonds: effect of bond twist and nitrogen pyramidalization. *The Journal of Physical Chemistry A*, *107*(13), 2304–2315. doi:10.1021/jp022014s

Morokuma, K. (1971). Molecular Orbital Studies of Hydrogen Bonds. III. C=O···H-O Hydrogen Bond in $H_2CO···H_2O$ and $H_2CO···2H_2O$. *The Journal of Chemical Physics*, *55*(3), 1236–1244. doi:10.1063/1.1676210

Mulliken, R. S. (1955). Electronic population analysis on LCAO MO molecular wave functions. I. *The Journal of Chemical Physics*, *23*(17), 1833–1840. doi:10.1063/1.1740588

Murray, J. S., Brinck, T., Grice, M. E., & Politzer, P. (1992). Correlations between molecular electrostatic potentials and some experimentally-based indices of reactivity. *Journal of Molecular Structure THEOCHEM, 256*, 29–45. doi:10.1016/0166-1280(92)87156-T

Murray, J. S., Lans, P., Brinck, T., & Politzer, P. (1991). Electrostatic potentials on the molecular surfaces of cyclic ureides. *Journal of Physical Chemistry, 95*(2), 844–848. doi:10.1021/j100155a066

Murray, J. S., & Politzer, P. (1988). Electrostatic potentials of amine nitrogens as a measure of the total electron-attracting tendencies of substituents. *Chemical Physics Letters, 152*(4-5), 364–370. doi:10.1016/0009-2614(88)80107-6

Murray, J. S., & Politzer, P. (1992). Relationship between solute hydrogen-bond acidity/basicity and the calculated electrostatic potential. *Journal of Chemical Research (S), 3*, 110–111.

Murray, J. S., & Politzer, P. J. (1991). Correlations between the solvent hydrogen-bond-donating parameter. alpha. and the calculated molecular surface electrostatic potential. Correlations between the solvent hydrogen-bond-donating parameter. alpha. and the calculated molecular surface electrostatic potential. *The Journal of Organic Chemistry, 56*(23), 6715–6717. doi:10.1021/jo00023a045

Murray, J. S., & Sen, K. D. (Eds.). (1996). *Molecular electrostatic potentials. Concepts and applications*. Amsterdam: Elsevier.

Naray-Szabo, G., & Ferenczy, G. (1995). Molecular electrostatics. *Chemical Reviews, 95*(4), 829–847. doi:10.1021/cr00036a002

Nesbitt, D. J. (1988). High-resolution infrared spectroscopy of weakly bound molecular complexes. *Chemical Reviews, 88*(6), 843–870. doi:10.1021/cr00088a003

Novakovic, S. B., Bogdanovic, G. A., Fraisse, B., Ghermani, N. E., Bouhmaida, N., & Spasojevic-de Bire, A. (2007). Topological features of both electron density and electrostatic potential in the bis(thiosemicarbazide)zinc(II) dinitrate complex. *The Journal of Physical Chemistry A, 111*(51), 13492–13505. doi:10.1021/jp075456i

Novakovic, S. B., Fraisse, B., Bogdanovic, G. A., & Spasojevic-de Bire, A. (2007). Experimental charge density evidence for the existence of high polarizability of the electron density of the free electron pairs on the sulfur atom of the thioureido group, $NH−C(=S)−NH_2$, induced by $N−H\cdots S$ and $C−H\cdots S$ interactions. *Crystal Growth & Design, 7*(2), 191–195. doi:10.1021/cg060497+

O'Hair, R. A. J., & Androutsopoulos, N. K. (2000). Can transacylation reactions occur via S_N2 pathways in the gas phase? Insights via ion−molecule reactions of N-acylpyridinium ions and *ab initio* calculations. *Organic Letters, 2*(17), 2567–2570. doi:10.1021/ol006060r

Parr, R. G., Szentpály, L. V., & Liu, S. (1999). Electrophilicity index. *Journal of the American Chemical Society, 121*(9), 1922–1924. doi:10.1021/ja983494x

Parr, R. G., & Yang, W. (1989). *Density functional theory of atoms and molecules*. New York: Oxford University Press.

Pearson, R. G. (1997). *Chemical hardness: Applications from molecules to Solids*. Weinheim, Germany: Wiley-VCH.

Politzer, P., & Truhlar, D. G. (Eds.). (1981). *Chemical applications of atomic and molecular electrostatic potentials*. New York: Plenum Press.

Rangelov, M. A., Vayssilov, G. N., Yomtova, V. M., & Petkov, D. D. (2005). Theoretical study of the o-OH participation in catechol ester ammonolysis. *Organic & Biomolecular Chemistry, 3*(5), 737–744. doi:10.1039/b417285j

Reed, A. E., Curtiss, L. A., & Weinhold, F. (1988). Intermolecular interaction from a natural bond orbital, donor–acceptor viewpoint. *Chemical Reviews, 88*(6), 899–926. doi:10.1021/cr00088a005

Sadlej-Sosnowska, N. (2007). Molecular similarity based on atomic electrostatic potential. *The Journal of Physical Chemistry A, 111*(43), 11134–11140. doi:10.1021/jp072748a

Sadlej-Sosnowska, N. (2007). Substituent active region – a gate for communication of substituent charge with the rest of a molecule: Monosubstituted benzenes. *Chemical Physics Letters, 447*(4-6), 192–196. doi:10.1016/j.cplett.2007.09.023

Sadlej-Sosnowska, N., & Murlowska, K. (2008). Similarity based on atomic electrostatic potential in heterocyclic molecules: Acidity of tetrazoles. *The Journal of Physical Chemistry A, 112*(40), 10017–10022. doi:10.1021/jp804100f

Scrocco, E., & Tomasi, J. (1973). *Topics in current chemistry*. Berlin: Springer-Verlag.

Sen, K. D., & Jorgersen, C. K. (Eds.). (1993). *Electronegativity, structure and bonding*. Berlin: Springer.

Sokolov, N. (1997). Electrostatic model of cooperative effects in hydrogen-bonded systems: cooperative effect of base and cation on the A---H stretching[1] vibrational frequency. *Journal of Molecular Structure, 436/437*, 201–211. doi:10.1016/S0022-2860(97)00210-X

Streitwieser, A. (1961). *Molecular orbital theory for organic chemists*. New York: Wiley.

Suresh, C. H., & Gadre, S. R. (1997). Electronic perturbations of the aromatic nucleus: Hammett constants and electrostatic potential topography. *The Journal of Organic Chemistry, 62*(8), 2625–2627. doi:10.1021/jo9616791

Suresh, C. H., & Gadre, S. R. (2007). Electrostatic potential minimum of the aromatic ring as a measure of substituent constant. *The Journal of Physical Chemistry A, 111*(4), 710–714. doi:10.1021/jp066917n

Taft, R. W. (1960). Sigma values from reactivities. *Journal of Physical Chemistry, 64*(12), 1805–1815. doi:10.1021/j100841a003

Tomasi, J., Bonaccorsi, R., & Cammi, R. (1990). *Theoretical methods of chemical bonding* (Maksic, Z. B., Ed.). *Vol. 3*). New York: Springer.

Toro-Labbe, A. (2006). *Theoretical aspects of chemical reactivity*. Amsterdam: Elsevier.

Um, I. H., Kim, K. H., Park, H. R., Fujio, M., & Tsuno, Y. (2004). Effects of amine nature and non-leaving group substituents on rate and mechanism in aminolyses of 2,4-dinitrophenyl X-substituted benzoates. *The Journal of Organic Chemistry, 69*(11), 3937–3942. doi:10.1021/jo049694a

Umeyama, H., & Morokuma, K. (1977). The origin of hydrogen bonding. An energy decomposition study. *Journal of the American Chemical Society, 99*(5), 1316–1332. doi:10.1021/ja00447a007

Van Bekkum, H., Verkade, P. E., & Wepster, B. M. (1959)... *Recueil des Travaux Chimique des Pays-Bas, 78*, 815. doi:10.1002/recl.19590781009

Wilson, E. B. (1962). Four dimensional electron density function. *The Journal of Chemical Physics, 36*(8), 2232–2233. doi:10.1063/1.1732864

Wladkowski, B. D., Wilbur, J. L., & Brauman, J. I. (1994). Intrinsic structure-reactivity relationships in gas-phase SN2 reactions: Identity exchange of substituted benzyl chlorides with chloride ion. *Journal of the American Chemical Society, 116*(6), 2471–2480. doi:10.1021/ja00085a030

Xiong, Y., & Zhan, C. (2006). Theoretical studies of the transition-state structures and free energy barriers for base-catalyzed hydrolysis of amides. *The Journal of Physical Chemistry A, 110*(46), 12644–12652. doi:10.1021/jp063140p

Yang, W., & Drueckhammer, D. G. (2000). Computational studies of the aminolysis of oxoesters and thioesters in aqueous solution. *Organic Letters, 2*(26), 4133–4136. doi:10.1021/ol0066911

Young, J. K., Pazhanisamy, S., & Schowen, R. L. (1984). Energetics of carbonyl addition and elimination. Kinetic manifestations of acyl substituent effects in anilide hydrolysis. *The Journal of Organic Chemistry, 49*(22), 4148–4152. doi:10.1021/jo00196a009

Zheng, W. X., Wong, N. B., & Li, W. K. (2004). Tri-*s*-triazine and its nitrogen isoelectronic equivalents: An ab initio study. *The Journal of Physical Chemistry A, 108*(52), 11721–11727. doi:10.1021/jp046909b

Zheng, W. X., Wong, N. B., & Tian, A. (2005). Anion–tri-s-triazine bonding: A case for anion recognition. *The Journal of Physical Chemistry A, 109*(9), 1926–1932. doi:10.1021/jp045827k

Zipse, H., Wang, L., & Houk, K. N. (1996). Polyether catalysis of ester aminolysis - a computational and experimental study. *Liebigs Annalen,* 1511–1522. doi:10.1002/jlac.199619961004

ADDITIONAL READING

Arnaut, L. G., Formosinho, S. J., & Burrows, H. (2006). *Chemical kinetics: From molecular structure to chemical reactivity.* Amsterdam: Elsevier.

Brown, R. S. (1999). *The amide linkage: selected structural aspects in chemistry, biochemistry, and materials science* (Breneman, C. M., Greenberg, A., & Liebman, J. F., Eds.). New York: Wiley Interscience.

Chattaraj, P. K., Sarkar, U., & Roy, D. R. (2006). Electrophilicity Index. *Chemical Reviews, 106*(6), 2065–2091. doi:10.1021/cr040109f

Chermette, H. J. (1999). Chemical reactivity indexes in density functional theory. *Journal of Computational Chemistry, 20*(1), 129–154. doi:10.1002/(SICI)1096-987X(19990115)20:1<129::AID-JCC13>3.0.CO;2-A

Geerlings, P., De Proft, F., & Langenaeker, W. (2003). Conceptual density functional theory. *Chemical Reviews, 103*(5), 1793–1874. doi:10.1021/cr990029p

Politzer, P., Murray, J. S., & Concha, M. (2002). The complementary roles of molecular surface electrostatic potentials and average local ionization energies with respect to electrophilic processes. *International Journal of Quantum Chemistry, 88*(1), 19–27. doi:10.1002/qua.10109

Sen, K. D. (Ed.). (2002). *Reviews of modern quantum chemistry.* Singapore: World Scientific.

Smith, M. B., & March, J. (2006). *March's advanced organic chemistry reactions, mechanisms and structure.* New York: Wiley. doi:10.1002/0470084960

Suresh, C. H., & Gadre, S. R. (1998). A novel electrostatic approach to substituent constants: Doubly substituted benzenes. *Journal of the American Chemical Society, 120*(28), 7049–7055. doi:10.1021/ja973105j

Chapter 14
An Epistemological Analysis of QSPR/QSAR Models

Jordi Vallverdú
Universitat Autònoma de Barcelona, Spain

ABSTRACT

Computer sciences have deeply changed the way by which we make science or produce knowledge. With the era of computers and the development of computer science, quantum chemists were among the first scientists to explore the potentialities of the new tool, and even to collaborate in its development. In this way, they also became participants in what many dubbed as the Second Instrumental Revolution in chemistry. Deeply involved into this research field, QSAR methods are powerful tools to create knowledge on toxicology and drug design, among others. There are several epistemological questions to be analyzed in order to understand the truth and scientific value of their research results (from in silico to wet laboratories and vice versa).

CHEMISTRY AND COMPUTING: A BRIEF HISTORICAL SKETCH

Computational Chemistry

Computer sciences have deeply changed the way by which we make science or produce knowledge, and this new change affects all different possible research fields (Vallverdu, 2009). When we look at

the history of chemistry and the specific moment in which computers came into, we should at the same time to explain the ideas that made possible to analyze chemistry with computers.

We must start explaining something elemental: before to have a computational chemistry, it was necessary to create a theoretical chemistry, that is, a mathematical description of chemistry. After, these mathematical models were automated and implemented on computers, leading to the computational chemistry.

DOI: 10.4018/978-1-60960-860-6.ch014

As part of the research in the toxicological field, in 1863 A.F.A. Cros noted his Ph.D. thesis that the relationship between the toxicity of primary aliphatic alcohols and their water solubility. After several improvements made by Dujardin-Beaumetz & Audigé (1875), who indicated that the toxicity of the alcohols mathematically followed their atomic composition, and Hans Horts Meyer & Fritz Baum (1899) discovered a relationship between the lipophilicity of general anaesthetics and their potency. They concluded that lipophilicity was the essential factor in the effectiveness of an anaesthetic. In 1916 Gilbert Newton Lewis proposed that chemical bonding - both the ionic and the homopolar type - could be explained in terms of shared electron pairs (Gavroglu & Simões, 1994). From Lewis research chemistry began its own quest for the elucidation of the nature of chemical bond and bonding.

But quantum mechanics was the key to understand this process. In 1925, Werner Heisenberg published the first paper on quantum mechanics (when we was only 23 years old!). Just one year later, Erwin Schrödinger wrote a series of papers published in the *Annalen der Physik*, where he created the basis for the future computational chemistry, with the great contribution of the so-called 'Schrödinger equation': $H\Psi = E\Psi$. This equation and his several consequences provided a method for calculating how molecules behave. Two years later, in 1927, the Heitler-London paper opened a new era in chemistry, after offering a complete theory on atom bonding, in a German view (reductionist) opposite to that of the Americans Mulliken and Pauling (inclinated towards semi-empirical methods) (Gavroglu & Simões, 1994). The next important step was made in the 1930s, by Nikolai Vasilyevich Lazarev in St. Petersburg who first demonstrated that different physiological and toxicological effects of molecules were correlated with their oil–water partition coefficient through formal mathematical equations in the form: $\log C = a \log_{P_{oil/water}} + b$ (Lipnick & Filov, 1992; Devillers, 2009). Louis

Plack Hammet, in 1935, gave rise to the so-called 'σ-π' culture, in the delineation of substituent effects on organic reactions. In this historical moment, at the 1930's end, there were different communities working on quantum chemistry: the pragmatic or trusters in rough semi-empirical approximations (Americans) and the mathematicians (British). The first generation of British quantum chemists, which included J.E. Lennard Jones (1894-1954), D. Hartree (1897-1958) and C.A. Coulson (1910-1974), perceived the problems of quantum chemistry first and foremost as problems in calculation, and by devising novel calculation methods tried to bring quantum chemistry within the realm of applied mathematics (Gavroglu & Simões, 1994, 2002). For the different epistemological approaches to chemistry views of quantum mechanics (valence bond theory –also called the Heitler-London-Slater-Pau method- and molecular orbital theory – the Hund-Mulliken method) read Shaik & Hiberty (2004). As happened also previously with molecular biology, physics came like an elephant into the chemists' culture. In this moment appeared a methodological question: the classic approach of modern chemistry, a 'paper & pencil' discipline, lost its visualization advantages when quantum chemistry appeared as an inherently non-visualizable field. Computers could change in a future this situation, helping human experts to work with fittest cognitive tools to create knowledge.

One decade later, Linus Pauling wrote his 1945 book *The Nature of the Chemical Bond*, affirming that should be possible to describe structural chemistry without the use of advanced mathematics, something that made much easier to apply computers to the chemical analysis (Goodman 2001). In fact, in the 1940's appeared the electronic computers that made possible to elaborate wave equations for complex atomic systems. ENIAC in the USA and Colossus in the UK were the first machines able to compute fast and powerfully large amounts of data (at least for the standards of that moment). As Ana

Simões (2007) has clearly explained, with the era of computers and the development of computer science, quantum chemists were among the first scientists to explore the potentialities of the new tool, and even to collaborate in its development. In this way, they also became participants in what many dubbed as the Second Instrumental Revolution in chemistry (Reinhardt, 2006).

Anyhow, it was in the 1970's when started the modern era of computational chemistry (Ma & Nussinov, 2004). The crucial point was the analysis of the methylene molecule. And in the next decades, with the new supercomputers, parallel processing and personal but powerful computing, was born the modern computational chemistry. Even if the definition of computational chemistry is somewhat arbitrary and subjective, (Ma, 1995), it deals with the more advanced ideas on chemistry research, always under an *in silico* experimental chemistry paradigm. With the advent of high performance computers, different *ab initio* and semi-empirical quantum-chemical methods have been implemented in theoretical drug design. However, many *ab initio* quantum chemical calculations are still not practicable in QSAR and modelling studies in view of the large computational requirements of these calculations. Instead of *ab initio* methods, semi-empirical quantum-chemical methods are often used for the calculation of many electronic descriptors of molecules and their constituent atoms. The most commonly used descriptor are different kinds of charge densities, atomic and molecular orbital (HOMO, LUMO) energies, σ and π orbital electron densities, σ- and π-bond orders, free-valences, electrophilic-, nucleophilic- and radical-superdelocalizabilities, atom-atom and molecular polarizabilities, dipole moments and a variety of energy indices. (Prabhakar & Gupta, 2008).

QSAR's History

Although exists some authors, previously quoted, who made introductory contributions into the

toxicological properties of substances, was in 1964 when Hansch and Fujita wrote the seminal paper of QSAR technique. They provided the method to make possible to analyze drug actions through a Quantitative Structure Activity Relationship (henceforth, QSAR). It is assumed that the geometric/steric/electronic structure of a molecule is directly related to its properties (physical, chemical and biological). The Hansch & Fujiya approach combined the hydrophobic constants with Hammet's electronic constants to yield the linear Hansch equation and its many extended forms (Gramatica, 2008).

Nevertheless there is an interesting and strong debate about which were the founders of modern QSAR techniques (Martin, 2001). The truth is that there was a second important approach: the Free-Wilson analysis (Kubinyi, 2002). Working on an independent research, Free and Wilson formulated a mathematical model to describe biological activities without considering its physicochemical properties, but the presence or absence of a certain constituent in a certain position. Easier to apply than Hansch-Fujita method but al the same time, more restricted (many parameters and less degrees of freedom in the statistical analysis).

Anyhow, both methods, Hansch-Fujita and Free-Wilson can be mixed to obtain a better method, creating a 'mixed approach'. At the end, both models were based in linear regression analyses for correlating biological activities of congeneric series of molecules with their physicochemical properties.

After this basic method, appeared thousands of Hansch-Fujiya's variations. In the early 1980s Konemann & Veith developed multi-class-based, hydrophobic-dependent models for industrial organic chemical, creating a strong revival of QSAR paradigm. The introduction of Partial Least Squares (PLS) regression analysis improved the classic Hansch-Fujita/Free-Wilson linear models and led to the extended 3D QSAR under the the Comparative Molecular Field Analysis (CoMFA) approach. Between the 1960's and 1980's were created some of the leading journals on the field[1], like: 1. Journal of Medicinal Chemistry (J. Med. Chem.) 1959; 2. QSAR & Combinatorial Science (QSAR Comb. Sci.) 1982; 3. Quantitative Structure-Activity Relationships (Quant. Struct.-Act. Relat.) 1982, 4. Quantitative Structure-Activity Relationships 1982-1997 (Quant. Struct.-Act. Relat.), 5. Journal of Chemometrics (J. Chemom.) 1987; 6. Journal of Chemometrics 1987-1995 (J. Chemom.), 7. Journal of Chemical Information and Modeling (J. Chem. Inf. Model.) 1961; 8. Journal of Chemical Information and Computer Sciences (J. Chem. Inf. Comput. Sci.); 9. Machine Learning (Machine Learning) 1986 and 10. Mini-Reviews in Medicinal Chemistry (Mini Reviews in Med. Chem.) 2001.

Finally, in the 1990s Artificial Neural Networks bursted on to the QSAR stage helping to the evolution of QSAR techniques and applications. In 1997, Hopfinger and his co-workers proposed the 4D-QSAR formalism, which includes the conformational flexibility and the freedom of alignment by ensemble averaging in the conventional three dimensional descriptors found in traditional 3D-QSAR methods. Thus, the "fourth dimension" of the method is ensemble sampling the spatial features of the members of a training set. Since 1997, the complexity and sophistication of QSAR models has been increasing constantly offering new dimensions methods. As a consequence, 3D-QSAR has been 'replaced' (or *updated*, or *increased in complexity…*) by 4D, 5D or even 6D-QSAR models. The truth is that 3-QSAR models refer to the real dimensions of our reality, while 4D, 5D, 6D…models include further dimensions that are more closely related to data characterizations that to spatial dimensions. An example: 5D-QSAR allows the model to include induced fit, which occurs during the binding of many ligands. Consequently, 5D-QSAR method allows for multiple conformation, orientation, and protonation state representation of ligand molecules. 5D-QSAR, due to the fact that model selection may vary throughout the entire simulation, yields less biased results than 4D-QSAR where only a single induced- fit model can be evaluated at a time (Vedani & Dobler, 2002).

While older methods draw on a richer variety of molecular and property descriptors than higher-dimension models, these latest are more automatable, and this characteristics increases efficiency and allows the processing of larger data sets. All these facts have made possible the existence of very successful Computer-Aided/Assisted Drug Design (CADD) or Computer-Aided/Assisted Molecular Design (CAMD) activities.

Finally, we should remark that the new *in silico* e-Science research paradigm applied to computational chemistry has also made possible the transnational research on line. For example, the International Virtual Collaboratory of Computational Chemical Toxicology puts together the efforts of investigations located in the USA (UNC-Chapel Hill, H. Zhu & A. Tropsha), France (University of Louis Pasteur, D. Fourches & A. Varnek), Italy (University of Insubria, E. Papa & P. Gramatica), Sweden (University of Kalmar, T. Öberg), Germany (Munich Information Center for Protein Sequences/Virtual Computational Chemistry Laboratory, I. Tetko) and Canada (University of British Columbia, A. Cherkasov).

QSAR's Taxonomy in a Nutshell

After our short historical analysis of QSAR techniques we are able now to provide something like the formal taxonomy of QSAR techniques, based on the number of dimensions implied in QSAR techniques[2]:

0D-QSAR (Classical): uses molecular descriptors such as molecular weight, no. of atoms, no. of non-H atoms, no. of bonds, no. of heteroatoms, no. of multiple bonds, no. of aromatic bonds, no. of functional groups, no. of rings, no. of circuits, no. of H-bond donors, no. of H-bond acceptors, chemical composition.

1D-QSAR: Affinity correlates with pKa, logP, etc.

2D-QSAR: Affinity correlates with a structural pattern (e.g., chemical connectivity).

3D-QSAR: Affinity correlates with the three-dimensional structure. Receptor modeling: QSAR based on the interactions of the ligands with a 3D receptor surrogate.

4D-QSAR: As with 3D, but with multiple representations of ligand conformation/orientation.

5D-QSAR: As with 4D, but with multiple representations of induced-fit scenarios.

6D-QSAR: As with 5D, but with multiple representations of solvation models.

Nevertheless, the previously summarized QSAR techniques could be also organized in two major groups according to their receptor properties (Andrade, 2010):

a. *receptor-independent (RI) QSAR analyses.* Either the geometry of the receptor is not available, or it is neglected in the QSAR analysis because of uncertainty in the receptor geometry and/or ligand binding mode. This group included the "classical" (zero-dimensional), one-dimensional (1D), two-dimensional (2D), three-dimensional (3D), and four-dimensional QSAR approaches. The calculated descriptors are recognizable molecular features, such as atom and molecular counts, molecular weight, sum of atomic properties (0D-QSAR); fragment counts (1D-QSAR); topological descriptors (2D-QSAR); geometrical, atomic coordinates, or energy grid descriptors (3D-QSAR); and the combination of atomic coordinates and sampling of conformations (RI-4D-QSAR)

b. *receptor-dependent (RD) QSAR analyses.* In the RD-QSAR analysis, models are derived from the 3D structure of the multiple ligand-receptor complex conformations. This approach provides an explicit simulation of the induced-fit process, using the structure of the ligand-receptor complex, where both ligand and receptor are allowed to be completely flexible by the use of molecular dynamics (MD) simulation. RD-QSAR is used to gather binding interaction energies, as descriptors, from the interaction between the analog molecules and the receptor.

THE EPISTEMOLOGY OF QSAR CHEMISTRY

From an epistemological point of view, QSAR methods try to understand chemical structures selecting their outstanding chemical descriptors and designing predictive computational models which find connections between structure and property or activity. After running the computational models (the virtual screening) and checking the results with a real chemical database, some compounds will be labelled as correct hits while others will be declared as inactive. It is something like a marriage of convenience between simulation and 'reality'. Nevertheless, we are never sure about the meaning and extension of our 'reality' and if we have chosen the best descriptors of the structures we are trying to know. In the middle of this process, we have also to deal with statistical correlations. So, perhaps computational chemistry, and specially QSAR methods, is the most interesting topic of research for philosophers of chemistry or computer sciences. To be honest, theorists of science have been only interested on physics (initially) and biology (later), while chemistry has not been a topic of intense research. Affortunately, there is a new change on this dynamics (Bhushan & Rosenfeld, 2000; Burguete, 2006).

Besides of a new interest of theoreticians of science into computational chemistry, there is also an epistemological turn towards visualization technologies (Vallverdú, 2010a), because *seeing, thinking* and *knowing* have common roots. Huge amounts of data must be analyzed and processed, and then, the virtual model reaches a different level of abstraction, but it is also a model. The crucial question is about the accuracy of the similitudes (and the successful final research) between the virtual model and the real world, not about the physical o digital nature of the studied object. The use on imaging and processing computational tools (data mining, expert systems, genetic algorithms,…) led not only to a direct animation, but also to the visualization of the *hidden* properties under real analysis, properties that would not be accessible to classical experimental observation. We can think in a certain way because of our visualization (smart) machines. Therefore, cognition is not a human-centered process, but also a machine-centered process. Although they are outside out bodies, contemporary visualization tools constitute part of our thoughts. The representation of data graphically as a means of gaining understanding and insight into the data, allows the researcher to gain insight into the system that is studied in ways previously impossible.

According to the scale of the analyzed objects, computational chemistry experts tend to use certain methods: *Ab Initio* for small systems of atoms, Semi-Empirical for medium-sized systems (hundreds of atoms) and Molecular Mechanics for large systems (thousands of atoms). Obviously, the size of the sample is not the only aspect implied into this choice but is a very important one. Only *ab initio* method is fully involved into computational quantum chemistry, while the other two deal with the formulation of analytical expressions for the properties of molecules and their reactions. Nevertheless, semi-empirical methods use approximations from previously existing experimental data to provide the input into the mathematical model and, therefore, they are also using quantum physics for their research purposes.

The epistemological problem, here, is that the kind of research and results we will obtain will differ according to the kind of experiment we are working to. The instruments that we use to find QSAR/QSPR properties are at the same time constrained by their specific methodological characteristics. Therefore, the observer modifies the observed/simulated/calculated event of the nature. Every QSAR method has simultaneously *pro* and *contra* skills. The trust into the reliability of the obtained results will depend on the degrees of confidence that the specialized community attributes to that technique. It is also true that, in order to be useful, a model and its target have to be isomorphic or, at least, partially isomorphic.

Reality and Experiments

Another important debate present into QSAR recent history is about the ontological role of QSAR techniques. By 'ontology' I mean "is the philosophical study of the nature of being, existence or reality *in general*, as well as the basic categories of being/existence/reality and their relations", and not the very much different computational meaning (a formal representation of knowledge as a set of concepts within a domain, and the relationships between those concepts). Ma & Nussinov (2004) have explained it very clearly: "Thus, the question arises as to whether computational biology today is in the similar state to that of computational chemistry 30 years ago: namely *interpret* rather than *discover* biological facts". Because of the deep relationships between computational chemistry and quantum mechanics (remember the case of the methylene molecule[3], and the success of theory *against* experiments), computational approaches acquired an epistemological status equivalent to that of experiments. Ontologically, both methodologies wet & in silico chemistry, were discovering the real truth of chemical molecules. That is, their ontological skills were co-equivalent. Despite of some problems we will analyze in next sections, there is no place now to affirmations like made by Alberte Pullman in the 1970's (Nye, 1993): 'While it is certainly indispensable that theoretical chemist constantly try to improve the values of the size they calculated and more and more approach exact energy values... quantum chemistry risk giving the impression that its essential goal is *reproducing by uncertain methods known results*, in contrast to all other sciences whose goal is to use well-defined methods for the research of unknown truths'.

Models

While talking on parsimony, the statistician G.E. Box told in his 1976 paper "Science and Statistics", page 792: **"Since all models are wrong the scientist cannot obtain a "correct" one by excessive elaboration. On the contrary, following William of Occam he should seek an economical description of natural phenomena. Just as the ability to devise simple but evocative models is the signature of the great scientist so overelaboration and overparameterization is often the mark of mediocrity"**. I certainly recommend the reading of this original paper, full of clever as well as critic ideas about the role of statistics into reaching scientific knowledge (and the better training for statisticians, Baskerville, 1981).

The truth is that the question of models is one of the most important epistemological aspects of philosophy of science. And more, since computers made possible to implement complex models into machines creating powerful simulations.

Statistics and Models

As remarks Kubinyi (2002), already in 1972 Costello & Topliss pointed out that the enormous number of variables and tested variables increased enormously the risk of chance correlations. Soon after Hansch method existed a few number of variables (log P, π, hydrophobicity values for f for lipophilicity some $\sigma/F/R$ scales for electronic properties, molar refractivity values as a measure of dispersion forces and E, values as steric parameters) but in the next years appeared a huge number of QSAR parameters, until 3000 (topological, connectivity, electrotopological state, WHIM,

EVA, BCUT,....). It was a nightmare situation where the whole QSAR approach could be collapsed by its own epistemological uncertainties. Trying to solve these problems, in 1973 Unger & Hansch defined 'good practice in QSAR', here summarized:

1. select independent variables.
2. justify the choice of the variables by statistical procedures.
3. apply the parsimony principle.
4. have a large number of objects, as compared to the number of variables
5. try to find a qualitative model of physicochemical and biochemical significance.

After this first attempt appeared several 'Best Practices in QSAR', one of the latest being that by Tropsha (2010), shown in Figure 1.

Again, quoting Box (1976), we must see that statistics has had two big problems: *Cookbookery* and *Mathematistry*. Cookbookery is a tendency to force all problems into the molds of one or two routine techniques, insufficient thought being given to the real objectives of the investigation or to the relevance of the assumptions implied by the imposed methods. On the other hand, mathematistry is characterized by development of theory for theory's sake, which since it seldom touches down with practice, has a tendency to redefine the problem rather than solve it. Typically, there has once been a statistical problem with scientific relevance but this has long since been lost sight of. Come back again the debate about the ontological and epistemological nature of computational chemistry. Hugo Kubinyi has considered seriously the statistical problems present into QSAR methods and has discussed them in several of his academic conferences[4] (Kubinyi, 2003). From his point of view, QSAR experts can derive good models (as statistically valid models), these models have internal predictivity (Q^2 values) without using scrambled or random data, and the total amount of variables implied are not so much.

Figure 1. Predictive QSAR modeling workflow (Adapted from Tropsha, 2010, p.479)

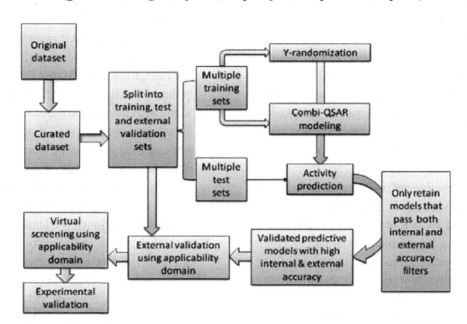

On the other hand, these models cannot predict a test set (r^2_{pred} value) nor offer any relationship between internal and external variables. This later fact was early noticed by Unger & Hansch (1973), when they wrote: "One must rely heavily on statistics in formulating a quantitative model but, at each critical step in constructing the model, one must set aside statistics and ask questions.... without a qualitative perspective one is apt to generate *statistical unicorns*, beasts that exist on paper but not in reality.... it has recently become all too clear that one can correlate a set of dependent variables using random numbers as dependent variables"(the emphasis is mine). Nice metaphor: statistical unicorns. Kubinyi (2003) suggest a possible solution focused on crossvalidation tools.

Error & Knowledge

There is another important aspect, the importance of cleaning data and the control of error rates (ranging in public as well as in private databases from 0.1 to 3.4%, according to Young, Martin,

Venkatapathy & Harten, 2008). Very recently, Hugo Kubinyi (2010) described an exhaustive list of possible statistical problems that we can find in QSAR studies: (1) inappropriate biological data; (2) wrong scaling of biological data, (3) data from different labs, (4) different binding modes, (5) mixed data (e.g. oral absorption and bioavailability), (6) different mechanism of action (e.g. toxicity data), (7) too few data points, (8) too many single points, (9) lack of chemical variation, (10) clustered data, (11) small variance of y values, (12) systematic error/s in y, (13) too large errors in y values, (14) outliers / wrong values, (15) wrong model selection, (16) inappropriate x variables, (17) too many x variables (Topliss): a) in the model selection and b) in the final model, (18) x variable scaling in CoMFA fields (19) interrelated x variables (20) singular matrix, (21) elimination of variables that are significant only with others, (22) insignificant model (F test), (23) insignificant x variables (t test), (24) no qualitative (biophysical) model, (25) no causal relationship (the storks), (26) extrapolation too far outside of observation space, (27) no validation method applied, (28) wrong validation method,.....

There is a huge list of methodological errors that should be fixed to obtain better QSAR models, as have pointed Golbraikh & Tropsha (2002), Johnson (2002), Maggiora (2006), Doweyko (2008), Dearden et al. (2009) or Scior et al. (2009). We should also take our attention to some statistical problems of QSAR methods:

a. *The Kubinyi paradox (*External vs. Internal Predictivity*)*: it is applied to a behavior observed by a number of workers in the field, and it was most prominently Hugo Kubinyi who coined its name and defined the problem with the next statement "the models that fit the best retrospectively tend to predict the worst prospectively". The fact is that, in general, there is no relationship between internal and external predictivity: high internal predictivity may result in low external predictivity and vice versa. The way to solve these problems is return to the recommendations of Topliss, Unger and Hansch to include only reasonable variables, selected from small numbers, and to generate only models that have a sound biophysical background.

b. **Predictability:** One of the keystones of modern science is the predictability power. Without it, the value of science, beyond the technological transformational capacities, would be nothing better than any other human activity. But science is the best human project to produce and predict knowledge. Conventional QSAR examines the structure of a drug or natural ligand without including interactions with the receptor, and only about half 3D-QSAR models published in the last decade made "reasonable" predictions about test compounds not used to create the model (Doweyko, 2008).

c. **Verification and Validation (V&V):** V&V is a fascinating moment of scientific prac-

tices, with strong relationships with epistemology (Maibaum, 2005). It is also one of the hottest topics in QSAR research, because it is also related to the access to large and open datasets. Besides, as Mager & Mager (1992) point, the validation of QSAR is a troublesome activity. Basically because of the lack of agreement inside the QSAR community about the meaning of the word 'validation'. And the point is that this problem relies not only in the statistical debate but also in the biological and physicochemical aspects of QSAR relationships. Under this triadic approach, the reproducibility and design of the experiments gains a more conflictive epistemological nature (as you can observe when you look towards the history of the risk assessment techniques).

And Golbraikh & Tropsha (2002) argued that only a small fraction of "predictive" training set models with LOO $q2 > 0.6$ is capable of making accurate predictions ($r2 > 0.6$) for the test sets. And LOO $q2$ is perhaps the most popular QSAR validation criteria. Often, a high value of this statistical characteristic ($q2 > 0.5$) is considered as a proof of the high predictive ability of the model. But this assumption is generally incorrect.

SELECTING QSPR/QSAR MODELS

In philosophy of science exists a concept that explains a basic debate into QSAR theories: the infradetermination of theories. According to this thesis, for any corpus of 'empirical evidence' there are always several theories compatible with it, and hence, selecting one of them will not be a question of logic alone, but will be based on other kinds of values (epistemic, social, or whatever). It is a very simple and powerful idea: the evidence available to us at a given time may be insufficient to determine what beliefs we should hold in response to it. The debate among statisticians about bayesian and frequentist approaches, or in AI experts between top-down and bottom-up approaches are examples of this fact (Vallverdú, 2010b). Nevertheless, infradetermination does not promotes relativism neither subjectivism. Philosophically, it has been called the 'Duhem-Quine Thesis'. The Duhem–Quine thesis (also called the Duhem–Quine problem) is that it is impossible to test a scientific hypothesis in isolation, because an empirical test of the hypothesis requires one or more background assumptions (also called *auxiliary assumptions* or *auxiliary hypotheses*). The hypothesis in question is by itself incapable of making predictions. Instead, the consequences of the hypothesis typically rest on background assumptions from which to derive predictions. This prevents a theory from becoming conclusively falsified through empirical means if the background assumptions are not proven (since background assumptions sometimes involve one or more scientific theories)[5].

When we are faced to QSAR methodologies the problem of infradetermination arises without any kind of doubt. So many possible combinatorial choices of basic approaches (1D-6D-QSAR), mathematical methods, variables selected, databases, biological targets (at least in toxicology, with the consequent intraspecies analogies…), makes very difficult, or at least nearly impossible, to find a common agreement about the best experiment design to obtain more reliable results.

Let me show you an example, based on mathematical models (Liu & Long, 2009). The mathematical tools used in QSAR studies, such as regression tools have been developing very quickly. Multiple Linear Regression, Partial Least Squares, Neural Networks or Support Vector Machine have been upgraded by improving the kernel algorithms or by combining them with other methods. At the same time have been added new techniques, like Gene Expression Programming, Project Pursuit Regression or Local Lazy Regression. When we talk about the advantages of these methods appear into the scene non-epistemic values such as 'simplicity', 'beauty', 'time consuming',… Do we really can show that parsimony in QSAR methods is a clear and objective way to choose among theories? Every QSAR method has inherent restrictions about datasets, calculation speed, kind of usable/significant descriptors, linearity/non-linearity capacities, data over/underfiting, radial basis functions choice (linear. Cubic, thin plate spline, Gaussian, multi-quadratic, inverse multi-quadratic,…), training times (for NN), reproducibility, complexity of produced equations, predictive ability..and so on! There is no a definitive and overall agreed way to choose among all these possibilities. And these are only basic methodological possibilities. Once chosen the specific methodology, the debate is reproduced at a different level: the design of the specific method. Even decide which is the 'simplest' solution' will led us to a long debate that surely will finish without general agreement among QSAR experts. Under this light, the power of QSAR techniques is that inferred from its successes, practical as well a s theoretical. Prediction, theory support, 'easiness' of application and coherence are values that make QSAR techniques so powerful in our days. All the differences in QSAR methods reflect the richness of this research field, its dynamical nature. And being a intensive computational discipline, QSAR methods are under the pressure and benefits of the increasingly complexity of computer machines and techniques. Computer software is the best example of this incessant activity: ADAPT, ATMOL, CODESA, SMILES, GAUSSIAN, IBMO, DRAGON, MolConnZ, POLYATOM...are diverse and possible ways to approach to same thing: the scientific truth. And, definitively, QSAR techniques are closer to chemical truth decade after decade, despite of several paradoxes, statistical problems or methodological disagreement into the field. A simple statement: if they were not useful (and true), surely not be applied by industries, a research sector without too many interest in pure theoretical research. Combined with wet experiments, but even as computational experiments,

QSAR methods are being useful for checking previous results, designing new experiments and calculations and to make possible to study some elusive experimental activities. Ab initio methods, for example, are better and powerful, more accurate, make better predictions.

CHEAP, FAST & ETHICAL? SOME SOCIAL REMARKS ABOUT QSPR/QSAR MODELS

QSAR methods have been successfully accepted not only by drug, food and chemistry industries but also for the civil society. The reason of this overwhelming acceptation is that that kind of computational method has reduced and replaced in the toxicological methods the animal testing.

A few months ago, Gilman D. Veith, the founder and president of the non-profit International QSAR Foundation (IQF: http://www.qsari.org/) received the Henry J. Heimlich Award for Innovative Medicine. According to Gilman, and the IQF own definition: "The International QSAR Foundation is the only non-profit research organization devoted solely to creating alternative methods for identifying chemical hazards without further laboratory testing. We develop, implement and support new QSAR technologies for use in regulation, research and education or wherever testing animals with chemicals is now required". But this is not a strong trend in the USA, but also in Europe. The recent Lisbon Treaty (was signed by the EU members states on 13 December 2007, and entered into force on 1 December 2009) includes as a primary goal the animal welfare, and it does mean that QSAR methods have a future in a life-protecting society.

Beyond social attitudes towards animal testing and the society of risk (including in this concept the risk assessment debates), there is also another important factor moral in QSAR studies: the privatization of knowledge. Patents and software are the keystones of this non-epistemic debate.

The new field of chemblaics is a good example of this new social framework[6]. Chemblaics is the science that uses computers to solve problems in chemistry, biochemistry and related fields. The big difference between chemblaics and areas such as chemoinformatics, chemometrics, computational chemistry, etc, is that chemblaics only uses *open source software, open data, and open standards*, making experimental results reproducible and validatable. The copyleft culture arrives also to the computational chemistry. It is a fact that the causes of this new trend are eminently conceptual and social, but at the same time, a different methodological approach can led to new ways to produce knowledge. On the other side, QSAR patents can stop as well as protect (and make possible its related research industry) QSAR progress. The debate among QSAR developers should be deeply analyzed by that community in the next years, when QSAR implementation will be still greater and extended among industries and academic research departments. Concerns over intellectual property hinder several QSAR attempts. Bayram believes, however, that such concerns can be overcome[7]. "Public databases should have a filter mechanism to anonymize the data. Compound names can be stripped and only the descriptor values along with the bioactivity values would be made public." In some ways, intellectual property protectionism reflects the fact that QSAR has come a long way. "Each step of the way has been paved with powerful mathematical tools designed to maximize the potential of the model to predict the activities or properties of novel molecules," Doweyko says. As in the past, the next steps will be defined by an unexpected combination of imagination and insight".

CONCLUSION: WHAT GOOD ARE QSAR MODELS?

From in silico to in vitro and in vivo models, QSAR techniques must deal with an increasing complexity and uncertainty. But, at the same time, QSAR models are the best, cheap and fast way to create scientific knowledge on quantitative structure-activity-relationships. Toxicology and drug design are the fields in which QSAR has made greater contributions. Nevertheless we must ask ourselves: have been all these results only a methodological way to obtain data or QSAR methods are also deeply involved into a better and new scientific methodology? From my humble point of view, QSAR techniques embrace a new approach to scientific practices and their epistemology: they are a new and powerful epistemological space situated in between classic wet experiments and full *in silico* simulations. Van Drie (2007) talks about a growth of CADD (Computer-assisted drug design (CADD), also called computer-assisted molecular design (CAMD)) QSAR studies in the next 20 years. Anyhow, there is a successful future for QSAR in the new paradigm of e-science if we are brave enough to face with the several conceptual debates listed in this chapter that make QSAR techniques even more strong. Computational minds will reach deeper knowledge.

ACKNOWLEDGMENT

Part of this research has been developed under the main activities of the TECNOCOG research group (UAB) into Cognition and Technological Environments, "El diseño del espacio en entornos de cognición distribuida: plantillas y affordances", MCI [FFI2008-01559/FISO], funded by MEC (Spain)].

REFERENCES

Andrade, C. H. (2010). 4D-QSAR: Perspectives in Drug Design. *Molecules (Basel, Switzerland)*, *15*, 3281–3294. doi:10.3390/molecules15053281

Baskerville, J. C. (1981). A Systematic Study of the Consulting Literature as an Integral Part of Applied Training in Statistics. *The American Statistician*, *35*(3), 121–123. doi:10.2307/2683974

Bhushan, N., & Rosenfeld, S. (Eds.). (2000). *Of Minds and Molecules: New Philosophical Perspectives on Chemistry*. Oxford, UK: Oxford University Press.

Box, G. E. P. (1976). Science and Statistics. *Journal of the American Statistical Association*, *71*, 791–799. doi:10.2307/2286841

Cros, A. F. A. (1863). *Action de l'alcool amylique sur l'organisme*. Ph.D. Thesis, University of Strasbourg, Strasbourg.

Dearden, J. C. (2009). How not to develop a QSAR/QSPR relationship. *SAR and QSAR in Environmental Research*, *20*, 241–266. doi:10.1080/10629360902949567

Devillers, J. (Ed.). (2009). *Endocrine Disruption Modeling, QSAR in Environmental and Health Sciences*. New York: CRC Press.

Doweyko, A. M. (2008). QSAR: dead or alive? *Journal of Computer-Aided Molecular Design*, *22*, 81–89. doi:10.1007/s10822-007-9162-7

Dujardin-Beaumetz & Audige. (1875). Recherches Expérimentales sur la puissance toxique des Alcools. *Comptes Rendus de l'Academie des Sciences*, *81*, 192.

Free, S. M. Jr, & Wilson, J. W. (1964). A Mathematical Contribution to Structure Activity Studies. *Journal of Medicinal Chemistry*, *7*, 395–399. doi:10.1021/jm00334a001

Gavroglu, K., & Simões, A. (1994). The Americans, the Germans, and the beginnings of quantum chemistry: The confluence of diverging traditions. *Historical Studies in the Physical Sciences*, *25*(1), 47–110.

Gavroglu, K., & Simões, A. (2002). Preparing the Ground for Quantum Chemistry in Great Britain: The Work of the Physicist R. H. Fowler and the Chemist N. V. Sidgwick. *British Journal for the History of Science, 35*(2), 187–212. doi:10.1017/S0007087402004673

Golbraikh & Tropsha. (2002). Beware of q2! *Journal of Molecular Graphics & Modelling, 20*, 269–276. doi:10.1016/S1093-3263(01)00123-1

Goodman, J. M. (2001). World Champion Chemists: People versus Computers. In Thompson, J. M. T. (Ed.), *Visions of the Future: Chemistry and Life Science* (pp. 43–57). Cambridge, UK: Cambridge University Press.

Gramatica, P. (2008). *A short history of QSAR evolution*. Electronic material downloadable at: http://www.qsarworld.com/ Temp_Fileupload/Shorthistoryofqsar.pdf

Hammet, L. P. (1935). Some relations between reaction rates and equilibrium Constants. *Chemical Reviews, 17*(1), 125–136. doi:10.1021/cr60056a010

Hansch, C., & Fujita, T. (1964). ρ-σ-π Analysis. A method for the correlation of biological activity and chemical structure. *Journal of the American Chemical Society, 86*, 1616–1625. doi:10.1021/ja01062a035

Heisenberg, W. (1925). Über quantentheorestische Umdeutung kinematischer und mechanischer Beziehungen. *Zeitschrift fur Physik, 33*, 879. doi:10.1007/BF01328377

Heitler, W., & London, F. (1927). Wechselwirkung neutraler Atome und homopolare Bindung nach der Quantenmechanik. *Zeitschrift fur Physik, 44*, 455. doi:10.1007/BF01397394

Hopfinger, A. (1997). Construction of 3D-QSAR models using the 4D-QSAR analysis Formalism. *Journal of the American Chemical Society, 119*, 10509–10524. doi:10.1021/ja9718937

Johnson, S. R. (2008). The trouble with QSAR (or how I learned to stop worrying and embrace fallacy). *Journal of Chemical Information and Modeling, 48*, 25–26. doi:10.1021/ci700332k

Kokowski (ed.) *The Global and the Local: The History of Science and the Cultural Integration of Europe*. Proceedings of the 2nd ICESHS (Cracow, Poland, September 6–9, 2006), 943-949.

Kubinyi, H. (2002). From Narcosis to Hyperspace: The History of QSAR. *Quantitative Structure-Activity Relationships, 21*, 348–356. doi:10.1002/1521-3838(200210)21:4<348::AID-QSAR348>3.0.CO;2-D

Kubinyi, H. (2003). 2D QSAR Models. Hansch and Free–Wilson Analyses. In Wilfried Langenaeker, H., Patrick, B., & Tollenaere, J. P. (Eds.), *Computational Medicinal Chemistry for Drug Discovery*. New York: CRC Press. doi:10.1201/9780203913390.ch21

Kubinyi, H. (2010). *The Long Road from QSAR to Virtual Screening*. Lecture at the 18th EuroQSAR, Rhodes, Greece, September 2010.

Lipnick, R. L., & Filov, V. A. (1992). Nikolai Vasilyevich Lazarev, toxicologist and pharmacologist, comes in from the cold. *Trends in Pharmacological Sciences, 13*, 56–60. doi:10.1016/0165-6147(92)90024-Z

Liu, P., & Wei Long, W. (2009). Current Mathematical Methods Used in QSAR/QSPR Studies. *International Journal of Molecular Sciences, 10*(5), 1978–1998. doi:10.3390/ijms10051978

Ma, B. (1995). *The Philosophy of Computational Quantum Chemistry*. Ph. Dissertation, University of Georgia.

Ma, B., & Nussinov, R. (2004). From computational quantum chemistry to computational biology: experiments and computations are (full) partners. *Physical Biology, 1*, 23–26. doi:10.1088/1478-3967/1/4/P01

Mager, H., & Mager, P. P. (1992). Validation of QSARs: Some Reflections. *Quantitative Structure-Activity Relationships, 11*(4), 518–521. doi:10.1002/qsar.2660110409

Maggiora, G. M. (2006). On outliers and activity cliffs - why QSAR often disappoints. *Journal of Chemical Information and Modeling, 46*, 1535. doi:10.1021/ci060117s

Maibaum, T.S.E. (2005). The Epistemology of Validation and Verification Testing. *Lecture Notes in Computer Science*, 3502/2005, 1-8.

Maria, C. (2006). The philosophy of computational chemistry II. In *M.* Burguete.

Martin, Y. (2001). Beginnings of QSAR, CADD?. *Newsletter. The QSAR and Modelling Society.* Issue No. 12, 12-20.

Meyer, H.H. & Baum, F. (1899). Zur Theorie der Alkoholnarkose (I-III). *Archiv für experimentelle Pathologie und Pharmakologie, 42*.

Nye, M. J. (1993). *From chemical philosophy to theoretical chemistry*. Berkeley, CA: University of California Press.

Prabhakar, Y. S., & Gupta, M. K. (2008). Chemical Structure Indices in *In Silico* Molecular Design. *Scientia Pharmaceutica, 76*, 101–132. doi:10.3797/scipharm.0804-12

Reinhardt, C. (2006). *Shifting and Rearranging: Physical Methods and the Transformation of Modern Chemistry*. Sagamore Beach, MA: Science History Publications.

Schrödinger, E. (1926a). Quantisierung als Eigenwertproblem. *Annalen der Physik, 79*, 361–376. doi:10.1002/andp.19263840404

Schrödinger, E. (1926b). Quantisierung als Eigenwertproblem. *Annalen der Physik, 79*, 489–527. doi:10.1002/andp.19263840602

Schrödinger, E. (1926c). Quantisierung als Eigenwertproblem. *Annalen der Physik, 80*, 437–490. doi:10.1002/andp.19263851302

Schrödinger, E. (1926d). Quantisierung als Eigenwertproblem. *Annalen der Physik, 81*, 109–139. doi:10.1002/andp.19263861802

Scior, T. (2009). How to recognize and workaround pitfalls in QSAR studies: a critical review. *Current Medicinal Chemistry, 16*, 4297–4313. doi:10.2174/092986709789578213

Shaik, S., & Hibert, P. C. (2004). Valence Bond Theory, Its History, Fundamentals, and Applications. In Kenny B. Lipkowitz, Raima Larter, Thomas R. Cundari (eds.), *Reviews in Computational Chemistry,* 20, 1-100. London: Wiley.

Simões, A. (2007). *Neighbours and Territories: The Evolving Identity of Chemistry*. Conference presented at 6TH INTERNATIONAL CONFERENCE ON THE HISTORY OF CHEMISTRY. Downloadable at: http://www.euchems.org/binaries/04_Ana_Simoes_tcm23-139346.pdf

Topliss, J. G., & Costello, R. J. (1972). Chance correlation in Structure-Activity Studies Using Multiple Regression Analysis. *Journal of Medicinal Chemistry, 15*, 1066–1068. doi:10.1021/jm00280a017

Tropsha, A. (2010). Best Practices for QSAR Model Development, Validation, and Exploitation. *Molecular Informatics, 29*, 476–488. doi:10.1002/minf.201000061

Unger, S. H., & Hansch, C. (1973). On Model Buildingin Structure-Activity Relationships. A Reexamination of Adrenergic Blocking Activity of β-Halo-β-arylalkylamines. *Journal of Medicinal Chemistry, 16*, 745–749. doi:10.1021/jm00265a001

Vallverdú, J. (2005). La evolución de la toxicología: de los venenos a la evaluación de Riesgos. *Revista Española de Toxicología, 22*(3), 153–161.

Vallverdú, J. (2009). Computational Epistemology and e-Science. A New Way of Thinking. *Minds and Machines*, *19*(4), 557–567. doi:10.1007/s11023-009-9168-0

Vallverdú, J. (2010a). Seeing for Knowing. The Thomas Effect and Computational Science. In Jordi Vallverdú (Ed.) *Thinking Machines and the Philosophy of Computer Science: Concepts and Principles, 280-293.* Hershey, PA: IGI Global Group.

Vallverdú, J. (2010b). *History of Probability / Schools of Statistical Reasoning. In the International Lexicon of Statistical Sciences.* New York: Springer.

Van Drie, J. H. (2007). Computer-aided drug design: the next 20 years. *Journal of Computer-Aided Molecular Design*, *21*, 591–601. doi:10.1007/s10822-007-9142-y

Vedani, A., & Dobler, M. (2002). 5D-QSAR: the key for simulating induced fit? *Journal of Medicinal Chemistry*, *45*(11), 2139–2149. doi:10.1021/jm011005p

Young, D. M., Martin, T. M., Venkatapathy, R., & Harten, P. (2008). Are the Chemical Structures in your QSAR Correct? *QSAR & Combinatorial Science*, *27*(11-12), 1337–1345. doi:10.1002/qsar.200810084

ENDNOTES

[1] A comprehensive QSAR journals List at: http://www.qsarworld.com/literature-qsar-journals.php?lm=1. In the list I've detailed above are included some of the most recent journals, although they clearly do not belong to the 1960-1980 period.

[2] (Source: Based on information provided by Biographics Laboratory 3R, http://www.biograf.ch/index.php?id=home.

[3] Following Ma and Nussinov (2004): "Between 1962 and 1970 there was essentially a universal scientific agreement that the methylene molecule was linear in its triplet ground state, as concluded by the brilliant spectroscopist Gerhard Herzberg (the father of modern spectroscopy) from experiments described in his Nobel Prize citation. In 1970, the theoretical treatment by Bender and Schaefer applied rigorous quantum mechanics to the triatomic molecule. Previously, the method had been applied only to atoms and diatomic molecules. Their theoretical result, which predicted that the methylene molecule was bent by, contradicted experiment. Yet, indirect experimental evidence for such a highly bent methylene molecule came out quickly, followed by a reinterpretation of the spectroscopic studies confirming the bent geometry predicted by theory. The reliability of a molecular quantum mechanical model for chemistry and a new role for theory, 'full partner with experiment' was charted. Since then, computational quantum chemistry advanced to a stage allowing us to reliably use computed results to calibrate or to substitute experiments in many small molecule systems".

[4] http://www.kubinyi.de/lectures.html

[5] See: http://plato.stanford.edu/entries/scientific-underdetermination/.

[6] http://chem-bla-ics.blogspot.com/2008/07/commercial-qsar-modeling-sorry-already.html. About QSAR patents, look at: http://www.freepatentsonline.com/result.html?query_txt=qsar&sort=relevance&srch=top&search=

[7] http://www.dddmag.com/qsar-prediction-beyond-the-fourth.aspx

Chapter 15
Computational Techniques in Binding Affinity Prediction of Drugs

Kshatresh Dutta Dubey
DDU Gorakhpur University, India

Rajendra Prasad Ojha
DDU Gorakhpur University, India

ABSTRACT

Computational techniques are widely used in the chemoinformatics and bioinformatics. Most of the drugs produce their effect by interacting with the target molecules via different interactions. However, these interactions are tough to be calculated without use of robotics techniques. The potentials of these drugs depend upon their binding affinity. Due to huge number of such drugs, the measurement of their relative potency is a hard task. In present chapter the authors have discussed about some most common techniques which are widely used in bioinformatics and chemoinformatics.

INTRODUCTION

Discovering and developing any new drug is a long and expensive process because the novel drug should not only produce optimum potency but it should exhibit minimum side effect. After the advancement in the development of high throughout screening and combinatorial techniques, the data of bioactivity and structure of a

DOI: 10.4018/978-1-60960-860-6.ch015

drug also increased abruptly. Therefore, analysis of bioactivity of such huge data becomes very ridiculous. A newly discovered drug may have to pass some filtering criterion like toxicity, selectivity and binding affinity. This explosion of data has increased the need for integration of chemical information with molecular modelling techniques. After the successful invention of a drug, the demands of discovery of lead series are also expected. A lead series comprises a set of related molecules that usually share some common structural features, and shows some variation in the activity as the structure is modified. However, discovering a novel lead series by experimental techniques becomes more complicated than discovery of a single molecule. For example, after discovery of penicillin by Alexander Fleming, pharmaceutical companies screened soil and other biological samples to find a new lead, but it was proved very difficult to extract and purify a lot of bioactive ingredient. However, presently, due to robotic techniques, high throughout screening is very common which enables high number of compound to be screened. In this way, the scope of chemoinformatics has increased drastically in the field of drug discovery. Presently, there are more than 5000 drugs approved according to the Drug Bank (www.drugbank.ca). The relative potency of these drugs for a selected target has vast scope for medicinal chemists and practitioners. Due to huge number of such drugs, it is very difficult to examine relative potentials by experimental techniques. Therefore the computational techniques are widely used for this purpose. Drug-receptor binding is the most fertile field of study for biochemists and bioinformatics. *Receptors* are the macromolecules involved in chemical signaling between and within cells. Molecules (drugs, DNA, proteins etc) that bind to a receptor are called *ligand*. Although the drugs are targeted for a specific receptor, most have relative selectivity. Selectivity is the degree to which a drug acts on a given site relative to other sites. The probability of a drug occupying the receptor bat any instant is known as *binding affinity*. In the present chapter we have discussed all popular methods which are used as binding affinity predictors.

BACKGROUND

In this section we will discuss about the commonly used techniques for the prediction of binding affinity of drug protein complexes.

Molecular Docking

In this section, we shall discuss computational methods for modeling the interaction of small molecule ligands with protein receptors in aqueous solution. Such interactions form the basis of the mechanism of the great majority of pharmaceutically active compounds. Figure 1 shows an example of the interaction by molecular docking. The ability to determine the structures and free energy of binding of protein ligand complexes is, therefore, the key objective of computational structure-based drug design. Molecular docking attempts to predict the structure of the intermolecular complex formed by two or more molecules. Docking is widely used to suggest the binding mode of bioactive inhibitors. Most docking algorithm is able to generate a large number of possible structures, and so they also require a means to score each structure to identify those of the most interest. Usually the docking algorithms generate different possible modes of binding of inhibitors for a selected target which are further ranked according to some filtering criteria which is known as docking score.

Theoretically a molecular dynamic simulation can be used to predict the free energy of a pharmaceutically active protein ligand complex, but due to large computational time and force field accuracy limitation, this method is ridiculous for straightforward usage. These considerations have led to the development of approximate methods that based on physical chemistry principles, endeavor to embody such principles in empirically optimized models and determine structures via specially designed conformational search algorithms. The optimized models are known as scoring function and conformational search algorithms are often called docking algorithm. When the scoring function is combined with docking algorithms, it constitutes docking program. Various docking programs have been developed to tackle the docking problem. The first docking program, DOCK (Kuntz et al. 1982), was developed in the

Figure 1. This shows the interaction of a well known drug STI-570 with c-Abl kinase using molecular docking. The docking is done with help of GLIDE.

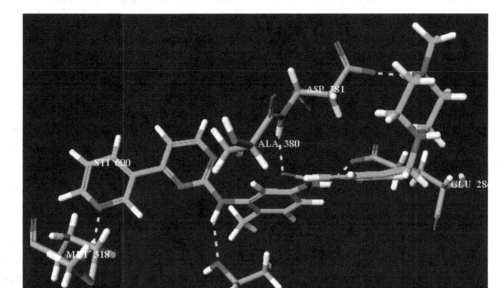

laboratory of Tack Kuntz at the University of California, San Francisco, and beginning in the early 1980s.

Requisites of Molecular Docking

The setup for the ligand docking approach needs: 1) a target protein structure with or without a ligand 2) the molecule of interest or a database containing existing or virtual compounds for the docking process and 3) A computational framework that allows the implementation of the desired docking and scoring procedure. The three dimensional structure of the protein ligand complexes has to be detailed at atomic resolutions. In many cases only the unbound form of the protein is determined without the bioactive conformations of the ligand. Docking can be done by placing rigid molecule into the protein active site using different approaches. Different docking program used different approaches. Presently there are three approaches widely used by different programs which

are clique-search, geometrical hashing, and pose clustering. DOCK, the basic docking program, uses the clique-search matches approach where matches are searched to describe the compatible characteristics of ligand and protein by means of a distance compatibility graph. A geometrical hashing function is created to describe geometric features like distance in two steps, the prepossessing phase and a recognition phase. This approach is very attractive regarding to its time efficacy and the option for partial matching of the ligand in the protein pocket (Fischer et al, 1993). The third approach, pose clustering is based on the matching of triplets of feature of the ligand with a triplet of the features of the protein. The features represent the interaction zones of the ligand and receptor. This approach is used in LUDI (Boehm 1992).

A more details of the summarized methods of the basic rigid docking algorithm is described elsewhere (Muegge et al. 2001, Halperien et al. 2002, R.J. Tame 1999, Waszkowyez et al 2002). Besides the accurate docking of the ligand, the preparation of the protein is of big importance. The correct assessment of the model system plays important role in correct docked pose. In the beginning of the protein preparation, the atomic resolution must be attended and the water molecule in the PDB structure must be regarded cautiously because it is subjective information given by a crystallographer from electron density map. Some remarks are also found in the PDB file indicating the problem found during the interpretation of the crystal structure. This data may be helpful in docking process and may enhance accuracy of docking.

On the account of flexibility of receptor there are also different approaches for ligand docking: the rigid receptor approach, where the receptor is kept fixed and there is no change in the conformation as well. Different poses are obtained by changing the orientations and conformations of ligand. This is most widely used approach. The DOCK program was the first of its kind, and continues to be used in both academia and industry. However, over the past decade a number of new programs have been developed, incorporating efforts to improve sampling algorithms, pose selection functions, and the scoring function for binding affinity. FLEXX (Rarey et al 1996 and 1997), GOLD (Jones et al 1995 and 1997), Glide(Schrodinger Inc) programs also account for rigid receptor docking. In the second approach receptor flexibility is also accounted. A study of Dubey and coworker (Dubey et al 2010) shows the effect of flexibility of target protein using GLIDE program. In this study eight kinase inhibitors are docked rigidly as well as flexible docking and their results were compared. In principle, flexible treatment of both ligand and receptor to produce an accurate prediction of the structure of a ligand-receptor complex is a straightforward problem in biomolecular simulation. One could; for example, use molecular dynamics (MD) methods with explicit solvation, starting with the ligand in solution, and under appropriate conditions with regard to effective ligand concentration, a sufficiently long

MD simulation should converge to the bound state as thermodynamic equilibrium is reached. In practice, such an approach would require far too much computation time to be practical.

Parameters Influencing the Docking Results

A critical issue is the multi-factorial dependence of docking results. Many efforts have been devoted to investigate, how and to what extend the outcome of the accuracy of a docking approach are influenced by different parameters. Aside from the docking algorithm and scoring function, binding site definition and the use of additional pharmacophore constraints are decisive (Schulz et al 2003). Also the nature of the biological target, the properties of the active site, crystallographic resolution, as well as ligand flexibility were found to influence the docking reliability. A study demonstrate that full force field runs give the highest success rate-success meaning a root mean square deviation (rmsd) between top ranked docking position and X-ray structure of less than 2 A. it also shows that the full force field minimization also gives good docking results. Hence the accurate parameterization of force field plays an important role in docking results. Another discussed parameter is ligand flexibility. A lower number of ratable bonds can clearly be connected with higher docking success, whereas molecular weight or binding affinity seem less differentiating for docking accuracy. Increasing the ligand sampling leads to improved accuracy, but not beyond a level of 50 replicas. Another study of Zavodaski (Zavodaski et al 2002), shows the importance of interaction representation and interaction for a ligand and protein for hydrophobic and hydrogen bond interactions. The detailed analysis of parameters influencing the docking accuracy is presented in an article by Perola et al (Perola et al 2004).

Docking Algorithms

Nowadays there is a vast pool of different docking scoring methodologies. Advantage and disadvantages of these methods and the target they are best suited for are critical and intensively investigated issues. A thorough study of comparison of docking algorithms in terms of accuracy in virtual screening, correct prediction of binding modes, and CPU time consumption is given by Kontoyianni (Kontoyianni et al 2004). In the study the authors compare the results obtained from new docking programs FRED (OpenEye Scientific Software) and GLIDE (Schrodinger Inc) with previous results obtained using FLEXX (Tripos Inc.) GLIDE and FRED separates conformational search of a molecule from its placement in the binding site while FLEXX docks a small, rigid fragment, capable of specific directed interaction with protein, at various favorable positions in the active site. Kontoyianni and coworker also investigated five very common docking programs (FLEXX, GOLD, DOCK, LigandFit and Glide) against 14 protein families in order to compare the strengths and limitations of these tools. Docking accuracy is detected via visual inspection and rmsd calculation between the docked and experimentally determined ligand conformations. In that study GOLD outperforms the other program in accordance with the crystal structure. While on behalf of docking results, ligand flexibility, active site topology, GLIDE shows the best results. DOCK is found preferable for rather hydrophobic sites while GLIDE does not seem efficient in this respect. A similar comparison study for eight docking programs (DOCK, FLEXX, FRED, GOLD, SLIDE, SURFLEX and QXP) can be seen in the work of Kellenberger (Kellenberger et al 2004).

Use of Docking in Chemoinformatics

Many research groups apply docking and scoring methods, when synthesis and experimental testing have already been performed in order to correlate the scores with the biological activity. Docking proves a reliable and fast filter in virtual screening (Jenkins et al 2003, Venkatchalam et al 2003), thereby providing a pool of ideas for novel lead structures. Docking score is frequently used for comparison of binding affinity of library of drugs which reduces much experimental time.

Future Trends in Docking

With increase of computational efficiency modern computational chemistry is relying mostly on the quantum chemical approaches. The present molecular docking algorithms use semi-empirical charge methods which do not give accurate assessment of charge in the protein or solvation. Therefore the use of quantum mechanics in docking algorithms is a time demanding task. Some software (GLIDE) have implemented this concept in Quantum Mechanical Polarized ligand Docking (QPLD) in their docking algorithms. These methods have shown a very fruitful result in docking accuracy of many protein ligand complexes. (Cho et al, Friesner et al). A recent study of Dubey et al 2010 showed the effect of ab initio charge calculation of ligand enhances the accuracy of docking pose relative to crystal structure.

Free Energy Methods

These are the most commonly methods for the prediction of binding affinity of drugs. Fee energy methods use conformational sampling to generate thermodynamic average, in contrast with docking methods, which focuses on a single bound conformation. The use of conformational sampling is advantageous because it removes sensitivity to details of the single representative conformation relied on docking methods. On the other hand free energy methods need more computer time in order to generate unambiguous, converged results. Before going into deep of the methods for calculations of free energy differences, we will discuss briefly about the concept of free energy.

Free energy is considered as the most important thermodynamical parameters for persons of bioinformatics. In thermodynamics, the free energy is usually expressed in terms of Helmholtz function (A) and Gibbs free energy (G). Helmholtz function A is mathematically given by A= U-TS. If A is a perfect differential then

dA =dU- d(TS) => dA= TdS - PdV - TdS – SdT= - PdV- SdT

For constant temperature and volume i.e. for NVT ensemble dV and dT will be zero, hence, dA=0. Therefore, Helmholtz free energy is appropriate for NVT ensemble. Similarly, Gibbs free energy is appropriate for NPT ensemble as it mathematically given by G =H-TS. Here H stands for the enthalpy, S for entropy, U for internal energy. The details of above can be easily found in any standard thermodynamics books. Since most experiments are conducted on constant P and V, Gibbs free energy has greater importance. Figure 2 shows the schematic diagram for Gibbs free energy in biochemistry.

LIE (Linear Interaction Energy) methods, MM-PB/SA(Molecular Mechanical Poisson Boltzmann Surface Area) methods and free energy perturbation (FEP) methods are widely used free energy methods.

LIE Methods

The linear interaction energy (LIE) method was originally given by Aqvist and co-workers (Aqvist et al. 1994) to calculate the binding affinity of protein ligand complexes. It is also known as linear response method and it is semi empirical method for estimating absolute free energies and requires just two simulations, one for the ligand in solution and other for the ligand in the protein binding site. The snapshots saved from the simulations represent Boltzmann ensembles of conformations and are used to compute the Boltzmann- averaged electrostatic and van der

Figure 2. This shows a schematic diagram of the binding free energy for a ligand

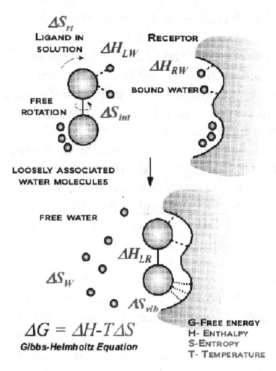

$$\Delta G = \Delta H - T\Delta S$$
Gibbs-Helmholtz Equation

G- Free Energy
H- Enthalpy
S- Entropy
T- Temperature

Waals interaction energies of the ligand with its environments in the bound and Free states. The binding free energy is estimated as -

$$\Delta G = \beta(<U^{elec}_{ligand-protein}> - <U^{elec}_{ligand-solvent}>) + \alpha (<U^{vdw}_{ligand-protein}> - <U^{vdw}_{ligand-solvent}>) + \gamma$$

As usual, the angle bracket indicates Boltzmann average, α and β are two parameters. To determine ΔG one thus needs to perform just to simulations, one of the ligand in solvent and other of the ligand in bounded form with the protein. The first term describes the electrostatic contributions in the ΔG according to the linear response approximation (LRA) theory (Lee et al 1992, Aqvist et al 1996, 1991). The second term in the above equation holds for the nonpolar contributions to ΔG. Its linear relationship with the surrounding van der Waals energy is based on the observation that solvation energies of non-polar compounds are linearly correlated with the surrounding van der

Waals energies (Hanson et al 1998 and Carlson et al 1995). γ is a constant that can be added to get a correct energy. In the initial implementation, β was fixed to ½ following the LRA approximation, while α was fitted empirically to a value of 0.16 to reproduce the experimental activity of four structurally related endothiapepsin inhibitors (Aquivst et al 1994). γ was kept to 0 to limit the over-parametrization. Although these parameters gave satisfying results for protein-ligand systems, it was found using FEP calculations that β could be considered has a function of the ligand nature. Values of 0.5, 0.43, 0.37, and 0.33 were suggested for ionic molecules, and neutral compounds with one, two, or more hydroxyl groups, respectively. (Aqvist et al 1994) A 0.18 value was found to be optimal for α. Non-zero values of γ can be necessary to reproduce ΔG for some systems.(Ljungberg et al 2001) More recently, it was suggested that γ could be expressed as a function of the buried solvent accessible surface area (SASA) of the ligand that is buried upon complexation,(Zhou et al 2001) leading to the modified equation-

$$\Delta G = \beta(<U^{elec}_{ligand-protein}> - <U^{elec}_{ligand-solvent}>)$$
$$+ \alpha (<U^{vdw}_{ligand-protein}> - <U^{vdw}_{ligand-solvent}>) +$$
$$\gamma(<SASA_{ligand-protein}> - <SASA_{ligand-solvent}>)$$

However, in the study of Aqvist et (2002,2001) the addition of this term is questioned since buried SASA is correlated with van der Waal term. Some efforts have been done to reduce the computational costs where the electrostatic terms are replaced by the function of Coulombic interaction between the ligand and the protein and the solvation reaction field energy (Zhou et al 2001, and Carlsson et al 2006). This variant is attractive due to reduced computational costs.

A study of the Alam(Alam et al 2009) proves tells that the accuracy of the LIE method in comparison to the most accurate approximation method as free energy perturbation methods. Here a training set of 76 podophyllotoxin analogues was used to build a binding affinity model for estimating the free energy of binding for 36 inhibitors (test set) with diverse structural modifications. Similar application were found by many studies (Singh et al, 2005, Bortolato et al 2007, Kyani et al 2009).

Limitations of LIE Methods

Several important contributions to molecular recognition are neglected in LIE, such as the conformational rearrangement upon complexation of the ligand and the receptor, the receptor desolvation energy, and the entropies. However, it has been argued that these terms are implicitly taken into account by the LRA approximation and the adjustable parameters of the model (Zhou et 2001, Aqvist et al). Nonetheless the quality of the results obtained by LIE methods is somewhat surprising, because the LIE method does not account explicitly for standard configurational entropy or the internal energy of the ligand. This method may be successful in part because it is generally used to compare ligands within a single chemical series.

MM-PB(GB)/SA Methods

A second approach, the MM-PBSA method along with its GB variant (MM-GBSA), uses MD simulations of the free ligand, free protein, and their complex as a basis for calculating their average potential and solvation free energy. In this approach ΔG is written in terms of gas phase contribution, energy diffence due to trtanslational and rotational motion, desolvation energy and entropic contributions. Therefore-

$$G = G + G^{tran/rot} + G^{sol} - TS^{ideal}$$

Here first term of RHS is gas phase contributions which is sum of the electrostatic energy, van der Waals energy and internal energy i.e. $G^{gas} = E^{vdw} + E^{ele} + E^{int}$ The second term of the RHS is the energy due to translational/ rotational motion. In classical mechanics this term is equal to 3RT which is generally omitted in MM-PB/SA calculations. The third term is the solvation energy term which is further composed of nonpolar solvation and polar solvation terms. The last term is the entropic contribution which depends upon the degree of freedom of the translational, rotational and vibrational motion of the molecular system. Theoretically, above formula is applicable for the ligand, protein and complex. The resultant binding free energy is expressed as -

$$\Delta G = G^{comp} - (G^{lig} + G^{protein})$$

which can be explained in details (Bren et al 2006 and 2007) as:

Unbound ligand free energy: The free energy for the ligand is given by

$$G(L) = E^{gas}(L^u) + G^{sol}(L^u) - TS^{ideal}(L^u)$$

where the superscript u indicates the unbound conformation of the ligand.

Unbound protein free energy: The protein is treated by classical mechanics during the simulation for unbound protein. Its free energy is composed of total intramolecular energy, E^{gas} [van der Waal interaction (E^{vdw}) + Coulombic interaction (E^{coul}) + bonding interaction (E^{bond})], solvation free energy (E^{solv}) and entropic contributions ($-TS^{ideal}$).

$$G(P) = E^{gas}(P^u) + G^{solv}(P^u) - TS^{ideal}(P^u)$$

Complex free energy: The complex is treated by both MM and QM methods and it contains the sum of energy terms corresponding to the protein and ligand in bound state and of the term for protein ligand interactions (P/L). The free energy of complex is composed of following terms:

$$G(C) = E^{gas}(P^b) + E^{gas}(L^b) + G^{solv}(C^b) + - TS^{ideal}$$

Here, E^{int} is decomposed as the sum of E^{bond}, E^{coul} and E^{vdw} and superscript 'b' denotes the bound form.

The binding free energy for the noncovalent association of two molecules, may be written as

$$\Delta G_{bind} = \Delta G(L+P \to C) = G(C) - G(L) - G(P)$$

or

$$\Delta G_{bind} = \Delta E^{int} + \Delta G^{solv} - T\Delta S^{ideal} + \alpha \Delta E^{vdw}(P/L)$$

Here,

$$\Delta E^{int} = E^{int}(P^b) - E^{int}(P^u);$$

$$\Delta G^{solv} = G^{solv}(C^b) - G^{sol}(L^u) - G^{solv}(P^u), \text{ and}$$

$$-T\Delta S^{ideal} = -TS^{ideal} + TS^{ideal}(L^u) + TS^{ideal}(P^u)$$

The empirical scaling factor α is introduced to balance the van der Waals energy relative to the electrostatic energy. It is obtained from the experimental results and here it is only used as a fitting parameter. ΔE^{int} is the change in protein intramolecular energy which is calculated by MM-PB/SA method. ΔG^{solv} (Gohlke et al 2004) is composed of nonpolar contribution and polar contribution. Nonploar solvation energy accounts for the unfavorable cavity formation and favorable van der Waals interaction between solute atoms and the solvent (Perdih et al 2009)

$$E^{solv,np} = \gamma A + b$$

where A stands for solvent accessible surface area (SASA).

γ and b are empirical constant which may have different values. The polar solvation energy is calculated using the linear Poisson- Boltzmann (PB) equation (Grochowaski et al 2007) that relates the charge density, $\rho(r)$, to the electrostatic potential, $\phi(r)$, in a medium with non uniform dielectric permittivity, $\varepsilon(r)$ which was used as 1 and 80 for the solute and the solvent respectively

$$\Delta \, \varepsilon(r) \, \Delta \, \phi(r) = -4\pi \, \rho(r) + \kappa^2 \, \varepsilon(r) \, \Delta \, \phi(r)$$

where κ is the Debye-Huckel screening parameter to take into account the electrostatic screening effect.

$T\Delta S$ arises from the change in translational, rotational and vibrational degrees of freedom in the system upon the protein ligand binding (Schwarzl et al 2002). The entropy term, due to the loss of degrees of freedom upon association, is decomposed into translational, S_{trans}, rotational, S_{rot}, and vibrational, S_{vib}, contributions. These terms are calculated using standard equations of statistical mechanics.(Tidor et al 1994), S_{rot} is a function of the moments of inertia of the molecule, whereas S_{trans} is a function of the mass and the solute concentration. S_{trans} is the only term in the free energy of an ideal solution that depends on solute concentration, leading to the concentration-dependence of the binding reactions. The vibrational entropy term is calculated with the quantum formula from a normal mode analysis (NMA). (Tidor et al 1994) A quasiharmonic analysis of the MD simulations is also possible. However, it has been found that it does not always yield convergent values, even using very long MD simulation trajectories, and also led to large deviations from the results obtained with NMA, giving an overall unreasonable entropic contribution. (Gohlke et al 2004)

Generally in MM-PBSA methods we run the MD simulation till 200- 500 frames in explicit solvent and trajectories of the MD simulations are averaged. The ions and the explicit solvent were striped before MM-PBSA analysis and periodic boundary conditions are also applied. A study in implicit solvent has been also performed by Pearlman and Rizzo (Pearlman 2005, Rizzo et al 2004). In study of Pearlman, it has been found that MM-PBSA yields better results with MD simulations restrained around the X-ray structure, compared to unrestrained simulations. There are two possibilities regarding to the MD simulation foe MM-PBSA. In first approach one should make three trajectories, one for the complex and each

of the isolated partners, and calculate the energy terms using the adequate simulation. However, a popular alternative consists in performing only one MD simulation for the complex. In this variant, the terms relative to one isolated partner are calculated after removing the atoms of the other partner in the frames extracted from the MD simulation of the complex. As a consequence, the reorganization energy of the molecules upon association is neglected ($\Delta H_{intra} = 0$). However, this variant is less CPU demanding and leads to increased convergence due to cancellation of errors, reduction of noise arising from flexible remote regions relative to the binding site, and conformational restraints imposed by the complex geometry. Thus, this one-simulation variant is attracting when ΔH_{intra} may be reasonably neglected. Comparisons between one- and three trajectories results can be found in the literature. The recent application of MM-PBSA method can be found in some recent study (Balasubrimaniam et al 2007, Agrawal et al 2008).

Future Scope of MM-PBSA
In MM-PB/SA approach, the entire protein and ligand are treated by classical mechanics. However, due to enrichment of computational efficiency the use quantum mechanics is demanding. Recently, a new method QM/MM-PB/SA is used by Dubey and Ojha (Dubey et al 2010) where the quantum mechanical approach is implemented successfully for the calculation of binding free energy. In this study, it is observed that implementation of QM method enhances the accuracy of free energy in respect to experimental results. Although this work is done on the AMBER molecular dynamics package, a similar strategy may be applicable for the other force fields.

Free Energy Perturbation Methods

Among all the known methods of binding free energy calculations this method gives the most promising results. However, due to large computational time, these methods are less applicable for huge system. A brief principle of this method is discussed below.

The change in free energy between two states of a system, such as before and after binding, can be written as $-RT\ln<e^{-\Delta U/RT}>$, where ΔU is the change in the energy function between the initial and final states, and the angle bracket indicates a Boltzmann average taken in the initial state. The change in the energy can be found by the interaction energy term and the Boltzmann average taken by a classical MD run. In reality, such a simulation is extraordinarily difficult to converge unless the initial and final states are simple. The FEP methods solves this problem by breaking the change into small steps δU (perturbations) and running a separate simulations for each resulting energy function U_i to obtain the stepwise free energy changes. Pathways (perturbation) methods can also be used to compute the standard binding free energy of a protein and ligand.

The free energy difference between two states A and B can formally be obtained from Zwanzig's formula (Zwanzig, 1954)

$$\Delta G = G_B - G_A = \beta^{-1}\ln<\exp(-\beta\Delta V)>_A$$

here $\beta = 1/KT$ and angular bracket denotes a MD generated ensemble average.

The main criterion for above equation to be practically useful is that the configurations sampled on the potential V_A should have a reasonable (at least non-vanishing) probability of occurring also on V_B. This essentially means that thermally accessible regions of the two potentials should have a significant degree of overlap. If not, the result will be a very slow convergence of the average. That convergence can, e.g., be assessed by interchanging the labels A and B and changing the sign of ΔG in above equation, thus applying the formula "backwards.

In order to solve the above convergence problem associated with the implementation of Eq. (1), a multistage approach is normally adopted.

A path between the states A and B is defined by introducing a set of intermediate potential energy functions that are usually constructed as linear combinations of the initial (A) and final (B) state potentials

$$V_m = (1 - \lambda_m) V_A + \lambda_m V_B$$

where λ_m varies from 0 to 1. In practice this path is thus discretized into a number of points ($m=1,...,n$), each represented by a separate potential energy function that corresponds to a given value of λ. This coupling parameter approach rests upon the fact that the free energy difference is uniquely defined by the initial and final states (i.e. a state function) and can be computed along any reversible path connecting those states. Now the total free energy change can be obtained by summing over the intermediate states along the λ variable

$$\Delta G = G_B - G_A = \beta^{-1}\ln<\exp[-\beta(V_{m+1} - V_m)]>_m$$

This approach is generally referred to as the free energy perturbation (FEP) method.

FEP methods can also be used to compute the standard binding free energy of a protein and ligand. Many successful application of these methods can be found elsewhere(Chandani et al. 2005, Lopez et al 1995)

QSAR Techniques

Quantitative Structure Activity Relationships (QSAR) attempt to correlate structural, molecular properties (descriptors) with function (activity, toxicity, physicochemical properties...) for a set of compounds using machine learning (statistical) methods. The QSAR relationship is expressed as a mathematical model that can be used to predict the properties of new molecules. QSAR models can either predict a continuous endpoint (regression), or classify molecules if the endpoint is categorical (classification). For example a regression model may predict the aqueous solubility of compounds while a classification molecule may predict whether the compounds are Soluble or Insoluble. Less complex, or quantitative, understanding of the role of structure to govern effects, i.e. that a fragment or sub-structure could result in a certain activity, is often simply termed a structure–activity relationship or SAR. Together SARs and QSARs can be referred to as (Q)SARs and fall within a range of techniques known as in silico approaches. Generally, although there is no formal definition, in silico includes SARs and QSARs, as well as the use of existing data (e.g. searching within databases), category formation and read-across. It also borders into various other areas of chemoinformatics and bioinformatics. Readers are referred to www.qsar.org for more study materials. This site contains a lot of books, journals, dictionaries related to the QSAR methods.

General Scheme of the QSAR Study

The chemoinformatic methods used in building QSAR models can be divided into three groups, i.e., extracting descriptors from molecular structure, choosing those informative in the context of the analyzed activity, and, finally, using the values of the descriptors as independent variables to define a mapping that correlates them with the activity in question. The chemical structures do not usually contain in an explicit form the information that relates to activity. This information has to be extracted from the structure. Various rationally designed molecular descriptors accentuate different chemical properties implicit in the structure of the molecule. Only those properties may correlate more directly with the activity. Such properties range from physicochemical and quantum-chemical to geometrical and topological features.

Molecular Descriptors

The foundation of QSAR study without description of molecular descriptors is absolutely worthless. Much research has focused on how to convert the information encoded in a molecular structure into mathematical representation that may be used to establish quantitative relationships between structures and properties. Molecular descriptors are numeric values derived from quantifying the chemical or structural information encoded in a molecule using a logical procedure. Molecular descriptors are derived by applying principles from several different theories, such as quantum chemistry, information theory, organic chemistry, graph theory.

2-D and 3-D QSAR descriptors are broadly used molecular descriptors which are distinguished according to structural information.

2-D Descriptors
These descriptors range from simple measures of entities constituting the molecule, through its topological and geometrical properties to computed electrostatic and quantum-chemical descriptors or advanced fragment-counting methods. 2-D descriptors have also vast variety depending upon different properties. Constitutional descriptors, topological descriptors, electrostatic and quantum chemical descriptors, 2-D geometrical descriptors are the subtypes of the 2-D molecular descriptors. Constitutional descriptors, as the name, based on the constituting properties like molecular weights and total number of atoms in molecules. Topological descriptors are based on the graph theory, molecular connectivity, and information about valence electrons. The electronic and quantum chemical descriptors deal about the net atomic and partial charge on atoms. The role of polarization and negative and positive character of atoms are also considered in this category. Geometrical descriptors are based on the spatial arrangement of atoms, molecular volume, moment of inertia

and gravitational indices. Total solvent accessible surface area is a broadly used geometrical descriptor.

3-D Descriptors

The 3-D molecular descriptors are relatively complicated than 2-D descriptors. The calculation of such descriptors involves many stages such as structure of the molecular system is either determined by experimental techniques or by molecular modelling. The structure refinement is done by energy minimization process. Though, this method is complicated but it is more attractive than 2-D. The first applicable 3D-QSAR method was proposed by Cramer et al. in 1986. His program, CoMFA, was a major breakthrough in the field of 3D-QSAR. The primary aim of 3D-QSAR methods is to establish a correlation of biological activities of a series of structurally and biologically characterized compounds with the spatial fingerprints of numerous field properties of each molecule, such as steric demand, lipophilicity, and electrostatic interactions. Typically, a 3D-QSAR analysis allows the identification of the pharmacophoric arrangement of molecular features in space and provides guidelines for the design of next-generation compounds with enhanced bioactivity or selectivity. The number of 3D-QSAR studies has increased exponentially over the last decade, since a variety of methods have been made commercially available in user friendly software (Cramer et al 1988, Klebe et al 1993, 1994). The alignment based 3-D QSAR descriptors, alignment independent based 3-D QSAR descriptors, weighted holistic invariant molecular descriptors, and quantum mechanical descriptors (HOMO-LUMO energy gap) are some main approaches of the 3-D QSAR descriptors. Recent progress in computational hardware and the development of efficient algorithms has assisted the routine development of molecular quantum-mechanical calculations. New semi empirical methods supply realistic quantum-chemical molecular quantities in a relatively short computational time frame.

Quantum chemical calculations are thus an attractive source of new molecular descriptors, which can, in principle, express all of the electronic and geometric properties of molecules and their interactions. Indeed, many recent QSAR/QSPR studies have employed quantum chemical descriptors alone or in combination with conventional descriptors. A review article by Karelson et al 1995 tells a detail study about the descriptor of this kind. A study of Katritzky et al 2002 discusses major softwares for QSAR study.

Future Trends in QSAR Study

The adoption of novel, more accurate QSAR modeling techniques does not reduce the responsibility of the investigator. On the contrary, the more complex and optimized is the model, the more caution it requires during its application. Combined with the increased complexity of the inspected datasets, this makes the QSAR analysis a challenging endeavor. The efforts should be done in enhancement of the accuracy of the predictions using QSAR methods. The advancement in computational enables to apply quantum mechanical approaches in QSAR predictions, which may increase the accuracy in the prediction of chemical properties.

CONCLUSION

The computational techniques in chemoinformatics have been developed very rapidly after their potential application in drug discovery was recognized. The binding affinity calculations using computational techniques have increased the rate of drug discovery. For a library of drugs and lead drug discovery, molecular docking and QSAR techniques play an important role. However, for the accuracy of results regarding to experimental values, one should use free energy methods for binding affinity calculations. Those methods which are more accurate, demand more computational time and those which are less accurate are computational cheaper i.e. a researcher have to compromise with one side. Therfore, more research should be done to get both aspects and a need of accurate and faster algorithm is always demanding.

REFERENCES

Agrawal, S., Ojha, R. P., & Maiti, S. (2008)... *The Journal of Physical Chemistry B, 112,* 6828–6836. doi:10.1021/jp7102676

Alam, M. A., & Naik, P. K. (2009)... *Journal of Molecular Graphics & Modelling, 27,* 930–947. doi:10.1016/j.jmgm.2009.02.003

Åqvist, J., & Hansson, T. (1996)... *Journal of Physical Chemistry, 100*(22), 9512–9521. doi:10.1021/jp953640a

Åqvist, J., Luzhkov, V. B., & Brandsdal, B. O. (2002)... *Accounts of Chemical Research, 35*(6), 358–36. doi:10.1021/ar010014p

Åqvist, J., & Marelius, J. (2001)... *Combinatorial Chemistry & High Throughput Screening, 4*(8), 613–626.

Åqvist, J., Medina, C., & Samuelsson, J. E. (1994)... *Protein Engineering, 7,* 385–391. doi:10.1093/protein/7.3.385

Balasubrimaniam, C., Ojha, R. P., & Maiti, S. (2007)... *Biochemical and Biophysical Research Communications, 355,* 1081–1086. doi:10.1016/j.bbrc.2007.02.084

Boehm, H. J. (1992)... *Journal of Computer-Aided Molecular Design, 6,* 593–606. doi:10.1007/BF00126217

Boehm, H. J. (1992)... *Journal of Computer-Aided Molecular Design, 6,* 61–78. doi:10.1007/BF00124387

Bortolato, A., & Moro, S. (2007)... *Journal of Chemical Information and Modeling, 47,* 572–582. doi:10.1021/ci600369n

Bren, M., Florian, J., Mavri, J., & Bren, U. (2007)... *Theoretical Chemistry Accounts, 117,* 535–540. doi:10.1007/s00214-007-0264-z

Bren, U., Martinek, V., & Florian, J. (2006)... *The Journal of Physical Chemistry B, 110,* 12782–12788. doi:10.1021/jp056623m

Carlson, H. A., & Jorgensen, W. L. (1995)... *Journal of Physical Chemistry, 99,* 10667–10673. doi:10.1021/j100026a034

Carlsson, J., Ander, M., Nervall, M., & Åqvist, J. (2006)... *The Journal of Physical Chemistry B, 110,* 12034–12041. doi:10.1021/jp056929t

Chandani, S., Lee, C. H., & Loecher, E. L. (2005)... *Chemical Research in Toxicology, 18,* 1108–1123. doi:10.1021/tx049646l

Cho, A. E., Gullar, V., Berne, B. J., & Friesner, R. (2005)... *Journal of Computational Chemistry, 26,* 915–931. doi:10.1002/jcc.20222

Cramer, R. D. III, Patterson, D. E., & Bunce, J. D. (1988)... *Journal of the American Chemical Society, 110,* 5959–5967. doi:10.1021/ja00226a005

Dubey, K. D.Chaubey, A.K. Ojha, R.P. (2011). *Medicinal Chemistry Research.* doi:.doi:10.1007/s00044-011-9617-1

Dubey, K. D., Chaubey, A. K., Paravin, A., & Ojha, R. P. (2010)... *J Biophy Struct Biol, 2,* 47–54.

Dubey, K. D., & Ojha, R. P. (2011)... *Journal of Biological Physics, 37,* 69–78. doi:10.1007/s10867-010-9199-z

Fischer, D., Norel, R., Wolfson, H. L., & Nussinov, R. (1993)... *Proteins, 16,* 278–292. doi:10.1002/prot.340160306

Folkers G, Merz A, Rognan D (1993). *ESCOM Science Publishers*

Friesner, R. A., & Gullar, V. (2005)... *Annual Review of Physical Chemistry*, *56*, 389. doi:10.1146/annurev.physchem.55.091602.094410

Gohlke, H., Kuhn, L. A., & Case, D. A. (2004)... *Proteins*, *56*(2), 322–337. doi:10.1002/prot.20116

Halperin, I., Ma, B., Wolfson, H., & Nussinov, R. (2002)... *Proteins*, *47*, 409–443. doi:10.1002/prot.10115

Hansson, T., Marelius, J., & Åqvist, J. (1998)... *Journal of Computer-Aided Molecular Design*, *12*, 27–35. doi:10.1023/A:1007930623000

Jenkins, J. L., Kao, R. Y. T., & Shapiro, R. (2003)... *Proteins*, *51*, 81–93.

Jones, G., Willett, P., & Glen, R. C. (1995)... *Journal of Computer-Aided Molecular Design*, *9*, 532–549. doi:10.1007/BF00124324

Jones, G., Willett, P., Glen, R. C., Leach, A. R., & Taylor, R. (1997)... *Journal of Molecular Biology*, *267*, 727–748. doi:10.1006/jmbi.1996.0897

Karelson, M., Lobanov, V. S., & Katritzky, A. R. (1996)... *Chemical Reviews*, *96*, 1027–1043. doi:10.1021/cr950202r

Katritzky, A. R., Fara, D. C., Petrukhin, R. O., Tatham, D. B., Maran, U., Lomaka, A., & Karelson, M. (2002)... *Current Topics in Medicinal Chemistry*, *2*, 1333–1356. doi:10.2174/1568026023392922

Kellenberger, E., Rodrigo, J., Muller, P., & Rognan, D. (2004)... *Proteins*, *57*, 225–242. doi:10.1002/prot.20149

Klebe, G., & Abraham, U. (1993)... *Journal of Medicinal Chemistry*, *36*, 70–80. doi:10.1021/jm00053a009

Klebe, G., Abraham, U., & Mietzner, T. (1994)... *Journal of Medicinal Chemistry*, *37*, 4130–4146. doi:10.1021/jm00050a010

Kontoyianni, M., & McClellan, L. M. (2004). Sokol. G.S.,(2004). *Journal of Medicinal Chemistry*, *47*, 588–565.

Kyani, A., & Goliaei, B. (2009)... *Journal of Molecular Structure*, *913*, 63–69. doi:10.1016/j.theochem.2009.07.018

Lee, F. S., Chu, Z. T., Bolger, M. B., & Warshel, A. (1992)... *Protein Engineering*, *5*(3), 215–222. doi:10.1093/protein/5.3.215

Ljungberg, K. B., Marelius, J., Musil, D., Svensson, P., Norden, B., & Åqvist, J. (2001)... *European Journal of Pharmaceutical Sciences*, *12*, 441–446. doi:10.1016/S0928-0987(00)00185-8

Lopex, M. A., & Kollman, P. A. (1993)... *Protein Science*, *2*, 1975–1986. doi:10.1002/pro.5560021119

Muegge, I., & Rarey, M. (2001)... *Reviews in Computational Chemistry*, *17*, 1–60. doi:10.1002/0471224413.ch1

Pearlman, D. A. (2005)... *Journal of Medicinal Chemistry*, *48*(24), 7796–7807. doi:10.1021/jm050306m

Perdih, A., Bren, U., & Solemajer, T. (2009)... *Journal of Molecular Modeling*, *15*, 983–996. doi:10.1007/s00894-009-0455-8

Perola, E., Walters, W. P., & Charifson, P. S. (2004)... *Proteins*, *56*, 235–249. doi:10.1002/prot.20088

Rarey, M., Kramer, B., & Lengauer, T. (1997)... *Journal of Computer-Aided Molecular Design*, *11*, 369–384. doi:10.1023/A:1007913026166

Rarey, M., Kramer, B., Lengauer, T., & Klebe, G. (1996)... *Journal of Molecular Biology*, *261*, 470–489. doi:10.1006/jmbi.1996.0477

Rizzo, R. C., Toba, S., & Kuntz, I. D. (2004)... *Journal of Medicinal Chemistry*, *47*, 3065–3074. doi:10.1021/jm030570k

Schulz-Gasch, T., & Stahl, M. (2003)... *Journal of Molecular Modeling, 9*, 47–57.

Singh, P., Mhaka, A. M., Christensen, S. B., Gray, J. J., Denmeade, S. R., & Isaacs, J. T. (2005)... *Journal of Medicinal Chemistry, 48*, 3005–3014. doi:10.1021/jm049319a

Tame, J. R. H. (1999)... *Journal of Computer-Aided Molecular Design, 13*, 99–108. doi:10.1023/A:1008068903544

Tidor, B., & Karplus, M. (1994)... *Journal of Molecular Biology, 238*, 405–414. doi:10.1006/jmbi.1994.1300

Venkatachalam, C. M., Jiang, X., Oldfield, T., & Waldman, M. (2003)... *Journal of Molecular Graphics & Modelling, 21*, 289–307. doi:10.1016/S1093-3263(02)00164-X

Waszkowycz, B. (2002)... *Curr Opi Drug Discov, 5*, 414–421.

Zavodaski, M., I., Sanschagrin, P.C., Korde, R.S., Kuhn, L.A (2002) *J Comp Aided Mol Des, 16*, 883-902. doi:10.1023/A:1023866311551

Zhou, R. H., Friesner, R. A., Ghosh, A., Rizzo, R. C., Jorgensen, W. L., & Levy, R. M. (2001)... *The Journal of Physical Chemistry B, 105*, 10388–10397. doi:10.1021/jp011480z

Zwanzig, R. W. (1954)... *The Journal of Chemical Physics, 22*, 1420–1426. doi:10.1063/1.1740193

Chapter 16

Symbolic Equation for the Instantaneous Amount of Substance in Linear Compartmental Systems:
Software Furnishing the Coefficients Involved in it

J. M. Villalba
Universidad de Castilla-la Mancha, Spain

R. Varón
Universidad de Castilla-la Mancha, Spain

E. Arribas
Universidad de Castilla-la Mancha, Spain

R. Diaz-Sierra
UNED, Spain

F. Garcia-Sevilla
Universidad de Castilla-La Mancha, Spain

F. Garcia-Molina
Universidad de Murcia, Spain

M. Garcia-Moreno
Universidad de Castilla-la Mancha, Spain

M. J. Garcia-Meseguer
Universidad de Castilla-la Mancha, Spain

ABSTRACT

The symbolic time course equations corresponding to a general model of a linear compartmental system, closed or open, with or without traps and with zero input are presented in this chapter. From here, the steady state equations are obtained easily from the transient phase equations by setting the time towards infinite. Special attention is given to the open systems, for which an exhaustive kinetic analysis has been developed to obtain important properties. Besides, the results are particularized to open systems without traps. The software COEFICOM, easy to use and with a user-friendly format of the input of data and the output of results, allows the user to obtain the symbolic expressions of the coefficients involved in the general symbolic equation and all the information necessary to derive the symbolic time course equations for closed or open systems as well as for the derivation of the mean residence times.

DOI: 10.4018/978-1-60960-860-6.ch016

INTRODUCTION

In the analysis of any linear compartmental system consisting of compartments $X_1, X_2, ... X_n$, there are two problems that must be solved: (1) The forward problem, i.e. to ascertain how the system behaves kinetically for given inputs, assuming connectivity between the compartments and that the values of the non-null fractional transfer coefficients, $K_{i,j}$ ($i,j = 1,2,...,n; i \neq j$), between compartments X_i and X_j are known, and (2) The inverse problem, i.e., to determine the structure connectivity of the system and to estimate the values of the fractional transfer coefficients (Anderson, 1983; Jacquez, 1996; Jacquez, 2002). Some illustrative contributions on the forward problem are those in references (Anderson, 1983; Chou, 1990; Garcia-Meseguer et al., 2001; Hearon, 1963; Lal & Anderson, 1990; Rescigno, 1956; Rescigno, 1999; Varon, Garcia-Meseguer, & Havsteen, 1995b; Varon, Garcia-Meseguer, Garcia-Canovas, & Havsteen, 1995a). A recent contribution on this inverse problem is that of Juillet et al (2009).

The solution of the forward problem, together with the specific inputs of the substance made, leads to knowledge of the kinetic behavior of the compartmental system under study, i.e. the time variation of the amount of substance in each compartment.

The forward problem requires choosing both a model of the connectivity structure of the compartmental system and a mathematical model to acquire the kinetic behavior of the system. Mathematical model may be the residence time concept or the corresponding set of differential equations (Weiss, 1992). The first mathematical model gives time-independent kinetic parameters such as *exit* and *transit times, MRT, occupancy, turnover time* and *half-life* (Anderson, 1983; Jacquez, 1985; Jacquez, 1999). The second mathematical model furnishes the time course of the amount of substance in any compartment of the system after a specific input in one or more compartments is made (Garcia-Meseguer et al.,

2001; Jacquez, 2002; Rescigno, 1956; Rescigno, 1999; Rescigno, 2004; Varon et al., 1995a). From the results obtained with the second mathematical model, the parameters provided by the first method can also be obtained (Anderson, 1983; Garcia-Meseguer et al., 2003; Jacquez, 1985; Jacquez, 1999; Varon, Garcia-Meseguer, Valero, Garcia-Moreno, & Garcia-Canovas, 1995). In this section the second mathematical model mentioned above is used.

The compartmental systems are considered closed if there is no interchange of substance between any compartment of the system and the environment; otherwise they are named open systems. A compartment or a set of interconnected compartment, from which substance cannot leave, is named a simple trap, i.e. material is "trapped" (Anderson, 1983; Jacquez, 1985).

From structural point of view of the compartmental systems and according to Rescigno (1956) one compartment X_i is precursor of another, X_j, if the variation in the concentration in the first compartment influences the concentration in the second one. Then X_j is called successor X_i. Naturally, a compartment is a precursor and a successor of itself.

In this way, one class is formed by all compartments of the system, such that any of them is a precursor of all the others, and each compartment of a system belongs to one and only to one class (Galvez & Varon, 1981). Therefore, a class is a component of the strongly connected system (Jacquez, 1985). A class of the system which neither transfer material to any other class of the system nor to the environment (in open systems) is designated a final class. The concept of the final class coincides with the definition of simple trap given by Jacquez (1985).

In closed systems without traps the whole system can be considered as a trap and the only existing class is a final class. Hence in systems, which are not strongly connected (with traps), more than one class exits. Next, the study of the closed systems and subsequently the open systems as particular cases of the former is presented.

BACKGROUND

There are numerous physical, chemical and biological systems which can be studied from the point of view of the mathematical compartment theory (Anderson, 1983; Jacquez, 1985; Juillet, Bos, Gaudichon, Tome, & Fouillet, 2009; Rescigno & Thakur, 1991; Rescigno, 1956; Varon et al., 1995a; Varon et al., 1995b; Watabe, Ikoma, Kimura, Naganawa, & Shidahara, 2006).

Compartmental systems are important to describe many aspects of biotechnology and several other biological sciences, e.g. pharmacokinetic process, i.e. drug absorption, drug distribution, drug elimination, metabolites, dosing times, etc. (Rescigno, 1999; Veng-Pedersen, 1989), enzyme kinetic (Arribas et al., 2008a; Arribas et al., 2008b; Garcia-Sevilla et al., 2010; Sines & Hackney, 1987; Varon et al., 2007), nuclear medicine (Li & Hoeschen, 2010; Nye et al., 2008), the study of basic nutritional process e.g. nutrient digestion, nutrient absorption, nutrient metabolism (de Graaf et al., 2009; Green, 1992), toxicokinetics (Bevan & Weyand, 1988), different aspects of cellular growth (Jacquez, 1996) and the growth of tumor cells (Moolgavkar & Luebeck, 1990).

The behaviour of most of these biological systems fits that of open systems due to the excretion of material to the environment. Besides, some of these open systems are open systems without traps since a trap is a set of connected compartments, from which the substance cannot leave. Therefore, in an open system without traps, all material is eliminated from the system eventually, described by drug elimination kinetics. Hence, the knowledge of different kinetic aspects of open systems with or without traps has created a great interest in the kinetics of life systems.

In general, these studies of biological systems require the application of compartmental analysis together with isotope tracer methods, parameter identification and the evaluation of their mean values. They require the total analysis of the model under study, including both the derivation of kinetic equations of the compartmental system as a function of its parameters and the evaluation of the mean parameters.

The global study of compartmental systems involves the application of determinants and matrices (Rescigno, 1956), the use of graphic methods (Chou, 1990), of iterative methods (Lal et al., 1990) or of other methods which require the inversion of matrices. For this reason, systems with a matrix that is not invertible has no general solution (Cheng, 1991; Gibaldi, 1991).

Varón et al (1995b) presented an analysis in terms of the model parameters (the initial amount of substance in each compartment and the fractional transfer coefficients corresponding to direct connections between the compartments) of a closed general n-compartment model without input (zero input), i.e. substance may be injected at t=0 into one or more of the compartments of the system simultaneously. This analysis circumvented many of the above difficulties by the introduction of algorithms which facilitate the derivation of the kinetic equations. The expressions of the coefficients in these equations have been obtained by procedures that require neither expansion of determinants, nor operations with matrices, nor graphics methods. In this way, explicit general equations, which describe the evolution of any closed compartmental system, have been achieved. Nevertheless, these equations can be further simplified.

Although these equations could also be applied to open systems by the application of a formalism, the mathematical theory has been developed specifically for closed systems (Varon et al., 1995a). The present formalism for the study of open systems only reaches the level of a general approach that involves the expansion of symbolic determinants and matrix. This fact renders much additional work necessary later if one wishes to apply the theory to a concrete open compartmental system.

A total analysis of the structure of the open systems from point of view of a system matrix has not been carried out yet. That study would reveal specific properties from the matrix associated with open compartmental system that would yield general time course equations for this system in a simplified and elaborated final form, which applies to any particular open system with or without traps. Besides, it would be possible to obtain alternative formulations for some kinetic parameters.

On the other hand, there are several computer programs based on different algorithms that provide the numerical solution of linear differential equation systems (Garcia-Sevilla et al., 2000; Garrido del Solo, Varon, & Garcia-Canovas, 1992) from the numerical inputs of its parameters but, to our knowledge, only one computer program exits that yields the kinetic equations as a function of the model parameters (Varon et al., 1995b). However, from point of view of the current necessity for kinetic studies of compartmental systems this computer program has some limitations: 1) It cannot save the results in a file and always needs a printer 2) It treats closed systems only 3) It does not permit the choice of those minors from polynomial characteristics that the user are interesting in; i.e. it always provides all possible values. Hence a large memory and long time are necessary to execute the program. 4) It does not allow changes in all of the initial conditions for the same compartmental system. Hence, it is necessary to enter the data again 5) The study of each new compartmental system requires that the program is started again.

A great part of the exposed problems were taken into account by Garcia-Meseguer et al (2001) and these authors carried out an analysis of the kinetics of linear compartmental systems, closed or open, with or without traps and with zero input. This analysis allowed to obtain a simple, general, symbolic kinetic equation furnishing the time course of the amount of substance in any linear compartmental systems and moreover they implemented a software giving the expressions of the coefficients involved in the above equation. The results obtained in this chapter have been the start point for ulterior contributions on mean residence times (Garcia-Meseguer et al., 2003; Villalba et al., 2010)

CLOSED SYSTEMS

The Model

The general compartmental model and notation used in this chapter has been described already (Varon et al., 1995a). It consists of a linear compartmental system, with zero input i.e. material may be injected at t=0 into one or more of the compartments simultaneously, which may be strongly connected (i.e. the whole system can be considered a trap or final class) or not. It is composed of n compartments denoted arbitrarily by X_i ($i = 1, 2,..., n$). $K_{i,j}$ denotes the fractional transfer coefficient corresponding to the direct connection between the compartments X_i and X_j. This coefficient may be zero (if no direct connection exits between the compartments X_i and X_j) or positive. We admit the possibility that two compartments, X_i and X_j, are directly connected in more than one way. In that case, we denote these fractional transfer coefficients as $K'_{i,j}, K_{i,j}''...$, and $K_{i,j}$ as their sum. The kinetics of the system of compartments is described by an ordinary, linear and homogeneous system of differential equations with constant coefficients. It is assumed that non-null eigenvalues of the matrix corresponding to the system, matrix **K**, are simple, which is the most probable situation in practice.

Let Ω be the set of subindices in the notation of the compartments, which contain substance at t=0, and X_k ($k \in \Omega$) each one of these compartments. The amount of material in the compartment X_k at this moment is denoted x_k^o ($k \in \Omega$).

Time Course Equations

The instantaneous amount of substance in the compartment X_i, x_i, is given by the following equations (1)-(3) (Garcia-Meseguer et al., 2001; Varon et al., 1995a):

$$x_i = A_{i,0} + \sum_{h=1}^{u} A_{i,h} e^{\lambda_h t} \qquad (i = 1, 2, ..., n)$$

(1)

$$A_{i,0} = \frac{(-1)^{n+i+1} \sum_{k \in \Omega} (-1)^k (a_{k,i})_u x_k^0}{F_u}$$

$$(i = 1, 2, ..., n; \quad h = 1, 2, ..., u)$$

(2)

$$A_{i,h} = \frac{(-1)^{i+c} \sum_{k \in \Omega} (-1)^k x_k^0 \left(\sum_{q=0}^{u} (a_{k,i})_q \lambda_h^{u-q} \right)}{\lambda_h \prod_{\substack{p=1 \\ p \neq h}}^{u} (\lambda_p - \lambda_h)}$$

$$(i = 1, 2, ..., n; \quad h = 1, 2, ..., u)$$

(3)

(If $u=1$, then the denominator is λ_1)

The parameters λ_1, λ_2,..., λ_u are the non-null roots of the characteristic polynomial of the matrix **K**, $D(\lambda)$. The values c and u are the number of null and non-null roots of $D(\lambda)$, respectively. Hence, $n=c+u$. The development of $D(\lambda)$ yields Eq. (4)

$$D(\lambda) = (-1)^n \lambda^c T(\lambda)$$

(4)

where

$$T(\lambda) = \sum_{q=0}^{u} F_q \lambda^{u-q} \qquad (F_0 = 1)$$

(5)

Note that λ_1, λ_2,..., λ_u coincide with the roots of the polynomial $T(\lambda)$. These roots are real and negative or complex with a negative real part (Hearon, 1963).

The expressions for F_q ($q = 0, 1, 2,..., u$) may be obtained by expanding the secular determinant $D(\lambda)$ and Eqs. (4) and (5) taking into account. However, this is not necessary, because the expressions for these coefficients may be obtained in an easy, systematic and recurrent way from combinations of the $K_{i,j}$'s *(Varon et al., 1995a)*.

The Meaning of the Coefficients $(a_{k,i})_q$ ($k \in \Omega$); i=1, 2,..., n; q=0, 1, 2,..., u)

Let $D_{k,i}(\lambda)$ ($k \in \Omega$ $i=1, 2,..., n$) be the resulting determinant, if the k-th row and the i-th column in the determinant $D(\lambda)$ are removed. The expansion of $D_{k,i}(\lambda)$ leads to:

$$D_{m,i}(\lambda) = \lambda^{c-1} \sum_{q=0}^{u} (a_{k,i})_q \lambda^{u-q}$$

$$(i = 1, 2, ..., n)$$

(6)

Thus, $(a_{k,i})_q$ ($k \in \Omega$; $i=1, 2,..., n$; $q=0, 1, 2,..., u$) is the coefficient of the term of the degree $n-q-1$ of the polynomial $D_{k,i}(\lambda)$. In the reference Varón et al (1995a) it is showed that

$$(a_{k,i})_q = (-1)^{n+i+k-1} (f_{k,i})_q$$

$$(k \in \Omega; q = 0, 1, ..., u; i = 1, 2, ..., n)$$

(7)

The coefficients $(f_{k,i})_q$ ($q = 0, 1,..., u$) may be zero or positive, whereas the coefficients $(a_{k,i})_q$ can be also negative. When they are not zero and $q \neq 0$, they consist of one term or of a sum of terms, which each is a product of qK's. The $(f_{k,i})_0$-values ($i=1, 2,..., n$) are:

$$(f_{k,i})_0 = \begin{cases} 1 & if \quad k = i \\ 0 & if \quad k \neq i \end{cases}$$

(8)

The coefficients $(f_{k,i})_q$ ($k \in \Omega$; $i = 1, 2,..., n$; $q = 0, 1, 2,..., u$) have the following additional characteristics: *a)* If the compartment X_i ($i = 1, 2,..., n$) does not belong to a final class, then the coefficient $(f_{k,i})_u = 0$. *b)* If compartment X_k ($k \in \Omega$) is not a precursor of compartment X_i ($i = 1, 2,..., n$), all the coefficients $(f_{k,i})_q$ ($q = 0, 1, 2,..., u$) are null, i.e. $(f_{k,i})_0 = (f_{k,i})_1 = ... = (f_{k,i})_u = 0$. *c)* If in a concrete compartmental system for two compartments X_k ($k \in \Omega$) and X_i ($i = 1, 2,..., n$) the coefficient $(f_{k,i})_u$ is null then, the coefficient $(f_{k,i})_{u-1}$ is non-null, except if X_k is not a precursor of X_i (Garcia-Meseguer, 1998).

A more suitable form of Eqs. (2) and (3). If Eq. (7) is inserted to Eqs. (2) and (3), the next expressions result:

$$A_{i,0} = \frac{\left(f_{k,i}\right)_u x_k^0}{F_u} \qquad (i = 1, 2, ..., n) \qquad (9)$$

$$A_{i,h} = \frac{(-1)^{u-1} \sum\limits_{k \in \Omega} x_k^0 \sum\limits_{q=0}^{u} \left(f_{k,i}\right)_q \lambda_h^{u-q}}{\lambda_h \prod\limits_{\substack{p=1 \\ p \neq h}}^{u} \left(\lambda_p - \lambda_h\right)}$$

$$(i = 1, 2, ..., n; \quad h = 1, 2, ..., u) \qquad (10)$$

(If $u = 1$, then the denominator is λ_1)

These expressions are more compact and the involved coefficients are always positive.

Some Particular Cases

The general expression (Eq. (1)) and the expressions of its coefficients (Eqs. (9) and (10)), which determine the progress of material in any compartment of a closed system, can acquire a more simplified form in some cases.

Case (a): *compartment X_i ($i = 1, 2,.., n$) is not successor of any compartment X_k ($k \in \Omega$. In this situation, all the coefficients $(f_{k,i})_q$ ($q = 0, 1, 2,..., u$) are null and from Eqs. (9) and (10) one deduces:

$$A_{i,0} = A_{i,h} = 0 \qquad (11)$$

Therefore, Eq. (1) is transformed in the following:

$$x_i = 0 \qquad (12)$$

Case (b): *compartment X_i is a successor of at least, one compartment X_k ($k \in \Omega$), and X_i does not belong to a final class, i.e. X_i does not belong to a simple trap.* In this case, all the coefficients $(f_{k,i})_u$ ($k \in \Omega$) all null and $A_{i,0} = 0$, i.e. Eq. (1) becomes:

$$x_i = \sum_{h=1}^{u} A_{i,h} e^{\lambda_n t}$$
$$(i = 1, 2, ..., n) \qquad (13)$$

Example 1. Figure 1 shows a closed compartmental system with traps that consists of 6 compartments ($n = 6$) denoted by $X_1, X_2,..., X_6$.

Figure 1.

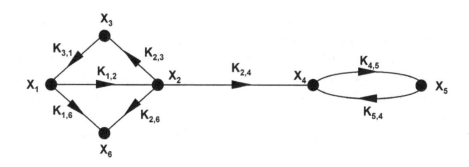

The fractional transfer coefficients corresponding to the flow of material between the compartments are given by $K_{1,2}, K_{1,6},..., K_{5,4}$.

To determine the expression of x_1 when material has been injected at t=0 into compartments X_1, X_3 and X_5, i.e. when $\Omega = \{X_1, X_3, X_5\}$, one must take into account that X_5 is not a precursor of X_1, that the compartment X_1 does not belong to a final class and that X_1 is a successor of X_1 and X_3, we are dealing with the case (b) and Eq. (13) can be applied, i.e.:

$$x_1 = \sum_{h=1}^{4} A_{1,h} e^{\lambda_h t} \qquad (i = 1, 2, ..., n) \qquad (14)$$

where

$$A_{1,h} = \frac{x_1^0 \sum_{q=0}^{4} (f_{1,1})_q \lambda_h^{4-q} + x_3^0 \sum_{q=0}^{4} (f_{3,1})_q \lambda_h^{4-q}}{\lambda_h \prod_{\substack{p=1 \\ p \neq h}}^{4} (\lambda_p - \lambda_h)}$$

$$(i = 1, 2, ..., n; \quad h = 1, 2, ..., n)$$

$$(15)$$

and λ_1, λ_2, λ_3 and λ_4 are the non null roots of the polynomial $\lambda^4 + F_1\lambda^3 + F_2\lambda^2 + F_3\lambda + F_4$.

The expressions of the coefficients involved in Eq. (15) and of the coefficients F_1, F_2, F_3 and F_4 are obtained in Appendix A.

OPEN SYSTEMS

The Model

Open systems can be treated formally as an hypothetical equivalent closed system from the kinetic point of view, where the environment is replaced by one compartment which receives all the excretions (Jacquez, 1985). However, a complete and systematic analysis that allows the treatment of the open compartmental systems by

their corresponding kinetically equivalent closed systems has not been done yet.

Notation and Definitions

In this section, some complementary definitions to the above mentioned for closed system, which are necessary to the analysis of open systems, have been included. As support, the example in Figure 2a shows the connectivity diagram corresponding to an open compartmental system with 5 compartments. $X_1,..., X_5$ denote the compartments, $K_{i,j}$ ($i,j = 1, 2,..., 5$) indicate the flow of material between them and $K_{i,o}$ ($i=1,2$) are the fractional excretion coefficients.

Figure 2b shows the directed graph corresponding to the closed compartmental system, which is kinetically equivalent to open compartment system shown in Figure 2a. The added hypothetical compartment that receives all the excretions has been denoted by X_6. The fractional excretion coefficients, $K_{i,o}$ ($i=1,2$) in Figure 2a have been replaced by the fractional transfer coefficients $K_{1,6}$ and $K_{2,6}$, respectively, in Figure 2b. Note that the closed compartmental system shown in Figure 2b coincides with the one in Figure 1.

Next, the general notation for open systems is presented.

- N: number of compartments of open system. In Figure 2a, $N = 5$.
- N-OLCS: Open linear compartmental system that consists of N compartments, X_1, X_2,..., X_N. The open system in Figure 2a is a 5-OLCS.
- $K_{i,o}$ ($i = 1, 2,..., N$): Fractional excretion coefficients describing the excretion of material from compartment X_i to the environment. Evidently, if no excretion from any compartment of the system to the environment occurs, all these coefficients are null and it would be a closed system. Therefore,

Figure 2.

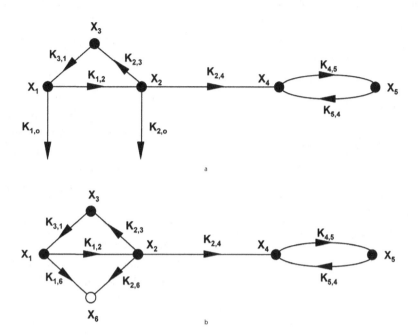

an open system has to have, at least a non-null fractional excretion coefficient.

- x_T^0 : Total amount of material in the system at t=0.

n-ECLCS: Closed linear compartmental system which is kinetically equivalent to the N-OLCS under study. This system consists of n compartments, X_1, X_2,..., X_N, X_{N+1} ($X_n \equiv X_{N+1}$) where X_n is the added hypothetical compartment to N-OLCS, that receives all the excretions. Thus, the application of this formalism yields:

$$K_{i,0} \equiv K_{i,n} \qquad \left(i = 1, 2, ..., N\right) \qquad (16)$$

Evidently:

$$n = N + 1 \qquad (17)$$

A: Matrix of the system of differential equations that describes the kinetics of the open compartmental system under study, N-OLCS. Besides, this matrix has been designated as the *compartmental system matrix* or the *system matrix*. The expressions of this matrix is:

$$A = \begin{vmatrix} K_{1,1} & K_{2,1} & . & . & . & K_{N,1} \\ K_{1,2} & K_{2,2} & . & . & . & K_{N,2} \\ . & . & . & . & . & . \\ . & . & . & . & . & . \\ . & . & . & . & . & . \\ K_{1,N} & K_{2,N} & . & . & . & K_{N,N} \end{vmatrix} \qquad (18)$$

where the elements of the main diagonal, $K_{i,i}$ ($i = 1,2,...,N$), have been defined by the next equation:

$$K_{i,i} = -\left(\sum_{\substack{j=1 \\ j \neq i}}^{N} K_{i,j} + K_{i,0}\right) \qquad (19)$$

In the example of Figure 2a, the compartmental system matrix, **A**, is:

$$A = \begin{vmatrix} K_{1,1} & 0 & K_{3,1} & 0 & 0 \\ K_{1,2} & K_{2,2} & 0 & 0 & 0 \\ 0 & K_{2,3} & K_{3,3} & 0 & 0 \\ 0 & K_{2,4} & 0 & K_{4,4} & K_{5,4} \\ 0 & 0 & 0 & K_{4,5} & K_{5,5} \end{vmatrix} \quad (20)$$

$A(\lambda)$: Characteristic determinant of the matrix **A**. Also denoted by the *characteristic determinant of the compartmental system*. The expression of this determinant is given by:

$$A(\lambda) = \begin{vmatrix} K_{1,1}-\lambda & K_{2,1} & \cdots & K_{N,n} \\ K_{1,2} & K_{2,2}-\lambda & \cdots & K_{N,2} \\ \cdot & \cdot & \cdots & \cdot \\ \cdot & \cdot & \cdots & \cdot \\ \cdot & \cdot & \cdots & \cdot \\ K_{1,N} & K_{2,N} & \cdots & K_{N,N}-\lambda \end{vmatrix}$$

$$(21)$$

The development of this determinant yields its polynomial form, i.e., the characteristic polynomial. In the following, $A(\lambda)$ can be named as a determinant or as a polynomial. For example, in the compartmental system in Figure 2a, this determinant is

$$A(\lambda) =$$

$$\begin{vmatrix} K_{1,1}-\lambda & 0 & K_{3,1} & 0 & 0 \\ K_{1,2} & K_{2,2}-\lambda & 0 & 0 & 0 \\ 0 & K_{2,3} & K_{3,3}-\lambda & 0 & 0 \\ 0 & K_{2,4} & 0 & K_{4,4}-\lambda & K_{5,4} \\ 0 & 0 & 0 & K_{4,5} & K_{5,5}-\lambda \end{vmatrix}$$

$$(22)$$

- λ_h ($h = 1, 2,..., N$): Eigenvalues the matrix **A**. These values are the same as the roots of the characteristic polynomial $A(\lambda)$.
- u: Number of non-null roots of the polynomial $A(\lambda)$, e.g., the number of non-null eigenvalues of matrix A.
- $\lambda_1, \lambda_2,..., \lambda_u$: Non-null roots of the polynomial $A(\lambda)$ and consequently the non-null eigenvalues of matrix **A**.
- c': Number of null roots of the polynomial $A(\lambda)$. The c' value can be positive or equal to zero.

$A_{k,i}(\lambda)$ ($k,i = 1, 2,..., N$): Minor of the order N-1 of $A(\lambda)$, which is obtained by removing the k-th row and the i-th column from $A(\lambda)$. For example, the determinant $A_{1,4}(\lambda)$ corresponding to the compartmental system in Figure 2a is the following:

$$A_{1,4}(\lambda) = \begin{vmatrix} K_{1,2} & K_{2,2}-\lambda & 0 & 0 \\ 0 & K_{2,3} & K_{3,3}-\lambda & 0 \\ 0 & K_{2,4} & 0 & K_{5,4} \\ 0 & 0 & 0 & K_{5,5}-\lambda \end{vmatrix}$$

$$(23)$$

Garcia-Meseguer et al. (2001) showed that:

$$A(\lambda) = (-1)^N \lambda^{c-1} \sum_{q=0}^{u} F_q \lambda^{u-q} \quad (F_0 = 1)$$

$$(24)$$

Where c and u are the number of null and no null roots, respectively, of the corresponding n-ECLCS

The coefficients of characteristic polynomial $A(\lambda)$ are the same as the coefficients of the characteristic polynomial $D(\lambda)$ of its equivalent closed system, i.e., of the *n*-ECLCS.

Some Properties of the Determinant $A_{k,i}(\lambda)$ (k,i =1,..., N) (29)

Garcia-Meseguer et al. (2001) showed that

$$A_{k,i}(\lambda) = (-1)^{N+i+k-1} \lambda^{c-2} \sum_{q=0}^{u} (f_{k,i})_q \lambda^{u-q}$$

$$(k, i = 1, 2, ..., N) \tag{25}$$

$$(f_{k,i})_o = 1 \text{ if } k = i; \quad (f_{k,i})_o = 0 \text{ si } k^1 i$$

The Eqs. (24) and (25) allow the expression of the characteristic determinant of the system matrix of any linear compartmental open system (and any of its minors of order N-1), as a function of parameters pertaining to the kinetically equivalent closed system. These parameters can be obtained by the procedure explained in Varón et al. (1995a) and Appendix A for closed systems. The non-null roots of the determinant $A(\lambda)$ associated with the N-OCLS under study, coincide with the non-null roots of the determinant $D(\lambda)$ corresponding to the n-ECLCS. Besides, the determinant $A(\lambda)$ has one null root fewer than $D(\lambda)$. Analogously, the non-null roots of the minor $A_{k,i}(\lambda)$ ($k,i = 1, 2,..., N$) of the determinant $A(\lambda)$ coincide with the non-null roots of the determinant $D_{k,i}(\lambda)$ ($k,i = 1, 2,..., N$). The minor $A_{k,i}(\lambda)$($k,i = 1, 2,..., N$) has one non-null root fewer than $D_{k,i}(\lambda)$ ($k,i=1,...,N$) (Garcia-Meseguer et al., 2001).

Time Course Equations

Due to the application of the formalism that allows the study of an open system through its corresponding kinetically equivalent closed system, the kinetic equations describing each of the N compartments, which belong to a N-OCLS, are the same as the kinetic equations pertaining to the compartments $X_1, X_2,..., X_N$ of the kinetically equivalent closed system (n-ECLCS). The addition of a hypothetical compartment a real system has no effect on the behavior of the progress of

material in the other compartments of the system. Therefore, the time course equation of the amount of material in any compartment of the open system is given by Eq. (1) (and the involved coefficients by Eqs. (9) and (10)), when it has been applied to any one of the compartments $X_1, X_2,..., X_N$ of the n-ECLCS. In this way the simplification of these expressions in the cases presented before can be performed in open compartmental systems.

$$x_i = A_{i,0} + \sum_{h=1}^{u} A_{i,h} e^{\lambda_h t} \qquad (i = 1, 2, ..., N) \tag{26}$$

where:

$$A_{i,0} = \frac{(f_{k,i})_u \, x_k^0}{F_u} \qquad (i = 1, 2, ..., N) \tag{27}$$

$$A_{i,h} = \frac{(-1)^{u-1} \sum_{k \in \Omega} x_k^0 \sum_{q=0}^{u} (f_{k,i})_q \lambda_h^{u-q}}{\lambda_h \prod_{\substack{p=1 \\ p \neq h}}^{u} (\lambda_p - \lambda_h)} \tag{28}$$

$$(i = 1, 2, ..., N; \quad h = 1, 2, ..., u)$$

(If u=1, then the denominator is λ_1)

Example 2. The scheme in Figure 2a corresponds to an open system, which we shall use as an example. Let us determine the time course equations for compartment X_1, i.e. x_1, under the same initial conditions as in the example in section 4.1. (i.e. $\Omega=\{X_1, X_3, X_5\}$). Since the kinetically equivalent closed compartmental system presented in Figure 2b coincides with the closed one presented in Figure 1 and since the initial conditions are the same, the expression of x_1 is given by Eq. (14) where $A_{1,h}$ is given by Eq. (15). The expressions of the coefficients involved also coincide with those presented in Appendix A if the fractional transfer coefficients $K_{1,6}$ and $K_{2,6}$ are replaced by the fractional excretion coefficients $K_{1,o}$ and $K_{2,o}$, respectively.

From a biological point of view, the most interesting open systems are the open ones without traps. In these particular open systems, all material is eventually excreted from the system to the environment through compartments with excretion. Hence, it is very interesting to apply the general results obtained before, which are valid for any open system with or without traps, to the particular case of open system without *traps*.

The Characteristic Determinant and its Minor of Order N-1

In open systems without traps, we have:

$$c' = 0 \tag{29}$$

$$\left(f_{k,i}\right)_N = 0 \tag{30}$$

Taking Eq. (17) and that $n=u+c$ into account, the following equations are valid:

$$u=N \tag{31}$$

$$c=1 \tag{32}$$

The development of the characteristic determinant $A(\lambda)$ according to Eq. (28), yields the next polynomial:

$$A(\lambda) = (-1)^N (\lambda^N + F_1 \lambda^{N-1} + \ldots + F_{N-1} \lambda + F_N) \tag{33}$$

where the coefficients in this expression can be obtained from the corresponding *n*-ECLCS by the procedure indicated before or by the development of the determinant that, in general, is more complicated.

In an analogous way and taking Eqs. (30)-(32) into account in Eq. (28), the following expression for minor $A_{k,i}(\lambda)$ has been obtained:

$$A_{k,i}(\lambda) = (-1)^{N+k+i+1} \left[\left(f_{k,i}\right)_0 \lambda^{N-1} + \left(f_{k,i}\right)_1 \lambda^{N-2} + \ldots + \left(f_{k,i}\right)_{N-1}\right] \quad (k,i = 1, 2, \ldots, N) \tag{34}$$

where the coefficients $\left(f_{k,i}\right)_q$ $(q = 0, 1, 2,\ldots, N\text{-}1)$ can be obtained easily from the corresponding *n*-ECLCS.

Simplified Time Course Equations

Since this kind of systems they are open, it is possible to apply Eqs. (1), (10) and (11), but more simplified expressions can be obtained by taking Eqs. (29) and (30) into account, i.e. that an open system without traps has not any null-root (Eq. (29)) and that all the compartments in an open system without traps $(X_1, X_2,\ldots, X_N)$ belong to non-final class in its corresponding kinetically equivalent closed system (Eq. (30)). Thus, the time progress of the amount of material in any compartment, which belongs to an open system without traps, is given by:

$$x_i = \sum_{h=1}^{N} A_{i,h} e^{\lambda_h t} \tag{35}$$

where:

$$A_{i,h} = \frac{(-1)^{N-1} \sum_{k\in\Omega} x_k^0 \left(\sum_{q=0}^{N-1} \left(f_{k,i}\right)_q \lambda_h^{N-q-1}\right)}{\prod_{\substack{p=1 \\ p\neq h}}^{N} \left(\lambda_p - \lambda_h\right)}$$

$$(i = 1,2,\ldots,n; \quad h = 1,2,\ldots,u) \tag{36}$$

if $N = 1$, then denominator of equation (36) is equal to λ_1, e.g., to $-F_1$.

COEFICOM: THE COMPUTER PROGRAM

The sequential and systematic character of the procedure proposed to employ the kinetic expressions, has allowed to implement a computer program which provides from data input:

1. The expressions of the coefficients $F_0, F_1, ...,$ F_u in the polynomial form of the characteristic determinant the matrix system ($D(\lambda)$ for closed systems or $A(\lambda)$ for open ones).
2. Optionally, the coefficients $(f_{k,i})_0, (f_{k,i})_1, ...,$ $(f_{k,i})_u$ in the development of the minors of characteristic determinant ($D_{k,i}(\lambda)$ for closed systems or $A_{k,i}(\lambda)$ for open ones)
3. The number of non-null roots, i.e. u, and of null roots of the characteristic polynomial (c for closed systems and c' for open ones).

The computer program has been written and compiled with the Microsoft Visual Basic for MS-DOS under the name COEFICOM. The main requirement is for a 32-bit Windows operating system such as Windows 2000, XP, Vista or Windows 7. The number of compartments of the system accepted by the program depends on the complexity of the compartmental system as well as on the characteristics of the computer used. We have resolved systems with up to 80 compartments. The software is available in http://oretano.iele-ab. uclm.es/~fgarcia/COEFICOM/. The correctness of the execution of the program has been checked using many different cases.

For simplicity, in the following we denote as υ the number of compartments of the system, i.e. $\upsilon = N$ for open systems and $\upsilon = n$ for closed ones.

Data Input

Once one has an open or closed particular linear system described as a connectivity diagram, the data necessary to obtain the number of non-null

roots, the expressions of coefficients $F_0, F_1, ..., F_u$ and $(f_{k,i})_0, (f_{k,i})_1, ..., (f_{k,i})_q$ ($q = 0, 1, ..., u; k, i = 1, 2, ..., \upsilon$) are the following:

1. The number of compartments, υ, which is directly obtained from the connectivity diagram of the system
2. The expressions of fractional transfer coefficients besides the expressions of the fractional excretion coefficients for open systems.
3. k-values and i-values in which the user is interested.

The program permits the user to give the compartmental system under study a name, which is saved in the file created by the program. If no name is given, then the *enter* key must be pressed directly. Next, the program requests the number of compartments of the system. Then, it asks for an arbitrary correlative numbering of these compartments as $X_1, X_2, ..., X_\upsilon$. After this, the user has to indicate if it is a closed or an open system by pressing 1 or 2 respectively (at the request of the program).

Now, the program needs the υ (υ-1) expressions of all of the fractional transfer coefficients $K_{i,j}$ ($i,j=1,2,..., \upsilon; i \neq j$) for closed systems or of all the (υ-1)^2 fractional transfer coefficients and fractional excretion coefficients $K_{i,j}$ ($i=1,2,..., \upsilon$; $j=o,1,2,..., \upsilon$) for open systems.

The possibility of choosing any expression for a fractional coefficient (transfer or excretion), besides $K_{i,j}$ itself, provides a greater versatility to the program (Figure 3). In this way, if for example the compartments of the system are identified with enzyme species, then, the expressions of the rate constants, i.e. the fractional transfer coefficients can include concentrations of ligand species or any other characteristics e.g. $k_{+1}[S]_0$, $k_{+1}[I]$, $k_3[I]$ etc. All characters in the expression of a fractional coefficient must be written on the same line, e.g. a rate constant such as $k_{+1}[S]_0$ must be entered as

Figure 3.

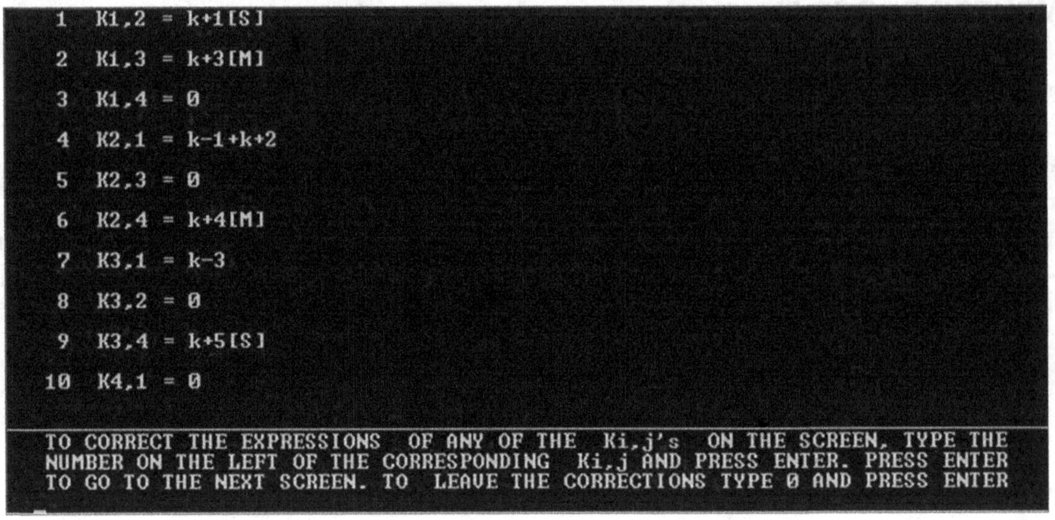

```
 1   K1,2  =  k+1[S]

 2   K1,3  =  k+3[M]

 3   K1,4  =  0

 4   K2,1  =  k-1+k+2

 5   K2,3  =  0

 6   K2,4  =  k+4[M]

 7   K3,1  =  k-3

 8   K3,2  =  0

 9   K3,4  =  k+5[S]

10   K4,1  =  0
```

```
TO CORRECT THE EXPRESSIONS  OF ANY OF THE  Ki,j's  ON THE SCREEN, TYPE THE
NUMBER ON THE LEFT OF THE CORRESPONDING  Ki,j AND PRESS ENTER. PRESS ENTER
TO GO TO THE NEXT SCREEN. TO  LEAVE THE CORRECTIONS TYPE 0 AND PRESS ENTER
```

k+1[S]0. If, in a compartmental system, more than one direct connection between X_i and X_j exits (the corresponding connectivity diagram will show only an arrow), then the expression for the corresponding fractional coefficient consists of a sum of terms; for example if between compartment X_i and compartment X_j two connections characterized by $K'_{i,j}$ and $K''_{i,j}$ constants exit, then, $K_{i,j} = K'_{i,j} + K''_{i,j}$. In these cases, $K_{i,j}$ can be entered as Ki,j or as $K'i,j + K''i,j$. Besides, if a fractional coefficient contains a superindex and subindex, e.g. $K'_{i,j}$, the input can be $K'i,j$ or Ki,j'. We limited the number of type characters for any fractional coefficient, $K_{i,j}$ or $K_{i,o}$, to 144 to improve the presentation on the computer screen.

The left side and the symbol = of each of the equations for the input of the different fractional coefficients $K_{i,j}$ are displayed automatically on the screen. If a fractional coefficient (transfer or excretion) is zero, then the input must be *0* or the *enter* key may be pressed directly. After the input of all of the fractional coefficients, the program offers the possibility of correction or modification of these constants (Figure 3).

Choice of the Options

After the data input, the program allows the user to select any of the following options:

1. Determination of coefficients $F_0, F_1,..., F_u$
2. Determination of coefficients $(f_{k,i})_0, (f_{k,i})_1,..., (f_{k,i})_u$
3. Both the coefficients $F_0, F_1,..., F_u$ and the coefficients $(f_{k,i})_0,..., (f_{k,i})_u$

Press 1, 2 or 3 to select the corresponding option. If the input is option 2 or option 3, all the possible k-values are displayed on the screen, i.e. 1, 2,..., v for choosing the values in which the user is interested. Next, all the possible i-values are displayed on the screen, i.e. 1, 2,..., v to be chosen by the user. The program allows the corrections of mistakes in the choice of k- and i-values.

Output File

The program creates an ASCII file named MARA-MAED, which can be changed by the user. This file can be handled like other ASCII files and it is suitable for adequate word processors. The file

Figure 4.

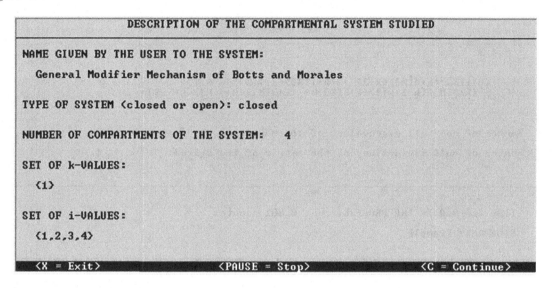

```
┌──────────────────────────────────────────────────────────────────────┐
│          DESCRIPTION OF THE COMPARTMENTAL SYSTEM STUDIED               │
├──────────────────────────────────────────────────────────────────────┤
│ NAME GIVEN BY THE USER TO THE SYSTEM:                                  │
│   General Modifier Mechanism of Botts and Morales                     │
│                                                                        │
│ TYPE OF SYSTEM (closed or open): closed                               │
│                                                                        │
│ NUMBER OF COMPARTMENTS OF THE SYSTEM:    4                            │
│                                                                        │
│ SET OF k-VALUES:                                                       │
│   (1)                                                                  │
│                                                                        │
│ SET OF i-VALUES:                                                       │
│   (1,2,3,4)                                                            │
│                                                                        │
│  (X = Exit)              (PAUSE = Stop)              (C = Continue)    │
└──────────────────────────────────────────────────────────────────────┘
```

content is divided in two parts: *description of the compartmental system studied* and *results*. At the end of the file the given name, the datum of the file creation and the time elapsed in the process appear. The first part, *description of the compartmental system studied*, consists of a presentation of all the data inputs and the choices of the options made (Figure 4). The second part, *results*, gives the symbolic expressions of coefficients corresponding to the option selected (Figure 5). Besides, the file contains always the number of non-null eigenvalues (i.e. u) and the number of null eigenvalues (denoted by c in closed systems and by c' in open ones) of the matrix of the system, which are determined by the computer program too.

Exit of the Program

It is possible to view on the screen the content of the output file and to repeat the process, to carry out a different analysis of the same compartmental system and/or to study a new compartmental system. Repetition of the process for the same system allows the user to modify the expressions of the fractional coefficients $K_{i,j}$ and/or to change one or more of the options which were selected. In the case of repetition of a compartmental system or for studying a new one, it is important, if one does not want to lose information, in each case to save the output file under a different name.

Correction of Possible Errors

The program prevents most of the errors in the input of the expressions of the fractional coefficients $K_{i,j}$'s involved in the compartmental system under study. Therefore, it does not accept any expression, which does not possess the required characteristics (commented in this chapter as well as in the instructions contained in the program). Nevertheless, as not all of the possible typing misprints due to deviation from the instructions are considered, it is advisable to follow the instructions carefully. Moreover, in the input of data as well as in the selection of the different options, the program permits a correction of other kinds of errors and/or to make modifications.

Acquisition of the Kinetic Equations and the Kinetic Parameters

The content of the second part of the output file (i.e. *results*) for the concrete compartmental sys-

Figure 5.

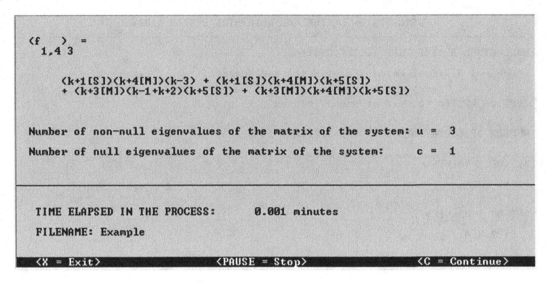

```
(f   ) =
  1,4 3


    (k+1[S])(k+4[M])(k-3) + (k+1[S])(k+4[M])(k+5[S])
    + (k+3[M])(k-1+k+2)(k+5[S]) + (k+3[M])(k+4[M])(k+5[S])



Number of non-null eigenvalues of the matrix of the system: u = 3
Number of null eigenvalues of the matrix of the system:     c = 1



TIME ELAPSED IN THE PROCESS:        0.001 minutes
FILENAME: Example
```

⟨X = Exit⟩	⟨PAUSE = Stop⟩	⟨C = Continue⟩

tem under study together with the general Eq. (1), (9)-(10) allow the user in all cases to include the kinetic equations desired.

EXAMPLES

In the following, COEFICOM is applied to two compartmental systems: A closed and an open one with traps. These examples cover most of the situations that a user will deal with since the open systems without traps have been studied in this chapter as a particular case of open systems.

Example 1: Closed Compartmental System

Compartmental System to be Studied

COEFICOM is applied to the example given in Figure 6 for obtaining the transient phase equation of all of the enzyme species. Denoting the enzyme species E, ES, EM and ESM as the compartments X_1, X_2, X_3 and X_4, respectively, then the directed graph corresponding to above mechanism is shown in Figure 7. It is assumed that at t=0 the only enzyme species in the system

is the free enzyme, X_1, the initial concentration has been denoted by $[E]_0$. It is also assumed that the concentrations of any ligand species which binds to an enzyme specie remains constant, while the time passes. Thus, under these conditions, this mechanism fits our model, because all of the steps are of first or pseudo-first order. The interaction with the program is as follows.

Data Input

One name of the mechanism under study could be: *General Modifier Mechanism of Botts and Morales (Botts & Morales, 1953)*. Any other name would be valid. When the program requests the number of compartments involved in the reaction

Figure 6.

$$E + S \underset{k_{-1}}{\overset{k_{+1}}{\rightleftharpoons}} ES \xrightarrow{k_{+2}} E + P$$

$$+ \qquad +$$

$$M \qquad M$$

$$k_{+3} \big\Vert k_{-3} \qquad k_{-4} \big\Vert k_{+4}$$

$$EM + S \underset{k_{-5}}{\overset{k_{+5}}{\rightleftharpoons}} EMS \xrightarrow{k_{+6}} EM + P$$

mechanism, the number 4 must be entered. Then, the program denotes arbitrarily the compartments as X_1, X_2, X_3 and X_4 and next, the program ask whether the compartmental system is closed or open, in this case, it could be entered closed.

Now the 4 x 3=12 expressions of the different $K_{i,j}$-expressions $(i,j=1,2,3,4; i \neq j)$ must be entered as:

$$K1,2 = k + 1[S]$$

$$K1,3 = k + 3[M]$$

$$K1,4 = 0$$

$$K2,1 = k \text{-} 1 + k + 2$$

$$K2,3 = 0$$

$$K2,4 = k + 4[M]$$

$$K3,1 = k \text{-} 3$$

$$K3,2 = 0$$

$$K3,4 = k + 5[S]$$

$$K4,1 = 0$$

$$K4,2 = k \text{-} 4$$

$$K4,3 = k \text{-} 5 + k + 6$$

(37)

The left side and the symbol = of each of the above equations for the input of the 12 fractional transfer coefficients $K_{i,j}$ are displayed automati-

cally on the screen. For the fractional transfer coefficients $K_{i,j}$ equal to zero, the input must be *0* or the *enter* key may be pressed directly.

Choice of the Options

Once the above 12 expressions for all the $K_{i,j}$'s have been entered, we select the option 3, i.e. both coefficients F_0, F_1,..., F_u and coefficients $(f_{k,i})_0$,..., $(f_{k,i})_u$. Now the k-values that may appear in the determinant $D_{k,i}(\lambda)$ are displayed on the screen and we select the number 1. After this, all the possible i-values of the determinant $D_{k,i}(\lambda)$ are displayed on the screen and we select all of them by pressing (*) or each of them, i.e. i=1, 2, 3, 4.

Output File

Once all the inputs have been made, the process begins and after a short time (indicated in this file) the output file is completed. The file name given automatically by the program is MARAMAED. This name can be changed by the user. One arbitrarily can rename the file as *Example 1*. Then, the content of the output file can be viewed on the screen on the request of the user. Finally, the *u*- and *c*- values are given (3 and 1 respectively). The content of this file is shown in Appendix B. Note, that the part of the output file named *Description of the compartmental system studied* summarises all the data input and options selected.

Exit of the Program

If one does not want to view the output file or if the view is finished, then the program offers the possibility of exiting or to carry out another kinetic analysis for the same compartmental system, key "N" must be pressed. Next, the program offers the possibility to carry out the kinetic analysis for another compartmental system. If someone wants to derive another kinetic analysis for the next example, it is not necessary to exit the program but press the key "Y".

Figure 7.

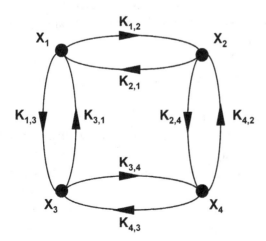

Example 2: Open Compartmental System with Traps

Compartmental System to be Studied

From open compartmental system represented in Figure 2a, the coefficients F_0, F_1, F_2, F_3, F_4 and F_5 of the characteristic polynomial $A(\lambda)$ (given by Eq. (22) for this example) and the coefficients involved in kinetic equations corresponding to the example studied in section 4.2 are going to be obtained using COEFICOM

Data Input

Initially, the program asks for the name given to the system under study, one possibility could be "*Example 2: open system*". After this, the program requests the number of compartments of the systems involved in the compartmental system and the number 5 must be entered. Then, the program denotes arbitrarily the compartments as X_1, X_2, X_3, X_4 and X_5; now the program asks whether the compartmental system is a closed or open one. We enter option 2 (open). Next, the program requires the 25 expressions of fractional coefficients, which include the transfer coefficients $K_{i,j}$ ($i,j = 1, 2,...,$ 5; $i \neq j$) and the excretion coefficients $K_{i,o}$ ($i = 1$, 2,..., 5). The following expression must be entered:

$$K1,2 = K1,2$$
$$K1,0 = K1,0$$
$$K2,3 = K2,3$$
$$K2,4 = K2,4$$
$$K2,0 = K2,0 \quad\quad (38)$$
$$K3,1 = K3,1$$
$$K4,5 = K4,5$$
$$K5,4 = K5,4$$

The left side and the symbol = of each of the above equations for the input of the 25 fractional coefficients $K_{i,j}$'s are displayed automatically on the screen. For the fractional coefficients $K_{i,j}$ equal to zero, the input must be *0* or the *enter* key may be pressed directly.

Choice of the Options

Once the above 25 expressions for all of the $K_{i,j}$'s have been entered, option 3 must be selected. Now the k-values that may appear in the determinant $A_{k,i}(\lambda)$ are displayed on the screen and numbers 1, 3 and 5 are selected. After this, all the possible i-values of determinant $A_{k,i}(\lambda)$ are displayed on the screen and we select number 1.

Output File

Once all the inputs have been made, the process begins and after a short time (indicated in this file) the output file is completed. The file name given automatically by the program is MARA-MAED. This name can be changed by the user. One could arbitrarily rename the file, e.g., as *Example 2*. Then, the content of the output file can be viewed on the screen on request of the user. Finally, u and c' (the number of non-null roots and of null roots, respectively, of the characteristic polynomial of 5-OLCS, $A(\lambda)$, and the c-value (the number of null roots of the characteristic polynomial of 6-ECLCS, $D(\lambda)$). The content of this file is shown in Appendix C as *Example 2*. Note, that the part of the output file named *Description of the compartmental system studied* summarises all the data input and options selected.

Exit of the Program

If one does not want to view the output file or if the view is finished, then the program offers the possibility of exiting or to carry out another kinetic analysis for the same compartmental system, key "N" must be pressed. Next, the program offers the possibility to carry out the kinetic analysis for another compartmental system. If someone does not want to derive any other kinetic analysis, the key "Y" must be pressed to exit the program.

FUTURE RESEARCH DIRECTIONS

Eq. (1) determines the progress of material in any compartment of a closed linear system, with the coefficients $A_{i,o}$ and $A_{i,h}$ given by the Eqs. (2) and (3). It is valid in a general way and it can be applied to any closed compartmental system that fits the model, regardless the compartment X_i considered as well as the compartments in which the matter is injected at t=0.

However, these equations have the limitation that all non-null fractional transfer coefficients involved in the system appear in them. This fact did not mean any limitation of these equations if they are simplified so as to eliminate the factors that haven't got influence. This simplification can be very laborious, requiring work time and being subjected to human errors. Thus, it would be more convenient to obtain, from Eqs. (1-3), simplified expressions where the fractional transfer coefficients listed, were the only ones that have an influence on the compartment X_i in the initial set conditions.

Therefore, if in the initial compartmental system, some of these coefficients are equal to zero and Eqs. (1-3) are applied to this modified system, an equation is obtained in which the parameters u and F_1, F_2, ..., F_u involved in this expression are not the same as those parameters corresponding to the initial compartmental system. These parameters also change, in general, according to the compartment X_i considered (keeping the initial conditions).

One of the future research direction could be the development of a computer program that determine the optimized expressions of general kinetic equations corresponding to any linear compartmental system with zero input, i.e. material may be injected at t=0 into one or more of its compartments, as well as the optimized general

kinetic equations, for the instantaneous concentration, from both enzyme species and ligand species, that fit the model or the incorporation of the rapid equilibrium approximation from the reversible stage to generate directly the corresponding kinetic equations or even include the possibility of giving numerical values for the fractional transfer coefficients and initial concentrations, which would yield a numerical expression for the instantaneous concentrations of the species involved in the mechanism.

CONCLUSION

In this chapter, it has presented and extended the global study of linear compartmental systems using a model, with zero input, which includes both open and closed systems with or without traps carry out essentially by Garcia-Meseguer et al. (2001). The open systems are treated as hypothetical kinetically equivalent closed systems by the application of an appropiate formalism. This formalism together with some properties of the matrix system is very useful because it allows to obtain general expressions in a final, simple form for the description of the kinetic evolution of the system as a function of the inputs and of the quantities, which are simple functions of the fractional coefficients [Eqs. (1), (9)-(10)]. The determination of these quantities can be greatly facilitated by the use of the versatile computer program (COEFICOM).

To determine the kinetic expressions of linear open systems of N compartments with or without traps, denoted as N-OLCS, the procedure used consisted on obtaining the kinetic equations of the kinetically equivalent closed system, n-ECLCS. The additional compartment, X_n, added to N-OLCS becomes n-ECLC, behaves as a trap, which collects all the excretions of material to the environment from any compartment of the initial original open system. Since the added compartment does not affect the kinetics of the rest of compartments of the open system, the time course equations obtained for these compartments in the *n*-ECLCS are the same as those corresponding to the above mentioned compartments in the original open system. This formalism had been proposed before (Jacquez, 1985) but, in our knowledge, it was not received any quantitative treatment until now.

Besides, if one wants to determine the kinetics of the elimination of material from the open system to the environment, one would only have to determine the instantaneous accumulation of material in the compartment X_n.

In addition, the general expressions can be particularized for an important case from the point of view of a biological system: open systems without traps [Eqs (35)-(36)].

The properties of the open *N*-OLCS allow the recast of the multiexponential time course equations to a form, which contains quantities that easily can be obtained from the non-null fractional coefficients, i.e. from the connectivity diagram. Another important aspect of this analysis is its circumvention of the symbolic expansion of determinants. The latter is a laborious task which is prone to human errors even for systems of no great complexity.

Applicability of the Equations

The time course equations derived here are applicable to a very general model. These equations are valid for the process of distribution of material between the compartments of a system, closed or open, in the transient phase and the steady state ($t \rightarrow \infty$). In the latter state, the general expression (Eq. (1)) becomes $x_i = A_{i,0}$ ($i = 1, 2,..., v$) in closed systems and open systems with traps, and $x_i = 0$ in open ones without traps, since the exponential terms can be neglected and since the λ_h's are negative or complex with the real part negative.

This analysis for linear compartmental systems with zero input is also useful for the analysis of systems with any input, since the analysis of the

latter requires the previous solution of the system assuming zero input (Anderson, 1983; Jacquez, 1985).

The kinetic equations presented here are valid irrespective of whether the λ_h's are real or complex. Nevertheless, in the case that complex roots exist, these equations can be also expressed in a more reliable form, i.e., when one or more pairs of roots λ_h ($h = 1, 2,..., u$) can be complex conjugate, Eq. (1) remains valid, but the sum of two exponential terms of the equation that contain seldom roots complex conjugate, λ_v y λ_w ($\lambda_v = a+bi$ and $\lambda_w = a-bi$, being a negative quantity), can be replaced, using the Euler relations, as follows:

$$A_{j,v}e^{\lambda_v t} + A_{j.w}e^{\lambda_n t} = \left(B\cos bt + C\,senbt\right)e^{at}$$

$$(39)$$

where:

$$B=A_{j,v}+A_{j,w} \qquad (40)$$

$$C = i(A_{j,v} - A_{j,w}) \quad i = \sqrt{-1} \qquad (41)$$

The examples shown in Figure 1 and Figure 2a, section 3.2. and 4.1., respectively, show the derivation of the time course equations by this procedure. The manual determination of the coefficients in these equations is shown in Appendix A.

The Computer Program (COEFICOM)

The formulation of the expressions of the coefficients F_q ($q = 0, 1, 2,..., u$) and of the coefficients $(f_{k,i})_q$ and the determination of the *u*-value (number of non-null eigenvalues of the matrix system) in Eqs. (1), (9), (10), (37) may be performed by the simple and efficient computer program. This program improves and extends a previous one implemented by Varón et al. (1995b).

The computer program COEFICOM only needs the following inputs:

1. The number of compartments of the system;
2. The indication of whether the system is open or closed;
3. The identification of the *k*- and *i*-values
4. The expressions of the fractional coefficients.

These inputs allow the choice of one of the three following options:

1. Determination of the expressions of the coefficients F_q.
2. Determination of the expressions of the coefficients $(f_{k,i})_q$.
3. The simultaneously determination of the expressions of both types of coefficients.

The result of the process is saved in a ASCII file, which is made automatically during the execution. This one allows its loading with any adequate text proccessor. Therefore, it is no longer necessary to apply any manual procedure to obtain the transient phase equations of compartmental system. Moreover, since $A_{i,o}$ ($i = 1, 2,...,$ υ) describes the amount of material into compartment X_i. This program is also valid for the derivation of the steady state equations and for evaluating mean residence times and other kinetic parameters in any linear compartmental system.

REFERENCES

Anderson, D. H. (1983). *Compartmental modelling and tracer kinetics*. Berlin: Springer Verlag.

Arribas, E., Bisswanger, H., Sotos-Lomas, A., Garcia-Moreno, M., Garcia-Canovas, F., & Donoso-Pardo, J. (2008a). A method, based on statistical moments, to evaluate the kinetic parameters involved in unstable enzyme systems. *Journal of Mathematical Chemistry, 44,* 379–404. doi:10.1007/s10910-007-9316-9

Arribas, E., Munoz-Lopez, A., Garcia-Meseguer, M. J., Lopez-Najera, A., Avalos, L., & Garcia-Molina, F. (2008b). Mean lifetime and first-passage time of the enzyme species involved in an enzyme reaction. Application to unstable enzyme systems. *Bulletin of Mathematical Biology, 70,* 1425–1449. doi:10.1007/s11538-008-9307-4

Bevan, D. R., & Weyand, E. H. (1988). Compartmental analysis of the disposition of benzo[a] pyrene in rats. *Carcinogenesis, 9,* 2027–2032. doi:10.1093/carcin/9.11.2027

Botts, J., & Morales, M. (1953). Analytical description of the effect of modifiers and of enzyme multivalency upon the steady state catalyzed reaction rate. *Transactions of the Faraday Society, 49,* 696–707. doi:10.1039/tf9534900696

Cheng, H. Y. (1991). A method for calculating the mean residence times of catenary metabolites. *Biopharmaceutics & Drug Disposition, 12,* 335–342. doi:10.1002/bdd.2510120503

Chou, K. C. (1990). Applications of graph theory to enzyme kinetics and protein folding kinetics. Steady and non-steady-state systems. *Biophysical Chemistry, 35,* 1–24. doi:10.1016/0301-4622(90)80056-D

de Graaf, A. A., Freidig, A. P., De, R. B., Jamshidi, N., Heinemann, M., & Rullmann, J. A. (2009). Nutritional systems biology modeling: from molecular mechanisms to physiology. *PLoS Computational Biology, 5,* e1000554. doi:10.1371/journal.pcbi.1000554

Galvez, J., & Varon, R. (1981). I. Transient phase kinetics of enzyme reactions. *Journal of Theoretical Biology, 89,* 1–17. doi:10.1016/0022-5193(81)90175-2

Garcia-Meseguer, M. J. (1998). *Análisis cinético de los sistemas lineales de compartimentos: aplicación a la evaluación de parámetros medios. Doctoral Thesis.* Cuenca, Spain: Servicio de publicaciones de la UCLM.

Garcia-Meseguer, M. J., Vidal de Labra, J. A., Garcia-Canovas, F., Havsteen, B. H., Garcia-Moreno, M., & Varon, R. (2001). Time course equations of the amount of substance in a linear compartmental system and their computerized derivation. *BioSystems*, *59*, 197–220. doi:10.1016/S0303-2647(01)00116-2

Garcia-Meseguer, M. J., Vidal de Labra, J. A., Garcia-Moreno, M., Garcia-Canovas, F., Havsteen, B. H., & Varon, R. (2003). Mean residence times in linear compartmental systems. Symbolic formulae for their direct evaluation. *Bulletin of Mathematical Biology*, *65*, 279–308. doi:10.1016/S0092-8240(02)00096-4

Garcia-Sevilla, F., Arribas, E., Bisswanger, H., Garcia-Moreno, M., Garcia-Canovas, F., & Gomez-Ladron de Guevara, R. (2010). wREFERASS: Rate Equations for Enzyme Reactions at Steady State under MS-Windows. *MATCH Commun.Math.Comput.Chem.*, *63*, 553–571.

Garcia-Sevilla, F., Garrido del Solo, C., Duggleby, R. G., Garcia-Canovas, F., Peyro, R., & Varon, R. (2000). Use of a windows program for simulation of the progress curves of reactants and intermediates involved in enzyme-catalyzed reactions. *Bio Systems*, *54*, 151–164. doi:10.1016/S0303-2647(99)00071-4

Garrido del Solo, C., Varon, R., & Garcia-Canovas, F. (1992). Programa de ordenador para simular el comportamiento cinético de las reacciones enzimáticas. *Anales de Química de la RSEQ*, *88*, 633–639.

Gibaldi, M. (1991). *Biopharmaceutics and clinical pharmacokinetics* (4th ed.). Londres: Lea and Febiger.

Green, M. H. (1992). Introduction to modelling. *The Journal of Nutrition*, *122*, 690–694.

Hearon, J. Z. (1963). Theorems on linear systems. *Ann.N.Y. Acad.Sci.*, *108*, 36–38. doi:10.1111/j.1749-6632.1963.tb13364.x

Jacquez, J. A. (1985). *Compartmental analysis in Biology and Medicine* (2nd ed.). Ann Arbor, Michigan.

Jacquez, J. A. (1996). *Compartmental analysis in Biology and Medicine.* (3 ed.) Dexter, Michigan: Thompson-Shore Inc.

Jacquez, J. A. (1999). *Modelling with Compartmets.* Ann Arbor, Michigan: Biomedware.

Jacquez, J. A. (2002). Density functions of residence times for deterministic and stochastic compartmental systems. *Mathematical Biosciences*, *180*, 127–139. doi:10.1016/S0025-5564(02)00110-4

Juillet, B., Bos, C., Gaudichon, C., Tome, D., & Fouillet, H. (2009). Parameter estimation for linear compartmental models--a sensitivity analysis approach. *Annals of Biomedical Engineering*, *37*, 1028–1042. doi:10.1007/s10439-009-9651-z

Lal, R., & Anderson, D. H. (1990). Calculation and utilization of component matrices in linear bioscience models. *Mathematical Biosciences*, *99*, 11–29. doi:10.1016/0025-5564(90)90136-M

Li, W. B., & Hoeschen, C. (2010). Uncertainty and sensitivity analysis of biokinetic models for radiopharmaceuticals used in nuclear medicine. *Radiation Protection Dosimetry*, *139*, 228–231. doi:10.1093/rpd/ncq064

Moolgavkar, S. H., & Luebeck, G. (1990). Two-event model for carcinogenesis: biological, mathematical, and statistical considerations. *Risk Analysis*, *10*, 323–341. doi:10.1111/j.1539-6924.1990.tb01053.x

Nye, J. A., Votaw, J. R., Jarkas, N., Purselle, D., Camp, V., & Bremner, J. D. (2008). Compartmental modeling of 11C-HOMADAM binding to the serotonin transporter in the healthy human brain. *Journal of Nuclear Medicine*, *49*, 2018–2025. doi:10.2967/jnumed.108.054262

Rescigno, A. (1956). A contribution to the theory of tracer methods. II. *Biochimica et Biophysica Acta, 21*, 111–116. doi:10.1016/0006-3002(56)90100-7

Rescigno, A. (1999). Compartmental analysis revisited. *Pharmacological Research, 39*, 471–478. doi:10.1006/phrs.1999.0467

Rescigno, A. (2004). On the use of pharmacokinetic models. *Physics in Medicine and Biology, 49*, 4657–4676. doi:10.1088/0031-9155/49/19/014

Rescigno, A., & Thakur, S. (1991). *New trends in pharmacokinetics (Vol. 221)*. New York: Plenum Press.

Sines, J. J., & Hackney, D. D. (1987). A residence-time analysis of enzyme kinetics. *The Biochemical Journal, 243*, 159–164.

Varon, R., Garcia-Meseguer, M. J., Garcia-Canovas, F., & Havsteen, B. H. (1995a). General linear compartment model with zero input: I. Kinetic equations. *Bio Systems, 36*, 121–133. doi:10.1016/0303-2647(95)01533-Q

Varon, R., Garcia-Meseguer, M. J., & Havsteen, B. H. (1995b). General linear compartment model with zero input: II. The computerized derivation of the kinetic equations. *Bio Systems, 36*, 135–144. doi:10.1016/0303-2647(95)01536-T

Varon, R., Garcia-Meseguer, M. J., Valero, E., Garcia-Moreno, M., & Garcia-Canovas, F. (1995). General linear compartment model with zero input: III. First passage residence time of enzyme systems. *Bio Systems, 36*, 145–156. doi:10.1016/0303-2647(95)01535-S

Varon, R., Masia-Perez, J., Garcia-Molina, F., Garcia-Canovas, F., Arias, E., & Arribas, E. (2007). An alternative analysis of enzyme systems based on the whole reaction time. Evaluation of the kinetic parameters and initial enzyme concentration. *Journal of Mathematical Chemistry, 42*, 789–813. doi:10.1007/s10910-006-9142-5

Veng-Pedersen, P. (1989). Mean time parameters dealing with the tissue distribution of drugs: limitations and extension. *Journal of Pharmaceutical Sciences, 78*, 264–266. doi:10.1002/jps.2600780320

Villalba, J. M., Barbero, A. J., Diaz-Sierra, R., Arribas, E., Garcia-Meseguer, M. J., Garcia-Sevilla, F. et al. (2010). Computerized evaluation of mean residence times in multicompartmental linear system and pharmacokinetics. *J. Comput. Chem.*

Watabe, H., Ikoma, Y., Kimura, Y., Naganawa, M., & Shidahara, M. (2006). PET kinetic analysis-compartmental model. *Annals of Nuclear Medicine, 20*, 583–588. doi:10.1007/BF02984655

Weiss, M. (1992). The relevance of residence time theory to pharmacokinetics. *European Journal of Clinical Pharmacology, 43*, 571–579. doi:10.1007/BF02284953

ADDITIONAL READING

Arias, E., Picazo, M., Garcia-Sevilla, F., Alberto, A., Arribas, E., & Varon, R. (2007). A Matlab-based software to obtain the time course equations of dynamic linear systems. *Applied Mathematical Sciences, 1*, 551–570.

Carson, E., & Cobelli, C. (2001). *Modelling methodology for physiology and medicine*. San Diego: Academic Press.

Diaz-Sierra, R., & Fairen, V. (2001). Simplified method for the computation of parameters of power-law rate equations from time-series. *Mathematical Biosciences, 171*, 1–19. doi:10.1016/S0025-5564(01)00051-7

Diaz-Sierra, R., Hernandez-Bermejo, B., & Fairen, V. (1999). Graph-theoretic description of the interplay between non-linearity and connectivity in biological systems. *Mathematical Biosciences, 156*, 229–253. doi:10.1016/S0025-5564(98)10068-8

Diaz-Sierra, R., Lozano, J. B., & Fairen, V. (1999). Deduction of chemical mechanism from the linear response around steady state. *Journal of Physical Chemistry*, *3*, 337–343.

Escribano, J., Garcia-Moreno, M., Garcia-Canovas, F., Garcia-Carmona, F., Varon, R., & Tudela, J. (1987). Kinetic study of the transient phase of a chemical reaction system coupled to an enzymatically catalyzed step. Application to the oxidation of epinine by tyrosinase. *Biophysical Chemistry*, *27*, 15–25. doi:10.1016/0301-4622(87)80043-1

Escribano, J., Tudela, J., Garcia-Carmona, F., & Garcia-Canovas, F. (1989). A kinetic study of the suicide inactivation of an enzyme measured through coupling reactions. Application to the suicide inactivation of tyrosinase. *The Biochemical Journal*, *262*, 597–603.

Garcia-Canovas, F., Tudela, J., Martinez-Madrid, C., Varon, R., Garcia-Carmona, F., & Lozano, J. A. (1987a). Kinetic study on the suicide inactivation of tyrosinase induced by catechol. *Biochimica et Biophysica Acta*, *912*, 417–423. doi:10.1016/0167-4838(87)90047-1

Garcia-Canovas, F., Tudela, J., Varon, R., & Vazquez, A. (1989). Experimental methods for kinetic study of suicide substrates. *Journal of Enzyme Inhibition*, *3*, 81–90. doi:10.3109/14756368909030367

Garcia-Canovas, F., Varon, R., Galvez, J., Garcia-Carmona, F., Tudela, J., & Garcia-Moreno, M. (1987b). Kinetic study about the transient phase of Michaelis-type enzymes with linear and hyperbolic inhibition. *An. Quim.*, *83*, 219–223.

Garcia-Molina, F., Munoz, J. L., Varon, R., Rodriguez-Lopez, J. N., Garcia-Canovas, F., & Tudela, J. (2007). An approximate analytical solution to the lag period of monophenolase activity of tyrosinase. *The International Journal of Biochemistry & Cell Biology*, *39*, 238–252. doi:10.1016/j.biocel.2006.08.007

Garcia-Molina, F., Penalver, M. J., Rodriguez-Lopez, J. N., Garcia-Canovas, F., & Tudela, J. (2005). Enzymatic method with polyphenol oxidase for the determination of cysteine and N-acetylcysteine. *Journal of Agricultural and Food Chemistry*, *53*, 6183–6189. doi:10.1021/jf050197k

Garcia-Moreno, M., Garcia-Canovas, F., Varon, R., Garcia-Carmona, F., Vazquez, A., & Valero, E. (1987). Kinetic-study of the transient phase of 3-substrate enzyme reaction with ordered ter-ter mechanisms – Kinetic data analysis. *An. Quim.*, *83*, 344–347.

Garcia-Moreno, M., Havsteen, B. H., Varon, R., & Rix-Matzen, H. (1991). Evaluation of the kinetic parameters of the activation of trypsinogen by trypsin. *Biochimica et Biophysica Acta*, *1080*, 143–147. doi:10.1016/0167-4838(91)90141-L

Garrido del Solo, C., Yago, J. M., Garcia-Moreno, M., Havsteen, B. H., Garcia-Canovas, F., & Varon, R. (2005). The kinetic effect of the inactivation of the enzyme-substrate complex in an enzymatic reaction with slow-binding inhibition. *Applied Mathematics and Computation*, *171*, 450–463. doi:10.1016/j.amc.2005.01.042

Havsteen, B. H., Garcia-Moreno, M., Valero, E., Manjabacas, M. C., & Varon, R. (1993). The kinetics of enzyme systems involving activation of zymogens. *Bulletin of Mathematical Biology*, *55*, 561–583.

Juillet, B., Bos, C., Gaudichon, C., Tome, D., & Fouillet, H. (2009). Parameter estimation for linear compartmental models--a sensitivity analysis approach. *Annals of Biomedical Engineering*, *37*, 1028–1042. doi:10.1007/s10439-009-9651-z

Peletier, L. A., Benson, N., & van der Graaf, P. H. (2010). Impact of protein binding on receptor occupancy: A two-compartment model. *Journal of Theoretical Biology*, *265*, 657–671. doi:10.1016/j.jtbi.2010.05.035

Rowland, M., & Tozer, N. (1989). *Clinical pharmacokinetics: concepts and applications* (2nd ed.). London: Lea & Febiger.

Tozer, T., & Rowland, M. (2006). *Introduction to Pharmacokinetics and Pharmacodynamics: The Quantitative Basis of Drug Therapy*. (1 ed.) Baltimore, MD 21201: Lippincott Williams & Wilkins.

Tudela, J., Garcia-Canovas, F., Varon, R., Jimenez, M., Garcia-Carmona, F., & Lozano, J. A. (1988). Kinetic study in the transient phase of the suicide inactivation of frog epidermis tyrosinase. *Biophysical Chemistry, 30*, 303–310. doi:10.1016/0301-4622(88)85025-7

Valero, E., Varon, R., & Garcia-Carmona, F. (1997). Mathematical model for the determination of an enzyme activity based on enzymatic amplification by substrate cycling. *Analytica Chimica Acta, 346*, 215–221. doi:10.1016/S0003-2670(97)00054-8

Varon, R., Fuentes, M. E., Garcia-Moreno, M., Garcia-Sevilla, F., Arias, E., & Valero, E. (2006). Contribution of the intra- and intermolecular routes in autocatalytic zymogen activation: application to pepsinogen activation. *Acta Biochimica Polonica, 53*, 407–420.

Varon, R., Garcia-Moreno, M., Garcia-Molina, F., Fuentes, M. E., Arribas, E., & Yago, J. M. (2005). Two new regulatory properties arising from the transient phase kinetics of monocyclic enzyme cascades. *Journal of Mathematical Chemistry, 38*, 437–450. doi:10.1007/s10910-004-6895-6

Varon, R., Garcia-Moreno, M., Valero, E., Fuentes, M. E., & Amo-Saus, M. Ll., Arias, E. et al. (2007a). Optimized derivation of transfer functions and a software giving it. Application to biological systems. *Applied Mathematics and Computation, 184*, 823–841. doi:10.1016/j.amc.2006.06.073

Varon, R., Havsteen, B. H., Valero, E., Garrido del Solo, C., Rodriguez-Lopez, J. N., & Garcia-Canovas, F. (1993). The kinetics of an enzyme catalyzed reaction in the presence of an unstable irreversible modifier. *The International Journal of Biochemistry, 25*, 1889–1895. doi:10.1016/0020-711X(88)90321-7

Varon, R., Havsteen, B. H., Vazquez, A., Garcia-Moreno, M., Valero, E., & Garcia-Canovas, F. (1990). Kinetics of the trypsinogen activation by enterokinase and trypsin. *Journal of Theoretical Biology, 145*, 123–131. doi:10.1016/S0022-5193(05)80538-7

Varon, R., Masia-Perez, J., Garcia-Molina, F., Garcia-Canovas, F., Arias, E., & Arribas, E. (2007b). An alternative analysis of enzyme systems based on the whole reaction time. Evaluation of the kinetic parameters and initial enzyme concentration. *Journal of Mathematical Chemistry, 42*, 789–813. doi:10.1007/s10910-006-9142-5

Varon, R., Picazo, M., Alberto, A., Arribas, E., Masia-Perez, J., & Arias, E. (2007c). General solution of the set of differential equations describing the time invariant linear dynamics systems. Application to enzyme systems. *Applied Mathematical Sciences, 1*, 281–300.

Yates, J. W. T., & Arundel, P. A. (2008). On the volume of distribution at steady state and its relationship with two-compartmental models. *Journal of Pharmaceutical Sciences, 97*, 111–122. doi:10.1002/jps.21089

KEY TERMS AND DEFINITIONS

Closed and Open Compartmental System: Compartmental systems are considered closed, if there is no interchange of substance between any compartments of the system with the environment. Otherwise, they are named open systems.

Compartment: A compartment may represent a real physical region or an abstract representation of the same.

Kinetic Equations: The time course equations of the amount of substance in any linear compartmental.

Mean Residence Time (MRT) of a Particle in a Compartment: The MRT of a particle in a compartmen X_i $(i=1,2,...,n)$, after its injection at t=0 in any compartment X_m $(m=1,2,...,n)$, of the system is defined as the mean time that the particle spends in compartment X_i before leaving it definitely.

Mean Residence Time (MRT) of a Particle in the Entire System: The MRT of a particle in the entire system after its injection at t=0 in any compartment X_m $(m=1,2,...,n)$ of the system is defined as the mean time that the particle spends in the entire system before leaving it.

Steady State: The steady state of an enzymatic reaction is the corresponding time interval in which the concentrations of the enzyme species involved can be considered constant

Transient Phase: The transient phase of an enzymatic reaction is the time from the beginning of the reaction until it reaches the steady state.

APPENDIX A. EXPRESSIONS OF COEFFICIENTS IN EQ. (15) (EXAMPLE A. FIGURE 1)

Expressions of Coefficients F_q (q=1, 2,..., u) (Procedure Explained in Varon et al. (1995b)

$$F_1 = K_{1,2} + K_{1,6} + K_{2,3} + K_{2,4} + K_{2,6} + K_{3,1} + K_{4,5} + K_{5,4} \tag{1}$$

$$\begin{aligned} F_2 = &K_{1,2}K_{2,3} + K_{1,2}K_{2,4} + K_{1,2}K_{2,6} + K_{1,2}K_{3,1} + K_{1,2}K_{4,5} + K_{1,2}K_{5,4} + K_{1,6}K_{2,3} + K_{1,6}K_{2,4} + K_{1,6}K_{2,6} + K_{1,6}K_{3,1} \\ &+ K_{1,6}K_{4,5} + K_{1,6}K_{5,4} + K_{2,3}K_{3,1} + K_{2,3}K_{4,5} + K_{2,3}K_{5,4} + K_{2,4}K_{3,1} + K_{2,4}K_{4,5} + K_{2,4}K_{5,4} + K_{2,6}K_{3,1} + K_{2,6}K_{4,5} + \\ &K_{2,6}K_{5,4} + K_{3,1}K_{4,5} + K_{3,1}K_{5,4} \end{aligned} \tag{2}$$

$$\begin{aligned} F_3 = &K_{1,2}K_{2,3}K_{4,5} + K_{1,2}K_{2,3}K_{5,4} + K_{1,2}K_{2,4}K_{3,1} + K_{1,2}K_{2,4}K_{4,5} + K_{1,2}K_{2,4}K_{5,4} + K_{1,2}K_{2,6}K_{3,1} + K_{1,2}K_{2,6}K_{4,5} + \\ &K_{1,2}K_{2,6}K_{5,4} + K_{1,2}K_{3,1}K_{4,5} + K_{1,2}K_{3,1}K_{5,4} + K_{1,6}K_{2,3}K_{3,1} + K_{1,6}K_{2,3}K_{4,5} + K_{1,6}K_{2,3}K_{5,4} + K_{1,6}K_{2,4}K_{3,1} + \\ &K_{1,6}K_{2,4}K_{4,5} + K_{1,6}K_{2,4}K_{5,4} + K_{1,6}K_{2,0}K_{3,1} + K_{1,6}K_{2,6}K_{4,5} + K_{1,6}K_{2,6}K_{5,4} + K_{1,6}K_{3,1}K_{4,5} + K_{1,6}K_{3,1}K_{5,4} + \\ &K_{2,3}K_{3,1}K_{4,5} + K_{2,3}K_{3,1}K_{5,4} + K_{2,4}K_{3,1}K_{4,5} + K_{2,4}K_{3,1}K_{5,4} + K_{2,6}K_{3,1}K_{4,5} + K_{2,6}K_{3,1}K_{5,4} \end{aligned} \tag{3}$$

$$\begin{aligned} F_4 = &K_{1,2}K_{2,4}K_{3,1}K_{4,5} + K_{1,2}K_{2,4}K_{3,1}K_{5,4} + K_{1,2}K_{2,6}K_{3,1}K_{4,5} + K_{1,2}K_{2,6}K_{3,1}K_{5,4} + K_{1,6}K_{2,3}K_{3,1}K_{4,5} + \\ &K_{1,6}K_{2,3}K_{3,1}K_{5,4} + K_{1,6}K_{2,4}K_{3,1}K_{4,5} + K_{1,6}K_{2,4}K_{3,1}K_{5,4} + K_{1,6}K_{2,6}K_{3,1}K_{4,5} + K_{1,6}K_{2,6}K_{3,1}K_{5,4} \end{aligned} \tag{4}$$

$$F_5 = F_6 = 0 \tag{5}$$

Since the last non-null coefficient of the polynomial $D(\lambda)$ is F_4 and since $n=u+c$, one obtains:

$$c = 2 \tag{6}$$

$$u = 4 \tag{7}$$

Expressions of Coefficients $(f_{1,1})_q$; $(f_{3,1})_q$ and $(f_{5,1})_q$ (q=1, 2, 3, 4)

The coefficients $(f_{k,i})_q$ ($k \in \Omega$; $i=1, 2,..., n$; $q=0, 1, 2,..., u$) may be obtained easily from the coefficient F_q with the same q-value. We will distinguish two cases: Case a) $k = i$. One deletes the terms, which contain any of the fractional transfer coefficients $K_{i,2}, K_{i,3},..., K_{i,n}$ as a factor. Case b) $k \neq i$. One proceeds as in case a) and then deletes those of the remaining terms that do not represent a connection between X_k and X_i, i.e. the terms, which do not contain a set of fractional transfer coefficients such as $K_{k,i}, K_{k,a}... K_{a,i}, K_{k,a}...K_{a,b}...K_{b,i}$, etc. If all terms of the corresponding F_q must be deleted, then $(f_{k,i})_q = 0$.

The application of this procedure to the example in Figure 1 and taking Eq. (8) into account yields the following expressions for the coefficients $(f_{1,1})_q$ ($q = 1, 2, 3, 4$).

$$(f_{1,1})_0 = 1 \tag{8}$$

$$(f_{1,1})_1 = K_{2,3} + K_{2,4} + K_{2,6} + K_{3,1} + K_{4,5} + K_{5,4} \tag{9}$$

$$(f_{1,1})_2 = K_{2,3}K_{3,1} + K_{2,3}K_{4,5} + K_{2,3}K_{5,4} + K_{2,4}K_{3,1} + K_{2,4}K_{4,5} + K_{2,4}K_{5,4} + K_{2,6}K_{3,1} + K_{2,6}K_{4,5} + K_{2,6}K_{5,4} + K_{3,1}K_{4,5}$$
$$+ K_{3,1}K_{5,4} \tag{10}$$

$$(f_{1,1})_3 = K_{2,3}K_{3,1}K_{4,5} + K_{2,3}K_{3,1}K_{5,4} + K_{2,4}K_{3,1}K_{4,5} + K_{2,4}K_{3,1}K_{5,4} + K_{2,6}K_{3,1}K_{4,5} + K_{2,6}K_{3,1}K_{5,4} \tag{11}$$

$$(f_{3,1})_1 = K_{3,1} \tag{12}$$

$$(f_{3,1})_2 = K_{2,3}K_{3,1} + K_{2,4}K_{3,1} + K_{2,6}K_{3,1} + K_{3,1}K_{4,5} + K_{3,1}K_{5,4} \tag{13}$$

$$(f_{3,1})_3 = K_{2,3}K_{3,1}K_{4,5} + K_{2,3}K_{3,1}K_{5,4} + K_{2,4}K_{3,1}K_{4,5} + K_{2,4}K_{3,1}K_{5,4} + K_{2,6}K_{3,1}K_{4,5} + K_{2,6}K_{3,1}K_{5,4} \tag{14}$$

$$(f_{1,1})_4 = (f_{3,1})_0 = (f_{3,1})_4 = (f_{5,1})_0 = (f_{5,1})_1 = (f_{5,1})_2 = (f_{5,1})_3 = (f_{5,1})_4 = 0 \tag{15}$$

APPENDIX B. CONTENT OF OUTPUT FILE OF EXAMPLE 1: CLOSED SYSTEM (FIGURE 7)

```
=====================================
DESCRIPTION OF THE COMPARTMENTAL SYSTEM STUDIED


_____

NAME GIVEN BY THE USER TO THE SYSTEM:
   General Modifier Mechanism of  Botts and Morales
 TYPE OF SYSTEM (closed or open): closed
 NUMBER OF COMPARTMENTS OF THE SYSTEM:   4
 SET OF k-VALUES:              {1}
 SET OF i-VALUES:        {1,2,3,4}
 EXPRESSIONS OF ALL NON-NULL Ki,j's:
   K1,2 = k+1[S]
   K1,3 = k+3[M]
   K2,1 = k-1+k+2
   K2,4 = k+4[M]
   K3,1 = k-3
   K3,4 = k+5[S]
   K4,2 = k-4
   K4,3 = k-5+k+6_____
 RESULTS

 _____

  F   = 1
   0
  (f  )  =  1
```

$$(f_{1,1}^0) = 0$$

$$(f_{1,2}^0) = 0$$

$$(f_{1,3}^0) = 0$$

$$F_1 =$$

$$(f_{1,1}^1) = (k+1[S]) + (k+3[M]) + (k-1+k+2) + (k+4[M]) + (k-3) + (k+5[S]) + (k-4) + (k-5+k+6)$$

$$(f_{1,2}^1) = (k-1+k+2) + (k+4[M]) + (k-3) + (k+5[S]) + (k-4) + (k-5+k+6)$$

$$(f_{1,3}^1) = (k+1[S])$$

$$(f_{1,4}^1) = (k+3[M])$$

$$= 0$$

$$F_2 =$$

$$(k+1[S])(k+4[M]) + (k+1[S])(k-3) + (k+1[S])(k+5[S]) + (k+1[S])(k-4) + (k+1[S])(k-5+k+6) + (k+3[M])(k-1+k+2) + (k+3[M])(k+4[M]) + (k+3[M])(k+5[S]) + (k+3[M])(k-4) + (k+3[M])(k-5+k+6) + (k-1+k+2)(k-3) + (k-1+k+2)(k+5[S]) + (k-1+k+2)(k-4) + (k-1+k+2)(k-5+k+6) + (k+4[M])(k-3) + (k+4[M])(k+5[S]) + (k+4[M])(k-5+k+6) + (k-3)(k-4) + (k-3)(k-5+k+6) + (k+5[S])(k-4)$$

$$(f_{1,1}^2) =$$

$$(k-1+k+2)(k-3) + (k-1+k+2)(k+5[S]) + (k-1+k+2)(k-4) + (k-1+k+2)(k-5+k+6) + (k+4[M])(k-3) + (k+4[M])(k+5[S]) + (k+4[M])(k-5+k+6) + (k-3)(k-4) + (k-3)(k-5+k+6) + (k+5[S])(k-4)$$

$$(f_{1,2}^2) =$$

$$(k+1[S])(k-3) + (k+1[S])(k+5[S]) + (k+1[S])(k-4) + (k+1[S])(k-5+k+6)$$

$$(f_{1,3}^2) =$$

$$(k+3[M])(k-1+k+2) + (k+3[M])(k+4[M]) + (k+3[M])(k-4) + (k+3[M])(k-5+k+6)$$

$$(f_{1,4}^2) =$$

$$(k+1[S])(k+4[M]) + (k+3[M])(k+5[S])$$

```
   F  =
    3
        (k+1[S])(k+4[M])(k-3) + (k+1[S])(k+4[M]) (k+5[S])       +       (k+1[S])
(k+4[M]) (k-5+k+6) + (k+1[S])(k-3)(k-4)  + (k+1[S])(k-3)(k-5+k+6) + (k+1[S])
(k+5[S])(k-4)   + (k+3[M])(k-1+k+2) (k+5[S])       +       (k+3[M])(k-1+k+2)
(k-4)      + (k+3[M])(k-1+k+2)(k-5+k+6)     +     (k+3[M]) (k+4[M])(k+5[S]) +
(k+3[M])(k+4[M])          (k-5+k+6)     +          (k+3[M])(k+5[S])(k-4)     +
(k-1+k+2)(k-3)(k-4)+(k-1+k+2)(k-3)(k-5+k+6)+
(k-1+k+2)(k+5[S])(k-4)     +    (k+4[M])(k-3) (k5+k+6)
   (f  )  =
    1,1 3
        (k-1+k+2)(k-3)(k-4)  +   (k-1+k+2)(k-3)   (k-5+k+6)  +   (k-1+k+2)
(k+5[S])(k-4)      + (k+4[M])(k-3)(k-5+k+6)
   (f  )  =
    1,2 3
        (k+1[S])(k-3)(k-4)    +    (k+1[S])(k-3)       (k-5+k+6) + (k+1[S])
(k+5[S])(k-4)
+ (k+3[M])(k+5[S])(k-4)
   (f  )  =
    1,3 3
        (k+1[S])(k+4[M])(k-5+k+6) + (k+3[M])(k-1+k+2)(k-4)
        + (k+3[M])(k-1+k+2)(k-5+k+6) + (k+3[M])(k+4[M])(k-5+k+6)
   (f  )  =
    1,4 3
(k+1[S])(k+4[M])(k-3)          + (k+1[S])(k+4[M])(k+5[S])    +
(k+3[M])(k-1+k+2)(k+5[S]) +  (k+3[M])(k+4[M])(k+5[S])
Number of non-null eigenvalues of the matrix of the system: u =  3
Number of null eigenvalues of the matrix of the system:    c =  1
```

```
TIME ELAPSED IN THE PROCESS:       0.002 minutes
FILENAME: Example1
DATE: 10-30-2010
TIME: 17:40:09
```

APPENDIX C. CONTENT OF THE OUTPUT FILE OF EXAMPLE 2: OPEN SYSTEM (FIGURE 2A)

```
DESCRIPTION OF THE COMPARTMENTAL SYSTEM STUDIED
```

```
NAME GIVEN BY THE USER TO THE SYSTEM:
```

```
    Example2
TYPE OF SYSTEM (closed or open): open
NUMBER OF COMPARTMENTS OF THE SYSTEM:    5
SET OF k-VALUES:    {1, 3, 5}
SET OF i-VALUES:       {1}
EXPRESSIONS OF ALL NON-NULL Ki,j's:
    K1,2 = K1,2
    K1,o = K1,0
    K2,3 = K2,3
    K2,4 = K2,4
    K2,o = K2,0
    K3,1 = K3,1
    K4,5 = K4,5
    K5,4 = K5,4
```

```
  RESULTS
```

```
  F  = 1
   0
   (f  )  =  1
    1,1 0
 (f  )  = 0
  3,1 0


 (f  )  = 0
   5,1 0
  F  =
   1
      K1,2 + K1,0 + K2,3 + K2,4 + K2,0 + K3,1 + K4,5 + K5,4
  (f  )  =
    1,1 1
      K2,3 + K2,4 + K2,0 + K3,1 + K4,5 + K5,4
 (f  )  =
   3,1 1
      K3,1
   (f  )  = 0
    5,1 1
   F  =
   2
K1,2K2,3 + K1,2K2,4 + K1,2K2,0 + K1,2K3,1 + K1,2K4,5 + K1,2K5,4 +
K1,0K2,3 + K1,0K2,4 + K1,0K2,0 + K1,0K3,1 + K1,0K4,5 + K1,0K5,4 +
K2,3K3,1 + K2,3K4,5 + K2,3K5,4 + K2,4K3,1 + K2,4K4,5 + K2,4K5,4 +
K2,0K3,1 + K2,0K4,5 + K2,0K5,4 + K3,1K4,5 + K3,1K5,4
   (f  )  =
```

$$(f_{1,1}^2) = K2,3K3,1 + K2,3K4,5 + K2,3K5,4 + K2,4K3,1 + K2,4K4,5 + K2,4K5,4 + K2,0K3,1 + K2,0K4,5 + K2,0K5,4 + K3,1K4,5 + K3,1K5,4$$

$$(f_{3,1}^2) = K2,3K3,1 + K2,4K3,1 + K2,oK3,1 + K3,1K4,5 + K3,1K5,4 = 0$$

$$F_{5,1}^2 = 3$$

$$(f_{1,1}^3) = K1,2K2,3K4,5 + K1,2K2,3K5,4 + K1,2K2,4K3,1 + K1,2K2,4K4,5 + K1,2K2,4K5,4 + K1,2K2,0K3,1 + K1,2K2,0K4,5 + K1,2K2,0K5,4 + K1,2K3,1K4,5 + K1,2K3,1K5,4 + K1,0K2,3K3,1 + K1,0K2,3K4,5 + K1,0K2,3K5,4 + K1,0K2,4K3,1 + K1,0K2,4K4,5 + K1,0K2,4K5,4 + K1,0K2,0K3,1 + K1,0K2,0K4,5 + K1,0K2,0K5,4 + K1,0K3,1K4,5 + K1,0K3,1K5,4 + K2,3K3,1K4,5 + K2,3K3,1K5,4 + K2,4K3,1K4,5 + K2,4K3,1K5,4 + K2,0K3,1K4,5 + K2,0K3,1K5,4$$

$$(f_{3,1}^3) = K2,3K3,1K4,5 + K2,3K3,1K5,4 + K2,4K3,1K4,5 + K2,4K3,1K5,4 + K2,0K3,1K4,5 + K2,0K3,1K5,4 +$$

$$= K2,3K3,1K4,5 + K2,3K3,1K5,4 + K2,4K3,1K4,5 + K2,4K3,1K5,4 + K2,oK3,1K4,5 + K2,oK3,1K5,4 = 0$$

$$F_{5,1}^3 = 4$$

$$(f_{1,1}^4) = K1,2K2,4K3,1K4,5 + K1,2K2,4K3,1K5,4 + K1,2K2,0K3,1K4,5 + K1,2K2,0K3,1K5,4 + K1,0K2,3K3,1K4,5 + K1,0K2,3K3,1K5,4 + K1,0K2,4K3,1K4,5 + K1,0K2,4K3,1K5,4 + K1,0K2,0K3,1K4,5 + K1,0K2,0K3,1K5,4 = 0$$

$$(f_{3,1}^4) = 0$$

$$(f_{5,1}^4) = 0$$

```
Number of non-null eigenvalues of the matrix of the system: u' =u =  4
u-value for the  6-ECLCS:  4
c-value for the  6-ECLCS:  2
```

```
TIME ELAPSED IN THE PROCESS:       0.320 minutes
FILENAME: Example2
DATE: 10-30-2010

TIME:09:32:24
```

Chapter 17
On Extended Topochemical Atom (ETA) Indices for QSPR Studies

Kunal Roy
Jadavpur University, India

Rudra Narayan Das
Jadavpur University, India

ABSTRACT

Development of predictive models has been accepted as an important strategy to aid in toxicity screening of chemicals, determination of physicochemical as well as other biological activity of new molecules, and also in the generation and optimization of lead compounds in rational drug discovery process. The journey of quantitative structure-property relationship (QSPR) modeling started with the development of various property-based and two-dimensional descriptors to model various physicochemical and biological properties (including toxicity). Topological descriptors contain significant information encoded in the molecular structure. Extended topochemical atom (ETA) indices, a relatively new class of topological descriptors, are the focus point in this chapter. ETA indices contain important information regarding the nature of the atoms, bonds, atomic electronic environment and consider the contribution of different functional groups, molecular fragments, and branching to the response as evidenced by different reports showing their successful application in modeling different endpoints including toxicity, drug activity, and physicochemical properties. Extensive research is still going on for the refinement of the ETA indices by the incorporation of some novel parameters, and future reports on ETA indices will include these new indices.

DOI: 10.4018/978-1-60960-860-6.ch017

1. INTRODUCTION

Use of chemicals for various purposes has been an inseparable event to human life since time immemorial. Starting from the ancient times to the modern world, the use of chemicals has increased to a great extent to fulfill different demands of mankind. Millions of chemicals are synthesized and released into the market now-a-days to meet the need of the modern industrialization. About 56 million organic and inorganic substances are reported to be present in the CAS registry and there is an addition of around 12,000 new numbers daily (http://en.wikipedia.org/wiki/CAS_registry_number). After synthesis and release of these chemicals, determination of their various physicochemical properties as well as biological activities (including toxicities) becomes essential for various needs. Now, individual assessment of this large number of chemicals for a particular property or a number of properties thereof is really troublesome and impracticable. Appropriate use of computational technique can help in this context to predict the desired property or activity of a large number of chemicals using the experimental values of comparatively lesser number of chemicals. In drug discovery and development, the ultimate main aim of research is to synthesize novel therapuetically and pharmacologically active molecules with minimum side effects and toxicity profile. Because of involvement of huge time and cost in drug discovery process, it is not possible to rely upon trial and error method. Suitable computational technique is very useful in guiding medicinal chemists for the proper selection of compounds. Use of quantitative structure–property/activity/toxicity relationship (QSPR/QSAR/QSTR) analysis makes the drug discovery and toxicological screening process more successful and economic as well (Choplin, 1990; Franke, 1984). Apart from this, development and use of computationally derived predictive models has also got other applications, namely in agriculture, forensic science etc. (Roy, 2004).

Regarding toxicity assessment of chemicals, the European Union has implemented Registration, Evaluation and Authorization of Chemicals (REACH) program which requires human and environmental hazard assessment of all chemicals produced or imported >1 ton per annum (tpa) in the European Union (Aptula & Roberts, 2006). In order to avoid toxicity testing in animals, use of alternative tools for the determination of potential hazardous effects of chemicals was prescribed in the European Union White Paper concerning a future of chemical policy (Christensen *et al.*, 2003). QSAR (QSTR) modeling has been proposed by the Office of Toxic Substances of the US Environmental Protection Agency (Auer *et al.*, 1990) and the Agency for Toxic Substances and Disease Registry (ATSDR) (El-Masri *et al.*, 2002) to aid toxicological screening.

Biological activity or toxicity shown by a molecule is a result of its interaction with the biological system or some specific biological receptor using basic physicochemical forces (Andrews & Tintelnot, 1990; Franke, 1984; Martin, 1989). The type and extent to which a compound undergoes such interaction is dependent on the structural properties of the compounds. Proper encoding of these structural features controlling activity and/ or property of a molecule in the form of numerical quantities called descriptors forms the basis for the development of predictive models in the form of QSPR/QSAR/QSTR. This study helps in optimizing compounds so as to get better analogues of a series of existing compounds exhibiting a particular activity or toxicity (lead optimization).

Topological indices are simple two dimensional descriptors which can be easily calculated and interpreted. These indices have been widely used by the QSAR community to represent chemical structures numerically (Jurs *et al.*, 1995). A large amount of novel research has been carried out on model development with topological descriptors for different endpoints from the past, and such approaches have been found to be fruitful in many instances. This chapter gives an overview of history of evolution of QSAR techniques and glimpses of different two-dimensional descriptors for effective model development and then specifically focuses on the generation, use and applicability of extended topochemical atom (ETA) indices which were originally derived based on refinement of the topochemically arrived unique (TAU) scheme indices developed in the eighties.

2. HISTORY OF EVOLUTION OF QSPR STUDIES

Quantitative structure-property relationship (QSPR) study refers to the development of predictive models assuming that structure of a molecule contains information which can be correlated with a desired property or activity of interest. Depending upon the desired endpoint to be modeled, the predictive models are named likewise, *e.g.*, for modeling any kind of biological activity of compounds like anti-arthritic, anti-oxidant, anti-malarial, anti-HIV activity etc., the technique is named quantitative structure-activity relationship (QSAR); similarly for modeling toxicity endpoints namely genotoxicity, hepatotoxicity, renal toxicity, ecotoxicitiy on different organisms etc., the used terminology is QSTR (quantitative structure -toxicity relationship) while the term QSPR is used when physicochemical properties (partition coefficient, water solubility, molar refractivity, melting point, boiling point, reaction rate, chromatographic retention time etc.) are modeled. The basic idea is that all these different types of responses or endpoints (biological activity, toxicity and physicochemical properties) represent property in general exerted by any molecule and hence QSPR covers all the endpoints modeled and include QSAR, QSTR and QSPR as a whole.

It has been found that QSAR/QSPR modeling has been a part of the toxicological field for more than 100 years. Different past as well as present toxicological literatures show the approach of finding relationship between chemical structure and toxicity of chemicals. Cros (1863) observed that a relationship existed between the toxicity of primary aliphatic alcohols and their water solubility in his thesis. The central maxim of QSTR was explained by this relationship which referred that toxicity of compounds was related to their property which could be again determined by their chemical structure. Hence, structure, properties, and toxicity are said to be interrelated (Gramatica).

Crum-Brown and Fraser (1868) first expressed the concept that physiological action of a compound in a biological system (Φ) can be expressed as a function of the chemical constitution (C) of the compound as given by the following expression:

$$\Phi = f\left(C\right) \tag{1}$$

Hence, changes in chemical constitution (ΔC) will produce changes in biological activity ($\Delta\Phi$). At that time, the term "chemical constitution" was not an appropriately defined terminology and it roughly referred to the elemental composition of a compound (Selassie *et al.* 2002). Meyer (1899) and Overton (1897) imparted transparency to Eq. (1) by providing predictive model of narcotic (depressant) action of a group of organic compounds with their corresponding olive oil/water partition coefficients. From then, QSPR studies have been accepted and used as a very essential tool for different modeling purposes. Many researchers have been working since the past in this field for further exploration. The next milestone discovery in QSPR analysis was by Hammett (1935, 1970) who showed the effect of the substituents (structural correlation) in determining reaction rate (a physicochemical property) and defined the famous term, Hammett's σ which was later modified by Taft (1952), who defined the polar effects introducing E_S (the first steric parameter) and separated polar, steric, and resonance contributions. The famous Hammett equation which gives relationship between the ionization constants of benzoic acid system and electronic effect of substituents is given below:

$$Log \frac{K_X}{K_H} = \sigma \qquad (2)$$

where K_X and K_H represent the ionization constants of substituted and unsubstituted benzoic acids respectively in water at 25°C and the term σ is defined as the substituent constant in a manner that electron withdrawing substituents are characterized by positive values of σ while negative values of σ indicate electron donating substituents. Eq. (2) was later modified to a more descriptive form and another term ρ (rho) was defined in the following manner:

$$Log \frac{K_X}{K_H} \ or \ log \frac{k_X}{k_H} = \rho\sigma \qquad (3)$$

where rate constants were incorporated (k_X and k_H) to cover the rate processes and ρ was the reaction constant, defined as a specific parameter for each reaction. The parameter ρ gave a measure of propensity of a chemical reaction to the electronic effects of substituents and this theory has led to the development of predictive models for many reactions in physical organic chemistry (Hammett, 1970; Hansch & Leo, 1995; Leffler & Grunwald, 1963; Shorter, 1973). Hammett's equation was modified by many researchers (Brown & Okamoto, 1958; Ehrenson *et al.*,1973; Grob, 1983; Hanch *et al.*, 1973, 1991; Holtz & Stock, 1964; Jaffe, 1953; Roberts & Moreland, 1953; Swain & Lupton 1968; Taft *et al.*, 1952, 1958, 1960, 1963; Yukawa *et al.*, 1966; Yukawa & Tsuno, 1959) to define new parameters which have been used successfully to develop QSPR models.

In a significant development made by Hansch *et al.* (1962), a QSPR model was reported for plant growth regulators with Hammett's constant

and hydrophobicity. Partition coefficient values of a series of compounds were measured by using octanol/water system and this led to the development of a new hydrophobic parameter π, which is a measure of relative hydrophobicity of a substituent. The parameter was defined in analogy to the definition of Hammett sigma (σ) (Klopman *et al.*, 1994):

$$\pi = \log P_X - \log P_H \qquad (4)$$

where P_X and P_H are the partition coefficients of a derivative and the parent molecule, respectively. After the introduction of hydrophobicity parameter, a number of computational techniques have emerged namely CLOGP, AlogP98, Alogp_atypes etc. (Ghose *et al.*, 1998) for the calculation of hydrophobicity of substituents as well as for the whole molecule.

Hansch and Fujita developed a QSAR/QSPR hypothesis combining Hammett's electronic constant along with the hydrophobic constants to give the comprehensive model (Hansch-Fujita equation) for the prediction of biological activity of a group of 'congeneric' chemical compounds. The Hansch equation can be described as (Hansch & Leo, 1995, pp. 1–68):

$$Log \frac{1}{C} = a\sigma + b\pi + k \qquad (5)$$

where C corresponds to the concentration of the compound of interest required to elicit a response in biological system, and the right hand side of Eq. (5) includes Hammett's electronic term σ, hydrophobicity term π and a constant term k. Parabolic form of Hansch equation was developed in order to meet the need for modeling of extended hydrophobicity values (Hansch, 1969):

$$Log \frac{1}{C} = a \times \log P - b \times (\log P)^2 + c\sigma + k$$

$$(6)$$

A large number of QSPR approaches have been made to model different property and biological activity endpoints with the help of Hansch equation and its modified forms. Kubinyi developed a bilinear model as an extension to the parabolic form of Hansch model, and it has been found to be better in many cases (Kubinyi, 1976):

$$Log \frac{1}{C} = a \times \log P - b \times (\log \beta P + 1) + k \tag{7}$$

Apart from Hansch approach of QSPR, several other methodologies were also developed of which the Free-Wilson approach had been famous in developing successful predictive models. The following equation explains the Free-Wilson approach (Free & Wilson, 1964):

$$BA = \sum a_i x_i + \mu \tag{8}$$

where BA corresponds to the Biological Activity of interest, μ is the average contribution of the parent moiety, a_i refers to the contribution of each structural fragment and x_i refers to the presence ($X_i=1$) or absence ($X_i=0$) of a particular molecular structural fragment. Refinement in this approach led to the development of Fujita-Ban equation described as below (Fujita & Ban, 1971):

$$LogBA = \sum G_i X_i \tag{9}$$

Here logarithmic scale of biological activity (response) has been considered, G_i corresponds to the biological activity contribution of a substituent (relative to the corresponding position of a reference compound) and X_i corresponds to the presence or absence of the particular substituent fragment. Klopman *et al* (1984) and Blake *et al.* (1990) have provided variation on this activity based theory.

Continuing from this, vast development has occurred in QSAR/QSPR modeling resulting in a wide number of new techniques as well as descriptors including three-dimensional ones developed till today with the goal of successful model development in various fields encompassing drug discovery, toxicity screening, agriculture. In the eighties, topological descriptors were introduced and since then they have become very popular. Topological descriptors can be calculated simply from molecular structure without need of any experimentation unlike physicochemical descriptors.

3. TOPOLOGICAL DESCRIPTORS FOR QSPR

An important evolution in computational molecular modelling has been the use of the mathematical technique named "Graph Theory" in chemistry (Milne, 1997). In this theory, molecular structures are represented as hydrogen suppressed graphs, also known as molecular graphs, where different atoms correspond to vertices while bonds are represented by edges. Depiction of an object that provides information regarding its composition in terms of the number of elements in it and their corresponding connectivities, is termed as the topological representation of that object. Use of molecular graph may be done for the topological representation of a molecule (Balaban & Ivanciuc, 1999; Gutman & Polansky, 1987; Trinajstic, 1992) and the corresponding index values are independent of the numbering pattern of the atoms in the graphs. Topological descriptors have been extensively subjected to model development covering QSAR, QSTR and QSPR as a whole (Balaban, 1997; Bonchev & Rouvray, 1991; Devillers & Balaban, 1999; Ivanciuc, 1998; Kier & Hall, 1976, 1986; Todeschini & Consonni, 2000).

There are two general ways for the representation of the structure of a chemical compound; the first approach includes topological representation where the identities of atoms and their connections are represented in the form of two dimensional points and covalent bonds respectively. In the second approach, various three dimensional aspects are considered namely size, shape, volume and surface area etc. Such representation is commonly referred to as the "Molecular Topography". It has been found in general that the properties shown by a compound depend upon the three dimensional structural geometry of the compounds. Conversely the molecular topography is dependent on the molecular topology, *i.e.,* the type of atoms and the bonded connection between them. It is envisaged that characteristics such as bond length, strength, polarity depends on the type of bonds formed by various atoms and hence it is reasonably postulated that bond properties are related to the topology, which can be extended to correlate different properties shown by a molecule (Kier & Hall, 1986).

For the two-dimensional numerical representation of chemical structures, various different types of matrices are used namely adjacency matrix, distance matrix, reciprocal distance matrix (Ivanciuc *et al.*, 1993), resistance distance matrix (Klein & Randic, 1993), distance path matrix (Diudea, 1996), distance complement matrix (Randic, 1997), reverse Wiener matrix (Balaban *et al.*, 2000), Szeged matrix (Diudea, 1997), Laplacian matrix (Pisanski & Shawe-Taylor, 2000), Burden matrix (Burden, 1989), Detour matrix (Ivanciuc & Balaban, 1994), etc.

Information regarding the conformational perspectives, i.e., bond lengths, bond angles and torsion angles, are not used in the graph theoretical approach. However, topological approach can give valuable numerical information on adjacency, branching, cyclicity and relative distance among different functionalities such that they can be used as predictor variables for modeling any biological or physicochemical property. The topological descriptors have gained popularity due to their reduced complexity and consumption of lesser computational time. A plethora of research has been performed on this approach and notable refinements have been published which include incorporation of parameters for heteroatom

and multiple bonds from the basics of different molecular matrices and graph theoretical basis (Roy, 2004).

Some commonly used topological descriptors are Wiener index (Wiener, 1947a, 1947b), molecular connectivity indices, E-state index (Kier & Hall, 1999), kappa shape index (Kier, 1989), Hosoya index (Hosoya, 1971), Balaban J index (Balaban, 1982), Szeged index (Khadikar *et al.*, 1995), information theory derived indices (Bonchev, 1983), Bonchev's index (Bonchev & Trinajstic, 1977), Schultz's index (Schultz, 1989), Kirchoff index (Klein & Randic, 1993) etc.

Considering the discovery period, nature and complexity, Balaban (Balaban & Ivanciuc, 1999; Balaban, 1995) guided the classification of the Topological Indices (TIs) into first, second and third generations. Table 1 shows a brief overview of selected topological indices.

a. **First generation TIs:** The first introduced indices include the Wiener index and the Platt index (Platt, 1947). After that Gordon & Scantlebury (1964) developed an index termed as N_2. Another set of topological descriptors was developed in the seventies and these are classed in the first generation including the Hoyosa Z, Zagreb Group indices (Gutman *et al.*, 1975), the Balaban centric indices (Balaban, 1979) and the Schultz index (MTI).

b. **Second generation TIs:** This group includes molecular connectivity index developed by Randić (1975) based on graph-theoretical algorithm. These indices were further explored by Kier & Hall (1976, 1986, 1989, 1999, 2000) to include the contribution of heteroatom and different subgraphs in a molecule and as a consequence the term valence molecular connectivity was introduced. The next parameter in this group was introduced by Balaban (1982) from a modification of Randić's molecular connectivity index and this index is known as Balaban J index. A few

Table 1. An overview of different two dimensional topological descriptors

Sl. No.	Name of Descriptor	Brief definition of the topological descriptors
1	Wiener index	The Wiener number, W, is the summation of the number of bond or edges connecting all pairs of atoms in a molecular graph. For a connected molecular graph G, it is defined as (Wiener, 1947a, 1947b): $W = \frac{1}{2}\sum_{i=1}^{N}\sum_{j=1}^{N}D_{ij}$ where N corresponds to the number of vertices and D_{ij} is the distance matrix of the shortest possible path between two vertices.
2	Hyper-Wiener index	It is expressed as the summation of Wiener index and the squared distances between pairs of vertices in a molecular graph (Li & Lin, 2003): $WW = \frac{1}{2}\sum_{i<j}\delta_{ij}^2 + \frac{1}{2}Weiner$
3	Platt index	It is the summation of the number of bonds adjacent to each of the bonds in the molecule and is defined as (Platt, 1947): $F = \sum_{j=1}^{A}e$ where e_j corresponds to the number of edges adjacent to the edge j.
4	N_2	It proposes the number of ways in which a path of length two can be subjected to superimposition on a molecular graph and is defined as (Gordon & Scantlebury 1964): $N_2 = \sum\left(P_2\right)_i$ where P_2 represents a path length of two edges.
5	Hosoya Z	It is defined as (Hosoya, 1971): $Z = \sum_{K} p\left(G,K\right)$ where, p (G, K) corresponds to the number of ways in which K edges from all bonds of a molecular graph G may be chosen so that no two of them are adjacent. For linear graphs only Z can also be defined as the summation of the absolute values of coefficients in the following polynomial: $P_H\left(G,x\right) = \sum\left(-1\right)^K \times p\left(G,K\right)x^{N-2K}$ where N is the number of atoms present in the molecule.
6	Zagreb group indices	It is defined as the summation of the squares of vertex valencies (Bonchev, 1983): $Zagreb = \sum_{i}\delta_i^2$, δ_i being the valency of vertex atom i.
7	Balaban centric indices	It is defined on the basis of sequences of numbers obtained as a result of 'pruning' an acyclic graph towards its center. Balaban developed five such indices of which the centric index is defined as (Balaban, 1979): $B = \sum_{i=1}^{N}d_i^2$ where, d_i is the number of vertices that undergoes deletion at each step of N atoms in a molecular graph.
8	Schultz index	It is called molecular topological index (MTI) and is defined as (Schultz, 1989): $MTI = \sum_{j=1}^{N}e_j$ and e_j is defined as: $e_j\sum_{i=1}^{N}v_i\left(A_{ij} + D_{ij}\right)$ where v_i is the valence of vertex i, and A_{ij} and D_{ij} are the elements of the adjacency and distance matrix respectively in a molecular graph.
9	Randic branching index (χ)	It is the defined as the summation of the weighted edges in a molecular graph (Randic, 1975). For a connected molecular graph: $^1\chi = \sum_{\substack{all \\ edges}}\left(\delta_i\delta_j\right)^{-0.5}$ where δ_i and δ_j are the number of other non-hydrogen atoms bonded to atoms (vertices) i and j constituting an edge ij.
10	Valence Molecular Connectivity	This is defined in terms of δ^v which deals with valence electron of an atom and also shares information about the identity of atom i: $^1\chi^v = \sum_{\substack{all \\ edges}}\left(\delta_i^v\delta_j^v\right)^{-0.5}$ where δ_i^v is defined as: $\delta_i^v = \left(Z_i^v - h_i\right)/\left(Z_i - Z_i^v - 1\right)$ and Z_i^v being the total number of valence electron and Z_i is the atomic number of atom i (Kier & Hall, 1976).

continued on following page

Table 1. Continued

Sl. No.	Name of Descriptor	Brief definition of the topological descriptors
11	Balaban J index	It is a connectivity index based on the summation of average-distance (Balaban, 1982). For a connected molecular graph G it is defined as: $J = \dfrac{M}{\mu+1} \sum\limits_{\substack{all \\ edges}} \left(D_i D_j\right)^{-0.5}$ where, M is the number of edges in G, μ is the cyclomatic number of G (on a polycyclic graph, μ is the minimum number of edges that must be removed before G becomes acyclic), and D_{ij} is expressed as: $D_i = \sum\limits_{j=1} D_{ij}$ where, D_{ij} corresponds to the distance matrix of the shortest paths between any two vertices for N vertices, and $D_{ij} = I_{ij}$, if, $i \neq j$ otherwise equal to zero, and I_{ij} is the shortest distance between vertices i and j.
12	Information theoretic indices	The information content of a system (I) consisting of N elements is defined as (Bonchev & Trinajstić, 1977): $I = N \log_2 N - \sum\limits_{i=1}^{n} N_i \log_2 N_i$ where n represents the number of different sets of elements and N_i is the number of elements present in the ith set. The logarithm considered here is at basis 2 to measure the information content in bits.
13	Charge indices	It is defined as (Galvez *et al.*, 1994): $G_k = \sum\limits_{i=1, j=i+1}^{i=N-1, j=N} \left|CT_{ij}\right| \delta\left(k, D_{ij}\right)$ where, N corresponds to the number of vertices in a molecular graph G, D_{ij} is the distance matrix, k is an index order of G, and CT_{ij} is the charge term and is defined as: $CT_{ij} = m_{ij} - m_{ji}$ where m represents the elements of the M matrix.
14	Kappa shape index	These indices are based on an assumption of comparison of the molecule graph with "minimal" and "maximal" graphs depending upon the order n. Here, a path variable ^mP is defined as the number of paths along adjacent bonds of length m. Different degree of kappa shape indices are denoted and defined as (Kier, 1985): $^1\kappa = \dfrac{2\,^1P_{max}\,^1P_{min}}{\left(^1P_i\right)^2}$; $^2\kappa = \dfrac{2\,^2P_{max}\,^2P_{min}}{\left(^2P_i\right)^2}$; $^1\kappa = \dfrac{2\,^3P_{max}\,^3P_{min}}{\left(^3P_i\right)^2}$ where, ^1P_i, ^2P_i and ^3P_i are the numbers of one, two, and three path lengths in a molecular graph. Again considering A to be the number of atoms, the maximum and minimum terms are defined as: $^1P_{max} = \left(A(A-1)\right)/2$ and $^1P_{min} = (A-1)$, and replacement of these values in the expression of Kappa will yield: $^1\kappa = \dfrac{A(A-1)^2}{\left(^1P_i\right)^2}$ $^2\kappa = \dfrac{(A-1)(A-2)^2}{\left(^2P_i\right)^2}$ and $^3\kappa = \dfrac{(A-1)(A-3)^2}{\left(^3P_i\right)^2}$ when A is odd, and $^3\kappa = \dfrac{(A-2)^2(A-3)}{\left(^3P_i\right)^2}$ when A is even.
15	E-state index	It is defined as the summation of an intrinsic state (I_i) and perturbation factor (ΔI_i) value (Kier & Hall, 1990): $S_i = I_i + \Delta I_i$, where I_i is an intrinsic state and is defined as: $I_i = \dfrac{\left[\left(^2\!/_N\right)^2 \delta^v + 1\right]}{\delta}$ where N is the principal quantum number, and the perturbation factor, $\Delta I_i = \sum\limits_{j=1}^{N} \dfrac{\left(I_i - I_j\right)}{r_{ij}^2}$ where r_{ij} is the number of atoms in the shortest path between atoms i and j.
16	Szeged Index	It is defined as (Khadikar *et al.*, 1995): $S_z(G) = \sum\limits_{e \in E(G)} n_1\left(e/G\right) n_2\left(e/G\right)$ where $n_1\left(e/G\right)$ and $n_2\left(e/G\right)$ are the numbers of vertices of molecular graph G present on two sides of the edge e and $E(G)$ represents the set of edge.
17	Kirchoff index (number)	It is designated as K_f and defined as (Klein & Randic, 1993): $K_f = \dfrac{1}{2}\sum\limits_i \sum\limits_j \Omega_{ij}$ where Ω_{ij} is the (i, j) element of resistance matrix.

more TIs including the information theoretic indices developed by Bonchev (Basak, 1981; Bonchev, 1977), charge indices (Galvez *et al.*, 1994) and the kappa shape indices (Kier, 1985) were developed in the late seventies and these are categorized in the second generation.

c. **Third generation TIs:** The new descriptors in this group are the hyper-Wiener index (Gutman, 1994; Li & Lin, 2003; Randić, 1993) and the most importantly E-state index (Kier & Hall, 1990, 1999; Hall & Kier, 1995). Some descriptors derived and reported by Trinajstić (Bogdanov *et al.*, 1989; Randić et al., 1990), Todeschini (Todeschini *et al.*, 1997) (MS-WHIM) are potential 3-D analogues of TIs that fall within this group.

Now-a-days, atom or fragment based descriptors have become an important domain of research for the exploration of QSAR/QSPR/QSTR analysis. Contributions of groups and atom types are found to be essential because they control the fundamental intermolecular interactions shown by a molecule and the atom-type indices provide better mechanistic explanations and diagnostic features over the global ones (Roy, 2004). Hence predictor variables like E-state index, AI index (Ren, 2003a, 2003b), TOPS-MODE (Estrada, 2001) and notably the extended topochemical atom (ETA) indices (Roy & Ghosh, 2003), etc. perform very well during predictive model development. In this chapter we will focus on the rationale for the development, use and applications of extended topochemical atom (ETA) indices in detail in the later sections.

4. TOPOCHEMICALLY ARRIVED UNIQUE (TAU) SCHEME INDICES

Successful development of a QSAR/QSPR/QSTR model needs three basic requirements:

1. a dataset of chemicals with their experimental biological activity (or toxicity) and/or property values.

2. numerical data called descriptors corresponding to the information encoded in structure of chemicals, and

3. suitable statistical methods for the development of models for the observed activity/toxicity data.

After the development of Kier's molecular connectivity indices (MCI), many researchers worked on that and reported high correlations between the MCI indices and various physico-chemical properties (Bojarski & Ekiert, 1983; Boyd *et al.*, 1982; Burda *et al.*, 1985; Buydens & Massart, 1981; Buydens *et al.* 1983; De Voogt & Govers, 1986; Doherty *et al.*, 1984; Funasaki *et al.*, 1986; Huang *et al.*, 1985; Hurtubise *et al.*, 1982; Kaliszan, 1986, Kaliszan & Foks, 1977; Karger *et al.*, 1976; Kier, 1976, 1980; Kier & Hall, 1979; Lehtonen 1983, 1984a, 1984b, 1985, 1986; Lurie & Allen, 1984; Michotte & Massart, 1977; Millership & Woolfson, 1978, 1982; Parker, 1978; Raymer *et al.*, 1985; Sabljic, 1984, 1985; Stead *et al.*, 1982; Wells *et al.*, 1981, 1982, 1986; Wells & Clark, 1982a, 1982b, Szasz *et al.*, 1983) as well as biological activities (De Voogt & Govers, 1986; Di Paolo, 1978; Kier, 1980; Kier & Glennon, 1978; Kier & Hall 1976; Richards & Kier, 1980) in many series of compounds. After such extensive work on molecular connectivity indices, many researchers provided modifications of Kier's index as well as developed some new parameters as mentioned earlier. In the eighties, Pal *et al.* (1989) argued that Kier's connectivity indices possess limited diagnostic power and interpretability, and they also added that it is possible to get the ideal value of $^{m}\chi^{v}$ by making suitable molecular adjustments of several compounds in a given dataset, which will lead to a varied group of compounds devoid of the desired optimum activity and/or property. The simple molecular connectivity indices were also unable to correspond to effects such as stereoisomerism and steric effects that are known to be important for QSAR studies and rational drug design (RDD).

Pal *et al.* (1988, 1989, 1990, 1992) showed that the definitions of χ and χ^v were erroneous with the following deficiencies:

a.   the definition of the vertex valency (δ^v) appears to be logically inconsistent when atoms of different quantum levels are considered;

b.   redundancy in δ^v values is shown by vertices corresponding to different atoms;

c.   valency of the vertex atoms is important for the calculation of the weight of the edges (as per the definitions of χ and χ^v) which are subsequently used for the calculation of the higher indices. But this definition holds practical graph theoretical meaning for $^1\chi$ and $^1\chi^v$ only and basically the higher order indices ($^m\chi^v$, m>1) show good correlation when the activity and/or property shows good correlation with $^1\chi^v$ value which resembles that the higher order indices are correlated with $^1\chi^v$ itself.

Kier & Hall (1983) showed that the inconsistency in the definition of δ^v may be overcome by providing a numerical modification such as $1\big/\delta^v = \left(Z - Z^v - 1\right)\big/\left(Z^v - h\right)$. It bears the same value for the first row (N=2) elements and for other row elements (N>2), it shows a little difference. However, it corresponds to a value of -1 for H atom (when hydrogen suppression does not prevail in the molecular graph) and it does not provide privilege for the vertex atomic entities (Table 2).

To overcome the deficiencies of Kier's connectivity (branching) index, Pal *et al.* (1988) attempted to define and develop a new topochemical scheme. As per this new scheme, an atom in a molecular graph (named as a vertex) was assumed to be consisted of i) a core and ii) a valence electronic environment. The core count (λ) was defined as the ratio of the number of core electrons to the number of valence electrons:

$$\lambda = \frac{Z - Z^v}{Z^v} \tag{10}$$

where Z is the atomic number (number of protons of an atom) and Z^v is the number of valence electrons of the atom (electrons of the outermost electronic shell), *i.e.*, number of positive charges not neutralized by the core electron of such an atom (screening effect not taken under consideration).

From the definition, it appears that $1/\lambda$ roughly denotes the strength of the positive field of an atomic core. From the Table 3 it is observed that the core count (λ) of some most prevalent atoms of organic compounds shows a regular change in λ when compared with the corresponding Pauling's electronegativity value (ε°) of the atoms, across the periods.

The authors (Pal *et al.*, 1988, 1989) divided the valence electronic environment into two components namely localized and mobile valence electrons. The localized valence electronic environment, termed as the VEL count (θ'), was defined as follows:

$$\theta' = 2h + 1.5\nu + 2l \tag{11}$$

where h is the number of H vertices deleted through hydrogen suppressed graph, ν is the number of simple edges in the H-suppressed graph, and l is the number of lone pair of electrons. The mobile valence electronic environment was termed as the VEM count (θ) and defined as:

$$\theta = 8 - \theta' = 8 - \left(2h + 1.5\nu + 2l\right) \tag{12}$$

The number eight is used, because 8 electrons take part in constituting the valence electronic environment around an atom after bonding. The λ value of hydrogen is zero and in hydrogen fused

Table 2. Different definitions of δ^v (Kier, 1980)

Quantum level	Vertices (atoms)	$1/\delta^v$
1	H	0
2	C, N, O, F	$1/(Z^v-H)$
>2	Cl, Br, I S, P and others	$(Z-Z^v)/(Z^v-H)$ Empirical or undefined.

$$h + l + \pi + \nu = 4 \tag{13}$$

where π is the number of pi bonds present in an unsaturated system. Hence, the expressions of the localized electrons felt by positive field of the atomic field (VEL) and the VEM become:

$$\theta' = 8 - \left(0.5\nu + 2\pi\right) \tag{14}$$

and

$$\theta = 0.5\nu + 2\pi \tag{15}$$

The VEM vertex valence of the ith vertex was denoted by V_i and defined as:

$$V_i = \frac{\lambda_i}{\theta_i} \tag{16}$$

graph, the hydrogen vertices are assumed to coincide with the nearest non-hydrogen vertex. Hence, the electron pair that is involved in the formation of covalent bond with a hydrogen atom, is assumed to be principally 'utilized' by the vertex (atom) to which it is bonded such that it behaves as a lone pair of electrons. The coefficient 2 for the number of suppressed hydrogens was used by Pal *et al.* (1988, 1989) to denote the mentioned electron pair that apparently corresponds to hyperconjugation. From an assumption of chemical bond formation that an atom enjoys fifty percent electron of the other sigma bonded atom (apart from hydrogen in this case), the coefficient of the edges ν (that corresponds to sigma bond) was taken 1.5. The mobile valence electron felt by the field of the core, VEM count, can be calculated from the following assumption. For organic atoms linked by covalent bonds:

The VEM edge weight (E_{ij}) of the edge formed by i^{th} and j^{th} vertices was defined as the geometric mean of the weight of the vertex:

$$E_{ij} = E_{ji} = \left(V_i \times V_j\right)^{\frac{1}{2}}; \text{ provided } i^1j \text{ and } i, j \text{ are connected} = 0, \text{ otherwise} \tag{17}$$

Table 3. Core count (λ) and Pauling's electronegativity ($\varepsilon°$) of some neutral atoms

Element	Period number	Core count (λ)	Pauling's electronegativity ($\varepsilon°$)
H	1	0.000	2.1
C	2	0.500	2.5
N	2	0.400	3.0
O	2	0.333	3.5
F	2	0.286	4.0
P	3	0.200	2.1
S	3	1.667	2.5
Cl	3	1.429	3.0
Br	4	4.000	2.8
I	5	6.571	2.5

and, finally the first order VEM molecular index (T) of a hydrogen suppressed molecular graph was proposed as the algebraic summation of all the VEM edge contributions, mathematically:

$$T = 0.5 \sum E_{ij} \tag{18}$$

and zero order composite VEM molecular index ($°T$) was defined as:

$$°T = 0.5 \sum V_i \tag{19}$$

For determination of VEL, the terms become:

$$V_i' = \frac{\lambda_i}{\theta_i'} \tag{20}$$

$$E_{ij}' = \left(V_i' \times V_j'\right)^{\frac{1}{2}}; \text{ provided i}^1\text{j and i, j are connected}$$
$$= 0, \text{ otherwise} \tag{21}$$

Similarly,

$$T' = 0.5 \sum E_{ij}' \tag{22}$$

and

$$°T' = 0.5 \sum V_i' \tag{23}$$

where, V', E', T' and $°T'$ indicate the terms for VEL contribution. The composite topochemical index in this scheme is defined as:

$$T = \sum_{i<j} E_{ij} = \sum_{i<j} \left(V_i \times V_j\right)^{0.5} \tag{24}$$

The vertex valence V used in the TAU scheme (Pal *et al.*, 1988, 1989) and δ^v values of different atomic entities are given in Table 4. The authors in this group (Pal *et al.*, 1988, 1989) additionally developed two more parameters called functionality parameter F and branching parameter B in order to incorporate information regarding the contributions of functional group and relative branchedness of the molecules respectively. Both the parameters are of first order and were defined as:

$$F = T_R - T \tag{25}$$

where T_R is the first order VEM molecular index of the reference alkane (hetero atoms replaced with carbon and multiple bonds with single bonds), and

$$B = T_N - T_R \tag{26}$$

where T_N is the first order VEM molecular index of the normal alkane.

The value of B becomes zero for *n*−alkanes and straight chain compounds and the overall relationship is:

$$T = T_R - F = T_N - B - F \tag{27}$$

A number of successful applications of this topologically arrived unique (TAU) formalism was made to model various activity/property/toxicity endpoints (Pal *et al.*, 1988, 1989, 1990, 1992; Roy *et al.*, 1999, 2001, 2004; Roy and Saha 2003a, 2003b, 2003c, 2004, 2005, 2006) confirming the acceptability of the TAU descriptors.

5. REFINEMENT OF TAU TO EXTENDED TOPOCHEMICAL ATOM (ETA) INDICES

The TAU descriptors have been claimed to show good analytical capability for revealing contributions of branching, functionality, shape and size factors related to molecular structure to the response being modeled, but later these have been found to be associated with some degree of incompleteness. For example, it was observed

Table 4. Vertex valences (V) in the TAU scheme (Pal et al.1989) and δ^v (Kier, 1980)

1/V	δ^v						
	1	2	3	4	5	6	7
1.00	$-CH_3$						
1.25			$-NH_2$				
1.50					$-OH$		
1.75							$-F$
2.00		$-CH_2-$					
2.50				$-NH-$			
3.00			$>CH-$			$-O-$	
3.75					$>N-$		
4.00				$>C<$			
5.00		$=CH_2$					
6.00			$-CH=$				
6.25				$=NH$			
7.00				$=C<$			
7.50					$=N-$	$=O$	
8.75					$=N-$ (nitro)		
9.00			$\equiv CH$				
10.00				$=C=$ $=C-$			
11.25					$\equiv N$		
12.50				$\equiv N \longrightarrow$			

that the λ values of different atoms increased disproportionately with increase in atomic number. Again, VEM vertex count of a vertex in a sigma bond with another atom of similar electronegativity was given the same value to that bonded to an atom of different electronegativity. Additionally, differentiation was not made among double bonds of different types (ordinary alkenes or alkynes, conjugated system, aromatic system, *etc.*). Moreover, it was felt that contribution of atoms or fragments to the response parameter could serve as an important tool to identify pharmacophore/toxicophore fragments. To fix all these problem associated with TAU indices, extended topochemical atom (ETA) indices were introduced by the present authors' group (Roy & Ghosh, 2003) by refining and modifying some of the basic TAU descrip-

tors and incorporating more specific information from the topological perspective of molecular structure of compounds. To show usefulness of ETA descriptors in modeling studies, these indices have been extensively applied in various QSAR/QSPR/QSTR studies (Roy & Das, 2010; Roy *et al.*, 2006a; Roy & Ghosh, 2004a, 2004b, 2004c, 2005, 2006a, 2006b, 2007, 2008, 2009a, 2009b, 2009c, 2010; Roy & Sanyal, 2006).

6. DEFINITION OF BASIC ETA INDICES

The ETA indices comprise of a number of parameters encoding different types of structural information required to explain a specific response

Table 5. List of values of TAU core count parameter (λ), ETA core count term (α), and ETA electronegativity term (ε) of some common neutral atoms present in organic compounds

Element	Period number	TAU Core count (λ)	ETA indices	
			Core count (α)	Electronegativity term (ε)
H	1	0.000	0.000	0.300
C	2	0.500	0.500	0.700
N	2	0.400	0.400	1.100
O	2	0.333	0.333	1.467
F	2	0.286	0.286	1.814
P	3	0.200	1.000	0.500
S	3	1.667	0.833	0.967
Cl	3	1.429	0.714	1.386
Br	4	4.000	1.333	0.767
I	5	6.571	1.643	0.457

(biological or physicochemical) of interest. The basic ETA indices are defined below with their mathematical expressions.

1. The core count (α) (Roy & Ghosh, 2003)

The core count of a non-hydrogen vertex (α) is defined as:

$$\alpha = \frac{Z - Z^V}{Z^V} \cdot \frac{1}{PN - 1} \qquad (28)$$

In Eq. (28), Z and Z^V correspond to the atomic number and valence electron number respectively, and PN denotes the period number of the corresponding atom. The value of α for hydrogen is taken as zero considering hydrogen atom as the reference. It has been interestingly observed that the α values of different atoms (which are commonly found in organic compounds) have a high correlation (r = 0.946) with (uncorrected) *van der Waals* volume (Roy & Ghosh, 2003).

2. The measure of electronegativity (EN; ε) (Roy & Ghosh, 2003):

This parameter is defined as follows:

$$\varepsilon = -\alpha + 0.3Z^V \qquad (29)$$

where, Z^V is the number of valence electrons of the vertex. The parameter ε shows good correlation (r = 0.937) with Pauling's EN scale (Roy & Ghosh, 2003). A list of values of TAU core count parameter (λ), ETA core count term (α), and ETA electronegativity term (ε) of some common neutral atoms present in organic compounds is given in Table 5.

3. The VEM count (β) (Roy & Ghosh, 2003):

The VEM count β of ETA scheme for a non-hydrogen vertex is defined as:

$$\beta = \Sigma x\sigma + \Sigma y\pi + \delta \qquad (30)$$

where δ is a correction factor having a value of 0.5 per atom with loan pair of electrons that can make resonance with an aromatic ring (e.g. nitrogen of aniline, oxygen of phenol, halogen atoms etc.). In Eq. (30), the parameters σ and π represent the number of sigma and pi bonds, respectively, related to the vertex in the hydrogen-suppressed graph. For the calculation of VEM count β, contribution of a sigma bond (x) between two atoms of similar electronegativity ($\Delta\varepsilon \leq 0.3$) is considered to be 0.5, and for a sigma bond between two atoms of different electronegativity ($\Delta\varepsilon > 0.3$) it is assumed to be 0.75. Again, in case of π bonds, depending on the type of the double bond, contributions (y) are considered:

a.   for π bond between two atoms of similar electronegativity ($\Delta\varepsilon \leq 0.3$), y is assumed to be 1;

b.   for π bond between two atoms of different electronegativity ($\Delta\varepsilon > 0.3$) or for conjugated (non–aromatic) π system, y is considered to be 1.5; and

c.   for aromatic π system, the value of y is taken as 2.

4.   The VEM vertex count (γ) (Roy & Ghosh, 2003):

The VEM vertex count γ_i of the ith vertex in a molecular graph is defined as:

$$\gamma_i = \frac{\alpha_i}{\beta_i} \qquad (31)$$

In Eq. (31), the term α_i denotes the alpha value for the ith vertex and β_i stands for the VEM count considering all bonds connected to the atom and lone pair of electrons (if any).

5.   The composite index (η) (Roy & Ghosh, 2003):

Finally, the composite index η is defined as given below:

$$\eta = \sum_{i<j} \left[\frac{\gamma_i \gamma_j}{r_{ij}^2} \right]^{0.5} \qquad (32)$$

In the above equation (Eq. 32), both the bonded and non-bonded interactions have been taken under consideration. The term r_{ij} corresponds to the topological distance between the ith and j^{th} atoms. Again, replacement of all hetero-atoms and multiple bonds in the molecular graph by carbon atom and single bond respectively, corresponds to a molecular graph that may be considered as the reference alkane and the corresponding composite index value is designated as η_R, the composite index for reference alkane.

6.   The functionality index (η'_F) (Roy & Ghosh, 2003):

If functionality is considered to be the presence of hetero-atoms (atoms other than carbon or hydrogen) and multiple bonds, functionality index η_F may be calculated as ($\eta_R - \eta$). In order to avoid dependence of functionality on vertex count or bulk, another term has been defined: η'_F as η_F / N_V.

7.   The atom level index (Roy & Ghosh, 2003):

For the determination of the contribution of a particular vertex or position (within the common substructure in a congeneric series) to functionality, following expression was used:

$$[\eta]_i = \sum_{j \neq i} \left[\frac{\gamma_i \gamma_j}{r_{ij}^2} \right]^{0.5} \qquad (33)$$

Here (Eq. 33), $[\eta]_i$ refers to the contribution of the ith vertex to η. In a similar way, the contribution of the ith vertex $[\eta_R]_i$ to η_R can be computed. Contribution of the ith vertex to functionality $[\eta_F]_i$ may be defined as $[\eta_R]_i - [\eta]_i$. To avoid dependence of this value on N_V, a related term $[\eta'_F]_i$ was defined as $[\eta_F]_i / N_V$.

8. The local index η^{local} (Roy & Ghosh, 2003):

When consideration is focused only on bonded interactions ($r_{ij}=1$), the corresponding composite index is expressed as η^{local} which is defined mathematically as follows:

$$\eta^{local} = \sum_{i<j,r_{ij}=1} \left(\gamma_i \gamma_j\right)^{0.5} \tag{34}$$

Similarly, the η_R^{local} value for the corresponding reference alkane can also be calculated. The local functionality contribution (without considering global topology), η_F^{local} is calculated as:

$$\eta_F^{local} = \eta_R^{local} - \eta^{local} \tag{35}$$

9. The branching index (η_B) (Roy & Ghosh, 2003):

The branching index η_B can be appropriately calculated by using the following expression:

$$\eta_B = \eta_N^{local} - \eta_R^{local} + 0.086 N_R \tag{36}$$

where, N_R represents the number of rings in the molecular graph of the reference alkane. The term N_R in the formula of branching index offers a correction factor for cyclicity. The term η_N^{local} represents the η value of the corresponding normal alkane (straight chain compound of same vertex count obtained from the structure of the reference alkane), which may be calculated conveniently as (when $N_V \geq 3$):

$$\eta_N^{local} = 1.414 + (N_V - 3)0.5 \tag{37}$$

The branching contribution of a molecule with $N_V \leq 3$ is obviously zero. The branching contribution relative to the molecular size can

be determined by calculating another term η'_B, which is defined as:

$$\eta'_B = \frac{\eta_B}{N_V} \tag{38}$$

10. The shape indices (Roy & Ghosh, 2003):

Following indices are defined as the shape parameters in the ETA scheme: $\dfrac{\left(\sum\alpha\right)_p}{\sum\alpha}$, $\dfrac{\left(\sum\alpha\right)_Y}{\sum\alpha}$, $\dfrac{\left(\sum\alpha\right)_X}{\sum\alpha}$. The parameters $(\Sigma\alpha)_p$, $(\Sigma\alpha)_Y$ and $(\Sigma\alpha)_X$ are the summation of α values of the vertices that are joined to one, three and four other non-hydrogen vertices, respectively.

Table 6 summarises the different ETA descriptors.

7. SAMPLE CALCULATION OF ETA INDICES

Different ETA indices namely η, η_R, η_F, η_B, and contributions of different vertices to η_F can be determined by calculating distance matrix and VEM vertex counts as inputs. Sample calculations of different ETA parameters for 3-hydroxybenzaldehyde are shown in Table 7.

An arbitrary numbering of the compound 3-hydroxybenzaldehyde and its corresponding reference alkane has been shown in Table 7.

8. APPLICATION OF ETA INDICES IN VARIOUS QSPR/QSTR STUDIES

Roy & Ghosh (2003) introduced the ETA formalism in the arena of two dimensional molecular descriptors resulting in a number of successful studies reporting predictive models for ecotoxic-

Table 6. Definitions of different ETA parameters used for the development of QSAR/QSPR/QSTR

Variables	Definitions
N_v	Vertex count (excluding hydrogen)
N	Total number of atoms including hydrogens
$\Sigma\alpha$	Sum of α values of all non-hydrogen vertices of a molecule
$[\Sigma\alpha]_P$	Sum of α values of all non-hydrogen vertices each of which is joined to only one other non-hydrogen vertex of the molecule
$[\Sigma\alpha]_X$	Sum of α values of all non-hydrogen vertices each of which is joined to four other non-hydrogen vertex of the molecule
$[\Sigma\alpha]_Y$	Sum of α values of all non-hydrogen vertices each of which is joined to three other non-hydrogen vertex of the molecule
η	The composite ETA index
η_R	The composite index for the reference alkane
$\Sigma\beta'_s$	Sum of β_s values of all non-hydrogen vertices of a molecule divided by N_v; $\Sigma\beta'_s$ is defined as $[\Sigma\beta_s]/N_v$ (with corrections for duplicate considerations of electrons).
$\Sigma\beta'_{ns}$	Sum of β_{ns} values of all non-hydrogen vertices of a molecule divided by N_v; $\Sigma\beta'_{ns}$ is defined as $[\Sigma\beta_{ns}]/N_v$ (with corrections for duplicate considerations of electrons).
$[\eta'_F]$	Total functionality contribution
$[\eta'_F]_X$	Functionality contribution for the atom/group/fragment X (*e.g.*, −F, −CN, −OH etc.)

ity of hazardous chemicals and toxicity of drugs substances (Roy & Das, 2010; Roy *et al.*, 2006a; Roy & Ghosh, 2004a, 2004b, 2004c, 2005, 2006a, 2006b, 2007, 2008, 2009a, 2009b, 2009c, 2010; Roy & Sanyal, 2006). Apart from toxicity, ETA indices have also been used to develop a number of QSPR models. In all the studies involving ETA indices, models were developed using multiple strategies for selection of descriptors, namely genetic function approximation (GFA) (Holland, 1975; Rogers & Hopfinger, 1994), stepwise regression with F value as the objective function (F to enter 4, F to remove 3.9) (Darlington, 1990) and principle component analysis (Franke & Gruska, 1995; Lewi, 1980). Multiple linear regression and partial least square (PLS) method were used as statistical tools for model development. The developed models have been subjected to rigorous validation by applying multiple validation strategies including internal [leave-one-out (LOO) cross-validated r^2 or Q^2] and/or external [Q^2_{ext} or R^2_{pred}] validation parameters. The developed ETA models have been compared with those obtained from various other non-ETA topological parameters calculated on the given dataset of compounds.

Attempt was also made to use a combined set of ETA and non-ETA descriptors for modeling the endpoints.

The journey with ETA descriptors started with modeling of a dataset of 50 substituted phenols for protozoa (*Tetrahymena pyriformis*) toxicity (Roy & Ghosh, 2003) and the corresponding results were of high statistical significance showing model R^2 and Q^2 values greater than 0.9. After this study, a number of other attempts was made to use ETA indices for modeling toxicity of diverse chemicals against various representation organisms for ectoxicity like algae (*Chlorella vulgaris*) (Roy & Ghosh, 2007), protozoa (*Tetrahymena pyriformis*) (Roy & Das, 2010; Roy & Ghosh, 2004b, 2009b) bacteria (*Vibrio fischeri*) (Roy & Ghosh, 2004c, 2005), tadpole (*Rana japonica*) (Roy & Ghosh, 2006a), fish (*Pimephales promelas*) (Roy & Ghosh, 2004a), yeast (*Saccharomyces cerevisiae*) (Roy & Sanyal, 2006), plant (*Cucumis sativus*) (Roy & Ghosh, 2006b), etc. Other than these, QSTR models for rat hepatocyte toxicity (Roy & Ghosh, 2009a), human toxicity (Roy & Ghosh, 2008), and hERG K$^+$ channel blocking activity (Roy & Ghosh, 2009c) of diverse functional

Table 7. Sample calculation of various ETA indices for the compound 3-hydroxy-benzaldehyde

3-Hydroxy-benzaldehyde (with arbitrary numbering)

Reference alkane (with arbitrary numbering)

Calculations for the individual vertices

3-Hydroxy-benzaldehyde (with arbitrary numbering)

Vertex	1	2	3	4	5	6	7	8	9
α_i	0.500	0.500	0.500	0.500	0.500	0.500	0.500	0.333	0.333
$[\beta_s]_i$	1.500	1.000	1.750	1.000	1.000	1.000	1.250	0.750	0.750
$[\beta_{ns}]_i$	2.000	2.000	2.000	2.000	2.000	2.000	1.500	1.500	0.500
β_i	3.500	3.000	3.750	3.000	3.000	3.000	2.750	2.250	1.250
γ_i	0.143	0.167	0.133	0.167	0.167	0.167	0.182	0.148	0.266
$[\eta]_i$	0.806	0.771	0.766	0.715	0.709	0.730	0.708	0.487	0.682
$[\eta_R]_i$	–	–	–	–	–	–	–	–	–
$[\eta'_F]_i$	0.156	0.172	0.157	0.161	0.161	0.164	0.168	0.182	0.176

Reference alkane (with arbitrary numbering)

Vertex	1	2	3	4	5	6	7	8	9
α_i	0.500	0.500	0.500	0.500	0.500	0.500	0.500	0.500	0.500
$[\beta_s]_i$	1.500	1.000	1.500	1.000	1.000	1.000	1.000	0.500	0.500
$[\beta_{ns}]_i$	0.000	0.000	0.000	0.000	0.000	0.000	0.000	0.000	0.000
β_i	1.500	1.000	1.500	1.000	1.000	1.000	1.000	0.500	0.500
γ_i	0.333	0.500	0.333	0.500	0.500	0.500	0.500	1.000	1.000
$[\eta]_i$	–	–	–	–	–	–	–	–	–
$[\eta_R]_i$	2.212	2.322	2.180	2.164	2.154	2.207	2.220	2.130	2.266
$[\eta'_F]_i$	–	–	–	–	–	–	–	–	–

Calculations for the whole molecule

	3-Hydroxy-benzaldehyde	Reference alkane
η	3.186	–
η'	0.354	–
η_R	–	9.929
η_F	6.743	–
η'_F	0.749	–
η^{local}	1.454	–
$[\eta']^{local}$	0.162	–
η_R^{local}	–	4.326
η_F^{local}	2.872	–

continued on following page

Table 2. Continued

$[\eta']^{local}_F$	0.319	–	–	–	–	–	–	–	–	–	–	–	–	–	–	–
η_N^{local}	–	–	–	–	–	–	–	–	4.414	–	–	–	–	–	–	–
η_B	0.174	–	–	–	–	–	–	–	–	–	–	–	–	–	–	–
η'_B	0.019	–	–	–	–	–	–	–	–	–	–	–	–	–	–	–
$\Sigma\alpha$	4.167	–	–	–	–	–	–	–	–	–	–	–	–	–	–	–
$\Sigma\alpha/N_v$	0.463	–	–	–	–	–	–	–	–	–	–	–	–	–	–	–
$\Sigma\varepsilon$	9.633	–	–	–	–	–	–	–	–	–	–	–	–	–	–	–
$\Sigma\varepsilon/N$	0.642	–	–	–	–	–	–	–	–	–	–	–	–	–	–	–
$\Sigma\beta_S$	5.000	–	–	–	–	–	–	–	–	–	–	–	–	–	–	–
$\Sigma\beta'_S$	0.556	–	–	–	–	–	–	–	–	–	–	–	–	–	–	–
$\Sigma\beta_{ns}$	8.000	–	–	–	–	–	–	–	–	–	–	–	–	–	–	–
$\Sigma\beta'_{ns}$	0.889	–	–	–	–	–	–	–	–	–	–	–	–	–	–	–
$\Sigma\beta$	13.000	–	–	–	–	–	–	–	–	–	–	–	–	–	–	–
$\Sigma\beta'$	1.444	–	–	–	–	–	–	–	–	–	–	–	–	–	–	–
$[\Sigma\alpha]_P$	0.666	–	–	–	–	–	–	–	–	–	–	–	–	–	–	–
$[\Sigma\alpha]_Y$	1.000	–	–	–	–	–	–	–	–	–	–	–	–	–	–	–
$[\Sigma\alpha]_X$	0.000	–	–	–	–	–	–	–	–	–	–	–	–	–	–	–
$[\Sigma\alpha]_P/\Sigma\alpha$	0.160	–	–	–	–	–	–	–	–	–	–	–	–	–	–	–
$[\Sigma\alpha]_Y/\Sigma\alpha$	0.240	–	–	–	–	–	–	–	–	–	–	–	–	–	–	–
$[\Sigma\alpha]_X/\Sigma\alpha$	0.000	–	–	–	–	–	–	–	–	–	–	–	–	–	–	–

Table 8. Different notations used in Dragon software (version 6) for the ETA indices

SL.	Notations used in Dragon (version 6.0)	Corresponding ETA indices
1	Eta_alpha	$\Sigma\alpha$
2	Eta_alpha_A	$\Sigma\alpha/N_v$
3	Eta_epsi	$\Sigma\varepsilon$
4	Eta_epsi_A	$\Sigma\varepsilon/N$
5	Eta_betaS	$\Sigma\beta_S$
6	Eta_betaS_A	$\Sigma\beta'_S (=\Sigma\beta_S/N_v)$
7	Eta_betaP	$\Sigma\beta_{ns}$
8	Eta_betaP_A	$\Sigma\beta'_{ns} (=\Sigma\beta_{ns}/N_v)$
9	Eta_beta	$\Sigma\beta$
10	Eta_beta_A	$\Sigma\beta' (=\Sigma\beta/N_v)$
11	Eta_C	η
12	Eta_C_A	$\eta' (=\eta/N_v)$
13	Eta_L	η^{local}
14	Eta_L_A	$[\eta']^{local} (=\eta^{local}/N_v)$
15	Eta_F	η_F
16	Eta_F_A	$\eta'_F (=\eta_F/N_v)$
17	Eta_FL	η_F^{local}
18	Eta_FL_A	$[\eta']_F^{local} (=\eta_F^{local}/N_v)$
19	Eta_B	η_B
20	Eta_B_A	$\eta'_B (=\eta_B/N_v)$
21	Eta_sh_p	$[\Sigma\alpha]_P/\Sigma\alpha$
22	Eta_sh_y	$[\Sigma\alpha]_Y/\Sigma\alpha$
23	Eta_sh_x	$[\Sigma\alpha]_X/\Sigma\alpha$

chemicals/drugs have been developed with ETA indices. Models were also developed to correlate bio-concentration factors of non-ionic organic compounds in fish and n-octanol/water partition coefficient of non-ionic organic compounds with ETA indices (Roy et al., 2006a, 200b). Comparison of the ETA models with non-ETA ones showed that the models derived from the ETA indices were comparable in statistical quality to that of the non-ETA models and in some cases the former models have proved to be better in terms of predictability than the latter models. The reported results showed that ETA indices, either alone or along with non-ETA descriptors, could produce robust QSAR models. In some cases, ETA indices improved the quality of the non-ETA models when used in combination. It has been concluded that ETA descriptors contain important information regarding molecular structure, and they are able to successfully model various properties and toxicities of organic chemicals.

9. FUTURE DIRECTIONS

The ETA parameters have been recently included in the book entitled "Molecular Descriptors for Chemoinformatics" by Todeschini & Consonni

(Mannhold *et al.*, 2009). The latest version of Dragon software (Dragon ver. 6 from TALETE srl, Italy, 2010) has incorporated some of the ETA descriptors among various other topological descriptors. The list of 23 basic ETA parameters included in Dragon 6 (http://www.talete.mi.it/products/dragon_molecular_descriptors.htm) is given in Table 8.

Extensive and fruitful research is being carried out on the ETA parameters for further improvement by incorporating some more indices that are able to explain the specific contributions of unsaturation, hydrogen bond acceptor groups, hydrogen bond donor groups and overall hydrogen bonding propensity of the molecules, lone pair of electrons entering into resonance with aromatic system, and influence of polar surface area. The performance of these novel parameters in modeling various endpoints is discussed elsewhere (Roy & Das, 2011a, 2011b).

It is generally believed that no descriptor(s) can be relied as universally perfect to describe any specific response of interest. What is always observed is the extent to which a descriptor is able to predict by means of modeling different datasets without any bias. The ETA descriptors have been applied for modeling of several datasets of relatively large number of compounds of diverse nature and hence the developed models are unbiased and can be relied as good predictors of respective biological activity or toxicity or physicochemical property. Molecular structure of any compound can contain a lot of information which controls the behavioral information (activity and/or property) shown by that compound. Development of appropriate predictor variables that can encode information at the atomic as well as molecular level is desired for predictive modeling research. The ETA descriptors have been much successful in this regard. Wider use of ETA descriptors in QSAR/QSPR/QSTR studies will further justify usefulness of these indices.

REFERENCES

Andrews, P. R., & Tintelnot, M. (1990). Intermolecular forces and molecular binding. In Hansch, C., Sammes, P. G., & Taylor, J. B. (Eds.), *Comprehensive Medicinal Chemistry* (*Vol. 4*, pp. 321–347). Oxford: Pergamon Press.

Aptula, A. O., & Roberts, D. W. (2006). Mechanistic applicability domains for non-animal based prediction of toxicological end points: general principles and application to reactive toxicity. *Chemical Research in Toxicology*, *19*(8), 1097–1105. doi:10.1021/tx0601004

Auer, C. M., Nabholz, J. V., & Baetcke, K. P. (1990). Mode of action and the assessment of chemical hazards in the presence of limited data: use of structure–activity relationships (SAR) under TSCA, Section 5. *Environmental Health Perspectives*, *87*, 183–197. doi:10.1289/ehp.9087183

Balaban, A. T. (1979)... *Theoretica Chimica Acta*, *5*, 239–261.

Balaban, A. T. (1982). Highly discriminating distance-based topological index. *Chemical Physics Letters*, *89*(5), 399–404. doi:10.1016/0009-2614(82)80009-2

Balaban, A. T. (1995). Chemical graphs: Looking back and glimpsing ahead. *Journal of Chemical Information and Computer Sciences*, *35*(3), 339–350. doi:10.1021/ci00025a001

Balaban, A. T. (Ed.). (1997). *From Chemical Topology to Three-Dimensional Geometry. New York*. Kluwer Academic Publishers.

Balaban, A. T., & Ivanciuc, O. (1999). Historical Development of Topological Indices. In Devillers, J., & Balaban, A. T. (Eds.), *Topological Indices and Related Descriptors in QSAR and QSPR* (pp. 21–57). Amsterdam: Gordon and Breach Science Publishers.

Balaban, A. T., Mills, D., Ivanciuc, O., & Basak, S. C. (2000). Reverse Weiner indices. *Croatica Chemica Acta, 73*(4), 923–941.

Basak, S.C., Raychaudhury, C., Roy, A.B., & Ghosh, J.J. (1990). *Indian Journal of Pharmacology*, (1981), *13*, 112–116.

Blake, B. W., Enslein, K., Gombar, V. K., & Borgstedt, H. H. (1990). Salmonella Mutagenicity and Rodent Carcinogenicity: Quantitative Structure-Activity-Relationships. *Mutation Research, 241*(3), 261–271. doi:10.1016/0165-1218(90)90023-U

Bogdanov, B., & Nikolic, S., & Trinajstić, N. (1989). On the three-dimensional wiener number. *Journal of Mathematical Chemistry, 3*(3), 299–309. doi:10.1007/BF01169597

Bojarski, J., & Ekiert, L. (1982). Relationship between molecular connectivity indices of barbiturates and chromatographic parameters. *Chromatographia, 15*(3), 172–176. doi:10.1007/BF02261534

Bojarski, J., & Ekiert, L. (1983). Evaluation of Modified Valence Molecular Connectivity Index for Correlations of Chromatographic Parameters. *Journal of Liquid Chromatography, 6*(1), 73–80. doi:10.1080/01483918308066871

Bonchev, D., & Trinajstić, N. (1977). Information theory, distance matrix and molecular branching. *The Journal of Chemical Physics, 67*(10), 4517–4533. doi:10.1063/1.434593

Bonchev, D. (1983). *Information Theoretic Indices for Characterization of Chemical Structure.* Chichester: Research Studies Press, Wiley.

Bonchev, D., & Rouvray, D. H. (Eds.). (1991). *Chemical Graph Theory. Introduction and Fundamentals.* New York: Academic Press.

Boyd, J. C., Millership, J. S., & Woolfson, A. D. (1982). The relationship between molecular connectivity and partition coefficients. *The Journal of Pharmacy and Pharmacology, 34*(6), 364–366. doi:10.1111/j.2042-7158.1982.tb04730.x

Brown, H. C., & Okamoto, Y. (1958). Electrophilic Substituent Constants. *Journal of the American Chemical Society, 80*(18), 4979–4987. doi:10.1021/ja01551a055

Burda, J., Kurans, M., Kriz, J., & Vodicka, L. (1985). Relationship between retention behaviour and molecular structure of alkanes in reversed phase high performance liquid chromatography. *Fresenius'. Journal of Analytical Chemistry, 321*(6), 549–552.

Burden, F. R. (1989). Molecular identification number for substructure searches. *Journal of Chemical Information and Computer Sciences, 29*(3), 225–227. doi:10.1021/ci00063a011

Buydens, L., Coomans, D., Vanbelle, M., Massart, D. L., & Driessche, R. V. (1983). Comparative study of topological and linear free energy-related parameters for the prediction of GC retention indices. *Journal of Pharmaceutical Sciences, 72*(11), 1327–1329. doi:10.1002/jps.2600721122

Buydens, L., & Massart, D. L. (1981). Prediction of gas chromatographic retention indices from linear free energy and topological parameters. *Analytical Chemistry, 53*(13), 1990–1993. doi:10.1021/ac00236a010

Choplin, F. (1990). Computers and the medicinal chemist. In Hansch, C., Sammes, P. G., & Taylor, J. B. (Eds.), *Comprehensive Medicinal Chemistry* (*Vol. 4*, pp. 33–58). Oxford: Pergamon Press.

Christensen, F. M., de Bruijn, J. H. M., Hansen, B. G., Munn, S. J., Sokull-Klüttgenm, B., & Pedersen, F. (2003). Assessment tools under the new European Union chemicals policy. GMI 41, 5–19, http://ecb.jrc.ec.europa.eu/ documents/ REACH/ PUBLICATIONS/ Assessment_tools_ REACH040122.pdf (last accessed on 19 November, 2010).

Cros (1863). Action de l'alcohol amylique sur l'organisme" at the Faculty of Medicine, University of Strasbourg, Strasbourg, France on January 9.

Crum-Brown, A., & Fraser, T. R. (1868). On the Connection between Chemical Constitution and Physiological Action. Part I. On the Physiological Action of the Salts of the Ammonium Bases, derived from Strychnine, Brucia, Thebaia, Codeia, Morphia, and Nicotia. *Journal of Anatomy and Physiology, 2*(2), 224–242.

Darlington, R. B. (1990). *Regression and Linear Models*. New York, NY: McGraw-Hill.

De Voogt, P., & Govers, H. (1986). Structural and chromatographic predictors of n-octanol/water partition coefficients. *Chemosphere, 15*(9–12), 1467–1472. doi:10.1016/0045-6535(86)90426-1

Di Paolo, T. (1978). Structure-activity relationships of anesthetic ethers using molecular connectivity. *Journal of Pharmaceutical Sciences, 67*(4), 564–566. doi:10.1002/jps.2600670436

Diudea, M. V. (1996). Walk numbers ^eW_M: Wiener-type numbers of higher rank. *Journal of Chemical Information and Computer Sciences, 36*(3), 535–540. doi:10.1021/ci950134+

Diudea, M. V. (1997). Indices of reciprocal properties or Harary indices. *Journal of Chemical Information and Computer Sciences, 37*(2), 292–299. doi:10.1021/ci960037w

Doherty, P. J., Hoes, R. M., Robbat, A. Jr, & White, C. M. (1984). Relationship between gas chromatographic retention indices and molecular connectivities of nitrated polycyclic aromatic hydrocarbons. *Analytical Chemistry, 56*(14), 2697–2701. doi:10.1021/ac00278a017

Dragon ver. 6 is a software from TELETE srl, Italy, 2010 http://www.talete.mi.it/products / dragon_description.htm (Last accessed date 8th July, 2011)

Ehrenson, S., Brownlee, R. T. C., & Taft, R. W. (1973). Generalized Treatment of Substituent Effects in the Benzene Series. Statistical Analysis by the Dual Substituent Parameter Equation (1). In Streitwieser, A., & Taft, R. W. (Eds.), *Progress in Physical Organic Chemistry* (*Vol. 10*, pp. 1–80). Germany: Wiley publishers. doi:10.1002/9780470171899.ch1

El-Masri, H. A., Mumtaz, M. M., Choudhary, G., Cibulas, W., & De Rosa, C. T. (2002). Application of computational toxicology methods at the Agency for Toxic Substances and Disease Registry. *International Journal of Hygiene and Environmental Health, 205*(1–2), 63–69. doi:10.1078/1438-4639-00130

Estrada, E., & Uriate, T. (2001). Quantitative structure–toxicity relationships using TOPS-MODE. 1. Nitrobenzene toxicity to *Tetrahymena pyriformis*. *SAR and QSAR in Environmental Research, 12*(3), 309–324. doi:10.1080/10629360108032919

Franke, R. (1984). *Theoretical Drug Design Methods*. Amsterdam: Elsevier.

Franke, R., & Gruska, A. (1995). Principal component and factor analysis. In van de Waterbeemd, H. (Ed.), *Chemometric Methods in Molecular Design* (*Vol. 2*, pp. 113–163). Weinheim: VCH. doi:10.1002/9783527615452.ch4

Free, S. M., & Wilson, J. W. (1964). A mathematical contribution to structure-activity studies. *Journal of Medicinal Chemistry, 7*(4), 395–399. doi:10.1021/jm00334a001

Fujita, T., & Ban, T. (1971). Structure-activity study of phenethylamines as substrates of biosynthetic enzymes of sympathetic transmitters. *Journal of Medicinal Chemistry*, *14*(2), 148–152. doi:10.1021/jm00284a016

Funasaki, N., Hada, S., & Neye, S. (1986). Prediction of retention times in reversed-phase high-performance liquid chromatography from the chemical structure. *Journal of Chromatography. A*, *361*(C), 33–45. doi:10.1016/S0021-9673(01)86891-6

Galvez, J., Garcia, R., Salabert, M. T., & Soler, R. (1994). Charge indexes. New topological descriptors. *Journal of Chemical Information and Computer Sciences*, *34*(3), 520–525. doi:10.1021/ci00019a008

Ghose, A. K., Viswanadhan, V. N., & Wendoloski, J. J. (1998). Prediction of hydrophobic (lipophilic) properties of small organic molecules using fragmental methods: An analysis of ALOGP and CLOGP methods. *Journal of Physical Chemistry*, *102*(21), 3762–3772.

Gordon, M., & Scantlebury, G. R. (1964). Non-random polycondensation: Statistical theory of the substitution effect. *Transactions of the Faraday Society*, *60*, 604–621. doi:10.1039/tf9646000604

Gramatica, P. A Short History of QSAR evolution, QSAR Research Unit in Environmental Chemistry and Ecotoxicology, DBSF, Insubria University, Varese, Italy; http://www.qsarworld.com/ Temp_Fileupload/ Shorthistoryofqsar.pdf (last accessed date 8th July 2011)

Grob, C. A. (1983). Inductivity and Bridging in Carbocations. *Accounts of Chemical Research*, *16*(12), 426–431. doi:10.1021/ar00096a001

Gutman, I. (1994). A formula for the Wiener number of trees and its extension to graphs containing cycles. *Graph Theory Notes New York*, *27*, 9–15.

Gutman, I., & Polansky, O. E. (1987). *Mathematical Concepts in Organic Chemistry*. Berlin: Springer-Verlag.

Gutman, I., & Ruscic, B., Trinajstić, N., & Wilcox, C. F. (1975). Graph theory and molecular orbitals. XII. Acyclic polyenes. *The Journal of Chemical Physics*, *62*(9), 3399–3409. doi:10.1063/1.430994

Hall, L. H., & Kier, L. B. (1995). Electrotopological state indices for atom types: A novel combination of electronic, topological, and valence state information. *Journal of Chemical Information and Computer Sciences*, *35*(6), 1039–1045. doi:10.1021/ci00028a014

Hammett, L. P. (1935). Some Relations between Reaction Rates and Equilibrium Constants. *Chemical Reviews*, *17*(1), 125–136. doi:10.1021/cr60056a010

Hammett, L. P. (1970). *Physical Organic Chemistry* (2nd ed.). New York: McGraw Hill.

Hansch, C. (1969). A quantitative approach to biochemical structure-activity relationships. *Accounts of Chemical Research*, *2*(8), 232–239. doi:10.1021/ar50020a002

Hansch, C., & Leo, A. (1995). In Heller, S. R. (Ed.), *Exploring QSAR Fundamentals and Applications in Chemistry and Biology* (pp. 1–68). Washington, DC: American Chemical Society.

Hansch, C., Leo, A., & Taft, R. W. (1991). A Survey of Hammett Substituent Constants and Resonance and Field Parameters. *Chemical Reviews*, *91*(2), 165–195. doi:10.1021/cr00002a004

Hansch, C., Leo, A., Unger, S. H., Kim, K. H., Nikaitani, D., & Lien, E. J. (1973). "Aromatic" Substituent Constants for Structure-Activity Correlations. *Journal of Medicinal Chemistry*, *16*(11), 1207–1216. doi:10.1021/jm00269a003

Hansch, C., Maloney, P. P., Fujita, T., & Muir, R. M. (1962). Correlation of biological activity of phenoxyacetic acids with Hammett substituent constants and partition coefficients. *Nature, 194,* 178–180. doi:10.1038/194178b0

Holland, J. (1975). *Adaptation in Artificial and Natural Systems.* Ann Arbor, MI: University of Michigan Press.

Holtz, H. D., & Stock, L. M. (1964). Dissociation Constants for 4-Substituted Bicyclo-[2.2.2]-Octane-1-Carboxylic Acids. Empirical and Theoretical Analysis. *Journal of the American Chemical Society, 86*(23), 5188–5194. doi:10.1021/ja01077a031

Hosoya, H. (1971). Topological index: A proposed quantity characterizing the topological nature of structural isomers of saturated hydrocarbons. *Bulletin of the Chemical Society of Japan, 44*(9), 2332–2339. doi:10.1246/bcsj.44.2332

http://en.wikipedia.org/wiki/CAS_registry_number (last accessed date 8th July 2011)

http://www.talete.mi.it/products/ dragon_molecular_descriptors.htm (last accessed date 8th July 2011)

Huang, J. X., Bouvier, E. S. P., Stuart, J. D., & Melander, W. R., & Horwath, Cs. (1985). High-performance liquid chromatography of substituted p-benzoquinones and p-hydroquinones. II. Retention behavior, quantitative structure-retention relationships and octanolwater partition coefficients. *Journal of Chromatography. A, 330*(C), 181–192. doi:10.1016/S0021-9673(01)81976-2

Hurtubise, R. J., Allen, T. W., & Silver, H. F. (1982). Comparison of molecular connectivity and a chromatographic correlation factor in reversed-phase high-performance liquid chromatography for polycyclic aromatic hydrocarbons. *Journal of Chromatography. A, 235*(2), 517–522. doi:10.1016/S0021-9673(00)85917-8

Ivanciuc, O. (1998). Structural similarity measures for database searching. In P. Schlayer, R. Van, N.L. Allinger, T. Clark, J. Gasteiger, P.A. Kollman, H.F. III Schaefer, & P.R. Schreiner (Eds.), *Encyclopedia of Computational Chemistry.* Chichester: Wiley.

Ivanciuc, O., & Balaban, A. T. (1994). Design of topological indices. Part 8. Path matrices and derived molecular graph invariants. [Communications in Mathematical and computational Chemistry]. *MATCH, 30,* 141–152.

Ivanciuc, O., Balaban, T. S., & Balaban, A. T. (1993). Design of topological indices. Part 4. Reciprocal distance matrix, related local vertex invariants and topological indices. *Journal of Mathematical Chemistry, 12*(1), 309–318. doi:10.1007/BF01164642

Ivanciuc, O., & Devillers, J. (1999). Algorithms and Software for the Computation of Topological Indices and Structure-Property Models. In Devillers, J., & Balaban, A. T. (Eds.), *Topological Indices and Related Descriptors in QSAR and QSPR* (pp. 779–804). The Netherlands: Gordon and Breach Science Publishers.

Jaffe, H. H. (1953). A Re-Examination of the Hammett Equation. *Chemical Reviews, 53*(2), 191–261. doi:10.1021/cr60165a003

Jurs, P. C., Dixon, S. L., & Eglof, L. M. (1995). Representations of molecules. In van de Waterbeemd, H. (Ed.), *Chemometric Methods in Molecular Design* (pp. 15–38). Weinheim: VCH. doi:10.1002/9783527615452.ch2

Kaliszan, R. (1986). Quantitative relationships between molecular structure and chromatographic retention. Implications in physical, analytical, and medicinal chemistry. *Critical Reviews in Analytical Chemistry, 16,* 323–383.

Kaliszan, R., & Foks, H. (1977). The relationship between the R_m values and the connectivity indices for pyrazine carbothioamide derivatives. *Chromatographia, 10*(7), 346–349. doi:10.1007/BF02274482

Karger, B. L., Gant, J. R., Hartkopf, A., & Weiner, P. H. (1976)... *Journal of Chromatography. A, 128,* 65–78. doi:10.1016/S0021-9673(00)84032-7

Khadikar, P. V., Deshpande, N. V., & Kale, P. P. (1995). The Szeged Index and an Analogy with the Wiener Index. *Journal of Chemical Information and Computer Sciences, 35*(3), 547–550. doi:10.1021/ci00025a024

Kier, L. B. (1980). Molecular connectivity as a description of structure for SAR analyses. In Yalkowsky, S. H., Sinkula, A. A., & Valvani, S. C. (Eds.), *Physical chemical properties of drugs* (pp. 277–319). New York: Marcel Dekker.

Kier, L. B. (1985). A shape index from molecular graphs. *Quantitative Structure-Activity Relationships, 4*(3), 109–116. doi:10.1002/qsar.19850040303

Kier, L. B. (1989). An index of flexibility from molecular shape descriptors. *Progress in Clinical and Biological Research, 291,* 105–109.

Kier, L. B., & Glennon, R. A. (1978). Psychotomimetic phenalkylamines as serotonin agonists: an sar analysis. *Life Sciences, 22*(18), 1589–1593. doi:10.1016/0024-3205(78)90053-X

Kier, L. B., & Hall, L. H. (1976). *Molecular Connectivity in Chemistry and Drug Research.* New York: Academic Press.

Kier, L. B., & Hall, L. H. (1979). Molecular connectivity analyses of structure influencing chromatographic retention indexes. *Journal of Pharmaceutical Sciences, 68*(1), 120–122. doi:10.1002/jps.2600680143

Kier, L. B., & Hall, L. H. (1983). General definition of valence delta-values for molecular connectivity. *Journal of Pharmaceutical Sciences, 72*(10), 1170–1173. doi:10.1002/jps.2600721016

Kier, L. B., & Hall, L. H. (1986). *Molecular Connectivity in Structure–Activity Analysis.* Lethchworth, England: Research Studies Press.

Kier, L. B., & Hall, L. H. (1990). An electro-topological-state index for atoms in molecules. *Pharmaceutical Research, 7*(8), 801–807. doi:10.1023/A:1015952613760

Kier, L. B., & Hall, L. H. (1999). *Molecular Structure Description: The Electrotopological State.* San Diego: Academic Press.

Kier, L. B., & Hall, L. H. (2000). Intermolecular Accessibility: The Meaning of Molecular Connectivity. *Journal of Chemical Information and Computer Sciences, 40*(3), 792–795. doi:10.1021/ci990135s

Klein, D. J., & Randic, M. (1993). Resistance distance. *Journal of Mathematical Chemistry, 12*(1), 81–95. doi:10.1007/BF01164627

Klopman, G. (1984). Artificial intelligence approach to structure-activity studies. Computer automated structure evaluation of biological activity of organic molecules. *Journal of the American Chemical Society, 106*(24), 7315–7321. doi:10.1021/ja00336a004

Klopman, G., Li, J. K., Wang, S., & Dimayuga, M. (1994). Computer Automated log *P* Calculations Based on an Extended Group Contribution Approach. *Journal of Chemical Information and Computer Sciences, 34,* 752–781. doi:10.1021/ci00020a009

Kubinyi, H. (1976). Quantitative structure activity relationships. IV. Non linear dependence of biological activity on hydrophobic character: a new model. *Arzneimittel-Forschung. Drug Research, 26*(11), 1991–1997.

Leffler, J. E., & Grunwald, E. (1963). *Rates and Equilibria of Organic Reactions.* New York: John Wiley.

Lehtonen, P. (1983). Reversed-phase liquid chromatographic elution characteristics of substituted N-ethylbenzamides. *Journal of Chromatography. A, 267*(C), 277–284. doi:10.1016/S0021-9673(01)90847-7

Lehtonen, P. (1984a). Reversed-phase retention behaviour of Dns-amides as a function of eluent composition and molecular structrure in ethanol-water and methanol-water. *Journal of Chromatography. A, 314*(C), 141–153. doi:10.1016/S0021-9673(01)97729-5

Lehtonen, P. (1984b). Use of molecular connectivity indices to predict LC retention of dansylamides in six different eluent systems. *Chromatographia, 19*(1), 316–321. doi:10.1007/BF02687762

Lehtonen, P. (1985). Properties of six octadecylsilane stationary phases for the separation of dansylamides. *Journal of Chromatography. A, 330*(C), 243–252. doi:10.1016/S0021-9673(01)81981-6

Lehtonen, P. (1986). Isolation and HPLC determination of amines in wine. *Zeitschrift fur Lebensmittel-Untersuchung und -Forschung, 183*(3), 177–181. doi:10.1007/BF01027442

Lewi, P. J. (1980). Multivariate data analysis in structure activity relationships. In Ariens, E. J. (Ed.), *Drug Design* (*Vol. 10*, pp. 307–342). New York: Academic Press.

Li, X., Zhang, T., Min, X., & Liu, P. (2010). Toxicity of aromatic compounds to Tetrahymena estimated by microcalorimetry and QSAR. *Aquatic Toxicology (Amsterdam, Netherlands), 98*(4), 322–327. doi:10.1016/j.aquatox.2010.03.002

Li, X. H., & Lin, J. J. (2003). The overall hyper-Wiener index. *Journal of Mathematical Chemistry, 33*(2), 81–89. doi:10.1023/A:1023299514399

Lurie, I. S., & Allen, A. C. (1984). Reversed-phase high-performance liquid chromatographic separation of fentanyl homologues and analogues. II. Variables affecting hydrophobic group contribution. *Journal of Chromatography. A, 292*(2), 283–294. doi:10.1016/S0021-9673(01)83609-8

Mannhold, R., Kubinyi, H., & Folkers, G. (Eds.). (2009). *Molecular Descriptors for Chemoinformatics*. Weinheim, Germany: Wiley-VCH.

Martin, Y. C. (1989). Theoretical basis of medicinal chemistry: Structure–activity relationships and three–dimensional structures of small and macromolecules. In Martin, Y. C., Kutter, E., & Anstel, V. (Eds.), *Modern Drug Research. Paths to Better and Safer Drugs* (pp. 161–216). New York: Marcel Dekker, Inc.

Meyer, H. (1899). Zur Theorie Der Alkolnarkose I. Welche Eigenschaft Der Anaesthetica Bedingt Jhre Narkotische Wirkuny? *Archiv fur Experimentalle Pathologie und Pharmakologie, 42*(2–4), 109–118. doi:10.1007/BF01834479

Michotte, Y., & Massart, D. L. (1977). Molecular connectivity and retention indexes. *Journal of Pharmaceutical Sciences, 66*(11), 1630–1632. doi:10.1002/jps.2600661134

Millership, J. S., & Woolfson, A. D. (1978). The relation between molecular connectivity and gas chromatographic retention data. *The Journal of Pharmacy and Pharmacology, 30*(8), 483–485. doi:10.1111/j.2042-7158.1978.tb13298.x

Millership, J. S., & Woolfson, A. D. (1982)... *The Journal of Pharmacy and Pharmacology, 32*, 610. doi:10.1111/j.2042-7158.1980.tb13015.x

Milne, G. W. A. (1997). Mathematics as a basis for chemistry. *Journal of Chemical Information and Computer Sciences, 37*(4), 639–644. doi:10.1021/ci960165k

Netzeva, T. H., Pavan, M., & Worth, A. P. (2008). Review of (quantitative) structure–activity relationships for acute aquatic toxicity. *QSAR & Combinatorial Science, 27*(1), 77–90. doi:10.1002/qsar.200710099

Overton, E. (1897). Osmotic Properties of Cells in the Bearing on Toxicology and Pharmacy. *Zeitschrift für Physikalische Chemie, 22*, 189–209.

Pal, D. K., Purkayastha, S. K., Sengupta, C., & De, A. U. (1992). Quantitative structure–property relationships with TAU indices: part I – research octane numbers of alkane fuel molecules. *Indian Journal of Chemistry, 31B*, 109–114.

Pal, D. K., Sengupta, C., & De, A. U. (1988). A new topochemical descriptor (TAU) in molecular connectivity concept: part I – aliphatic compounds. *Indian Journal of Chemistry, 27B*, 734–739.

Pal, D. K., Sengupta, C., & De, A. U. (1989). Introduction of a novel topochemical index and exploitation of group connectivity concept to achieve predictability in QSAR and RDD. *Indian Journal of Chemistry, 28B*, 261–267.

Pal, D. K., Sengupta, M., Sengupta, C., & De, A. U. (1990). QSAR with TAU (τ) indices: part I – polymethylene primary diamines as amebicidal agents. *Indian Journal of Chemistry, 29B*, 451–454.

Parker, G. R. (1978). Correlation of log P with molecular connectivity in hydroxyureas: Influence of conformational system on log P. *Journal of Pharmaceutical Sciences, 67*(4), 513–516. doi:10.1002/jps.2600670419

Pisanski, T., & Shawe-Taylor, J. (2000). Characterizing graph drawing with eigen vectors. *Journal of Chemical Information and Computer Sciences, 40*(3), 567–571. doi:10.1021/ci9900938

Platt, J. R. (1947). Influence of Neighbor Bonds on Additive Bond Properties in Paraffins. *The Journal of Chemical Physics, 15*(6), 419–420. doi:10.1063/1.1746554

Randić, M. (1975). On characterization of molecular branching. *Journal of the American Chemical Society, 97*(23), 6609–6615.

Randić, M. (1997). Linear combinations of path numbers as molecular descriptors. *New Journal of Chemistry, 21*(9), 945–951.

Randić, M., Guo, X., Oxley, T., & Krishnapriyan, H. (1993). Wiener matrix: source of novel graph invariants. *Journal of Chemical Information and Computer Science, 33*(5), 709–716.

Randić, M., Jerman-Blazic, B., & Trinajstić, N. (1990). Development of 3-dimensional molecular descriptors. *Computers & Chemistry, 14*(3), 237–246.

Raymer, J., Wiesler, D., & Novotny, M. (1985). Structure-retention studies of model ketones by capillary gas chromatography. *Journal of Chromatography. A, 325*(C), 13–22. doi:10.1016/S0021-9673(00)96003-5

Ren, B. (2003a). Atom-level-based AI topological descriptors for structure–property correlations. *Journal of Chemical Information and Computer Sciences, 43*(1), 161–169. doi:10.1021/ci020382n

Ren, B. (2003b). Atom-Type-Based AI Topological Descriptors: Application of structure–boiling point correlations of oxo organic compounds. *Journal of Chemical Information and Computer Sciences, 43*(4), 1121–1131. doi:10.1021/ci025651o

Richards, A. J., & Kier, L. B. (1980). Structure activity analysis of hydrazide monoamine oxidase inhibitor using molecular connectivity. *Journal of Pharmaceutical Sciences, 69*(1), 124–126. doi:10.1002/jps.2600690143

Roberts, J. D., & Moreland, W. T. Jr. (1953). Electrical Effects of Substituent Groups in Saturated Systems. Reactivities of 4-Substituted Bicyclo-[2.2.2]-Octane-1-Carboxylic Acids. *Journal of the American Chemical Society, 75*(9), 2167–2173. doi:10.1021/ja01105a045

Rogers, D., & Hopfinger, A. J. (1994). Application of genetic function approximation to quantitative structure–activity relationships and quantitative structure–property relationships. *Journal of Chemical Information and Computer Sciences, 34*(4), 854–866. doi:10.1021/ci00020a020

Roy, K. (2004). Topological descriptors in drug design and modeling studies. *Molecular Diversity*, 8(4), 321–323. doi:10.1023/B:MODI.0000047519.35591.b7

Roy, K., & Das, R. N. (2010). QSTR with extended topochemical atom (ETA) indices. 14. QSAR modeling of toxicity of aromatic aldehydes to *Tetrahymena pyriformis*. *Journal of Hazardous Materials*, 183(1–3), 913–922. doi:10.1016/j.jhazmat.2010.07.116

Roy, K., & Das, R. N. (2011a). On some novel extended topochemical atom (ETA) parameters for effective encoding of chemical information and modeling of fundamental physicochemical properties. *SAR and QSAR in Environmental Research*, http://dx.doi.org/10.1080/1062936X.2011.569900.

Roy, K., & Das, R. N. (2011b, Unpublished results). QSTR with extended topochemical atom (ETA) indices. 15. Development of predictive models for toxicity of organic chemicals against fathead minnow. (communicated).

Roy, K., & Ghosh, G. (2003). Introduction of extended topochemical atom (ETA) Indices in the valence electron mobile (VEM) environment as tools for QSAR/QSPR studies. *Internet Electronic Journal of Molecular Design*, 2(9), 599–620, http://www.biochempress.com/.

Roy, K., & Ghosh, G. (2004a). QSTR with extended topochemical atom indices. 2. Fish toxicity of substituted benzenes. *Journal of Chemical Information and Computer Sciences*, 44(2), 559–567. doi:10.1021/ci0342066

Roy, K., & Ghosh, G. (2004b). QSTR with extended topochemical atom indices. 3. Toxicity of nitrobenzenes to *Tetrahymena pyriformis*. *QSAR & Combinatorial Science*, 23(2–3), 99–108. doi:10.1002/qsar.200330864

Roy, K., & Ghosh, G. (2004c). QSTR with extended topochemical atom indices. 4. Modeling of the acute toxicity of phenylsulfonyl carboxylates to *Vibrio fischeri* using principal component factor analysis and principal component regression analysis. *QSAR & Combinatorial Science*, 23(7), 526–535. doi:10.1002/qsar.200430891

Roy, K., & Ghosh, G. (2005). QSTR with extended topochemical atom indices. Part 5. Modeling of the acute toxicity of phenylsulfonyl carboxylates to *Vibrio fischeri* using genetic function approximation. *Bioorganic & Medicinal Chemistry*, 13(4), 1185–1194. doi:10.1016/j.bmc.2004.11.014

Roy, K., & Ghosh, G. (2006a). QSTR with extended topochemical atom (ETA) indices. VI. Acute toxicity of benzene derivatives to tadpoles (*Rana japonica*). *Journal of Molecular Modeling*, 12(3), 306–316. doi:10.1007/s00894-005-0033-7

Roy, K., & Ghosh, G. (2006b). QSTR with extended topochemical atom (ETA) indices. 8. QSAR for the inhibition of substituted phenols on germination rate of *Cucumis sativus* using chemometric tools. *QSAR & Combinatorial Science*, 25(10), 846–859. doi:10.1002/qsar.200510211

Roy, K., & Ghosh, G. (2007). QSTR with extended topochemical atom (ETA) indices. 9. Comparative QSAR for the toxicity of diverse functional organic compounds to *Chlorella vulgaris* using chemometric tools. *Chemosphere*, 70(1), 1–12. doi:10.1016/j.chemosphere.2007.07.037

Roy, K., & Ghosh, G. (2008). QSTR with Extended Topochemical Atom Indices. 10. Modeling of Toxicity of Organic Chemicals to Humans Using Different Chemometric Tools. *Chemical Biology & Drug Design*, 72(5), 383–394. doi:10.1111/j.1747-0285.2008.00712.x

Roy, K., & Ghosh, G. (2009a). QSTR with extended topochemical atom (ETA) indices. 11. Comparative QSAR of acute NSAID cytotoxicity in rat hepatocytes using chemometric Tools. *Molecular Simulation*, 35(8), 648–659. doi:10.1080/08927020902744664

Roy, K., & Ghosh, G. (2009b). QSTR with extended topochemical atom (ETA) indices. 12. QSAR for the toxicity of diverse aromatic compounds to *Tetrahymena pyriformis* using chemometric tools. *Chemosphere, 77*(7), 999–1009. doi:10.1016/j.chemosphere.2009.07.072

Roy, K., & Ghosh, G. (2009c). QSTR with extended topochemical atom (ETA) Indices. 13. Modeling of hERG K^+ channel blocking activity of diverse functional drugs using different chemometric tools. *Molecular Simulation, 35*(15), 1256–1268. doi:10.1080/08927020903015379

Roy, K., & Ghosh, G. (2010). Exploring QSARs with Extended Topochemical Atom (ETA) Indices for Modeling Chemical and Drug Toxicity. *Current Pharmaceutical Design, 16*(24), 2625–2639. doi:10.2174/138161210792389270

Roy, K., Pal, D. K., De, A. U., & Sengupta, C. (1999). Comparative QSAR with molecular negentropy molecular connectivity, STIMS and TAU indices: part I. Tadpole narcosis of diverse functional acyclic compounds. *Indian Journal of Chemistry, 38B*(6), 664–671.

Roy, K., Pal, D. K., De, A. U., & Sengupta, C. (2001). Comparative QSAR studies with molecular negentropy, molecular connectivity, STIMS and TAU indices. Part II: general anaesthetic activity of aliphatic hydrocarbons, halocarbons and ethers. *Indian Journal of Chemistry, 40B*(2), 129–135.

Roy, K., & Saha, A. (2003a). Comparative QSPR studies with molecular connectivity, molecular negentropy and TAU Indices. Part I: molecular thermochemical properties of diverse functional acyclic compounds. *Journal of Molecular Modeling, 9*(4), 259–270. doi:10.1007/s00894-003-0135-z

Roy, K., & Saha, A. (2003b). Comparative QSPR studies with molecular connectivity, molecular negentropy and TAU indices. Part 2: lipid–water partition coefficient of diverse functional acyclic compounds. *Internet Electronic Journal of Molecular Design, 2*(5), 288–305.

Roy, K., & Saha, A. (2003c). QSPR with TAU indices: water solubility of diverse functional acyclic compounds. *Internet Electronic Journal of Molecular Design, 2*(7), 475–491.

Roy, K., & Saha, A. (2004). QSPR with TAU indices: boiling points of sulfides and thiols. *Indian Journal of Chemistry, 43A*(7), 1369–1376.

Roy, K., & Saha, A. (2005). QSPR with TAU indices: molar refractivity of diverse functional acyclic compounds. *Indian Journal of Chemistry, 44B*(8), 1693–1707.

Roy, K., & Saha, A. (2006). QSPR with TAU indices: Part 5. Liquid heat capacity of diverse functional organic compounds. *Journal of the Indian Chemical Society, 83*(4), 351–355.

Roy, K., Saha, A., Chakroborty, S., & Ghosh, C. C. (2004). QSPR with TAU indices: molar thermochemical properties of diverse functional acyclic compounds. *Journal of the Indian Chemical Society, 81*(2), 115–125.

Roy, K., & Sanyal, I. (2006). QSTR with extended topochemical atom indices. 7. QSAR of substituted benzenes to *Saccharomyces cerevisiae*. *QSAR & Combinatorial Science, 25*(4), 359–371. doi:10.1002/qsar.200530172

Roy, K., Sanyal, I., & Ghosh, G. (2006a). QSPR of n-octanol/water partition coefficient of non-ionic organic compounds using extended topochemical atom (ETA) indices. *QSAR & Combinatorial Science, 26*(5), 629–646. doi:10.1002/qsar.200610112

Roy, K., Sanyal, I., & Roy, P. P. (2006b). QSPR of the bioconcentration factors of non-ionic organic compounds in fish using extended topo-chemical atom (ETA) indices. *SAR and QSAR in Environmental Research, 17*(6), 563–582. doi:10.1080/10629360601033499

Sabljic, A. (1984). Calculation of retention indices by molecular topology: chlorinated alkanes. *Journal of Chromatography. A, 314*(C), 1–12. doi:10.1016/S0021-9673(01)97719-2

Sabljic, A. (1985). Calculation of retention indices by molecular topology. Chlorinated benzenes. *Journal of Chromatography. A, 319*(C), 1–8. doi:10.1016/S0021-9673(01)90533-3

Schultz, H. P. (1989). Topological organic chemistry. 1. Graph theory and topological indices. *Journal of Chemical Information and Computer Sciences, 29*(3), 227–228. doi:10.1021/ci00063a012

Selassie, C. D., Mekapati, S. B., & Verma, R. P. (2002). QSAR: Then and Now. *Current Topics in Medicinal Chemistry, 2*(12), 1357–1379. doi:10.2174/1568026023392823

Seward, J. R., Hamblen, E. L., & Schultz, T. W. (2002). Regression comparisons of *Tetrahymena pyriformis* and *Poecilia reticulata* toxicity. *Chemosphere, 47*(1), 93–101. doi:10.1016/S0045-6535(00)00473-2

Shorter, J. (1973). *Correlation Analysis in Organic Chemistry*. Cambridge: Cambridge University Press.

Stead, A. H., Gill, R., Evans, A. T., & Moffat, A. C. (1982). Predictions of gas chromatographic retention characteristics of barbiturates from molecular structure. *Journal of Chromatography. A, 234*(2), 277–283. doi:10.1016/S0021-9673(00)81866-X

Swain, C. G., & Lupton, E. C. Jr. (1968). Field and Resonance Components of Substituent Effects. *Journal of the American Chemical Society, 90*(16), 4328–4337. doi:10.1021/ja01018a024

Szasz, Gy., Papp, O., Vamos, J., Hanko-Novak, K., & Kier, L. B. (1983). Relationships between molecular connectivity indices, partition coefficients and chromatographic parameters. *Journal of Chromatography. A, 269*(C), 91–95. doi:10.1016/S0021-9673(01)90789-7

Taft, R. W. Jr. (1952). Linear Free-Energy Relationships from Rates of Esterification and Hydrolysis of Aliphatic and Ortho-Substituted Benzoate Esters. *Journal of the American Chemical Society, 74*(11), 2729–2732. doi:10.1021/ja01131a010

Taft, R. W. Jr. (1960). Sigma Values from Reactivities. *Journal of Physical Chemistry, 64*(12), 1805–1815. doi:10.1021/j100841a003

Taft, R. W. Jr, & Lewis, I. C. (1958). The General Applicability of a Fixed Scale of Inductive Effects. II. Inductive Effects of Dipolar Substituents in the Reactivities of m- and p-Substituted Derivatives of Benzene. *Journal of the American Chemical Society, 80*(10), 2436–2443. doi:10.1021/ja01543a023

Taft, R. W. Jr, Price, E., Fox, I. R., Lewis, I. C., Anderson, K. K., & Davis, G. T. (1963). Fluorine Nuclear Magnetic Resonance Shielding in Meta-Substituted Fluorobenzenes. The Effect of Solvent on the Inductive Order. *Journal of the American Chemical Society, 85*(6), 709–724. doi:10.1021/ja00889a015

Todeschini, R., & Consonni, V. (2000). *Handbook of Molecular Descriptors*. Weinheim, Germany: Wiley-VCH.

Todeschini, R., Vighi, M., Finizio, A., & Gramatica, P. (1997). 30-Modelling and Prediction by WHIM Descriptors. Part 8. Toxicity and Physico-chemical Properties of Environmental Priority Chemicals by 2D-TI and 3D-WHIM Descriptors. *SAR and QSAR in Environmental Research, 7*(1–4), 173–193. doi:10.1080/10629369708039130

Trinajstić, N. (1992). *Chemical Graph Theory*. Boca Raton, FL, USA: CRC Press.

Wang, X. D., Sun, C., Wang, Y., & Wang, L. S. (2002). Quantitative structure–activity relationships for the inhibition toxicity to root elongation of *Cucumis sativus* of selected phenols and interspecies correlation with *Tetrahymena pyriformis*. *Chemosphere*, *46*(2), 153–161. doi:10.1016/S0045-6535(01)00133-3

Wells, M. J. M., & Clark, C. R. (1982a). Investigation of N-alkylbenzamides by reversed-phase liquid chromatography. IV. The study of a homologous series of N-alkylbenzamides using the solvophobic theory and molecular connectivity. *Journal of Chromatography. A*, *243*(2), 263–267. doi:10.1016/S0021-9673(00)82417-6

Wells, M. J. M., & Clark, C. R. (1982b). Investigation of N-alkylbenzamides by reversed-phase liquid chromatography. V. Charateristics of some tertiary alkylbenzamides. *Journal of Chromatography. A*, *244*(2), 231–240. doi:10.1016/S0021-9673(00)85686-1

Wells, M. J. M., Clark, C. R., & Patterson, R. M. (1981). Correlation of reversed-phase capacity factors for barbiturates with biological activities, partition coefficients, and molecular connectivity indices. *Journal of Chromatographic Science*, *19*(11), 573–582.

Wells, M. J. M., Clark, C. R., & Patterson, R. M. (1982). Investigation of N-alkylbenzamides by reversed-phased liquid chromatography. III. Correlation of chromatographic parameters with molecular connectivity indices for the C1C5 N-alkylbenzamides. *Journal of Chromatography. A*, *235*(1), 61–74. doi:10.1016/S0021-9673(00)95789-3

Wells, M. J. M., Clark, C. R., & Patterson, R. M. (1986). Structure-retention relationship analysis for some mono- and polycyclic aromatic hydrocarbons in reversed-phase liquid chromatography using molecular connectivity. *Analytical Chemistry*, *58*(8), 1625–1633. doi:10.1021/ac00121a008

Wiener, H. (1947a). Correlation of heats of isomerization, and differences in heats of vaporization of isomers, among the paraffin hydrocarbons. *Journal of the American Chemical Society*, *69*(11), 2636–2638. doi:10.1021/ja01203a022

Wiener, H. (1947b). Structural determination of paraffin boiling points. *Journal of the American Chemical Society*, *69*(1), 17–20. doi:10.1021/ja01193a005

Yukawa, Y., & Tsuno, Y. (1959). Resonance Effect in Hammett Relation. II. Sigma Constants in Electrophilic Reactions and their Intercorrelation. *Bulletin of the Chemical Society of Japan*, *32*, 965–971. doi:10.1246/bcsj.32.965

Yukawa, Y., Tsuno, Y., & Sawada, M. (1966). Resonance Effect In Hammett Relation. IV. Linear Free Energy Based on the Normal Substituent Constants. *Bulletin of the Chemical Society of Japan*, *39*, 2274–2286. doi:10.1246/bcsj.39.2274

Compilation of References

Abboud, J.-L. M., & Notario, R. (1999). Critical compilation of scales of solvent parameters. Part I. Pure, non-hydrogen bond donor solvents. *Pure and Applied Chemistry*, *71*(4), 645–718. doi:10.1351/pac199971040645

Abidi, N., Hequet, E., Tarimala, S., & Dai, L. L. (2007). Cotton fabric surface modification for improved UV radiation protection using sol-gel process. *Journal of Applied Polymer Science*, *104*, 111–117. doi:10.1002/app.24572

Abraham, M. H., Berthelot, M., Laurence, C. H., & Taylor, P. J. (1998). Analysis of hydrogen-bond complexation constants in 1,1,1-trichloroethane: the α_2^H and β_2^H relationship. *Journal of the Chemical Society, Perkin Transactions 2: Physical Organic Chemistry*, *1*, 187–191. doi:10.1039/a702326j

Abraham, M. H., Duce, P. P., Prior, D. V., Barrat, D. G., Morris, J. J., & Taylor, P. J. J. (1989). Hydrogen bonding. Part 9. Solute proton donor and proton acceptor scales for use in drug design. *Journal of the Chemical Society, Perkin Transactions 2: Physical Organic Chemistry*, *10*, 1355–1375. doi:10.1039/p29890001355

ACD/Labs. (1996). Retrieved from http://www.acdlabs.com.

Adalstensson, H., & Bruice, T. C. (1998). What is the mechanism of catalysis of ester aminolysis by weak amine bases? Comparison of experimental studies and theoretical investigation of the aminolysis of substituted phenyl esters of quinoline-6- and -8-carboxylic acids. *Journal of the American Chemical Society*, *120*(14), 3440–3447. doi:10.1021/ja972162+

Agrawal, S., Ojha, R. P., & Maiti, S. (2008)... *The Journal of Physical Chemistry B*, *112*, 6828–6836. doi:10.1021/jp7102676

Aguero-Chapin, G., Antunes, A., Ubeira, F. M., Chou, K.-C., & González-Díaz, H. (2008). Comparative Study of Topological Indices of Macro/Supramolecular RNA Complex Networks. *Journal of Chemical Information and Modeling*, *48*, 2265–2277. doi:10.1021/ci8001809

Ahmad, M. K., Halid, M. L. M., Rasheid, N. A., Ahmed, A. Z., Abdullah, S., & Rusop, M. (2010). Effect of annealing temperatures on surface morphology and electrical properties of titanium dioxide thin films prepared by sol-gel method. *Journal of Sustainable Energy & Environment*, *1*, 17–20.

Ahn, Y. U., Kim, E. J., Kim, H. T., & Hahn, S. H. (2003). Variation of structural and optical properties of sol-gel TiO_2 thin films with catalyst concentration and calcination temperature. *Materials Letters*, *57*, 4660–4666. doi:10.1016/S0167-577X(03)00380-X

Aiello, L. C., & Collard, M. (2001). Our newest oldest ancestor? *Nature*, *410*, 526–527. doi:10.1038/35069164

Akers, K. S., Sinks, G. D., & Schultz, T. W. (1999). Structure-toxicity relationships for selected halogenated aliphatic chemicals. *Environmental Toxicology and Pharmacology*, *7*, 33–39. doi:10.1016/S1382-6689(98)00048-9

Akporiaye, D. E., Dahl, I. M., Karlsson, A., & Wendelbo, R. (1998)... *Angewandte Chemie International Edition*, *37*(5), 609–611. doi:10.1002/(SICI)1521-3773(19980316)37:5<609::AID-ANIE609>3.0.CO;2-X

Alam, M. A., & Naik, P. K. (2009)... *Journal of Molecular Graphics & Modelling*, *27*, 930–947. doi:10.1016/j.jmgm.2009.02.003

Albery, W. J., & Knowles, J. R. (1976). Evolution of enzyme function and the development of the catalytic efficiency. *Biochem.*, *15*, 5631–5640. doi:10.1021/bi00670a032

Alia, J. M., & Edwards, H. G. (2005). Vibrational spectroscopic properties of hydrogen bonded acetonitrile studied by DFT. *The Journal of Physical Chemistry A, 109*(35), 7977–7987. doi:10.1021/jp051892y

Alia, J. M., & Edwards, H. G. (2007). Vibrational dynamics of hydrogen-bonded HCN complexes with OH and NH acids: Computational DFT systematic study. *International Journal of Quantum Chemistry, 107*(5), 1170–1180. doi:10.1002/qua.21235

Allen, M. J., & Rushton, N. (1994). Use of the CytoTOX 96(TM) assay in routine biocompatibility testing in vitro. *Promega Notes Magazine, 45*, 7–10.

Alper, K. O., Singla, M., Stone, J. L., & Bagdassarian, C. K. (2001). Correlated conformational fluctuations during enzymatic catalysis: Implications for catalytic rate enhancement. *Protein Science, 10*, 1319–1330. doi:10.1110/ps.220101

Al-Shahrour, F. (2006). BABELOMICS: A systems biology perspective in the functional annotation of genome-scale experiments. *Nucleic Acids Research, 34*, W472–W476. doi:10.1093/nar/gkl172

Al-Shahrour, F., Díaz-Uriarte, R., & Dopazo, J. (2004). FatiGO: A web tool for finding significant associations of gene ontology terms with groups of genes. *Bioinformatics (Oxford, England), 20*, 578–580. doi:10.1093/bioinformatics/btg455

Al-Shahrour, F., Díaz-Uriarte, R., & Dopazo, J. (2005). Discovering molecular functions significantly related to phenotypes by combining gene expression data and biological information. *Bioinformatics (Oxford, England), 21*, 2988–2993. doi:10.1093/bioinformatics/bti457

Al-Shahrour, F., Minguez, P., Vaquerizas, J. M., Conde, L., & Dopazo, J. (2005). Babelomics: A suite of web-tools for functional annotation and analysis of group of genes in high-throughput experiments. *Nucleic Acids Research, 33*, W460–W464. doi:10.1093/nar/gki456

Al-Shahrour, F., Arbiza, L., Dopazo, H., Huerta, J., Minguez, P., Montaner, D., Dopazo, J. (2007). From genes to functional classes in the study of biological systems. *BMC Bioinformatics, 8*, 114-1–17.

Alvarez de Andrés, S. (2005). A predictor based on the somatic changes of the BRCA1/2 breast cancer tumors identifies the non-BRCA1/2 tumors with BRCA1 promoter hypermethylation. *Clinical Cancer Research, 11*, 1146–1153.

Anderson, D. H. (1983). *Compartmental modelling and tracer kinetics*. Berlin: Springer Verlag.

Andrade, C. H. (2010). 4D-QSAR: Perspectives in Drug Design. *Molecules (Basel, Switzerland), 15*, 3281–3294. doi:10.3390/molecules15053281

Andrews, P. R., & Tintelnot, M. (1990). Intermolecular forces and molecular binding. In Hansch, C., Sammes, P. G., & Taylor, J. B. (Eds.), *Comprehensive Medicinal Chemistry* (Vol. 4, pp. 321–347). Oxford: Pergamon Press.

Aptula, A. O., & Roberts, D. W. (2006). Mechanistic applicability domains for non-animal based prediction of toxicological end points: general principles and application to reactive toxicity. *Chemical Research in Toxicology, 19*(8), 1097–1105. doi:10.1021/tx0601004

Åqvist, J., & Hansson, T. (1996)... *Journal of Physical Chemistry, 100*(22), 9512–9521. doi:10.1021/jp953640a

Åqvist, J., Luzhkov, V. B., & Brandsdal, B. O. (2002)... *Accounts of Chemical Research, 35*(6), 358–36. doi:10.1021/ar010014p

Åqvist, J., & Marelius, J. (2001)... *Combinatorial Chemistry & High Throughput Screening, 4*(8), 613–626.

Åqvist, J., Medina, C., & Samuelsson, J. E. (1994)... *Protein Engineering, 7*, 385–391. doi:10.1093/protein/7.3.385

Aragues, R., Sali, A., Bonet. J., Marti-Renom. M.A,, Oliva, B. (2007). Characterization of protein hubs by inferring interacting motifs from protein interactions. *PLoS Comput Biol, 3*, e178-1–11.

Aranda, M. A., Fraile, A., Dopazo, J., Malpica, J. M., & García-Arenal, F. (1997). Contribution of mutation and RNA recombination to the evolution of a plant pathogenic RNA. *Journal of Molecular Evolution, 44*, 81–88. doi:10.1007/PL00006124

Arbiza, L. (2006). Selective pressures at a codon-level predict deletereous mutations in human disease genes. *Journal of Molecular Biology, 358*, 1390–1404. doi:10.1016/j.jmb.2006.02.067

Arbiza, L., Dopazo, J., Dopazo, H. (2006). Positive selection, relaxation, and acceleration in the evolution of the human and chimp genomes. *PLoS Comp Biol, 2*, e38-1–13.

Ariel, P. D. (2010). Homotopy perturbation method and natural convection flow of a third grade fluid through a circular tube. *Nonlinear. Sci. Lett, 1*, 43–52.

Arissawa, M., Taft, C. A., & Felcman, J. (2003). Investigation of nucleoside analogs with anti-HIV activity. *International Journal of Quantum Chemistry, 93*, 422–432. doi:10.1002/qua.10580

Arribas, E., Bisswanger, H., Sotos-Lomas, A., Garcia-Moreno, M., Garcia-Canovas, F., & Donoso-Pardo, J. (2008a). A method, based on statistical moments, to evaluate the kinetic parameters involved in unstable enzyme systems. *Journal of Mathematical Chemistry, 44*, 379–404. doi:10.1007/s10910-007-9316-9

Arribas, E., Munoz-Lopez, A., Garcia-Meseguer, M. J., Lopez-Najera, A., Avalos, L., & Garcia-Molina, F. (2008b). Mean lifetime and first-passage time of the enzyme species involved in an enzyme reaction. Application to unstable enzyme systems. *Bulletin of Mathematical Biology, 70*, 1425–1449. doi:10.1007/s11538-008-9307-4

Astumian, R. D., Chock, P. B., Tsong, T. Y., & Westerhoff, H. V. (1989). Effects of oscillations and energy-driven fluctuations on the dynamics of enzyme catalysis and free-energy transduction. *Physical Review A., 39*, 6416–6435. doi:10.1103/PhysRevA.39.6416

Auer, C. M., Nabholz, J. V., & Baetcke, K. P. (1990). Mode of action and the assessment of chemical hazards in the presence of limited data: use of structure–activity relationships (SAR) under TSCA, Section 5. *Environmental Health Perspectives, 87*, 183–197. doi:10.1289/ehp.9087183

Avise, J. C., Neigel, J. E., & Arnold, J. (1984). Demographic influences on mitochondrial DNA lineage survivorship in animal populations. *Journal of Molecular Evolution, 20*, 99–105. doi:10.1007/BF02257369

Bader, R. F. W. (1990). *Atoms in molecules: A quantum theory*. Oxford, UK: Oxford University Press.

Bahnson, B. J., & Klinman, J. P. (1995). Hydrogen tunneling in enzyme catalysis. *Methods in Enzymology, 249*, 373–397. doi:10.1016/0076-6879(95)49042-6

Bailey-Kellogg, N. Ramakrishnan.(2003). *Proc. 17th Int. Workshop on Qualitative Reasoning*, pp. 23-30.\

Bajorath, J. (2002). Integration of virtual and high-throughput screening. *Nature Reviews. Drug Discovery, 1*(11), 882–894. doi:10.1038/nrd941

Bala, P., Grochowski, P., Lesyng, B., & McCammon, J. A. (1996). Quantum-classical molecular dynamics simulation of proton transfer processes in molecular complexes and in enzymes. *Journal of Physical Chemistry, 100*, 2535–2545. doi:10.1021/jp952642s

Balaban, A. T., Oniciu, D. C., & Katrizky, A. R. (2004). Aromaticity as a Cornerstone of Heterocyclic Chemistry. *Chemical Reviews, 104*, 2777–2812. doi:10.1021/cr0306790

Balaban, A. T. (1979)... *Theoretica Chimica Acta, 5*, 239–261.

Balaban, A. T. (1982). Highly discriminating distance-based topological index. *Chemical Physics Letters, 89*(5), 399–404. doi:10.1016/0009-2614(82)80009-2

Balaban, A. T. (1995). Chemical graphs: Looking back and glimpsing ahead. *Journal of Chemical Information and Computer Sciences, 35*(3), 339–350. doi:10.1021/ci00025a001

Balaban, A. T. (Ed.). (1997). *From Chemical Topology to Three-Dimensional Geometry. New York*. Kluwer Academic Publishers.

Balaban, A. T., Mills, D., Ivanciuc, O., & Basak, S. C. (2000). Reverse Weiner indices. *Croatica Chemica Acta, 73*(4), 923–941.

Balaban, A. T., & Ivanciuc, O. (1999). Historical Development of Topological Indices. In Devillers, J., & Balaban, A. T. (Eds.), *Topological Indices and Related Descriptors in QSAR and QSPR* (pp. 21–57). Amsterdam: Gordon and Breach Science Publishers.

Balasubrimaniam, C., Ojha, R. P., & Maiti, S. (2007)... *Biochemical and Biophysical Research Communications, 355*, 1081–1086. doi:10.1016/j.bbrc.2007.02.084

Bally, A. (1999). *Electronic properties of nano-crystaline titanium dioxide thin films*. Lausanne: École Polytechnique Fédérale de Lausanne.

Banerjee, S., Gopal, J., Muraleedharan, P., Tyagi, A. K., & Raj, B. (2006). Physics and chemistry of photocatalytic titanium dioxide: visualization of bactericidal activity using atomic force microscopy. *Current Science, 90*(10), 1378–1383.

Barati, N., & Faghihi Sani, M. A. (2009). Coating of titania nanoparticles on stainless steel using an alkoxide precursor. *Progress in Color. Colorants and Coatings, 2*, 71–78.

Barlow, S. E., Van Doren, J. M., & Bierbaum, V. M. (1988). The gas phase displacement reaction of chloride ion with methyl chloride as a function of kinetic energy. *Journal of the American Chemical Society, 110*(21), 7240–7242. doi:10.1021/ja00229a064

Barry, D. A., Culligan-Hensley, P. J., & Barry, S. J. (1995). Real values of the W-function. *Assoc. Comput. Machinery Trans. Math. Software, 21*, 161–171. doi:10.1145/203082.203084

Barry, D. A., Parlange, J.-Y., Li, L., Prommer, H., Cunningham, C. J., & Stagnitti, F. (2000). Analytical approximations for real values of Lambert W-function. *Mathematics and Computers in Simulation, 53*, 95–103. doi:10.1016/S0378-4754(00)00172-5

Barry, D. A., Parlange, J.-Y., Sander, G. C., & Sivaplan, M. (1993). A class of exact solutions for Richards' equation. *Journal of Hydrology (Amsterdam), 142*, 29–46. doi:10.1016/0022-1694(93)90003-R

Barta, A., Dorner, S., & Polacek, N. (2001). Mechanism of ribosomal peptide bond formation. *Science, 291*, 203a–204. doi:10.1126/science.291.5502.203a

Bartlett, R. J., & Purvis, G. D. (1978). Many-body perturbation theory, coupled-pair many-electron theory, and the importance of quadruple excitations for the correlation problem. *International Journal of Quantum Chemistry, 14*(5), 561–581. doi:10.1002/qua.560140504

Basak, S.C., Raychaudhury, C., Roy, A.B., & Ghosh, J.J. (1990). *Indian Journal of Pharmacology*, (1981), *13*, 112–116.

Baskerville, J. C. (1981). A Systematic Study of the Consulting Literature as an Integral Part of Applied Training in Statistics. *The American Statistician, 35*(3), 121–123. doi:10.2307/2683974

Basran, J., Sutcliffe, M. J., & Scrutton, N. S. (1999). Enzymatic H-transfer requires vibration-driven extreme tunneling. *Bichem., 38*, 3218–3222. doi:10.1021/bi982719d

Battiston, G. A., Gerbasi, R., Porchia, M., & Marigo, A. (1994). Influence of substrate on structural properties of TiO_2 thin films obtained via MOCVD. *Thin Solid Films, 239*, 186–191. doi:10.1016/0040-6090(94)90849-4

Baumes, L. A. (2006)... *Journal of Combinatorial Chemistry, 8*(3), 304–314. doi:10.1021/cc050130+

Baumes, L. A., & Collet, P. (2009). [New York: Elsevier.]. *Computational Materials Science, 45*(1), 27–40. doi:10.1016/j.commatsci.2008.03.051

Baumes, L. A., Farruseng, D., Lengliz, M., & Mirodatos, C. (2004)... *QSAR & Combinatorial Science, 29*(9), 767–778. doi:10.1002/qsar.200430900

Baumes, L. A., Gaudin, R., Serna, P., Nicoloyannis, N., & Corma, A. (2008)... *Combinatorial Chemistry & High Throughput Screening, 11*(4), 266–282. doi:10.2174/138620708784246068

Baumes, L. A., Jimenez, S., Kruger, F., Maitre, O., Collet, P., & Corma, A. (n.d.). How gaming industry fosters crystal structure prediction? [PCCP]. *Physical Chemistry Chemical Physics*.

Baumes, L. A., Moliner, M., & Corma, A. (2006)... *QSAR & Combinatorial Science, 26*(2), 255–272. doi:10.1002/qsar.200620064

Baumes, L. A., Moliner, M., & Corma, A. (2008)... *CrystEngComm, 10*, 1321–1324. doi:10.1039/b812395k

Baumes, L. A., Moliner, M., & Corma, A. (2009)... *Chemistry (Weinheim an der Bergstrasse, Germany), 15*, 4258–4269. doi:10.1002/chem.200802683

Baumes, L. A., Serna, P., & Corma, A. (in press). Merging traditional and high throughput approaches results in efficient design, synthesis and screening of catalysts for an industrial process. *Applied Catalysis A*.

Baumes, L. A., Serra, J. M., Serna, P., & Corma, A. (2006)... *Journal of Combinatorial Chemistry, 8*(4), 583–596. doi:10.1021/cc050093m

Baumes, L. A., Blansché, A., Serna, P., Tchougang, A., Lachiche, N., P. Collet & A. Corma (2009). *Materials and Manufacturing Processes*, [REMOVED HYPERLINK FIELD]*24* (3), 282 – 292.

Baumes, L. A., Jimenez, S., & Corma, A. (in press). *hITeQ: A new workflow-based computing environment for streamlining discovery.* In L.A. Baumes, D. Farruseng, F. Ausfelder (eds). *Application in materials science.* Catalysis Today, Special Issue "EuroCombiCat 2009" Conf.

Baumes, L. A., Jouve, P., Farrusseng, D., Lengliz, M., Nicoloyannis, N., & Mirodatos, C. (2003). *7th Int. Conf. on Knowledge-Based Intelligent Information & Engineering Systems (KES'2003).* Lecture Notes in AI (LNCS/LNAI series). Sept. 3-5. Univ. of Oxford, UK: Springer-Verlag

Baumes, L.A., Farruseng, D., Ausfelder, F. (2009). *Catalysis Today.* Special Issue "EuroCombiCat 2009" conference.

Baykoucheva, S. (2007). A new era in chemical information: PubChem, DiscoveryGate, and chemistry central. *Online (Wilton, Connecticut), 31*(5), 16–20.

Becke, A. D. (1998). Density-functional exchange-energy approximation with correct asymptotic behavior. *Physical Review A., 38*, 3098–3100. doi:10.1103/PhysRevA.38.3098

Beganskienė, A., Šakirzanovas, S., Melninkaitis, A., Sirutkaitis, V., & Kareiva, A. (2006). Sol-gel derived optical coating with controlled parameters. *Materials Science, 12*(4), 283–286.

Bellera, C. L., Talevi, A., & Bruno-Blanch, L. E. (2007). Aplicación de Análisis Lineal Discriminante en la Búsqueda de Drogas Antiepileptogénica. *Latin American Journal of Pharmacy, 26*(2), 244–252.

Bem, D. S., Erlandson, E. J., Gillespie, R. D., Harmon, L. A., Schlosser, S. G., & Vayda, A. J. (2003). *Experimental design for combinatorial and high throughput materials development*, 89-107. Hoboken, NJ: Wiley and sons.

Ben Amor, S., Baud, G., Jacquet, M., & Pichon, N. (1998). Photoprotective titania coatings on PET substrates. *Surface and Coatings Technology, 102*, 63–72. doi:10.1016/S0257-8972(97)00558-6

Bender, A., Mussa, H. Y., & Glen, R. C. (2004). Molecular similarity searching using atom environments, information-based feature selection, and a naïve bayesian classifier. *Journal of Chemical Information and Computer Sciences, 44*(1), 170–178. doi:10.1021/ci034207y

Bender, M. L. (1960). Mechanisms of catalysis of nucleophilic reactions of carboxylic acid derivatives. *Chemical Reviews, 60*(1), 53–113. doi:10.1021/cr60203a005

Benedix, R., Dehn, F., Quaas, J., & Orgass, M. (2000). Application of titanium dioxide photocatalysis to create self-cleaning building materials. *Leipzig Annual Civil Engineering Report, 5*(157).

Benzecri, J.-P. (1984). *L'analyse des données (Vol. 1).* Paris: Dunod.

Bernstein, F. C. (1977). The Protein Data Bank: A computer-based archival file for macromolecular structures. *Journal of Molecular Biology, 112*, 535–542. doi:10.1016/S0022-2836(77)80200-3

Besalu, E., de Julian-Ortiz, J. V., Iglesias, M., & Pogliani, L. (2006). An Overlooked Property of Plot Methods. *Journal of Mathematical Chemistry, 39*, 475–484. doi:10.1007/s10910-005-9035-z

Besalu, E., de Julian-Ortiz, J. V., & Pogliani, L. (2006). Some Plots Are not that Equivalent. *MATCH Communications in Mathematical and Computer Chemistry, 55*, 281–286.

Besalu, E., de Julian.Ortiz, J. V., & Pogliani, L. (2007). Trends and Plot Methods in MLR Studies. *Journal of Chemical Information and Modeling, 47*, 751–760. doi:10.1021/ci6004959

Besalu, E., de Julian.Ortiz, J. V., & Pogliani, L. (2010). Ordinary and Orthogonal Regressions in QSAR/QSPR and Chemistry-Related Studies. *MATCH Communications in Mathematical and Computer Chemistry, 63*, 573–583.

Besalu, E. de Julian.Ortiz, J.V., Pogliani, L. (2010). On Plopts QSAR/QSPR Methodologies. In M. Putz (Ed.) *Quantum Frontiers of Atoms and Molecules in Physics, Chemistry, and Biology* (pp. 581-598). New York: Nova Publishing Inc.

Besler, B. H., Merz, K. M., & Kollman, P. A. (1990). Atomic charges derived from semiempirical methods. *Journal of Computational Chemistry, 11*(4), 431–439. doi:10.1002/jcc.540110404

Bevan, D. R., & Weyand, E. H. (1988). Compartmental analysis of the disposition of benzo[a]pyrene in rats. *Carcinogenesis, 9*, 2027–2032. doi:10.1093/carcin/9.11.2027

Bhushan, N., & Rosenfeld, S. (Eds.). (2000). *Of Minds and Molecules: New Philosophical Perspectives on Chemistry.* Oxford, UK: Oxford University Press.

Biazar, J., & Ghazvini, H. (2009). He's homotopy- perturbation method for solving systems of Volterra integral equations. *Chaos, Solitons, and Fractals, 39*, 770. doi:10.1016/j.chaos.2007.01.108

Binkley, J. S., & Pople, J. A. (1975). Møller–Plesset theory for atomic ground state energies. *International Journal of Quantum Chemistry, 9*(2), 229–236. doi:10.1002/qua.560090204

Bisson, G. (2000). *La similarité: une notion symbolique/numérique. Apprentissage symbolique-numérique (Vol. 2*, pp. 169–201). Eds Moulet, Brito. Editions Cépadues.

Blake, C. C. F., Mair, G. A., North, A. C. T., Phillips, D. C., & Sarma, V. R. (1967). On the conformation of the hen egg-white lysozyme molecule. *Proceedings of the Royal Society of London. Series B. Biological Sciences, 167*, 365–385. doi:10.1098/rspb.1967.0034

Blake, B. W., Enslein, K., Gombar, V. K., & Borgstedt, H. H. (1990). Salmonella Mutagenicity and Rodent Carcinogenicity: Quantitative Structure-Activity-Relationships. *Mutation Research, 241*(3), 261–271. doi:10.1016/0165-1218(90)90023-U

Blancourgoiti, B., Sanchez, F., Desanroman, C. P., Dopazo, J., & Ponz, F. (1998). Potato-virus-Y group-C isolates are a homogeneous pathotype but 2 different genetic strains. *The Journal of General Virology, 79*, 2037–2042.

Blancourgoiti, B., Sanchez, F., Dopazo, J., & Ponz, F. (1996). A strain-type clustering of potato-virus-Y based opn the genetic-distance between isolates calculated by RFLP analysis of the amplified coat. *Archives of Virology, 141*, 2425–2442. doi:10.1007/BF01718641

Blickle, T., & Thiele, L. (1995). *6th Int. Conf. on Genetic Algorithms.* San Mateo, CA: Morgan Kaufmann.

Bobadova-Parvanova, P., & Galabov, B. (1998). Ab initio molecular-orbital study of hydrogen-bonded complexes of carbonyl aliphatic compounds and hydrogen fluoride. *The Journal of Physical Chemistry A, 102*(10), 1815–1819. doi:10.1021/jp9710852

Boehm, H. J. (1992)... *Journal of Computer-Aided Molecular Design, 6*, 61–78. doi:10.1007/BF00124387

Boeker, E. A. (1984). Integrated rate equations for enzyme-catalyzed first-order and second-order reactions. *The Biochemical Journal, 223*, 15–22.

Boeker, E. A. (1985). Integrated rate equations for irreversible enzyme-catalysed first-order and second-order reactions. *The Biochemical Journal, 226*, 29–35.

Boeker, E. A. (1987). Analytical methods for fitting integrated rate equations. A discontinuous assay. *The Biochemical Journal, 245*, 67–74.

Bogdanov, B., & Nikolic, S., & Trinajstić, N. (1989). On the three-dimensional wiener number. *Journal of Mathematical Chemistry, 3*(3), 299–309. doi:10.1007/BF01169597

Bojarski, J., & Ekiert, L. (1982). Relationship between molecular connectivity indices of barbiturates and chromatographic parameters. *Chromatographia, 15*(3), 172–176. doi:10.1007/BF02261534

Bojarski, J., & Ekiert, L. (1983). Evaluation of Modified Valence Molecular Connectivity Index for Correlations of Chromatographic Parameters. *Journal of Liquid Chromatography, 6*(1), 73–80. doi:10.1080/01483918308066871

Bonchev, D., & Trinajstić, N. (1977). Information theory, distance matrix and molecular branching. *The Journal of Chemical Physics, 67*(10), 4517–4533. doi:10.1063/1.434593

Bonchev, D. (1983). *Information Theoretic Indices for Characterization of Chemical Structure.* Chichester: Research Studies Press, Wiley.

Bonchev, D., & Rouvray, D. H. (Eds.). (1991). *Chemical Graph Theory. Introduction and Fundamentals.* New York: Academic Press.

Borchers, A. T., Keen, C. L., & Gershwin, M. E. (2002). The influence of yogurt/*Lactobacillus* on the innate and acquired immune response. *Clinical Reviews in Allergy & Immunology, 22*, 207–230. doi:10.1007/s12016-002-0009-7

Bortolato, A., & Moro, S. (2007)... *Journal of Chemical Information and Modeling, 47*, 572–582. doi:10.1021/ci600369n

Botts, J., & Morales, M. (1953). Analytical description of the effect of modifiers and of enzyme multivalency upon the steady state catalyzed reaction rate. *Transactions of the Faraday Society, 49*, 696–707. doi:10.1039/tf9534900696

Boussie, T. R. (2003)... *Journal of the American Chemical Society, 125*, 4306–4317. doi:10.1021/ja020868k

Box, G., & Draper, N. (1987). *Empirical model-building and response surfaces*. New York: John Wiley and Sons.

Box, G. E. P. (1976). Science and Statistics. *Journal of the American Statistical Association, 71*, 791–799. doi:10.2307/2286841

Boyd, J. C., Millership, J. S., & Woolfson, A. D. (1982). The relationship between molecular connectivity and partition coefficients. *The Journal of Pharmacy and Pharmacology, 34*(6), 364–366. doi:10.1111/j.2042-7158.1982.tb04730.x

Boys, S. F., & Bernardi, F. (1970). The calculation of small molecular interactions by differences of separate total energies - some procedures with reduced errors. *Molecular Physics, 19*(4), 553–566. doi:10.1080/00268977000101561

Bozzi, A., Yuranova, T., Guasaquillo, I., Laub, D., & Kiwi, J. (2005). Self-cleaning of modified cotton textiles by TiO_2 at low temperatures under daylight irradiation. *Journal of Photochemistry and Photobiology A Chemistry, 174*, 156–164. doi:10.1016/j.jphotochem.2005.03.019

Braun, G. H., Jorge, D. M., Ramos, H. P., Alves, R. M., da Silva, V. B., & Giuliatti, S. (2008). Molecular dynamics, flexible docking, virtual screening, ADMET predictions, and molecular interaction field studies to design novel potential MAO-B inhibitors. *Journal of Biomolecular Structure & Dynamics, 25*(4), 347–355.

Braydich-Stolle, L., Hussain, S., Schlager, J. J., & Hofmann, M.-C. (2005). In vitro cytotoxicity of nanoparticles in mammalian germline stem cells. *Toxicological Sciences, 88*(2), 412–419. doi:10.1093/toxsci/kfi256

Breiman, L. (2001). Random Forests. *Machine Learning, 45*, 5–32. doi:10.1023/A:1010933404324

Bren, M., Florian, J., Mavri, J., & Bren, U. (2007)... *Theoretical Chemistry Accounts, 117*, 535–540. doi:10.1007/s00214-007-0264-z

Bren, U., Martinek, V., & Florian, J. (2006)... *The Journal of Physical Chemistry B, 110*, 12782–12788. doi:10.1021/jp056623m

Breneman, C. M., & Wiberg, K. B. (1990). Determining atom-centered monopoles from molecular electrostatic potentials. The need for high sampling density in formamide conformational analysis. *Journal of Computational Chemistry, 11*(3), 361–373. doi:10.1002/jcc.540110311

Bricker, M. L., Sachtler, J. W. A., Gillespie, R. D., McGoneral, C. P., Vega, H., Bem, D. S., & Holmgren, J. S. (2004)... *Applied Surface Science, 223*(1-3), 109–117. doi:10.1016/S0169-4332(03)00893-6

Brinker, C. J., & Harrington, M. S. (1981). Sol-gel derived antireflective coatings for silicon. *Solar Energy Materials, 5*, 159–172. doi:10.1016/0165-1633(81)90027-7

Brinker, K. (2003). In Proc. of the 20th Int. Conf. on Machine Learning (ICML'03), pp. 59-66.

Brodin, A., Nyquist-Mayer, A., & Wadstein, T. (1984). Phase diagram and aqueous solubility of the lidocaine–prilocaine binary system. *Journal of Pharmaceutical Sciences, 73*, 481–484. doi:10.1002/jps.2600730413

Brown, A. J. (1902). Enzyme Action. *Journal of the Chemical Society Transactions, 81*, 373–388. doi:10.1039/ct9028100373

Brown, R. S., Bennet, A. J., & Slebocka-Tilk, H. (1992). Recent perspectives concerning the mechanism of H3O+- and hydroxide-promoted amide hydrolysis. *Accounts of Chemical Research, 25*(11), 481–488. doi:10.1021/ar00023a001

Brown, H. C., & Okamoto, Y. (1958). Electrophilic Substituent Constants. *Journal of the American Chemical Society, 80*(18), 4979–4987. doi:10.1021/ja01551a055

Bruice, T. C., & Benkovic, S. J. (1966). *Bioorganic mechanisms*. New York: W.A. Benjamin Inc.

Bruno, W. J., & Bialek, W. (1992). Vibrationally enhanced tunneling as a mechanism for enzymatic hydrogen transfer. *Biophysical Journal*, *63*, 689–699. doi:10.1016/S0006-3495(92)81654-5

Burda, J., Kurans, M., Kriz, J., & Vodicka, L. (1985). Relationship between retention behaviour and molecular structure of alkanes in reversed phase high performance liquid chromatography. *Fresenius'. Journal of Analytical Chemistry*, *321*(6), 549–552.

Burden, F. R., Ford, M. G., Whitley, D. C., & Winkler, D. A. (2000). Use of automatic relevance determination in QSAR studies using Bayesian neural networks. *Journal of Chemical Information and Computer Sciences*, *40*(6), 1423–1430. doi:10.1021/ci000450a

Burden, F. R. (1989). Molecular identification number for substructure searches. *Journal of Chemical Information and Computer Sciences*, *29*(3), 225–227. doi:10.1021/ci00063a011

Buydens, L., Coomans, D., Vanbelle, M., Massart, D. L., & Driessche, R. V. (1983). Comparative study of topological and linear free energy-related parameters for the prediction of GC retention indices. *Journal of Pharmaceutical Sciences*, *72*(11), 1327–1329. doi:10.1002/jps.2600721122

Buydens, L., & Massart, D. L. (1981). Prediction of gas chromatographic retention indices from linear free energy and topological parameters. *Analytical Chemistry*, *53*(13), 1990–1993. doi:10.1021/ac00236a010

Buyevskaya, O. V., Bruckner, A., Kondratenko, E. V., Wolf, D., & Baerns, M. (2001)... *Catalysis Today*, *67*, 369–378. doi:10.1016/S0920-5861(01)00329-7

Buzea, C., Pacheco Blandino, I. I., & Robbie, K. (2007). Nanomaterials and nanoparticles: Sources and Toxicity. *Biointerphases*, *2*(4), MR17–MR172. doi:10.1116/1.2815690

Caballero, J., Fernandez, L., Abreu, J. I., & Fernandez, M. (2006). Amino acid sequence autocorrelation vectors and ensembles of Bayesian-regularized genetic neural networks for prediction of conformational stability of human lysozyme mutants. *Journal of Chemical Information and Modeling*, *46*, 1255–1268. doi:10.1021/ci050507z

Caffrey, M. (2003). Membrane protein crystallization. *Journal of Structural Biology*, *142*(1), 108–132. doi:10.1016/S1047-8477(03)00043-1

Cai, X. C., Wu, W. Y., & Li, M. S. (2006). Approximate period solution for a kind of nonlinear oscillator by He's perturbation method. *Int. J. Nonlinear. Sci. Numer. Simulation*, *7*(1), 109–117. doi:10.1515/IJNSNS.2006.7.1.109

Cai, Y. D., & Chou, K. C. (2005). Predicting enzyme subclass by functional domain composition and pseudo amino acid composition. *Journal of Proteome Research*, *4*, 967–971. doi:10.1021/pr0500399

Cai, Y. D., & Lin, S. L. (2003). Support vector machines for predicting rRNA-, RNA-, and DNA-binding proteins from amino acid sequence. *Biochimica et Biophysica Acta*, *1648*, 127–133.

Calvo, D., Dopazo, J., & Vega, M. A. (1995). Cd36, CLA-1 (Cd36L1), and limpii (Cd36L2) gene family – Cellular-distribution, chromosomal location, and genetic evolution. *Genomics*, *25*, 100–106. doi:10.1016/0888-7543(95)80114-2

Canfield, R. E. (1963). The amino acid sequence of egg white lysozyme. *The Journal of Biological Chemistry*, *238*, 2698–2707.

Cann, R. L., Stoneking, M., & Wilson, A. C. (1987). Mitochondrial DNA and human evolution. *Nature*, *325*, 31–36. doi:10.1038/325031a0

Cantor, C. R., & Schimmel, P. R. (1980). *Biophysical Chemistry. Part III: The Behavior of Biological Macromolecules*. San Francisco: Freeman & Co.

Capriotti, E., Arbiza, L., Casadio, R., Dopazo, J., Dopazo, H., & Marti-Renom, M. A. (2008). The use of estimated evolutionary strength at the codon level improves the prediction of disease related protein mutations in human. *Human Mutation*, *29*, 198–204. doi:10.1002/humu.20628

Capriotti, E., & Marti-Renom, M. A. (2008). Computational RNA structure prediction. *Curr Bioinformatics*, *3*, 32–45. doi:10.2174/157489308783329823

Carey, F. A., & Sanders, R. J. (2000). *Advanced organic chemistry Part A, Structure and mechanisms*. New York: Springer.

Cargas, M. L., & Seybold, P.G., Andersen. (1988). M. E. Modeling the tissue solubilities and metabolic rate constant (V$_{max}$) of halogenated compounds. *Toxicology Letters, 43*, 235–256. doi:10.1016/0378-4274(88)90031-8

Carley, D. W. (2005). Drug repurposing: Identify, develop and commercialize new uses for existing or abandoned drugs. Part II. *IDrugs, 8*(4), 310–313.

Carlson, H. A., & Jorgensen, W. L. (1995)... *Journal of Physical Chemistry, 99*, 10667–10673. doi:10.1021/j100026a034

Carlsson, L., Ahlberg Helgee, E., & Boyer, S. (2009). Interpretation of nonlinear QSAR models applied to Ames mutagenicity data. *Journal of Chemical Information and Modeling, 49*(11), 2551–2558. doi:10.1021/ci9002206

Carlsson, J., Ander, M., Nervall, M., & Åqvist, J. (2006)... *The Journal of Physical Chemistry B, 110*, 12034–12041. doi:10.1021/jp056929t

Caruthers, J. M., Lauterbach, J. A., Thomson, K. T., Venkatasubramanian, V., Snively, C. M., & Bhan, A. (2003)... *Journal of Catalysis, 216*, 98. doi:10.1016/S0021-9517(02)00036-2

Casañola-Martín, G. M., Marrero-Ponce, Y., Khan, M. T. H., Ather, A., Sultan, S., Torrens, F., & Rotondo, R. (2007). TOMOCOMD-CARDD descriptors-based virtual screening of tyrosinase inhibitors. Evaluation of different classification model combinations using bond-based linear indices. *Bioorganic & Medicinal Chemistry, 15*(3), 1483–1503. doi:10.1016/j.bmc.2006.10.067

Casañola-Martín, G. M., Marrero-Ponce, Y., Tareq Hassan Khan, M., Torrens, F., Pérez-Giménez, F., & Rescigno, A. (2008). Atom- and bond-based 2D TOMOCOMD-CARDD approach and ligand-based virtual screening for the drug discovery of new tyrosinase inhibitors. *Journal of Biomolecular Screening, 13*(10), 1014–1024. doi:10.1177/1087057108326078

Cascón, A. (2005). A novel candidate region linked to development of both pheochromocytoma and head/neck paraganglioma. *Genes, Chromosomes & Cancer, 42*, 260–268. doi:10.1002/gcc.20139

Castellano, G., & Torrens, F. (2009). Local anaesthetics classified using chemical structural indicators. *Nereis, 2*, 7–17.

Castillo-Garit, J. A., Vega, M. C., Rolon, M., Marrero-Ponce, Y., Kouznetsov, V. V., & Torres, D. F. A. (2010). Computational Discovery of novel trypanosomicidal drug-like Chemicals by using bond-based non-stochastic and stochastic quadratic maps and linear discriminant analysis. *European Journal of Pharmaceutical Sciences, 39*(1-3), 30–36. doi:10.1016/j.ejps.2009.10.007

Castro, E. A., Torrens, F., Toropov, A. A., Nesterov, I. V., & Nabiev, O. M. (2004). QSAR Modeling Anti-HIV-1 Activities by Optimization of Correlation Weights of Local Graph Invariants. *Molecular Simulation, 30*, 691–696. doi:10.1080/08927020412331272449

Castro, E. A., Ruiz, M. G., Salinas, S., & Santos, J. G. (1999). Kinetics and mechanism of the aminolysis of phenyl and 4-nitrophenyl chloroformates in aqueous solution. *The Journal of Organic Chemistry, 64*(13), 4817–4820. doi:10.1021/jo990146k

Câteau, H., & Tanaka, S. (2002). Kinetic analysis of multisite phosphorylation using analytic solutions to Michaelis-Menten equation. *Journal of Theoretical Biology, 217*, 1–14. doi:10.1006/jtbi.2002.3024

Cavalli Sforza, L. L., Piazza, A., Menozzi, P., & Mountain, J. (1988). Reconstruction of human evolution: Bringing together genetic, archaeological, and linguistic data. *Proceedings of the National Academy of Sciences of the United States of America, 85*, 6002–6006. doi:10.1073/pnas.85.16.6002

Cawse, J. N., Baerns, M., & Holena, M. (2004)... *Journal of Chemical Information and Computer Sciences, 44*(1), 143–146. doi:10.1021/ci034171+

Cawse, J. N., & Wroczynski, R. (2003). Experimental design for combinatorial and high throughput materials development, 109-127. Hoboken, NJ: Wiley and sons.

Cebra, J. J. (1999). Influences of microbiota on intestinal immune system development. *The American Journal of Clinical Nutrition, 69*, 1046S–1051S.

Cedervall, T., Lynch, I., Lindman, S., Berggard, T., Thulin, E., & Nilsson, H. (2007). Understanding the nanoparticle–protein corona using methods to quantify exchange rates and affinities of proteins for nanoparticles. *Proceedings of the National Academy of Sciences of the United States of America, 104*(7), 2050–2055. doi:10.1073/pnas.0608582104

Cedillo, A., Contreras, R., Galvan, M., Aizman, A., Andres, J., & Safont, V. S. (2007). Nucleophilicity index from perturbed electrostatic potentials. *The Journal of Physical Chemistry A, 111*(12), 2442–2447. doi:10.1021/jp068459o

Cha, Y., Murray, C. J., & Klinman, J. P. (1989). Hydrogen tunneling in enzyme reaction. *Science, 143,* 1325–1330. doi:10.1126/science.2646716

Chakravarti, L., & Roy, H. L. (1967). John Wiley and Sons. pp. 392-394.

Chalk, A. J., Worth, C. L., Overington, J. P., & Chan, A. W. (2004). PDBLIG: classification of small molecular protein binding in the Protein Data Bank. *Journal of Medicinal Chemistry, 47,* 3807–3816. doi:10.1021/jm040804f

Chalmet, S., Harb, W., & Ruiz-Lopez, M. F. (2001). Computer simulation of amide bond formation in aqueous solution. *The Journal of Physical Chemistry A, 105*(51), 11574–11581. doi:10.1021/jp0135656

Chaloner, K., & Verdinelli, I. (1995)... *Statistical Science, 10*(3), 273–304. doi:10.1214/ss/1177009939

Chandani, S., Lee, C. H., & Loecher, E. L. (2005)... *Chemical Research in Toxicology, 18,* 1108–1123. doi:10.1021/tx049646l

Chattaraj, P. K., Chakraborty, A., & Giri, S. (2009). Net electrophilicity. *The Journal of Physical Chemistry A, 113,* 10068. doi:10.1021/jp904674x

Chattaraj, P. K., & Giri, S. (2009). Electrophilicity index within a conceptual DFT framework. *Annu. Rep. Prog. Chem. Sect. C., 105,* 13–39. doi:10.1039/b802832j

Chattaraj, P. K., Maiti, B., & Sarkar, U. (2003). Philicity: A unified treatment of chemical reactivity and selectivity. *The Journal of Physical Chemistry A, 107,* 4973–4975. doi:10.1021/jp034707u

Chattaraj, P. K., & Roy, D. R. (2007). Update 1 of: Electrophilicity index. *Chemical Reviews, 107,* PR46–PR74. doi:10.1021/cr078014b

Chattaraj, P. K., Roy, D. R., Giri, S., Mukherjee, S., Subramanian, V., & Parthasarathi, R. (2007). An atom counting and electrophilicity based QSTR approach. *Journal of Chemical Sciences, 119,* 475–488. doi:10.1007/s12039-007-0061-1

Chattaraj, P. K., Sarkar, U., & Roy, D. R. (2006). Electrophilicity index. *Chemical Reviews, 106,* 2065–2091. doi:10.1021/cr040109f

Chattaraj, P. K. (Ed.). (2009). *Chemical reactivity theory. A density functional view.* Boca Raton, FL: CRS Press. doi:10.1201/9781420065442

Chattaraj, P. K., Nath, S., & Maiti, B. (2003). Reactivity descriptors. In Tollenaere, J., Bultinck, P., Winter, H. D., & Langenaeker, W. (Eds.), *Computational Medicinal Chemistry for Drug Discovery* (pp. 295–322). New York: Marcel Dekker.

Chatterjee, S., Price, B., & Hadi, A. S. (1999). *Regression Analysis by Example. Wiley Series in Probability and Statistics* (3rd ed.). New York: John Wiley & Sons.

Chen, D., Eulenstein, O., & Fernández-Baca, D. (2004). Rainbow: A toolbox for phylogenetic supertree construction and analysis. *Bioinformatics (Oxford, England), 20,* 2872–2873. doi:10.1093/bioinformatics/bth313

Chen, W., Liao, B., Xiang, X., & Zhu, W. (2009). An improved binary representation of DNA sequences and its applications. *MATCH Commun Math Comput Chem, 61,* 767–780.

Chen, W., & Zhang, Y. (2009). Comparisons of DNA sequences based on dinucleotide. *MATCH Commun Math Comput Chem, 61,* 533–540.

Chen, W., & Zhang, Y. (2009). Three distances for rapid similarity analysis of DNA sequences. *MATCH Commun Math Comput Chem, 61,* 781–788.

Chen, B.-X., Wilson, S. R., Das, M., Couglin, D. J., & Erlanger, B. F. (1998)... *Proceedings of the National Academy of Sciences of the United States of America, 95,* 10809–10813. doi:10.1073/pnas.95.18.10809

Chen, H.-W., Su, S.-F., Chien, C.-T., Lin, W.-H., Yu, S.-L., & Chou, C.-C. (2006). Titanium dioxide nanoparticles induce emphysema-like lung injury in mice. *The FASEB Journal, 20*(13), 2393–2395. doi:10.1096/fj.06-6485fje

Chen, S. Z., Zhang, P. Y., Zhu, W. P., Chen, L., & Xu, S. M. (2006). Deactivation of TiO_2 photocatalytic films loaded on aluminium: XPS and AFM analyses. *Applied Surface Science, 252,* 7532–7538. doi:10.1016/j.apsusc.2005.09.023

Cheng, H. Y. (1991). A method for calculating the mean residence times of catenary metabolites. *Biopharmaceutics & Drug Disposition, 12*, 335–342. doi:10.1002/bdd.2510120503

Chermette, H. (1999). Chemical reactivity indexes in Density Functional Theory. *Journal of Computational Chemistry, 20*, 129–154. doi:10.1002/(SICI)1096-987X(19990115)20:1<129::AID-JCC13>3.0.CO;2-A

Cheshmedzhieva, D., Ilieva, S., Hadjieva, B., & Galabov, B. (2009). The mechanism of alkaline hydrolysis of amides: a comparative computational and experimental study of the hydrolysis of N-methylacetamide, N-methylbenzamide, and acetanilide. *Journal of Physical Organic Chemistry, 22*(6), 619–631. doi:10.1002/poc.1492

Cheshmedzhieva, D., Ilieva, S., Hadjieva, B., Trayanova, T., & Galabov, B. (2009). Reactivity of acetanilides in the alkaline hydrolysis reaction: Theory vs. experiment. *Molecular Physics, 107*(8), 1187–1192. doi:10.1080/00268970902799890

Chiang, B. L., Sheih, Y. H., Wang, L. H., Liao, C. K., & Gill, H. S. (2000). Enhancing immunity by dietary consumption of a probiotic lactic acid bacterium (*Bifidobacterium lactis HN019*): Optimization and definition of cellular immune responses. *European Journal of Clinical Nutrition, 54*, 849–855. doi:10.1038/sj.ejcn.1601093

Chiu, T.-L., & So, S.-S. (2003). Genetic neural networks for functional approximation. *QSAR & Combinatorial Science, 22*(5), 519–526. doi:10.1002/qsar.200310004

Cho, A. E., Gullar, V., Berne, B. J., & Friesner, R. (2005)... *Journal of Computational Chemistry, 26*, 915–931. doi:10.1002/jcc.20222

Choi, S.-J., Oh, J.-M., & Choy, J.-H. (2008). Human-related application and nanotoxicology of inorganic particles: complementary aspects. *Journal of Materials Chemistry, 18*(6), 615–620. doi:10.1039/b711208d

Choplin, F. (1990). Computers and the medicinal chemist. In Hansch, C., Sammes, P. G., & Taylor, J. B. (Eds.), *Comprehensive Medicinal Chemistry* (*Vol. 4*, pp. 33–58). Oxford: Pergamon Press.

Chou, K. C., & Cai, Y. D. (2003). Predicting protein quaternary structure by pseudo amino acid composition. *Proteins, 53*, 282–289. doi:10.1002/prot.10500

Chou, K. C., & Cai, Y. D. (2005). Prediction of membrane protein types by incorporating amphipathic effects. *Journal of Chemical Information and Modeling, 45*, 407–413. doi:10.1021/ci049686v

Chou, K. C., & Shen, H. B. (2006). Predicting protein subcellular location by fusing multiple classifiers. *Journal of Cellular Biochemistry, 99*, 517–527. doi:10.1002/jcb.20879

Chou, K. C., & Shen, H. B. (2007). MemType-2L: A web server for predicting membrane proteins and their types by incorporating evolution information through Pse-PSSM. *Biochemical and Biophysical Research Communications, 360*, 339–345. doi:10.1016/j.bbrc.2007.06.027

Chou, K. C. (1990). Applications of graph theory to enzyme kinetics and protein folding kinetics. Steady and non-steady-state systems. *Biophysical Chemistry, 35*, 1–24. doi:10.1016/0301-4622(90)80056-D

Chowdhury, M. S. H., & Hashim, I. (2007). Solutions of time- dependent Emden-Fowler type equations by homotopy- perturbation method. *Physics Letters. [Part A], 368*, 305–313. doi:10.1016/j.physleta.2007.04.020

Christensen, F. M., de Bruijn, J. H. M., Hansen, B. G., Munn, S. J., Sokull-Klüttgenm, B., & Pedersen, F. (2003). Assessment tools under the new European Union chemicals policy. GMI 41, 5–19, http://ecb.jrc.ec.europa.eu/ documents/REACH/ PUBLICATIONS/Assessment_tools_REACH040122.pdf (last accessed on 19 November, 2010).

Chrysicopoulou, P., Davazoglou, D., Trapalis, C., & Kordas, G. (1998). Optical properties of very thin (<100 nm) sol-gel TiO_2 films. *Thin Solid Films, 323*, 188–193. doi:10.1016/S0040-6090(97)01018-3

Chun, H. Y., Park, S. S., You, S. H., Kang, G. H., Bae, W. T., & Kim, K. W. (2009). Preparation of a transparent hydrophilic TiO_2 thin film photocatalyst. *Journal of Ceramic Processing Research, 10*(2), 219–223.

Ciccarelli, F. D., Doerks, T., von Mering, C., Creevey, C. J., Snel, B., & Bork, P. (2006). Toward automatic reconstruction of a highly resolved tree of life. *Science, 311*, 1283–1287. doi:10.1126/science.1123061

Claros, M. G. (2003). *BioROM 2003*. Málaga: Sociedad Española de Bioquímica y Biología Molecular–Roche Diagnostics.

Claros, M. G. (2004). *BioROM 2005*. Málaga: Sociedad Española de Bioquímica y Biología Molecular–Universidad Miguel Hernández–Universidad del País Vasco.

Claros, M. G. (2006). *BioROM 2007*. Málaga: Sociedad Española de Bioquímica y Biología Molecular–Pearson Educación.

Claros, M. G., Fernández-Fernández, J. M., González-Mañas, J. M., Herráez, Á., Sanz, J. M., & Urdiales, J. L. (2001). *BioROM 1.0 y 1.1*. Málaga: Sociedad Española de Bioquímica y Biología Molecular.

Claros, M. G et al. (2002). *BioROM 2002. Sociedad Española de Bioquímica y Biología Molecular.* Málaga

Claude, N. (2009). Reducing the use of laboratory animals. *Bulletin de l'Académie Nationale de Médicine, 193*(8), 1767–1772.

Cohen, E., Gamliel, A., & Katan, J. (1988). The fungitoxicity of chlorophenols to the pathogenic fungi.Fusarium oxysporum and Rhizoctonia solani: A structure-activity relationship study. *Pesticide Science, 24*, 139–146. doi:10.1002/ps.2780240205

Cohn, D., Atlas, L., & Ladner, R. (1990). *Advances in Neural Information Processing Systems 2*. San Francisco: Morgan Kaufmann.

Cohn, D. A., Ghahramani, Z., & Jordan, M. I. in G. Tesauro, D. Touretzky, J. Alspector,(1995). *Advances in Neural Information Processing Systems 7*. San Francisco: Morgan Kaufmann.

Conde, L. (2004). PupaSNP Finder: A web tool for finding SNPs with putative effect at transcriptional level. *Nucleic Acids Research, 32*, W242–W248. doi:10.1093/nar/gkh438

Conde, L. (2006). PupaSuite: Finding functional SNPs for large-scale genotyping purposes. *Nucleic Acids Research, 34*, W621–W625. doi:10.1093/nar/gkl071

Conde, L., Mateos, Á., Herrero, J., & Dopazo, J. (2003). Improved class prediction in DNA microarray gene expression data by unsupervised reduction of the dimensionality followed by supervised learning with a perceptron. *J VLSI Signal Processing-Syst Signal, Image. Video Technol, 35*, 245–253.

Conde, L., Montaner, D., Burguet-Castell, J., Tárraga, J., Al-Shahrour, F., & Dopazo, J. (2007). Functional profiling and gene expression analysis of chromosomal copy number alterations. *Bioinformation, 1*, 432–435.

Conde, L., Montaner, D., Burguet-Castell, J., Tárraga, J., Medina, I., Al-Shahrour, F., & Dopazo, J. (2007). ISACGH: A web-based environment for the analysis of Array CGH and gene expression which includes functional profiling. *Nucl Acids Res*, 35, W81–W85. Al-Shahrour, F., Minguez, P., Tárraga, J., Medina, I., Alloza, E., Montaner, D., Dopazo, J. (2007). FatiGO+: A functional profiling tool for genomic data. Integration of functional annotation, regulatory motifs and interaction data with microarray experiments. *Nucleic Acids Research, 35*, W91–W96.

Conde, L., Vaquerizas, J. M., Ferrer-Costa, C., Orozco, M., & Dopazo, J. (2005). PupasView: A visual tool for selecting suitable SNPs, with putative pathologic effect in genes, for genotyping purposes. *Nucleic Acids Research, 33*, W501–W505. doi:10.1093/nar/gki476

Conesa, A., & Götz, S. (2008). Blast2GO: A comprehensive suite for functional analysis in plant genomics. *International Journal of Plant Genomics, 2008*, 619832-1–12. doi:10.1155/2008/619832

Cooper, A., Mourer-Chauviré, C., Chambers, G. K., von Haeseler, A., Wilson, A. C., & Pääbo, S. (1992). Independent origins of New Zealand moas and kiwis. *Proceedings of the National Academy of Sciences of the United States of America, 89*, 8741–8744. doi:10.1073/pnas.89.18.8741

Copeland, R. A. (2000). *Enzymes*. New York: Wiley-VCH. doi:10.1002/0471220639

Corless, R. M., Gonnet, G. H., Hare, D. E. G., Jeffrey, D. J., & Knuth, D. E. (1996). On the Lambert W function. *Advances in Computational Mathematics, 5*, 329–359. doi:10.1007/BF02124750

Corless, R. M., & Jeffrey, D. J. (2002). The right ω function. In Calmet, J., Benhamou, B., Caprotti, O., Henocque, L., & Sorge, V. (Eds.), *Artificial Intelligence, Automated Reasoning, and Symbolic Computation* (pp. 76–89). Berlin: Springer. doi:10.1007/3-540-45470-5_10

Corma, A., Moliner, M., Serra, J. M., Serna, P., Díaz-Cabañas, M. J., & Baumes, L. A. (2006)... *Chemistry of Materials, 18*(14), 3287–3296. doi:10.1021/cm060620k

Corma, A., Serra, J. M., & Chica, A. (2002). *Principles and methods for accelerated catalyst design and testing.*

Corriou, J. P., Iordache, O., & Tondeur, D. (1991). Classification of biomolecules by information entropy. *Journal de Chimie Physique, 88,* 2645–2652.

Covino, B. G. (1972). Local anesthesia. *The New England Journal of Medicine, 286,* 975–983. doi:10.1056/NEJM197205042861805

Covino, B. G. (1980). Local anesthetic agents for peripheral nerve blocks. *Der Anaesthesist, 29*(7), 33–37.

Covino, B. G. (1986). Pharmacology of local anaesthetic agents. *British Journal of Anaesthesia, 58,* 701–716. doi:10.1093/bja/58.7.701

Cramer, R. D. III, Patterson, D. E., & Bunce, J. D. (1988)... *Journal of the American Chemical Society, 110,* 5959–5967. doi:10.1021/ja00226a005

Crittenden, D. L., Chebib, M., & Jordan, M. J. (2005). Stabilization of zwitterions in solution: GABA analogues. *The Journal of Physical Chemistry A, 109*(18), 4195–4201. doi:10.1021/jp050320a

Cronin, M. T. D., & Schultz, W. (2001). Development of quantitative structure-activity relationships for the toxicity of aromatic compounds to Tetrahymina pyriformis: Comparative assessment of methodologies. *Chemical Research in Toxicology, 14,* 1284–1295. doi:10.1021/tx0155202

Cronin, M. T. D. (1996). The use of cluster significance analysis to identify asymmetric QSAR data sets in toxicology. An example with eye irritation data. *SAR and QSAR in Environmental Research, 5*(3), 167–175. doi:10.1080/10629369608032987

Cros (1863). Action de l'alcohol amylique sur l'organisme" at the Faculty of Medicine, University of Strasbourg, Strasbourg, France on January 9.

Cros, A. F. A. (1863). *Action de l'alcool amylique sur l'organisme.* Ph.D. Thesis, University of Strasbourg, Strasbourg.

Crosby, A. W. (2003). *America's forgotten pandemic: The influenza of 1918.* Cambridge, UK: Cambridge University.

Crum-Brown, A., & Fraser, T. R. (1868). On the Connection between Chemical Constitution and Physiological Action. Part I. On the Physiological Action of the Salts of the Ammonium Bases, derived from Strychnine, Brucia, Thebaia, Codeia, Morphia, and Nicotia. *Journal of Anatomy and Physiology, 2*(2), 224–242.

Curry, S. H. (2008). Translational science: past, present and future. *BioTechniques, 44*(2), 2–8. doi:10.2144/000112749

Da Rocha Pita, S. S., Cirino, J. J. V., de Alencastro, R. B., Castro, H. C., Rodrigues, C. R., & Albuquerque, M. G. (2009). Molecular docking of a series of peptidomimetics in the trypanothione binding site of *T. cruzi* Trypanothione Reductase. *Journal of Molecular Graphics & Modelling, 28*(4), 330–335. doi:10.1016/j.jmgm.2009.08.011

Da Silva, C. H. T. P., Almeida, P., & Taft, C. A. (2004). Density functional and docking studies of retinoids for cancer treatment. *Journal of Molecular Modeling, 10,* 38–43. doi:10.1007/s00894-003-0167-4

Da Silva, C. H. T. P., Carvalho, I., & Taft, C. A. (2005). Homology modeling and molecular interaction field studies of α-glucosidases as a guide to structure-based design of novel proposed anti-HIV inhibitors. *Journal of Computer-Aided Molecular Design, 19,* 83–92. doi:10.1007/s10822-005-1486-6

Da Silva, C. H. T. P., Carvalho, I., & Taft, C. A. (2006). Molecular dynamics, docking, density functional, and ADMET studies of HIV-1 reverse transcriptase inhibitors. *Journal of Theoretical and Computational Chemistry, 5,* 579–586. doi:10.1142/S0219633606002441

Da Silva, C. H. T. P., del Ponte, G., Neto, A. F., & Taft, C. A. (2005). Rational design of novel diketoacid-containing ferrocene inhibitors of HIV-1 integrase. *Bioorganic Chemistry, 33,* 274–284. doi:10.1016/j.bioorg.2005.03.001

Da Silva, C. H. T. P., & Taft, C. A. (2004). Computer-aided molecular design of novel glucosidase inhibitors for AIDS treatment. *Journal of Biomolecular Structure & Dynamics, 22,* 59–64.

Da Silva, C. H. T. P., & Taft, C. A. (2005). Molecular dynamics, database screening, density functional and docking studies of novel RAR ligands in cancer chemotherapy. *Biophysical Chemistry, 117*, 73–77. doi:10.1016/j.bpc.2005.02.006

Da Silva, C. H. T. de P., da Silva, V. B., Resende, J., Rodrigues, P. F., Bononi, F. C., Benevenuto, C. G., & Taft, C. A. (2010). Computer-aided drug design and ADMET predictions for identification and evaluation of novel potential farnasyltransferase inhibitors in cancer therapy. *Journal of Molecular Graphics & Modelling, 28*(6), 513–523. doi:10.1016/j.jmgm.2009.11.011

Da Silva, V. B., Kawano, D. F., Gomes, A. S., Carvalho, I., Taft, C. A., & da Silva, C. H. T. de P. (2008). Molecular dynamics, density functional, ADMET predictions, virtual screening, and molecular interaction field studies for identification and evaluation of novel potential CDK2 inhibitors in cancer therapy. *The Journal of Physical Chemistry A, 112*(38), 8902–8910. doi:10.1021/jp8011969

Dai, Q., Liu, X.-Q., Wang, T.-M., & Vukicevic, D. (2007). Linear regression model of DNA sequences and its application. *Journal of Computational Chemistry, 28*, 1434–1445. doi:10.1002/jcc.20556

Damchan, J., Sikong, L., Kooptarnond, K., & Niyomwas, S. (2008). Contact angle of glass substrate coated with TiO_2/SiO_2 thin film. *Journal of Natural Sciences, 7*(1), 19.

Daoud, W. A., & Xin, J. H. (2004). Low temperature sol-gel processed photocatalytic titania coating. *Journal of Sol-Gel Science and Technology, 29*, 25–29. doi:10.1023/B:JSST.0000016134.19752.b4

Darlington, R. B. (1990). *Regression and Linear Models.* New York, NY: McGraw-Hill.

Daylight Chemical Information Systems. (2008). Retrieved from http://www.daylight.com.

De Clercq, E. (2002). New developments in anti-HIV chemotherapy. *Biochimica et Biophysica Acta, 1587*, 258–275.

de Graaf, A. A., Freidig, A. P., De, R. B., Jamshidi, N., Heinemann, M., & Rullmann, J. A. (2009). Nutritional systems biology modeling: from molecular mechanisms to physiology. *PLoS Computational Biology, 5*, e1000554. doi:10.1371/journal.pcbi.1000554

De Jong, K. A. (n.d.). Doctoral dissertation, univ. of Michigan. *Dissertation Abstract International, 36*(10), 5140(B). Univ. of Michigan Microfilms No. 76-9381

De la Fraga, L. G., Dopazo, J., & Carazo, J. M. (1995). Confidence-limits for resolution estimation in image averaging by random subsampling. *Ultramicroscopy, 60*, 385–391. doi:10.1016/0304-3991(95)00080-1

De Voogt, P., & Govers, H. (1986). Structural and chromatographic predictors of n-octanol/water partition coefficients. *Chemosphere, 15*(9–12), 1467–1472. doi:10.1016/0045-6535(86)90426-1

Dean-Ross, D., & Rahimi, M. (1995). Toxicity of phenolic compounds to sediment bacteria. *Bulletin of Environmental Contamination and Toxicology, 55*, 245–250. doi:10.1007/BF00203016

Dearden, J. C., & Ghafourian, T. (1999). Hydrogen bonding parameters for QSAR: Comparison of indicator variables, hydrogen bond counts, molecular orbital and other parameters. *Journal of Chemical Information and Computer Sciences, 39*, 231–235. doi:10.1021/ci980065+

Dearden, J. C. (2009). How not to develop a QSAR/QSPR relationship. *SAR and QSAR in Environmental Research, 20*, 241–266. doi:10.1080/10629360902949567

Debeljak, Ž., Marohnić, V., Srečnik, G., & Medić-Šarić, M. (2005). Novel approach to evolutionary neural network based descriptor selection and QSAR model development. *Journal of Computer-Aided Molecular Design, 19*, 835–855. doi:10.1007/s10822-005-9022-2

Debeljak, Ž., Škrbo, A., Jasprica, I., Mornar, A., Plečko, V., Banjanac, M., & Medić-Šarić, M. (2007). QSAR study of antimicrobial activity of some 3-nitrocoumarins and related compounds. *Journal of Chemical Information and Modeling, 47*, 918–926. doi:10.1021/ci600473z

Della, G. M., Monaco, P., Pinto, G., Pollio, A., Previtera, L., & Temussi, F. (2001). Phytotoxicity of low-molecular-weight phenols from olive mill wastewaters. *Bulletin of Environmental Contamination and Toxicology, 67*, 352–359. doi:10.1007/s001280132

Deming, S. N., & Morgan, S. L. (1993). *Experimental design: A chemometric approach* (2nd ed.). Amsterdam: Elsevier Science Publishers B.V.

Deng, W., Maust, B. S., Nickle, D. C., Learn, G. H., Liu, Y., & Heath, L. (2010). DIVEIN: A web server to analyze phylogenies, sequence divergence, diversity, and informative sites. *BioTechniques, 48*, 405–408. doi:10.2144/000113370

Deng, W., Breneman, C., & Embrechts, M. J. (2004). Predicting protein-ligand binding affinities using novel geometrical descriptors and machine-learning methods. *Journal of Chemical Information and Computer Sciences, 44*, 699–703. doi:10.1021/ci034246+

Derouane, E., Parmon, V., Lemos, F., & Ribeir, F. (2002). *Book Series: NATO SCIENCE SERIES: II: Mathematics, Physics and Chemistry* (Vol. 69, pp. 101–124). Dordrecht, Netherlands: Kluwer Academic Publishers.

Derouane, E. G., Parmon, V., Lemos, F., & Ribeiro, F. R. (Eds.). Kluver Academic Publishers: Dordrecht, The Netherlands, pp 153-172.

DeSimone, C., Vesely, R., Negri, R., Bianchi-Salvadori, B., Zanzoglu, S., Cilli, A., & Lucci, L. (1987). Enhancement of immune response of murine Peyer's patches by a diet supplemented with yogurt. *Immunopharmacology and Immunotoxicology, 9*, 87–100. doi:10.3109/08923978709035203

DeVault, D., & Chance, B. (1966). Studies of photosynthesis using a pulsed laser. I. Temperature dependence of cytochrome oxidation rate in chromatium. Evidence for tunneling. *Biophysical Journal, 6*, 825–847. doi:10.1016/S0006-3495(66)86698-5

Devillers, J., & Chambon, P. (1986). Acute toxicity and QSAR of chlorophenols on Daphnia magna. *Bulletin of Environmental Contamination and Toxicology, 37*, 599–605. doi:10.1007/BF01607810

Devillers, J., & Chambon, P. (1986). Toxicité aiguë chlorophénols sur *Daphnia magna* et *Brachydanio rerio. J. Fr. Hydrol., 17*, 111–120. doi:10.1051/water/19861702111

Devillers, J., & Balaban, A. T. (1999). *Topological Indices and Related Descriptors in QSAR/QSPR*. Amsterdam: Gordon and Breach.

Devillers, J. (Ed.). (2009). *Endocrine Disruption Modeling, QSAR in Environmental and Health Sciences*. New York: CRC Press.

Di Paolo, T. (1978). Structure-activity relationships of anesthetic ethers using molecular connectivity. *Journal of Pharmaceutical Sciences, 67*(4), 564–566. doi:10.1002/jps.2600670436

Di Rienzo, A., & Wilson, A. C. (1991). Branching pattern in the evolutionary three for human mitochondrial DNA. *Proceedings of the National Academy of Sciences of the United States of America, 88*, 1597–1601. doi:10.1073/pnas.88.5.1597

Díez-Sales, O., Copoví, A., Casabó, V. G., & Herráez, M. (1991). A modelistic approach showing the importance of the stagnant aqueous layers in in vitro diffusion studies, and in vitro-in vivo correlations. *International Journal of Pharmaceutics, 77*, 1–11. doi:10.1016/0378-5173(91)90295-Y

Díez-Sales, O., López-Castellano, A., Maiques-Lacer, F. J., & Herráez-Domínguez, M. (1993). An in vitro percutaneous absorption study of non-ionic compounds across human skin. *Die Pharmazie, 48*, 684–686.

Díez-Sales, O., Pérez-Sayas, E., Martín-Villodre, A., & Herráez-Domínguez, M. (1993). The prediction of percutaneous absorption: I. Influence of the dermis on in vitro permeation models. *International Journal of Pharmaceutics, 100*, 1–7. doi:10.1016/0378-5173(93)90068-Q

Díez-Sales, O., Watkinson, A.C., Herráez-Domínguez, M., & Javaloyes, C., Hadgraf,t J. (1996). A mechanistic investigation of the in vitro human skin permeation enhancing effect of Azone®. *International Journal of Pharmaceutics, 129*, 33–40. doi:10.1016/0378-5173(95)04237-7

Díez-Sales, O., Guzmán, D., Cano, D., Martín, A., Sánchez, E., Herráez, M. (1991) A comparative in vitro study of permeability with different synthetic and biological membranes. *Eur J Drug Metab Pharmacokinet* (Spec 3), 441–446.

Dimasi, J. A., Hansen, R. W., & Grabowsky, H. G. (2003). The price of innovation: new estimates of drug development costs. *Journal of Health Economics, 22*(2), 151–185. doi:10.1016/S0167-6296(02)00126-1

Dimitriev, Y., Ivanova, Y., & Iordanova, R. (2008). History of sol-gel science and technology [review]. *Journal of the University of Chemical Technology and Metallurgy, 43*(2), 181–192.

Dimitrov, S. D., Mekenyan, O. G., Sinks, G. D., & Schultz, T. W. (2003). Global modeling of narcotic chemicals: ciliate and fish toxicity. *Journal of Molecular Structure THEOCHEM, 622,* 63–70. doi:10.1016/S0166-1280(02)00618-8

Dimitrova, M., Ilieva, S., & Galabov, B. (2004). Reactivity descriptors for the hydrogen bonding ability of pyridine bases. *SAR and QSAR in Environmental Research, 15*(4), 311–319. doi:10.1080/10629360410001724914

Dimitrova, V., Ilieva, S., & Galabov, B. (2002). Electrostatic potential at atomic sites as a reactivity descriptor for hydrogen bonding. Complexes of monosubstituted acetylenes and ammonia. *The Journal of Physical Chemistry A, 106*(48), 11801–11805. doi:10.1021/jp026203m

Dimitrova, V., Ilieva, S., & Galabov, B. (2003). Electrostatic potential at nuclei as a reactivity index in hydrogen bond formation. Complexes of ammonia with C–H, N–H and O–H proton donor molecules. *Journal of Molecular Structure THEOCHEM, 637*(1), 73–80. doi:10.1016/S0166-1280(03)00402-0

Dislich, H., & Hinz, P. (1982). History and principles of the sol-gel process, and some new multicomponent oxide coatings. *Journal of Non-Crystalline Solids, 48,* 11–16. doi:10.1016/0022-3093(82)90242-3

Diudea, M. V. (Ed.). (2000). *Studies by Molecular Descriptors.* New York: Nova Science Publishing.

Diudea, M. V. E. (2001). *QSPR/QSAR Studies by Molecular Descriptors.* New York: Nova Science Publishers.

Diudea, M. V. (1996). Walk numbers ^eW_M: Wiener-type numbers of higher rank. *Journal of Chemical Information and Computer Sciences, 36*(3), 535–540. doi:10.1021/ci950134+

Diudea, M. V. (1997). Indices of reciprocal properties or Harary indices. *Journal of Chemical Information and Computer Sciences, 37*(2), 292–299. doi:10.1021/ci960037w

Djurisic, A. B., Fritz, T., & Leo, K. (1999). Determination of optical constants of thin absorbing films from normal incidence reflectance and transmittance measurements. *Optics Communications, 166,* 35–42. doi:10.1016/S0030-4018(99)00246-1

Dobson, P. D., & Doig, A. J. (2005). Predicting enzyme class from protein structure without alignments. *Journal of Molecular Biology, 345,* 187–199. doi:10.1016/j.jmb.2004.10.024

Doherty, P. J., Hoes, R. M., Robbat, A. Jr, & White, C. M. (1984). Relationship between gas chromatographic retention indices and molecular connectivities of nitrated polycyclic aromatic hydrocarbons. *Analytical Chemistry, 56*(14), 2697–2701. doi:10.1021/ac00278a017

Donets, V. V., Melnichenko, L. Y., Shaykevich, I. A., & Lomakina, O. V. (2009). Determination of refractive index dispersion and thickness of thin antireflection films TiO_2 and Si_3N_4 on surfaces of silicon photoelectric converters. *Journal of Semiconductor Physics. Quantum Electronics & Optoelectronics, 12,* 162–164.

Dopazo, H., Santoyo, J., & Dopazo, J. (2004). Phylogenomics and the number of characters required for obtaining an accurate phylogeny of eukaryote model species. *Bioinformatics (Oxford, England), 20,* 116–121. doi:10.1093/bioinformatics/bth902

Dopazo, J. (1997). A new index to find regions showing an unexpected variability or conservation in sequence alignments. *Computer Applications in the Biosciences, 13,* 313–317.

Dopazo, J. (2006). Bioinformatics and cancer: An essential alliance. *Clinical & Translational Oncology, 8,* 409–415. doi:10.1007/s12094-006-0194-6

Dopazo, J. (2006). Functional interpretation of microarray experiments. *OMICS: A Journal of Integrative Biology, 10,* 398–410. doi:10.1089/omi.2006.10.398

Dopazo, J. (2001). Annotated draft genomic sequence from a *Streptococcus pneumoniae* type 19F clinical isolate. *Microbial Drug Resistance (Larchmont, N.Y.), 7,* 99–125. doi:10.1089/10766290152044995

Dopazo, J., & Carazo, J. M. (1997). Phylogenetic reconstruction using an unsupervised growing neural network that adopts the topology of a phylogenetic tree. *Journal of Molecular Evolution, 44,* 226–233. doi:10.1007/PL00006139

Dopazo, J., Zanders, E., Dragoni, I., Amphlett, G., & Falciani, F. (2001). Methods and approaches in the analysis of gene expression data. *Journal of Immunological Methods*, *250*, 93–112. doi:10.1016/S0022-1759(01)00307-6

Dopazo, H, Dopazo, J. (2005). Genome-scale evidence of the nematode arthropod clade. *Genome Biol*, 6, R41-1–10.

Dopazo, J., Aloy, P. (2006). Discovery and hypothesis generation through bioinformatics. *Genome Biol*, 7, 307-1–3.

Doweyko, A. M. (2008). QSAR: dead or alive? *Journal of Computer-Aided Molecular Design*, *22*, 81–89. doi:10.1007/s10822-007-9162-7

Downs, G. M., Willett, P., & Fisanick, W. (1994). Similarity Searching and Clustering of Chemical-Structure Databases Using Molecular Property Data. *Journal of Chemical Information and Computer Sciences*, *34*, 1094–1102. doi:10.1021/ci00021a011

Dragon ver. 6 is a software from TELETE srl, Italy, 2010 http://www.talete.mi.it/products/dragon_description.htm (Last accessed date 8th July, 2011)

Dragos, H., Gilles, M., & Alexandre, V. (2009). Predicting the predictability: a unified approach to the applicability domain problem of QSAR models. *Journal of Chemical Information and Modeling*, *49*(7), 1762–1776. doi:10.1021/ci9000579

Dubey, K. D. Chaubey, A.K. Ojha, R.P. (2011). *Medicinal Chemistry Research*. doi:.doi:10.1007/s00044-011-9617-1

Dubey, K. D., Chaubey, A. K., Paravin, A., & Ojha, R. P. (2010)... *J Biophy Struct Biol*, *2*, 47–54.

Dubey, K. D., & Ojha, R. P. (2011)... *Journal of Biological Physics*, *37*, 69–78. doi:10.1007/s10867-010-9199-z

Duchowicz, P. R., & Castro, E. A. (2008). Partial Order Theory Applied to QSPR-QSAR Studies. In Brueggemann, R. (Ed.), *Combinatorial Chemistry and High Throughput Screening (special issue)* (pp. 783–793). New York: Bentham Science Publishers.

Duchowicz, P. R., Fernández, F. M., & Castro, E. A. (2009b). The Employment of Orthogonalization Methods in QSPR-QSAR Studies. In Pandalai, S. G., & Castro, E. A. (Eds.), *QSPR-QSAR Studies on Desired Properties for Drug Design*. New York: Research Signpost/Transworld Research Network.

Duchowicz, P. R., & Castro, E. A. (2009a). Application of the Fuzzy Logic Theory to QSAR/QSPR Studies. In Putz, M. (Ed.), *Quantum Frontiers of Atoms and Molecules in Physics, Chemistry and Biology*. Cairo, Egypt: Hindawi Publishing Corp.

Duffin, R., Tran, L., Brown, D., Stone, V., & Donaldson, K. (2007). Proinflammogenic Effects of Low-Toxicity and Metal Nanoparticles In Vivo and In Vitro: Highlighting the Role of Particle Surface Area and Surface Reactivity. *Inhalation Toxicology*, *19*(10), 849–856. doi:10.1080/08958370701479323

Duggleby, R. G. (1986). Progress-curve analysis in enzyme kinetics. Numerical solution of integrated rate equations. *The Biochemical Journal*, *235*, 613–615.

Duggleby, R. G. (2001). Quantitative analysis of the time courses of enzyme-catalyzed reactions. *Methods (San Diego, Calif.)*, *24*, 168–174. doi:10.1006/meth.2001.1177

Duggleby, R. G., & Morrison, J. F. (1977). The analysis of progress curves for enzyme-catalysed reactions by non-linear regression. *Biochimica et Biophysica Acta*, *481*, 297–312.

Duggleby, R. G., & Morrison, J. F. (1978). Progress curve analysis in enzyme kinetics: model discrimination and parameter estimation. *Biochimica et Biophysica Acta*, *526*, 398–409.

Duggleby, R. G., & Morrison, J. F. (1979). The use of steady-state rate equations to analyse progress curve data. *Biochimica et Biophysica Acta*, *568*, 357–362.

Duggleby, R. G., & Wood, C. (1989). Analysis of progress curves for enzyme-catalysed reactions. Automatic construction of computer programs for fitting integrated equations. *The Biochemical Journal*, *258*, 397–402.

Dujardin-Beaumetz & Audige. (1875). Recherches Expérimentales sur la puissance toxique des Alcools. *Comptes Rendus de l'Academie des Sciences*, *81*, 192.

Duzhko, V., Timoshenko, V. Y., Koch, F., & Dittrich, T. (2001). Photovoltage in nanocrystalline porous TiO_2. *Physical Review B: Condensed Matter and Materials Physics*, *64*, 1–7. doi:10.1103/PhysRevB.64.075204

Edelstein, A. S., & Cammarata, R. C. (1998). *Nanomaterials: Synthesis, Properties and Applications*. New York: CRC Press.

Edwards, B. S., Bologa, C., Young, S. M., Balakin, K. V., Prossnitz, E. R., & Savchuck, N. P. (2005). Integration of virtual screening with high-throughput flow cytometry to identify novel small molecule formylpeptide receptor antagonists. *Molecular Pharmacology, 68*(5), 1301–1310. doi:10.1124/mol.105.014068

Ehrenson, S., Brownlee, R. T. C., & Taft, R. W. (1973). Generalized Treatment of Substituent Effects in the Benzene Series. Statistical Analysis by the Dual Substituent Parameter Equation (1). In Streitwieser, A., & Taft, R. W. (Eds.), *Progress in Physical Organic Chemistry* (Vol. 10, pp. 1–80). Germany: Wiley publishers. doi:10.1002/9780470171899.ch1

Elena, S., Dopazo, J., de la Peña, M., Flores, R., Diener, T. O., & Moya, A. (2001). Phylogenetic analysis of viroid and viroid-like satellite RNAs from plants: A reassessment. *Journal of Molecular Evolution, 53*, 155–159.

Ellis, R. W. (1999). New technologies for making vaccines. *Vaccine, 17*, 1596–1604. doi:10.1016/S0264-410X(98)00416-2

El-Masri, H. A., Mumtaz, M. M., Choudhary, G., Cibulas, W., & De Rosa, C. T. (2002). Application of computational toxicology methods at the Agency for Toxic Substances and Disease Registry. *International Journal of Hygiene and Environmental Health, 205*(1–2), 63–69. doi:10.1078/1438-4639-00130

Ergün, O., KarslioĞlu, O., Yilmaz, A., & Üner, D. (2007). Preparation and characterization of ordered TiO_2 photocatalysts: films and mesoporous structures. *Turkish Journal of Chemistry, 31*, 501–508.

Eriksson, L., Johansson, E., Muller, M., & Wold, S. J. (2000). On the Selection of Training Set in Environmental QSAR when Compounds are Clustered. *Chemometrics, 14*, 599–616. doi:10.1002/1099-128X(200009/12)14:5/6<599::AID-CEM619>3.0.CO;2-8

Eriksson, S. O. (1968). Hydrolysis of anilides. IV. Hydroxylaminolysis, hydrazinolysis, and general acid-catalysed alkaline hydrolysis of trifluoroacetanilide. *Acta Chemica Scandinavica, 22*, 892–906. doi:10.3891/acta.chem.scand.22-0892

Ertl, G., Knözinger, H., & Weitkamp, J. (1997). *Handbook of Heterogeneous Catalysis*. New York: Whiley-VCH. doi:10.1002/9783527619474

Escarmis, C., Dopazo, J., Davila, M., Palma, E. L., & Domingo, E. (1995). Large deletions in the 5'-untranslated region of foot-and-mouth-disease virus of serotype-C. *Virus Research, 35*, 155–167. doi:10.1016/0168-1702(94)00091-P

Estrada, E. (2001). Recent advances on the role of topological indices in drug discovery research. *Current Medicinal Chemistry, 8*, 1573–1588.

Estrada, E. (2001). Generalization of topological indices. *Chemical Physics Letters, 336*, 248–252. doi:10.1016/S0009-2614(01)00127-0

Estrada, E. (2003). Application of a novel graph-theoretic folding degree index to the study of steroid-DB3 antibody binding affinity. *Computational Biology and Chemistry, 27*, 305–313. doi:10.1016/S1476-9271(02)00078-6

Estrada, E., & Uriate, T. (2001). Quantitative structure–toxicity relationships using TOPS-MODE. 1. Nitrobenzene toxicity to *Tetrahymena pyriformis. SAR and QSAR in Environmental Research, 12*(3), 309–324. doi:10.1080/10629360108032919

Eswar N, et al. (2007).Comparative protein structure modeling using MODELLER. *Cur. Protocols Prot Sci S50*, 2-9-1–31.

Euler, L. (1779). *De serie Lambertina plurimisque eius insignibus proprietatibus*. 1921 reprinted at B.G. Teubner, Leipzig and Berlin in *Opera Omnia*, series 1, *6*, 350-369.

European Commission. Linking science to technology bibliographic references in patents (2002). *DG Research project report*.

European Federation of Pharmaceutical Industries and Associations (2007). *The pharmaceutical industry in figures*.

Euvananont, C., Doungratsamee, J., Junin, C., Tippo, T., & Thanachayanont, C. (2008). Microstructures of dip-coated TiO_2 thin film capacitor. *Journal of Microscopy Society of Thailand, 22*, 34–36.

Euvananont, C., Junin, C., Inpor, K., Limthongkul, P., & Thanachayanont, C. (2008). TiO_2 optical coating layers for self-cleaning applications. *Ceramics International, 34*, 1067–1071. doi:10.1016/j.ceramint.2007.09.043

Exner, O. (1978). *Correlation Analysis in Chemistry* (Chapman, N. B., & Shorter, J., Eds.). London: Plenum.

Faith, D. P., Lozupone, C. A., Nipperess, D., & Knight, R. (2009). The cladistic basis for the phylogenetic diversity (PD) measure links evolutionary features to environmental gradients and supports broad applications of microbial ecology's "phylogenetic beta diversity" framework. *International Journal of Molecular Sciences, 10*, 4723–4741. doi:10.3390/ijms10114723

Falaras, P., & Xagas, A. P. (2002). Roughness and fractality of nanostructured TiO_2 films prepared via sol-gel technique. *Journal of Materials Science, 37*, 3855–3860. doi:10.1023/A:1019686902277

Farruseng, D., Baumes, L. A., & Mirodatos, C. (2003). Data Management For Combinatorial Heterogeneous Catalysis: Methodology And Development Of Advanced Tools. In Potyrailo, R. A., & Amis, E. J. (Eds.), *High-Throughput Analysis: A Tool for Combinatorial Materials Science* (pp. 551–579). Boston: Kluwer Academic/Plenum Publishers.

Farrusseng, D., Klanner, C., Baumes, L. A., Lengliz, M., Mirodatos, C., & Schüth, F. (2005)... *QSAR & Combinatorial Science, 24*, 78–93. doi:10.1002/qsar.200420066

Farrusseng, D., Baumes, L. A., Hayaud, C., Vauthey, I., Denton, P., & Mirodatos, C. (2001). Nato series. In E. Derouane (ed). Proc. NATO Advanced Study Institute on Principles and Methods for Accelerated Catalyst Design, Preparation, Testing and Development. Vilamoura, Portugal, 15-28 July 2001. Boston: Kluwer Academic Publisher.

Fawcett, J. P., Kennedy, J. M., Kumar, A., Ledger, R., Kumara, G. M., Patel, M. J., & Zacharias, M. (2002). Comparative efficacy and pharmacokinetics of racemic bupivacaine and S-bupivacaine in third molar surgery. *Journal of Pharmacy & Pharmaceutical Sciences, 5*, 199–204.

Fayyad, U., Piatetsky-Shapiro, G., & Smyth, P. (1996). *From Data Mining to Knowledge Discovery in Databases.*

Fedorov, V. V. (1972). *Theory of optimal experiments.* New York: Acad. Press.

Feldheim, D. L. (2001). *Metal Nanoparticles: Synthesis, Characterization, and Applications.* New York: CRC Press.

Felsenstein, J. (1983). Parsimony in systematics: Biological and statistical issues. *Annual Review of Ecology and Systematics, 14*, 313–333. doi:10.1146/annurev.es.14.110183.001525

Felsenstein, J. (1988). Phylogenies and quantitative characters. *Annual Review of Ecology and Systematics, 19*, 445–471. doi:10.1146/annurev.es.19.110188.002305

Felsenstein, J. (1988). Phylogenies from molecular sequences: Inference and reliability. *Annual Review of Genetics, 22*, 521–565. doi:10.1146/annurev.ge.22.120188.002513

Fernández, L., Caballero, J., Abreu, J. I., & Fernández, M. (2007). Amino acid sequence autocorrelation vectors and Bayesian regularized genetic neural networks for modeling protein conformational stability: Gene V protein mutants. *Proteins, 67*, 834–852. doi:10.1002/prot.21349

Fersht, A. (1999). *Structure and mechanism in protein science.* New York: W.H. Freeman and Company.

Fiorito, S. (2007). Carbon nanoparticles: benefits and risks for human health. In Zhao, Y., & Nalwa, H. S. (Eds.), *Nanotoxicology, Interactions of Nanomaterials with Biological Systems* (pp. 167–180). New York: American Scientific Publishers.

Fischer, D., Norel, R., Wolfson, H. L., & Nussinov, R. (1993)... *Proteins, 16*, 278–292. doi:10.1002/prot.340160306

Foley, R. (1987). Hominid species and stone-tool assemblages: How are they related? *Antiquity, 61*, 380–392.

Folkers G, Merz A, Rognan D (1993). *ESCOM Science Publishers*

Fouchécourt, M.-O., Béliveau, M., & Krishnan, K. (2001). Quantitative structure-pharmacokinetic modeling. *The Science of the Total Environment, 274*, 125–135.

Franke, R. (1984). *Theoretical Drug Design Methods.* Amsterdam: Elsevier.

Franke, R., & Gruska, A. (1995). Principal component and factor analysis. In van de Waterbeemd, H. (Ed.), *Chemometric Methods in Molecular Design* (*Vol. 2*, pp. 113–163). Weinheim: VCH. doi:10.1002/9783527615452.ch4

Franklin, N. M., Rogers, N. J., Apte, S. C., Batley, G. E., Gadd, G. E., & Casey, P. S. (2007). Comparative Toxicity of Nanoparticulate ZnO, Bulk ZnO, and $ZnCl_2$ to a Freshwater Microalga (Pseudokirchneriella subcapitata): The Importance of Particle Solubility. *Environmental Science & Technology*, *41*(24), 8484–8490. doi:10.1021/es071445r

Free, S. M. Jr, & Wilson, J. W. (1964). A Mathematical Contribution to Structure Activity Studies. *Journal of Medicinal Chemistry*, *7*, 395–399. doi:10.1021/jm00334a001

Free, S. M., & Wilson, J. W. (1964). A mathematical contribution to structure-activity studies. *Journal of Medicinal Chemistry*, *7*(4), 395–399. doi:10.1021/jm00334a001

Freitas, R. F., Prokopczyk, I. M., Zottis, A., Oliva, G., Andricopulo, A. D., & Trevisan, M. T. S. (2009). Discovery of novel Trypanosoma cruzi glyceraldehyde-3-phosphate deshydrogenase inhibitors. *Bioorganic & Medicinal Chemistry*, *17*(6), 2476–2482. doi:10.1016/j.bmc.2009.01.079

Fretwell, R., & Douglas, P. (2001). An active, robust and transparent nanocrystalline anatase TiO_2 thin film-preparation, characterization and the kinetics of photodegradation of model pollutants. *Journal of Photochemistry and Photobiology A Chemistry*, *143*, 229–240. doi:10.1016/S1010-6030(01)00526-3

Friedman, P. M., Fogelman, J. P., Nouri, K., Levine, V. J., & Ashinoff, R. (1999). Comparative study of the efficacy of four topical anesthetics. *Dermatologic Surgery*, *25*, 950–954. doi:10.1046/j.1524-4725.1999.99138.x

Friedman, P. M., Mafong, E. A., Friedman, E. S., & Geronemus, R. G. (2001). Topical anesthetics update: EMLA and beyond. *Dermatologic Surgery*, *27*, 1019–1026. doi:10.1046/j.1524-4725.2001.01855.x

Friedman, S. H., Decamp, D. L., Sijbesma, R. P., Srdanov, G., Wudl, F., & Kenyon, G. L. (1993)... *Journal of the American Chemical Society*, *115*, 6506–6509. doi:10.1021/ja00068a005

Friedman, S. H., Ganapathi, P. S., Rubin, Y., & Kenyon, G. L. (1998). Optimizing the Binding of Fullerene Inhibitors of the HIV-1 Protease through Predicted Increases in Hydrophobic Desolvation. *Journal of Medicinal Chemistry*, *41*(13), 2424–2429. doi:10.1021/jm970689r

Friesner, R. A., & Gullar, V. (2005)... *Annual Review of Physical Chemistry*, *56*, 389. doi:10.1146/annurev.physchem.55.091602.094410

Frisch, M. J., Trucks, G. W., Schlegel, H. B., Scuseria, G. E., Robb, M. A., Cheeseman, J. R., & Zakrzewski, V. G. ...Pople, J. A. (1998). *Gaussian 98*, revision A.7. Pittsburg, PA: Gaussian, Inc.

Frisch, M. J., Trucks, G. W., Schlegel, H. B., Scuseria, G. E., Robb, M. A., Cheeseman, J. R., et al. (2004). *Gaussian 03, Revision C.02*. Wallingford, CT: Gaussian, Inc.

Fritsch, F. N., Shafer, R. E., & Crowley, W. P. (1973). Algorithm 443: solution of the transcendental equation $we^w = x$. *Communications of the ACM*, *16*, 123–124. doi:10.1145/361952.361970

Fujita, T., & Ban, T. (1971). Structure-activity study of phenethylamines as substrates of biosynthetic enzymes of sympathetic transmitters. *Journal of Medicinal Chemistry*, *14*(2), 148–152. doi:10.1021/jm00284a016

Fukui, K. (1975). *Theory of orientation and stereoselection. Reactivity and structure concepts in organic chemistry* (*Vol. 2*). Berlin: Springer.

Funasaki, N., Hada, S., & Neye, S. (1986). Prediction of retention times in reversed-phase high-performance liquid chromatography from the chemical structure. *Journal of Chromatography. A*, *361*(C), 33–45. doi:10.1016/S0021-9673(01)86891-6

Gabaldón, T. (2005). Evolution of proteins and proteomes: A phylogenetics approach. Evol. *Bioinformatics Online*, *1*, 51–61.

Gabaldón, T. (2006). Computational approaches for the prediction of protein function in the mitochondrion. *American Journal of Physiology. Cell Physiology*, *291*, C1121–C1128. doi:10.1152/ajpcell.00225.2006

Gabaldón, T., Peretó, J., Montero, F., Gil, R., Latorre, A., & Moya, A. (2007). Structural analysis of a hypothetical minimal metabolism. *Philos Trans R Soc B*, *362*, 1751–1762. doi:10.1098/rstb.2007.2067

Gabaldón, T &Huynen, M.A. (2007). From endosymbiont to host-controlled organelle: The hijacking of mitochondrial protein synthesis and metabolism. *PLoS Comp Biol*, 3, e219-1–10.

Gabaldón, T., Snel, B., van Zimmeren, F., Hemrika, W., Tabak, H., Huynen, M.A. (2006). Origin and evolution of the peroxisomal proteome. *Biol Direct*, 1,8-1–14,

Gadre, S. R., Kulkarni, S. A., & Srivastava, I. H. (1992). Molecular electrostatic potentials: A topographical study. *The Journal of Chemical Physics*, 96(7), 5253–5260. doi:10.1063/1.462710

Gajewicz, A., Puzyn, T., Rasulev, B., Leszczynska, D., & Leszczynski, J. (2011). Metal Oxide Nanoparticles: Size-Dependence of Quantum-Mechanical Properties. *Nanoscience & Nanotechnology-Asia*, 1, 53–58. doi:10.2174/2210681211101010053

Galabov, B., & Bobadova-Parvanova, P. (1999). Molecular electrostatic potential as reactivity index in hydrogen bonding: Ab initio molecular orbital study of complexes of nitrile and carbonyl compounds with hydrogen fluoride. *The Journal of Physical Chemistry A*, 103(34), 6793–6799. doi:10.1021/jp984313g

Galabov, B., & Bobadova-Parvanova, P. (2000). Molecular electrostatic potential as reactivity index in hydrogen bond formation: an HF/6-31+G(d) study of hydrogen-bonded $(HCN)_n$ clusters, n=2,3,4,5,6,7. *Journal of Molecular Structure*, 550, 93–98. doi:10.1016/S0022-2860(00)00383-5

Galabov, B., Cheshmedzhieva, D., Ilieva, S., & Hadjieva, B. (2004). Computational study of the reactivity of N-phenylacetamides in the alkaline hydrolysis reaction. *The Journal of Physical Chemistry A*, 108(51), 11457–11462. doi:10.1021/jp046199+

Galabov, B., Ileiva, S., & Schaefer, H. F. (2006). An efficient computational approach for the evaluation of substituent constants. *The Journal of Organic Chemistry*, 71(17), 6382–6387. doi:10.1021/jo0605288

Galabov, B., Ilieva, S., Hadjieva, B., Atanasov, Y., & Schaefer, H. F. (2008). Predicting reactivities of organic molecules. theoretical and experimental studies on the aminolysis of phenyl acetates. *The Journal of Physical Chemistry A*, 112(29), 6700–6707. doi:10.1021/jp8007514

Galabov, B., Nikolova, V., Wilke, J. J., Schaefer, H. F., & Allen, W. D. (2008). Origin of the S_N2 benzylic effect. *Journal of the American Chemical Society*, 130(30), 9887–9896. doi:10.1021/ja802246y

Galindo, J. F., Bermudez, C. I., & Daza, E. E. (2006). tRNA structure from a graph and quantum theoretical perspective. *Journal of Theoretical Biology*, 240, 574–582. doi:10.1016/j.jtbi.2005.10.017

Galvez, J., & Varon, R. (1981). I. Transient phase kinetics of enzyme reactions. *Journal of Theoretical Biology*, 89, 1–17. doi:10.1016/0022-5193(81)90175-2

Galvez, J., Garcia, R., Salabert, M. T., & Soler, R. (1994). Charge indexes. New topological descriptors. *Journal of Chemical Information and Computer Sciences*, 34(3), 520–525. doi:10.1021/ci00019a008

Gan, H. H., Pasquali, S., & Schlick, T. (2003). Exploring the repertoire of RNA secondary motifs using graph theory; implications for RNA design. *Nucleic Acids Research*, 31, 2926–2943. doi:10.1093/nar/gkg365

Gancia, E., Montana, J. G., & Manallack, D. T. (2001). Theoretical hydrogen bonding parameters for drug design. *Journal of Molecular Graphics & Modelling*, 19(3-4), 349–362. doi:10.1016/S1093-3263(00)00084-X

Gandía, M. (2007). Transcriptional response of *Citrus aurantifolia* to infection by *Citrus tristeza virus*. *Virology*, 367, 298–306. doi:10.1016/j.virol.2007.05.025

Gao, H., Katzenellenbogen, J. A., Garg, R., & Hansch, C. (1999). Comparative QSAR Analysis of Estrogen Receptor Ligands. *Chemical Reviews*, 99, 723–744. doi:10.1021/cr980018g

Gao, Q., Yang, L., & Zhu, Y. (2010). Pharmacophore based drug design approach as a practical process in drug discovery. *Current Computer-aided Drug Design*, 6(1), 37–49. doi:10.2174/157340910790980151

García-Domenech, R., Gálvez, J., de Julián-Ortiz, J. V., & Pogliani, L. (2008). Some New Trends in Chemical Graph Theory. *Chemical Reviews*, 108, 1127–1169. doi:10.1021/cr0780006

García-Doménech, R., Gálvez, J., de Julián Ortiz, J. V., & Pogliani, I. (2008). Some new trends in chemical graph theory. *Chemical Reviews*, 108(3), 1127–1169. doi:10.1021/cr0780006

Garcia-Meseguer, M. J., Vidal de Labra, J. A., Garcia-Canovas, F., Havsteen, B. H., Garcia-Moreno, M., & Varon, R. (2001). Time course equations of the amount of substance in a linear compartmental system and their computerized derivation. *Bio Systems*, *59*, 197–220. doi:10.1016/S0303-2647(01)00116-2

Garcia-Meseguer, M. J., Vidal de Labra, J. A., Garcia-Moreno, M., Garcia-Canovas, F., Havsteen, B. H., & Varon, R. (2003). Mean residence times in linear compartmental systems. Symbolic formulae for their direct evaluation. *Bulletin of Mathematical Biology*, *65*, 279–308. doi:10.1016/S0092-8240(02)00096-4

Garcia-Meseguer, M. J. (1998). *Análisis cinético de los sistemas lineales de compartimentos: aplicación a la evaluación de parámetros medios. Doctoral Thesis.* Cuenca, Spain: Servicio de publicaciones de la UCLM.

Garcia-Sevilla, F., Arribas, E., Bisswanger, H., Garcia-Moreno, M., Garcia-Canovas, F., & Gomez-Ladron de Guevara, R. (2010). wREFERASS: Rate Equations for Enzyme Reactions at Steady State under MS-Windows. *MATCH Commun. Math. Comput. Chem.*, *63*, 553–571.

Garcia-Sevilla, F., Garrido del Solo, C., Duggleby, R. G., Garcia-Canovas, F., Peyro, R., & Varon, R. (2000). Use of a windows program for simulation of the progress curves of reactants and intermediates involved in enzyme-catalyzed reactions. *Bio Systems*, *54*, 151–164. doi:10.1016/S0303-2647(99)00071-4

Garg, R., Kapur, S., & Hansch, C. (2001). Radical toxicity of phenols: a reference point for obtaining perspective in the formulation of QSAR. *Medicinal Research Reviews*, *21*, 73–82. doi:10.1002/1098-1128(200101)21:1<73::AID-MED3>3.0.CO;2-5

Garrick, R. C., Caccone, A., & Sunnucks, P. (2010). Inference of population history by coupling exploratory and model-driven phylogeographic analyses. *International Journal of Molecular Sciences*, *11*, 1190–1227. doi:10.3390/ijms11041190

Garrido del Solo, C., Varon, R., & Garcia-Canovas, F. (1992). Programa de ordenador para simular el comportamiento cinético de las reacciones enzimáticas. *Anales de Química de la RSEQ*, *88*, 633–639.

Gavernet, L., Talevi, A., Castro, E. A., & Bruno-Blanch, L. E. (2008). A combined virtual screening 2D and 3D QSAR methodology for the selection of new anticonvulsant candidates from a natural products library. *QSAR & Combinatorial Science*, *27*(9), 1120–1129. doi:10.1002/qsar.200730055

Gavroglu, K., & Simões, A. (1994). The Americans, the Germans, and the beginnings of quantum chemistry: The confluence of diverging traditions. *Historical Studies in the Physical Sciences*, *25*(1), 47–110.

Gavroglu, K., & Simões, A. (2002). Preparing the Ground for Quantum Chemistry in Great Britain: The Work of the Physicist R. H. Fowler and the Chemist N. V. Sidgwick. *British Journal for the History of Science*, *35*(2), 187–212. doi:10.1017/S0007087402004673

Gazquez, J. L., Cedillo, A., & Vela, A. (2007). Electrodonating and electro accepting powers. *The Journal of Physical Chemistry A*, *111*, 1966–1970.

Geerlings, P., De Proft, F., & Langenaeker, W. (2003). Conceptual Density Functional Theory. *Chemical Reviews*, *103*, 1793–1873. doi:10.1021/cr990029p

Ghasemi, M., Tavassoli Kajani, M., & Babolian, E. (2007). Numerical solutions of nonlinear Volterra-Fredholm integral equations by using homotopy- perturbation method. *Applied Mathematics and Computation*, *188*, 446–449. doi:10.1016/j.amc.2006.10.015

Ghodsi, F. E. (2005). Determination of the optical constants and thickness of semitransparent thin films using successive interference fringes of transmission spectra. *Surface Review and Letters*, *12*(3), 1–7. doi:10.1142/S0218625X05007256

Ghodsi, F. E., Tepehan, F. Z., & Tepehan, G. G. (1997). Optical properties of Ta_2O_5 thin films deposited using the spin coating process. *Thin Solid Films*, *295*, 11–15. doi:10.1016/S0040-6090(96)09509-0

Ghodsi, F. E., Tepehan, F. Z., & Tepehan, G. G. (1999). Optical and electrochromic properties of sol-gel made CeO_2-TiO_2 thin films. *Electrochimica Acta*, *44*, 3127–3136. doi:10.1016/S0013-4686(99)00030-4

Ghodsi, F. E., Tepehan, F. Z., & Tepehan, G. G. (2006). Atomic force microscopy and spectroscopy studies of annealed Ce/Ti/Zr mixed oxide thin films prepared by sol-gel process. *Surface Science, 600,* 4361–4364. doi:10.1016/j.susc.2006.02.078

Ghodsi, F. E., Tepehan, F. Z., & Tepehan, G. G. (2008a). Electrochromic properties of heat-treated thin films of CeO_2-TiO_2-ZrO_2 prepared by sol-gel route. *Solar Energy Materials and Solar Cells, 92,* 234–239. doi:10.1016/j.solmat.2007.02.026

Ghodsi, F. E., Tepehan, F. Z., & Tepehan, G. G. (2008b). Optical and structural properties of sol-gel made Ce/Ti/Zr mixed oxide thin films as transparent counter electrode for electrochromic devices. *Optical Materials, 31,* 63–67. doi:10.1016/j.optmat.2008.01.014

Ghori, Q. K., Ahmed, M., & Siddiqui, A. M. (2007). Application of homotopy perturbation method to squeezing flow of a Newtonian fluid. *Int. J. Nonlinear Sci. Numer. Simulat., 8*(2), 179–184. doi:10.1515/IJNSNS.2007.8.2.179

Ghose, A. K., Viswanadhan, V. N., & Wendoloski, J. J. (1998). Prediction of hydrophobic (lipophilic) properties of small organic molecules using fragmental methods: An analysis of ALOGP and CLOGP methods. *Journal of Physical Chemistry, 102*(21), 3762–3772.

Gibaldi, M. (1991). *Biopharmaceutics and clinical pharmacokinetics* (4th ed.). Londres: Lea and Febiger.

Gill, S., Lobenberg, R., Ku, T., Azarmi, Sh., Roa, W., & Prenner, E. J. (2007). Nanoparticles: characteristics, mechanisms of action, and toxicity in pulmonary drug delivery - a review. *Journal of Biomedical Nanotechnology, 3*(2), 107–119. doi:10.1166/jbn.2007.015

Giri, S., Roy, D. R., Bultinck, P., Subramanian, V., & Chattaraj, P. K. (2008). An Atom counting QSPR protocol. *QSAR & Combinatorial Science, 27,* 208–230. doi:10.1002/qsar.200730109

Glasstone, S., Laidler, K. J., & Eyring, H. (1941). *The theory of the rate processes.* New York: McGraw-Hill.

Gnyba, M., Kozanecki, M., & Wierzba, P. (2005). Spectroscopic studies of sol-gel derived thin-film structures for integrated optics. *Journal of Molecular and Quantum Acoustics, 26,* 81–89.

Gohlke, H., Kuhn, L. A., & Case, D. A. (2004)... *Proteins, 56*(2), 322–337. doi:10.1002/prot.20116

Golbabai, A., & Keramati, B. (2008). Modified homotopy- perturbation method for solving Fredholm integral equations. *Chaos, Solitons, and Fractals, 37,* 1528. doi:10.1016/j.chaos.2006.10.037

Golbraikh & Tropsha. (2002). Beware of q2! *Journal of Molecular Graphics & Modelling, 20,* 269–276. doi:10.1016/S1093-3263(01)00123-1

Gombar, V. K., & Kapoor, V. K. (1990). Quantitative structure-activity relationship studies: β-adrenergic blocking activity of 1-(2,4-disubstituted phenoxy)-3-aminopropan-2-ols. *European Journal of Medicinal Chemistry, 25,* 689–695. doi:10.1016/0223-5234(90)90134-O

Gong, L. L., Fang, L. H., Peng, J. H., Liu, A. L., & Du, G. H. (2010). Integration of virtual screening with high-throughput screening for the identification of novel Rho-kinase I inhibitors. *Journal of Biotechnology, 145*(3), 295–303. doi:10.1016/j.jbiotec.2009.12.003

Goñi, J.R., Vaquerizas, J.M., Dopazo, J., Orozco, M. (2006). Exploring the reasons for the large density of triplex-forming oligonucleotide target sequences in the human regulatory regions. *BMC Genomics, 7,* 63-1–10.

Gonzales, J. M., Allen, W. D., & Schaefer, H. F. (2005). Model identity S_N2 reactions $CH_3X + X^-$ (X = F, Cl, CN, OH, SH, NH_2, PH_2): Marcus theory analyzed. *The Journal of Physical Chemistry A, 109*(46), 10613–10628. doi:10.1021/jp054734f

González-Díaz, H., Agüero-Chapin, G., Varona, J., Molina, R., Delogu, G., & Santana, L. (2007a). 2D-RNA-coupling numbers: A new computational chemistry approach to link secondary structure topology with biological function. *Journal of Computational Chemistry, 28,* 1049–1056. doi:10.1002/jcc.20576

González-Díaz, H., Aguero-Chapin, G., Varona-Santos, J., Molina, R., de la Riva, G., & Uriarte, E. (2005). 2D RNA-QSAR: assigning ACC oxidase family membership with stochastic molecular descriptors; isolation and prediction of a sequence from Psidium guajava L. *Bioorganic & Medicinal Chemistry Letters, 15,* 2932–2937. doi:10.1016/j.bmcl.2005.03.017

González-Díaz, H., Cruz-Monteagudo, M., Vina, D., Santana, L., Uriarte, E., & De Clercq, E. (2005a). QSAR for anti-RNA-virus activity, synthesis, and assay of anti-RSV carbonucleosides given a unified representation of spectral moments, quadratic, and topologic indices. *Bioorganic & Medicinal Chemistry Letters, 15*, 1651–1657. doi:10.1016/j.bmcl.2005.01.047

González-Díaz, H., de Armas, R. R., & Molina, R. (2003a). Markovian negentropies in bioinformatics. 1. A picture of footprints after the interaction of the HIV-1 Psi-RNA packaging region with drugs. *Bioinformatics (Oxford, England), 19*, 2079–2087. doi:10.1093/bioinformatics/btg285

González-Díaz, H., de Armas, R. R., & Molina, R. (2003b). Vibrational Markovian modelling of footprints after the interaction of antibiotics with the packaging region of HIV type 1. *Bulletin of Mathematical Biology, 65*, 991–1002. doi:10.1016/S0092-8240(03)00064-8

González-Díaz, H., Ferino, G., Podda, G., & Uriarte, E. (2008a). Discriminating prostate cancer patients from control group with connectivity indices. *ECSOC, 12*, 1–10.

González-Díaz, H., González-Díaz, Y., Santana, L., Ubeira, F. M., & Uriarte, E. (2008b). Proteomics, networks and connectivity indices. *Proteomics, 8*, 750–778. doi:10.1002/pmic.200700638

González-Díaz, H., Molina, R., & Uriarte, E. (2005b). Recognition of stable protein mutants with 3D stochastic average electrostatic potentials. *FEBS Letters, 579*, 4297–4301. doi:10.1016/j.febslet.2005.06.065

González-Díaz, H., Pérez-Bello, A., Cruz-Monteagudo, M., González-Díaz, Y., Santana, L., & Uriarte, E. (2007b). Chemometrics for QSAR with Low Sequence Homology: Mycobacterial Promoter Sequences Recognition with 2D-RNA Entropies. *Chemometrics and Intelligent Laboratory Systems, 85*, 20–26. doi:10.1016/j.chemolab.2006.03.005

González-Díaz, H., Perez-Bello, A., Uriarte, E., & González-Díaz, Y. (2006a). QSAR study for mycobacterial promoters with low sequence homology. *Bioorganic & Medicinal Chemistry Letters, 16*, 547–553. doi:10.1016/j.bmcl.2005.10.057

González-Díaz, H., Pérez-Castillo, Y., Podda, G., & Uriarte, E. (2007c). Computational chemistry comparison of stable/nonstable protein mutants classification models based on 3D and topological indices. *Journal of Computational Chemistry, 28*, 1990–1995. doi:10.1002/jcc.20700

González-Díaz, H., Prado-Prado, F., Pérez-Montoto, L. G., Duardo-Sánchez, A., & López-Díaz, A. (2009). QSAR Models for Proteins of Parasitic Organisms, Plants and Human Guests: Theory, Applications, Legal Protection, Taxes, and Regulatory Issues. *Current Proteomics, 6*, 214–227. doi:10.2174/157016409789973789

González-Díaz, H., Sanchez-González, A., & González-Díaz, Y. (2006b). 3D-QSAR study for DNA cleavage proteins with a potential anti-tumor ATCUN-like motif. *Journal of Inorganic Biochemistry, 100*, 1290–1297. doi:10.1016/j.jinorgbio.2006.02.019

González-Díaz, H., & Uriarte, E. (2005c). Proteins QSAR with Markov average electrostatic potentials. *Bioorganic & Medicinal Chemistry Letters, 15*, 5088–5094. doi:10.1016/j.bmcl.2005.07.056

González-Díaz, H., Uriarte, E., & Ramos de Armas, R. (2005d). Predicting stability of Arc repressor mutants with protein stochastic moments. *Bioorganic & Medicinal Chemistry, 13*, 323–331. doi:10.1016/j.bmc.2004.10.024

González-Díaz, H., Vilar, S., Santana, L., & Uriarte, E. (2007d). Medicinal Chemistry and Bioinformatics-Current Trends in Drugs Discovery with Networks Topological Indices. *Current Topics in Medicinal Chemistry, 7*, 1015–1029. doi:10.2174/156802607780906771

Good, A. C., Hermsmeier, M. A., & Hindle, S. A. (2004). Measuring CAMD technique performance: a virtual screening case study in the design of validation experiments. *Journal of Computer-Aided Molecular Design, 18*(7-9), 529–536. doi:10.1007/s10822-004-4067-1

Good, A. C., & Kuntz, I. D. (1995). Investigating the extension of pairwise distance pharmacophore measures to triplet-based descriptors. *Journal of Computer-Aided Molecular Design, 9*(4), 373–379. doi:10.1007/BF00125178

Goodarzi, M., Duchowicz, P. R., Wu, C. H., Fernández, F. M., & Castro, E. A. (2009). New Hybrid Genetic Based Support Vector Regression as QSAR Approach for Analyzing Flavonoids-GABA(A) Complexes. *Journal of Chemical Information and Modeling, 49*, 1475–1485. doi:10.1021/ci900075f

Goodman, A. F., Bellato, C. M., & Khidr, L. (2005). The uncertain future for central dogma. *Scientist (Philadelphia, Pa.)*, *19*, 20–21.

Goodman, J. M. (2001). World Champion Chemists: People versus Computers. In Thompson, J. M. T. (Ed.), *Visions of the Future: Chemistry and Life Science* (pp. 43–57). Cambridge, UK: Cambridge University Press.

Gorder, P. F. (2005). Computing life's family tree. *Computing in Science & Engineering*, *7*(3), 3–6. doi:10.1109/MCSE.2005.48

Gordon, M., & Scantlebury, G. R. (1964). Non-random polycondensation: Statistical theory of the substitution effect. *Transactions of the Faraday Society*, *60*, 604–621. doi:10.1039/tf9646000604

Gorer, A. (2004). U.S. Patent 6.723.678, to Symyx Technologies Inc.

Goudar, C. T., Harris, S. K., McInerney, M. J., & Suflita, J. M. (2004). Progress curve analysis for enzyme and microbial kinetic reactions using explicit solutions based on the Lambert W function. *Journal of Microbiological Methods*, *59*, 317–326. doi:10.1016/j.mimet.2004.06.013

Goudar, C. T., Sonnad, J. R., & Duggleby, R. G. (1999). Parameter estimation using a direct solution of the integrated Michaelis-Menten equation. *Biochimica et Biophysica Acta*, *1429*, 377–383. doi:10.1016/S0167-4838(98)00247-7

Graham, L. D., Haggett, K. D., Hayes, P. J., Schober, P. A., Jennings, P. A., & Whittaker, R. G. (1994). A new library of alpha-lytic protease S1 mutants generated by combinatorial random substitution. *Biochemistry and Molecular Biology International*, *32*, 831–839.

Gramatica, P. (2008). *A short history of QSAR evolution*. Electronic material downloadable at: http://www.qsarworld.com/ Temp_Fileupload/ Shorthistoryofqsar.pdf

Gramatica, P. A Short History of QSAR evolution, QSAR Research Unit in Environmental Chemistry and Ecotoxicology, DBSF, Insubria University, Varese, Italy; http://www.qsarworld.com/ Temp_Fileupload/ Shorthistoryofqsar.pdf (last accessed date 8th July 2011)

Grant, K. L., & Klinman, J. P. (1989). Evidence that protium and deuterium undergo significant tuneling in the reaction catalyzed by bovine serum amine oxidase. *Biochem.*, *28*, 6597–6605. doi:10.1021/bi00442a010

Grätzel, M. (2003). Dye-sensitized solar cells. *Journal of Photochemistry and Photobiology C, Photochemistry Reviews*, *4*, 145–153. doi:10.1016/S1389-5567(03)00026-1

Gray, P. (1988). Instabilities and oscillations in chemical reactions in closed and open systems. *Proceedings of the Royal Society of London*, *415*, 1–34. doi:10.1098/rspa.1988.0001

Green, M. H. (1992). Introduction to modelling. *The Journal of Nutrition*, *122*, 690–694.

Grob, C. A. (1983). Inductivity and Bridging in Carbocations. *Accounts of Chemical Research*, *16*(12), 426–431. doi:10.1021/ar00096a001

Grubert, G., Kondratenko, E. V., Kolf, S., Baerns, M., van Geem, P., & Parton, R. (2003)... *Catalysis Today*, *81*, 337–345. doi:10.1016/S0920-5861(03)00132-9

Guang-Lei, T., Hong-Bo, H., & Jian-Da, S. (2005). Effect of microstructure of TiO_2 thin films on optical band gap energy. *Chemical Physics Letters*, *22*(7), 1787–1789. doi:10.1088/0256-307X/22/7/062

Gupta, A., Chakraborty, A., Giri, S., Subramanian, V., & Chattaraj, P. K. (2010). (in press). Toxicity of halogen, sulfur and chlorinated aromatic compounds: A quantitative-structure-activity-relationship(QSTR). *International Journal of Chemoinformatics and Chemical Engineering*.

Gupta, S. P. (1991). QSAR Studies on Local Anesthetics. *Chemical Reviews*, *91*, 1109–1119. doi:10.1021/cr00006a001

Gupta, S. P., Singh, P., & Bindal, M. C. (1983). QSAR Studies on Hallucinogens. *Chemical Reviews*, *83*, 633–648. doi:10.1021/cr00058a003

Gupta, K. K., Jassal, M., & Agrawal, A. K. (2008). Sol-gel derived titanium dioxide finishing of cotton fabric for self-cleaning. *Indian Journal of Fiber & Textile Research*, *33*, 443–450.

Gutman, I. (1994). A formula for the Wiener number of trees and its extension to graphs containing cycles. *Graph Theory Notes New York*, *27*, 9–15.

Gutman, I., & Polansky, O. E. (1987). *Mathematical Concepts in Organic Chemistry*. Berlin: Springer-Verlag.

Gutman, I., & Ruscic, B., Trinajstić, N., & Wilcox, C.F. (1975). Graph theory and molecular orbitals. XII. Acyclic polyenes. *The Journal of Chemical Physics*, *62*(9), 3399–3409. doi:10.1063/1.430994

Guyon, I., & Elisseeff, A. (2003). An Introduction to Variable and Feature Selection. *Journal of Machine Learning Research*, *3*, 1157–1182. doi:10.1162/153244303322753616

Ha, C. L., Lee, J. H., Zhou, H. R., Ustunol, Z., & Pestka, J. J. (1999). Effects of yogurt ingestion on mucosal and systemic cytokine gene expression in the mouse. *Journal of Food Protection*, *62*, 181–188.

Habibi, M. H., Talebian, N., & Choi, J. H. (2007). The effect of annealing on photocatalytic properties of nanostructured titanium dioxide thin films. *Dyes and Pigments*, *73*, 103–110. doi:10.1016/j.dyepig.2005.10.016

Hage-Melim, L. I. da S., da Silva, C. H. T de P., Semighini, E. P., Taft, C. A., & Sampaio, S. V.Computer-aided drug design of novel PLA2 inhibitor candidates for treatment of snakebite. *Journal of Biomolecular Structure & Dynamics*, *27*(1), 27–36.

Halder, A. K., Adhikari, N., & Jha, T. (2009). Comparative QSAR modelling of 2-phenylindole-3-carbaldehyde derivatives as potential antimitotic agents. *Bioorganic & Medicinal Chemistry Letters*, *19*, 1737–1739. doi:10.1016/j.bmcl.2009.01.081

Halder, A. K., & Jha, T. (2010). Validated predictive QSAR modeling of *N*-aryl-oxazolidinone-5-carboxamides for anti-HIV protease activity. *Bioorganic & Medicinal Chemistry Letters*, *20*, 6082–6087. doi:10.1016/j.bmcl.2010.08.050

Hall, L. H., & Kier, L. B. (1995). Electrotopological state indices for atom types: A novel combination of electronic, topological, and valence state information. *Journal of Chemical Information and Computer Sciences*, *35*(6), 1039–1045. doi:10.1021/ci00028a014

Haller, D., Blum, S., Bode, C., Hammes, W. P., & Schiffrin, E. J. (2000). Activation of human peripheral blood mononuclear cells by nonpathogenic bacteria in vitro: Evidence of NK cells as primary targets. *Infection and Immunity*, *68*, 752–759. doi:10.1128/IAI.68.2.752-759.2000

Halperin, I., Ma, B., Wolfson, H., & Nussinov, R. (2002)... *Proteins*, *47*, 409–443. doi:10.1002/prot.10115

Halpern, G. M., Vruwink, K. G., van de Water, J., Keen, C. L., & Gershwin, M. E. (1991). Influence of long-term yoghurt consumption in young adults. *International Journal of Immunotherapy*, *7*, 205–210.

Hambäck, P. A. (1998). Seasonality, optimal foraging, and prey coexistence. *American Naturalist*, *152*, 881–895. doi:10.1086/286215

Hamid, M. A., & Rahman, I. A. (2003). Preparation of titanium dioxide (TiO$_2$) thin films by sol-gel dip coating method. *Malaysian Journal of Chemistry*, *5*(1), 86–91.

Hammett, L. P. (1937). The effect of structure upon the reactions of organic compounds. Benzene derivatives. *Journal of the American Chemical Society*, *59*(1), 96–103. doi:10.1021/ja01280a022

Hammett, L. P. (1938). Linear free energy relationships in rate and equilibria phenomena. *Transactions of the Faraday Society*, *34*, 156–165. doi:10.1039/tf9383400156

Hammett, L. P. (1935). Some Relations between Reaction Rates and Equilibrium Constants. *Chemical Reviews*, *17*(1), 125–136. doi:10.1021/cr60056a010

Hammett, L. P. (1970). *Physical Organic Chemistry* (2nd ed.). New York: McGraw Hill.

Han, L., Cui, J., Lin, H., Ji, Z., Cao, Z., Li, Y., & Chen, Y. (2006). Recent progresses in the application of machine learning approach for predicting protein functional class independent of sequence similarity. *Proteomics*, *6*, 4023–4037. doi:10.1002/pmic.200500938

Hanak, J. J. (2004)... *Applied Surface Science*, *223*, 1–8. doi:10.1016/S0169-4332(03)00902-4

Hansch, C., Hoekman, D., Leo, A., Weininger, D., & Selassie, C. (2002). Chem-Bioinformatics: Comparative QSAR at the Interface between Chemistry and Biology. *Chemical Reviews*, *102*, 783–812. doi:10.1021/cr0102009

Hansch, C., Leo, A., & Taft, R. W. (1991). A Survey of Hammett Substituent Constants and Resonance and Field Parameters. *Chemical Reviews*, *91*, 165–195. doi:10.1021/cr00002a004

Hansch, C., Maloney, P. P., Fujita, T., & Muir, R. M. (1962). Correlation of Biological Activity of Phenoxyacetic Acids with Hammett Substituent Constants and Partition Coefficients. *Nature*, *194*, 178–180. doi:10.1038/194178b0

Hansch, C., Muir, R. M., Fujita, T., Maloney, P. P., Geiger, F., & Streich, M. (1963). The correlation of biological activity of plant growth regulators and chloromycetin derivatives with Hammett constants and partition coefficients. *Journal of the American Chemical Society*, *85*(18), 2817–2824. doi:10.1021/ja00901a033

Hansch, C., & Fujita, T. (1964). ρ-σ-π Analysis. A method for the correlation of biological activity and chemical structure. *Journal of the American Chemical Society*, *86*, 1616–1625. doi:10.1021/ja01062a035

Hansch, C. (1969). A quantitative approach to biochemical structure-activity relationships. *Accounts of Chemical Research*, *2*(8), 232–239. doi:10.1021/ar50020a002

Hansch, C., Leo, A., & Taft, R. W. (1991). A Survey of Hammett Substituent Constants and Resonance and Field Parameters. *Chemical Reviews*, *91*(2), 165–195. doi:10.1021/cr00002a004

Hansch, C., Leo, A., Unger, S. H., Kim, K. H., Nikaitani, D., & Lien, E. J. (1973). "Aromatic" Substituent Constants for Structure-Activity Correlations. *Journal of Medicinal Chemistry*, *16*(11), 1207–1216. doi:10.1021/jm00269a003

Hansch, C., & Leo, A. (1995). In Heller, S. R. (Ed.), *Exploring QSAR Fundamentals and Applications in Chemistry and Biology* (pp. 1–68). Washington, DC: American Chemical Society.

Hansson, T., Marelius, J., & Åqvist, J. (1998)... *Journal of Computer-Aided Molecular Design*, *12*, 27–35. doi:10.1023/A:1007930623000

Harary, F., & Read, R. (1977). *Proc. Graphs and Combinatorics Conference*. New York: George Washington University, Springer. Cited in, Barrow, J.D. (2000). *The Book of Nothing* (p.155). New York: Vintage Books.

Hariharan, P. C., & Pople, J. A. (1973). The influence of polarization functions on molecular orbital hydrogenation energies. *Theoretica Chimica Acta*, *28*, 213–222. doi:10.1007/BF00533485

Harmon, L. A. (2003)... *Journal of Materials Science*, *38*, 4479–4485. doi:10.1023/A:1027325400459

Hartwell, L. (2005). How to build a cancer sensor system. *Scientist (Philadelphia, Pa.)*, *19*, 18–19.

Hasan, M. M., Haseeb, A. S. M. A., Saidur, R., & Masjuki, H. H. (2008). Effects of annealing treatment on optical properties of anatase TiO_2 thin films. *International Journal of Chemical and Biomolecular Engineering*, *1*(2), 93–97.

Hättig, C., & Hald, K. (2002). Implementation of RI-CC2 triplet excitation energies with an application to trans-azobenzene. *Physical Chemistry Chemical Physics*, *4*, 2111–2118. doi:10.1039/b110847f

Haupt, R. L., & Haupt, S. E. (1998). *Practical genetic algorithms*. New York: John Wiley & Sons, Inc.

Hayasaka, K., Gojobori, T., & Horai, S. (1988). Molecular phylogeny and evolution of primate mitochondrial DNA. *Molecular Biology and Evolution*, *5*, 626–644.

Hayes, B. (2005). Why W? *American Scientist*, *93*, 104–108.

He, J. H. (1999). Homotopy perturbation technique. *Comput. Math. Appl. Mech. Eng.*, *178*, 257–262. doi:10.1016/S0045-7825(99)00018-3

He, J. H. (2003). Homotopy perturbation method: A new nonlinear analyticaltechnique. *Applied Mathematics and Computation*, *135*, 73–79. doi:10.1016/S0096-3003(01)00312-5

He, J. H. (2003). A simple perturbation approach to Blasius equation. *Applied Mathematics and Computation*, *140*, 217–222. doi:10.1016/S0096-3003(02)00189-3

He, J. H. (2006). Homotopy- perturbation method for solving boundary value problems. *Physics Letters. [Part A]*, *350*, 87–88. doi:10.1016/j.physleta.2005.10.005

He, J. H. (2006). Some asymptotic methods for strongly nonlinear equations. *International Journal of Modern Physics B*, *20*(10), 1141–1199. doi:10.1142/S0217979206033796

Hearon, J. Z. (1963). Theorems on linear systems. *Ann. N.Y. Acad. Sci.*, *108*, 36–38. doi:10.1111/j.1749-6632.1963.tb13364.x

Heisenberg, W. (1925). Über quantentheorestische Umdeutung kinematischer und mechanischer Beziehungen. *Zeitschrift fur Physik*, *33*, 879. doi:10.1007/BF01328377

Heitler, W., & London, F. (1927). Wechselwirkung neutraler Atome and homopolare Bindung nach der Quantenmechanik. *Zeitschrift fur Physik, 44*, 455. doi:10.1007/BF01397394

Hellmann, T. (2007). The role of patents for bridging the science to market gap. *Journal of Economic Behavior & Organization, 63*(4), 624–647. doi:10.1016/j.jebo.2006.05.013

Hemissi, M., & Amardjia-Adnani, H. (2007). Optical and structural properties of titanium oxide thin films prepared by sol-gel method. *Digest Journal of Nanomaterials and Biostructures, 2*(4), 299–305.

Hemmateenejad, B., Akhond, M., Miri, R., & Shamsipur, M. (2003). Genetic algorithm applied to the selection of factors in principal component-artificial neural networks: application to QSAR study of calcium channel antagonist activity of 1,4-dihydropyridines (Nifedipine Analogous). *Journal of Chemical Information and Computer Sciences, 43*(4), 1328–1334. doi:10.1021/ci025661p

Hendlich, M. (1998). Databases for Protein–Ligand Complexes. *Acta Crystallographica. Section D, Biological Crystallography, 54*, 1178–1182. doi:10.1107/S0907444998007124

Henri, V. (1901). Über das gesetz der wirkung des invertins. *Zeitschrift für Physikalische Chemie, 39*, 194–216.

Herias, M. V., Hessle, C., Telemo, E., Midtvedt, T., Hanson, L. A., & Wold, A. E. (1999). Immunomodulatory effects of *Lactobacillus plantarum* colonizing the intestine of gnotobiotic rats. *Clinical and Experimental Immunology, 116*, 283–290. doi:10.1046/j.1365-2249.1999.00891.x

Hermann, J., & Jollès, J. (1970). The primary structure of duck egg-white lysozyme II. *Biochimica et Biophysica Acta, 200*, 178–179.

Hernández P, et al. (2007). Evidence for systems-level molecular mechanisms of tumorigenesis. *BMC Genomics, 8*, 115-1–12.

Herráez, Á. (2006). Biomolecules in the computer: Jmol to the rescue. *Biochemistry and Molecular Biology Education, 34*, 255–261. doi:10.1002/bmb.2006.494034042644

Herrero, J. (2003). GEPAS, a web-based resource for microarray gene expression data analysis. *Nucleic Acids Research, 31*, 3461–3467. doi:10.1093/nar/gkg591

Herrero, J. (2004). New challenges in gene expression data analysis and the extended GEPAS. *Nucleic Acids Research, 32*, W485–W491. doi:10.1093/nar/gkh421

Herrero, J., Díaz-Uriarte, R., & Dopazo, J. (2003). An approach to inferring transcriptional regulation among genes form large-scale expression data. *Comparative and Functional Genomics, 4*, 148–154. doi:10.1002/cfg.237

Herrero, J., Díaz-Uriarte, R., & Dopazo, J. (2003). Gene expression data preprocessing. *Bioinformatics (Oxford, England), 19*, 655–656. doi:10.1093/bioinformatics/btg040

Herrero, J., & Dopazo, J. (2002). Combining hierarchical clustering and self-organizing maps for exploratory analysis of gene expression patterns. *Journal of Proteome Research, 1*, 467–470. doi:10.1021/pr025521v

Herrero, J., Valencia, A., & Dopazo, J. (2001). A hierarchical unsupervised growing neural network for clustering gene expression patterns. *Bioinformatics (Oxford, England), 17*, 126–136. doi:10.1093/bioinformatics/17.2.126

Hillis, D. M., Bull, J. J., White, M. E., Badgett, M. R., & Molineux, I. J. (1992). Experimental phylogenetics: generation of a known phylogeny. *Science, 255*, 589–592. doi:10.1126/science.1736360

Hinch, R., & Schnell, S. (2004). Mechanism equivalence in enzyme-substrate reactions: distributed differential delay in enzyme kinetics. *Journal of Mathematical Chemistry, 35*, 253–264. doi:10.1023/B:JOMC.0000033258.42803.60

Hirs, C. H. W. (1967). *Methods Enzymol. 11 (Enzyme Structure)*. New York: Academic Press.

Hirshfeld, F. L. (1977). Bonded-atom fragments for describing molecular charge densities. *Theoretica Chimica Acta, 44*, 129–138. doi:10.1007/BF00549096

Hoef-Emden, K. (2005). Molecular phylogenetic analyses and real-life data. *Computing in Science & Engineering, 7*(3), 86–91. doi:10.1109/MCSE.2005.55

Hoffmann, R., Dopazo, J., Cigudosa, J. C., & Valencia, A. (2005). HCAD, closing the gap between breakpoints and genes. *Nucleic Acids Research, 33*, D511–D513. doi:10.1093/nar/gki061

Hoffmann, C., & Wolf, A. & F. SchMth. (1999). *Angew. Chem.* 111, 2971. *Angewandte Chemie International Edition*, *38*, 2800. doi:10.1002/(SICI)1521-3773(19990917)38:18<2800::AID-ANIE2800>3.3.CO;2-0

Hohenberg, P., & Kohn, W. (1964). Inhomogeneous Electron Gas. *Physical Review*, *136*, 864–871. doi:10.1103/PhysRev.136.B864

Holena, M., & Baerns, M. (2003)... *Catalysis Today*, *81*, 485–494. doi:10.1016/S0920-5861(03)00147-0

Holland, J. (1975). *Adaptation in Artificial and Natural Systems*. Ann Arbor, MI: University of Michigan Press.

Holmgren, J., Bem, D., Bricker, M., Gillespie, R., Lewis, G., & Akporiaye, D. (2001)... *Studies in Surface Science and Catalysis*, *135*, 461–470.

Holtz, H. D., & Stock, L. M. (1964). Dissociation Constants for 4-Substituted Bicyclo-[2.2.2]-Octane-1-Carboxylic Acids. Empirical and Theoretical Analysis. *Journal of the American Chemical Society*, *86*(23), 5188–5194. doi:10.1021/ja01077a031

Hong, Y., Li, D., Zheng, J., & Zou, G. (2006). Sol-gel growth of titania from electrospun polyacrylonitrile nanofibres. *Nanotechnology*, *17*, 1986–1993. doi:10.1088/0957-4484/17/8/032

Hooper, L. V., Wong, M. H., Thelin, A., Hansson, L., Falk, P. G., & Gordon, J. I. (2001). Molecular analysis of commensal host-microbial relationships in the intestine. *Science*, *291*, 881–884. doi:10.1126/science.291.5505.881

Hop, C. E. (2008). High throughput ADME screening: practical considerations, impact on the portfolio and enabler of in silico ADME models. *Current Drug Metabolism*, *9*(9), 847–853. doi:10.2174/138920008786485092

Hopfinger, A. (1997). Construction of 3D-QSAR models using the 4D-QSAR analysis Formalism. *Journal of the American Chemical Society*, *119*, 10509–10524. doi:10.1021/ja9718937

Hori, K., Kamimura, A., Ando, K., Mizumura, M., & Ihara, Y. (1988). *Ab initio* molecular orbital study on the mechanism of amide hydrolysis dependent on leaving groups. *Tetrahedron*, *53*(12), 4317–4330. doi:10.1016/S0040-4020(97)00158-0

Hosoya, H. (1971). Topological index: A proposed quantity characterizing the topological nature of structural isomers of saturated hydrocarbons. *Bulletin of the Chemical Society of Japan*, *44*(9), 2332–2339. doi:10.1246/bcsj.44.2332

http://en.wikipedia.org/wiki/CAS_registry_number (last accessed date 8th July 2011)

http://www.talete.mi.it/products/dragon_molecular_descriptors.htm (last accessed date 8th July 2011)

Hua, D., Cheuk, K., Wei-ning, Z., Chen, W., & Chang-fa, X. (2007). Low temperature preparation of nano TiO_2 and its application as antibacterial agents. *Transactions of Nonferrous Metals Society of China*, *17*, 700–703.

Huang, H. Y., & Niemann, C. (1951). The Kinetics of the α-Chymotrypsin Catalyzed Hydrolysis of Acetyl- and Nicotinyl-L-tryptophanamide in Aqueous Solutions at 25° and *p*H 7.9. *Journal of the American Chemical Society*, *73*, 1541–1548. doi:10.1021/ja01148a040

Huang, J. X., Bouvier, E. S. P., Stuart, J. D., & Melander, W. R., & Horwath, Cs. (1985). High-performance liquid chromatography of substituted p-benzoquinones and p-hydroquinones. II. Retention behavior, quantitative structure-retention relationships and octanolwater partition coefficients. *Journal of Chromatography. A*, *330*(C), 181–192. doi:10.1016/S0021-9673(01)81976-2

Huerta-Cepas, J., Bueno, A., Dopazo, J., & Gabaldón, T. (2008). PhylomeDB: A database for complete collections of gene phylogenies. *Nucleic Acids Research*, *36*, D491–D496. doi:10.1093/nar/gkm899

Huerta-Cepas, J., Dopazo, H., Dopazo, J., Gabaldón, T. (2007). The human phylome. *Genome Biol*, *8*, R109-1–16.

Hur, J., & Wild, D. J.(n.d.). PubChemSR: A search and retrieval tool for PubChem. *Chemistry Central Journal*, *2*, 11.

Hurtubise, R. J., Allen, T. W., & Silver, H. F. (1982). Comparison of molecular connectivity and a chromatographic correlation factor in reversed-phase high-performance liquid chromatography for polycyclic aromatic hydrocarbons. *Journal of Chromatography. A*, *235*(2), 517–522. doi:10.1016/S0021-9673(00)85917-8

Hussain, S. M., Hess, K. L., Gearhart, J. M., Geiss, K. T., & Schlager, J. J. (2005). In vitro toxicity of nanoparticles in BRL 3A rat liver cells. *Toxicology In Vitro, 19*(7), 975–983. doi:10.1016/j.tiv.2005.06.034

Hwang, J.-K., & Warshel, A. (1996). How important are quantum mechanical nuclear motion in enzyme catalysis? *Journal of the American Chemical Society, 118*, 11745–11751. doi:10.1021/ja962007f

Ilieva, S., Galabov, B., Musaev, D. G., Morokuma, K., & Schaefer, H. F. (2003). Computational study of the aminolysis of esters. The reaction of methylformate with ammonia. *The Journal of Organic Chemistry, 68*(4), 1496–1502. doi:10.1021/jo0263723

Ingman, M., Kaessmann, H., Pääbo, S., & Gyllensten, U. (2000). Mitochondrial genome variation and the origin of moden humans. *Nature, 408*, 708–713. doi:10.1038/35047064

Iordache, O., Corriou, J. P., Garrido-Sánchez, L., Fonteix, C., & Tondeur, D. (1993). Neural network frames. Application to biochemical kinetic diagnosis. *Computers & Chemical Engineering, 17*, 1101–1113. doi:10.1016/0098-1354(93)80091-Z

Irwin, J. J., & Shoichet, B. K. (2005). Zinc – A free database of commercially available compounds for virtual screening. *Journal of Chemical Information and Modeling, 45*(1), 177–182. doi:10.1021/ci049714+

Isolauri, E., Juntunen, M., Rautanen, T., Sillanaukee, P., & Koivula, T. (1991). A human *Lactobacillus* strain (*Lactobacillus casei sp. strain GG*) promotes recovery from acute diarrhea in children. *Pediatrics, 88*, 90–97.

Ivanciuc, O., & Balaban, A. T. (1994). Design of topological indices. Part 8. Path matrices and derived molecular graph invariants. [Communications in Mathematical and computational Chemistry]. *MATCH, 30*, 141–152.

Ivanciuc, O., Balaban, T. S., & Balaban, A. T. (1993). Design of topological indices. Part 4. Reciprocal distance matrix, related local vertex invariants and topological indices. *Journal of Mathematical Chemistry, 12*(1), 309–318. doi:10.1007/BF01164642

Ivanciuc, O., & Devillers, J. (1999). Algorithms and Software for the Computation of Topological Indices and Structure-Property Models. In Devillers, J., & Balaban, A. T. (Eds.), *Topological Indices and Related Descriptors in QSAR and QSPR* (pp. 779–804). The Netherlands: Gordon and Breach Science Publishers.

Ivanciuc, O. (1998). Structural similarity measures for database searching. In P. Schlayer, R. Van, N.L. Allinger, T. Clark, J. Gasteiger, P.A. Kollman, H.F. III Schaefer, & P.R. Schreiner (Eds.), *Encyclopedia of Computational Chemistry*. Chichester: Wiley.

Ivanova, T., Harizanova, A., & Surtchev, M. (2002). Formation and investigation of sol-gel TiO_2-V_2O_5 system. *Materials Letters, 55*, 327–333. doi:10.1016/S0167-577X(02)00387-7

Jacquez, J. A. (1985). *Compartmental analysis in Biology and Medicine* (2nd ed.). Ann Arbor, Michigan.

Jacquez, J. A. (1999). *Modelling with Compartmets*. Ann Arbor, Michigan: Biomedware.

Jacquez, J. A. (2002). Density functions of residence times for deterministic and stochastic compartmental systems. *Mathematical Biosciences, 180*, 127–139. doi:10.1016/S0025-5564(02)00110-4

Jacquez, J. A. (1996). *Compartmental analysis in Biology and Medicine*. (3 ed.) Dexter, Michigan: Thompson-Shore Inc.

Jaffe, A., & Trajtenberg, M. (2002). *Patents, citations and innovations: A window on the knowledge economy*. Cambridge, MA: MIT Press.

Jaffe, H. H. (1953). A Re-Examination of the Hammett Equation. *Chemical Reviews, 53*(2), 191–261. doi:10.1021/cr60165a003

Jahromi, H. S., Taghdisian, H., Afshar, S., & Tasharrofi, S. (2009). Effects of pH and polyethylene glycol on surface morphology of TiO_2 thin film. *Surface and Coatings Technology, 203*, 1991–1996. doi:10.1016/j.surfcoat.2009.01.034

Jakubik, W. P. (2006). Investigations of thin film of titanium dioxide (TiO_2) in a surface acoustic wave gas sensor system. *Molecular and Quantum Acoustics, 27*, 133–139.

Jandeleit, B., Schaefer, D. J., Powers, T. S., Turner, H. W., & Weinberg, W. H. (1999)... *Angewandte Chemie International Edition*, *38*, 2494–2532. doi:10.1002/(SICI)1521-3773(19990903)38:17<2494::AID-ANIE2494>3.0.CO;2-#

Jaworska, J., Nikolova-Jeliazkova, N., & Aldenberg, T. (2005). QSAR applicability domain estimation by projection of the training set in descriptor space: a review. *Alternative to Laboratoy Animals: ATLA*, *33*(5), 445–459.

Jencks, W. P. (1969). *Catalysis in chemistry and enzymology*. New York: McGraw Hill.

Jenkins, F. A., & White, H. E. (1981). *Fundamentals of optics. Ackland*. McGraw-Hill.

Jenkins, J. L., Kao, R. Y. T., & Shapiro, R. (2003)... *Proteins*, *51*, 81–93.

Jennings, R. R., & Niemann, C. (1953). The Kinetics of the α-Chymotrypsin Catalyzed Hydrolysis of Acetyl-L-hexahydrophenylalaninamide in Aqueous Solutions at 25° and pH 7.9. *Journal of the American Chemical Society*, *75*, 4687–4692. doi:10.1021/ja01115a020

Jennings, R. R., & Niemann, C. (1955). The Evaluation of the Kinetic Constants of Enzyme-catalyzed Reactions by Procedures Based upon Integrated Rate Equations. *Journal of the American Chemical Society*, *77*, 5432–5433. doi:10.1021/ja01625a077

Jiang, K., Zakutayev, A., Stowers, J., Anderson, M. D., Tate, J., & McIntyre, D. H. (2009). Low-temperature, solution processing of TiO_2 thin films and fabrication of multilayer dielectric optical elements. *Solid State Sciences*, *11*, 1692–1699. doi:10.1016/j.solidstatesciences.2009.05.026

Jiménez González, A. E., & Gelover Santiago, S. (2007). Structural and optoelectronic characterization of TiO_2 films prepared using the sol-gel technique. *Semiconductor Science and Technology*, *22*, 709–716. doi:10.1088/0268-1242/22/7/006

Jing, C., Zhao, X., Han, J., Zhu, K., Liu, A., & Tao, H. (2003). A new method of fabricating internally sol-gel coated capillary tubes. *Surface and Coatings Technology*, *162*, 228–233. doi:10.1016/S0257-8972(02)00568-6

Johnson, M. A., & Maggiora, G. M. (1990). *Concepts and Applications of Molecular Similarity*. New York: John Wiley & Sons.

Johnson, S. R. (2008). The trouble with QSAR (or how I learned to stop worrying and embrace fallacy). *Journal of Chemical Information and Modeling*, *48*, 25–26. doi:10.1021/ci700332k

Jollès, J., Hermann, J., Niemann, B., & Jollès, P. (1967). Differences between the chemical structures of duck and hen egg-white lysozymes. *European Journal of Biochemistry*, *1*, 344–346. doi:10.1111/j.1432-1033.1967.tb00079.x

Jones, P. S. (1998). Strategies for antiviral drug discovery. *Antiviral Chemistry & Chemotherapy*, *9*, 283–302.

Jones, G., Willett, P., & Glen, R. C. (1995)... *Journal of Computer-Aided Molecular Design*, *9*, 532–549. doi:10.1007/BF00124324

Jones, G., Willett, P., Glen, R. C., Leach, A. R., & Taylor, R. (1997)... *Journal of Molecular Biology*, *267*, 727–748. doi:10.1006/jmbi.1996.0897

Jonsson, T., Edmondson, D. E., & Klinman, J. P. (1994). Hydrogen tunneling in the flavoenzyme monoamine oxidase B. *Biochem.*, *33*, 14871–14878. doi:10.1021/bi00253a026

Jonsson, T., Glickman, M. H., Sun, S., & Klinman, J. P. (1996). Experimental evidence for extensive tunneling of hydrogen in the lipoxygenase reaction: implication for enzyme catalysis. *Journal of the American Chemical Society*, *118*, 10319–10320. doi:10.1021/ja961827p

Juillet, B., Bos, C., Gaudichon, C., Tome, D., & Fouillet, H. (2009). Parameter estimation for linear compartmental models--a sensitivity analysis approach. *Annals of Biomedical Engineering*, *37*, 1028–1042. doi:10.1007/s10439-009-9651-z

Jurs, P. C., Dixon, S. L., & Eglof, L. M. (1995). Representations of molecules. In van de Waterbeemd, H. (Ed.), *Chemometric Methods in Molecular Design* (pp. 15–38). Weinheim: VCH. doi:10.1002/9783527615452.ch2

Juszczak, P., & Duin, R. P. W. (2004). *Proc. 17th Int. Conf. on Pattern Recognition*. IEEE Comp. Soc., Los Alamitos, CA.

Kalate, R. N., Tambe, S. S., & Kulkarni, B. D. (2003). Artificial neural networks for prediction of mycobacterial promoter sequences. *Computational Biology and Chemistry*, *27*, 555–564. doi:10.1016/j.compbiolchem.2003.09.004

Kaliszan, R. (1986). Quantitative relationships between molecular structure and chromatographic retention. Implications in physical, analytical, and medicinal chemistry. *Critical Reviews in Analytical Chemistry, 16*, 323–383.

Kaliszan, R., & Foks, H. (1977). The relationship between the R_m values and the connectivity indices for pyrazine carbothioamide derivatives. *Chromatographia, 10*(7), 346–349. doi:10.1007/BF02274482

Kamlet, M. J., Abboud, J. L. M., Abraham, M. H., & Taft, R. W. (1983). Linear solvation energy relationships. 23. A comprehensive collection of the solvatochromic parameters. pi.*. alpha., and. beta., and some methods for simplifying the generalized solvatochromic equation. *The Journal of Organic Chemistry, 48*(17), 2877–2887. doi:10.1021/jo00165a018

Kamlet, M. J., Doherty, R. M., Abboud, J. L. M., Abraham, M. H., & Taft, R. W. (1986). Linear solvation energy relationships. 36. Molecular properties governing solubilities of organic nonelectrolytes in water. *Journal of Pharmaceutical Sciences, 75*, 338–349. doi:10.1002/jps.2600750405

Kaneda, M., Kato, T., Tominaga, N., Chitani, K., & Narita, K. (1969). The amino acid sequence of quail lysozyme. *Journal of Biochemistry, 66*, 747–749.

Karakoti, A. S., Hench, L. L., & Seal, S. (2006). The potential toxicity of nanomaterials - The role of surfaces. *JOM, 58*(7), 77–82. doi:10.1007/s11837-006-0147-0

Karelson, M., Lobanov, V. S., & Katritzky, A. R. (1996). Quantum-Chemical Descriptors in QSAR/QSPR Studies. *Chemical Reviews, 96*, 1027–1043. doi:10.1021/cr950202r

Karelson, M., Lobanov, V. S., & Katritzky, A. R. (1996)... *Chemical Reviews, 96*, 1027–1043. doi:10.1021/cr950202r

Karger, B. L., Gant, J. R., Hartkopf, A., & Weiner, P. H. (1976)... *Journal of Chromatography. A, 128*, 65–78. doi:10.1016/S0021-9673(00)84032-7

Karpfen, A., & Kryachko, E. S. (2005). Strongly blue-shifted C–H stretches: Interaction of formaldehyde with hydrogen fluoride clusters. *The Journal of Physical Chemistry A, 109*(39), 8930–8937. doi:10.1021/jp050408o

Karwasz, G. P., Miotello, A., Zomer, E., Brusa, R. S., Kościelska, B., & Armellini, C. (2005). Structural studies of titanium oxide multilayers. *Acta Physica Polonica A, 107*(6), 977–982.

Karzynski, M., Mateos, Á., Herrero, J., & Dopazo, J. (2003). Using a genetic algorithm and a perceptron for feature selection and supervised clase learning in DNA microarray data. *Artificial Intelligence Review, 20*, 39–51. doi:10.1023/A:1026032530166

Kasai, N., Mizushina, Y., Sugawara, F., & Sakaguchi, K. (2002). Three-dimensional structural model analysis of the binding site of an inhibitor, nervonic acid, of both DNA polymerase β and HIV-1 reverse transcriptase. *Journal of Biochemistry, 132*, 819–828.

Kash, J. C. (2004). Global host immune response: Pathogenesis and transcriptional profiling of type A influenza viruses expressing the hemagglutinin and neuraminidase genes from the 1918 pandemic virus. *Journal of Virology, 78*, 9499–9511. doi:10.1128/JVI.78.17.9499-9511.2004

Katritzky, A. R., & Goordeva, E. V. (1993). Traditional Topological Indices vs. Electronic, Geometrical, and Combined Molecular Descriptors in QSAR/QSPR Research. *Journal of Chemical Information and Computer Sciences, 33*, 835–857. doi:10.1021/ci00016a005

Katritzky, A. R., Lobanov, V. S., & Karelson, M. (1995). QSPR: the correlation and quantitative prediction of chemical and physical properties from structure. *Chemical Society Reviews, 24*, 279–287. doi:10.1039/cs9952400279

Katritzky, A. R., Fara, D. C., Petrukhin, R. O., Tatham, D. B., Maran, U., Lomaka, A., & Karelson, M. (2002)... *Current Topics in Medicinal Chemistry, 2*, 1333–1356. doi:10.2174/1568026023392922

Kaufmann, A. (1975). *Introduction à la théorie des sous-ensembles flous, vol. 3 Paris*. Masson.

Kearsley, S. K., Sallamack, S., Fluder, E. M., Andose, J. D., Mosley, R. T., & Sheridan, R. P. (1996). Chemical Similarity Using Physicochemical Property Descriptors. *Journal of Chemical Information and Computer Sciences, 36*, 118–127. doi:10.1021/ci950274j

Kędzierski, P., Wielgus, P., Sikora, A., Sokalski, W. A., & Leszczyński, J. (2004). Visualization of the differential transition state stabilization within the active site environment. *International Journal of Molecular Sciences*, 5, 186–195. doi:10.3390/i5040186

Kellenberger, E., Rodrigo, J., Muller, P., & Rognan, D. (2004)... *Proteins*, 57, 225–242. doi:10.1002/prot.20149

Kenny, P. W. (1994). Prediction of hydrogen basicity from computed molecular electrostatic properties: Implications for Comparative Molecular Field Analysis. *Journal of the Chemical Society, Perkin Transactions 2: Physical Organic Chemistry*, 2, 199–202. doi:10.1039/p29940000199

Khadikar, P. V., Deshpande, N. V., & Kale, P. P. (1995). The Szeged Index and an Analogy with the Wiener Index. *Journal of Chemical Information and Computer Sciences*, 35(3), 547–550. doi:10.1021/ci00025a024

Khakar, P. S. (2010). Two-dimensional (2D) in silico models for absorption, distribution, metabolism, excretion and toxicity (ADME/T) in drug discovery. *Current Topics in Medicinal Chemistry*, 10(1), 116–126. doi:10.2174/156802610790232224

Kier, L. B., & Hall, L. H. (1986). *Molecular Connectivity in Structure-Activity Analysis*. New York: Wiley.

Kier, L. B., & Hall, L. H. (1999). *Molecular Structure Description. The Electrotopological State*. New York: Academic Press.

Kier, L. B. (1985). A shape index from molecular graphs. *Quantitative Structure-Activity Relationships*, 4(3), 109–116. doi:10.1002/qsar.19850040303

Kier, L. B. (1989). An index of flexibility from molecular shape descriptors. *Progress in Clinical and Biological Research*, 291, 105–109.

Kier, L. B., & Glennon, R. A. (1978). Psychotomimetic phenalkylamines as serotonin agonists: an sar analysis. *Life Sciences*, 22(18), 1589–1593. doi:10.1016/0024-3205(78)90053-X

Kier, L. B., & Hall, L. H. (1976). *Molecular Connectivity in Chemistry and Drug Research*. New York: Academic Press.

Kier, L. B., & Hall, L. H. (1979). Molecular connectivity analyses of structure influencing chromatographic retention indexes. *Journal of Pharmaceutical Sciences*, 68(1), 120–122. doi:10.1002/jps.2600680143

Kier, L. B., & Hall, L. H. (1983). General definition of valence delta-values for molecular connectivity. *Journal of Pharmaceutical Sciences*, 72(10), 1170–1173. doi:10.1002/jps.2600721016

Kier, L. B., & Hall, L. H. (1986). *Molecular Connectivity in Structure–Activity Analysis*. Lethchworth, England: Research Studies Press.

Kier, L. B., & Hall, L. H. (1990). An electrotopological-state index for atoms in molecules. *Pharmaceutical Research*, 7(8), 801–807. doi:10.1023/A:1015952613760

Kier, L. B., & Hall, L. H. (1999). *Molecular Structure Description: The Electrotopological State*. San Diego: Academic Press.

Kier, L. B., & Hall, L. H. (2000). Intermolecular Accessibility: The Meaning of Molecular Connectivity. *Journal of Chemical Information and Computer Sciences*, 40(3), 792–795. doi:10.1021/ci990135s

Kier, L. B. (1980). Molecular connectivity as a description of structure for SAR analyses. In Yalkowsky, S. H., Sinkula, A. A., & Valvani, S. C. (Eds.), *Physical chemical properties of drugs* (pp. 277–319). New York: Marcel Dekker.

Kim, C. K., Li, H. G., Lee, H. W., Sohn, C. K., Chun, Y. I., & Lee, I. (2000). Ab initio study of the X^- + RCOY displacement reactions with R = H, CH_3 and X, Y = Cl, Br. *The Journal of Physical Chemistry A*, 104(17), 4069–4076. doi:10.1021/jp994238p

King, B. F., & Weinhold, F. (1995). Structure and spectroscopy of $(HCN)_n$ clusters: Cooperative and electronic delocalization effects in C–H□□□N hydrogen bonding. *The Journal of Chemical Physics*, 103(1), 333–347. doi:10.1063/1.469645

Kireev, D. B., Raevsky, O. A., & Fetisov, V. I. (1993). QSAR H-bonding descriptors. In Wermuth, C. G. (Ed.), *Trends in QSAR and molecular modelling 92*. Leiden: ESCOM.

Kitaura, K., & Morokuma, K. (1976). A new energy decomposition scheme for molecular interactions within the Hartree-Fock approximation. *International Journal of Quantum Chemistry, 10*(2), 325–340. doi:10.1002/qua.560100211

Klabunde, K. J. (2001). *Nanoscale Materials in Chemistry.* New York: John Wiley & Sons, Inc. doi:10.1002/0471220620

Klanner, C., Farrusseng, D., Baumes, L. A., Lengliz, M., Mirodatos, C., & Schüth, F. (2004)... *Angewandte Chemie International Edition, 43*(40), 5347–5349. doi:10.1002/anie.200460731

Klanner, C., Farrusseng, D., Baumes, L. A., Mirodatos, C., & Schüth, F. (2003)... *QSAR & Combinatorial Science, 22*, 729–736. doi:10.1002/qsar.200320003

Klebe, G., & Abraham, U. (1993)... *Journal of Medicinal Chemistry, 36*, 70–80. doi:10.1021/jm00053a009

Klebe, G., Abraham, U., & Mietzner, T. (1994)... *Journal of Medicinal Chemistry, 37*, 4130–4146. doi:10.1021/jm00050a010

Klein, J., Lehmann, C. W., Schmidt, H. W., & Maier, W. F. (1999)... *Angewandte Chemie International Edition, 38*, 3369. doi:10.1002/(SICI)1521-3773(19990712)38:13/14<2057::AID-ANIE2057>3.0.CO;2-G

Klein, D. J., & Randic, M. (1993). Resistance distance. *Journal of Mathematical Chemistry, 12*(1), 81–95. doi:10.1007/BF01164627

Kleinert, H., Pelster, A., & Putz, M. V. (2002). Variational perturbation theory for Markov processes. *Phys. Rev. E, 65*, 066128/1-7.

Klopman, G. (Ed.). (1974). *Chemical reactivity and reaction paths.* New York: Wiley.

Klopman, G. (1984). Artificial intelligence approach to structure-activity studies. Computer automated structure evaluation of biological activity of organic molecules. *Journal of the American Chemical Society, 106*(24), 7315–7321. doi:10.1021/ja00336a004

Klopman, G., Li, J. K., Wang, S., & Dimayuga, M. (1994). Computer Automated log P Calculations Based on an Extended Group Contribution Approach. *Journal of Chemical Information and Computer Sciences, 34*, 752–781. doi:10.1021/ci00020a009

Kohavi, R., & John, G: H. (1997). Wrappers for feature subset selection. *Artificial Intelligence Journal, 97*(1-2), 273–324. doi:10.1016/S0004-3702(97)00043-X

Kohen, A., Jonsson, T., & Klinman, J. P. (1997). Effects of protein glycosylation on catalysis: changes in hydrogen tunneling and enthalpy of activation in the glucose oxidase reaction. *Biochem., 36*, 2603–2611. doi:10.1021/bi962492r

Kohonen, T. (1982). Self-organized formation of topologically correct feature maps. *Biological Cybernetics, 43*, 59–69. doi:10.1007/BF00337288

Koinuma, H., & Takeuchi, I. (2004)... *Nature Materials, 3*, 429–438. doi:10.1038/nmat1157

Kokowski (ed.) *The Global and the Local: The History of Science and the Cultural Integration of Europe.* Proceedings of the 2nd ICESHS (Cracow, Poland, September 6–9, 2006), 943-949.

Koleva, G., Galabov, B., Wu, I. J., Schaefer, H. F., & Schleyer, P. V. R. (2009). Electrophile affinity: A reactivity measure for aromatic substitution. *Journal of the American Chemical Society, 131*(41), 14722–14727. doi:10.1021/ja902194y

Kollman, P., McKelvey, J., Johansson, A., & Rothenberg, S. (1975). Theoretical studies of hydrogen-bonded dimers. Complexes involving HF, H2O, NH3, CH1, H2S, PH3, HCN, HNC, HCP, CH2NH, H2CS, H2CO, CH4, CF3, H, C2H2, C2H4, C6H6, F- and H3O+. *Journal of the American Chemical Society, 97*(5), 955–965. doi:10.1021/ja00838a001

Kontoyianni, M., & McClellan, L. M. (2004). Sokol. G.S.,(2004). *Journal of Medicinal Chemistry, 47*, 588–565.

Koopmans, T. A. (1933). Über die Zuordnung von Wellenfunktionen und Eigenwerten zu den Einzelnen Elektronen Eines Atoms. *Physica, 1*, 104. doi:10.1016/S0031-8914(34)90011-2

Kościelska, B., Murawski, L., & Wicikowski, L. (2005). Electrical and mechanical properties of nitrided sol-gel derived TiO_2 and SiO_2-TiO_2 films. *Materials Science-Poland, 23*(1), 93–100.

Kozłowska, K., Łukowiak, A., Szczurek, A., Dudek, K., & Maruszewski, K. (2005). Sol-gel coatings for electrical gas sensors. *Optica Applicata, XXXV*(4), 783–790.

Krasavin, M., Rufanov, K. A., Sosnov, A. V., Karapetian, R., Godovykh, E., Soldatkina, O., Lavrovsky, Y., Gakh, A. A (2010). Discovery and SAR exploration of *N*-aryl-*N*-(3-aryl-1,2,4-oxadiazol-5-yl)amines as potential therapeutic agents for prostate cancer. *Chem Central J, 4*, 4-1–7.

Krings, M., Stone, A., Schmitz, R. W., Krainitzki, H., Stoneking, M., & Pääbo, S. (1997). Neanderthal DNA sequences and the origin of modern humans. *Cell, 90*, 19–30. doi:10.1016/S0092-8674(00)80310-4

Kruger, F., Baumes, L. A., Lachiche, N., & Collet, P. (2010). In *Lecture Notes in Computer Science*, Publisher Springer Berlin / Heidelberg. Proc. Int. Conf. EvoStar 2010, 7th - 9th April 2010, Istanbul Technical University, Istanbul, Turkey.

Kubinyi, H. (2008). *QSAR: Hansch Analysis and Related Approaches*. New York: Wiley-Interscience.

Kubinyi, H. (2002). The design of combinatorial libraries. *Drug Discovery Today, 7*(9), 503–504. doi:10.1016/S1359-6446(02)02274-2

Kubinyi, H. (2002). From Narcosis to Hyperspace: The History of QSAR. *Quantitative Structure-Activity Relationships, 21*, 348–356. doi:10.1002/1521-3838(200210)21:4<348::AID-QSAR348>3.0.CO;2-D

Kubinyi, H. (1976). Quantitative structure activity relationships. IV. Non linear dependence of biological activity on hydrophobic character: a new model. *Arzneimittel-Forschung. Drug Research, 26*(11), 1991–1997.

Kubinyi, H. (2003). 2D QSAR Models. Hansch and Free-Wilson Analyses. In Wilfried Langenaeker, H., Patrick, B., & Tollenaere, J. P. (Eds.), *Computational Medicinal Chemistry for Drug Discovery*. New York: CRC Press. doi:10.1201/9780203913390.ch21

Kubinyi, H. (2010). *The Long Road from QSAR to Virtual Screening*. Lecture at the 18th EuroQSAR, Rhodes, Greece, September 2010.

Kuno, M., Palangsuntikul, R., & Hannongbua, S. (2003). Investigation on an orientation and interaction energy of the water molecule in the HIV-1 reverse transcriptase active site by quantum chemical calculations. *Journal of Chemical Information and Computer Sciences, 43*, 1584–1590. doi:10.1021/ci0203850

Kurakula, S. R. (2007). *Studies on the electrical properties of titanium dioxide thin film dielectrics for microelectronic applications*. Bangalore: Indian Institute of Science.

Kušić, H., Rasulev, B., Leszczynska, D., Leszczynski, J., & Koprivanac, N. (2009). Prediction of Rate Constants for Radical Degradation of Aromatic Pollutants in Water Matrix: A QSAR Study. *Chemosphere, 75*, 1128–1134. doi:10.1016/j.chemosphere.2009.01.019

Kuwahara, R. T., & Skinner, R. B. Jr. (2001). EMLA versus ice as a topical anesthetic. *Dermatologic Surgery, 27*, 495–496. doi:10.1046/j.1524-4725.2001.00343.x

Kyani, A., & Goliaei, B. (2009)... *Journal of Molecular Structure, 913*, 63–69. doi:10.1016/j.theochem.2009.07.018

Lacrămă, A.-M., Putz, M. V., & Ostafe, V. (2008). Designing a Spectral Structure-Activity Ecotoxico-Logistical Battery. In Putz, M. V. (Ed.), *Advances in Quantum Chemical Bonding Structures* (pp. 389–419). Kerala, India: Transworld Research Network.

Laidler, K. J. (1955). Theory of transient phase in kinetics, with special reference to enzyme systems. *Canadian Journal of Chemistry, 33*, 1614–1624. doi:10.1139/v55-195

Lal, R., & Anderson, D. H. (1990). Calculation and utilization of component matrices in linear bioscience models. *Mathematical Biosciences, 99*, 11–29. doi:10.1016/0025-5564(90)90136-M

Lao, C., Chuai, Y., Su, L., Liu, X., Huang, L., & Cheng, H. (2005). Mix-solvent-thermal method for the synthesis of anatase nanocrystalline titaniumdioxide used in dye-sensitized solar cell. *Solar Energy Materials and Solar Cells, 85*, 457–465. doi:10.1016/j.solmat.2004.10.002

Largo, C. (2006). Identification of overexpressed genes in frequently gained/amplified chromosome regions in multiple myeloma. *Haematologica, 91*, 184–191.

LaRue, J. N., & Speck, J. C. Jr. (1969)... *Federation Proceedings, 28*, 662–662.

Leach, A. R., & Gillet, V. J. (2003). *An Introduction to Chemoinformatics*. Dordrecht: Kluwer.

Lee, C., Yang, W., & Parr, R. G. (1988). Local softness and chemical reactivity in the molecules CO, SCN- and H_2CO. *Journal of Molecular Structure THEOCHEM, 163*, 305–313. doi:10.1016/0166-1280(88)80397-X

Lee, C., Yang, W., & Parr, R. G. (1988). Development of the Colle-Salvetti correlation- energy formula into a functional of the electron density. *Physical Review B: Condensed Matter and Materials Physics, 37*, 785–789. doi:10.1103/PhysRevB.37.785

Lee, J.-K., & Cho, M. H. (2006). Toxicity and Tissue Distribution of Magnetic Nanoparticles in Mice. *Toxicological Sciences, 89*(1), 338–347.

Lee, F. S., Chu, Z. T., Bolger, M. B., & Warshel, A. (1992)... *Protein Engineering, 5*(3), 215–222. doi:10.1093/protein/5.3.215

Leffler, J. E., & Grunwald, E. (1963). *Rates and Equilibria of Organic Reactions*. New York: John Wiley.

Legendre, P., & Legendre, L. (1998). *Numerical ecology*. Amsterdam: Second English Edition, Elsevier.

Lehtonen, P. (1983). Reversed-phase liquid chromatographic elution characteristics of substituted N-ethylbenzamides. *Journal of Chromatography. A, 267*(C), 277–284. doi:10.1016/S0021-9673(01)90847-7

Lehtonen, P. (1984a). Reversed-phase retention behaviour of Dns-amides as a function of eluent composition and molecular structrure in ethanol-water and methanol-water. *Journal of Chromatography. A, 314*(C), 141–153. doi:10.1016/S0021-9673(01)97729-5

Lehtonen, P. (1984b). Use of molecular connectivity indices to predict LC retention of dansylamides in six different eluent systems. *Chromatographia, 19*(1), 316–321. doi:10.1007/BF02687762

Lehtonen, P. (1985). Properties of six octadecylsilane stationary phases for the separation of dansylamides. *Journal of Chromatography. A, 330*(C), 243–252. doi:10.1016/S0021-9673(01)81981-6

Lehtonen, P. (1986). Isolation and HPLC determination of amines in wine. *Zeitschrift fur Lebensmittel-Untersuchung und -Forschung, 183*(3), 177–181. doi:10.1007/BF01027442

Leinen, D., Fernández, L. A., Espinós, J. P., Belderrain, T. R., & González-Elipe, A. R. (1994). Ion beam induced chemical vapor deposition for the preparation of thin film oxides. *Thin Solid Films, 241*, 198–201. doi:10.1016/0040-6090(94)90425-1

Lemmen, C., & Lengauer, T. (2000). Computational methods for the structural alignment of molecules. *Journal of Computer-Aided Molecular Design, 14*(3), 215–232. doi:10.1023/A:1008194019144

Leonard, J. T., & Roy, J. (2008). Exploring molecular shape analysis of styrylquinoline derivatives as HIV-1 integrase inhibitors. *European Journal of Medicinal Chemistry, 43*, 81–92. doi:10.1016/j.ejmech.2007.02.021

Leonard, J. T., & Roy, K. (2003). QSAR modeling of anti-HIV activities of alkenyldiarylmethanes using topological and physicochemical descriptors. *Drug Design and Discovery, 18*, 165–180. doi:10.1080/10559610390484221

Leonard, J. T., & Roy, K. (2004). Classical QSAR modeling of HIV-1 reverse transcriptase inhibitor 2-amino-6-arylsulfonylbenzonitriles and congeners. *QSAR & Combinatorial Science, 23*, 23–35. doi:10.1002/qsar.200330845

Leonard, J. T., & Roy, K. (2004). Classical QSAR modeling of CCR5 receptor binding affinity of substituted benzylpyrazoles. *QSAR & Combinatorial Science, 23*, 387–398. doi:10.1002/qsar.200430871

Leonard, J. T., & Roy, K. (2006). QSAR by LFER model of HIV protease inhibitory data of mannitol derivatives using FA-MLR, PCRA and PLS techniques. *Bioorganic & Medicinal Chemistry, 14*, 1039–1046. doi:10.1016/j.bmc.2005.09.022

Leonard, J. T., & Roy, K. (2006). The HIV entry inhibitors revisited. *Current Medicinal Chemistry, 13*, 911–934. doi:10.2174/092986706776361030

Levêque, D., Michallat, A. C., Schaller, C., & Ranc, M. (2005). Off label drug use in adult patients treated by anti-cancer chemotherapy. *Bulletin du Cancer, 92*(5), 498–500.

Levin, A. M. (2007). Spatial differentiation in the vegetative mycelium of *Aspergillus niger. Eukaryotic Cell, 6*, 2311–2322. doi:10.1128/EC.00244-07

Lewi, P. J. (1980). Multivariate data analysis in structure activity relationships. In Ariens, E. J. (Ed.), *Drug Design* (*Vol. 10*, pp. 307–342). New York: Academic Press.

Lewinski, N., Colvin, V., & Drezek, R. (2008). Cytotoxicity of nanoparticles. *Small*, *4*(1), 26–49. doi:10.1002/smll.200700595

Li, M., Badger, J. H., Chen, X., Kwong, S., Kearney, P., & Zhang, H. (2001). An information-based sequence distance and its application to whole mitochondrial genome phylogeny. *Bioinformatics (Oxford, England)*, *17*, 149–154. doi:10.1093/bioinformatics/17.2.149

Li, X., & Gutman, I. (2006). *Mathematical Aspects of Randić-Type Molecular Structure Descriptors. MCM 7.* Kragujevac: University of Kragujevac Press.

Li, Z., Qiu, N., & Yang, G. (2009). Effects of synthesis parameters on the microstructure and phase structure of porous 316L stainless steel supported TiO_2 membranes. *Journal of Membrane Science*, *326*, 533–538. doi:10.1016/j.memsci.2008.10.035

Li, W. B., & Hoeschen, C. (2010). Uncertainty and sensitivity analysis of biokinetic models for radiopharmaceuticals used in nuclear medicine. *Radiation Protection Dosimetry*, *139*, 228–231. doi:10.1093/rpd/ncq064

Li, X., Zhang, T., Min, X., & Liu, P. (2010). Toxicity of aromatic compounds to Tetrahymena estimated by microcalorimetry and QSAR. *Aquatic Toxicology (Amsterdam, Netherlands)*, *98*(4), 322–327. doi:10.1016/j.aquatox.2010.03.002

Li, X. H., & Lin, J. J. (2003). The overall hyper-Wiener index. *Journal of Mathematical Chemistry*, *33*(2), 81–89. doi:10.1023/A:1023299514399

Liao, B., Liao, L., Yue, G., Wu, R., & Zhu, W. (2010). A vertical and horizontal method for constructing phylogenetic tree. *MATCH Commun Math Comput Chem*, *63*, 691–700.

Liao, B., Zhu, W., & Liu, Y. (2006). 3D graphical representation of DNA sequence without degeneracy and its applications in constructing phylogenic tree. *MATCH Commun Math Comput Chem*, *56*, 209–216.

Liao, B., & Ding, K. (2005). Graphical approach to analyzing DNA sequences. *Journal of Computational Chemistry*, *26*, 1519–1523. doi:10.1002/jcc.20287

Liao, B., & Wang, T. M. (2004). Analysis of similarity/dissimilarity of DNA sequences based on nonoverlapping triplets of nucleotide bases. *Journal of Chemical Information and Computer Sciences*, *44*, 1666–1670. doi:10.1021/ci034271f

Liao, B., Xiang, X., & Zhu, W. (2006). Coronavirus phylogeny based on 2D graphical representation of DNA sequence. *Journal of Computational Chemistry*, *27*, 1196–1202. doi:10.1002/jcc.20439

Liau, L. C. K., & Chiang, P. I. (2007). Multiple nano-TiO_2 layers to prevent dye/nano-TiO_2 from photodegradation under a UV-exposure environment. *Applied Surface Science*, *253*, 3982–3986. doi:10.1016/j.apsusc.2006.08.031

Lin, I. H., Hsu, C. C., Wang, S. H., Hsieh, H. P., & Sun, Y. C. (2010). Comparative molecular field analysis of antitubulin agents with indole ring binding at the colchicine binding site. *Journal of Theoretical and Computational Chemistry*, *9*, 279–291. doi:10.1142/S0219633610005657

Lin, S. H., & Guidotti, G. (2009). Chapter 35. Purification of membrane proteins. *Methods in Enzymology*, *463*, 619–629. doi:10.1016/S0076-6879(09)63035-4

Lin, H., Uchino, T., Kozuka, H., & Yoko, T. (1997). Electrical properties of transparent doped titania films by sol-gel method. *ICR Annual Report*, *4*, 22–23.

Linden, F. Weber.(1993). Proc. 2ᵈ Int. Conf. on Simulation of Adaptive Behavior. Cambridge, MA: MIT Press.

Ling. *Journal of Chemical Information and Computer Sciences*, *43*, 1947–1958.

Link-Amster, H., Rochat, F., Saudan, K. Y., Mignot, O., & Aeschlimann, J. M. (1994). Modulation of a specific humoral immune response and changes in intestinal flora mediated through fermented milk intake. *FEMS Immunology and Medical Microbiology*, *10*, 55–63. doi:10.1111/j.1574-695X.1994.tb00011.x

Lipnick, R. L., & Filov, V. A. (1992). Nikolai Vasilyevich Lazarev, toxicologist and pharmacologist, comes in from the cold. *Trends in Pharmacological Sciences*, *13*, 56–60. doi:10.1016/0165-6147(92)90024-Z

Liu, D., Thomson, K., & Kaiser, K. L. E. (1982). Quantitative structure-toxicity relationship of halogenated phenols on bacteria. *Bulletin of Environmental Contamination and Toxicology*, *29*, 130–136. doi:10.1007/BF01606140

Liu, Z., Liao, B., & Zhu, W. (2009). A new method to analyze the similarity based on dual nucleotides of the DNA sequence. *MATCH Commun Math Comput Chem, 61*, 541–552.

Liu, H., Yao, X., Zhang, R., Liu, M., Hu, Z., & Fan, B. (2005). Accurate quantitative structure-property relationship model to predict the solubility of C_{60} in various solvents based on a novel approach using a least-squares support vector machine. *The Journal of Physical Chemistry B, 109*, 20565–20571. doi:10.1021/jp052223n

Liu, K., Feng, J., & Young, S. S. (2005). PowerMV: A software environment for molecular viewing, descriptor generation, data analysis and hit evaluation. *Journal of Chemical Information and Modeling, 45*(2), 515–522. doi:10.1021/ci049847v

Liu, W. m., Chen, Y. x., Kou, G. T., Xu, T., & Sun, D. C. (2003). Characterization and mechanical/tribological properties of nano Au-TiO$_2$ composite thin films prepared by a sol–gel process. *Wear, 254*, 994–1000. doi:10.1016/S0043-1648(03)00305-3

Liu, P., & Wei Long, W. (2009). Current Mathematical Methods Used in QSAR/QSPR Studies. *International Journal of Molecular Sciences, 10*(5), 1978–1998. doi:10.3390/ijms10051978

Ljungberg, K. B., Marelius, J., Musil, D., Svensson, P., Norden, B., & Åqvist, J. (2001)... *European Journal of Pharmaceutical Sciences, 12*, 441–446. doi:10.1016/S0928-0987(00)00185-8

Löbl, P., Huppertz, M., & Mergel, D. (1994). Nucleation and growth in TiO$_2$ films prepared by sputtering and evaporation. *Thin Solid Films, 251*, 72–79. doi:10.1016/0040-6090(94)90843-5

Lopex, M. A., & Kollman, P. A. (1993)... *Protein Science, 2*, 1975–1986. doi:10.1002/pro.5560021119

Lopez, X., Mujika, J. I., Blackburn, G. M., & Karplus, M. (2003). Alkaline hydrolysis of amide bonds: effect of bond twist and nitrogen pyramidalization. *The Journal of Physical Chemistry A, 107*(13), 2304–2315. doi:10.1021/jp022014s

López, A., Faus, V., Díez-Sales, O., & Herráez, M. (1998). Skin permeation model of phenyl alcohols: Comparison of experimental conditions. *International Journal of Pharmaceutics, 173*, 183–191. doi:10.1016/S0378-5173(98)00231-2

López, A., Morant, M. J., Guzmán, D., Borrás-Blasco, J., Díez-Sales, O., & Herráez, M. (1996). Skin permeation model of phenylalkylcarboxylic homologous acids and their enhancer effect on percutaneous penetration of 5-fluorouracil. *International Journal of Pharmaceutics, 139*, 205–213. doi:10.1016/0378-5173(96)04628-5

López, A., Pellett, M. A., Llinares, F., Díez-Sales, O., Herráez, M., & Hadgraft, J. (1997). The enhancer effect of several phenyl alcohols on percutaneous penetration of 5-fluorouracil. *Pharmaceutical Research, 14*, 681–685. doi:10.1023/A:1012177717336

Lucic, B., & Trinajstic, N. (1999). Multivariate regression outperforms several robust architectures of neural networks in QSAR modeling. *Journal of Chemical Information and Computer Sciences, 39*, 121–132. doi:10.1021/ci980090f

Lurie, I. S., & Allen, A. C. (1984). Reversed-phase high-performance liquid chromatographic separation of fentanyl homologues and analogues. II. Variables affecting hydrophobic group contribution. *Journal of Chromatography. A, 292*(2), 283–294. doi:10.1016/S0021-9673(01)83609-8

Ma, B., & Nussinov, R. (2004). From computational quantum chemistry to computational biology: experiments and computations are (full) partners. *Physical Biology, 1*, 23–26. doi:10.1088/1478-3967/1/4/P01

Ma, B. (1995). *The Philosophy of Computational Quantum Chemistry*. Ph. Dissertation, University of Georgia.

Macher, B. A., & Yen, T. Y. (2007). Proteins at membrane surfaces – a review of approaches. *Molecular BioSystems, 3*(10), 705–713. doi:10.1039/b708581h

Mager, H., & Mager, P. P. (1992). Validation of QSARs: Some Reflections. *Quantitative Structure-Activity Relationships, 11*(4), 518–521. doi:10.1002/qsar.2660110409

Maggiora, G. M. (2006). On outliers and activity cliffs - why QSAR often disappoints. *Journal of Chemical Information and Modeling, 46*, 1535. doi:10.1021/ci060117s

Mahé, P., & Vert, J. P. (2007). *Virtual screening with support vector machines and structure kernels* (Technical report HAL-00166188), Paris: Ecole des Mines de Paris, Centre de Bioinformatique.

Mahltig, B., Fiedler, D., & Böttcher, H. (2004). Antimicrobial sol-gel coatings. *Journal of Sol-Gel Science and Technology, 32*, 219–222. doi:10.1007/s10971-004-5791-7

Maibaum, T.S.E. (2005). The Epistemology of Validation and Verification Testing. *Lecture Notes in Computer Science, 3502/2005*, 1-8.

Maier, W. F. (2004)... *Polymeric Materials Science and Engineering, 90*, 652–653.

Maitre, O., & Lachiche, N. P., Baumes, L. A., Corma, A. & P. Collet.(2009). In *Lecture Notes in Computer Science*, Publisher Springer Berlin / Heidelberg Vol. 5704/2009 Euro-Par **2009** Parallel Processing, 974-985.

Maitre, O., Baumes, L. A., Lachiche, N., & Collet, P. Corma, A. (2009). *Proc. of the 11th Annual conf. on Genetic and evolutionary computation.* Montreal, Québec, Canada, Session: Track 12: parallel evolutionary systems, 1403-1410. New York: Association for Computing Machinery.

Makarenkov, V., & Lapointe, F. J. (2004). A weighted least-squares approach for inferring phylogenies from incomplete distance matrices. *Bioinformatics (Oxford, England), 20*, 2113–2121. doi:10.1093/bioinformatics/bth211

Malin, M., Suomalainen, H., Saxelin, M., & Isolauri, E. (1996). Promotion of IgA immune response in patients with Crohn's disease by oral bacteriotherapy with *Lactobacillus GG. Annals of Nutrition & Metabolism, 40*, 137–145. doi:10.1159/000177907

Malvezzi, A., de Rezende, L., Izidoro, M. A., Cezari, M. H. S., Juliano, L., & Amaral, A. T. d. (2008). Uncovering false positives on a virtual screening search for cruzain inhibitors. *Bioorganic & Medicinal Chemistry Letters, 18*(1), 350–354. doi:10.1016/j.bmcl.2007.10.068

Mannhold, R., Kubinyi, H., & Folkers, G. (Eds.). (2009). *Molecular Descriptors for Chemoinformatics.* Weinheim, Germany: Wiley-VCH.

Marchant, T. R. (2002). Cubic autocatalytic reaction–diffusion equations: semi-analytical solutions. *Proceedings of the Royal Society of London. Series A, 458*, 873–888. doi:10.1098/rspa.2001.0899

Marcorin, G. L., Da Ros, T., Castellano, S., Stefancich, G., Bonin, I., Miertus, S., & Prato, M. (2000). Design and Synthesis of Novel C[60] Fullerene Derivatives as Potential HIV Aspartic Protease Inhibitors. *Organic Letters, 2*(25), 3955–3958. doi:10.1021/ol000217y

Marcus, R.A., Electron-transfer reactions in chemistry- theory and experiment (Nobel lecture). (1993). *Angew. Chem. Int. Ed., 32*, 1111-1121. doi:10.1002/anie.199311113

Mardare, D., & Rusu, G. I. (2004). Comparison of the dielectric properties for doped and undoped TiO_2 thin films. *Journal of Optoelectronics and Advanced Materials, 6*(1), 333–336.

Maria, C. (2006). The philosophy of computational chemistry II. In *M.* Burguete.

Marrero Ponce, Y., Castillo Garit, J. A., & Nodarse, D. (2005). Linear indices of the 'macromolecular graph's nucleotides adjacency matrix' as a promising approach for bioinformatics studies. Part 1: prediction of paromomycin's affinity constant with HIV-1 psi-RNA packaging region. *Bioorganic & Medicinal Chemistry, 13*, 3397–3404. doi:10.1016/j.bmc.2005.03.010

Marrero-Ponce, Y. (2005). A computer-based approach to the rational discovery of new trichomonacidal drugs by atom-type linear indices. *Current Drug Discovery Technologies, 2*, 245–265. doi:10.2174/157016305775202955

Marrero-Ponce, Y. (2006). Predicting antitrichomonal activity: A computational screening using atom-based bilinear indices and experimental proofs. *Bioorganic & Medicinal Chemistry, 14*, 6502–6524. doi:10.1016/j.bmc.2006.06.016

Marrero-Ponce, Y. (2008). Bond-based linear indices in QSAR: Computational discovery of novel anti-trichomonal compounds. *Journal of Computer-Aided Molecular Design, 22*, 523–540. doi:10.1007/s10822-008-9171-1

Marrero-Ponce, Y., Medina-Marrero, R., Castillo-Garit, J. A., Romero-Zaldivar, V., Torrens, F., & Castro, E. A. (2005). Protein linear indices of the 'macromolecular pseudograph alpha-carbon atom adjacency matrix' in bioinformatics. Part 1: prediction of protein stability effects of a complete set of alanine substitutions in Arc repressor. *Bioorganic & Medicinal Chemistry, 13,* 3003–3015. doi:10.1016/j.bmc.2005.01.062

Marrero-Ponce, Y., Medina-Marrero, R., Castro, E. A., Ramos de Armas, R., González, H., Romero, V., & Torrens, F. (2004a). Protein quadratic indices of the "macromolecular pseudograph's a-carbon atom adjacency Matrix". 1. prediction of Arc repressor alanine-mutant's stability. *Molecules (Basel, Switzerland), 9,* 1124–1147. doi:10.3390/91201124

Marrero-Ponce, Y., Nodarse, D., González-Díaz, H., Ramos de Armas, R., Romero-Zaldivar, V., Torrens, F., & Castro, E. A. (2004b). Nucleic acid quadratic indices of the "macromolecular graph's nucleotides adjacency matrix" modeling of footprints after the interaction of paromomycin with the HIV-1 C-RNA packaging region. *International Journal of Molecular Sciences, 5,* 276–293. doi:10.3390/i5110276

Marrero-Ponce, Y., et al.. (n.d.). Atom, atom-type and total molecular linear indices as a promising approach for bioorganic and medicinal chemistry: theoretical and experimental assessment of a novel method for virtual screening and rational design of new lead anthelmintic. *Bioorganic and Medicinal Chemistry, 13*(4), 1005-1020.

Marteau, P.R, de Vrese, M, Cellier, C.J, Schrezenmeir, J. (2001). Protection from gastrointestinal diseases with the use of probiotics. *Am J Clin Nutr, 73*(Supl 2),430S–436S.

Martin, N., Rousselot, C., Savall, C., & Palmino, F. (1996). Characterizations of titanium oxide films prepared by radio frequency magnetron sputtering. *Thin Solid Films, 287,* 154–163. doi:10.1016/S0040-6090(96)08782-2

Martín, M. J., González-Candelas, F., Sobrino, F., & Dopazo, J. (1995). A method for determining the position and size of optimal sequence regions for phylogenetic analysis. *Journal of Molecular Evolution, 41,* 1128–1138. doi:10.1007/BF00173194

Martín, M. J., Herrero, J., Mateos, Á., & Dopazo, J. (2003). Comparing bacterial genomes through conservation profiles. *Genome Research, 15,* 991–998. doi:10.1101/gr.678303

Martín, M. J., Núñez, J. I., Sobrino, F., & Dopazo, J. (1998). A procedure for detecting selection in highly variable viral genomes – Evidence of positive selection in antigenic regions of capsid protein VP1 of foot-and-mouth-disease virus. *Journal of Virological Methods, 74,* 215–221. doi:10.1016/S0166-0934(98)00088-3

Martin, Y. C. (1989). Theoretical basis of medicinal chemistry: Structure–activity relationships and three–dimensional structures of small and macromolecules. In Martin, Y. C., Kutter, E., & Anstel, V. (Eds.), *Modern Drug Research. Paths to Better and Safer Drugs* (pp. 161–216). New York: Marcel Dekker, Inc.

Martin, Y. (2001). Beginnings of QSAR, CADD?. *Newsletter. The QSAR and Modelling Society.* Issue No. 12, 12-20.

Martinez, I., Dopazo, J., & Melero, J. A. (1997). Antigenic structure of the human respiratory syncytial virus G-glycoprotein and relevance of hypermutation events for the generation of antigenic variants. *The Journal of General Virology, 78,* 2419–2429.

Martínez-Delgado, B. (2004). Expression profiling of T-cell lymphomas differentiates peripheral and lymphoblastic lymphomas and defines survival related genes. *Clinical Cancer Research, 10,* 4971–4982. doi:10.1158/1078-0432.CCR-04-0269

Marti-Renom, M. A. (2007). DBAli tools: Mining the protein structural space. *Nucleic Acids Research, 35,* W393–W397. doi:10.1093/nar/gkm236

Marti-Renom, M.A., Rossi, A., Al-Shahrour, F., Davis, F.P., Pieper, U., Dopazo, J., Sali, A. (2007). The AnnoLite and AnnoLyze programs for comparative annotation of protein structures. *BMC Bioinformatics, 8,*S4-1–12.

Mason, J. S., Morize, I., Menard, P. R., Cheney, D. L., Hulne, C. C., & Labaudinieres, R. F. (1999). New 4-Point Pharmacophore Method for Molecular Similarity and Diversity Applications: Overview of the Method and Applications, Including a Novel Approach to the Design of Combinatorial Libraries Containing Privileged Substructures. *Journal of Medicinal Chemistry, 42*(17), 3251–3264. doi:10.1021/jm9806998

Mason, J. S., & Cheney, D. L. (1999). Ligand-receptor 3-D similarity studies using multiple 4-point pharmacophores. *Pacific Symposium on Biocomputing, 4*, 456-467.

Mateos, Á., Dopazo, J., Jansen, R., Tu, Y., Gerstein, M., & Stolovitzky, G. (2002). Systematic learning of gene functional classes from DNA array expression data by using multilayer perceptrons. *Genome Research, 12*, 1703–1715. doi:10.1101/gr.192502

Matsuzaki, T., Yamazaki, R., Hashimoto, S., & Yokokura, T. (1998). The effect of oral feeding of *Lactobacillus casei strain Shirota* on immunoglobulin E production in mice. *Journal of Dairy Science, 81*, 48–53. doi:10.3168/jds.S0022-0302(98)75549-3

Maynard, A. T., Huang, M., Rice, W. G., & Covell, D. G. (1998). Reactivity of the HIV-1 nucleocapsid protein p7 zinc finger domains from the perspective of density-functional theory. *Proceedings of the National Academy of Sciences of the United States of America, 95*, 11578–11583. doi:10.1073/pnas.95.20.11578

MDL. (2007). *Program Chime*. San Leandro, CA: MDL Information Systems.

Medina, I., Montaner, D., Tárraga, J., & Dopazo, J. (2007). Prophet, a web-based tool for class prediction using microarray data. *Bioinformatics (Oxford, England), 23*, 390–391. doi:10.1093/bioinformatics/btl602

Medina, C., Santos-Martinez, M. J., Radomski, A., Corrigan, O. I., & Radomski, M. W. (2007). Pharmacological and toxicological significance of nanoparticles. *British Journal of Pharmacology, 150*(5), 552–558. doi:10.1038/sj.bjp.0707130

Medina-Valtierra, J., Sánchez-Cárdenas, M., Frausto-Reyes, C., & Calixto, S. (2006). Formation of smooth and rough TiO_2 thin films on fiberglass by sol-gel method. *Journal of the Mexican Chemical Society, 50*(1), 8–1.

Meena, A., & Rajendran, L. (2010). Mathematical modeling of amperometric and potentiometric biosensors and systems of non-linear equations - homotopy- perturbation method. *Journal of Electroanalytical Chemistry, 644*, 50–59. doi:10.1016/j.jelechem.2010.03.027

Meléndez, B. (2004). Gene expression analysis on chromosomal regions of gain or loss in genetic material detected by comparative genomic hybridization. *Genes, Chromosomes & Cancer, 41*, 353–365. doi:10.1002/gcc.20105

Meneses, A. (2005). A linear discrimination analysis based virtual screening of trichomonacidal lead-like compounds. Outcomes of *in silico* studies supported by experimental results. *Bioorganic & Medicinal Chemistry Letters, 17*, 3838–3843. doi:10.1016/j.bmcl.2005.05.124

Meneses, A., Rojas, L., Sifontes, R. S., López, Y., & Sariego, R. I. (2001). Aplicación de un método alternativo al conteo en cámara de Neubauer para determinar concentración de *Trichomonas vaginalis*. *Revista Cubana de Medicina Tropical, 53*, 180–188.

Meneses-Marcel, A., Marrero-Ponce, Y., Machado-Tugores, Y., Montero-Torres, A., Pereira, D. M., & Escario, J. A. (2005). A linear discrimination analysis virtual screening of trichomonacidal lead-like compounds: outcomes of in silico studies supported by experimental results. *Bioorganic & Medicinal Chemistry, 15*(17), 3838–3843. doi:10.1016/j.bmcl.2005.05.124

Merlot, C., Domine, D., Cleva, C., & Church, D. J. (2003). Chemical substructures in drug discovery. *Drug Discovery Today, 8*(13), 594–602. doi:10.1016/S1359-6446(03)02740-5

Meyer, H. (1899). Zur Theorie Der Alkolnarkose I. Welche Eigenschaft Der Anaesthetica Bedingt Jhre Narkotische Wirkuny? *Archiv fur Experimentalle Pathologie und Pharmakologie, 42*(2–4), 109–118. doi:10.1007/BF01834479

Meyer, H.H. & Baum, F. (1899). Zur Theorie der Alkoholnarkose (I-III). *Archiv für experimentelle Pathologie und Pharmakologie, 42*.

Michaelis, L., & Menten, M. L. (1913). Die kinetik der invertinwirkung. *Biochemische Zeitschrift, 49*, 333–369.

Michotte, Y., & Massart, D. L. (1977). Molecular connectivity and retention indexes. *Journal of Pharmaceutical Sciences, 66*(11), 1630–1632. doi:10.1002/jps.2600661134

Mihalić, Z., Nikolić, S., & Trinajstić, N. (1992). Comparative study of molecular descriptors derived from the distance matrix. *Journal of Chemical Information and Computer Sciences, 32,* 28–37. doi:10.1021/ci00005a005

Miki, T., Nishizawa, K., Suzuki, K., & Kato, K. (2004). Preparation of thick TiO_2 film with large surface area using aqueous sol with poly(ethylene glycol). *Journal of Materials Science, 39,* 699–701. doi:10.1023/B:JMSC.0000011535.89376.93

Millership, J. S., & Woolfson, A. D. (1978). The relation between molecular connectivity and gas chromatographic retention data. *The Journal of Pharmacy and Pharmacology, 30*(8), 483–485. doi:10.1111/j.2042-7158.1978.tb13298.x

Millership, J. S., & Woolfson, A. D. (1982)... *The Journal of Pharmacy and Pharmacology, 32,* 610. doi:10.1111/j.2042-7158.1980.tb13015.x

Milne, G. W. A. (1997). Mathematics as a basis for chemistry. *Journal of Chemical Information and Computer Sciences, 37*(4), 639–644. doi:10.1021/ci960165k

Mine, R. L. (2006). ERCC4 associated with breast cancer risk: A two-stage case-control study using high-throughput genotyping. *Cancer Research, 66,* 9420–9427. doi:10.1158/0008-5472.CAN-06-1418

Ming-Fang, X., Shan, L., Xin-Man, C., & Yan-Zhi, P. (2006). Studies on characteristics of nanostructure of N-TiO_2 thin films and photo-bactericidal action. *Journal of Zhejiang University. Science. B., 7*(7), 586–590. doi:10.1631/jzus.2006.B0586

Minguez, P., Al-Shahrour, F., Montaner, D., & Dopazo, J. (2007). Functional profiling of microarray experiments using text-mining derived bioentities. *Bioinformatics (Oxford, England), 23,* 3098–3099. doi:10.1093/bioinformatics/btm445

Miró, M. J., Méndez, M. T., Raposo, R., Herráez, Á., Barrero, B., & Palacios, E. (2007). Desarrollo de una asignatura virtual de tercer ciclo como un espacio de enseñanza-aprendizaje que permite la participación activa del alumno. In *III Jornada Campus Virtual UCM* (pp. 304–306). Madrid: Innovación en el Campus Virtual, Metodologías y Herramientas. Complutense.

Mitra, I., Roy, P. P., Kar, S., Ojha, P. K., & Roy, K. (2010). On further application of r_m^2 as a metric for validation of QSAR models. *Journal of Chemometrics, 24,* 22–33. doi:10.1002/cem.1268

Mlinaric, A., Kreft, S., Umek, A., & Strukelj, B. (2000). Screening of selected plant extracts for *in vivo* inhibitory activity on HIV-1 reverse transcriptase (HIV-1 RT). *Die Pharmazie, 55,* 75–77.

Monev, V. (2004). Introduction to Similarity Searching in Chemistry. *Match-Communications in Mathematical and in Computer Chemistry, 51,* 7–38.

Monier, A., Claverie, J.M., Ogata, H. (2008). Taxonomic distribution of large DNA viruses in the sea. *Genome Biol,* 9,R106-1–15.

Montaner, D. (2006). Next station in microarray data analysis: GEPAS. *Nucleic Acids Research, 34,* W486–W491. doi:10.1093/nar/gkl197

Montero, A. (2005). A novel non-stochastic quadratic fingerprints-based approach for the *in silico* discovery of new antitrypanosomal compounds. *Bioorganic & Medicinal Chemistry, 13,* 6264–6275. doi:10.1016/j.bmc.2005.06.049

Montero-Conde, C. (2008). Molecular profiling related to poor prognosis in thyroid carcinoma. Combining gene expression data and biological information. *Oncogene, 27,* 1554–1561. doi:10.1038/sj.onc.1210792

Montero-Torres, A. (2006). Non-stochastic quadratic fingerprints and LDA-based QSAR models in hit and lead generation through virtual screening: Theoretical and experimental assessment of a promising method for the discovery of new antimalarial compounds. *European Journal of Medicinal Chemistry, 41,* 483–493. doi:10.1016/j.ejmech.2005.12.010

Montgomery, D. C. (1991). *Design and analysis of experiments* (3rd ed.). New York: Wiley.

Montgomery, D. C. (1997). *Design and Analysis of Experiments* (4th ed.). New York: John Wiley & Sons Inc.

Moolgavkar, S. H., & Luebeck, G. (1990). Two-event model for carcinogenesis: biological, mathematical, and statistical considerations. *Risk Analysis, 10,* 323–341. doi:10.1111/j.1539-6924.1990.tb01053.x

Moore, M. N. (2006). Do nanoparticles present ecotoxicological risks for the health of the aquatic environment? *Environment International, 32*(8), 967–976. doi:10.1016/j.envint.2006.06.014

Moreno-Bueno, G. (2003). Differential gene expression profile in endometrioid and nonendometrioid endometrial carcinoma: *STK15* is frequently overexpressed and amplified in nonendometrioid carcinomas. *Cancer Research, 63*, 5697–5702.

Moss, O. R., & Wong, V. A. (2006). When nanoparticles get in the way: impact of projected area on in vivo and in vitro macrophage function. *Inhalation Toxicology, 18*(10), 711–716. doi:10.1080/08958370600747770

Mozziconacci, J. C (2003). *Développement et application de méthodes de drug design: Combinaison des approches de docking-scoring et de QSAR*. Unpublished doctoral dissertation, Orleans University, Orleans.

Muegge, I., & Oloffa, S. (2006). Advances in virtual screening. *Drug Discovery Today. Technologies, 3*(4), 405–411. doi:10.1016/j.ddtec.2006.12.002

Muegge, I., & Rarey, M. (2001)... *Reviews in Computational Chemistry, 17*, 1–60. doi:10.1002/0471224413.ch1

Mulliken, R. S. (1955). Electronic population analysis on LCAO MO molecular wave functions. I. *The Journal of Chemical Physics, 23*(17), 1833–1840. doi:10.1063/1.1740588

Murray, J. D. (1990). *Mathematical Biology*. Berlin: Springer Verlag.

Murray, J. S., Brinck, T., Grice, M. E., & Politzer, P. (1992). Correlations between molecular electrostatic potentials and some experimentally-based indices of reactivity. *Journal of Molecular Structure THEOCHEM, 256*, 29–45. doi:10.1016/0166-1280(92)87156-T

Murray, J. S., Lans, P., Brinck, T., & Politzer, P. (1991). Electrostatic potentials on the molecular surfaces of cyclic ureides. *Journal of Physical Chemistry, 95*(2), 844–848. doi:10.1021/j100155a066

Murray, J. S., & Politzer, P. (1988). Electrostatic potentials of amine nitrogens as a measure of the total electron-attracting tendencies of substituents. *Chemical Physics Letters, 152*(4-5), 364–370. doi:10.1016/0009-2614(88)80107-6

Murray, J. S., & Politzer, P. (1992). Relationship between solute hydrogen-bond acidity/basicity and the calculated electrostatic potential. *Journal of Chemical Research (S), 3*, 110–111.

Murray, J. S., & Politzer, P. J. (1991). Correlations between the solvent hydrogen-bond-donating parameter. alpha. and the calculated molecular surface electrostatic potential. Correlations between the solvent hydrogen-bond-donating parameter. alpha. and the calculated molecular surface electrostatic potential. *The Journal of Organic Chemistry, 56*(23), 6715–6717. doi:10.1021/jo00023a045

Murray, J. S., & Sen, K. D. (Eds.). (1996). *Molecular electrostatic potentials. Concepts and applications*. Amsterdam: Elsevier.

Nakano, M., Fukuda, K., & Taniguchi, H. (2009). Appropriate probe search method to specify groups in higher taxonomic ranks. *Journal of Basic Microbiology, 49*, 100–108. doi:10.1002/jobm.200800211

Nandy, A. (1994). Recent investigations into global characteristics of long DNA sequences. *Indian Journal of Biochemistry & Biophysics, 31*, 149–155.

Nandy, A. (1996). Two-dimensional graphical representation of DNA sequences and intron-exon discrimination in intronrich sequences. *Computer Applications in the Biosciences, 12*, 55–62.

Nandy, A., Harle, M., & Basak, S. C. (2006). Mathematical descriptors of DNA sequences: Development and applications. *ARKIVOC, 9*, 211–238.

Naray-Szabo, G., & Ferenczy, G. (1995). Molecular electrostatics. *Chemical Reviews, 95*(4), 829–847. doi:10.1021/cr00036a002

Nasr-Esfahani, M., & Habibi, M. H. (2009). A comparative study on physicochemical properties and photocatalytic behavior of two different nanostructure composite TiO_2 films coated on glass substrate. *Desalination and Water Treatment, 3*, 64–72. doi:10.5004/dwt.2009.441

MATLAB (1999) The Math Works, Inc.:Natick U.S.A.

Navarro, E., Fenude, E., & Celda, B. (2002). Solution structure of a D,L-alternating oligonorleucine as a model of doublestranded antiparallel beta-helix. *Biopolymers, 64*, 198–209. doi:10.1002/bip.10172

Navarro, E., Fenude, E., & Celda, B. (2004). Conformational and structural analysis of the equilibrium between single- and double-strand beta-helix of a D,L-alternating oligonorleucine. *Biopolymers*, *73*, 229–241. doi:10.1002/bip.10549

Needham, D. E., Wei, I.-C., & Seybold, P. G. (1988). Molecular modeling of the physical properties of the alkanes. *Journal of the American Chemical Society*, *110*, 4186–4194. doi:10.1021/ja00221a015

Nesbitt, D. J. (1988). High-resolution infrared spectroscopy of weakly bound molecular complexes. *Chemical Reviews*, *88*(6), 843–870. doi:10.1021/cr00088a003

Netzeva, T. H., Pavan, M., & Worth, A. P. (2008). Review of (quantitative) structure–activity relationships for acute aquatic toxicity. *QSAR & Combinatorial Science*, *27*(1), 77–90. doi:10.1002/qsar.200710099

Nicolaides, D. (2005)... *QSAR & Combinatorial Science*, 24.

Niraikulam, A., Hyungdon, Y., & Natarajan, S. (2010). Protein coding genes for better resolution of phylogenetic analysis. *Res J Biotechnol*, *5*, 74–74.

Nixon, A. E., Ostermeier, M., & Benkovic, S. J. (1998). Hybrid enzymes: manipulating enzyme design. *Trends in Biotechnology*, *16*, 258–264. doi:10.1016/S0167-7799(98)01204-9

Novakovic, S. B., Bogdanovic, G. A., Fraisse, B., Ghermani, N. E., Bouhmaida, N., & Spasojevic-de Bire, A. (2007). Topological features of both electron density and electrostatic potential in the bis(thiosemicarbazide)zinc(II) dinitrate complex. *The Journal of Physical Chemistry A*, *111*(51), 13492–13505. doi:10.1021/jp075456i

Novakovic, S. B., Fraisse, B., Bogdanovic, G. A., & Spasojevic-de Bire, A. (2007). Experimental charge density evidence for the existence of high polarizability of the electron density of the free electron pairs on the sulfur atom of the thioureido group, NH−C(=S)−NH$_2$, induced by N−H···S and C−H···S interactions. *Crystal Growth & Design*, *7*(2), 191–195. doi:10.1021/cg060497+

Nueda, M. J., Conesa, A., Westerhuis, J. A., Hoefsloot, H. C., Smilde, A. K., Talón, M., & Ferrer, A. (2007). Discovering gene expression patterns in time course microarray experiments by ANOVA-SCA. *Bioinformatics (Oxford, England)*, *23*, 1792–1800. doi:10.1093/bioinformatics/btm251

Núñez, J. I. (2001). Identification of optimal regions for phylogenetic studies on VP1 gene of foot-and-mouth disease virus: Analysis of types A and O Argentinean viruses. *Veterinary Research*, *32*, 31–45. doi:10.1051/vetres:2001107

Núñez, J. I., Blanco, E., Hernandez, T., Dopazo, J., & Sobrino, F. (1998). RT-PCR in foot-and-mouth-disease diagnosis. *The Veterinary Quarterly*, *20*, S34–S36.

Núñez, J. I., Blanco, E., Hernandez, T., Gomez-Tejedor, G., Martín, M. J., Dopazo, J., & Sobrino, F. (1998). A RT-PCR assay for the differential-diagnosis of vesicular viral diseases of swine. *Journal of Virological Methods*, *72*, 227–235. doi:10.1016/S0166-0934(98)00032-9

Nye, M. J. (1993). *From chemical philosophy to theoretical chemistry*. Berkeley, CA: University of California Press.

Nye, J. A., Votaw, J. R., Jarkas, N., Purselle, D., Camp, V., & Bremner, J. D. (2008). Compartmental modeling of 11C-HOMADAM binding to the serotonin transporter in the healthy human brain. *Journal of Nuclear Medicine*, *49*, 2018–2025. doi:10.2967/jnumed.108.054262

O'Hair, R. A. J., & Androutsopoulos, N. K. (2000). Can transacylation reactions occur via S_N2 pathways in the gas phase? Insights via ion−molecule reactions of N-acylpyridinium ions and *ab initio* calculations. *Organic Letters*, *2*(17), 2567–2570. doi:10.1021/ol006060r

Oberdörster, G., Oberdörster, E., & Oberdörster, J. (2005). Nanotoxicology: An Emerging Discipline Evolving from Studies of Ultrafine Particles. *Environmental Health Perspectives*, *13*(7), 823–839. doi:10.1289/ehp.7339

Odibat, Z., & Momani, S. (2007). A reliable treatment of homotopy- perturbation method for Klein-Gordon equations. *Physics Letters. [Part A]*, *365*, 351–357. doi:10.1016/j.physleta.2007.01.064

Ojha, P. K., & Roy, K. (2010). Chemometric modelling of antimalarial activity of aryltriazolylhydroxamates. *Molecular Simulation*, *36*, 939–952. doi:10.1080/08927022.2010.492835

Olivares, I., Menendez-Arias, L., Rodriguez-Bernabe, A., Martín, M. J., Dopazo, J., & Lopez-Galindez, C. (1995). Sequence-analysis of HIV-1 vif gene in Spanish isolates. *Virus Genes*, *9*, 283–288. doi:10.1007/BF01702884

Oloff, S., Mailman, R. B., & Tropsha, A. (2005). Application of validated QSAR models of D1 dopaminergic antagonists for database mining. *Journal of Medicinal Chemistry*, *48*(23), 7322–7332. doi:10.1021/jm049116m

Omata, K., Umegaki, T., Watanabe, Y., & Yamada, M. (2003). [New York: Elsevier Sci. B.V.]. *Studies in Surface Science and Catalysis*, 291–294. doi:10.1016/S0167-2991(03)80217-3

Organization for Economic Co-operation and Development (2007). *OECD Science*, Technology and Industry Scoreboard 2007.

Organization for Economic Co-operation and Development (2010). *Main Science and Technology Indicators (MSTI): 2010/1 edition.*

Ormsby, J. L., & King, B. T. (2004). Clar valence bond representation of π-bonding in carbon nanotubes. *The Journal of Organic Chemistry*, *69*, 4287–4291. doi:10.1021/jo035589+

Otu, H. H., & Sayood, K. (2003). A new sequence distance measure for phylogenetic tree construction. *Bioinformatics (Oxford, England)*, *19*, 2122–2130. doi:10.1093/bioinformatics/btg295

Ouzounis, C. A., & Valencia, A. (2003). Early bioinformatics: The birth of a discipline–A personal view. *Bioinformatics (Oxford, England)*, *19*, 2176–2190. doi:10.1093/bioinformatics/btg309

Ovchinnikov, I. V., Götherström, A., Romanova, G. P., Kharitonov, V. M., Lidén, K., & Goodwin, W. (2000). Molecular analysis of Neanderthal DNA from the Northern Caucasus. *Nature*, *404*, 490–493. doi:10.1038/35006625

Overton, E. (1897). Osmotic Properties of Cells in the Bearing on Toxicology and Pharmacy. *Zeitschrift für Physikalische Chemie*, *22*, 189–209.

Ozis, T., & Yildirim, A. (2007). A comparative study of He's homotopy- perturbation method for determining frequency-amplitude relation of a nonlinear oscillator with discontinuities. *Int. J. Nonlinear Sci. Numer. Simulation*, *8*(2), 243–248. doi:10.1515/IJNSNS.2007.8.2.243

Padmanabhan, J., Parthasarathi, R., Subramanian, V., & Chattaraj, P. K. (2006). Group philicity and electrophilicity as possible descriptors for modeling ecotoxicity applied to chlorophenols. *Chemical Research in Toxicology*, *19*, 356–364. doi:10.1021/tx050322m

Paez, L. R., & Matoušek, J. (2004). Properties of sol-gel TiO_2 layers on glass substrate. *Ceramics-Silikáty*, *48*(2), 66–71.

Painter, G. R., Andrews, C. W., & Furman, P. A. (2000). Conformation and local environment of nucleotides bound to HIV type 1 reverse transcriptase (HIV-1 RT) in the ground state. *Nucleosides, Nucleotides & Nucleic Acids*, *19*, 13–29. doi:10.1080/15257770008032994

Pal, D. K., Purkayastha, S. K., Sengupta, C., & De, A. U. (1992). Quantitative structure–property relationships with TAU indices: part I – research octane numbers of alkane fuel molecules. *Indian Journal of Chemistry*, *31B*, 109–114.

Pal, D. K., Sengupta, C., & De, A. U. (1988). A new topochemical descriptor (TAU) in molecular connectivity concept: part I – aliphatic compounds. *Indian Journal of Chemistry*, *27B*, 734–739.

Pal, D. K., Sengupta, C., & De, A. U. (1989). Introduction of a novel topochemical index and exploitation of group connectivity concept to achieve predictability in QSAR and RDD. *Indian Journal of Chemistry*, *28B*, 261–267.

Pal, D. K., Sengupta, M., Sengupta, C., & De, A. U. (1990). QSAR with TAU (τ) indices: part I – polymethylene primary diamines as amebicidal agents. *Indian Journal of Chemistry*, *29B*, 451–454.

Palacios, J. (2005). Phenotypic characterization of BRCA1 and BRCA2 tumors based in a tissue microarray study with 37 immunohistochemical markers. *Breast Cancer Research and Treatment*, *90*, 5–14. doi:10.1007/s10549-004-1536-0

Pandolfini, C., & Bonati, M. (2005). A literature review on off-label drug use in children. *European Journal of Pediatrics*, *164*(9), 552–558. doi:10.1007/s00431-005-1698-8

Parker, G. R. (1978). Correlation of log P with molecular connectivity in hydroxyureas: Influence of conformational system on log P. *Journal of Pharmaceutical Sciences*, *67*(4), 513–516. doi:10.1002/jps.2600670419

Parr, R. G., Donnelly, R. A., Levy, M., & Palke, W. E. (1978). Electronegativity: the density functional viewpoint. *The Journal of Chemical Physics, 68*, 3801–3807. doi:10.1063/1.436185

Parr, R. G., & Pearson, R. G. (1983). Absolute hardness: companion parameter to absolute electronegativity. *Journal of the American Chemical Society, 105*, 7512–7516. doi:10.1021/ja00364a005

Parr, R. G., & Yang, W. (1989). *Density Functional Theory of Atoms and Molecules*. Oxford, UK: Oxford University Press.

Parr, C. S., Lee, B., Campbell, D., & Bederson, B. B. (2004). Visualizations for taxonomic and phylogenetic trees. *Bioinformatics (Oxford, England), 20*, 2997–3004. doi:10.1093/bioinformatics/bth345

Parr, R. G., Szentpály, L. V., & Liu, S. (1999). Electrophilicity index. *Journal of the American Chemical Society, 121*(9), 1922–1924. doi:10.1021/ja983494x

Parr, R. G., & Yang, W. (1989). *Density functional theory of atoms and molecules*. New York: Oxford University Press.

Parthasarathi, R., Padmanabhan, J., Elango, M., Subramanian, V., & Chattaraj, P. K. (2004). Intermolecular reactivity through the generalized philicity concept. *Chemical Physics Letters, 394*, 225–230. doi:10.1016/j.cplett.2004.07.002

Parthasarathi, R., Padmanabhan, J., Subramanian, V., Maiti, B., & Chattaraj, P. K. (2003). Chemical reactivity profiles of two selected polychlorinated biphenyls. *The Journal of Physical Chemistry A, 107*, 10346–10352. doi:10.1021/jp035620b

Parthasarathi, R., Padmanabhan, J., Subramanian, V., Sarkar, U., Maiti, B., & Chattaraj, P. K. (2003). Toxicity analysis of benzidine through chemical reactivity and selectivity profiles: A DFT approach. *Internet Electron J. Mol. Des., 2*, 798–813.

Parthasarathi, R., Subramanian, V., Roy, D. R., & Chattaraj, P. K. (2004). Electrophilicity index as a possible descriptor of biological activity. *Bioorganic & Medicinal Chemistry, 12*, 5533–5543. doi:10.1016/j.bmc.2004.08.013

Paul, J. S., Janssens, R., Joeri, J. F. M., Baron, G. V., & Jacobs, P. A. (2005). [ACS.]. *Journal of Combinatorial Chemistry, 7*(3), 407–413. doi:10.1021/cc0500046

Pauling, L. (1946). Molecular architecture and biological reactions. *Chemical and Engineering News, 24*, 1375–1377. doi:10.1021/cen-v024n010.p1375

Pearlman, D. A. (2005). ... *Journal of Medicinal Chemistry, 48*(24), 7796–7807. doi:10.1021/jm050306m

Pearson, R. G. (1997). *Chemical hardness: Applications from molecules to Solids*. Weinheim, Germany: Wiley-VCH.

Pelto, L., Isolauri, E., Lilius, E. M., Nuutila, J., & Salminen, S. (1998). Probiotic bacteria down-regulate the milk-induced inflammatory response in milk-hypersensitive subjects but have an immunostimulatory effect in healthy subjects. *Clinical and Experimental Allergy, 28*, 1474–1479. doi:10.1046/j.1365-2222.1998.00449.x

Penrose, R. (1955). A Generalized inverse for matrices. *Proceedings of the Cambridge Philosophical Society, 51*, 406–413. doi:10.1017/S0305004100030401

Perdigon, G., Rachid, M., de Budeguer, M. V., & Valdez, J. C. (1994). Effect of yogurt feeding on the small and large intestine associated lymphoid cells in mice. *The Journal of Dairy Research, 61*, 553–562. doi:10.1017/S002202990002848X

Perdih, A., Bren, U., & Solemajer, T. (2009). ... *Journal of Molecular Modeling, 15*, 983–996. doi:10.1007/s00894-009-0455-8

Pereira, D. A., & Williams, J. A. (2007). Origin and evolution of high throughput screening. *British Journal of Pharmacology, 152*(1), 53–61. doi:10.1038/sj.bjp.0707373

Perera, V. P. S., Jayaweera, P. V. V., Pitigala, P. K. D. D. P., Bandaranayake, P. K. M., Hastings, G., & Perera, A. G. U. (2004). Construction of a photovoltaic device by deposition of thin films of the conducting polymer polythiocyanogen. *Synthetic Metals, 143*, 283–287. doi:10.1016/j.synthmet.2003.12.018

Perola, E., Walters, W. P., & Charifson, P. S. (2004)... *Proteins, 56*, 235–249. doi:10.1002/prot.20088

Pescarmona, P. P., Rops, J. J. T., van der Waal, J. C., Jansen, J. C., & Maschmeyer, T. (2002)... *J. Mol. Chem. A, 182-183*, 319–325. doi:10.1016/S1381-1169(01)00494-0

Peterangelo, S. C., & Seybold, P. G. (2004). Synergistic Interactions among QSAR Descriptors. *International Journal of Quantum Chemistry*, *96*, 1–9. doi:10.1002/qua.10591

Petrova, T., Rasulev, B. F., Toropov, A. A., Leszczynska, D., & Leszczynski, J. (2011). Improved Model for Fullerene C_{60} Solubility in Organic Solvents Based on Quantum-Chemical and Topological Descriptors. *Journal of Nanoparticle Research*, *2011*. doi:.doi:10.1007/s11051-011-0238-x

Piatetsky-Shapiro, G., & Frawley, W. (1991). *Knowledge discovery in databases*. Menlo Park, CA: AAAI/MIT Press.

Pickar, D., Vinik, J., & Bartko, J. J. (2008). Pharmacotherapy of schizophrenic patients: preponderance of off-label drug use. *PLoS ONE*, *3*(9), e3150. doi:10.1371/journal.pone.0003150

Pisanski, T., & Shawe-Taylor, J. (2000). Characterizing graph drawing with eigen vectors. *Journal of Chemical Information and Computer Sciences*, *40*(3), 567–571. doi:10.1021/ci9900938

Pitkethly, M. J. (2004). Nanomaterials – the driving force. *Materials Today*, *7*(12), 20–29. doi:10.1016/S1369-7021(04)00627-3

Platt, J. R. (1947). Influence of Neighbor Bonds on Additive Bond Properties in Paraffins. *The Journal of Chemical Physics*, *15*(6), 419–420. doi:10.1063/1.1746554

Poelman, D., & Frederic, S. P. (2003). Methods for the determination of the optical constants of thin films from single transmission measurements. *Journal of Physics. D, Applied Physics*, *36*, 1850–1857. doi:10.1088/0022-3727/36/15/316

Pogliani, L. (1992). Molecular Connectivity Model for Determination of Isoelectric Point of Amino Acids. *Journal of Pharmaceutical Sciences*, *81*, 334–336. doi:10.1002/jps.2600810407

Pogliani, L. (2000). From Molecular Connectivity Indices to Molecular Connectivity Terms. Recent Trends in Graph Theoretical Descriptors. *Chemical Reviews*, *100*, 3827–3858. doi:10.1021/cr0004456

Pogliani, L. (2002). Topics in Molecular Modeling: Dual Indices, Quality of Modeling and Missing Information, Truncation. *THEOCHEM*, *581*, 87–109. doi:10.1016/S0166-1280(01)00746-1

Pogliani, L. (2004). Encoding the Core Electrons with Graph Concepts. *Journal of Chemical Information and Computer Sciences*, *44*, 42–49. doi:10.1021/ci0341262

Pogliani, L. (2005). A Natural Graph-Theoretical Model for the Partition and Kinetic Coefficients. *New Journal of Chemistry*, *29*, 1082–1088. doi:10.1039/b506091p

Pogliani, L. (2005). Model of Physical Properties of Halides with Complete Graph based Indices. *International Journal of Quantum Chemistry*, *102*, 38–52. doi:10.1002/qua.20295

Pogliani, L. (2006). The Hydrogen Perturbation in Molecular Connectivity Computations. *Journal of Computational Chemistry*, *27*, 869–882. doi:10.1002/jcc.20375

Pogliani, L. (2007). Implementing the Molecular connectivity theory, a Basic Tool in Modeling Drugs. *Journal of Pharmaceutical Sciences*, *96*, 1856–1871. doi:10.1002/jps.20862

Pogliani, L. (2008). Graphs and Thermodynamics. *Journal of Mathematical Chemistry*, *46*, 15–23. doi:10.1007/s10910-008-9452-x

Pogliani, L. (2010). Model of Twelve Properties of a Set of Organic Solvents with Graph-Theoretical and/or Experimental Parameters. *Journal of Computational Chemistry*, *31*, 295–307.

Pogliani, L., & de Julian-Ortiz, J. V. (2004). Plot Methods in Quantitative Structure-Property Studies. *Chemical Physics Letters*, *393*, 327–330. doi:10.1016/j.cplett.2004.06.066

Pogliani, L., & de Julián-Ortiz, J. V. (2005). Residual plots and the quality of a model. *MATCH Communications in Mathematical and Computer Chemistry*, *53*, 175–180.

Pogliani, L. (2010). Novel Molecular Connectivity Indices: Pseudoconnectivity, Dual, *cis-trans* Indices and Indices based on a New Valence Delta. In Gutman, I., & Furtula, B. (Eds.), *Novel Molecular Structure Descriptors - Theory and Applications I, MCM 8* (pp. 39–72). Kragujevac: University of Kragujevac Press.

Pogliani, L. (2010/2011). Two QSPR Methodologies, The Random, and The Super-Descriptors, *MATCH Communications in Mathematical and Computer Chemistry*, in print.

Pogliani, L. (2011). The E and S Thermodynamic Directed Graphs. *International Journal of Chemical Modeling* (special issue for Eduardo Castro's anniversary), in print.

Politzer, P., & Truhlar, D. G. (Eds.). (1981). *Chemical applications of atomic and molecular electrostatic potentials*. New York: Plenum Press.

Pomoni, K., Vomvas, A., & Trapalis, C. (2005). Transient photoconductivity of nanocrystalline TiO_2 sol-gel thin films. *Thin Solid Films*, *479*, 160–165. doi:10.1016/j.tsf.2004.12.005

Ponce, M. A., Parra, R., Savu, R., Joanni, E., Bueno, P. R., & Cilense, M. (2009). Impedance spectroscopy analysis of TiO_2 thin film gas sensors obtained from water-based anatase colloids. *Sensors and Actuators. B, Chemical*, *139*, 447–452. doi:10.1016/j.snb.2009.03.066

Poppi, R. J., & Massart, D. L. (1998). The optimal brain surgeon for pruning neural network architecture applied to multivariate calibration. *Analytica Chimica Acta*, *375*, 187–195. doi:10.1016/S0003-2670(98)00462-0

Porto, L. C., Souza, E. S., Da Silva, J. B., Yunes, R. A., & Heinzen, V. E. F. (2008). Semi-empirical topological index: Development of QSPR/QSRR and optimization for alkylbenzenes. *Talanta*, *76*, 407–412. doi:10.1016/j.talanta.2008.03.023

Pourmand, M., & Taghavinia, N. (2008). TiO_2 nanostructured films on mica using liquid phase deposition. *Materials Chemistry and Physics*, *107*, 449–455. doi:10.1016/j.matchemphys.2007.08.011

Powers, K. W., Palazuelos, M., Moudgil, B. M., & Roberts, S. M. (2007). Characterization of the size, shape, and state of dispersion of nanoparticles for toxicological studies. *Nanotoxicology*, *1*(1), 42–51. doi:10.1080/17435390701314902

Prabhakar, Y. S., & Gupta, M. K. (2008). Chemical Structure Indices in *In Silico* Molecular Design. *Scientia Pharmaceutica*, *76*, 101–132. doi:10.3797/scipharm.0804-12

Prado-Prado, F. J., González-Díaz, H., de la Vega, O. M., Ubeira, F. M., & Chou, K. C. (2008). Unified QSAR approach to antimicrobials. Part 3: first multi-tasking QSAR model for input-coded prediction, structural back-projection, and complex networks clustering of antiprotozoal compounds. *Bioorganic & Medicinal Chemistry*, *16*(11), 5871–5880. doi:10.1016/j.bmc.2008.04.068

Prieto, J. J., Talevi, A., & Bruno-Blanch, L. E. (2006). Application of linear discriminant analysis in the virtual screening of trypanothione reductase inhibitors and redox cycling agents. *Molecular Diversity*, *10*(3), 361–375. doi:10.1007/s11030-006-9044-2

Prüfer, K., Stenzel, U., Hofreiter, M., Pääbo, S,. Kelso, J., Green, R.E. (2010). Computational challenges in the analysis of ancient DNA. *Genome Biol*, 11,R47-1–15.

Pucher, P., Benmami, M., Azouani, R., Krammer, G., Chhor, K., & Bocquet, J. F. (2007). Nano-TiO_2 sols immobilized on porous silica as new efficient photocatalyst. *Applied Catalysis A, General*, *332*, 297–303. doi:10.1016/j.apcata.2007.08.031

Puri, P., Rattan, A., Bijlani, R. L., Mahapatra, S. C., & Nath, I. (1996). Splenic and intestinal lymphocyte proliferation response in mice fed milk or yogurt and challenged with *Salmonella typhimurium*. *International Journal of Food Sciences and Nutrition*, *47*, 391–398. doi:10.3109/09637489609006952

Putz, M. V. (2011). On reducible character of Haldane-Radić enzyme kinetics to conventional and logistic michaelis-menten models. *Molecules (Basel, Switzerland)*, *16*, 3128–3145. doi:10.3390/molecules16043128

Putz, M. V., & Lacrămă, A.-M. (2007). Enzymatic control of the bio-inspired nanomaterials at the spectroscopic level. *Journal of Optoelectronics and Advanced Materials*, *9*, 2529–2534.

Putz, M. V., Lacrămă, A.-M., & Ostafe, V. (2006). Full analytic progress curves of the enzymic reactions in vitro. *International Journal of Molecular Sciences*, *7*, 469–484. doi:10.3390/i7110469

Putz, M. V., Lacrămă, A.-M., & Ostafe, V. (2007). Introducing logistic enzyme kinetics. *Journal of Optoelectronics and Advanced Materials*, *9*, 2910–2916.

Puzyn, T., Leszczynska, D., & Leszczynski, J. (2009). Toward the Development of "Nano-QSARs": Advances and Challenges. *Small*, *5*, 2494–2509. doi:10.1002/smll.200900179

Puzyn, T., Rasulev, B., Gajewicz, A., Hu, X., Dasari, T. P., & Michalkova, A. (2011). Using Nano-QSAR to predict the cytotoxicity of metal oxide nanoparticles. *Nature Nanotechnology*, *6*, 175–178. doi:10.1038/nnano.2011.10

Puzyn, T., Leszczynski, J., & Cronin, M. T. (2009). *Recent Advances in QSAR Studies: Methods and Applications*. New York: Springer.

Puzyn, T., Gajewicz, A., Leszczynska, D., & Leszczynski, J. (2010). Nanomaterials - the Next Great Challenge for QSAR Modelers. In Puzyn, T., Leszczynski, J., & Cronin, M. T. (Eds.), *Recent Advances in QSAR Studies: Methods and Applications. New York*. London, New York: Springer. doi:10.1007/978-1-4020-9783-6_14

Quinones-Mateu, M., Holguin, A., Dopazo, J., Najera, I., & Domingo, E. (1996). Point mutant frequencies in the pol gene of human-immunodeficiency-virus type-1 are 2-fold to 3-fold lower than those of env. *AIDS Research and Human Retroviruses*, *12*, 1117–1128. doi:10.1089/aid.1996.12.1117

Quinones-Mateu, M. E., Dopazo, J., Este, J. A., Rota, T. R., & Domingo, E. (1995). Molecular characterization of human-immunodeficiency-virus type-1 isolates from Venezuela. *AIDS Research and Human Retroviruses*, *11*, 605–616. doi:10.1089/aid.1995.11.605

Ramakrishnany, N., Bailey-Kellogg, C., Tadepalliy, S., & Pandeyy, V. N. (2005). *SIAM Int. Conf. on Data Mining, SDM 2005*. Newport Beach, CA, USA.

Rammal, R., Toulouse, G., & Virasoro, M. A. (1986). Ultrametricity for physicists. *Reviews of Modern Physics*, *58*, 765–788. doi:10.1103/RevModPhys.58.765

Ramos de Armas, R., González-Díaz, H., Molina, R., Pérez-Gonzalez, M., & Uriarte, E. (2004a). Stochastic-based descriptors studying peptides biological properties: Modeling the bitter tasting threshold of dipeptides. *Bioorganic & Medicinal Chemistry*, *12*, 4815–4822. doi:10.1016/j.bmc.2004.07.017

Ramos de Armas, R., González-Díaz, H., Molina, R., & Uriarte, E. (2004b). Markovian Backbone Negentropies: Molecular descriptors for protein research. I. Predicting protein stability in Arc repressor mutants. *Proteins*, *56*, 715–723. doi:10.1002/prot.20159

Ramsden, J. J. (2005). What is nanotechnology? *Nanotechnology Perceptions*, *1*, 3–17.

Randic, M., & Balaban, A. T. (2003). On a four-dimensional representation of DNA primary sequences. *Journal of Chemical Information and Computer Sciences*, *43*, 532–539. doi:10.1021/ci020051a

Randic, M., Guo, X., & Basak, S. C. (2001). On the characterization of DNA primary sequences by triplet of nucleic acid bases. *Journal of Chemical Information and Computer Sciences*, *41*, 619–626. doi:10.1021/ci000120q

Randic, M., Lers, N., Plavsic, D., Basak, S., & Balaban, A. T. (2005). Four-color map representation of DNA or RNA sequences and their numerical characterization. *Chemical Physics Letters*, *407*, 205–208. doi:10.1016/j.cplett.2005.03.086

Randic, M., Vracko, M., Nandy, A., & Basak, S. C. (2000). On 3-D graphical representation of DNA primary sequences and their numerical characterization. *Journal of Chemical Information and Computer Sciences*, *40*, 1235–1244. doi:10.1021/ci000034q

Randic, M., Zupan, J., & Vikic-Topic, D. (2007). On representation of proteins by star-like graphs. *Journal of Molecular Graphics & Modelling*, *26*, 290–305. doi:10.1016/j.jmgm.2006.12.006

Randić, M. (1975). On characterization of molecular branching. *Journal of the American Chemical Society*, *97*, 6609–6615. doi:10.1021/ja00856a001

Randić, M. (1991). Resolution of ambiguities in Structure-Property studies by use of orthogonal descriptors. *Journal of Chemical Information and Computer Sciences*, *31*, 311–320. doi:10.1021/ci00002a018

Randić, M. (1991). Orthogonal molecular descriptors. *New Journal of Chemistry*, *15*, 517–525.

Randić, M. (2003). Aromaticity of polyciclic conjugated hydrocarbons. *Chemical Reviews*, *103*, 3449–3605. doi:10.1021/cr9903656

Randić, M., & Basak, S. C. (2001). On use of the variable connectivity index $^1\chi^f$ in QSAR: toxicity of aliphatic ethers. *Journal of Chemical Information and Computer Sciences, 41*, 614–618. doi:10.1021/ci000114u

Randić, M., & Trinajstić, N. (1994). Notes on some less known early contributions to chemical graph theory. *Croatica Chemica Acta, 67*, 1–35.

Randić, M. (1975). On characterization of molecular branching. *Journal of the American Chemical Society, 97*(23), 6609–6615.

Randić, M. (1997). Linear combinations of path numbers as molecular descriptors. *New Journal of Chemistry, 21*(9), 945–951.

Randić, M., Guo, X., Oxley, T., & Krishnapriyan, H. (1993). Wiener matrix: source of novel graph invariants. *Journal of Chemical Information and Computer Science, 33*(5), 709–716.

Randić, M., Jerman-Blazic, B., & Trinajstić, N. (1990). Development of 3-dimensional molecular descriptors. *Computers & Chemistry, 14*(3), 237–246.

Rangelov, M. A., Vayssilov, G. N., Yomtova, V. M., & Petkov, D. D. (2005). Theoretical study of the o-OH participation in catechol ester ammonolysis. *Organic & Biomolecular Chemistry, 3*(5), 737–744. doi:10.1039/b417285j

Rarey, M., Kramer, B., & Lengauer, T. (1997)... *Journal of Computer-Aided Molecular Design, 11*, 369–384. doi:10.1023/A:1007913026166

Rarey, M., Kramer, B., Lengauer, T., & Klebe, G. (1996)... *Journal of Molecular Biology, 261*, 470–489. doi:10.1006/jmbi.1996.0477

Rasmussen, E. (2008). Government instruments to support the commercialization of university research: Lessons from Canada. *Technovation, 28*(8), 506–517. doi:10.1016/j.technovation.2007.12.002

Rasulev, B. F., Kušic, H., Lesczynska, D., Leszczynski, J., & Koprivanac, N. (2010). QSAR modeling of acute toxicity on mammals for aromatic compounds: the case study using oral LD_{50} for rats. *Journal of Environmental Monitoring, 12*(5), 1037–1044. doi:10.1039/b919489d

Rasulev, B. F., Saidkhodzhaev, A. I., Nazrullaev, S. S., Akhmedkhodzhaeva, K. S., Khushbaktova, Z. A., & Leszczynski, J. (2007). Molecular modeling and QSAR analysis of the estrogenic activity of terpenoids isolated from Ferula plants. *SAR and QSAR in Environmental Research, 18*(7-8), 663–673. doi:10.1080/10629360701428631

Raymer, J., Wiesler, D., & Novotny, M. (1985). Structure-retention studies of model ketones by capillary gas chromatography. *Journal of Chromatography. A, 325*(C), 13–22. doi:10.1016/S0021-9673(00)96003-5

Reed, A. E., Curtiss, L. A., & Weinhold, F. (1988). Intermolecular interaction from a natural bond orbital, donor–acceptor viewpoint. *Chemical Reviews, 88*(6), 899–926. doi:10.1021/cr00088a005

Reid, A. H., & Taubenberger, J. K. (2003). The origin of the 1918 pandemic influenza virus: A continuing enigma. *The Journal of General Virology, 84*, 2285–2292. doi:10.1099/vir.0.19302-0

Reinhardt, C. (2006). *Shifting and Rearranging: Physical Methods and the Transformation of Modern Chemistry.* Sagamore Beach, MA: Science History Publications.

Ren, B. (2003a). Atom-level-based AI topological descriptors for structure–property correlations. *Journal of Chemical Information and Computer Sciences, 43*(1), 161–169. doi:10.1021/ci020382n

Ren, B. (2003b). Atom-Type-Based AI Topological Descriptors: Application of structure–boiling point correlations of oxo organic compounds. *Journal of Chemical Information and Computer Sciences, 43*(4), 1121–1131. doi:10.1021/ci025651o

Rescigno, A. (1956). A contribution to the theory of tracer methods. II. *Biochimica et Biophysica Acta, 21*, 111–116. doi:10.1016/0006-3002(56)90100-7

Rescigno, A. (1999). Compartmental analysis revisited. *Pharmacological Research, 39*, 471–478. doi:10.1006/phrs.1999.0467

Rescigno, A. (2004). On the use of pharmacokinetic models. *Physics in Medicine and Biology, 49*, 4657–4676. doi:10.1088/0031-9155/49/19/014

Rescigno, A., & Thakur, S. (1991). *New trends in pharmacokinetics* (*Vol. 221*). New York: Plenum Press.

Reumers, J. (2008). Joint annotation of coding and non-coding single nucleotide polymorphisms and mutations in the 5 SNPeffect and PupaSuite databases. *Nucleic Acids Research, 36*, D825–D829. doi:10.1093/nar/gkm979

Ribo, J. M., & Kaiser, J. L. E. (1983). Effects of selected chemicals to photoluminescent bacteria and their correlations with acute and sublethal effects on other organisms. *Chemosphere, 12*, 1421–1442. doi:10.1016/0045-6535(83)90073-5

Richards, A. J., & Kier, L. B. (1980). Structure activity analysis of hydrazide monoamine oxidase inhibitor using molecular connectivity. *Journal of Pharmaceutical Sciences, 69*(1), 124–126. doi:10.1002/jps.2600690143

Rico, D., Vaquerizas, J.M., Dopazo, H., Boscá, L. (2007). Identification of conserved domains in the promoter regions of nitric oxide synthase 2: Implications for the species-specific transcription and evolutionary differences. *BMC Genomics, 8*, 271-1–10.

Rigby, P. W. J., Burleigh, B. D., & Hartley, B. S. (1974). Gene duplication in experimental enzyme evolution. *Nature, 251*, 200–204. doi:10.1038/251200a0

Ringe, D., & Petsko, G. A. (1999). Quantum enzymology: Tunnel vision. *Nature, 399*, 417–418. doi:10.1038/20819

Rivera-Borroto, O. M. (2009). Discovery of novel trichomonacidals using LDA-driven QSAR models and bond-based bilinear indices as molecular descriptors. *QSAR & Combinatorial Science, 28*, 9–26. doi:10.1002/qsar.200610165

Rizzo, R. C., Toba, S., & Kuntz, I. D. (2004)... *Journal of Medicinal Chemistry, 47*, 3065–3074. doi:10.1021/jm030570k

Roberts, J. D., & Moreland, W. T. Jr. (1953). Electrical Effects of Substituent Groups in Saturated Systems. Reactivities of 4-Substituted Bicyclo-[2.2.2]-Octane-1-Carboxylic Acids. *Journal of the American Chemical Society, 75*(9), 2167–2173. doi:10.1021/ja01105a045

Roberts, E., Eargle,J., Wright, D., Luthey-Schulten, Z. (2006). MultiSeq: Unifying sequence and structure data for evolutonary analysis. *BMC Bioinformatics, 7*, 382-1–11.

Rodemerck, U., Baerns, M., Holena, M., & Wolf, D. (2004)... *Applied Surface Science, 223*, 168. doi:10.1016/S0169-4332(03)00919-X

Rodrigo, M. J., & Dopazo, J. (1995). Evolutionary analysis of the picornavirus family. *Journal of Molecular Evolution, 40*, 362–371. doi:10.1007/BF00164022

Rodríguez-Perales, S. (2004). Cloning of a new familial t(3;8) translocation associated with conventional renal cell carcinoma reveals a 5 kb microdeletion and no gene involved in the rearrangement. *Human Molecular Genetics, 13*, 983–990. doi:10.1093/hmg/ddh111

Rogers, D., & Hopfinger, A. J. (1994). Application of genetic function approximation to quantitative structure–activity relationships and quantitative structure–property relationships. *Journal of Chemical Information and Computer Sciences, 34*(4), 854–866. doi:10.1021/ci00020a020

Rojas, J. M., Dopazo, J., Santana, M., Lopez-Galindez, C., & Tabares, E. (1995). Comparative-study of the genetic-variability in thymidine kinase and glycoprotein-B genes of herpes-simplex viruses by the RNase-A mismatch cleavage method. *Virus Research, 35*, 205–214. doi:10.1016/0168-1702(94)00097-V

Root, M. J., Kay, M. S., & Kim, P. S. (2001). Protein design of an HIV-1 entry inhibitor. *Science, 291*, 884–888. doi:10.1126/science.1057453

Ross, G., Loverix, S., De Proft, F., Wyns, L., & Geerlings, P. (2003). A computational and conceptual DFT study of the reactivity of anionic compounds: implications for enzymatic catalysis. *The Journal of Physical Chemistry A, 107*, 6828–6836. doi:10.1021/jp034376l

Ross, J., Schreiber, I., & Vlad, M. O. (2006). *Determination of Complex Reaction Mechanisms: Analysis of Chemical, Biological and Genetic Networks*. Oxford, UK: Oxford University Press.

Rotello, V. M. (2004). *Nanoparticles: Building Blocks for Nanotechnology* (Lockwood, D. J., Ed.). New York: Springer.

Roy, D. R., Giri, S., & Chattaraj, P. K. (2009). Arsenic toxicity: an atom counting and electrophilicity-based protocol. *Molecular Diversity, 13*, 551. doi:10.1007/s11030-009-9133-0

Roy, D. R., Pal, N., Mitra, A., Bultinck, P., Parthasarathi, R., Subramanian, V., & Chattaraj, P. K. (2007). An atom counting strategy towards analyzing the biological activity of sex hormones. *European Journal of Medicinal Chemistry, 42*, 1365–1369. doi:10.1016/j.ejmech.2007.01.028

Roy, D. R., Parthasarathi, R., Maiti, B., Subramanian, V., & Chattaraj, P. K. (2005). Electrophilicity as a possible descriptor of toxicity prediction. *Bioorganic & Medicinal Chemistry*, *13*, 3405–3412. doi:10.1016/j.bmc.2005.03.011

Roy, D. R., Parthasarathi, R., Subramanian, V., & Chattaraj, P. K. (2006). An electrophilicity based analysis of toxicity of aromatic compounds towards Tetrahymena Pyriformis. *QSAR & Combinatorial Science*, *25*, 114–122. doi:10.1002/qsar.200530146

Roy, D. R., Sarkar, U., Chattaraj, P. K., Mitra, A., Padmanabhan, J., & Parthasarathi, R. (2006). Analyzing toxicity through electrophilicity. *Molecular Diversity*, *10*, 119–131. doi:10.1007/s11030-005-9009-x

Roy, K., & Leonard, J. T. (2004). QSAR modeling of HIV-1 reverse transcriptase inhibitor 2-amino-6-arylsulfonylbenzonitriles and congeners using molecular connectivity and E-state parameters. *Bioorganic & Medicinal Chemistry*, *12*, 745–754. doi:10.1016/j.bmc.2003.11.009

Roy, K., & Leonard, J. T. (2005). Classical QSAR modeling of anti-HIV 2,3-diaryl-1,3-thiazolidin-4-ones. *QSAR & Combinatorial Science*, *24*, 579–592. doi:10.1002/qsar.200430901

Roy, K., & Leonard, J. T. (2005). QSAR by LFER model of cytotoxicity data of anti-HIV 5-phenyl-1-phenylamino-1*H*-imidazole derivatives using principal component analysis and genetic function approximation. *Bioorganic & Medicinal Chemistry*, *13*, 2967–2973. doi:10.1016/j.bmc.2005.02.003

Roy, K., & Leonard, J. T. (2005). QSAR analyses of 3-(4-benzylpiperidin-1-yl)-*N*-phenyl-propylamine derivatives as potent CCR5 antagonists. *Journal of Chemical Information and Modeling*, *45*, 1352–1368. doi:10.1021/ci050205x

Roy, K., & Leonard, J. T. (2006). Topological QSAR modeling of cytotoxicity data of anti-HIV 5-phenyl-1-phenylamino-1*H*-imidazole derivatives using GFA, G/PLS, FA and PCRA techniques. *Indian J Chem Sect A*, *45*, 126–137.

Roy, K. (2004). Topological descriptors in drug design and modeling studies. *Molecular Diversity*, *8*(4), 321–323. doi:10.1023/B:MODI.0000047519.35591.b7

Roy, K., & Das, R. N. (2010). QSTR with extended topochemical atom (ETA) indices. 14. QSAR modeling of toxicity of aromatic aldehydes to *Tetrahymena pyriformis*. *Journal of Hazardous Materials*, *183*(1–3), 913–922. doi:10.1016/j.jhazmat.2010.07.116

Roy, K., & Ghosh, G. (2004a). QSTR with extended topochemical atom indices. 2. Fish toxicity of substituted benzenes. *Journal of Chemical Information and Computer Sciences*, *44*(2), 559–567. doi:10.1021/ci0342066

Roy, K., & Ghosh, G. (2004b). QSTR with extended topochemical atom indices. 3. Toxicity of nitrobenzenes to *Tetrahymena pyriformis*. *QSAR & Combinatorial Science*, *23*(2–3), 99–108. doi:10.1002/qsar.200330864

Roy, K., & Ghosh, G. (2004c). QSTR with extended topochemical atom indices. 4. Modeling of the acute toxicity of phenylsulfonyl carboxylates to *Vibrio fischeri* using principal component factor analysis and principal component regression analysis. *QSAR & Combinatorial Science*, *23*(7), 526–535. doi:10.1002/qsar.200430891

Roy, K., & Ghosh, G. (2005). QSTR with extended topochemical atom indices. Part 5. Modeling of the acute toxicity of phenylsulfonyl carboxylates to *Vibrio fischeri* using genetic function approximation. *Bioorganic & Medicinal Chemistry*, *13*(4), 1185–1194. doi:10.1016/j.bmc.2004.11.014

Roy, K., & Ghosh, G. (2006a). QSTR with extended topochemical atom (ETA) indices. VI. Acute toxicity of benzene derivatives to tadpoles (*Rana japonica*). *Journal of Molecular Modeling*, *12*(3), 306–316. doi:10.1007/s00894-005-0033-7

Roy, K., & Ghosh, G. (2006b). QSTR with extended topochemical atom (ETA) indices. 8. QSAR for the inhibition of substituted phenols on germination rate of *Cucumis sativus* using chemometric tools. *QSAR & Combinatorial Science*, *25*(10), 846–859. doi:10.1002/qsar.200510211

Roy, K., & Ghosh, G. (2007). QSTR with extended topochemical atom (ETA) indices. 9. Comparative QSAR for the toxicity of diverse functional organic compounds to *Chlorella vulgaris* using chemometric tools. *Chemosphere*, *70*(1), 1–12. doi:10.1016/j.chemosphere.2007.07.037

Roy, K., & Ghosh, G. (2008). QSTR with Extended Topochemical Atom Indices. 10. Modeling of Toxicity of Organic Chemicals to Humans Using Different Chemometric Tools. *Chemical Biology & Drug Design*, *72*(5), 383–394. doi:10.1111/j.1747-0285.2008.00712.x

Roy, K., & Ghosh, G. (2009a). QSTR with extended topochemical atom (ETA) indices. 11. Comparative QSAR of acute NSAID cytotoxicity in rat hepatocytes using chemometric Tools. *Molecular Simulation*, *35*(8), 648–659. doi:10.1080/08927020902744664

Roy, K., & Ghosh, G. (2009b). QSTR with extended topochemical atom (ETA) indices. 12. QSAR for the toxicity of diverse aromatic compounds to *Tetrahymena pyriformis* using chemometric tools. *Chemosphere*, *77*(7), 999–1009. doi:10.1016/j.chemosphere.2009.07.072

Roy, K., & Ghosh, G. (2009c). QSTR with extended topochemical atom (ETA) Indices. 13. Modeling of hERG K^+ channel blocking activity of diverse functional drugs using different chemometric tools. *Molecular Simulation*, *35*(15), 1256–1268. doi:10.1080/08927020903015379

Roy, K., & Ghosh, G. (2010). Exploring QSARs with Extended Topochemical Atom (ETA) Indices for Modeling Chemical and Drug Toxicity. *Current Pharmaceutical Design*, *16*(24), 2625–2639. doi:10.2174/138161210792389270

Roy, K., Pal, D. K., De, A. U., & Sengupta, C. (1999). Comparative QSAR with molecular negentropy molecular connectivity, STIMS and TAU indices: part I. Tadpole narcosis of diverse functional acyclic compounds. *Indian Journal of Chemistry*, *38B*(6), 664–671.

Roy, K., Pal, D. K., De, A. U., & Sengupta, C. (2001). Comparative QSAR studies with molecular negentropy, molecular connectivity, STIMS and TAU indices. Part II: general anaesthetic activity of aliphatic hydrocarbons, halocarbons and ethers. *Indian Journal of Chemistry*, *40B*(2), 129–135.

Roy, K., & Saha, A. (2003a). Comparative QSPR studies with molecular connectivity, molecular negentropy and TAU Indices. Part I: molecular thermochemical properties of diverse functional acyclic compounds. *Journal of Molecular Modeling*, *9*(4), 259–270. doi:10.1007/s00894-003-0135-z

Roy, K., & Saha, A. (2003b). Comparative QSPR studies with molecular connectivity, molecular negentropy and TAU indices. Part 2: lipid– water partition coefficient of diverse functional acyclic compounds. *Internet Electronic Journal of Molecular Design*, *2*(5), 288–305.

Roy, K., & Saha, A. (2003c). QSPR with TAU indices: water solubility of diverse functional acyclic compounds. *Internet Electronic Journal of Molecular Design*, *2*(7), 475–491.

Roy, K., & Saha, A. (2004). QSPR with TAU indices: boiling points of sulfides and thiols. *Indian Journal of Chemistry*, *43A*(7), 1369–1376.

Roy, K., & Saha, A. (2005). QSPR with TAU indices: molar refractivity of diverse functional acyclic compounds. *Indian Journal of Chemistry*, *44B*(8), 1693–1707.

Roy, K., & Saha, A. (2006). QSPR with TAU indices: Part 5. Liquid heat capacity of diverse functional organic compounds. *Journal of the Indian Chemical Society*, *83*(4), 351–355.

Roy, K., Saha, A., Chakroborty, S., & Ghosh, C. C. (2004). QSPR with TAU indices: molar thermochemical properties of diverse functional acyclic compounds. *Journal of the Indian Chemical Society*, *81*(2), 115–125.

Roy, K., & Sanyal, I. (2006). QSTR with extended topochemical atom indices. 7. QSAR of substituted benzenes to *Saccharomyces cerevisiae*. *QSAR & Combinatorial Science*, *25*(4), 359–371. doi:10.1002/qsar.200530172

Roy, K., Sanyal, I., & Ghosh, G. (2006a). QSPR of n-octanol/water partition coefficient of non-ionic organic compounds using extended topochemical atom (ETA) indices. *QSAR & Combinatorial Science*, *26*(5), 629–646. doi:10.1002/qsar.200610112

Roy, K., Sanyal, I., & Roy, P. P. (2006b). QSPR of the bioconcentration factors of non-ionic organic compounds in fish using extended topochemical atom (ETA) indices. *SAR and QSAR in Environmental Research*, *17*(6), 563–582. doi:10.1080/10629360601033499

Roy, K., & Das, R. N. (2011a). On some novel extended topochemical atom (ETA) parameters for effective encoding of chemical information and modeling of fundamental physicochemical properties. *SAR and QSAR in Environmental Research*, http://dx.doi.org/10.1080/1062936X.2011.569900.

Roy, K., & Das, R. N. (2011b, Unpublished results). QSTR with extended topochemical atom (ETA) indices. 15. Development of predictive models for toxicity of organic chemicals against fathead minnow. (communicated).

Roy, K., & Ghosh, G. (2003). Introduction of extended topochemical atom (ETA) Indices in the valence electron mobile (VEM) environment as tools for QSAR/QSPR studies. *Internet Electronic Journal of Molecular Design, 2*(9), 599–620, http://www.biochempress.com/.

Rubinow, S. I. (1975). *Introduction to Mathematical Biology*. New York: Wiley.

Ruiz-Llorente, S.MTC Clinical Group. (2007). Association study of 69 genes in the ret pathway identifies low penetrance loci in sporadic medullary thyroid carcinoma. *Cancer Research, 67*, 9561–9567. doi:10.1158/0008-5472.CAN-07-1638

Ruvolo, M., Disotell, T. R., Allard, M. W., Brown, W. M., & Honeycutt, R. L. (1991). Resolution of the African hominoid trichotomy by use of a mitochondrial gene sequence. *Proceedings of the National Academy of Sciences of the United States of America, 88*, 1570–1574. doi:10.1073/pnas.88.4.1570

Rzhetsky, A., Dopazo, J., Snyder, E., Dangler, C. A., & Ayala, F. J. (1996). Assessing Dissimilarity of genes by comparing their RNase-A mismatch cleavage patterns. *Genetics, 144*, 1975–1983.

Sabljic, A. (1984). Calculation of retention indices by molecular topology: chlorinated alkanes. *Journal of Chromatography. A, 314*(C), 1–12. doi:10.1016/S0021-9673(01)97719-2

Sabljic, A. (1985). Calculation of retention indices by molecular topology. Chlorinated benzenes. *Journal of Chromatography. A, 319*(C), 1–8. doi:10.1016/S0021-9673(01)90533-3

Sadlej-Sosnowska, N. (2007). Molecular similarity based on atomic electrostatic potential. *The Journal of Physical Chemistry A, 111*(43), 11134–11140. doi:10.1021/jp072748a

Sadlej-Sosnowska, N. (2007). Substituent active region – a gate for communication of substituent charge with the rest of a molecule: Monosubstituted benzenes. *Chemical Physics Letters, 447*(4-6), 192–196. doi:10.1016/j.cplett.2007.09.023

Sadlej-Sosnowska, N., & Murlowska, K. (2008). Similarity based on atomic electrostatic potential in heterocyclic molecules: Acidity of tetrazoles. *The Journal of Physical Chemistry A, 112*(40), 10017–10022. doi:10.1021/jp804100f

Saiz, J. C. (1998). The prognostic relevance of the nonstructural 5A gene interferon sensibility determining region is different in infections with genotype 1B and 3A isolates of hepatitis-C virus. *The Journal of Infectious Diseases, 177*, 839–847.

Saiz-Urra, L., González-Díaz, H., & Uriarte, E. (2005). Proteins Markovian 3D-QSAR with spherically-truncated average electrostatic potentials. *Bioorganic & Medicinal Chemistry, 13*, 3641–3647. doi:10.1016/j.bmc.2005.03.041

Sakka, S. (2005). *Handbook of sol-gel science and technology*. Boston: Kluwer Academic Publishers.

Sammut, C., & Cribb, J. (1990). *7th Int. Machine Learning Conf.* Austin, TX: Morgan Kaufmann.

Sánchez-Moyano, E., Seco, C., Santolaria, A., Fabra-Campos, S., Herráez, M., & Martín-Villodre, M. (1992). Partition behavior of anilines in bulk-phase and high-performance liquid chromatographic systems: Influence on correlation with biological constants. *Journal of Pharmaceutical Sciences, 81*, 720–725. doi:10.1002/jps.2600810727

Sanchez-Palomino, S., Dopazo, J., Olivares, I., Martín, M. J., & Lopez-Galindez, C. (1995). Primary genetic-characterization of HIV-1 isolates from WHO-sponsored vaccine evaluation sites by the RNase-A mismatch method. *Virus Research, 39*, 251–259. doi:10.1016/0168-1702(95)00096-8

Sankar, S., & Gopchandran, K. G. (2009). Effect of annealing on the structural, electrical and optical properties of nanostructured TiO_2 thin films. *Crystal Research and Technology, 44*(9), 989–994. doi:10.1002/crat.200900073

Santoyo, J., Vaquerizas, J. M., & Dopazo, J. (2005). Highly specific and accurate selection of siRNAs for high-throughput functional assays. *Bioinformatics (Oxford, England), 21*, 1376–1382. doi:10.1093/bioinformatics/bti196

Sarich, V. M., & Wilson, A. C. (1967). Immunological time scale for hominid evolution. *Science, 158,* 1200–1203. doi:10.1126/science.158.3805.1200

Sasani Ghamsari, M., & Bahramian, A. R. (2008). High transparent sol-gel derived nanostructured TiO_2 thin film. *Materials Letters, 62,* 361–364. doi:10.1016/j.matlet.2007.05.053

Sayle, R. A., & Milner-White, E. J. (1995). RASMOL: Biomolecular graphics for all. *Trends in Biochemical Sciences, 20,* 374–376. doi:10.1016/S0968-0004(00)89080-5

Schein, A. I., Sandler, S. T., & Ungar, L. H. (2004). *Univ. of Pennsylvania, Dpt. of Comp. & Information Sci. Tech.* Report No. MS-CIS-04-08.

Schiffrin, E. J., Rochat, F., Link-Amster, H., Aeschlimann, J. M., & Donnet-Hughes, A. (1995). Immunomodulation of human blood cells following the ingestion of lactic acid bacteria. *Journal of Dairy Science, 78,* 491–497. doi:10.3168/jds.S0022-0302(95)76659-0

Schluter, A. (2007). PeroxisomeDB: A database for the peroxisomal proteome, functional genomics and disease. *Nucleic Acids Research, 35,* D815–D822. doi:10.1093/nar/gkl935

Schmidhuber, J., & Storck, J. (1993). *Tech.* Report, Fakultat fur Informatik. Technische Universitat Munchen.

Schnell, S., & Maini, P. K. (2003). A Century of enzyme kinetics: reliability of the K_M and v_{max} estimates. *Comments on Theoretical Biology, 8,* 169–187. doi:10.1080/08948550302453

Schnell, S., & Mendoza, C. (1997). Closed form solution for time-dependent enzyme kinetics. *Journal of Theoretical Biology, 187,* 207–212. doi:10.1006/jtbi.1997.0425

Schnell, S., & Mendoza, C. (2000). Enzyme kinetics of multiple alternative substrates. *Journal of Mathematical Chemistry, 27,* 155–170. doi:10.1023/A:1019139423811

Schnell, S., & Mendoza, C. (2000). Time-dependent closed form solution for fully competitive enzyme reactions. *Bulletin of Mathematical Biology, 62,* 321–336. doi:10.1006/bulm.1999.0156

Schrödinger, E. (1926a). Quantisierung als Eigenwertproblem. *Annalen der Physik, 79,* 361–376. doi:10.1002/andp.19263840404

Schrödinger, E. (1926b). Quantisierung als Eigenwertproblem. *Annalen der Physik, 79,* 489–527. doi:10.1002/andp.19263840602

Schrödinger, E. (1926c). Quantisierung als Eigenwertproblem. *Annalen der Physik, 80,* 437–490. doi:10.1002/andp.19263851302

Schrödinger, E. (1926d). Quantisierung als Eigenwertproblem. *Annalen der Physik, 81,* 109–139. doi:10.1002/andp.19263861802

Schultz, T. W. (1997). *Tetrahymina pyriformis* population growth impairment endpoint: a surrogate for fish lethality. *Toxicology Methods, 7,* 289–309. doi:10.1080/105172397243079

Schultz, H. P. (1989). Topological organic chemistry. 1. Graph theory and topological indices. *Journal of Chemical Information and Computer Sciences, 29*(3), 227–228. doi:10.1021/ci00063a012

Schulze, K., & Kirstein, S. (2005). Layer-by-layer deposition of TiO_2 nanoparticles. *Applied Surface Science, 246,* 415–419. doi:10.1016/j.apsusc.2004.11.064

Schulz-Gasch, T., & Stahl, M. (2003)... *Journal of Molecular Modeling, 9,* 47–57.

Schuster, D., Laggner, C., & Langer, T. (2005). Why drugs fail – A study on side effects of new chemical entities. *Current Pharmaceutical Design, 11*(27), 3545–3559. doi:10.2174/138161205774414510

Schwab, C. H., & Gasteiger, J. (2006). *AdrianaCode software version 2.0.* Germany: Molecular Networks GmbH Computerchemie.

Schwarz, J. A., & Contescu, C. I. (1999). Surfaces of Nanoparticles and Porous Materials. In *Surfactant Science, 78.* New York: CRC Press.

Scior, T. (2009). How to recognize and work-around pitfalls in QSAR studies: a critical review. *Current Medicinal Chemistry, 16,* 4297–4313. doi:10.2174/092986709789578213

Scrocco, E., & Tomasi, J. (1973). *Topics in current chemistry.* Berlin: Springer-Verlag.

Seaton, A. (2007). Nanotoxicology: Hazard and risk. *NanoBiotechnology, 3,* 316.

Seatona, A., & Donaldson, K. (2005). Nanoscience, nanotoxicology, and the need to think small. *Lancet, 365*(9463), 923–924. doi:10.1016/S0140-6736(05)71061-8

Seddon, A. M., Curnow, P., & Booth, P. J. (2004). Membrane proteins, lipids and detergents: not just soap opera. *Biochimica et Biophysica Acta, 1666*(1-2), 105–117. doi:10.1016/j.bbamem.2004.04.011

Segel, L. A., & Slemrod, M. (1989). The quasy-steady-state assumption: a case study in perturbation. *SIAM Review, 31*, 446–477. doi:10.1137/1031091

Segura-Cabrera, A., & Rodriguez-Perez, M. A. (2008). Structure-based prediction of Mycobacterium tuberculosis shikimate kinase inhibitors by high-throughput virtual screening. *Bioorganic & Medicinal Chemistry Letters, 18*(11), 3152–3157. doi:10.1016/j.bmcl.2008.05.003

Selassie, C. D., Mekapati, S. B., & Verma, D. P. (2002). QSAR: Then and Now. *Current Topics in Medicinal Chemistry, 2*, 1357–1379. doi:10.2174/1568026023392823

Sen, K. D., & Jorgersen, C. K. (Eds.). (1993). *Electronegativity, structure and bonding*. Berlin: Springer.

Senkan, S. (2001)... *Angewandte Chemie International Edition, 40*(2), 312–329. doi:10.1002/1521-3773(20010119)40:2<312::AID-ANIE312>3.0.CO;2-I

Serna, P., Baumes, L. A., Moliner, M., & Corma, A. (2008)... *Journal of Catalysis, 1*(258), 25–34. doi:10.1016/j.jcat.2008.05.033

Serra, J. M. (2003)... *Catalysis Today, 81*(3), 425–436. doi:10.1016/S0920-5861(03)00142-1

Serra, J. M., Baumes, L. A., Moliner, M., Serna, P., & Corma, A. (2007)... *Combinatorial Chemistry & High Throughput Screening, 10*, 13–24. doi:10.2174/138620707779802779

Serra, J. M., Chica, A.& Corma, A. (2003). *Appl. Catal., A. 239*, 35-42.

Seung, H. S., Opper, M., & Sompolinsky, H. (1992). Proc. of the 5th Annual Workshop on Computational Learning Theory, pp. 287-294.

Seward, J. R., Hamblen, E. L., & Schultz, T. W. (2002). Regression comparisons of *Tetrahymena pyriformis* and *Poecilia reticulata* toxicity. *Chemosphere, 47*(1), 93–101. doi:10.1016/S0045-6535(00)00473-2

Shaik, S., & Hibert, P. C. (2004). Valence Bond Theory, Its History, Fundamentals, and Applications. In Kenny B. Lipkowitz, Raima Larter, Thomas R. Cundari (eds.), *Reviews in Computational Chemistry, 20*, 1-100. London: Wiley.

Shannon, C. E. (1948). A mathematical theory of communication: Part I, discrete noiseless systems. *The Bell System Technical Journal, 27*, 379–423.

Shannon, C. E. (1948). A mathematical theory of communication: Part II, the discrete channel with noise. *The Bell System Technical Journal, 27*, 623–656.

Sharma, B., Kaushik, N., Singh, K., Kumar, S., & Pandey, V. N. (2002). Substitution of conserved hydrodynamic residues in motifs B and C of HIV-1 RT alters the geometry of its catalytic pocket. *Biochemistry, 41*, 15685–15697. doi:10.1021/bi026311z

Shen, P. (2000). Population genetic implications from sequence variation in four Y chromosome genes. *Proceedings of the National Academy of Sciences of the United States of America, 97*, 7354–7359. doi:10.1073/pnas.97.13.7354

Sheridan, R. P., & Kearsley, S. K. (2002). Why do we need so many chemical similarity search methods? *Drug Discovery Today, 7*(17), 903–911. doi:10.1016/S1359-6446(02)02411-X

Sheridan, R. P., Feuston, B. P., Maiorov, V. N., & Kearsley, S. K. (2004). Similarity to molecules in the training set is a good discriminator for prediction accuracy in QSAR. *Journal of Chemical Information and Computer Sciences, 44*(6), 1912–1928. doi:10.1021/ci049782w

Shibata, N., Kajikawa, Y., & Sakata, I. (2010). Extracting the commercialization gap between science and technology – Case study of a solar cell. *Technological Forecasting and Social Change, 77*(7), 1146–1155. doi:10.1016/j.techfore.2010.03.008

Shindyalov, I. N., & Bourne, P. E. (1995). *WPDB* – PC Windows-based interrogation of macromolecular structure. *Journal of Applied Crystallography, 28*, 847–852. doi:10.1107/S0021889895005723

Shindyalov, I. N., & Bourne, P. E. (1997). Protein data representation and query using optimized data decomposition. *CABIOS, 13*, 487–496.

Shorter, J. (1973). *Correlation Analysis in Organic Chemistry*. Cambridge: Cambridge University Press.

Sibley, C. G., & Ahlquist, J. E. (1984). The phylogeny of the hominoid primates, as indicated by DNA–DNA hybridization. *Journal of Molecular Evolution, 20,* 2–15. doi:10.1007/BF02101980

Sicheritz-Pontén, T., & Andersson, S. G. E. (2001). A phylogenomic approach to microbial evolution. *Nucleic Acids Research, 29,* 545–552. doi:10.1093/nar/29.2.545

Sijbesma, R., Srdanov, G., Wudl, F., Castoro, J. A., Wilkens, C., & Friedman, S. H. (1993)... *Journal of the American Chemical Society, 115,* 6510–6514. doi:10.1021/ja00068a006

Simões, A. (2007). *Neighbours and Territories: The Evolving Identity of Chemistry*. Conference presented at 6TH INTERNATIONAL CONFERENCE ON THE HISTORY OF CHEMISTRY. Downloadable at: http://www.euchems.org/ binaries/04_Ana_Simoes_ tcm23-139346.pdf

Sines, J. J., & Hackney, D. D. (1987). A residence-time analysis of enzyme kinetics. *The Biochemical Journal, 243,* 159–164.

Singh, P., Mhaka, A. M., Christensen, S. B., Gray, J. J., Denmeade, S. R., & Isaacs, J. T. (2005)... *Journal of Medicinal Chemistry, 48,* 3005–3014. doi:10.1021/jm049319a

Sjöblom, J., Creaser, D., & Papadakis, K. (2004). *Proc. 11th Nordic Symposium on Catalysis*. Oulu, Finland

Slater, J. C. (1951). A Simplification of the Hartree-Fock Method. *Physical Review, 81,* 385–390. doi:10.1103/PhysRev.81.385

Snedecor, G. W., & Cochran, W. G. (1989). *Iowa State Univ* (8th ed.). Press.

Sohn, K. S., Seo, S. Y., & Park, H. D. (2001)... *Electrochemical and Solid-State Letters, 4,* H26–H29. doi:10.1149/1.1398560

Sokolov, N. (1997). Electrostatic model of cooperative effects in hydrogen-bonded systems: cooperative effect of base and cation on the A---H stretching[1] vibrational frequency. *Journal of Molecular Structure, 436/437,* 201–211. doi:10.1016/S0022-2860(97)00210-X

Solis-Pereyra, B., Aattouri, N., & Lemonnier, D. (1997). Role of food in the stimulation of cytokine production. *The American Journal of Clinical Nutrition, 66,* 521S–525S.

Souvannavong, F., Mérialdo, B., & Huet, B. (2004). *WIAMIS'04, 5th Int. Workshop on Image Analysis for Multimedia Interactive Services*. Inst. Sup. Técnico, Lisboa, Portugal. Apr. 21-23.

Srivastava, D., Menon, M., & Cho, K. (2001). Computational Nanotechnology Withcarbon Nanotubes and Fullerenes. *Computing in Science & Engineering, 3*(4), 42–55. doi:10.1109/5992.931903

Stanley, W. A., Fodor, K., Marti-Renom, M. A., Schliebs, W., & Wilmanns, M. (2007). Protein translocation into peroxisomes by ring-shaped import receptors. *FEBS Letters, 581,* 4795–4802. doi:10.1016/j.febslet.2007.09.001

Stead, A. H., Gill, R., Evans, A. T., & Moffat, A. C. (1982). Predictions of gas chromatographic retention characteristics of barbiturates from molecular structure. *Journal of Chromatography. A, 234*(2), 277–283. doi:10.1016/S0021-9673(00)81866-X

Steel, M. (1992). The complexity of reconstructing trees from qualitative characters and subtrees. *J Classification, 9,* 91–116. doi:10.1007/BF02618470

Stemmer, W. P. C. (1994). Rapid evolution of a protein in vitro by DNA shuffling. *Nature, 370,* 389–391. doi:10.1038/370389a0

Stephens, M. A. (1974)... *Journal of the American Statistical Association, 69,* 730–737. doi:10.2307/2286009

Stewart, C. B. (1993). The powers and pitfalls of parsimony. *Nature, 361,* 603–607. doi:10.1038/361603a0

Stewart, J. J. P. (1990). Semiempirical molecular orbital methods. In Lipkowitz, K. B., & Boyd, D. B. (Eds.), *Reviews in Computational Chemistry* (Vol. 1, pp. 45–81). New York: VCH Publishers. doi:10.1002/9780470125786.ch2

Streitwieser, A. (1961). *Molecular orbital theory for organic chemists*. New York: Wiley.

Strotmann, U. J., & Eglsaer, H. (1995). The toxicity of substituted phenols in the nitrification inhibition test and luminescent bacteria test. *Ecotoxicology and Environmental Safety, 30,* 269–273. doi:10.1006/eesa.1995.1030

Suarez, P., Zardoya, R., Martín, M. J., Prieto, C., Dopazo, J., Solana, A., & Castro, J. M. (1996). Phylogenetic-relationships of European strains of porcine reproductive and respiratory syndrome virus (PRRSV) inferred from DNA-sequences of putative ORF-5 and ORF-7 genes. *Virus Research, 42*, 159–165. doi:10.1016/0168-1702(95)01305-9

Suciu, R. C., Indrea, E., Silipas, T. D., Dreve, S., Rosu, M. C., & Popescu, V. (2009). TiO$_2$ thin films prepared by sol-gel method. *Journal of Physics: Conference Series, 182*, 1–4. doi:10.1088/1742-6596/182/1/012080

Sun, H. (2008). Pharmacophore-based virtual screening. *Current Medicinal Chemistry, 15*(10), 1018–1024. doi:10.2174/092986708784049630

Sun, H., Wang, C., Pang, S., Li, X., Tao, Y., & Tang, H. (2008). Photocatalytic TiO$_2$ films prepared by chemical vapor deposition at atmosphere pressure. *Journal of Non-Crystalline Solids, 354*, 1440–1443. doi:10.1016/j.jnoncrysol.2007.01.108

Sun, Y., & Wu, D. (2008). A RELIEF based feature extraction algorithm, In M. J. Zaki, K. Wang, C. Apte, & H. Park (Eds.), *8th SIAM International Conference on Data Mining* (pp. 188–195). Philadelphia, PA: SIAM.

Sung, Y. M., & Kim, H. J. (2007). Sputter deposition and surface treatment of TiO$_2$ films for dye-sensitized solar cells using reactive RF plasma. *Thin Solid Films, 515*, 4996–4999. doi:10.1016/j.tsf.2006.10.079

Suresh, C. H., & Gadre, S. R. (1997). Electronic perturbations of the aromatic nucleus: Hammett constants and electrostatic potential topography. *The Journal of Organic Chemistry, 62*(8), 2625–2627. doi:10.1021/jo961679l

Suresh, C. H., & Gadre, S. R. (2007). Electrostatic potential minimum of the aromatic ring as a measure of substituent constant. *The Journal of Physical Chemistry A, 111*(4), 710–714. doi:10.1021/jp066917n

Sutcliffe, M., & Scrutton, N. (2000). Enzymology takes a quantum leap forward. *Philosophical Transactions of the Royal Society of London. Series A: Mathematical and Physical Sciences, 358*, 367–386. doi:10.1098/rsta.2000.0536

Svetnik, V., Liaw, A., Tong, C., Culberson, J. C., Sheridan, R. P., & Feuston, B. P. (2003) Random Forest: A classification and regression tool for compound classification and QSAR mode

Swain, C. G., & Lupton, E. C. Jr. (1968). Field and Resonance Components of Substituent Effects. *Journal of the American Chemical Society, 90*(16), 4328–4337. doi:10.1021/ja01018a024

Swanepoel, R. (1983). Determination of the thickness and optical constants of amorphous silicon. *Journal of Physics. E, Scientific Instruments, 16*, 1214–1222. doi:10.1088/0022-3735/16/12/023

Szasz, Gy., Papp, O., Vamos, J., Hanko-Novak, K., & Kier, L. B. (1983). Relationships between molecular connectivity indices, partition coefficients and chromatographic parameters. *Journal of Chromatography. A, 269*(C), 91–95. doi:10.1016/S0021-9673(01)90789-7

Taberner, A., Dopazo, J., & Castanera, P. (1997). Genetic-characterization of populations of a *de-novo* arisen sugar-beet pest, *Aubeonymus-mariaefranciscae* (coleoptera, curculionidae), by Rapd-analysis. *Journal of Molecular Evolution, 45*, 24–31. doi:10.1007/PL00006195

Taft, R. W. Jr. (1952). Linear Free-Energy Relationships from Rates of Esterification and Hydrolysis of Aliphatic and Ortho-Substituted Benzoate Esters. *Journal of the American Chemical Society, 74*(11), 2729–2732. doi:10.1021/ja01131a010

Taft, R. W. Jr. (1960). Sigma Values from Reactivities. *Journal of Physical Chemistry, 64*(12), 1805–1815. doi:10.1021/j100841a003

Taft, R. W. Jr, & Lewis, I. C. (1958). The General Applicability of a Fixed Scale of Inductive Effects. II. Inductive Effects of Dipolar Substituents in the Reactivities of m- and p-Substituted Derivatives of Benzene. *Journal of the American Chemical Society, 80*(10), 2436–2443. doi:10.1021/ja01543a023

Taft, R. W. Jr, Price, E., Fox, I. R., Lewis, I. C., Anderson, K. K., & Davis, G. T. (1963). Fluorine Nuclear Magnetic Resonance Shielding in Meta-Substituted Fluorobenzenes. The Effect of Solvent on the Inductive Order. *Journal of the American Chemical Society, 85*(6), 709–724. doi:10.1021/ja00889a015

Takagi, A., Matsuzaki, T., Sato, M., Nomoto, K., Moro-tomi, M., & Yokokura, T. (2001). Enhancement of natural killer cytotoxicity delayed murine carcinogenesis by a probiotic microorganism. *Carcinogenesis*, *22*, 599–605. doi:10.1093/carcin/22.4.599

Talevi, A., Bellera, C. L., Castro, E. A., & Bruno-Blanch, L. E. (2006). Application of molecular topology in descriptor-based virtual screening for the discovery of new anticon-vulsant agents. *Drugs of the Future*, *31*(Suppl. A), 188.

Talevi, A., Bellera, C. L., Castro, E. A., & Bruno-Blanch, L. E. (2007). A successful virtual screening application: Prediction of anticonvulsant activity in the MES test of widely used pharmaceutical and food preservatives methylparaben and propylparaben. *Journal of Computer-Aided Molecular Design*, *21*(9), 527–538. doi:10.1007/s10822-007-9136-9

Talevi, A., Gavernet, L., & Bruno-Blanch, L. E. (2009). Combined virtual screening strategies. *Current Computer-aided Drug Design*, *5*(1), 23–37. doi:10.2174/157340909787580854

Talevi, A., Sella-Cravero, M., Castro, E. A., & Bruno-Blanch, L. E. (2007). Discovery of Anticonvulsant Activity of Abietic Acid through Application of Linear Discriminant Analysis. *Bioorganic & Medicinal Chemistry Letters*, *17*(6), 1684–1690. doi:10.1016/j.bmcl.2006.12.098

Tamames, J., Clark, D., Herrero, J., Dopazo, J., Blaschke, C., & Fernández, J. M. (2002). Bioinformatics methods for the analysis of expression arrays: Data clustering and information extraction. *Journal of Biotechnology*, *98*, 269–283. doi:10.1016/S0168-1656(02)00137-2

Tame, J. R. H. (1999)... *Journal of Computer-Aided Molecular Design*, *13*, 99–108. doi:10.1023/A:1008068903544

Tárraga, J., Medina, I., Arbiza, L., Huerta, J., Gabaldón, T., Dopazo, J., & Dopazo, H. (2007). Phylemon: A suite of web tools for molecular evolution, phylogenetics and phylogenomics. *Nucleic Acids Research*, *35*, W38–W42. doi:10.1093/nar/gkm224

Taubenberger, J. K., Reid, A. H., Lourens, R. M., Wang, R., Jin, G., & Fanning, T. G. (2005). Characterization of the 1918 influenza virus polymerase genes. *Nature*, *437*, 889–893. doi:10.1038/nature04230

Tavares, C. J., Vieira, J., Rebouta, L., Hungerford, G., Coutinho, P., & Teixeira, V. (2007). Reactive sputtering deposition of photocatalytic TiO$_2$ thin films on glass substrates. *Materials Science and Engineering B*, *138*, 139–143. doi:10.1016/j.mseb.2005.11.043

Tchougang, A., Blansché, A., Baumes, L. A., Lachiche, N., & Collet, P. (2008). *Lecture Notes in Computer Science* 599-609, Volume 5199. In Rudolph, G., Jansen, T., Lucas, S. M., Poloni, C. & Beume, N. (eds). *Parallel Problem Solving from Nature – PPSN X*. Berlin: Springer.

Tejada-Simon, M. V., & Pestka, J. J. (1999). Proinflam-matory cytokine and nitric oxide induction in murine macrophages by cell wall and cytoplasmic extracts of lactic acid bacteria. *Journal of Food Protection*, *62*, 1435–1444.

Terstappen, G. C., & Reggiani, A. (2001). *In silico* research in drug discovery. *Trends in Pharmacological Sciences*, *22*(1), 23–26. doi:10.1016/S0165-6147(00)01584-4

Thrun, S., & Moller, K. (1992). *Advances in Neural Information Processing Systems 4*. San Francisco: Morgan Kaufmann.

Tidor, B., & Karplus, M. (1994)... *Journal of Molecular Biology*, *238*, 405–414. doi:10.1006/jmbi.1994.1300

Tobinick, E. L. (2009). The value of drug reposi-tioning in the current pharmaceutical market. *Drug News & Perspectives*, *22*(2), 119–125. doi:10.1358/dnp.2009.22.2.1343228

Todeschin, R., Consonni, V., Mauri, A., & Pavan, M. (2005). Dragon software version 5.3, Milano, Italy.

Todeschini, R., & Consonni, V. (2000). *Handbook of Molecular Descriptors*. Weinheim, Germany: Wiley-VCH.

Todeschini, R., & Consonni, V. (2002). *Handbook of molecular descriptors*. Weinstein, Germany: Wiley-VCH.

Todeschini, R., & Consonni, V. (2009). *Molecular Descriptors for Chemoinformatics*. Weinheim: Wiley-VCH.

Todeschini, R., Vighi, M., Finizio, A., & Gramatica, P. (1997). 30-Modelling and Prediction by WHIM Descriptors. Part 8. Toxicity and Physico-chemical Properties of Environmental Priority Chemicals by 2D-TI and 3D-WHIM Descriptors. *SAR and QSAR in Environmental Research*, *7*(1–4), 173–193. doi:10.1080/10629369708039130

Todeschini, R., & Consonni, V. (2000). *Handbook of Molecular Descriptors*. New York: Wiley-VCH 11, pp. 667.

Todeschini, R., Consonni, V. (2003). *DRAGON software for the calculation of molecular descriptors Version 3.0.*

Tokuyama, H., Yamago, S., Nakamura, E., Shiraki, T., & Suguira, Y. (1993)... *Journal of the American Chemical Society, 115,* 7918–7923. doi:10.1021/ja00070a064

Tomasi, J., Bonaccorsi, R., & Cammi, R. (1990). *Theoretical methods of chemical bonding* (Maksic, Z. B., Ed.). *Vol. 3*). New York: Springer.

Tondeur, D., & Kvaalen, E. (1987). Equipartition of entropy production. An optimality criterion for transfer and separation processes. *Industrial & Engineering Chemistry Fundamentals, 26,* 50–56.

Tong, S., & Koller, D. (2001)... *Journal of Machine Learning Research, 2,* 45–66. doi:10.1162/153244302760185243

Topliss, J. G., & Costello, R. J. (1972). Chance correlation in Structure-Activity Studies Using Multiple Regression Analysis. *Journal of Medicinal Chemistry, 15,* 1066–1068. doi:10.1021/jm00280a017

Toro-Labbe, A. (2006). *Theoretical aspects of chemical reactivity*. Amsterdam: Elsevier.

Toropov, A., Leszczynska, D., & Leszczynski, J. (2007). Predicting water solubility and octanol- water partition coefficient for carbon nanotubes based on the chiral vector. *Computational Biology and Chemistry, 31,* 127–128. doi:10.1016/j.compbiolchem.2007.02.002

Toropov, A., & Leszczynski, J. (2006). A new approach to the characterization of nanomaterials: Predicting Young's modulus by correlation weighting of nanomaterials codes. *Chemical Physics Letters, 433,* 125–129. doi:10.1016/j.cplett.2006.11.010

Toropov, A., Nesmerak, K., Raska, I. Jr, Waisser, K., & Palat, K. (2006). QSPR modeling of the half-wave potentials of benzoxazines by optimal descriptors calculated with the SMILES. *Computational Biology and Chemistry, 30,* 434–437. doi:10.1016/j.compbiolchem.2006.09.003

Toropov, A., Rasulev, B., Leszczynska, D., & Leszczynski, J. (2007). Additive SMILES based optimal descriptors: QSPR modeling of fullerene C_{60} solubility in organic solvents. *Chemical Physics Letters, 444,* 209–214. doi:10.1016/j.cplett.2007.07.024

Toropov, A., Rasulev, B., Leszczynska, D., & Leszczynski, J. (2008). Multiplicative SMILES Based Optimal Descriptors: QSPR Modeling of Fullerene C_{60} Solubility in Organic Solvents. *Chemical Physics Letters, 457,* 332–336. doi:10.1016/j.cplett.2008.04.013

Toropov, A., Toropova, A., Benfenati, E., Leszczynska, D., & Leszczynski, J. (2009). Additive InChI-based optimal descriptors: QSPR modeling of fullerene C_{60} solubility in organic solvents. *Journal of Mathematical Chemistry, 46*(4), 1232–1251. doi:10.1007/s10910-008-9514-0

Toropov, A., Toropova, A., Rasulev, B., Puzyn, T., Hu, X., & Hwang, H.-M. (2011). (in press). QSAR model of toxicity towards E.coli bacteria for nanosized oxides by SMILES-based optimal descriptors. *Chemical Biology & Drug Design.*

Toropov, A. A., & Benfenati, E. (2007). SMILES as an alternative to the graph in QSAR modelling of bee toxicity. *Computational Biology and Chemistry, 31,* 57–60. doi:10.1016/j.compbiolchem.2007.01.003

Toropov, A. A., Leszczynska, D., & Leszczynski, J. (2007). QSPR study on solubility of fullerene C_{60} in organic solvents using optimal descriptors calculated with SMILES. *Chemical Physics Letters, 441,* 119–122. doi:10.1016/j. cplett.2007.04.094

Toropov, A. A., Toropova, A. P., Mukhamedzhanova, D. V., & Gutman, I. (2005). Simplified molecular input line entry system (SMILES) as an alternative for constructing quantitative structure-property relationships (QSPR). *Indian Journal of Chemistry A, 44,* 1545–1552.

Torrens, F. (2000). Análisis fractal de la estructura terciaria de las proteínas. *Encuentros en la Biología, 8*(64), 4–6.

Torrens, F. (2000). Fractal hybrid orbitals in biopolymer chains. *Zh Fiz Khim, 74,* 125–131.

Torrens, F. (2000). Fractal hybrid orbitals in biopolymer chains. [Engl Transl]. *Russian Journal of Physical Chemistry, 74,* 115–120.

Torrens, F. (2000). Filogénesis de los simios antropoides. *Encuentros en la Biología, 8*(60), 3–5.

Torrens, F. (2002). Computing the Kekulé structure count for alternant hydrocarbons. *International Journal of Quantum Chemistry, 88,* 392–397. doi:10.1002/qua.10176

Torrens, F. (2002). Computing the permanent of the adjacency matrix for fullerenes. *Internet Electron J Mol Des, 1*, 351–359.

Torrens, F. (2002). Fractal hybrid orbitals analysis of the tertiary structure of protein molecules. *Molecules (Basel, Switzerland), 7*, 26–37. doi:10.3390/70100026

Torrens, F. (2003). Principal component analysis of structural parameters for fullerenes. *Internet Electron J Mol Des, 2*, 96–111.

Torrens, F. (2003). Principal component analysis of new structural parameters for fullerenes. *Internet Electron J Mol Des, 2*, 546–563.

Torrens, F. (2003). New structural parameters of fullerenes for principal component analysis. *Theoretical Chemistry Accounts, 110*, 371–376. doi:10.1007/s00214-003-0490-y

Torrens, F. (2004). Table of periodic properties of fullerenes based on structural parameters. *Journal of Chemical Information and Computer Sciences, 44*, 60–67. doi:10.1021/ci030029x

Torrens, F. (2004). Table of periodic properties of fullerenes based on structural parameters. *Journal of Molecular Structure THEOCHEM, 709*, 135–142. doi:10.1016/j.theochem.2003.10.076

Torrens, F. (2004). Fractal dimension of transdermal-delivery drug models. *Lebanese Science Journal, 5*(1), 61–70.

Torrens, F., & Castellano, G. (2005). Cluster origin of the solubility of single-wall carbon nanotubes. *Computing Letters, 1*, 331–336. doi:10.1163/157404005776611303

Torrens, F., & Castellano, G. (2006). Periodic classification of local anaesthetics (procaine analogues). *International Journal of Molecular Sciences, 7*, 12–34. doi:10.3390/i8010012

Torrens, F., & Castellano, G. (2007). Cluster origin of the transfer phenomena of single-wall carbon nanotubes. *J Comput Theor Nanosci, 4*, 588–603.

Torrens, F., & Castellano, G. (2007). Effect of packing on the cluster nature of C nanotubes: An information entropy analysis. *Microelectronics Journal, 38*, 1109–1122. doi:10.1016/j.mejo.2006.04.004

Torrens, F., & Castellano, G. (2007). Asymptotic analysis of coagulation–fragmentation equations of carbon nanotube clusters. *Nanoscale Research Letters, 2*, 337–349. doi:10.1007/s11671-007-9070-8

Torrens, F., & Castellano, G. (2010). Table of periodic properties of human immunodeficiency virus inhibitors. *Int J Comput Intelligence Bioinf Syst Biol, 1*, 246–273.

Torrens, F., & Castellano, G. (in press). Information entropy and the table of periodic properties of local anaesthetics. *Int J Chemoinf Chem Eng.*

Torrens, F., Ortí, E., & Sánchez-Marín, J. (1991). Representación de propiedades moleculares en la didáctica de la química. In *Colloquy University Pedagogy. Horsori* (pp. 375–379). Barcelone.

Torrens, F., & Castellano, G. (2007). Cluster nature of the solvation features of single-wall carbon nanotubes. In Columbus, F. (Ed.), *Progress in Nanotechnology Research* (pp. 1–28). Hauppauge, NY: Nova.

Torrens, F., & Castellano, G. (2009). Classification of complex molecules. In Hassanien, A. E., & Abragam, A. (Eds.), *Foundations of Computational Intelligence* (Vol. 5, pp. 243–315). Berlin: Springer. doi:10.1007/978-3-642-01536-6_11

Torrens, F., Sánchez-Marín, J., & Nebot-Gil, I. (1998). Fractals for hybrid orbitals in protein models. In Laxminarayan, S. (Ed.), *Information Technology Applications in Biomedicine* (pp. 1–6). Washington, DC: IEEE.

Torrens, F. (2001). Fractal hybrid orbitals analysis of tertiary structure of protein molecule. In Lin, S.-K. (Ed.), *Kappe O, Merino P, Marzinzik A, Wennemers H, Wirth T, vanden Eynde J-J* (pp. 1–11). Basel: Synthetic Organic Chemistry V. MDPI.

Torrens, F. (2003). Fractal dimension of transdermal-delivery drug models. In Mastorakis, N., Er, M. J., & D'Attelis, C. (Eds.), *Non-linear Analysis, Non-linear Systems and Chaos* (pp. 1–6). Athens: WSEAS.

Torrens, F., Sánchez-Marín, J., & Sánchez-Pérez, E. (1989). Didàctica empírica de la congelació de l'aigua. In Riera, S. (Ed.), *Actes del II Sympòsium sobre l'Ensenyament de les Ciències Naturals. Documents No. 11* (pp. 595–600). Eumo, Vic.

Torrens, F., Sánchez-Marín, J., & Sánchez-Pérez, E. (1989). Estudi interdisciplinari de la congelació de l'aigua. In Riera, S. (Ed.), *Actes del II Sympòsium sobre l'Ensenyament de les Ciències Naturals. Documents No. 11* (pp. 669–669). Eumo, Vic.

Torrens, F., & Castellano, G. (2009). Periodic classification of human immunodeficiency virus inhibitors. In Sidhu, A. S., Dillon, T., & Bellgard, M. (Eds.), *Biomedical Data Applications*. Berlin: Springer.

Torrens, F. (2001). Fractals for hybrid orbitals in protein models. *Complexity Int 8*, torren01-1–13.

Torrens, F. (2005). Partition of solvents and co-solvents of nanotubes: proteins and cyclopyranoses. In Caldwell, G.W., Atta-ur-Rahman, B.A. (Eds.), *Frontiers in Drug Design and Discovery I*, (pp. 231–268). Hilversum, Holland: Springer.

Torrens, F., & Castellano, G. (2006). Cluster origin of the solubility of single-wall carbon nanotubes. In Maroulis, G. (ed) *Structures and Properties of Clusters: From a few Atoms to Nanoparticles*. (Lecture Series on Computer and Computational Sciences No. 5. Brill, Leiden, pp 187–192).

Torrens, F., & Castellano, G. (2006). Effect of packing on cluster solvation of nanotubes. InBandyopadhyay S, Cahay M (eds), *Nanotechnology VI. Institute of Electrical and Electronics Engineers*, Piscataway (NJ) pp 1–4.

Torrens, F., & Castellano, G. (2008). Nuevo diseño y aproximaciones no ortodoxas con nanotubos de carbono. In García-Breijo E, et al.(eds). Workshop on Sensors: A Local Approach. Valencia, Spain: Universidad Politécnica de Valencia, pp. 409-415.

Torrens, F., Castellano, G. (2009). Modelling of complex multicellular systems: Tumour–immune cells competition. *Chem Central J 3(Suppl. I)*, 75-1–1.

Torrens, F., Castellano, G. (2011). Molecular classification of thiocarbamates with cytoprotection activity against human immunodeficiency virus. *Int J Chem Model*, 3(3), 8-1–48

Torrens, F., Sánchez-Pérez, E., & Sánchez-Marín, J. (1989). Didáctica empírica de la forma molecular. *Enseñanza de las Ciencias Extra-III Congreso*(1), 267–268.

Tracey, L. (2002). Identification of genes involved in resistance to Interferon-α in cutaneous T-cell lymphoma. *American Journal of Pathology, 161*, 1825–1837. doi:10.1016/S0002-9440(10)64459-8

Trah, H.-P., Franz, J., & Marek, J. (1999). Physics of semiconductor sensores. *Advances in Solid State Physics, 39*, 25–36. doi:10.1007/BFb0107462

Trelles, O., Ceron, C., Wang, H. C., Dopazo, J., & Carazo, J. M. (1998). New phylogenetic venues opened by a novel implementation of the DNAml algorithm. *Bioinformatics (Oxford, England), 14*, 544–545. doi:10.1093/bioinformatics/14.6.544

Trelles-Salazar, O., Zapata, E. L., Dopazo, J., Coulson, A. F. W., & Carazo, J. M. (1995). An image-processing approach to dotplots – An X-Window-based program for interactive analysis of dotplots derived from sequence and structural data. *Computer Applications in the Biosciences, 11*, 301–308.

Triballeau, N., Acher, F., Brabet, I., Pin, P., & Bertrand, H. O. Virtual screening workflow development guided by the "Receiver Operating Characteristic" Curve approach. Application to high-throughput docking on metabotropic glutamate receptor subtype 4. *Journal of Medicinal Chemistry, 48*(7), 2534–2547. doi:10.1021/jm049092j

Tribus, M., & Sconyi, G. (1989). An alternative view of the Taguchi approach. *Quality Progress, 22*, 46–48.

Trinajstić, N. (1992). *Chemical graph theory* (2nd ed.). Boca Raton, FL: CRC Press.

Trinajstić, N. (1992). *Chemical Graph Theory*. Boca Raton, FL, USA: CRC Press.

Tropsha, A. (2010). Best Practices for QSAR Model Development, Validation, and Exploitation. *Molecular Informatics, 29*, 476–488. doi:10.1002/minf.201000061

Trouiller, P., Olliaro, P., Torreele, E., Orbinski, J., Laing, R., & Ford, N. (2002). Drug development for neglected diseases: a deficient market and a public-health policy failure. *Lancet, 359*(9324), 2188–2194. doi:10.1016/S0140-6736(02)09096-7

Truhlar, D. G., & Gordon, M. S. (1990). From force-fields to dynamics – classical and quantal paths. *Science, 249*, 491–498. doi:10.1126/science.249.4968.491

Tsai, C. S. (2001). A computer-assisted tutorial on protein structure. *Journal of Chemical Education, 78*, 837–839. doi:10.1021/ed078p837

Tsaneva, G., Kozhukharov, V., Kozhukharov, S., Ivanova, M., Gerwann, J., & Schem, M. (2008). Functional nanocomposite coatings for corrosion protection of aluminum alloy and steel. *Journal of the University of Chemical Technology and Metallurgy, 43*(2), 231–238.

Tsuji, J. S., Maynard, A. D., Howard, P. C., James, J. T., Lam, C.-W., Warheit, D. B., & Santamaria, A. B. (2006). Research Strategies for Safety Evaluation of Nanomaterials, Part IV: Risk Assessment of Nanoparticles. *Toxicological Sciences, 89*(1), 42–50. doi:10.1093/toxsci/kfi339

Tumpey, T. M. (2005). Characterization of the reconstructed 1918 Spanish influenza pandemic virus. *Science, 310*, 77–79. doi:10.1126/science.1119392

Turabekova, M. A., Rasulev, B. F., & Dzhakhangirov, F. N. Salikhov, Sh. I. (2008). *Aconitum* and *Delphinium* alkaloids. "Drug-likeness" descriptors related to toxic mode of action. *Environmental Toxicology and Pharmacology, 25*, 310–320. doi:10.1016/j.etap.2007.10.035

Turchet, P., Laurenzano, M., Auboiron, S., & Antoine, J. M. (2003). Effect of fermented milk containing the probiotic *Lactobacillus casei DN-114001* on winter infections in free-living elderly subjects: A randomised, controlled pilot study. *The Journal of Nutrition, Health & Aging, 7*, 75–77.

Tyagi, R., Lee, Y.-T., Guddat, L. W., & Duggleby, R. G. (2005). Probing the mechanism of the bifunctional enzyme ketol-acid reductoisomerase by site-directed mutagenesis of the active site. *The FEBS Journal, 272*, 593–602. doi:10.1111/j.1742-4658.2004.04506.x

Um, I. H., Kim, K. H., Park, H. R., Fujio, M., & Tsuno, Y. (2004). Effects of amine nature and nonleaving group substituents on rate and mechanism in aminolyses of 2,4-dinitrophenyl X-substituted benzoates. *The Journal of Organic Chemistry, 69*(11), 3937–3942. doi:10.1021/jo049694a

Umeyama, H., & Morokuma, K. (1977). The origin of hydrogen bonding. An energy decomposition study. *Journal of the American Chemical Society, 99*(5), 1316–1332. doi:10.1021/ja00447a007

Unger, S. H., & Hansch, C. (1973). On Model Buildingin Structure-Activity Relationships. A Reexamination of Adrenergic Blocking Activity of β-Halo-β-arylalkylamines. *Journal of Medicinal Chemistry, 16*, 745–749. doi:10.1021/jm00265a001

Unofficial InChI FAQ. University of Cambridge, Cambridge, CB2 1EW (2011). Retrieved from http://wwmm.ch.cam.ac.uk/inchifaq/

Valls, J. (2008). CLEAR-test: Combining inference for differential expression and variability in microarray data analysis. *Journal of Biomedical Informatics, 41*, 33–45. doi:10.1016/j.jbi.2007.05.005

Vallverdú, J. (2005). La evolución de la toxicología: de los venenos a la evaluación de Riesgos. *Revista Española de Toxicología, 22*(3), 153–161.

Vallverdú, J. (2009). Computational Epistemology and e-Science. A New Way of Thinking. *Minds and Machines, 19*(4), 557–567. doi:10.1007/s11023-009-9168-0

Vallverdú, J. (2010b). *History of Probability / Schools of Statistical Reasoning. In the International Lexicon of Statistical Sciences.* New York: Springer.

Vallverdú, J. (2010a). Seeing for Knowing. The Thomas Effect and Computational Science. In Jordi Vallverdú (Ed.) *Thinking Machines and the Philosophy of Computer Science: Concepts and Principles, 280-293.* Hershey, PA: IGI Global Group.

Van Bekkum, H., Verkade, P. E., & Wepster, B. M. (1959)... *Recueil des Travaux Chimique des Pays-Bas, 78*, 815. doi:10.1002/recl.19590781009

van de Waterbeemd, H., & Gifford, E. (2003). ADMET in silico modelling: towards prediction paradise? *Journal of Chemical Information and Computer Sciences, 2*(3), 192–204.

Van de Waterbeemd, H. (2005). From in vivo to in vitro/in silico ADME: progress and challenges. *Expert Opinion on Drug Metabolism & Toxicology, 1*(1), 1–4. doi:10.1517/17425255.1.1.1

Van Drie, J. H. (2007). Computer-aided drug design: the next 20 years. *Journal of Computer-Aided Molecular Design, 21*, 591–601. doi:10.1007/s10822-007-9142-y

Vaquerizas, J. M. (2005). Gepas an experiment-oriented pipeline for the analysis of microarray gene expression data. *Nucleic Acids Research, 33,* W616–W620. doi:10.1093/nar/gki500

Vaquerizas, J. M., Dopazo, J., & Díaz-Uriarte, R. (2004). DNMAD: Web-based diagnosis and normalization for microarray data. *Bioinformatics (Oxford, England), 20,* 3656–3658. doi:10.1093/bioinformatics/bth401

Varmuza, K. (1980). *Pattern recognition in chemistry.* New York: Springer.

Varon, R., Garcia-Meseguer, M. J., Garcia-Canovas, F., & Havsteen, B. H. (1995a). General linear compartment model with zero input: I. Kinetic equations. *Bio Systems, 36,* 121–133. doi:10.1016/0303-2647(95)01533-Q

Varon, R., Garcia-Meseguer, M. J., & Havsteen, B. H. (1995b). General linear compartment model with zero input: II. The computerized derivation of the kinetic equations. *Bio Systems, 36,* 135–144. doi:10.1016/0303-2647(95)01536-T

Varon, R., Garcia-Meseguer, M. J., Valero, E., Garcia-Moreno, M., & Garcia-Canovas, F. (1995). General linear compartment model with zero input: III. First passage residence time of enzyme systems. *Bio Systems, 36,* 145–156. doi:10.1016/0303-2647(95)01535-S

Varon, R., Masia-Perez, J., Garcia-Molina, F., Garcia-Canovas, F., Arias, E., & Arribas, E. (2007). An alternative analysis of enzyme systems based on the whole reaction time. Evaluation of the kinetic parameters and initial enzyme concentration. *Journal of Mathematical Chemistry, 42,* 789–813. doi:10.1007/s10910-006-9142-5

Varón, R., Sevilla, F. G., García-Moreno, M., García-Cánovas, F., Peyro, R., & Duggleby, R. G. (1997). Computer program for the equations describing the steady state of enzyme reactions. *Computer Applications in the Biosciences, 13,* 159–167.

Vedani, A., & Dobler, M. (2002). 5D-QSAR: the key for simulating induced fit? *Journal of Medicinal Chemistry, 45*(11), 2139–2149. doi:10.1021/jm011005p

Vega, M. C. (2006). New ligand-based approach for the discovery of antitrypanosomal compounds. *Bioorganic & Medicinal Chemistry Letters, 16,* 1898–1904. doi:10.1016/j.bmcl.2005.12.087

Veng-Pedersen, P. (1989). Mean time parameters dealing with the tissue distribution of drugs: limitations and extension. *Journal of Pharmaceutical Sciences, 78,* 264–266. doi:10.1002/jps.2600780320

Venkatachalam, C. M., Jiang, X., Oldfield, T., & Waldman, M. (2003)... *Journal of Molecular Graphics & Modelling, 21,* 289–307. doi:10.1016/S1093-3263(02)00164-X

Venkatraman, V., Rowland Dalby, A., & Rong Yang, Z. (2004). Evaluation of mutual information and genetic programming for feature selection in QSAR. *Journal of Chemical Information and Computer Sciences, 44*(5), 1686–1692. doi:10.1021/ci049933v

Verma, U., Sharma, R., Gupta, P., Kapoor, V., Bano, G., & Swahney, B. (2005). New uses for old drugs: Novel therapeutic options. *Indian Journal of Pharmacology, 37*(5), 279–287. doi:10.4103/0253-7613.16850

Veronovski, N., Rudolf, A., Sfiligoj Smole, M., Kreže, T., & Geršak, J. (2009). Self-cleaning and handle properties of TiO_2-modified textiles. *Fibers and Polymers, 10*(4), 551–556. doi:10.1007/s12221-009-0551-5

Verschueren, K. (1996). *Handbook of Environmental Data on Organic Chemicals* (3rd ed.). New York: Van Nostrand Reinhold Company.

Viana, M. M., Mohallem, T. D. S., Nascimento, G. L. T., & Mohallem, N. D. S. (2006). Nanocrystalline titanium oxide thin films prepared by sol-gel process. *Brazilian Journal of Physics, 36*(3B), 1081–1083. doi:10.1590/S0103-97332006000600075

Vidal, D., Thormann, M., & Pons, M. (2005). LINGO, an efficient holographic text based method to calculate biophysical properties and intermolecular similarities. *Journal of Chemical Information and Modeling, 45*(2), 386–393. doi:10.1021/ci0496797

Villalba, J. M., Barbero, A. J., Diaz-Sierra, R., Arribas, E., Garcia-Meseguer, M. J., Garcia-Sevilla, F. et al. (2010). Computerized evaluation of mean residence times in multicompartmental linear system and pharmacokinetics. *J. Comput. Chem.*

Voet, D., & Voet, J. G. (1995). *Biochemistry* (2nd ed.). New York: John Wiley and Sons, Inc.

Walters, P., & Stahl, M. (1996). *Program BABEL.* Tucson, AZ: University of Arizona.

Wang, H. C., Dopazo, J., & Carazo, J. M. (1998). Self-organizing tree growing network for classifying amino acids. *Bioinformatics (Oxford, England)*, *14*, 376–377. doi:10.1093/bioinformatics/14.4.376

Wang, H. C., Dopazo, J., de la Fraga, L. G., Zhu, Y. P., & Carazo, J. M. (1998). Self-organizing tree-growing network for the classification of protein sequences. *Protein Science*, *7*, 2613–2622. doi:10.1002/pro.5560071215

Wang, Z., Helmersson, U., & Käll, P. O. (2002). Optical properties of anatase TiO$_2$ thin films prepared by aqueous sol-gel process at low temperature. *Thin Solid Films*, *405*, 50–54. doi:10.1016/S0040-6090(01)01767-9

Wang, X. D., Sun, C., Wang, Y., & Wang, L. S. (2002). Quantitative structure–activity relationships for the inhibition toxicity to root elongation of *Cucumis sativus* of selected phenols and interspecies correlation with *Tetrahymena pyriformis*. *Chemosphere*, *46*(2), 153–161. doi:10.1016/S0045-6535(01)00133-3

Warheit, D. B., Borm, P. J. A., Hennes, C., & Lademann, J. (2007). Testing Strategies to Establish the Safety of Nanomaterials: Conclusions of an ECETOC Workshop. *Inhalation Toxicology*, *19*(8), 631–643. doi:10.1080/08958370701353080

Waszkowycz, B. (2002)... *Curr Opi Drug Discov*, *5*, 414–421.

Watabe, H., Ikoma, Y., Kimura, Y., Naganawa, M., & Shidahara, M. (2006). PET kinetic analysis-compartmental model. *Annals of Nuclear Medicine*, *20*, 583–588. doi:10.1007/BF02984655

Watanabe, Y., Umegaki, T., Hashimoto, M., Omata, K., & Yamada, M. (2004). [New York: Elsevier Sci. B.V.]. *Catalysis Today*, *89*(4), 455–464. doi:10.1016/j.cattod.2004.02.001

Watanabe, T., Nakajima, A., Wang, R., Minabe, M., Koizumi, S., & Fujishima, A. (1999). Photocatalytic activity and photoinduced hydrophilicity of titanium dioxide coated glass. *Thin Solid Films*, *351*, 260–263. doi:10.1016/S0040-6090(99)00205-9

Webb, C., Dernis, H., Harhoff, D., & Hoisl, K. (2005). Analyzing European and International Patent Citations—A set of EPO patent database building blocks. *STI Working Paper 2005/9*, OECD, Paris.

Weber, J. (1996). Neutralization serotypes of human-immunodeficiency-virus type-1 field isolates are not predicted by genetic subtype. *Journal of Virology*, *70*, 7827–7832.

Wegner, K., Barborini, E., Piseri, P., & Milani, P. (2006). Gas-phase synthesis of nanostructured particulate films. *Journal of KONA Powder and Particle*, *24*, 54–64.

Wei, D. (2010). Dye Sensitized Solar Cells. *International Journal of Molecular Sciences*, *11*, 1103–1113. doi:10.3390/ijms11031103

Weigend, F., Häser, M., Patzelt, H., & Ahlrichs, R. (1998). RI-MP2: optimized auxiliary basis sets and demonstration of efficiency. *Chemical Physics Letters*, *294*(1-3), 143–152. doi:10.1016/S0009-2614(98)00862-8

Weiss, M. (1992). The relevance of residence time theory to pharmacokinetics. *European Journal of Clinical Pharmacology*, *43*, 571–579. doi:10.1007/BF02284953

Wells, M. J. M., & Clark, C. R. (1982a). Investigation of N-alkylbenzamides by reversed-phase liquid chromatography. IV. The study of a homologous series of N-alkylbenzamides using the solvophobic theory and molecular connectivity. *Journal of Chromatography. A*, *243*(2), 263–267. doi:10.1016/S0021-9673(00)82417-6

Wells, M. J. M., & Clark, C. R. (1982b). Investigation of N-alkylbenzamides by reversed-phase liquid chromatography. V. Charateristics of some tertiary alkylbenzamides. *Journal of Chromatography. A*, *244*(2), 231–240. doi:10.1016/S0021-9673(00)85686-1

Wells, M. J. M., Clark, C. R., & Patterson, R. M. (1981). Correlation of reversed-phase capacity factors for barbiturates with biological activities, partition coefficients, and molecular connectivity indices. *Journal of Chromatographic Science*, *19*(11), 573–582.

Wells, M. J. M., Clark, C. R., & Patterson, R. M. (1982). Investigation of N-alkylbenzamides by reversed-phased liquid chromatography. III. Correlation of chromatographic parameters with molecular connectivity indices for the C1C5 N-alkylbenzamides. *Journal of Chromatography. A*, *235*(1), 61–74. doi:10.1016/S0021-9673(00)95789-3

Wells, M. J. M., Clark, C. R., & Patterson, R. M. (1986). Structure-retention relationship analysis for some mono- and polycyclic aromatic hydrocarbons in reversed-phase liquid chromatography using molecular connectivity. *Analytical Chemistry*, *58*(8), 1625–1633. doi:10.1021/ac00121a008

Wen, T., Gao, J., & Shen, J. (2001). Preparation and characterization of TiO_2 thin films by the sol-gel process. *Journal of Materials Science*, *36*, 5923–5926. doi:10.1023/A:1012989012840

Wendy Warr & Associates. (2011). Retrieved from http://www.warr.com/

Wermuth, C. G., Ganellin, C. R., Lindberg, P., & Mitscher, L. A. (1998). Glossary if terms used in medicinal chemistry (IUPAC Recommendations 1997). *Annual Reports in Medicinal Chemistry*, *33*, 385–395. doi:10.1016/S0065-7743(08)61101-X

Wetchakun, N., & Phanichphant, S. (2008). Effect of temperature on the degree of anatase-rutile transformation in titanium dioxide nanoparticles synthesized by the modified sol-gel method. *Current Applied Physics*, *8*, 343–346. doi:10.1016/j.cap.2007.10.028

White, H. (1989)... *AI Expert*, *12*, 48–48.

Whitehead, S. (1991). *A study of cooperative mechanisms for reinforcement learning. TR-365, Dpt. of comp. sci.* Rochester, NY: Rochester Univ.

Whitley, D., Mathias, K., Rana, S., & Dzubera, J. (1996)... *Artificial Intelligence*, *85*(1-2), 245–276. doi:10.1016/0004-3702(95)00124-7

Wiener, H. (1947a). Correlation of heats of isomerization, and differences in heats of vaporization of isomers, among the paraffin hydrocarbons. *Journal of the American Chemical Society*, *69*(11), 2636–2638. doi:10.1021/ja01203a022

Wiener, H. (1947b). Structural determination of paraffin boiling points. *Journal of the American Chemical Society*, *69*(1), 17–20. doi:10.1021/ja01193a005

Willet, P. (2006). Similarity-based virtual screening using 2D fingerprints. *Drug Discovery Today*, *11*(23-24), 1046–1053. doi:10.1016/j.drudis.2006.10.005

Willett, P. (1998). Chemical Similarity Searching. *Journal of Chemical Information and Computer Sciences*, *38*, 983–996. doi:10.1021/ci9800211

Williams, D. F. (Ed.). (1986). *Techniques of Biocompatibility Testing (Vol. II)*. Boca Raton, FL: CRC Press.

Wilson, E. B. (1962). Four dimensional electron density function. *The Journal of Chemical Physics*, *36*(8), 2232–2233. doi:10.1063/1.1732864

Wladkowski, B. D., Wilbur, J. L., & Brauman, J. I. (1994). Intrinsic structure-reactivity relationships in gas-phase SN2 reactions: Identity exchange of substituted benzyl chlorides with chloride ion. *Journal of the American Chemical Society*, *116*(6), 2471–2480. doi:10.1021/ja00085a030

Wolber, G., Seidel, T., Bendix, F., & Langer, T. (2008). Molecule-pharmacophore superpositioning and pattern matching in computational drug design. *Drug Discovery Today*, *13*(1-2), 23–29. doi:10.1016/j.drudis.2007.09.007

Wolf, D.; Buyevskaya, O. V.; Baerns, M. (2000). *Appl. Catal. A*, 63-77.

Wood, B. (1992). Origin and evolution of the genus *Homo*. *Nature*, *355*, 783–790. doi:10.1038/355783a0

Wright, E. M. (1959). Solution of the equation $z\exp(z)=a$. *Proc. R. Soc. Edinburgh A*, *65*, 193–203.

Wu, R., Li, R., Liao, B., & Yue, G. (2010). A novel method for visualizing and analyzing DNA sequences. *MATCH Commun Math Comput Chem*, *63*, 679–690.

Wu, D., Long, M., Zhou, J., Cai, W., Zhu, X., & Chen, C. (2009). Synthesis and characterization of self-cleaning cotton fabrics modified by TiO_2 through a facile approach. *Surface and Coatings Technology*, *203*, 3728–3733. doi:10.1016/j.surfcoat.2009.06.008

Wu. M., Eisen, J.A. (2008). A simple, fast, and accurate method of phylogenomic inference. *Genome Biol*, *9*, R151-1–11.

Xiang, X. D., & Takeuchi, I. (2003). *Combinatorial Materials Science*. New York: Dekker. doi:10.1201/9780203912737

Xin, J. H., Daoud, W. A., & Kong, Y. Y. (2004). A new approach to UV-blocking treatment for cotton fabrics. *Textile Research Journal*, *74*(2), 97–100. doi:10.1177/004051750407400202

Xiong, Y., & Zhan, C. (2006). Theoretical studies of the transition-state structures and free energy barriers for base-catalyzed hydrolysis of amides. *The Journal of Physical Chemistry A*, *110*(46), 12644–12652. doi:10.1021/jp063140p

Yago, J. M., Sevilla, F. G., de Solo, C. G., Duggleby, R. G., & Varón, R. (2006). A Windows program for the derivation of steady-state equations in enzyme systems. *Applied Mathematics and Computation*, *181*, 837–852. doi:10.1016/j.amc.2006.02.016

Yang, W., & Mortier, W. J. (1986). The use of global and local molecular parameters for the analysis of the gas-phase basicity of amines. *Journal of the American Chemical Society*, *108*, 5708–5711. doi:10.1021/ja00279a008

Yang, W., & Parr, R. G. (1984). Density functional approach to the frontier-electron theory of chemical reactivity. *Journal of the American Chemical Society*, *106*, 4049–4050. doi:10.1021/ja00326a036

Yang, S. Y. (2010). Pharmacophore modeling and applications in drug discovery: challenges and recent advances. *Drug Discovery Today*, *15*(11-12), 444–450. doi:10.1016/j.drudis.2010.03.013

Yang, C., Fan, H., Xi, Y., Chen, J., & Li, Z. (2008). Effects of depositing temperatures on structure and optical properties of TiO_2 film deposited by ion beam assisted electron beam evaporation. *Applied Surface Science*, *254*, 2685–2689. doi:10.1016/j.apsusc.2007.10.006

Yang, W., & Wolden, C. A. (2006). Plasma-enhanced chemical vapor deposition of TiO_2 thin films for dielectric applications. *Thin Solid Films*, *515*, 1708–1713. doi:10.1016/j.tsf.2006.06.010

Yang, W., & Drueckhammer, D. G. (2000). Computational studies of the aminolysis of oxoesters and thioesters in aqueous solution. *Organic Letters*, *2*(26), 4133–4136. doi:10.1021/ol0066911

Yao, Y. H., Dai, Q., Nan, X. Y., He, P. A., Nie, Z. M., Zhou, S. P., & Zhang, Y. Z. (2008). Analysis of similarity/dissimilarity of DNA sequences based on a class of 2D graphical representation. *Journal of Computational Chemistry*, *29*, 1632–1639. doi:10.1002/jcc.20922

Yao, F., & Wanghe, C. (2006). Preparation of transparent TiO2 nanocrystalline film for UV sensor. *Chinese Science Bulletin*, *51*(14), 1657–1661. doi:10.1007/s11434-006-2022-3

Ye, Q., Liu, P. Y., Tang, Z. F., & Zhai, L. (2007). Hydrophilic properties of nano-TiO_2 thin films deposited by RF magnetron sputtering. *Vacuum*, *81*, 627–631. doi:10.1016/j.vacuum.2006.09.001

Yeow, Y. L., Pokethitiyook, P., Cheah, M. Y., Dang, H. D. T., & Law, C. K. P. (2004). An alternative way of analyzing the progress curves of enzyme-catalyzed reactions. *Biochemical Engineering Journal*, *21*, 1–10. doi:10.1016/j.bej.2004.04.009

Yoon, K. H., Noh, J. S., Kwon, C. H., & Muhammed, M. (2006). Photocatalytic behavior of TiO_2 thin films prepared by sol-gel process. *Materials Chemistry and Physics*, *95*, 79–83. doi:10.1016/j.matchemphys.2005.06.001

Young, J. K., Pazhanisamy, S., & Schowen, R. L. (1984). Energetics of carbonyl addition and elimination. Kinetic manifestations of acyl substituent effects in anilide hydrolysis. *The Journal of Organic Chemistry*, *49*(22), 4148–4152. doi:10.1021/jo00196a009

Young, D. M., Martin, T. M., Venkatapathy, R., & Harten, P. (2008). Are the Chemical Structures in your QSAR Correct? *QSAR & Combinatorial Science*, *27*(11-12), 1337–1345. doi:10.1002/qsar.200810084

Yu, J. F., Wang, J. H., & Sun, X. (2010). Analysis of similarities/dissimilarities of DNA sequences based on a novel graphical representation. *MATCH Commun Math Comput Chem*, *63*, 493–512.

Yu, Z. G., Zhan, X. W., Han, G. S., Wang, R. W., Anh, V., & Chu, K. H. (2010). Proper distance metrics for phylogenetic analysis using complete genomes without sequence alignment. *International Journal of Molecular Sciences*, *11*, 1141–1154. doi:10.3390/ijms11031141

Yu, J., Zhao, X., & Zhao, Q. (2001). Photocatalytic activity of nanometer TiO_2 thin films prepared by the sol-gel method. *Materials Chemistry and Physics*, *69*, 25–29. doi:10.1016/S0254-0584(00)00291-1

Yu, J. C., Tang, H. Y., Yu, J., Chan, H. C., Zhang, L., & Xie, Y. (2002). Bactericidal and photocatalytic activities of TiO$_2$ thin films prepared by sol-gel and reverse micelle methods. *Journal of Photochemistry and Photobiology A Chemistry, 153*, 211–219. doi:10.1016/S1010-6030(02)00275-7

Yuan, Z., Zhang, J., Li, B., & Li, J. (2007). Effect of metal ion dopants on photochemical properties of anatase TiO$_2$ films synthesized by a modified sol-gel method. *Thin Solid Films, 515*, 7091–7095. doi:10.1016/j.tsf.2007.02.101

Yukawa, Y., & Tsuno, Y. (1959). Resonance Effect in Hammett Relation. II. Sigma Constants in Electrophilic Reactions and their Intercorrelation. *Bulletin of the Chemical Society of Japan, 32*, 965–971. doi:10.1246/bcsj.32.965

Yukawa, Y., Tsuno, Y., & Sawada, M. (1966). Resonance Effect In Hammett Relation. IV. Linear Free Energy Based on the Normal Substituent Constants. *Bulletin of the Chemical Society of Japan, 39*, 2274–2286. doi:10.1246/bcsj.39.2274

Zainal, Z., Lee, C. Y., Hussein, M. Z., & Kassim, A. (2004). Photoelectrochemical properties of sol-gel derived TiO$_2$ thin films in aqueous sodium oxalate solution. *Materials Science-Poland, 22*(2), 99–110.

Zarycka, A., Ilczuk, J., & Czekaj, D. (2003). Application of the sol-gel method to deposition of thin films. *Materials Science, 21*(4), 439–443.

Zavodaski, M., I., Sanschagrin, P.C., Korde, R.S., Kuhn, L.A (2002) *J Comp Aided Mol Des, 16*, 883-902. doi:10.1023/A:1023866311551

Zeeman, M., Auer, C. M., Clements, R. G., Nabholz, J. V., & Boethling, R. S. (1995). U.S. EPA regulatory perspectives on the use of QSAR for new and existing chemical evaluations. *SAR and QSAR in Environmental Research, 3*, 179–201. doi:10.1080/10629369508234003

Zhang, S., & Wang, T. (2010). Phylogenetic analysis of protein sequences based on conditional LZ complexity. *MATCH Commun Math Comput Chem, 63*, 701–716.

Zhang, X., Luo, J., & Yang, L. (2007). New invariant of DNA sequence based on 3DD-curves and its application on phylogeny. *Journal of Computational Chemistry, 28*, 2342–2346. doi:10.1002/jcc.20760

Zhang, Y., & Chen, W. (2008). A new approach to molecular phylogeny of primate mitochondrial DNA. *MATCH Commun Math Comput Chem, 59*, 625–634.

Zhang, S., Golbraikh, A., & Tropsha, A. (2006). Development of quantitative structure-binding affinity relationship models based on novel geometrical chemical descriptors of the protein-ligand interfaces. *Journal of Medicinal Chemistry, 49*, 2713–2724. doi:10.1021/jm050260x

Zhang, O., & Muegge, I. (2006). Scaffold hopping through virtual screening using 2D and 3D similarity descriptors: ranking, voting, and consensus scoring. *Journal of Medicinal Chemistry, 49*(5), 1536–1548. doi:10.1021/jm050468i

Zhang, W., Chen, Y., Yu, S., Chen, S., & Yin, Y. (2006). Preparation, characterization and photocatalytic activity of in situ Fe-doped TiO$_2$ thin films. *Thin Solid Films, 496*(2), 273–280. doi:10.1016/j.tsf.2005.08.352

Zheng, W. X., Wong, N. B., & Li, W. K. (2004). Tri-*s*-triazine and its nitrogen isoelectronic equivalents: An ab initio study. *The Journal of Physical Chemistry A, 108*(52), 11721–11727. doi:10.1021/jp046909b

Zheng, W. X., Wong, N. B., & Tian, A. (2005). Anion–tri-s-triazine bonding: A case for anion recognition. *The Journal of Physical Chemistry A, 109*(9), 1926–1932. doi:10.1021/jp045827k

Zhou, R. H., Friesner, R. A., Ghosh, A., Rizzo, R. C., Jorgensen, W. L., & Levy, R. M. (2001)... *The Journal of Physical Chemistry B, 105*, 10388–10397. doi:10.1021/jp011480z

Zhu, W., Liao, B., & Li, R. (2010). A method for constructing phylogenetic tree based on a dissimilarity matrix. *MATCH Commun Math Comput Chem, 63*, 483–492.

Zipse, H., Wang, L., & Houk, K. N. (1996). Polyether catalysis of ester aminolysis - a computational and experimental study. *Liebigs Annalen*, 1511–1522. doi:10.1002/jlac.199619961004

Zulkarnain, Z., & Yong, L. C. (2005). Properties of sol-gel derived TiO$_2$ thin films prepared with different dip-coating layers. *Materials Science (Medžiagotyra), 11*(2), 97–100.

Zwanzig, R. W. (1954)... *The Journal of Chemical Physics, 22*, 1420–1426. doi:10.1063/1.1740193

About the Contributors

Eduardo A. Castro's career was launched by studying Physical Chemistry at the Faculty of Chemistry of the La Plata National University of La Plata, Buenos Aires, Argentina, during 1963-70. His diploma work to get his PhD Degree was on calculation of HMO and related semi empirical methods of beta-carotene for analyze chemical reactivity and electronic spectrum. Incidentally, his only available computational resource on that time was a diagonalization subroutine for symmetric matrices and his only disposable instruction book was Andrew Streitwieser's on Theoretical Organic Chemistry. From 1971-72 he performed his Ph.D. work at the Physics Department of the National La Plata University, working under supervision of Manuel Sorarrain. After that we find him as a research scientist at the Theoretical and Applied Research Institute located at La Plata National University where he founded the Group for Theoretical Chemistry in 1974. Then, he was appointed as a member of the Scientific Researcher Career in the Argentina National Research Council, and he continues up to the present time as a Superior Researcher.

A. K. Haghi holds a BSc in urban and environmental engineering from University of North Carolina (USA), a MSc in mechanical engineering from North Carolina A&T State University (USA), a DEA in applied mechanics, acoustics, and materials from Université de Technologie de Compiègne (France), and a PhD in engineering sciences from Université de Franche-Comté (France). He is the author and editor of 45 books, as well as 650 papers in various journals and conference proceedings. Dr. Haghi has received several grants, consulted for a number of major corporations, and is a frequent speaker to national and international audiences. Since 1983, he served as professor in several universities. He is currently Editor-in-chief of International Journal of Chemoinformatics and Chemical Engineering and on the Editorial Boards of many International journals. He is also faculty member of Universityof Guilan (Iran).

* * *

Abdelmalek Amine received an engineering degree in computer Science from the Computer Science department of Djillali Liabes University of Sidi-Belabbes-Algeria, received the Magister diploma in Computational Science and PhD from Djillali Liabes University co-supervised with Joseph Fourier University of Grenoble-France. Dr. Amine is member of Evolutionary Engineering and Distributed Information Systems laboratory at U.D.L University-Algeria, and associate professor at Computer Science department of UTM University of Saida-Algeria. He also collaborates with the "knowledge base and database" team of the TIMC laboratory at the Joseph Fourier University of Grenoble.

Laurent A. Baumes obtained his B.Sc. in Applied Mathematics and Econometrics from the University of Montpellier I in 2000. In 2001, he specialized in Artificial Intelligence, Modelling, Data mining and Statistics with a M.Sc. from the University Lyon II. End of 2001, he started a Ph.D. in Applied Mathematics and Computer science (Modelling and Optimization of Heterogeneous Catalysts using Combinatorial and High-Throughput Experimentation Approach), and joined the IRCeLyon (Institut de Recherches sur la Catalyse et l'Environnement de Lyon), at the University Lyon I under the supervision of Prof. Claude Mirodatos and Prof. Ferdi Schüth from the Max Planck Institute für Kohlenforschung at Mulheim, Germany. In January 2005, he started as researcher at the Instituto de Tecnología Química (ITQ) CSIC-UPV under the supervision of Prof. Avelino Corma. He published 40 articles in high-impact journals dealing with various domains (heterogeneous catalysis, microporous crystalline materials, supramolecular sensors, new algorithmic approaches, massive calculations, chemometrics), edited 1 book, wrote 3 book chapters, attended 45 international conferences, 3 as invited speaker. His h-index is 14.

Luis Bruno-Blanch received his degree in Chemistry from the National University of La Plata (UNLP, Argentina) and his PhD in Chemistry from that same institution in 1990. He held a full research associate position in Case Western Reserve University, under the advice of Prof. Giles Klopman, between 1990 and 1991. He was Visiting Professor at the Center of Drug Discovery from the University of Florida between 1991 and 1992, in 1995, 1997 and 2000, at the University of Rio de Janeiro in 2001 and at University of Valencia in 2002. He has specialized in the integrated research of new anticonvulsant agents, including drug design, organic synthesis and pharmacological evaluation. He has published over 50 articles in national and international journals. He has obtained a US Patent of novel myo-inositol antiepileptic derivatives. He is Full time Professor of Medicinal Chemistry at the Faculty of Exact Sciences, UNLP since 1992.

Gloria Castellano is associate professor of experimental sciences at the Universidad Católica de Valencia San Vicente Mártir. After obtaining a PhD in the study of the regioselectivity of the oxyfunctionalization reactions of C–H bonds deactivated with dioxiranes from the Universitat de València, Dr. Castellano undertook postdoctoral research with Professor Torrens at the Universitat de València, and has collaborated on projects with him. Major research projects include molecular modelling and chemistry-computer applications for the description and prediction of molecular properties and starting an electronic journal of scientific-technological and gender spreading. Dr. Castellano is editor-in-chief of the journal Nereis. BSc, Universitat de València, 1986, MSc, 1987, PhD, 1997, 30 courses, assistant professor Universidad Católica de Valencia, 2004, 88 articles, 676 presentations.

Arindam Chakraborty obtained his PhD degree in Theoretical Chemistry from University of Kalyani in 2007 under the supervision of Prof. Dulal C. Ghosh. Soon he joined the research group of Prof. Pratim K. Chattaraj, FNA at IIT, Kharagpur in 2008 as a Post-Doctoral Research Associate and has been working with the Chattaraj group till date. During his research career Dr. Chakraborty has worked on the various facets of application of theoretical chemistry and Conceptual Density Functional Theory (CDFT). The topics include self-consistent field localized MO study towards understanding the structure and bonding in molecules, all-metal aromaticity and its implementation towards assessing the bonding and stability of metal/non-metal cluster motifs, development of some conceptual DFT based reactivity descriptors and their role in constructing fruitful QSAR/QSTR based models, designing of novel molecular clusters as effective hydrogen storage materials. As a graduate student of Presidency College, Calcutta, Arindam Chakraborty has won the Presidency College Chemistry Alumni (PCCA) award in 1995 for showing academic excellence in pursuing a scientific career.

P. K. Chattaraj: After obtaining his B.Sc. and M.Sc. degrees from Burdwan University and his Ph. D. degree from Indian Institute of Technology (Bombay), Pratim Kumar Chattaraj joined the faculty of Indian Institute of Technology (Kharagpur). He is now a professor and the Head of the Department of Chemistry and also the Convener of the Center for Theoretical Studies there. In the meantime, he visited the University of North Carolina (Chapel Hill) as a postdoctoral research associate and several other universities throughout the world as a visiting professor. Apart from teaching, Professor Chattaraj is involved in research on density functional theory, the theory of chemical reactivity, aromaticity in metal clusters, ab initio calculations, quantum trajectories, and nonlinear dynamics. He has been invited to deliver special lectures at several international conferences and to contribute chapters to many edited volumes. Professor Chattaraj is a member of the editorial board of J. Mol. Struct. (Theochem) and J.Chem. Sci. among others. He is a council member of the Chemical Research Society of India and a Fellow of the Indian Academy of Sciences (Bangalore), the Indian National Science Academy (New Delhi), the National Academy of Sciences, India (Allahabad) and the West Bengal Academy of Science and Technology. He is a J. C. Bose National Fellow. He has edited three books on "Chemical reactivity theory: A density functional view", "Aromaticity and metal clusters" and "Quantum trajectories" published by Taylor and Francis Books, Inc./CRC Press, Boca Raton, FL and a special issue each of J. Chem. Sci. (on "Chemical reactivity") and J. Mol. Struct. (Theochem) (with Professor A. J. Thakkar, on "Conceptual aspects of electron densities and density functionals").

Hamid Dadvar was graduated in Bachelor and Master of Science both in Solid State Physics from Guilan University in 2007 and 2010, respectively. His research interests now include the sol-gel process as well as the development of special substrates such as steel, aluminum, mica, soda lime, glass, and nanofibrous mat coated with TiO_2 nanofilms. Currently he is working on funded project at Guilan University as an investigation of antimicrobial properties of the special substrates coated with TiO_2 nanofilms doped by various dopants.

Saeed Dadvar was awarded the degree of Bachelor of Science from Guilan University, Rasht, Iran in 2008 and obtained his Master of Science degree from Isfahan University of Technology, Isfahan, Iran in 2010 both in Textile Engineering (Textile Chemistry and Fiber Sciences). He has nearly four years of academic research experience in fields of ultraviolet protection and photocatalytic characteristics of TiO_2 sol-gel coated nanofibrous mats, antibacterial nanofinishing of textiles based on silver nanoparticles, and toxic gas physiochemical absorbing capability of the metal oxide composite activated carbon nanofibers. His research interests now include electrospinning and the sol-gel process as well as the development of industrial composite activated carbon nanofiber technologies.

Rudra Narayan Das is presently pursuing his research on quantitative structure-toxicity relationship using extended topochemical atom (ETA) indices under the guidance of Dr. Kunal Roy in the Department of Pharmaceutical Technology, Jadavpur University, Kolkata, India. He has to his credit two research papers in the area of ecotoxicological QSARs.

Željko Debeljak is a medical biochemistry specialist at Clinical Hospital Center Osijek, Croatia and a former analytical development scientist at PLIVA d.d. Zagreb, Croatia (today a part of Teva Pharmaceutical Industries Ltd). He is academically affiliated with the Department of Medicinal Chemistry, Faculty of Pharmacy and Biochemistry, Zagreb University and with the Department of Pharmacology, J.J. Strossmayer University in Osijek, Croatia. His research interests are related to the analytical chemistry, laboratory diagnostics and a computer-aided drug design.

Kshatresh Dutta Dubey is presently a senior research fellow in department of Physics of DDU Gorakhpur University, U.P. India. He is presently working with Prof. Rajendra Prasad Ojha. He has many publications in high impact international journals. He has also authored some books for graduate students. He has participated as speaker in many national and international conferences and meetings. His area of research is Molecular dynamics simulations, free energy and thermo-chemical study, conformational and structural study of proteins and enzymes, 2D and 3D QSAR study, Quantum chemical computations using ab initio calculations, molecular docking, pharmacophore modeling and chemoinformatics.

Pablo R. Duchowicz is a researcher from the National Council of Scientific and Technical Researches of Argentina (CONICET), and teaches Physical Chemistry at the National University of La Plata. He is an expert in the field of QSAR-QSPR Theory and also works in Theoretical and Computational Chemistry.

Zakaria Elberrichi received his Master degree in computer science from the California State University in addition to PGCert in higher education and received his PhD in Computer Science from the university Djillali Liabes, Sidi-Belabbes, Algeria. He has more than 20 years of experience in teaching both BSc and MSc levels in computer science and planning and leading Data Mining related projects. Dr. Elberrichi is currently an associate professor in computer science and a researcher at Evolutionary Engineering and Distributed Information Systems Laboratory, EEDIS at the university Djillali Liabes.

Boris Galabov received Ph. D. degree from the University of Sofia in 1975. In 1980 he was habilitated as associate professor and in 1989 as full professor of chemistry at the University of Sofia. His other academic appointments include visiting lecturer at University of Salford, U. K., visiting professor at the University of South Carolina (1986/1987), visiting scholar (Vanderbilt University, 1991), visiting professor (Center for Computational Chemistry, University of Georgia, Athens, 2002 - 2011). Prof. Galabov served as Vice Rector for Academic Affairs at the University of Sofia (1991-1993). During the period 1993 – 1995 he was Deputy Minister at the Ministry of Education and Science in Bulgaria, responsible for the higher education and research sectors. Boris Galabov has published over 150 refereed scientific publications. His scientific research is in two principal areas: (1) Physical organic chemistry; (2) Vibrational spectroscopy. His studies have been presented as plenary or invited lectures at 37 international scientific meetings and over 40 seminars in foreign universities and research institutions. In 1996 Elsevier Science published the monograph of B. Galabov and T. Dudev "Vibrational Intensities". In physical organic chemistry his principal work is in the field of theoretical description of chemical reactivity and in the elucidation of organic reaction mechanisms by applying quantum mechanical methods. The computational work is supplemented by experimental kinetic measurements. Boris Galabov is a member of the editorial boards of Journal of Molecular Structure, Asian Journal of Spectroscopy, and The Open Spectroscopy Journal. In 1986 he was awarded the Dr. Sci. degree by the Bulgarian National Research Evaluation Commission. He was the first recipient of the Grand Science Prize of Sofia University (2008), established on the occasion of the 120th anniversary of the university, for his studies in physical organic chemistry.

Santanab Giri received his B. Sc. (Chemistry Honors) and M. Sc. (Chemistry) degrees from the Vidyasagar University, West Bengal. Then he joined the research group of Professor P. K. Chattaraj for Ph.D. degree in the Department of Chemistry, Indian Institute of Technology, Kharagpur as an Institute Fellow. At present he is a Senior Research Fellow in a CSIR (Government of India) scheme. He is a recipient of two national awards (Professor Santi Ranjan Palit award and Sir P. C. Ray award).

Farhad E. Ghodsi received a BSc honours degree in Physics Engineering from Istanbul Technical University (Turkey), Faculty of Sciences and Letters, in 1992 and an MSc degree in the same department, in 1995. He obtained his PhD from Istanbul Technical University, in Physics Engineering, in 1999. He joined the Department of Physics, University of Guilan, Iran, as an assistant professor in 1999, and was promoted to associate professor in 2008. His main research interests are in optical, structural, and morphological properties of thin films, and electrochromic devices, particularly sol-gel derived films. He has published over 25 papers and presented over 50 papers to regional and international conferences and meetings.Corresponding author. E-mail: feghodsi@guilan.ac.ir.

Ashutosh Gupta received his M.Sc. degree in chemistry from Indian Institute of Technology (IIT), Bombay (India) and Ph.D degree from V.B.S. Purvanchal University, Jaunpur (INDIA) in 2007. He has been an assistant professor of chemistry at the Udai Pratap Autonomous College, Varanasi since 2003. Dr. Gupta has been visiting scientist at IIT Kanpur, IIT Kharagpur and JNCASR, Bangalore. He is currently a BOYSCAST Fellow, Govt. of India (2010-2011) at the Center for Computational Chemistry, University of Georgia, USA. His primary research interests lie in the area of theoretical biochemistry.

Sonia Ilieva was born in Deventzy, Bulgaria, in 1961. She obtained her M.Sc. (1985) and Ph.D. (1993) degrees from the University of Sofia, Bulgaria. She subsequently specialized at the University of Coimbra, Department of Chemistry, Portugal (2000), University of Georgia, Center for Computational Quantum Chemistry, Athens, Georgia, USA (2000), Emory University, Emerson Center for Scientific Computations, Atlanta, Georgia, USA (2001), and as a Fulbright Fellow at the University of Minnesota, Chemistry Department and Supercomputing Institute, Minneapolis, USA (2005). In 1993 she was appointed Assistant Professor at the Department of Chemistry, University of Sofia, and in 2004 promoted to Associate Professor. In 2010 she was awarded the scientific degree "Doctor Habilis in Chemical Sciences". She is a recipient of the Grand Science Prize of the University of Sofia for her research on chemical kinetics, reaction mechanisms and on quantifying reactivity of organic molecules. Her research interests are in the area of physical organic chemistry: application of ab initio quantum mechanical calculations and molecular spectroscopy methods for studying reactivity, organic reactions mechanisms, quantitative structure-activity relationship.

Danuta Leszczynska is a Professor of environmental engineering and environmental science in the Department of Civil and Environmental Engineering at the Jackson State University, Jackson, MS. Her research focuses on the environmental assessment, impact, and interactions of metallic, organic, and nanoscale contaminations in water matrices. Her recent projects include experimental and computational study of the possible interactions of different chemical classes of nanoparticles with organic compounds. Dr. Leszczynska is also internationally active as a Fulbright Scholar, providing information about new, affordable environmental management and treatment technologies, and assisting with the development and implementation of on-line classes.

Jerzy Leszczynski, Professor of chemistry and President's Distinguished Fellow at Jackson State University (JSU) is a computational quantum chemist whose areas of interest include the nature of chemical bonds, theoretical predictions of molecular potential energy surfaces and vibrational spectra, structures and properties of molecules with heavy elements, DNA fragments, and nanomaterials. He also applies computational chemistry methods to environmental problems, surface chemistry and atmospheric chemistry. He directs the Interdisciplinary NSF Nanotoxicity CREST Center at JSU. He is the recipient of numerous awards and distinctions, among them the White House Millennium Award for Teaching and Research Excellence in Mathematics, Science, and Engineering 2001; Guest Professorship, Chinese Academy of Sciences, Shanghai, 2002; Honorary Doctorate, Dnepropetrovsk National University, 2003, Honorary Professorship, Wroclaw University of Technology, 2004; Maria Sklodowska-Curie's Medal, Polish Chemical Society, 2007, and USA Presidential Award for Excellence in Science, Mathematics, and Engineering Mentoring, 2009.

Rajendra Prasad Ojha is presently a Professor in department of Physics of DDU Gorakhpur University, U.P., India. He did his Ph.D in 1985. He is one of the premier researchers of India in molecular dynamic simulations. He has more than fifty research publications in reputed international journals. He has earned many national and international awards. He has been deputed as visiting faculty many times for various international universities. He has supervised many students who are at reputed places in their fields. His area of research are Molecular Dynamics simulations, Conformational study of DNA and protein-ligand complexes, free energy and thermo-chemical study of biomolecules, QM-MM calculations, ab-initio calculations and spectroscopic study like NMR and CD of biomolecules. He has many collaboration with national and international organizations.

Ramakrishnan Parthasarathi works in an area of research that involves physical, chemical and biological sciences and addresses important issues in noncovalent interactions in clusters, biomolecules and their structure-reactivity relationship. He received a Ph.D. Degree from the University of Madras in 2007 under the supervision of Dr V Subramanian, CLRI investigating the nature and perspective of hydrogen bonding interactions. He has also contributed to the development and application of conceptual DFT based reactivity descriptors towards accurate prediction of biological activity and toxicity. As a postdoctoral fellow, he worked with Prof. Krishnan Raghavachari on the fundamental insights in peptide chemistry at Indiana University in 2007-2009. Dr. Parthasarathi became Young Associate of Indian Academy of Sciences in 2008. At present working as a Directors Fellow, in Theoretical Biology and Biophysics, Los Alamos National Laboratory, in the broad area of research focuses on Bio-Nano interactions, nanotoxicity, biofuels and molecular recognition on pathogenesis.

Lionello Pogliani is Professor in physical chemistry, at the University of Calabria, Italy. He graduated in Chemistry at the UniversityUniversity of Calabria, Italy. He graduated in Chemistry at the University of Firenze, Italy. He received his postdoctoral training at the department of Molecular Biology of the C. E. A. (Centre d'Etudes Atomiques) of Saclay,France, at the Physical Chemistry Institute of the Technical and Free University of Berlin, and at the Pharmaceutical Department of the University of California, San Francisco, CA. Here, he coauthored an experimental work, which was awarded with the GM Neural Trauma Research Award. He spent his sabbatical years at the Centro de Quý´mica-Fý´sica Molecular of the Technical University of Lisbon (Portugal) and at the Department of Physical Chemistry of the Faculty of Pharmacy of the University of Valencia-Burjassot (Spain). He contributed around 180 papers in experimental, theoretical, and didactical fields of physical chemistry, including chapters in specialized books, and made more than 40 symposium presentations. Recently, he published a book on numbers 0, 1, 2, and 3. He is a member of the International Academy of Mathematical Chemistry.

Mihai V. Putz is Associate Professor PhD in Chemistry at Chemistry Department of West University of Timisoara; with multiple international post-doctorate stages in physics (Free University of Berlin) and chemistry (University of Calabria), is author and co-author of about 100 papers, 15 monographs in the fields of quantum and computational physical-chemistry of atoms and molecules. MVP is member of many international scientific societies, among which American Chemical Society, as well as author and referee of premier journals of Am. Chem. Soc., Springer, Elsevier, Wiley. MVP is the founder and Editor-in-Chief of International Journal of Chemical Modeling (at Nova Science Publishers, New York) and of International Journal of Environmental Sciences (at Serials Publications, New Delhi). He is currently Guest-Editor of the special issue of „Atoms in Molecules and in Nanostructures" at International Journal of Molecular Sciences (by Molecular Diversity Preservation International-MDPI, Basel). In 2008 MVP was declared the Eminent Researcher of Timisoara by Romanian Government Agency of Scientific Research, while in 2010 he was declared by a nationwide competition the Best Researcher of the Year at Romanian Gala of Education.

Ana-Maria Putz is researcher PhD in Chemistry at Timisoara Institute of Chemistry of the Romanian Academy; with graduation in chemical-biology, master in biochemistry and doctorate in ecotoxicology, AMP is author and co-author of about 30 papers, communications and monographs in the field of enzyme kinetics, QSAR, with special interest in ionic liquids. AMP was research director of a national grant and she is currently the first researcher of a national grant dedicated to bio-, eco- and pharmacology chemoinformatics studies. Member of Romanian Chemical Society she activates as the Editor-Assistant of the *International Journal of Environmental Sciences* (at Serials Publications, New Delhi).

Ali Rahmouni received PhD from Strasbourg University, France. He is the head of the Laboratory of Modelling and Computational Methods at UTM University of Saida-Algeria. He supervises many master and PhD students in theoretical and computational chemistry. Dr. Rahmouni is currently a professor of theoretical and computational chemistry at UTM University of Saida-Algeria.

Bakhtiyor Rasulev is Research Associate in Interdisciplinary Center for Nanotoxicity at Jackson State University. He received his PhD degree in Chemistry from the Institute of the Chemistry of Plant substances, Tashkent, Uzbekistan in 2002. He joined the group of Prof. Jerzy Leszczynski in 2004 as a postdoctoral research associate. He leads the QSAR studies in the group. Dr. Rasulev researches a range of topics in structure-activity relationship studies, dealing with biological activity prediction of natural compounds, organic compounds, physico-chemical and toxicity prediction of various chemicals, including nanoparticles (metal oxides and carbon nanoparticles). For this purpose he develops computational methods for assessing the physico-chemical properties, biological activity, toxicity and environmental risk of studied chemicals. He is the author of many contributions devoted to QSAR modeling and quantum-chemical applications. Dr. Rasulev has closely collaborated with the Instituto di Ricerche Farmacologiche Mario Negri (Milano, Italy), University of Zagreb (Zagreb, Croatia), Johns Hopkins University (USA) and etc. His accomplishments have been widely recognized. He is permanent reviewer of more than 10 peer-reviewed journals. Dr. Rasulev has received many scholarships and awards, including Scholarship of Drew University for participating in Residential School of Medicinal Chemistry (Madison, NJ), Young Investigators Travel Award from Toxicological Division of American Chemical Society, Travel Grant of CRDF Foundation, Scholarship for short-term visit of the Institute of Desert study of Ben-Gurion University (Israel).

Kunal Roy (http://sites.google.com/site/kunalroyindia/) is an Asociate Professor in the Department of Pharmaceutical Technology, Jadavpur University, Kolkata 700 032, India. He is an Associate Editor of the Springer Journal Molecular Diversity and a member of the Editorial Board, Journal of Enzyme Inhibition and Medicinal Chemistry (Informa). He has been a Commonwealth Academic Staff Fellow in University of Manchester (UK) during 2007-08. The field of his research interest is QSAR and Molecular Modeling. Dr. Roy has published more than 150 research papers in refereed journals (http://sites. google.com/site/kunalroyindia/home/krlistofpublications). Dr. Roy has been a recipient of Bioorganic and Medicinal Chemistry Most Cited Paper 2003-2006, 2004-2007 and 2006-2009 Awards (Elsevier), Bioorganic and Medicinal Chemistry Letters Most Cited Paper 2006-2009 Award (Elsevier), AICTE Career Award (AICTE, New Delhi) etc. He is a reviewer of QSAR papers in different journals like Journal of Molecular Modeling (Springer), Journal of Chemical Information and Modeling (ACS), European Journal of Medicinal Chemistry (Elsevier), Bioorganic and Medicinal Chemistry Letters (Elsevier), Journal of Computational Chemistry (Wiley), Chemosphere (Elsevier), QSAR and Combinatorial Science (Wiley), etc. Dr. Roy is also a member of the Cheminformatics and QSAR Society.

Debesh Ranjan Roy obtained his M.Sc. degree (Physics) from the Visva-Bharati University, Santiniketan and Ph.D. (Science) degree under the supervision of Prof. P. K. Chattaraj from the Department of Chemistry, Indian Institute of Technology, Kharagpur. Subsequently, he did his postdoctoral research with Prof. S. N. Khanna in the Department of Physics, Virginia Commonwealth University, USA. Currently, Dr. Roy working as a Lecturer of Physics in the Department of Applied Physics, S. V. National Institute of Technology, Surat. His primary research interest includes density functional theory & physics and chemistry of clusters and cluster assembled materials. Dr. Roy is a member of American Physical Society and American Chemical Society. He has co-authored more than 40 research publication in referred journals and book chapters which are cited over 600 times with h-index of 12.

Marica Medic-Saric, PhD is head of Department of Medicinal Chemistry and a full professor on Faculty of Pharmacy and Biochemistry University of Zagreb, Croatia. She is course leader on the Pharmaceutical chemistry and Biochemistry of Drugs. She established the group for theoretical chemistry and developed novel modeling strategies in drug design. She is currently training the next generation of pharmacists. Her research interests are related to methabolism of drugs, the methods of optimization in chromatography analysis and a computer-aided drug design.

Michel Simonet received PhD from Joseph Fourier University of Grenoble, France. He is the head of the knowledge base and database team of the TIMC laboratory at the Joseph Fourier University of Grenoble. His group works on two main projects: a database and knowledge base management system, named OSIRIS, and a system for database conception and reverse engineering based on original concepts and a new methodology. Dr. Simonet managed in the recent years the European ASIA-ITC GENNERE with China and has been responsible of ontology enrichment in the European IP project Noesis, a platform for wide-scale integration and visual representation of medical intelligence.

Alan Talevi was born in November 1980. He obtained his degree in Pharmacy and Pharmaceutical Sciences from the National University of La Plata (UNLP, Argentina) in 2004. In 2007 he received his PhD in Biological Sciences –in the field of computer assisted drug design- from the National University of La Plata.. He was a doctoral and postdoctoral fellowship holder from the Argentinean National Council of Scientific and Technological Research (CONICET). At present, he holds a permanent position as Assistant researcher at CONICET, where he works in the development of computational models to predict affinity to MDR1 protein, and works as Chief Teaching Assistant of the Biopharmaceutics course at the Faculty of Exact Sciences, UNLP. He received the Enrique Herrero Ducloux award to the best thesis in Theoretical Chemistry from the Argentinean Chemical Society in 2008, and a Young Scholar award in Pacifichem 2010. He has obtained travel and accommodation grants from UNLP, TWAS and Bibliotheca Alexandrina, ICGEB, and the European Federation for Medicinal Chemistry. He has published 24 articles in national and international journals.

Francisco Torrens is lecturer in physical chemistry at the Universitat de València. After obtaining a PhD in molecular associations in azines and macrocycles from the Universitat de València, Dr. Torrens undertook postdoctoral research with Professor Rivail at the Université de Nancy I. More recently, Dr. Torrens has collaborated on projects with Professor Tomás-Vert. Major research projects include characterization of the electronic structure of electrically conductive organic materials, theoretical study of new electrically conductive organic materials, protein modelling, electronic correlation, development and applications of high-precision mono and multi referential electronic correlation methods, development and application of high-precision quantum methods, methodological developments and applications of quantum methods, molecular modelling and chemistry-computer applications for the description and prediction of molecular properties, development and integration of a computational system for the discovery of active drugs against AIDS, cancer pandemics and other microbial diseases of high social impact, starting an electronic journal of scientific-technological and gender spreading, computational design, chemical obtaining and biological evaluation of new antiprotozoal and anticancer drugs, prediction of the environmental impact of chemical substances using chemobioinformatics tools, discovery of new inhibitors of tyrosinase: computational design, synthesis, characterization and experimental corroboration, search for new antimicrobial agents that inhibit the synthesis of the bacterial cell wall and minimal active domains of proteins of the Bcl 2 family. His scientific accomplishments include the first implementation in a computer at the Universitat de València of a program for the elucidation of crystallographic structures, and the construction of the first computational-chemistry program adapted to a vector-facility supercomputer in a Spanish university. BSc, Universitat de València, 1984, MSc, 1987, PhD, 1990, PhD talent prize, 1991, PhD grant, 1987 91, 74 congress organizations, editor-in-chief of Meeting in Science, Technology, Education and Gender, editor of Molecules, MATCH Communications in Mathematical and in Computer Chemistry, Research Journal of BioTechnology, Research & Reviews in BioSciences, Asian Journal of Biochemistry, Asian Journal of Scientific Research, Biotechnology, International Journal of Biological Chemistry, Current Drug Discovery Technologies, Journal of WSCG, African Journal of Biochemistry Research, Molecular Diversity, African Journal of Pure and Applied Chemistry, African Journal of Pharmacy and Pharmacology, International Journal of Liquid State Sciences, International Journal on Analytical Proteomics, Research in Pharmaceutical Biotechnology, IETE Technical Review, Der Pharma Chemica, Journal of Nanoscience and Nanotechnology, Journal of Electromagnetic Analysis and Applications, Journal of Integrated OMICS, Nereis and Journal of Life Sciences. 62 scientific societies, 26 research projects, 6 visitor professor responsible, assistant professor U. V., 1990-95, chargé de recherche C.N.R.S., 1991, lecturer U. V., 1995-present, Head of the Research Grup Modelucar Modelling, Computer-Aided Drug Design and Development of the Research Unit Theoretical Chemistry of the Institut Universitari de Ciència Molecular, 1 book, 260 articles, 1200 presentations. Advisor of 2 Ph. D. and 1 M. Sc.

Jordi Vallverdú, Ph.D., M.A., B.Mus, is Lecturer Professor at Universitat Autònoma de Barcelona (Catalonia, Spain), where he teaches Philosophy and History of Science and Computing. He holds a Ph.D. in philosophy of science (UAB) and a Master in History of Sciences (UAB). His research is dedicated to the epistemological, ethical, gender, and educational aspects of Philosophy of Computing and Science. He is Editor-in-chief of the *International Journal of Synthetic Emotions* (IJSE), and as researcher is member of the E-CAP, Convergent Science Network of Biomimetic and Biohybrid systems Net member, member of the Spanish Society of Logic, Methodology and Philosophy of Science, member of the GEHUCT (Grup d'Estudis Interdisciplinaris sobre Ciència i Tecnologia) research project, member of the TECNOCOG (Philosophy, Technology and Cognition Research Group), member of EUCogII, Main researcher of SETE (Synthetic Emotions in Technological Environments), and Expert of the Biosociety Research (European Commission: http://ec.europa.eu/research/biosociety/index_en.htm). He has written 5 books as author or editor: (2007) *Una ética de las emociones,* (2009) *Bioética computacional,* (2009) *Handbook of Research on Synthetic Emotions and Sociable Robotics: New Applications in Affective Computing and Artificial Intelligence,* (2010) *Thinking Machines and the Philosophy of Computer Science: Concepts and Principle and* (2011) *¡Hasta la vista Baby! Un ensayo sobre los tecnopensamientos.* Very recently he has won a prestigious japanese JSPS fellowship to make his research on computational HRI interfaces at Kyoto University.

Index